# THE LEGAL ENVIRONMENT
# OF
# BUSINESS

# THE LEGAL ENVIRONMENT OF BUSINESS

Victor D. López, J.D.

*Prentice Hall*
*Upper Saddle River, NJ 07458*

**Library of Congress Cataloging-in-Publication Data**

López, Victor D.
    The legal environment of business / by Victor D. López. — 1st ed.
        p.      cm.
    Includes index.
    ISBN 0-13-125386-7
        1. Business law—United States.    I.    Title.
KF889.L67 1997
346.73'07—dc20                                              95-53338
[347.3067]                                                  CIP

Acquisitions editor: Elizabeth Sugg
Editorial/production supervision and interior design: Tally Morgan,
    WordCrafters Editorial Services, Inc.
Cover Director: Jayne Conte
Prepress/manufacturing buyer: Ed O'Dougherty
Managing editor: Mary Carnis
Director of production and manufacturing: Bruce Johnson

© 1997 by Prentice-Hall, Inc.
A Simon & Schuster Company
Upper Saddle River, NJ 07458

Printed in the United States of America
10  9  8  7  6  5  4  3  2  1

ISBN   0-13-125386-7

Prentice-Hall International (UK) Limited, *London*
Prentice-Hall of Australia Pty, Limited, *Sydney*
Prentice-Hall Canada Inc., *Toronto*
Prentice-Hall Hispanoamericana, S.A., *Mexico*
Prentice-Hall of India Privated Limited, *New Delhi*
Prentice-Hall of Japan, Inc., *Tokyo*
Simon & Schuster Asia Pte. Ltd., *Singapore*
Editora Prentice-Hall do Brasil, Ltda., *Rio de Janeiro*

# Dedication

For my wife and best friend, Alice Z. López,
without whom life would be . . . unthinkable.

# CONTENTS

# PREFACE

*The Legal Environment of Business* was designed to be used as a text in Legal Environment of Business and related introductory law courses offered to freshmen and sophomores in business and legal studies programs. *The Legal Environment of Business* provides an overview of the major areas of the law that shape the environment in which business and individuals operate. Unlike many leading Legal Environment textbooks, however, this book was not designed to be equally usable in undergraduate and graduate courses. Thus, while subject matter coverage of this text is analogous to that of other leading textbooks, the material has been adapted to meet the needs of undergraduate students and faculty. An effort has been made to present technically accurate material in as straightforward a manner as possible. In addition, inclusion of ancillary material has been kept to a minimum; it is my firm belief that the popular pedagogical devices such as charts, graphs, pictures, sidebars, illustrative case briefs, marginal definitions, marginal overviews or encapsulations of main concepts and the like more often serve to confuse students than to illuminate difficult concepts. Overuse of such devices by well intentioned authors also inflates the already high cost of college textbooks for students. Clear, accessible prose and logical organization need few enhancements. I have attempted to provide in this (and previous) texts what I hope is readable, interesting prose that will help the student to absorb difficult concepts with a minimum of effort; the extent to which I have succeeded is for you to judge.

# ABOUT THE AUTHOR

Victor D. López is a tenured associate professor of business at the State University of New York, College of Technology at Delhi, where he has taught since 1990. He has been teaching at the college level since 1986 at urban, suburban and rural colleges. López earned a Juris Doctor degree from St. John's University School of Law, and a B.A. from Queens College, C.U.N.Y. in English. He was admitted to the New York State Bar in 1984 and has been a member of the New York State Bar Association since 1984. He is also a member of the North East Academy of Legal Studies in Business and is an acting senior articles editor for the North East Journal of Legal Studies for the 1995–96 academic year. Previous books published include *Free and User-Supported Software for the IBM PC: A Resource Guide for Libraries and Individuals* (with Kenneth J. Ansley, McFarland & Co., 1990) and *Business Law: An Introduction* (Irwin/Mirror Press, 1993). A native of Buenos Aires, Argentina, López immigrated with his parents, Felipe and Manuela López (natives of Galicia, Spain), to the United States in 1967, at the age of 9. He lived in Woodside, Queens (N.Y.C.) until 1990, when he married his wife, Alice, and relocated to the peaceful, snowy college town of Oneonta in the rural southern tier of New York State.

UNIT

# I

# INTRODUCTION TO LAW AND THE LEGAL SYSTEM

Throughout the ages, philosophers, jurists, political scientists, leaders and common people from all walks of life have defined law in a number of ways. Cicero viewed law as "nothing but a correct principle drawn from the inspiration of the gods, commanding what is honest, and forbidding the contrary." According to the eminent British jurist William Blackstone, law could be defined as "a rule of civil conduct, prescribed by the supreme power in a state, commanding what is right and prohibiting what is wrong." St. Thomas Aquinas, on the other hand, defined law as "an ordinance of reason for the common good, made by him who has care of the community." Whatever our working definition, law is often what Justice Felix Frankfurter described as "all we have standing between us and the tyranny of mere will."

At its simplest, law can be defined as the rules of behavior that a government imposes on its people for the benefit of society as a whole. As such, it represents the governing body's subjective views of what is best for that society. And even though most legal systems attempt to protect society and promote the common good, there can be radical differences in the law from one country to another, and even in different regions within countries; this is inevitable, given that, as we will explore further in Chapter 3 on Ethics and Public Policy, such ethereal concepts as *fairness, justice* and *the public good* can have different meanings depending on which ethical system one uses as a reference. Thus, for the good of society, the laws of Holland tolerate drug use and prostitution, but those of Iran exact the death penalty for the same behavior. Likewise, a seven-year-old can drink wine and buy cigarettes in Italy or Spain, while that behavior is limited to twenty-one-year-olds in New York and is prohibited to all in Saudi Arabia. Reasonable people can debate (often heatedly) the relative good to society inherent in the diametrically opposed viewpoints expressed in these countries' laws; but philosophical discourse aside, travelers to these jurisdictions had better know the law, for

1

they will be subject to penalties for its violation; it is a universal precept that, with very few exceptions, ignorance of the law does not excuse its breach.

Businesses have always been faced with the practical problem of conflicting laws in sovereign jurisdictions. This is particularly the case in the United States, where, as we will explore in the next chapter, we have no unified legal system and must contend with separate federal, state and local laws. When you further consider the realities of the modern global economy and the trend towards freer international trade as evidenced by the North American Free Trade Agreement (NAFTA) and similar treaties that seek to lower trade barriers and encourage international trade, the implications for business are staggering. A company needs to be familiar with the laws in every state and country in which it conducts business. Larger companies have in-house legal departments or have access to the expertise of large law firms. Small businesses, on the other hand, often operate with minimal access to legal counsel—a practice somewhat akin to Russian roulette. Regardless of size, any business can benefit greatly from employing people at all levels who have at least a basic understanding of the law and a solid grasp of essential legal principles so that they can recognize potential legal problems and refer them to the legal department or outside counsel before they become costly catastrophes.

While no textbook can become a comprehensive hands-on guide to American law (the legal encyclopedias that attempt to do so run well beyond ten thousand pages and still do not comprehensively cover all aspects of the law), it is the purpose of this text to provide an accurate, easy to understand, useful guide to some areas of the law that have the greatest impact on business. A *Legal Environment of Business* course will provide students with the skills to recognize and apply the proverbial ounce of prevention to their business careers and personal lives that can prove more useful to employers and themselves than pounds of competent, costly lawyers called too late to remedy a problem that should never have arisen.

In this unit, we will begin our excursion into the practical application of the law by examining the sources of American law and the American legal system. We will then delve into government regulation of business and explore some of the issues involved in business ethics and the policy considerations involved in the regulatory environment of business in general. Finally, we will begin our exploration of substantive law by examining administrative law, criminal law, torts and the law of negligence and strict liability.

CHAPTER

# 1

# SOURCES OF THE LAW

While the laws of sovereign states can vary widely, all law can be traced at its most basic level to roots in one of two distinct legal traditions: civil law and common law. A brief examination of each system is a useful way to begin our journey through the legal environment of business, for it can give us useful clues to the basic philosophies that underlie legal systems, and allow us to explore some strengths and weaknesses inherent in different systems of law.

## CIVIL-LAW SYSTEMS . . . . . . . . . . . . . . . . . . . . . . . . . . . . . . . .

Civil law is the oldest and most common system of law. It traces its roots to a tradition that dates back to the Code of Hammurabi in 2100 B.C., and is based on the precept that all laws should be reduced to codes of conduct and written down and made public so that they could be understood and followed by all citizens. This tradition was continued in 450 B.C., in the Twelve Tables of Roman law, in which twelve bronze tablets specifying a code of law applicable to all Roman citizens were attached to the orator's platform on the Roman Forum in an attempt to make the law accessible to all Roman citizens. The tradition of codifying the law found its greatest expression in 533 A.D., when the Byzantine Emperor Justinian I integrated a thousand years of existing law into a single code that he called *Corpus Juris Civilis*—"the body of civil law," which became known as the Justinian Code. The Justinian Code is still studied today in civil-law jurisdictions as the most important pillar of jurisprudence upon which all modern civil law is based. The most notable attempt in modern times to codify the law into a comprehensive civil code was carried out by a commission appointed by Napoleon Bonaparte in 1800, and resulted in the 1804 *Code Civil*, more commonly referred to as the *Napoleonic Code*. Using the Justinian Code as a guide, the Napoleonic Code is divided into three parts. The first part deals with civil rights, marital rights, personal property and education; the second part deals with real-property ownership and the government's rights under eminent domain; the third part of the code concerns *inter vivos* and

3

testamentary gifts, as well as contractual rights. The code was supplemented by additional codes between 1807 and 1811 on civil procedure, commercial law, criminal procedure and criminal law. Taken together, this extensive body of law forms the basis of many modern legal systems in Europe, Central and South America and Quebec. The Napoleonic Code was also very influential in Louisiana, where a modified form of the code is still in effect today as the basis of that state's law.

The defining characteristic of civil law is the attempt at codifying the law—of reducing all law into a written form that ideally can be both understood and applied by the common citizenry. Perhaps the most tangible benefit of civil law is its efficiency and stability: the administration of justice is swift and, because civil law leaves little room for judicial interpretation, the application of the law is highly predictable and the law itself is very slow to change. The swift administration of justice is also aided by the fact that jury trials are generally unavailable in civil-law jurisdictions; a single judge or a panel of judges, depending on the nature and seriousness of the case, acts as a trier of both fact and law. This greatly speeds up trials and lowers their cost to litigants. In addition, because judges have relatively little power to interpret the law in civil-law jurisdictions, the outcome in many civil and criminal disputes is highly predictable—another factor that results in less litigation. Finally, the nature of civil law as a codified and accessible system reduces the need for attorneys in civil-law jurisdictions; since relatively little expertise is needed to interpret the law, many tasks that can be performed only by licensed attorneys in common-law jurisdictions can be performed by lesser-trained and less-expensive paralegals. In civil-law jurisdictions, *paralegals* (often called *notaries*) can legally perform routine, uncomplicated legal tasks and give limited legal advice in certain areas, such as will preparation, preparation of affidavits, and execution of powers of attorneys. In common-law jurisdictions, all of these tasks can be performed only by an attorney or by a paralegal under the direct supervision of an attorney.

## COMMON-LAW SYSTEMS

The common-law system has its roots in England. Under the feudal system, the king as supreme authority and landholder granted large tracts of land to favorite barons, each of whom in turn granted small tracts of land to his knights. Each baron became the arbiter of legal disputes within the boundaries of his land, subject only to the will of the king. Each manor eventually developed its own court to settle disputes between serfs, and higher courts were also developed by powerful barons to settle disputes between their knights. The law developed in these courts was based on regional customs and traditions. Not surprisingly, then, there was little uniformity from one manor to another in the application of the law.

During the Norman Conquest of 1066 A.D., William I attempted to consolidate English law into a single body of law that could be applied throughout England. He established the King's Court (*Curia Regis*) as an advisory body to the barons. The court had both legislative and judicial powers that eventually led to the development of Parliament and the English court system.

By the latter part of the twelfth century, the influence of the King's Court was extended into the local and regional courts by royal justices who visited these local courts periodically at set intervals of time, traveling along a set route or *circuit*. As these visits from royal judges increased in frequency, the power of the local courts was slowly eroded and the law in England began to be unified in a single common law that slowly erased regional differences in law and established greater uniformity throughout the realm. The law was still largely based on custom and tradition—the custom and tradition held in common by the King's Court judges. It was these judges who first began writing down their decisions to serve as guidelines for local magistrates and themselves in future cases. This tradition of writing down decisions to serve as guidelines for deciding future cases formed the basis for our modern common-law system.

While royal judges wielded great power in the shaping of early English common law, the king and Parliament retained the right to overturn court decisions and amend legal precedent by the issuance of *statutes*—written pronouncements on the law that courts were bound to follow.

After the invention of the printing press in the fifteenth century, it became possible to publish court decisions to serve as resources for lawyers and judges in researching the law. The first truly useful court reporters began appearing in the mid-eighteenth century.

The stability of common law is dependent on judges following legal precedent, guided by the doctrine of *stare decisis*. *Legal precedent* is the body of court decisions relating to a legal issue. The system of common law is based upon judges following the reasoning in previously decided cases when they decide cases currently before them. This gives the law its stability and allows legal practitioners to predict how a given case will be decided by examining how similar cases were decided in the past. Precedent can be *binding* or merely *persuasive*. Legal precedent is binding when a court has no choice but to follow it, and is merely persuasive when a court is free to follow or ignore it; for example, the decision of a state's highest court is binding precedent on that state's lower courts, who must follow it, but is merely persuasive precedent on the highest courts of other states, which are free to follow or ignore it. A state's highest court is always free to follow its own established legal precedents or to change them. The doctrine of *stare decisis* (to abide or stand by decided cases) states that courts should stand by decided cases and not overrule established precedent lightly. Under the principle of *stare decisis*, a court should follow established legal precedent unless there is a compelling reason not to do so. This principle is crucial to the stability of the common law; if judges did not follow established precedent, there would be little predictability to the law; attorneys would have no solid guidelines upon which to base the advice they give to clients and no stable guideposts on which to base legal arguments and chart legal strategies for arguing cases in court.

## SOURCES OF AMERICAN LAW · · · · · · · · · · · · · · · · · · · · · · · · · · · · ·

American law is based on the English common-law system. When the early Pilgrims emigrated to America, they brought with them their legal system, along with their customs, traditions and values. It is these that helped to give shape to our legal system. It is in the nature of common law, however, that it adapts to the customs, traditions and needs of a people. Thus, despite its English roots, American law has evolved to fit the needs of our federalist system, and reflects regional differences and values. As a result, law in the United States today more closely resembles early English common law with its differences between the various manors than it does the relatively unified law of modern-day Great Britain. We have a splintered system of federal, state and local laws to contend with which, while sharing many similarities, can often be quite different.

It is a common misconception to think of the law as a set of rules written in dusty rows of books in law libraries. While such an analogy might be somewhat accurate with regard to civil law, it is wholly inaccurate in our common-law system. It is true that printed court reports and statutes for the fifty states and commonwealths and for the federal system are collected in thousands of volumes in law libraries and provide an invaluable resource for legal research. But American law is far more than a collection of court decisions and the text of statutes; it is a vibrant, flowing river fed by many tributaries and streams. It is neither stagnant nor static, but ever-changing (albeit slowly) over time. In addition to the court decisions of the various federal and states' courts, sources of the law include constitutional law, statutory law and administrative law.

## CONSTITUTIONAL LAW

A country's or state's constitution is the most fundamental source of law. It delineates in general terms the sovereign state's form of government and provides the basic framework for its laws. Article VI, Section 2 of the U.S. Constitution specifically sets the U.S. Constitution as the "supreme law of the land." As such, no other law passed by a state or the federal government can conflict with it; any law that does is unconstitutional and void.

Constitutions are of necessity broad documents. In the United States, the job of interpreting the federal constitution and that of every state is left to the courts. Both state and federal courts have the power to interpret the U.S. Constitution, but the final word on the analysis of the federal constitution is reserved to the U.S. Supreme Court, whose interpretation of the Constitution is binding precedent for all lower state and federal courts.

But even the U.S. Constitution is not static. Both Congress and the states have the power to amend it in any way they choose. Under Article V of the Constitution, Congress may propose a constitutional amendment by a two-thirds vote by the House of Representatives and the Senate. If a proposed amendment is approved by Congress, it then goes to all the states' legislatures. If three-quarters of the states' legislatures approve the amendment, it becomes part of the Constitution and the preeminent law of the land. States may also propose to Congress amendments to the Constitution on their own initiative by votes for such a proposal in two-thirds of the states' legislatures. If the states make the initiative, Congress must decide whether to allow ratification by constitutional conventions in three-quarters of the states; if the states initiate the amendment, it also becomes law upon approval by three-quarters of the states' legislatures, by a constitutional convention in three-quarters of the states or by a vote for ratification by three-quarters of the states' legislatures. Other than the right to each state's equal representation in the Senate, there is no limit to what changes can be written into the Constitution. To date, the Constitution has been amended twenty-seven times. The latest attempt to amend the Constitution has been the Equal Rights Amendment, which has failed to obtain ratification by the necessary three-quarters margin in states' legislatures.

The U.S. Constitution serves as an important source of law in the areas of governmental power. It empowers states and the federal government to pass and enforce laws that regulate people's interactions with one another and with their government, while it sets limits on government's ability to legislate in certain areas.

Under our Constitution, the federal government is one of limited powers. Congress has the power to legislate only in areas that it has been specifically granted the power to regulate by the U.S. Constitution. The powers of Congress are enumerated in Article I, Section 8, and include the power to:

- collect taxes and import duties;
- borrow money;
- regulate commerce with foreign nations, among the states and with American Indian tribes;
- establish rules for naturalization and bankruptcy;
- coin money, regulate its value and fix a standard of weights and measures;
- punish counterfeiting;
- establish post offices and post roads;
- issue patents and copyrights;
- set up federal courts inferior to the U.S. Supreme Court;
- define and punish crimes on the high seas and crimes against the United States;
- declare war, grant *letters of marque and reprisal* (allowing the seizure of property belonging to other nations under extreme circumstances, such as the seizure of outlaw nations' assets in the United States or the seizure of foreign nationals' property on the high seas when other remedies are unavailable to satisfy claims against such persons or nations by the United States) and make rules regarding the seizure of property under letters of marque and reprisal;
- raise and support armies;
- create a navy;
- regulate the armed forces; and
- exercise control over the territory encompassing the seat of government (e.g., Washington, D.C.).

Although the enumerated powers of Congress may seem impressive at first glance, they are, in fact, very limited. There is, for example, no general police power specifically given to Congress by the Constitution, nor is there a general power to legislate for the common good. Nowhere in these enumerated powers does Congress have the right to enact a national health-care plan, or a social security plan, or a civil rights act. Because the federal government is one of limited powers, it can legislate in an area only if it can show a constitutional grant of power to do so. Where, then, does Congress find the power to pass social legislation? The answer lies in a very broad interpretation of the commerce clause by the U.S. Supreme Court, which has given Congress the power to regulate nearly any area that has a potential impact on interstate commerce. All social legislation can trace its roots to the commerce clause. If Congress can make an argument that an area it wishes to regulate has the potential to affect interstate commerce, then it can pass legislation to regulate the area; as an example, it can be shown that employees without health insurance can have a negative impact on interstate commerce, since ill health can result in absenteeism from work, resulting in lost productivity to business and a potential decrease in interstate commerce. Thus, Congress can implement a comprehensive plan for national health care under the theory that it will keep commerce flowing smoothly. Such reasoning may seem a bit forced, but it forms the constitutional basis of all social legislation.

Under the Constitution, states are free to legislate any area not specifically reserved to the federal government. Thus, states can adopt any laws they wish within their borders, as long as they do not conflict with a duly enacted federal law or transgress upon a constitutionally protected right.

While the Constitution gives broad regulatory powers to states and the federal government, it also serves to preserve the rights of the individual. The most significant body of constitutional law concerns itself with the prohibitions on governmental powers provided in the Constitution—in particular, the guarantees provided to individuals by the Bill of Rights (the first ten amendments to the U.S. Constitution), the Fourteenth Amendment and the U.S. Supreme Court's interpretation of the broad language in which they are framed. Much of the constitutional law that flows from the U.S. Supreme Court has centered upon the high court's interpretation of several key amendments, including:

- the First Amendment's guarantees of freedom of speech, religion and assembly, as well as the prohibition on the establishment of a national religion;
- the Fourth Amendment's protection against unreasonable searches and seizures and the requirement of probable cause before a search or arrest warrant is issued;
- the Fifth Amendment's requirement of grand-jury indictment for capital crimes and most felonies; protection against double jeopardy; privilege against self-incrimination; guarantees of due process before any deprivation of life, liberty or property; and guarantee of just compensation for any property taken for public use;
- the Sixth Amendment's guarantee of a speedy public trial by jury for criminal offenses; the rights of accused persons to be informed of the charges against them

and to confront their accusers; the rights of accused persons to be represented by counsel and to subpoena witnesses;

- the Seventh Amendment's guarantee of jury trials in most civil cases;
- the Eighth Amendment's prohibitions on excessive bail, excessive fines and cruel and unusual treatment;
- the Ninth Amendment's guarantee that rights not specifically granted by the Constitution are not by their mere omission abridged but rather retained by the people; and
- the Fourteenth Amendment's prohibition against abridging the privileges and immunities of any citizen of the United States, and its prohibition on states depriving any citizen of life, liberty or property without due process of law.

## STATUTORY LAW

Statutes enacted by federal, state and local legislative bodies make up another important source of law. At the federal level, Congress can legislate over a broad range of areas, as we've already seen, by relying on its power to regulate interstate commerce as well as through the exercise of its constitutionally granted powers. Whenever Congress legislates within its area of constitutionally granted power, the resulting legislation has the force of law. The Internal Revenue Code, the Americans with Disabilities Act and the 1964 Civil Rights Act are examples of statutory law enacted by Congress. The same is true of treaties that are negotiated by the president and ratified by the Senate, such as the North American Free Trade Agreement.

At the state level, each state has its own legislature that is usually patterned after Congress. These legislatures enact state laws in a wide range of areas, including civil and criminal law and procedure, business regulation and, of course, taxation. The power of state legislatures to regulate both business and private conduct is far greater than that of the state, since most states reserve to themselves in their state constitutions broad powers to legislate in all areas touching on the welfare of their citizens. In general, states have the right to regulate all areas of private or public life as long as they do not infringe on any right protected by the U.S. Constitution. In general, state and local legislation that does not infringe on a constitutionally protected right is valid as long as it can pass the relatively flexible *rational relationship test*, which simply means that any state law that is rationally related to the preservation of a valid societal interest is valid. This litmus test of constitutionality is a simple one to pass, since nearly any law can be rationally justified as serving some valid purpose. The test, however, is somewhat more stringent when a vital interest or suspect classification is involved; in such instances, the state must pass a *strict scrutiny test* of constitutionality, wherein the courts weigh the state's interest against the infringement of protected rights in determining the validity of a statute. For purposes of the strict scrutiny test, a vital interest can be defined as any constitutionally protected right, such as the rights enumerated under the Bill of Rights. A suspect classification would include a law that makes distinctions based on race, sex, color, religion or national origin. The following examples should illustrate:

- *The legislature of the state of Moot enacts a statute that requires all citizens to cover their mouths when they sneeze and subjects violators of the statute to a $50 fine. Since sneezing with one's mouth uncovered is not a constitutionally protected right, the courts would defer to the state's legislature and enforce the statute as long as there is a rational basis for the legislation. Since preventing the spread of germs is a rational basis for the statute, the statute is probably valid.*

- *The state of Moot passes a statute that prohibits the use of the word God in public and subjects violators to a $50 fine. This statute would be subject to the strict scrutiny test because it deals with two constitutionally protected rights: free speech and religious expression. It is unlikely that the state would be able to show a compelling enough reason for adopting the statute despite its infringement on constitutionally protected rights, and the statute would almost certainly be struck down as unconstitutional.*

Finally, city councils and various town boards and planning commissions also have the power to legislate in areas allowed them by their local charters. These local ordinances also carry the weight of law and form a part of the state's statutory law.

With all of these legislative bodies producing volumes of new statutory law every year, one might well think that the difference between civil law and common law has become blurred. But in reality, it has not. The distinguishing characteristic of common law is the broad power to interpret and invalidate statutes that is reserved to the courts. No matter how clear the language of a statute or how plain its import, it is generally impossible in a common-law jurisdiction to interpret a statute, or even a constitution, at face value. Ultimately, the validity of any statute is determined by the courts, as is its meaning. A case in point is the Second Amendment to the U.S. Constitution, which reads: "A well-regulated militia being necessary to the security of a free state, the right of the people to keep and bear arms shall not be infringed." Any reasonable interpretation of that amendment, particularly when viewed from the inherent distrust of government of its revolutionary framers, would lead one to believe that the U.S. Constitution guarantees the right of citizens to own and carry guns. Nevertheless, the amendment has been interpreted to mean *only* that individual states can raise their own militias (e.g., national guards) if they so choose. Regardless of the wisdom of such an interpretation, one message is clear: any statute, including the U.S. Constitution, means only what the courts ultimately decide it means.

## ADMINISTRATIVE LAW

The increase of government regulation of business in the twentieth century, in addition to the increasingly expansive social engineering role of the federal and state governments during the same time period, has given birth to what is often referred to as the fourth branch of government—the administrative agency system. Administrative agencies are empowered either by the executive or legislative branches of the state and federal governments to assist them in carrying out necessary governmental functions that they lack either the time or expertise to carry out themselves. When Congress decided to regulate nuclear energy, for example, it created the Nuclear Regulatory Commission and empowered it with the ability to both create and enforce rules for the safe civil use of nuclear energy. Although Congress could have created and enforced these rules itself, individual members of Congress have neither the necessary expertise nor the time to engage in such micromanagement of the regulatory environment. The same holds true for other agencies whose primary purpose is the regulation of business and industry, including the Federal Aviation Administration, the Securities and Exchange Commission, the National Labor Relations Board, the Equal Employment Opportunity Commission and the Federal Communications Commission. At the state level, state legislatures and governors can also set up administrative agencies to help them regulate business and carry out other important governmental functions. Taken together, the rules that all federal and state agencies promulgate have the force of law and form the most important component of administrative law. Like statutes, however, most administrative rules and many administrative agency decisions are subject to *judicial review*, the process whereby statutes, administrative rules and administrative agency decisions are reviewed by courts when challenged. (See Chapter 5 for a full discussion of administrative agencies.)

Taken together, federal and state court decisions, federal and state constitutions, federal and state statutes and federal and state administrative agency rules and decisions all represent primary sources of law. To these must be added secondary sources of law, such as legal encyclopedias, model acts, compiled restatements of law, legal treatises, law review articles and articles published in other scholarly journals, as well as textbooks on the law—all of which offer persuasive but nonbinding authority and insight on the law for lawyers and judges alike. In order to know what the law is in any given state, then, one must know the legal precedent represented in the state's case law, as well as the state's constitutional, statutory and administrative law and its interpretation by the courts. The same holds true for federal law. It should come as no surprise that the United States has more lawyers per capita and more litigation than any other nation on earth; it is an inevitable result, given the complexities and uncertainties inherent in one of the most complex legal systems any country has ever known. Keep this in mind when you hear absurd comparisons that stress the numbers of lawyers or lawsuits in, say, Japan or France as opposed to the United States, when both foreign countries employ a unified civil-law system. Even comparisons to Great Britain are unfair, since the United Kingdom does not need to contend with more than fifty-one different major court systems, each with its own laws.

# QUESTIONS . . . . . . . . . . . . . . . . . . . . . . . . . . . . . . .

   1. Define the term *law*.
   2. What are some potential problems that conflicting state laws pose for businesses?
   3. "A business with a good legal department does not need employees to be familiar with basic legal principles." Do you agree or disagree with this statement? Why?

4. What are the main sources of law in our common-law system?

5. What is the basic difference between common law and civil law?

## H Y P O T H E T I C A L    C A S E S

1. The legislature of the state of Moot enacts a statute that reads as follows: "In recognition of the spiritual importance of the Sabbath, citizens of the state of Moot are henceforth forbidden to engage upon any work-related activity on Sundays. Any citizen who violates this statute will be subject to a fine not to exceed $500 and/or imprisonment for up to thirty days in the county jail."
   a. If this statute is challenged, will the court use the strict scrutiny or the rational relationship test when reviewing the statute's constitutionality? Explain.
   b. Should the statute be enforced or struck down as unconstitutional? Explain.

2. Your local state legislature enacts the following statute. "Because of the inherent dangers represented to public health by the smoking of cigarettes, such activity will henceforth be prohibited to everyone under the age of thirty-five."
   a. If this statute is challenged, will the court use the strict scrutiny or the rational relationship test when reviewing the statute's constitutionality? Explain.
   b. Should the statute be enforced or struck down as unconstitutional? Explain.

3. Congress passes a bill prohibiting discrimination in hiring, promotion or housing based on a person's sexual preference. The bill is challenged in court on the basis that Congress lacks the power to pass such a bill under the U.S. Constitution.
   a. Does Congress have the power to pass and enforce such a statute? Explain.
   b. Would such a bill be constitutional? Explain.

4. Congress passes a bill that restricts the sale of music that promotes or condones violence to persons under the age of twenty-one. The statute is challenged in court and is ultimately struck down by the U.S. Supreme Court as an unconstitutional infringement of First Amendment free speech rights. What, if anything, can Congress do if it is unhappy with the high court's decision?

CHAPTER

# THE COURT SYSTEM

The U.S. court system is made up of two distinct federal and state systems. Ours is a system of fifty-one courts sharing the power and responsibility for the administration of justice. Fortunately, there are more similarities than differences between the federal system and that of each of the fifty sovereign states. This is so because most state court systems are patterned after the federal model that we will explore momentarily. But first, it is important to grasp some basic principles relating to the way our court systems operate.

## JURISDICTION · · · · · · · · · · · · · · · · · · · · · · · · · · · · · · · · · · · · · · · · · · ·

*Jurisdiction* can be defined as a court's power to hear and decide (or *adjudicate*) a case. The types of jurisdiction with which we must be familiar include personal jurisdiction, subject matter jurisdiction, original jurisdiction and appellate jurisdiction.

### PERSONAL AND SUBJECT MATTER JURISDICTION

*Personal jurisdiction* (also referred to as *in personam* jurisdiction) is the power of a court to decide a case between the specific litigants involved. *Subject matter jurisdiction* (also referred to as *in rem* jurisdiction) is the power of a court to adjudicate the type of case, or subject matter, before it. To put it another way, personal jurisdiction relates to a court's ability to decide a case between the litigants involved, while subject matter jurisdiction relates to a court's power to hear the type of case brought before it.

A court must have both personal jurisdiction over all litigants and subject matter jurisdiction over the type of matter in controversy before it can agree to hear and decide a case. As an example, a state's traffic court can hear all cases relating to traffic violations (its subject matter jurisdiction) allegedly committed by anyone in that state (over whom it has personal jurisdiction). It cannot, however, hear a divorce case between citizens of that state, nor can it hear cases about traffic violations allegedly committed in other states.

The subject matter jurisdiction of a court depends upon what power was reserved to it in the statute that created it. For the federal courts, the limits on subject matter and personal jurisdiction can be found in the U.S. Constitution under Article III, Section 2. The federal courts are limited to hearing cases involving the following criteria:

- cases involving the U.S. Constitution, federal laws or federal treaties;
- cases involving ambassadors, other public ministers and consuls;
- cases involving admiralty and maritime law;
- cases in which the United States is a party;
- cases between two or more states, between a state and the citizens of another state or between citizens of different states (when the amount in controversy exceeds $50,000 under Title 28 of the U.S. Code); and
- cases between citizens of the same state involving lands under grants by different states and cases between states or the citizens of states and foreign countries or foreign citizens.

For the state courts, their jurisdiction is set by the state constitution or other state statute creating the court system. Generally speaking, access to the state courts is greater than that of the federal courts. This is because states have the power to adjudicate any and all cases and controversies arising out of a state's laws and federal laws for its citizens and others who have sufficient contacts with the state. Most states impose subject matter jurisdiction limits on their court systems for the sake of expediency, setting up specialized courts with limited subject matter jurisdiction to handle routine matters. (See Figure 2.3.)

Generally speaking, state courts' personal jurisdiction extends only to persons who have *substantial contacts* with the state. Although state laws vary somewhat as to what constitutes a substantial contact with the state, in general, litigants who meet any one of the following criteria are deemed to have sufficient contact with a state so as to allow its courts to adjudicate matters in which they are a party:

- being present in the state when they are served with notice that they are being sued;
- living in the state;
- doing business in the state (e.g., working or conducting business in the state on a regular basis);
- committing a crime or tort in the state;
- owning real or personal property in the state (but if property ownership is the only contact with the state, then courts in the state may only issue judgments against the property owner up to the value of the property itself). When personal jurisdiction is based on property ownership in the state, it is referred to as *quasi in rem* jurisdiction; or

- voluntarily agreeing to allow the state to exert personal jurisdiction by personally appearing before the court as a *plaintiff* (one who institutes a lawsuit) or *defendant* (one who defends oneself against a lawsuit initiated by another).

Most states have enacted *long-arm statutes* that allow them to extend personal jurisdiction to people who do not meet any of the noted jurisdictional criteria. Typically, states' long-arm statutes allow states to exert personal jurisdiction over anyone who drives in the state or commits any act outside of the state that results in foreseeable injury to a person in the state. Under a state's long-arm statute, for example, a person who drives from Rhode Island to Florida can be forced to appear and defend himself in lawsuits brought by citizens of any East Coast state he drove through on the way for accidents or traffic violations alleged to have been committed by him while driving through those states, even if he has absolutely no other contact with those states. Likewise, a citizen of Nevada who mails a letter bomb to a citizen of California can be sued in California for any civil or criminal damages stemming from that act, even if she has no other contacts with that state.

Most types of cases that can be brought in federal court can also be brought in state court. With few exceptions, such as cases relating to bankruptcy which can be brought only in the appropriate federal court, state courts are free to hear cases relating to federal laws and the U.S. Constitution. Ultimately, the final word on the interpretation of all federal law, however, rests with the U.S. Supreme Court, which can hear appeals relating to cases involving federal law or the U.S. Constitution from any lower federal court or from any state's highest court.

### ORIGINAL AND APPELLATE JURISDICTION

State and federal courts can be classified into two basic types: those that can hear and adjudicate disputes for the first time and those that can hear cases only on appeal. Courts with the power to hear cases for the first time have *original jurisdiction*, while courts that can hear cases only on appeal have *appellate jurisdiction*. The U.S. Supreme Court is one of the few courts that has both original and appellate jurisdiction in certain cases. Under Article III, Section 2 of the U.S. Constitution, the U.S. Supreme Court is given original jurisdiction "[i]n all Cases affecting Ambassadors, other public Ministers and Consuls, and those in which a State shall be Party." Nevertheless, the highest court very seldom exercises its original jurisdiction, and the limited types of cases over which it has original jurisdiction are generally tried in the lower federal courts.

## THE FEDERAL COURT SYSTEM . . . . . . . . . . . . . . . . . . . . . . . . . .

The federal courts are organized into a system of four types of courts that includes specialized courts with limited original jurisdiction, courts of general original jurisdiction, intermediate appellate courts and the U.S. Supreme Court—the highest federal appeals court (see Figure 2.1). The federal courts of general original jurisdiction and the intermediate appellate courts are divided into thirteen federal circuits. These include eleven circuits, each of which contains numerous states and/or dependencies, as

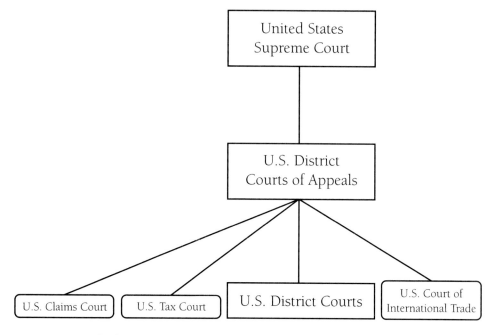

**FIGURE 2.1** The federal court system

well as the federal circuit and the District of Columbia circuit. (See Figure 2.2 for the current makeup of the federal districts.)

## SPECIALIZED COURTS

There are a number of federal courts with limited original jurisdiction. These include the U.S. Tax Court (which hears cases relating to federal income tax law), the U.S. Claims Court (in which lawsuits against the federal government must be filed) and the U.S. Court of International Trade (which adjudicates matters relating to foreign commerce). Appeals from these courts may generally be taken to the federal district court of appeals that has personal jurisdiction over the litigants.

## U.S. DISTRICT COURTS

The district courts are the federal courts of original general jurisdiction. These are the federal trial courts that have the power to adjudicate civil and criminal matters relating to federal law, subject to the limits of Article III, Section 1, on the federal courts discussed previously. As is true of all trial courts, the purpose of the district courts is to provide a forum for the resolution of civil and criminal disputes. Parties present their cases and the trier of fact (usually a jury, unless the parties agree to waive a jury trial, in which case the judge acts as trier of fact) decides whether the plaintiff or the defendant should prevail.

**First Circuit**
- Maine
- Massachusetts
- New Hampshire
- Rhode Island
- Puerto Rico

**Second Circuit**
- Connecticut
- New York
- Vermont

**Third Circuit**
- Delaware
- New Jersey
- Pennsylvania
- Virgin Islands

**Fourth Circuit**
- Maryland
- North Carolina
- South Carolina
- Virginia
- West Virginia

**Fifth Circuit**
- Louisiana
- Mississippi
- Texas

**Sixth Circuit**
- Kentucky
- Michigan
- Ohio
- Tennessee

**Seventh Circuit**
- Illinois
- Indiana
- Wisconsin

**Eighth Circuit**
- Arkansas
- Louisiana
- Minnesota
- Missouri
- Nebraska
- North Dakota
- South Dakota

**Ninth Circuit**
- Alaska
- Arizona
- California
- Hawaii
- Idaho
- Montana
- Nevada
- Oregon
- Washington
- Guam
- N. Mariana Is.

**Tenth Circuit**
- Colorado
- Kansas
- New Mexico
- Oklahoma
- Utah
- Wyoming

**Eleventh Circuit**
- Alabama
- Florida
- Georgia

**Federal Circuit**

**District of Columbia**

FIGURE 2.2   The thirteen circuits that make up the federal court system

## U.S. DISTRICT COURTS OF APPEAL

The district courts of appeals are the federal intermediate appeals courts. These courts hear appeals from a number of sources, including specialized federal courts, federal agencies and the district courts. As is the case for all appellate courts, these courts are concerned only with issues of law, not of fact. The losing party in a civil or criminal trial in a federal court of original jurisdiction can appeal to a district court of appeals only if he or she can show that an error was made in the trial court judge's application of the law. Questions of fact are not reviewable on appeal; only material errors in the application of the law by a trial court are grounds for reversing the judgment of that court. Examples of errors in the application of law that can lead to an appeal would include a judge giving improper instructions to a jury or incorrectly ruling on what evidence could be introduced at trial. Contrary to popular opinion, most lower court decisions are not appealable; a plaintiff or defendant can never appeal simply because he or she is unhappy with the trial's outcome. With very few exceptions (such as capital convictions that may carry an automatic appeal), the district courts of appeals decide for themselves whether to grant petitions for appeal. When a district court of appeals, in exercising its discretion, believes there is sufficient evidence of a possible reversible error having been committed in the lower trial court, it can grant the petitioner's request to hear oral arguments as to the error or errors allegedly committed by the lower court. Federal district courts are composed of three judges who are appointed by the president and confirmed by the Senate. Federal judgeships are lifetime appointments; federal judges serve until retirement, death or impeachment based on a conviction of treason, bribery or other high crimes and misdemeanors. (U.S. Constitution, Article II, Section 4)

## UNITED STATES SUPREME COURT

This country's highest court, the U.S. Supreme Court, can hear appeals from all district courts of appeals and all states' highest courts (as long as a question of federal law or the U.S. Constitution is involved). As is the case with the district courts of appeals, the U.S. Supreme Court decides for itself whether or not to hear cases on appeal. The highest court receives more than five thousand appeals each year, and grants approximately three hundred *writs of certiorari*—demands to lower courts at the state or federal levels to forward to it all transcripts of trials it wishes to review. The U.S. Supreme Court is made up of nine justices who, like all federal judges, are appointed by the president and serve for life terms.

# THE STATE COURT SYSTEM · · · · · · · · · · · · · · · · · · · · · · · · · · · ·

Although there are significant differences in the court systems of the fifty states, most states' systems are patterned on the federal court system and include a system of specialized courts of limited original jurisdiction, courts of general original jurisdiction, intermediate appeals courts and the highest appellate court in the state (usually called the state supreme court). (See Figure 2.3.)

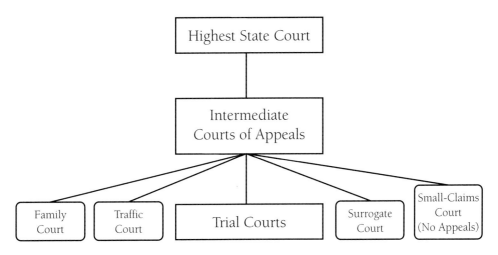

**FIGURE 2.3**    Typical state court system

## SPECIALIZED COURTS

Most state court systems include some or all of the following courts of limited original jurisdiction:

- Small-claims court: These courts have broad jurisdiction to try nearly any civil case that does not exceed a set dollar amount. The typical maximum amount that a plaintiff can sue for in a small-claims court varies from state to state, but a $5,000 limit is common. The benefit of these courts is that they provide an expeditious and inexpensive means for private individuals and businesses to litigate minor claims in a relatively informal setting in which attorneys are usually not needed and often not allowed to represent litigants. These courts help to channel away some litigation from the state's general trial courts, which are usually overburdened. They provide an important forum for dispute resolution for people who would not otherwise be able to avail themselves of the courts for reasons of time or expense. Cases can be heard by a small-claims judge in weeks, contrasted to the years it takes to litigate civil cases in most states' trial courts; the cost to litigants who represent themselves is a modest filing fee (usually under $5), contrasted with the many thousands of dollars it takes to litigate a trial in the traditional trial courts. The disadvantage of these courts is that there is often no appeal allowed from them.
- Traffic court: Many larger cities provide specialized courts to handle the large volume of litigation that arises out of traffic violations each year. Where these courts are available, they usually share subject matter jurisdiction with the state's general trial courts. Serious criminal traffic-related offenses, such as driving while intoxicated, vehicular manslaughter or reckless endangerment and similar offenses

that can result in incarceration of more than one year are typically not handled by traffic court, but rather by the state's general trial courts.

- Justice-of-the-peace court: Minor offenses that subject the accused to fines or short prison terms are often handled by these tribunals. In many jurisdictions, these tribunals serve as the criminal analog to the small-claims court in handling minor matters that would otherwise exacerbate the overcrowded calendars of states' general trial courts.
- Surrogate court: These courts handle matters relating to trusts and estates.
- Family court: The subject matter jurisdiction of these courts relates to matters pertaining to marriage and family life. Divorce, child custody, separation agreements and (often, but not always) criminal offenses committed by minors are all subject matters within this court's jurisdiction. In many states, family court jurisdiction is not exclusive; in such states, cases can be brought either before family court or in the state's court of general original jurisdiction (the state's trial court).

## GENERAL TRIAL COURTS

The trial courts are a state's courts of general original jurisdiction. Most civil or criminal cases can be adjudicated in these tribunals, which have very broad subject matter jurisdiction. In many states, the trial courts share jurisdiction with specialized courts of limited jurisdiction, so that it may be possible for a plaintiff to sue a defendant for redress of a civil wrong in more than one court. For example, a person who wishes to bring a lawsuit for $5,000 in property damages arising out of an automobile accident can sue in the state's small-claims court or in the state's general trial court. Likewise, a divorce action can often be brought either at a state's family court or the state's general trial court. The expense and time needed to gain access to specific courts, as well as important procedural differences in practicing before different courts, are crucial considerations weighed by attorneys when deciding on the best tribunal in which to bring a specific client's lawsuit—especially in cases when a variety of federal and state courts may have appropriate jurisdiction to adjudicate a dispute.

## INTERMEDIATE COURTS OF APPEAL

Most state court systems include an intermediate court of appeals. Typically, intermediate appeals courts are composed of three justices, even though this number can vary from state to state. These courts entertain appeals from losing parties in the state's trial courts who allege that the trial court judge has made one or more significant errors in the application of the law at trial. Common errors by lower court judges which form the basis of successful appeals include misinterpretation of state statutes, improper jury instructions, erroneous rulings on the types of evidence allowed to be presented by parties at trial, improper rulings on attorneys' motions and objections throughout the trial and any other misapplication of substantive or procedural law at trial that, in the appellate court's judgment, materially impaired the jury's ability to render a valid verdict.

If the court feels that there is sufficient evidence to believe that a *reversible error* (a mistake by the lower court judge that is serious enough to warrant overruling his or her decision and ordering a new trial) has occurred, it agrees to listen to oral arguments by the *appellant* (the losing party at trial who now seeks to overturn the lower court's decision) and the *respondent* (the winning party at trial who seeks to defend the lower court's application of the law).

### HIGHEST STATE COURT

Every state has a state court of final appeal, usually referred to as the *state supreme court*. This court is analogous to the U.S. Supreme Court and has the final word on the application of state law and the interpretation of state statutes. Losing parties at the intermediate appeals court level can seek to have the state's highest court review the case. In cases where that court disagrees with the lower appellate court's interpretation of the law, it can reverse that court's judgment and *remand* (order back to the trial court) the case for a new trial. The number of justices that sit on a state's highest court varies, but five or seven is common.

For most cases, there is no further appeal possible after the state's highest court has either ruled on it or refused to hear an appeal. But if the matter in controversy relates to federal law or the U.S. Constitution, then appeal is possible even from the highest state courts to the U.S. Supreme Court.

## QUESTIONS . . . . . . . . . . . . . . . . . . . . . . . . . . . . . . . . . . . . . . . .

1. Define the term *jurisdiction* and briefly discuss the kinds of jurisdiction available.
2. What kinds of cases may a federal court adjudicate?
3. What is a long-arm statute?
4. What types of jurisdiction may the U.S. Supreme Court exercise?
5. Name at least three state and three federal courts of limited original jurisdiction (also known as specialized courts).
6. What are the federal courts of general original jurisdiction called?
7. What is the highest court in each state usually called?

## H Y P O T H E T I C A L    C A S E S

1. John, a resident of New York who has no significant ties to Pennsylvania, gets into an automobile accident in Pennsylvania with Jane, a resident of Pennsylvania, and Jenine, a resident of New Jersey also traveling in Pennsylvania.
   a. In which states may Jane sue John?
   b. In which states can Jenine, the New Jersey resident, sue John?
   c. If Jane, the Pennsylvania resident, wants to sue Jenine, the New Jersey resident, in which states may she do so?

d. Assume that all three parties decide to sue each other for $100,000 in alleged personal injury and property damage. May this lawsuit be brought in federal court? Would your answer be the same if each party were suing for $10,000 in property damage?

2. Wanda, a resident of New York City, wants to purchase a handgun for personal protection. After doing some research on the subject, she comes to the conclusion that it is nearly impossible for her to obtain a gun permit legally due to New York City's tough gun laws. She has also read the U.S. Constitution, and she believes that New York City's laws are unconstitutional since they infringe on her right to keep and bear arms guaranteed by the Second Amendment. Certain of her rights, she purchases a handgun for personal protection from her local illegal gun dealer for $300. The next day, she is arrested when an undercover police officer sees her fending off a mugger with her illegally obtained gun. She is arrested and booked on a charge of illegal gun possession—which carries a minimum one-year mandatory jail sentence upon conviction in New York City. Her defense is the unconstitutionality of the law under which she was arrested. What result?

a. Assume that she is tried and convicted in State Supreme Court—New York's oddly named trial court of general original jurisdiction. Can she appeal? Explain.

b. Assume for the moment that she can appeal. To what court should she appeal?

c. Assume that she can and does appeal. What court in the **state** will have the final say on interpreting the U.S. Constitution?

d. Assume, for the sake of argument, that she exhausts her appeals to the state courts and none agree to hear her case, or, hearing her case, rule against her. Is there anything further she can do?

e. Assume that Wanda loses all her appeals and serves her one-year sentence for illegal gun possession. If she is convinced that the law is unfair and wants to fight it, is there any way she can do so?

3. Veronica suffers minor burns while dining at Richard's restaurant when a waiter trips and drops a plate of hot soup on her dress. Richard agrees to pay for the dry cleaning of the dress, but refuses to pay for pain and suffering that Veronica alleges she suffered as a result of the incident. After several discussions, Richard won't budge from his position and Veronica decides to sue. Her uncle is a justice in the intermediate appeals court in her state, so she would like to institute her lawsuit in that court, trusting her uncle to issue a fair verdict.

a. May she do so? Explain.

b. Assume that she cannot bring the lawsuit in her uncle's court. Which courts in her state have the appropriate jurisdiction to hear the case?

c. Under the circumstances, which court do you believe best suited to hear the case if she decides to sue for $2,500 in damages?

# CHAPTER

# 3

# ETHICS, PUBLIC POLICY AND THE REGULATORY ENVIRONMENT

## ETHICS . . . . . . . . . . . . . . . . . . . . . . . . . . . . . . . . . . . . .

*Ethics* is the branch of philosophy that concerns itself with the study of morality. Ethical inquiry centers around studying concepts such as good and evil, or right and wrong, in an attempt to ascertain whether they have any meaning that can be discovered through philosophical inquiry. Thousands of years of philosophical inquiry into the field of ethics have produced numerous conflicting theories by noted classical and contemporary philosophers. Not surprisingly, however, no general agreement has emerged as to which theory is most valid. While this may not be surprising, it is troubling, since law is closely tied to the fragile, ephemeral principles that are at the heart of ethics. By definition, law concerns itself with issues of right and wrong, good and evil and the administration of justice. Those who help shape the law need valid ethical reference points in order to steer the law in the direction of the common good. Legislators, judges, presidents, governors and regular citizens who help to shape the law through their official capacity or through the exercise of the right to vote may not consciously engage in the study of ethics in shaping their views on what constitutes justice or how best to promote the common good. Nevertheless, most of us act in accordance with certain principles that we may commonly think of as "values." Whether we acknowledge it or not, the guiding principles by which we steer our lives and which form the basis for our basic ideas about right and wrong are an expression of our ethical philosophy. The names of the ethical systems we adhere to, and the notable philosophers who espouse them, are not as important as the views themselves, for these shape our government and mold our laws. Regardless of what ethical philosophy or values a government and its laws are based on, it is healthy to examine the validity of those ethical views and values from time to time. Ethics forms the cornerstone of every society, its system of government and its laws. Any society whose basic values cannot stand up to objective examination and free debate rests on precarious ground.

# ETHICAL PHILOSOPHIES . . . . . . . . . . . . . . . . . . . . . . . . . . . . .

The quest to discover ethical truths has led Western philosophers on some very different paths throughout the past 2,500 years. Because law inevitably reflects a society's ethical views, even a brief glimpse at some of the leading theories of ethics can be very useful in understanding the development of law and the legal philosophies upon which differing legal systems rest.

## ETHICAL ABSOLUTISM

*Ethical absolutism* is an ethical philosophy with many diverse branches all tied in to the central idea that there are certain universal standards by which to measure morality. Under this philosophy, concepts such as good and evil, right and wrong and justice have a separate existence that can be discovered and understood by human beings through philosophical inquiry and introspection. Proponents of this broad branch of ethics represent a very wide variety of schools of thought that often include diametrically opposed world views and systems of ethics. Plato (428 BC–347 BC), St. Thomas Aquinas (1224–1274) and Karl Marx (1818–1883) all believed in ethical absolutism, despite the fact that the overall philosophies and world views of each man were quite different.

## RELIGIOUS FUNDAMENTALISM

Like ethical absolutism, *religious fundamentalism* as a theory of ethics relies on the existence of certain immutable truths. Unlike ethical absolutism, however, which requires that these values be discovered through philosophical inquiry and, for Plato and St. Thomas Aquinas, at least, through introspection, ethical norms under religious fundamentalism can be found by studying the lives and writings of prophets or by consulting holy scriptures. Under this philosophy, living a moral life depends upon strict adherence to religious principles and values. Proponents of religious fundamentalism include not only well known classical figures such as John Calvin (1509–1564) and Richard Baxter (1615–1691), but the myriad ultraconservative religious sects commonly found in the major religions in the United States and throughout the world.

## UTILITARIANISM

*Utilitarianism* has as its ethical base the assignment of value to actions based upon their outcome. Under utilitarianism, the ultimate good is defined as actions intended to bring about the greatest happiness (or greatest good) for the greatest number. Thus, moral action for a utilitarian requires the constant evaluation of actions based upon their intended result. Actions that bring about the greatest good to the greatest number are ethical, or good, while actions that fall short of that goal are unethical, or wrong. To put it another way, utilitarianism does not recognize an intrinsic value to actions, but rather assigns a positive or negative moral judgment to actions only in view of their result. The most notable proponents of this philosophy were the British philosophers Jeremy Bentham (1748–1832) and John Stuart Mill (1806–1873).

## ETHICAL RELATIVISM

Like utilitarianism, *ethical relativism* denies the existence of absolute moral values, and holds that moral judgments cannot be made in a vacuum. Unlike utilitarianism, however, the yardstick by which to measure the morality of an act is not the common good, but rather the circumstances surrounding the person committing an act at the time that an act is committed. It is a precept of this philosophy that a person's actions cannot be judged other than by placing oneself in the same situation that the person faced in committing the act in question; stealing to feed one's hungry child, for example, is not necessarily wrong. On a societal level, ethical relativism acknowledges that there are differences between cultures and that what is considered wrong or even hateful in one culture may be acceptable in another, depending on its particular circumstances. Human sacrifice, cannibalism, infanticide and ethnic cleansing are all at least arguably justifiable for some cultures. Notable proponents of relativistic theories include W. G. Sumner (1849–1910) in the U.S. and E. A. Westermarck (1862–1939) in the United Kingdom.

## DEONTOLOGY

*Deontology* is a duty-based ethical theory whose principal proponent was the German philosopher Immanuel Kant (1724–1804). According to Kant, an act's morality is dependent upon the actor's motive, and the only unconditionally good motive is duty. Therefore, for an act to be moral or good, it must be undertaken out of a sense of duty. Kant also held that the concept of *duty* finds its expression in *categorical imperatives*, a set of rules of behavior derived from practical reason and tested through a filter of universal application. A basic categorical imperative arrived at through practical reasoning, such as "You should not steal," is valid if you can justify the whole world living up to the rule. In other words, moral behavior can be defined as acting in accordance with rules that you would be willing to impose on the whole world as a valid code of conduct. A person acts morally whenever he or she follows a categorical imperative out of a sense of duty. Merely engaging in right action of itself is not moral conduct; refraining from stealing because one feels the obligation not to steal is moral conduct; but refraining from stealing out of fear of getting caught would not rise to the level of moral conduct.

## ETHICS AND PUBLIC POLICY · · · · · · · · · · · · · · · · · · · · · · · · · · · · ·

The political implications that flow from even a brief overview of differing ethical systems should not be ignored. Whether by design or by default, the ethical values held by political leaders and lawmakers invariably become a part of the political system. We need not look far to see examples of the influence of ethical systems on public policy and on the politics of nations. The influence of religious fundamentalism can readily be seen today in a number of countries, particularly in the Middle East, where militant religious fundamentalists are engaged in armed struggles to overthrow what they perceive to be immoral secular governments that are instilling in their people false moral values. If one believes that the only true source of morality is religion, it is logical to believe that the best form of moral government is a *theocracy*, a government based upon religious principles. Ethical absolutism is also readily observable in its secular form in past and present nonreligious totalitarian regimes. All totalitarian regimes, be they Marxist, Communist or Fascist, are based upon principles of ethical absolutism. Taken to their logical conclusion, absolutist ideals can be used to justify totalitarianism; if there are certain knowable, immutable truths that are valid for all time, then the only moral form of government, the argument goes, is one that educates (or indoctrinates) the people to recognize those truths and ensures that they conform to the moral conduct that those truths dictate.

If totalitarian regimes are based on ethical absolutism or religious fundamentalism, it is clear that democratic governments lean toward nonfundamentalist ethical principles. The assumption that a variety of plausible views exist on even essential ethical principles is central to a democratic form of government. The principle of majority rule inevitably leads to the adoption of some type of moral relativism as the guiding ethical principle. The very notion that right and wrong are subject to a vote institutionalizes ethical relativism in all democracies; issues such as the death penalty, abortion and pornography, with the strong emotions and endless debate they elicit, illustrate our relativistic ethics. The fact that laws relating to these and other issues are subject to change and do undergo changes slowly over time underscores that societal definitions of ethical conduct change as well. Individuals in democracies are free to reject ethical relativism, and many do. They can also lobby their government for change, arguing for the adoption of their points of view. But a democratic system that completely abandons ethical relativism cannot remain a democracy for long.

It can be argued that the ethical principles of a society are reflected even in the type of legal system it chooses. The civil-law system, with its intricate codes that carefully delineate individual rights and responsibilities in minute detail, its swift administration of justice and limited power of judicial interpretation, tends toward an absolutist ethical philosophy. In effect, governments with such systems demand strict adherence to set codes of behavior and leave little room for deviation from the established norm by their citizens. Common-law systems such as ours, on the other hand, leave the judiciary with wide latitude for interpreting the governmental edicts found in legislative enactments. In addition, a multilayered system of appeals courts is available for further review of court judgments, and determinations of fact are usually left to the interpretation of juries. In short, civil law leaves little room for arguing the validity or meaning of the law, while common law allows great latitude to litigants to do both. This underscores a fundamental difference in the legal philosophies of both systems, which is closely linked to the ethical bases upon which they are built: civil law springs from an absolutist ethical view (we will tell you what the law is and you will obey it without argument), while common law is based more on a relativistic ethical view (we will tell you what the law is, but you can argue both its meaning and its validity and even if you lose, we'll allow you other opportunities to argue your interpretation on appeal).

## PROBLEM AREAS

The obvious problem we face when trying to impose an ethical system is in deciding what system to use. While it can be argued that government should not legislate morality, all governments do so. Criminal law is largely based on prohibiting and punishing antisocial behavior; as such, criminal law inevitably reflects society's ethical standards and attempts to discourage behavior that society deems immoral. Ultimately, questions of ethics come down to personal belief. Depending on the philosophical system applied, nearly any moral point of view is defensible; unfortunately, one person's ethical conduct is frequently another's mortal sin. In a political context, ethical debate often hinges on irreconcilable differences. On the abortion issue, for example, the pro-choice and pro-life groups have philosophical differences that cannot be reconciled. The same is true of people on opposite sides of the perpetual debate on the death penalty, gun control, legalization of drugs, animal research and innumerable other issues. Very often, groups on either side of a political controversy believe themselves to be morally right, and, by definition, believe that people on the opposite side of the issue are morally wrong. The strength of a democracy is in its ability to incorporate differing points of view and to obtain a functional compromise on most issues. But some issues leave no room for compromise, and it is in those arenas that the battle for the minds—and votes—of citizens is often fought. But regardless of what group wins and what opinion manages to weave itself into the fiber of the law, issues of ethics cannot be resolved by majority rule for most people, and spirited debates continue, sometimes escalating into violence and death both in this country and abroad.

## THE REGULATORY ENVIRONMENT OF BUSINESS

One of the areas in which government tries to legislate ethical conduct, and which has been vigorously debated over the years, is the ethical accountability of business. Many people today feel that business has a responsibility to society as a whole to act in a responsible manner and to work for the betterment of society as the price for being allowed to do business and make a profit. Others feel that the sole social responsibility of business is to obey the law and turn a profit for investors. Although the issue is by no means settled, the current trend is to increase the amount of government regulation of business at both the federal and state levels. Primarily through the establishment of administrative agencies (see Chapter 4), the federal and state governments have put in place wide-reaching regulations in an attempt to ensure that business is conducted in a responsible manner. Some of the more notable areas in which the federal government actively regulates business include antitrust, securities, labor and consumer protection laws. Increasingly, legislatures and the courts at both the state and federal levels are also addressing ethical concerns about U.S. companies doing business abroad. Conduct that was once seen as acceptable, such as the bribery of foreign officials in the regular course of business in some foreign countries, now brings criminal penalties. A debate is also currently taking place about the responsibility of American firms selling products in foreign countries that cannot be sold in the United States due to health and safety regulations, but whose sale is not prohibited in foreign countries. This battle is likely to be fought largely in civil courts in the United States and abroad as foreign nationals sue American companies for selling allegedly unsafe products. In the past, such claims have been made with regard to a wide range of products, including baby formula, pharmaceutical products and pesticides.

## QUESTIONS . . . . . . . . . . . . . . . . . . . . . . . . . . . . . . . . . . .

1. Define the term *ethics*.
2. What is the central idea behind ethical absolutism?
3. What defines moral conduct under religious fundamentalism?
4. How does one define ethical conduct under utilitarian principles?
5. "You cannot judge a man until you have walked a mile in his shoes" is a statement that is best linked to which philosophy of ethics?
6. Who was the principal proponent of duty-based (deontological) ethics?
7. What is the basic problem in trying to legislate ethical behavior?

## H Y P O T H E T I C A L     C A S E S

1. XYZ Pharmaceuticals develops a new drug that causes the abortion of female fetuses up to the first trimester of pregnancy and does not affect male fetuses. The drug has no known side effects for women who take it, and seems perfectly safe to use. While awaiting FDA approval of the drug, a process that takes several years, XYZ receives very negative press, and numerous groups call for a boycott of the manufacturer. Because of the negative reaction to the drug by the general public, XYZ decides to scrap plans to market the drug in the United States, but wants to market it abroad in a number of countries where it expects the drug to be well received. There is nothing in U.S. law, or in the laws of the countries where the company intends to market the drug, to prevent its sale. Make an ethical argument either for or against the drug's sale abroad. Justify your argument with sound reasoning.

2. Most jurisdictions still have on their books laws that make certain kinds of conduct illegal based on religious principles. Such laws are commonly referred to as *blue laws* because they were traditionally written on blue paper. Such laws commonly prohibit the conducting of business on Sunday, the traditional Christian Sabbath, as well as many kinds of sexual practices such as sodomy—even between consenting, married, heterosexual adults. Should such laws be enforced or overturned in your view? Justify your answer through legal or ethical arguments.

3. Some argue that government needs to increase its regulation of business for the good of society as a whole, while others believe that the marketplace is self-regulating and that government intervention through needless regulation places an unfair, costly burden on business. What role do you feel government should play through regulation to ensure ethical conduct by business?

4. Large corporations often spend significant amounts of money every year on charitable contributions to a number of causes. While this long-established practice continues, so does the debate in some quarters as to its ethical value. Some people believe it is not just the right, but the social duty of corporations and other businesses to contribute money to worthy causes as a means of giving back something of tangible value for the profits it reaps from society as a whole. Others believe that corporate contributions are an improper use of money that rightfully should be distributed to shareholders as dividends from corporate profits, and that making such charitable gifts without shareholder consent constitutes misuse of corporate assets. What do you think? Explain your answer fully.

# ADMINISTRATIVE LAW

## ADMINISTRATIVE AGENCIES . . . . . . . . . . . . . . . . . . . . . . . . . . . .

Administrative law governs and defines the powers of government agencies. A number of political and technological factors have led to a veritable explosion in the growth of government since the turn of the century, at both the federal and state levels. This growth has given rise to what has come to be commonly referred to as the fourth branch of government: administrative agencies.

### PURPOSE OF FEDERAL AGENCIES

Beginning in the 1930s, the federal government has been steadily expanding its regulatory powers over business and individuals. Although Congress has the power to regulate nearly any matter that has an impact on interstate commerce under the U.S. Supreme Court's broad interpretation of the commerce clause, the 535 men and women that make up Congress have neither the time nor the expertise to become involved in the specifics of drafting regulatory rules for each federal agency. What Congress does instead is create administrative agencies to oversee or carry out specific governmental functions, and then empower those agencies to create the rules by which they will operate. When an agency is created, Congress gives it the power to draft its own *agency rules*—the guidelines under which the agency operates and which must be followed by persons over whom the agency is given regulatory powers. When federal agencies enact rules, they must follow the guidelines set forth in the *Administrative Procedures Act* (APA), which specifies the procedures agencies must follow in promulgating new rules. As long as the agency creates rules in accordance with the APA, such rules have the force of law.

Agencies have two main purposes: assisting in carrying out vital government functions and exerting regulatory control. They are the instrument through which Congress and the president institute policies and implement government regulation. As both government and its regulation have steadily grown throughout the twentieth century, agencies have likewise swelled in size and power. While the titular seat of power may rest with the 535 members of Congress and the president, neither branch of government can exercise its power without the assistance of federal agencies. Congress and the president lack the time and expertise to formulate policies and pass legislation affecting every area of government. Therefore, much of the actual running of government is entrusted to administrative agencies created by the legislative and executive branches.

## INDEPENDENT FEDERAL AGENCIES

Federal agencies fall into two basic categories: *independent* and *executive*. Independent agencies are created by Congress to assist it in exerting regulatory control or to carry out governmental administration. Once created, these agencies are headed by a director who is appointed by the president and confirmed by the Senate. In order to distance these agencies from the political process, independent agency directors serve for set terms that are staggered so as to prevent any given administration from having too great an impact on such agencies through presidential appointments of agency heads.

Independent agencies can wield tremendous power. Congress often imbues these agencies with quasi-judicial, quasi-legislative and quasi-executive powers: they create their own rules (a legislative power), enforce these rules and conduct investigations (an executive power) and adjudicate disputes relating to these rules or their applications in administrative hearings similar to trials (a judicial power).

Agencies perform a vital function in areas where specific expertise is a requirement in order to perform a governmental function or regulate a specific business. Independent federal agencies include the Central Intelligence Agency, the Environmental Protection Agency, the Equal Employment Opportunity Commission, the Federal Communications Commission, the Interstate Commerce Commission, the Federal Trade Commission, the Nuclear Regulatory Commission and the Securities and Exchange Commission, among many others. While Congress may have the right to regulate aviation (it affects interstate commerce), civilian and military use of nuclear energy and intelligence gathering, few senators or representatives have the highly specialized knowledge necessary to regulate any of these areas effectively. But agencies can be staffed with experts who can promulgate rules by relying on their superior knowledge of their respective fields.

## EXECUTIVE AGENCIES

Federal agencies have also been created to assist the executive branch in carrying out its responsibilities. Notable executive agencies include the Federal Bureau of Investigation (Justice Department), the U.S. Customs Service (Treasury Department), the Food and Drug Administration and the Social Security Administration (Health and Human Services Department), the Bureau of Indian Affairs (Interior Department), the Immigration and Naturalization Service (Justice Department), the Secret Service (Treasury Department), and the Federal Aviation Administration (Transportation Department), to name only a few.

Unlike independent agencies, executive agencies are under the control of the president who can appoint and remove their directors at will. These agencies are, therefore, much more responsive to political issues and subject to the winds of political change, at least at the top levels. But one must keep in mind that most agency workers are civil servants, not political appointees, and enjoy the relative job security that their status conveys. Thus, while the heads of executive agencies may come and go, the bureaucracy itself is well entrenched and grows yearly as new agencies are created and existing agencies are expanded to implement new government goals and programs.

## STATE AGENCIES

The appeal of agencies as a means of implementing necessary regulation and providing vital services is not limited to the federal government. States also use agencies to assist with such matters as the administration of workers' compensation, social services, and tax collection. As is true for federal agencies, state agencies can be created by either the state legislature or the state's chief executive (the governor).

# THE ADMINISTRATIVE PROCEDURES ACT . . . . . . . . . . . . . . . . . .

Independent federal agencies are created through an act of Congress that establishes the agency and empowers it to perform whatever duties Congress specifically delegates to it. The actual creation of the agency and the scope of its authority are detailed in the *enabling legislation*—the act of Congress that creates the agency. The details of the agency's operation are left to the agency, which creates its own rules in accordance with the guidelines set out in the 1946 Administrative Procedures Act (APA). The APA gives agencies broad rule-making powers, as long as they act within the guidelines that the APA provides. Federal executive agencies are usually created by presidential order. Like independent agencies, executive agencies are also subject to the guidelines of the APA.

Under the APA, agencies have the power to create rules that have the force of law, provided that the guidelines of the APA are observed. The basic requirements that all federal agencies must observe in rule-making are as follows:

- giving notice to the general public that a new rule or a rule change is being considered (this is almost always accomplished through publication of the proposed rule in the *Federal Register*);
- providing an opportunity for all interested parties to participate in the rule-making process by conducting public hearings and giving all interested parties a reasonable opportunity to voice their views on the proposed rule or rule change; and
- publishing in the *Federal Register* a draft containing the essential factors relating to the proposed rule and its purpose at least thirty days before the rule is to take effect.

Once the requirements of the APA have been met, the proposed rule takes effect on its proposed effective date and has the force of law.

## LIMITS ON ADMINISTRATIVE AGENCIES . . . . . . . . . . . . . . . . . . . . .

As previously noted, federal agencies have far-reaching powers within the areas that they oversee. A congressional grant of authority to an agency often includes the ability to carry out investigations, create rules that are the functional equivalent of law, hold hearings to adjudicate alleged violation of agency rules and assess punishment (usually by way of fines) to those judged in violation of the agency's rules. Agencies with such powers, such as the Internal Revenue Service, can act as legislator, police, judge, jury and executioner. While this concentration of power leads to the swift administration of justice, the average citizen facing an administrative hearing may take comfort in the knowledge that both agency rules and most agency decisions are subject to judicial review on any of the following grounds:

- The agency acted beyond the scope of its authority under the agency's enabling act;
- The agency misinterpreted federal law (including its enabling act) in its rule-making or in the adjudication of any matter before the agency;
- Agency action violates the U.S. Constitution or any federal law; or
- Agency rules or the findings of administrative law judges are arbitrary or capricious.

Agency rules and procedures, as well as the adjudications by administrative law judges of agency hearings conducted as informal trials, are upheld by the courts as long as they meet the noted requirements.

## QUESTIONS . . . . . . . . . . . . . . . . . . . . . . . . . . . . . . . . . . . . . .

1. What is the basic purpose of government agencies?
2. What are the two basic categories of federal agencies?
3. How do directors of independent agencies come to power?
4. What is the purpose of state administrative agencies?
5. What are the basic requirements that the Administrative Procedures Act requires agencies to observe in rule-making?
6. What are the grounds for overturning agency action in the courts?

## H Y P O T H E T I C A L    C A S E S

1. The Federal Aviation Administration (FAA) wants to institute new safety regulations relating to the use of drugs and alcohol by pilots in civil aviation. After conducting a study, the agency decides that it would be in the best interest of the general public to begin random drug testing of all airline pilots effective immediately. Under the authority of the agency director, the FAA sends out notices to all

airlines that a new drug-testing program is now in effect. Is this regulation valid under the facts given? Explain.

2. The Nuclear Regulatory Commission (NRC), concerned about safety in the nation's nuclear power-generating stations, wishes to impose new safety regulations affecting such power-generating plants. After issuing a notice to the general public that it is considering safety rule changes, the agency conducts hearings from interested persons from the industry as well as from the general public for a period of sixty days. At the conclusion of these hearings, the agency decides that it would be in the best interest of the industry to ban the sale of alcoholic beverages in counties where nuclear generating plants are located. It then publishes a copy of the proposed regulation, as well as a general statement of the need for such regulation, in the *Federal Register* thirty days before the regulation is to take effect. After the regulation takes effect, it is challenged in a federal district court of appeals by liquor store owners in affected counties.
   a. What result?
   b. Assume that the NRC follows the same procedure to promulgate a rule that forbids nuclear generating plant workers from working with a blood alcohol level of .005 percent, subjecting violators to a fine of $5,000. Is such a regulation likely to be upheld if it is challenged in court? Explain.

3. The Federal Communications Commission (FCC), concerned with the increasing violence and hatred depicted in the popular media, decides to consider new rules affecting the broadcasting of material of a violent, sexual or hateful nature. After following the established procedures for rule-making under the APA, the FCC promulgates the following new rules:
   a. Material of a violent or sexual nature can be broadcast only between the hours of 12:00 A.M. and 6:00 A.M.;
   b. Music videos that advocate physical violence, degradation of women or racial bigotry cannot be broadcast at any time.
   Will these two regulations withstand court challenges? Explain.

CHAPTER

# 5

# CRIMINAL LAW

*Criminal law* is the branch of law that concerns itself with the punishment of prohibited behavior seen as harmful to society as a whole. In a criminal trial, a *prosecutor* (a government representative who is charged with proving the guilt at trial of individuals accused of committing crimes) sues a person suspected of committing a crime, called a *criminal defendant*, in order to have that person punished by having to pay a fine, being sentenced to jail or both. Thus the nature of criminal law is punitive in nature, with the intended result of a successful conviction being the punishment of the criminal for having committed the prohibited act.

Although criminal law in both England and the Unites States was developed at common law based on custom and tradition, today all states have extensive criminal codes that enumerate a wide range of prohibited conduct and specify its punishment. As is often the case in our legal system, there are important differences in criminal-law statutes at the state and federal levels, in terms of both the kinds of conduct that are prohibited and the kinds of punishment such criminal conduct is subject to. Despite these differences, there are still many similarities in the kinds of conduct that are prohibited in each of the fifty states and by the federal government, since all criminal statutes trace their roots to common law. In this chapter, we will focus on areas of criminal law that are fairly standard in most states. Keep in mind, however, that the law is fluid and subject to constant revision and change; this is particularly true in the area of criminal law, where legislatures are constantly making changes both to the types of conduct deemed criminal and to the punishment for such conduct in order to reflect changing societal values.

## ELEMENTS OF A CRIME · · · · · · · · · · · · · · · · · · · · · · · · · · · ·

There are two elements to every crime that the prosecution must prove before a criminal defendant can be found guilty of having committed a crime: (1) a criminal *act* or *omission* by the accused, and (2) the existence of a wrongful *state of mind* or *intent* at the

35

time of the commission of the wrongful act or omission. If a criminal act or omission is carried out with the required criminal intent, then a crime is complete; but criminal intent alone or a harmful act that was not committed with the required criminal intent do not rise to the level of a crime. A few examples should help to illustrate:

> *Jane wishes Josh were dead. She spends every waking moment hoping for his demise and imagining ingenious ways of bringing it about. One day, Josh is struck by lightning and killed, much to Jane's delight. Jane is guilty of no crime, since she committed no act to help bring about Josh's death.*

> *Jane wishes Josh were dead. She takes a butcher knife and plunges it into Josh, intending to kill him. Josh dies. Jane is guilty of a crime (murder) since she undertook a criminal act (plunging the knife into Josh) while possessing the necessary criminal intent (intending to kill him).*

> *Jane, while deer hunting, sees the luckless Josh in the woods 100 yards away. He is wearing a tan deerskin coat and hat and is crawling on all fours looking for a lost contact lens. Mistaking Josh for a deer, Jane shoots and kills him. Jane is not guilty of a crime under the facts given, despite the fact that a criminal act was committed (homicide), since she lacked the required criminal intent (the criminal act was caused by a mistake rather than an evil intent).*

In general, failure to act will not result in criminal liability *unless the accused had a duty to act.* In our society, individuals are free to stand by and do nothing when others are faced with danger *unless* (1) there is a special relationship that by its nature requires the bystander to come to the assistance of the person in danger, or (2) the dangerous situation was caused or contributed to by the bystander. When criminal liability is predicated on *the failure to act*, or on a *criminal omission*, rather than on the commission of a criminal act, the situation in question is one in which the criminal defendant had an affirmative duty to act but failed to exercise that duty. The following example will illustrate:

> *Sam, a sadistic sociopath who enjoys others' suffering, watches as a blind stranger crosses a busy intersection while a tractor-trailer approaches her at fifty-five miles per hour. He does not warn the stranger of the danger or move to assist her. If the truck is unable to stop in time and causes the woman's death, Sam will not be guilty of any crime. As a stranger, he has no duty to warn or assist another in danger. His failure to do so is clearly monstrous and morally reprehensible, but since he did not place the woman in the dangerous situation and owed her no legal duty, he is guilty of no crime in failing to assist her through word or deed. Sam would, however, have had an affirmative duty to act to at least warn the woman if he had a close familial relationship to her, such as husband, son or father, and likewise if Sam were a police officer whose job required him to take some affirmative steps to preserve the victim's well-being.*

It is possible to be guilty of a crime without having the required criminal intent in a few kinds of special cases. There are certain types of behavior that legislatures want to prevent regardless of the intent of the person engaging in the behavior, usually because of its dangerous nature. Such criminal offenses are termed *strict liability* crimes. Whenever a strict liability crime is involved, the only issue is whether the act was committed; the mental state of the person committing the act is irrelevant. Typical strict liability offenses include traffic violations and driving while under the influence of alcohol or other drugs. If a person is accused of speeding or running a red light, for example, all that needs to be shown by the prosecutor is that the act occurred; it is irrelevant that the accused did not intend to speed or did not see the red light before crossing it. What is punishable is the act itself. Likewise with driving while under the influence or driving with impaired ability; it is irrelevant that the accused may not have intended the violation, or was so intoxicated that he or she lacked the ability to form criminal intent.

## CLASSIFICATION OF CRIMES . . . . . . . . . . . . . . . . . . . . . . . . . . . .

Traditionally, crimes have been classified into three basic categories based upon their seriousness: felonies, misdemeanors and violations. Felonies are the most serious crimes and are punishable by more than one year of imprisonment in a state or federal penitentiary. Misdemeanors are less serious criminal offenses that can carry a maximum penalty of one year of imprisonment. Violations are minor offenses that typically are punishable by a fine or short prison sentence (typically not to exceed thirty days).

Felonies and misdemeanors are typically further subdivided into other categories based upon the maximum penalty by which they are punishable. The following example is typical:

- First degree felony: Punishable by death or imprisonment from fifteen years to life, and/or a fine of up to $10,000.
- Second degree felony: Punishable by imprisonment of up to fifteen years and/or a fine of up to $10,000.
- Third Degree Felony: Punishable by imprisonment of up to five years and/or a fine of up to $5,000.
- Class A misdemeanor: Punishable by up to one year's imprisonment and/or up to a $1,000 fine.
- Class B misdemeanor: Punishable by up to six months' imprisonment and/or up to a $1,000 fine.
- Class C misdemeanor: Punishable by up to three months' imprisonment and/or up to a $1,000 fine.

Violations are also classed by their type and the maximum sentence or fine to which violators can be subjected. Common violations include minor traffic infractions as well as such offenses as littering and spitting on the sidewalk. The maximum fine for each violation is typically $500 or less.

## SPECIFIC CRIMES . . . . . . . . . . . . . . . . . . . . . . . . . . . . . . . . . .

Although a comprehensive study of criminal law is beyond the scope of our text, an examination of conduct punishable as criminal in all states is a useful exercise for two reasons: first, practical knowledge of basic criminal-law principles can be an important tool to average citizens in their business and private lives; second, even a cursory examination of criminal-law principles can show government efforts at legislating morality and highlight some basic societal values worthy of intellectual inquiry and discussion.

The following sections will present brief examinations of specific crimes in three basic categories: crimes against persons, crimes against property, and crimes against the judicial process.

## CRIMES AGAINST PERSONS

The first category of crimes that we will examine is crimes against persons. The law recognizes the rights of individuals in our society to be left alone. Undue interference with that right through physical or mental means often leads to criminal liability, as the following types of crimes illustrate.

**Murder**    The unjustified taking of a human life with malice aforethought constitutes the crime of *murder*, a first-degree felony. For a homicide to rise to the level of murder, it must be committed on purpose or knowingly. A homicide that occurs under circumstances that demonstrate extreme indifference to human life, or any homicide that results from the commission or attempted commission of another felony, also constitutes murder.

**Manslaughter**    The unjustified taking of a human life under circumstances that would constitute murder can result in the lesser crime (second-degree felony) of *manslaughter* if it is committed under extreme emotional distress. A homicide resulting from reckless conduct also constitutes manslaughter.

> *Harriet stabs her husband, Harold, to death after learning he has been unfaithful. She is probably guilty of manslaughter, since the crime is likely to have been committed under extreme emotional distress. (As we'll see shortly, she might be able to use a valid insanity defense depending on the circumstances.)*
>
> *Jack drives his hot rod in a school zone at ninety-five miles per hour, not intending to harm anyone but merely to impress the kindergartners. He accidentally kills a crossing guard when he loses control of his car. Despite his lack of intent to commit the homicide, Jack is guilty of manslaughter because a death resulted from his reckless conduct.*

**Negligent homicide**    *Negligent homicide*, a third-degree felony, results from the negligent taking of a human life. This type of homicide results from *carelessness*, or the failure to exercise the care that a reasonably prudent person would exercise under similar circumstances.

> *Melinda accidentally fires a handgun while cleaning it, not realizing it is loaded. The bullet strikes and kills a houseguest. She is guilty of criminally negligent homicide.*

**Aggravated assault**    An attempt to cause severe bodily harm to another, or the actual causing of such injuries, constitutes *aggravated assault* (a second-degree felony) if such an attempt is made intentionally or with extreme indifference to human life. The attempt to cause *any* injury (serious or not), through the use of a deadly weapon, in itself constitutes third-degree felony aggravated assault.

**Simple assault**    *Simple assault* consists of any one of the following offenses:

1. attempting to cause or actually causing *any* bodily injury to another, either intentionally or recklessly;
2. negligently causing an injury to another through the use of a firearm; or
3. attempting to place another in fear of impending serious physical harm through physical threats. Simple assault is usually a class A or B misdemeanor, or a class C misdemeanor if it results from a physical confrontation voluntarily entered into by the parties involved.

**Reckless endangerment**    Engaging in conduct that recklessly places another in danger of death or serious injury constitutes the misdemeanor of *reckless endangerment*. Under the Model Penal Act (§ 211.2), merely pointing a firearm in the general direction of any person constitutes reckless endangerment, whether or not the person pointing the gun believes it to be loaded.

**Kidnapping**    The unlawful taking of a person or confinement of a person in a place of isolation constitutes the crime of *kidnapping* if it is done for any of the following purposes:

1. to hold the victim for ransom or as a hostage;
2. to facilitate the commission of any felony or to facilitate escape after a felony is committed;
3. to inflict bodily injury or to place the victim or another in fear of imminent serious bodily injury to the victim; or
4. to interfere with the performance of any governmental or political function.

Kidnapping is a first-degree felony, but it is reduced to a second-degree felony if the victim is voluntarily released alive prior to the kidnapper's trial.

**False imprisonment**    The unjustified, intentional interference with the right of another to move about freely constitutes the crime of *false imprisonment*, a misdemeanor. It is not necessary that the restraint be physical. Threats directed at the victim or at another can constitute a sufficient interference with the person's right to move about freely if the person at whom the threats are directed reasonably believes that they may be carried out.

False imprisonment is a crime of particular concern to retail merchants who hold shoplifting suspects for questioning. A suspected shoplifter can lawfully be restrained for questioning, provided that there is sufficient evidence to believe that the person has stolen merchandise belonging to the store. Even when such evidence exists however, as is the case when the shoplifting is witnessed by a store employee, the suspect can be restrained only for a reasonable length of time for questioning or until police arrive on the scene.

**Rape**    *Rape* is defined both at common law and by the Model Penal Code (§ 213.1) as sexual intercourse (requiring some anal or vaginal penetration) by a male with a female who is not his wife when:

1. he compels her to submit by force or by the threat of imminent death, serious injury, extreme pain or kidnapping directed at the victim or any third party;
2. he has intentionally overcome the female's resistance by administering drugs or alcohol;
3. the female is unconscious; or
4. the female is under the age of consent in the state (the legal age of consent for sex is often under eighteen).

Rape is a second-degree felony, but can rise to a first-degree felony if the rapist inflicts serious physical injury during the rape, or if the victim was not a social companion of the rapist at the time of the crime and had not had previous sexual relations with the attacker.

Generally, whenever rape is predicated on the age of the victim (*statutory rape*), that the woman gave her consent freely or that the man might not have reasonably been able to know that the woman was below the legal age of consent are both irrelevant. This is a strict liability crime in nearly every state, where the only question is whether the act was committed (and, obviously, whether the woman was below the age of consent).

Note that at common law, a husband cannot be guilty of rape, and in most states as well as under the Model Penal Act, parties who live together as a traditional husband and wife are considered to be husband and wife for purposes of rape. Also notice that rape is a male-specific crime. At common law, a husband who forces his wife to submit to sexual intercourse is at most guilty of simple assault.

There is, however, a movement today in most states towards criminalizing marital rape as a separate (yet *still* usually *lesser*) criminal offense.

## CRIMES AGAINST PROPERTY

Crimes against property include offenses that result in the destruction of property or the permanent or temporary deprivation of the owner's right to exclusively use and enjoy real or personal property.

**Arson**    At common law, *arson* was defined as intentionally burning the dwelling place of another. Today, the definition of arson has been substantially expanded in the criminal-law statutes of most jurisdictions to include the intentional burning of another's occupied structure, or the intentional burning down of any property, including one's own, for the purpose of collecting insurance. For purposes of arson, an *occupied structure* is usually defined as any personal or real property that is constructed so as to permit overnight accommodation of persons or the conducting of business therein, whether or not the structure is actually occupied at the time that it is burned. Thus, all homes and businesses are subject to arson, as are mobile homes or trailers that are set up for human occupancy. Arson is typically a second-degree felony.

**Criminal mischief**    Damaging the personal or real property of another purposely, recklessly or by negligence in the use of explosives, fire or other dangerous means constitutes *criminal mischief*, which can be a third-degree felony; a class A, B or

C misdemeanor; or a violation, depending on the nature and extent of the damage caused. Under Section 220.3, Paragraph 2 of the Model Penal Code, for example, criminal mischief is a third-degree felony if damage in excess of $5,000 is caused, a misdemeanor if more than $100 in damage is caused and a petty misdemeanor if more than $25 in damage is caused, but only a violation if $25 or less in damage is caused by the criminal mischief.

**Burglary**    At common law, *burglary* was defined as breaking and entering into the dwelling house of another at night with the intent to commit a serious crime inside. As is the case with arson, modern criminal-law statutes have liberalized the definition to be less restrictive. A common definition of burglary today is *breaking and entering* any occupied structure with the intent of committing a crime inside. The requirement of a breaking is fulfilled whenever the burglar exerts any amount of force to gain access to a building; turning a doorknob or gently pushing in a door that is unlocked both constitute a sufficient breaking in most states. The requirement of entering is satisfied by the intrusion of any part of a person or any tool in his or her control into the occupied structure. The crime is complete as soon as the breaking and entering are accomplished, provided that the burglar intended to commit a crime once inside. The following three examples constitute the crime of burglary:

- *Bob Burglar kicks in a door and enters Victoria Victim's home in order to steal her valuables. Once inside, he is scared off by Victoria wielding a shotgun before he has a chance to take anything of value.*

- *Belinda Burglar pushes an unlocked door and walks into Vince Victim's apartment in order to physically assault him.*

- *Ben Burglar slides open a window to Victoria's home and, using a fishing pole, manages to hook and reel in valuable jewelry from her bureau as she sleeps.*

Bob, Belinda and Ben are all guilty of burglary, since the requirement of breaking and entering with criminal intent is met in all three cases. Notice that in the third case, Ben never physically enters Victoria's home; nevertheless, when he casts the fishing line through the window, it is the same as if he had entered himself. Notice also that sliding open an unlocked window constitutes a sufficient breaking, and the crime is complete as soon as the line is cast through the window with the intent to commit a crime (stealing the jewelry), even if he misses the jewelry after several casts and goes away empty-handed. Burglary is usually a third-degree felony, but it can be raised to a second-degree felony in many states if the crime is committed at night, if anyone is injured during the commission of the crime, or if the burglar carries deadly weapons during the burglary.

**Criminal trespass**    Anyone who knowingly enters real property owned by another without permission to do so is guilty of *criminal trespass*, a misdemeanor. Entering any building not open to the general public without permission constitutes criminal trespass, as does the entering into posted land that warns intruders not to trespass, or the entering into land that the trespasser knows or reasonably should have known belongs to another. Failure to leave another's property when instructed to do so also constitutes trespass, even if the trespasser originally was given permission to enter the land by its owner or tenant.

**Larceny**    The intentional taking and carrying away of the property of another with the intent to permanently deprive the owner of its use constitutes the crime of *larceny*. Larceny can be either a third-degree felony or a misdemeanor, depending upon the nature of the property stolen and its worth.

**Robbery**    A larceny that is accomplished through either the use of force or the threat of force against the property's owner constitutes *robbery*. Robbery is usually a second-degree felony, but it can become a first-degree felony if the perpetrator inflicts or attempts to inflict serious bodily harm during the course of the robbery.

**Embezzlement**    The misappropriation of property in one's care belonging to another constitutes the crime of *embezzlement*, which is typically punishable the same as other theft.

**Receiving stolen property**    A person who purchases or otherwise acquires stolen property is guilty of the crime of *receiving stolen property*, which is usually punishable exactly the same as theft, provided that the property is received with actual knowledge that it was stolen, or under circumstances that should have made the receiver suspicious that it might be stolen.

**Theft of services**    A person who knowingly receives the benefit of services that are available for compensation, through the use of deception or any physical means to avoid paying for such services, is guilty of *theft of services*, a crime punishable exactly as any other theft. Common examples of theft of services include using slugs in telephones, vending machines or parking meters, obtaining illegal hookups to cable services and using illegal descramblers to obtain scrambled satellite broadcasts.

**Forgery**    Any material alteration to a written document issued by another that is made in order to defraud or mislead anyone constitutes the crime of *forgery*, which can be a felony or a misdemeanor depending on the nature of the offense.

Altering government or commercial enterprise instruments that purport to have monetary value, such as currency, stamps, stocks, bonds and similar instruments represents a second-degree felony. Altering documents that affect legal relationships, such as wills, trusts, deeds, contracts and claims releases, is a felony in the third degree. Any other forgery, such as the material alteration of the date in a driver's license, is a misdemeanor.

**Issuing a bad check**    It is a misdemeanor to *issue a bad check*—for example, a check for which one no longer has an account in the bank on which it is drawn, or a check for which one has a valid account which lacks sufficient funds for the check's payment when it is presented within thirty days of the date of issue. A person may avoid criminal liability for bounced checks by promptly paying the due amount in many states (e.g., within ten days of the notice of dishonor).

**Credit-card fraud**    Using a forged or stolen credit card to obtain goods, services or cash advances, or using a credit card after it has been canceled or recalled, constitutes *credit-card fraud*, typically a third-degree felony if the amount of the fraudulent charge exceeds $500, or a misdemeanor if the amount is $500 or less.

## CRIMES AGAINST THE JUDICIAL PROCESS

In order to ensure fairness in the administration of justice and in the normal conduct of business, the criminal statutes of every state prohibit conduct that seeks to interfere with fair business practices or the impartial administration of justice.

**Bribery of a public official**    At common law, the crime of *bribery* consisted of promising to give something of value in exchange for a public official's official conduct. Soliciting, accepting and promising to give or accept a bribe are all equally punishable as a misdemeanor. The consideration involved need not be monetary; a promise of sexual favors made to a judge, police officer or housing inspector for favorable official action constitutes bribery just as much as a promise to exchange money or goods for such action.

**Commercial bribery**    It is a misdemeanor in most states to solicit, accept or agree to accept anything of value in exchange for violating a duty of fidelity owed to one's employer, client or company as an employee, officer of a corporation, partner, trustee or guardian or member of a profession. Commercial bribery is applicable in a wide variety of settings, including each of the following:

- a promise by parents to pay a Little League umpire $100 if he does not call a child out on strikes;
- a promise to give the CEO of XYZ Company an executive position in ZYX Company if she discloses trade secrets;
- an offer by a plaintiff's attorney to a defendant's attorney in a civil suit to pay him $100,000 if he loses the case;
- an offer of a new car by an unqualified applicant to Ivy League University to the Director of Admissions if she is accepted as a student; and
- an offer of a new suit by a failing student to Professor Scruffy in exchange for a passing grade.

**Extortion**    Under federal criminal law, extortion is defined as "the obtaining of property from another, with his consent, induced by wrongful use of actual or threatened force, violence, or fear, or under color of official right." (18 USC § 1951) Extortion is only a crime under federal law if it interferes with commerce. Under state law, extortion typically finds an even broader definition. Nearly any threat made to induce someone to turn over his or her property can form the basis of a prosecution for extortion. Thus, the statement "unless you pay me $100 a week I will kill you" constitutes extortion if the money is paid out of fear that the threat will be carried out. Likewise, the statement "I will not tell your wife about your recent affair if you give me your watch" also constitutes extortion if the watch is given by the victim and accepted by the person making the threat. But the statement "if you break up with me, I will destroy your car" will not constitute the basis of a prosecution for extortion, since the threat is not made to induce the turning over of property from the victim to the person making the threat.

**Threatening a public official**    *Threatening a public official* with harm in order to influence official action is a misdemeanor. Making similar threats to influence a judicial or administrative proceeding, however, is a third-degree felony. Members of a jury are deemed public officials for purposes of this crime.

**Influence peddling**    It is a misdemeanor to solicit, receive or agree to receive any consideration for the trading of political influence by a public servant. The crime of *influence peddling* includes soliciting, giving or receiving a political endorsement by a public official in exchange for something of value.

**Perjury**    Making a material misrepresentation while under oath or through a sworn statement (such as an affidavit) constitutes the crime of *perjury*, a third-degree felony. A misrepresentation is material if it can affect the course or outcome of a proceeding.

**Tampering with public records**    It is a misdemeanor to knowingly falsify, destroy or attempt to hide any official government record or document. The crime includes creating or using falsified documentation issued by the government, such as using a false social security or alien registration card. If *tampering with public records* is done to defraud or injure anyone, then the offense is a third-degree felony. Simply carrying a false social security card, for example, is a misdemeanor, but using it to attempt to obtain social services that you are not entitled to, thereby defrauding the government, is a third-degree felony.

**Obstructing justice**    Any intentional interference with the administration of justice in a person's official or private conduct is a misdemeanor, regardless of whether such interference is obtained through physical force or official action. Physically interfering with an arrest, disrupting courtroom proceedings, or giving false information that misleads police in an investigation are all examples of *obstructing justice*.

**Aiding in the commission of a crime**    Any assistance rendered to the commission of a crime, or to the hiding or converting the proceeds of criminal activity, is punishable as a misdemeanor. If the underlying crime was a first- or second-degree felony, however, then facilitating its commission is a third-degree felony.

## ATTEMPTED CRIMES AND CRIMINAL CONSPIRACY

The law punishes not only completed criminal acts, but also attempted commission of a crime that for some reason is not completed. In addition, conspiring to commit a crime, whether or not the crime is ultimately committed, is a separate offense.

**The crime of attempt**    Under the Model Penal Code and the criminal codes of most states, the *attempt* to commit a crime that is not ultimately carried out is punishable to the same degree that the crime itself would have been punishable if completed. In general, in order to convict a criminal defendant for attempting the commission of a crime, all that is necessary is for the defendant to have taken a *substantial step* toward committing the criminal act, and for the defendant to have acted with the required criminal intent. The penalty for attempting a crime is the same as that for committing the crime attempted, with the exception that first-degree crimes become second-degree attempted crimes. For example, attempted murder is a second-degree felony, because murder is a first-degree felony. But attempted robbery is a second-degree felony just as is robbery, and attempted larceny is either a third-degree felony or a misdemeanor depending on the value of the goods, exactly as is the case with larceny itself.

It must be noted that a defendant can be tried and convicted for *either* the attempt to commit a crime or the crime itself, but not both.

**Criminal conspiracy**    Either agreeing to commit a crime with others or agreeing to assist others in the commission of a crime results in the crime of *criminal conspiracy*. Criminal conspiracy, like the crime of attempt, is subject to the same punishment as the underlying crime that the conspirators intend to perpetrate. As is the case with the crime of attempt, criminal conspiracies to commit crimes that are first-degree felonies are second-degree felonies, and the punishment for conspiring to commit any second-degree felony or lower crime is exactly the same as for the underlying crime itself.

The crime of conspiracy is a completely separate crime from the underlying crime that the conspirators intend to commit. Therefore, persons found guilty of criminal conspiracy can also be found guilty of the underlying crime that the conspirators perpetrated, or of its attempt if the crime was not fully carried out. The following example will illustrate:

- *Tom, Dick and Harriet agree to kill Bill Billionaire and to steal the valuables from his home. Tom agrees to buy a gun from a local illegal dealer that specializes in untraceable weapons, Dick agrees to drive the car and disable Bill's alarm system, and Harriet agrees to do the actual killing. On the appointed day, the three thugs arrive at Bill's home and break in, and all three stand by as Harriet attempts to shoot Bill several times; but the gun misfires. The three panic and run out, only to be arrested a short time later. They are tried for burglary and criminal conspiracy to commit murder, and Harriet is also charged with attempted murder. Under the facts given, the three are guilty of all counts.*

Despite the fact that there was a criminal conspiracy to commit more than one crime in the last example (burglary and murder), there can be only a single conviction for any conspiracy that is ongoing. In this case, the conspiracy charge would be based on attempted murder rather than burglary, since murder is the more serious charge. Similarly, if a group of bank robbers plans and executes a dozen successful robberies, they can be charged with twelve separate counts of bank robbery but only a single count of conspiracy to commit bank robbery, since the criminal affiliation was ongoing and subject to the same agreement by the parties to commit the crimes.

# DEFENSES TO CRIMINAL LIABILITY · · · · · · · · · · · · · · · · · · · · · · · ·

As previously noted, there are two prerequisites to criminal liability: a criminal act and criminal intent. Unless both are present, there can be no criminal liability unless the offense charged is a strict liability crime. It stands to reason, then, that a criminal defendant can avoid a conviction by showing *either* that a criminal act did not occur, or if it did occur, that the defendant lacked the required intent for criminal culpability. To put it another way, criminal defense attorneys have two basic avenues on which to base their defense: that the act in question was not committed by the criminal defendant, or if the act was committed, that the defendant did not possess the requisite criminal intent. In addition, behavior that is normally criminal may be justifiable under certain circumstances, such as the intentional infliction of bodily harm to another in self-defense.

In a criminal trial, the prosecutor must establish *beyond a reasonable doubt* both that a criminal act occurred and that the defendant committed the act with the required criminal intent. All that counsel for the defense needs to do in order to be entitled to an acquittal is to establish that a *reasonable doubt exists* that either the defendant committed the alleged act or that defendant acted with the required criminal intent. Even in situations when the defense cannot effectively raise a reasonable doubt as to a defendant's guilt, there are some *affirmative defenses* that the defense can raise to excuse criminal liability. When any of the affirmative defenses is raised at trial, the burden of proof is on the defendant's attorney to prove to the jury that the defense being raised applies in that particular case. The following example will illustrate:

> Andrew Angry runs up to Don Dunderhead, a candidate for political office in his state, yelling, "I'm going to punch your lights out, you blundering idiot! I've been listening to your meandering speeches for months and have yet to hear you say a single thing that makes any sense!" Andrew then jumps onto the speaker's platform and beats Don silly. At his trial for aggravated assault, Andrew's attorney won't be able to deny either the act or the intent, since both were broadcast for a week over every television news program. But he or she might be able to assert a defense of insanity or intoxication to win Andrew's acquittal.

Specific defenses to criminal liability include: insanity, intoxication, infancy, self-defense, defense of others, defense of property and entrapment.

## INSANITY

The basic premise behind the insanity defense is that a person who, due to some mental illness or deficiency, commits a criminal act that he or she would not otherwise commit should not be held responsible for such an act. A defendant who effectively raises an insanity defense in fact proves to the satisfaction of the jury that even though he or she committed the criminal act as charged, the act was committed without the requisite criminal intent. In other words, whenever the insanity defense is successfully used, the jury believes the defense argument that although a criminal act was committed, the defendant was not motivated by any evil criminal intent, but rather acted out of some mental infirmity.

Tests for establishing a valid insanity defense vary from state to state, but most states use one of the following four standard tests:

- M'Naghten Rule: Defendants who suffer from a mental illness that prevent them at the time of committing a criminal act from either knowing the wrongfulness of their actions or understanding the nature of their actions are excused from criminal liability. Under this rule, it is not enough that a defendant may be suffering from mental illness; the test is whether such illness prevents him or her from understanding the wrongfulness of his of her actions.
- Irresistible Impulse Test: Defendants who establish that they acted as a result of an irresistible impulse due to mental illness are entitled to acquittal.
- The New Hampshire Rule: Under the New Hampshire rule (also known as the Durham rule), defendants cannot be found criminally liable if they establish that their crime was a *product* of a mental defect or disease. For a crime to be the product of mental illness, it must be shown that the crime would not have been committed *if not for* the mental illness. This test is much broader than the M'Naghten and New Hampshire tests, and is currently used by very few jurisdictions.
- Model Penal Code Test: The Model Penal Code test adopted by the American Law Institute excuses criminal conduct when defendants suffer from a mental disease or defect that prevents them from recognizing the wrongfulness of their conduct *or* prevents them from conforming their conduct to the requirements of the law. This is the most commonly used test of insanity today, and essentially combines the M'Naghten and irresistible impulse tests.

## INTOXICATION

The defense of intoxication is very similar to the insanity defense in that it seeks to exculpate criminal behavior by showing that at the time the behavior took place, the criminal defendant was incapable of forming criminal intent due to being intoxicated. If the intoxication is involuntary, it is treated in exactly the same manner as insanity. If, for example, a state subscribes to the Model Penal Code definition of insanity, then a person who is involuntarily intoxicated cannot be found guilty of a crime if the intoxication prevented the defendant at the time of committing the criminal act from recognizing the wrongfulness of his or her conduct or from conforming his or her conduct to the requirements of the law. In order to qualify for involuntary intoxication, the defendant must have been tricked or forced into taking the intoxicating substance.

In cases of voluntary intoxication, where the defendant took the intoxicating substance freely, the effect on the defense varies depending on the nature of the crime. If the crime is one that requires a finding of willful criminal intent in order to prove culpability, as is the case with such offenses as murder, rape or robbery, then it makes no difference whether the intoxication was voluntary or involuntary. Voluntary intoxication will not be a valid defense, however, when the crime is one that does not require willful criminal intent, such as a strict liability crime (driving while intoxicated or general traffic offenses, for example) or a crime based on negligence or recklessness (reckless endangerment or negligent homicide, for example). The following two examples will illustrate:

- *Juan, while at a party, eats several cookies that, unknown to him, have been laced with LSD. An hour later, while his world seems to melt about him, Juan burns down his college's administration building and drives away in the college president's car (without permission). He then drives the car at ninety-five miles per hour in a 15-mph school zone, killing a pedestrian. He is charged with arson, vehicular manslaughter, larceny of the auto, speeding and driving while intoxicated. In most states, he has a valid defense of involuntary intoxication to all charges, since none of the offenses would have been committed if not for the intoxication.*

- *Juan commits the offenses in the previous example after voluntarily drinking a fifth of vodka while at the party. His voluntary intoxication is a valid defense in most states to the arson and larceny charges, for they require willful intent, but not to the manslaughter, speeding or driving while intoxicated, since these are offenses based on recklessness and strict liability.*

## INFANCY

At common law, a child under the age of seven was deemed incapable of forming the necessary criminal intent to commit a crime, and a child between the ages of seven and fourteen was presumed incapable of forming criminal intent, but that presumption could be overcome by a prosecutor. The assumption was that, as a matter of law, a child under seven could not understand the difference between right and wrong, and a child between seven and fourteen probably did not understand the difference between right and wrong (but a prosecutor could show that a particular child did understand the difference).

Today, most states retain the common-law defense of infancy with little change in their criminal statutes, but have made provisions for dealing with youthful offenders through other means (usually by having the family court adjudicate such offenses during defendants' minority). The basic assumption is that minors who commit crimes need to be treated differently from adults; the emphasis is less on punishment and more on rehabilitation, counseling and training. Many states provide an option for courts to treat violent youthful offenders as adults if they fall within a certain age (such as fourteen to eighteen), subjecting them to the same harsh punishment as adults when they commit such violent crimes as rape and murder.

## SELF-DEFENSE

A person is free to use reasonable force in defense to an unprovoked attack. A person may use any necessary force to repel a physical attack or the threat of an attack. A person faced with an attack that he or she reasonably believes may cause death or serious bodily injury may use any physical force to repel such a threat or attack, up to and including *deadly physical force* (force that may reasonably be expected to cause death or life-threatening injury). The key to the justification of the use of force is the reasonableness of the perceived danger in the mind of the victim. If, for example, a mugger pulls a realistic-looking toy gun on a victim who shoots the mugger with a real gun in response, the victim would be justified in repelling the attack, even if the mugger is killed in the process, *provided* that the victim reasonably feared death or serious injury before fending off the attack. If the mugger's gun in the last example is clearly visible to the victim as a transparent neon-green water pistol, the shooting in self-defense would not be justified.

## DEFENSE OF OTHERS

In every state, a person who rushes to the aid of another who is being victimized may use as much force in defending the person as the victim could use in his or her own defense. Thus, if Susan, a passerby, sees Sam being held up by a gunman threatening to kill him, she can use any force against the assailant that Sam himself could use (she can kill the assailant in this example, since Sam is clearly in danger of death or serious bodily injury).

A problem arises for good Samaritans when, as is often the case, things are not what they seem. Consider the following example:

> Mohammed, a passerby, notices Carla, who is dressed as a police officer, being held at gunpoint by Frank, whom he hears saying, "If you move, I'll shoot." Sure that a police officer is in danger, Mohammed tackles Frank, wrestles with him for the gun and shoots him in the scuffle. Later, he learns that Frank was an undercover police officer attempting to arrest Carla, who had held up a convenience store while impersonating a police officer.

Mohammed's fate as a mistaken good Samaritan depends upon the state where the action occurred. In some states, Mohammed's actions would be judged simply on their reasonableness under the circumstances; if a reasonable person would have believed that Carla was a police officer in danger, then Mohammed's actions would be justified and would not subject him to criminal liability. In other states, however, good Samaritans are held to "stand in the shoes" of the people they try to defend; in such states, a person can use only as much force as the perceived victim *had a legal right to use* against the perceived attacker. In a state with such a rule, Mohammed would be criminally liable for the injury inflicted on Frank (the undercover police officer) since Carla, the person he perceived to be a victim, in fact had no right to defend herself under the circumstances.

## DEFENSE OF PROPERTY

All states recognize the right of an individual to protect property from being taken, misused or damaged by another. Any force short of deadly physical force may be used to protect one's property. In other words, you may threaten, restrain, or physically prevent another from harming or taking your property, but you may not kill or seriously wound another merely to protect your property. Keep in mind that you *may* use deadly physical force if you reasonably feel threatened with death or serious bodily injury. For example, you may use deadly force to protect yourself from a carjacking during the course of which you are threatened with serious injury, but you may not use deadly force to prevent your car from being stolen from your driveway by shooting the thief from inside your home when you are not directly being threatened.

### ENTRAPMENT

A person who is enticed or convinced to commit a crime by law enforcement agents when he or she is not otherwise predisposed to commit such a crime can escape criminal liability by asserting the defense of entrapment. In order to assert the defense successfully, the criminal defendant must prove two things: (1) that the commission of the crime was instigated or enticed by a law enforcement agent, and (2) that the crime would not have been committed were it not for the enticement or instigation of the law enforcement agent.

It is not enough for a defendant to show that police provided the opportunity for the crime to occur or that police suggested the crime's commission; the defendant must also show that he or she was not predisposed to commit the crime. Let's look at two examples for the sake of clarification:

- *Lina, an undercover police officer, offers to purchase a vial of crack cocaine from Freddy, a drug dealer. Freddy sells Lina the crack and Lina immediately arrests him.*

- *Lyssandra, an FBI agent, offers Rosalie, a state legislator, $10,000 to transport one kilogram of heroin from a contact in Mexico. Rosalie initially refuses, but Lyssandra manages to convince her following a hard sell over a period of several weeks. When Rosalie delivers the drugs, Lyssandra arrests her for drug trafficking.*

Freddy, in the first example, will not be able to assert the defense of entrapment. Even though he was approached by a police officer, he was clearly predisposed to commit the crime and was not in any way convinced to do so. In the second example, however, Rosalie will be able to assert the defense of entrapment successfully, since it is clear from the facts given that she was not predisposed to commit the crime, but was convinced to do so by Lyssandra. In the real world, the more pressure a police officer needs to exert on a criminal defendant to agree to commit the illegal act, the likelier it is that the defendant will be able to assert the defense of entrapment successfully. A criminal defendant who offers little or no resistance to the suggestion of committing a crime will not be successful in asserting the defense of entrapment. One of the key elements for prosecutors trying to overcome the defense when it is raised is the criminal predisposition of the defendant to commit the crime. Predisposition is usually shown by a pattern of previous behavior; thus, persons who are enticed by police to commit criminal acts that they are known to have committed in the past have a very difficult time in raising the defense of entrapment, since their previous acts will point to a predisposition to commit the crime with which they are charged.

## QUESTIONS . . . . . . . . . . . . . . . . . . . . . . . . . . . . . . . . . . .

1. What is the basic concern of criminal law?
2. What are the elements of a crime?

3. Can a failure to act lead to criminal liability? Explain.

4. In general, is there a legal duty for citizens in our society to come to the assistance of those in need? Should there be one? Explain fully.

5. What are the three basic classifications of crimes?

6. What is the difference between a first-degree and a third-degree felony?

7. Define *murder, manslaughter* and *negligent homicide.*

8. What is the difference between simple assault and aggravated assault?

9. What is the difference between larceny and embezzlement?

10. List the major affirmative defenses to criminal liability covered in this chapter.

# H Y P O T H E T I C A L    C A S E S

1. Ralph, a thirteen-year-old boy, mistakenly takes another's bicycle from a bike rack at school, thinking the bike to be his own. He is arrested and tried for larceny. You agree to represent Ralph, having just passed the bar exam in your state. What will be your defense? Be specific and thorough in your arguments.

2. Rowena, a gun collector, jokingly points a gun she believes to be unloaded at her best friend, Mark. The gun accidentally discharges and Mark is instantly killed. What crimes, if any, could Rowena be charged with?

3. Barbara, while shopping at her local department store, absentmindedly walks out of the store holding a folding umbrella she had grabbed a half-hour earlier, intending to pay for it on her way out of the store. A store security officer stops her just outside of the store and asks her to accompany him back inside. Barbara, realizing her mistake, apologizes profusely and attempts to pay for the umbrella, but the security guard refuses to release her and accuses her of shoplifting. Barbara becomes enraged and slaps the security guard when he tells her that he will call the police to have her arrested. The security guard then physically restrains her until police arrive, while Barbara continues to slap and kick him from time to time. When police arrive to arrest her, she resists arrest and demands that the security guard be arrested for false imprisonment. On the way to the police station, she offers the arresting officer $500 to "let me go and forget the whole thing."

   a. What crimes, if any, can Barbara be charged with?

   b. Assuming that she can convince the trier of fact that she intended to pay for the umbrella at her trial for larceny, will she be convicted of the crime? Explain.

   c. What should be the determination of all other criminal charges based on the facts given?

   d. Can she assert the defense of self-defense against any of the charges?

   e. Should the guard be charged with false imprisonment?

4. Ben sets fire to a grain silo on his neighbor's farm after a heated argument. Fortunately, the silo is not attached to the neighbor's house or barn, and the damage does not spread beyond the destruction of the silo and its contents. The next day,

Ben is arrested and charged with arson. Should he be convicted of the crime if the prosecutor can show that he purposely set the fire? Explain.

5. Spark and Flash, malicious but less-than-brilliant arsonists, agree to burn down a number of apartment buildings in exchange for a fee from landlords eager to collect insurance on unprofitable rent-controlled apartment buildings. When they arrive at the first site, they slosh several gallons of gasoline only to discover that they neglected to bring matches or a lighter. Housing police arrest the two after observing them going from door to door asking tenants for matches. What crime or crimes, if any, can they be charged with, and what is the maximum penalty they face for each crime or crimes?

## ETHICS AND THE LAW: QUESTIONS FOR FURTHER STUDY   . . . . . . .

1. We have seen in this chapter that an attempt to commit a crime, even if unsuccessful, is generally punishable the same as if the crime had been successfully committed. This may seem a bit unfair at first glance. What do you think is the purpose of such a rule? Do you agree with it? Explain.

2. The common-law differentiation of youthful offenders from adults was largely based on a paternalistic view of children by the courts. The underlying rationale for treating youthful offenders differently from adults is that children are inherently good, innocent and incapable of forming criminal intent until they grow into adulthood and are somehow hardened by the "ways of the world." The law tends to view children in an idealistic way reminiscent of William Blake's *Songs of Innocence*. It can be argued that Blake's *Songs of Experience*, however, are more directly applicable. Statistics today unequivocally show that most violent crimes, including murder, rape and aggravated assault, are committed by young adults and by children under the age of eighteen. Yet the violent crimes of youthful offenders are usually handled by states' family courts, with the emphasis on rehabilitation and training, as opposed to punishment. How do you feel about this issue? What do you think are the causes of juvenile crime? What can society do to reverse this troubling trend?

3. Although the emphasis of criminal law is fundamentally on punishment, there has been a gradual shift in the philosophical base of our penal institutions away from punishment and towards rehabilitation as a means of fighting crime. Whether one views crime as resulting primarily from external causes such as poverty, lack of education, bigotry, sexism or any number of other societal causes, or whether one believes that most crime results from innate human flaws and human weaknesses, can have a fundamental impact on the approach one takes to combating it. What do you believe to be the most important cause of crime in society (internal causes, external causes, a combination of the two or something else entirely)? Based on your view, what do you think is the best way to deal with the issue of crime? How is your answer influenced by your view of ethics? Your political philosophy? Your religious views?

CHAPTER

# 6

# INTENTIONAL TORTS

*Tort* law (from the Latin *torquere* and *tortus,* meaning "to twist" and "twisted," respectively) is the branch of law that governs civil wrongs that members of a society inflict on one another. The purpose of tort law is to provide just compensation to injured parties for civil injuries that they suffer at the hands of others.

At first glance, it is easy to confuse tort law with criminal law, because both attempt to exact a penalty for wrongful conduct. Such confusion is exacerbated by the fact that many crimes are also torts. What distinguishes a crime from a tort, however, is the nature of the offense: As we've seen in Chapter 5, criminal law concerns itself with wrongs against society as a whole and is punitive in nature, while tort law concerns itself with wrongs against individuals and is primarily compensatory in nature. To put it another way, crimes are wrongs against society while torts are offenses against individuals.

Tort law is grounded on the principle that individuals in a free society have the right to be left alone—to live free of unreasonable interference from others. While not every action that an individual may consider objectionable may rise to the level of an *actionable tort* (a recognized civil wrong for which a court may grant civil relief), tort law as it has developed from early common law through today recognizes a large number of specific torts that individuals can inflict on one another. This chapter will provide an overview of the most common intentional torts against persons and property. Negligence and strict liability torts will be the subject of Chapter 7.

## BREACH OF DUTY AS A PREREQUISITE TO TORT LIABILITY ● ● ● ● ● ● ● ● ● ● ● ● ● ● ● ● ● ● ● ● ● ● ● ● ● ● ● ● ● ● ● ● ●

Tort liability is based upon the breach of a civil duty owed by one person to another. All persons in a society have the responsibility, for example, not to cause injury to one another either on purpose or carelessly. Thus, purposely hitting a stranger with a stone thrown at him or her is a tort (battery), as is carelessly hitting a person's car with a stone carelessly thrown from a rooftop without the intention of doing any harm (negligence). It is also possible to breach a duty of care owed another, and be thus guilty of a tort, by failing to act when one has a duty to act. A person who fails to step on the brakes when approaching a red light breaches an affirmative duty to act, as does a parent who fails to stop a minor child from destroying another's property while under his or her direct care. Automobile drivers have an affirmative duty to observe the rules of the road, and parents have an affirmative duty to supervise children in their care to prevent them from harming themselves or others.

Where no duty to act exists, individuals are free to act or refuse to act in order to prevent harm to the persons or property of others as they see fit. Thus, a passerby who sees another in a dangerous situation generally has no duty to lift a finger to help, and can merely stand by and watch events unfold without incurring criminal or tort liability. The following example will illustrate:

> *Mark Meany, a sadistic sociopath, sees a young, lost child playing next to the lion's cage at the zoo just before feeding time. He looks around and notices no other adults in the area. Deciding that this scene has some entertainment potential for him, he sits down and waits as the child plays about the cage, hoping that he will eventually squeeze through the bars. A half-hour later, Mark gets his wish as the child slips through the cage and is promptly pounced on by the lion. (Don't worry: The child escapes after suffering only a very small scratch on one knee.) If the parents of the child want to have Mark arrested for endangering the safety of a minor (a crime) and for the torts of battery, intentional infliction of emotional distress and negligence, will they succeed?*

Mark is clearly an immoral, monstrous individual. Nevertheless, he has committed no crime or tort, since he was not responsible for placing the child in danger and had no duty to intervene on the child's behalf. If, on the other hand, Mark were a close relative of the child, a police officer or a firefighter, a duty to act would have been imposed on him by nature of his familial ties to the infant or the duties of his job.

## INTENTIONAL TORTS AGAINST PERSONS · · · · · · · · · · · · · · · · · · ·

The first type of torts that we will explore is intentional torts against persons. While we explore the most common torts of this type, keep in mind that each of the following torts comes into existence only if a duty owed by the *tort feasor* (the person who perpetrates a tort) to the victim is breached. When intentional torts against persons are involved, the duty typically breached is the duty to refrain from undue interference with the rights of others to be left alone.

### BATTERY

*Battery* can be defined as an *unconsented-to touching* that is either harmful or offensive. Any intentional touching that has not been consented to can give rise to the tort, whether or not serious injury occurs; the extent of the injury is relevant only in determining the monetary damages that the victim is entitled to. For purposes of the tort, a touching is deemed to be offensive if a reasonable person would object to the touching under similar circumstances. Punching someone on the nose without provocation is clearly a battery. But so is kissing a stranger without permission, since a reasonable person would likely find such an unconsented-to touching objectionable.

## ASSAULT

The tort of *assault* consists of placing someone in fear of an imminent battery. For the tort to be complete, all that is required is that the victim believe that he or she is about to be battered. It is not necessary that a battery actually take place or that the tort feasor intend to batter the victim. The tort seeks to compensate the victim for the apprehension of fearing a battery, and all that is required is that the apprehension be reasonable for the tort to be complete. Thus, the words, "I am going to kill you" can constitute assault if the hearer reasonably believes that he or she is about to be harmed. Likewise, pointing a gun at someone constitutes assault if the person at whom the gun is aimed reasonably believes that he or she may be shot. But pointing a gun at someone's back is not assault unless the person is aware that he or she is being targeted. Also, individuals who learn *after the fact* that they had been placed in danger are not the victims of assault, since they are not placed in fear of immediate or imminent danger.

## INTENTIONAL INFLICTION OF EMOTIONAL DISTRESS

Intentionally causing someone to suffer extreme emotional distress by engaging in extremely cruel, outrageous conduct constitutes the tort of *intentional infliction of emotional distress*. Like assault, this tort attempts to compensate victims for the apprehension that they are subjected to by the willful acts of others.

In order for this tort to arise, the conduct of the tort feasor must be outrageous and shockingly cruel. Conduct that is merely unkind will not give rise to the tort, regardless of the pain that such conduct causes the person at whom it is directed. Telling someone, "You're ugly and stupid," for example, will not give rise to the tort, regardless of the devastation these words may cause for the person hearing them; the statement may be unkind, antisocial and mean-spirited, but it is not sufficiently shocking to constitute intentional infliction of emotional distress. Calling up someone at 4:00 A.M every day for a month to say, "You're ugly and stupid," however, probably is sufficiently outrageous conduct to give rise to the tort.

## FALSE IMPRISONMENT

Intentionally interfering with a person's right to freely move about without just cause constitutes the tort of *false imprisonment*. The restriction can be physical or psychological in nature. Tying a person to a chair clearly constitutes the tort, but so does threatening a person with recrimination if he or she leaves—even if no physical restraint is used.

In business, this tort is of particular interest to retailers who frequently question suspected shoplifters. Holding someone for questioning who is reasonably suspected of shoplifting is permissible, provided that the length of time the person's movements are restrained is reasonable, and further provided that the retailer has reasonable suspicion for suspecting the person to be a shoplifter. A customer who is unreasonably detained or who is questioned for an unreasonable length of time can sue successfully for false imprisonment.

## INVASION OF PRIVACY

Tort law recognizes an individual's fundamental right to privacy, and provides four distinct torts to compensate persons whose right to privacy is violated. *Invasion of privacy* as a tort encompasses the following four distinct torts.

**Appropriation of a person's name or likeness for commercial use**    It is a tort to use a person's name or likeness for commercial purposes without permission. The law recognizes the right of individuals to profit from the use of their name or likeness, as well as to prevent others from using their name or likeness for commercial purposes without consent. Thus, if Joan Smith, a famous athlete, eats Brand X cereal, the makers of Brand X cannot state that fact (even though it is true) in promotional material without her consent, nor can they use her picture on a cereal box unless she authorizes it. A newspaper, magazine or television newscast *can* use her name and likeness without her consent for a newsworthy purpose, however; such use does not constitute a commercial purpose in the eyes of the law.

**Intrusion into seclusion**    It is a tort to willfully observe the private conduct of others under circumstances where an expectation of privacy exists. Before the tort arises, three conditions must be met: (1) the conduct observed must be private, not public, (2) the intrusion must be willful, and (3) the nature of the intrusion must be such that it is objectionable to a reasonable person. A passerby who glances into an open ground-level window from the street is not invading anyone's privacy, regardless of the private nature of the acts observed inside, since there can be no reasonable expectation of privacy for persons who carry out their business in plain view. But a passerby who climbs a telephone pole to look into a second-floor window is clearly guilty of invasion of privacy.

**False light**    It is a tort to place persons in a false light by publishing true facts about them in such a way that unpopular views or actions are attributed to them. In order for the tort to arise, the views or actions that are attributed to the victim through false light must be objectionable to a reasonable person. The following example should illustrate:

> *Jane Doe, a prominent politician, stops to give assistance to the victims of an automobile accident. She helps to extricate five people from their car and leaves after an ambulance arrives. She later learns that the five individuals, whom she had not previously met, happen to be members of the American Communist Party when she reads the following headline in the next morning's paper: "Doe seen driving away from accident site after meeting with 5 Communists." If Jane sues, what result?*

Jane wins, of course, since the headline clearly places her in a false light—making it appear that she had unlawfully left the site of an accident, and further making it seem as though she had had an official meeting with known Communists.

**Public disclosure of private facts**    Publication of private facts that a reasonable person would find objectionable can also result in a valid invasion-of-privacy tort. For this tort to arise, the facts disclosed must be private in nature and must be objectionable to a reasonable person. Note that truth is *not* a defense to this tort, as long as the truth disclosed is not generally known and a reasonable person would object to its disclosure.

## DEFAMATION

The tort of defamation consists of publishing false statements about a person that cause damage to the person's reputation. Defamation takes two forms: *libel*, if the false statements are printed or broadcast over the commercial airways (radio or television), and *slander* if the false statements are spoken.

In a successful defamation suit, the following three requirements must be established: (1) the statement must be false, (2) it must have a negative effect on the person's reputation, and (3) it must be published (communicated to at least one third party).

If the person or company suing for defamation is a private person, the only issue remaining once defamation is proven is that of damages—what monetary sum will compensate the person or company for the damage to the reputation made by the false statements. If the person suing is a *public figure* (a person who has either thrust himself or herself into the public eye or who has been thrust into the limelight by events outside of his or her control), a fourth requirement must be met before a successful defamation action can be brought: It must be shown that the false, damaging statements made about the person were made with *malice*. For the purpose of the tort, *malice* is defined as making a false statement with the actual knowledge that it is false, or with reckless disregard for its truth or falsity. While the wisdom of making a distinction between private individuals and public figures can be debated, the reason for treating public figures differently from private individuals is a recognition by the law that public figures are likely to be scrutinized by media and others. The double standard is an answer to the dilemma posed by conflicting interests: freedom of speech versus the individual's right to privacy.

Whether a person is a private or public figure, the tort of defamation requires that damage to the person's reputation made by the false statement be shown. Merely showing that a false statement was made is not enough; the plaintiff must also show actual damage to his or her reputation. Such damage can include loss of business as a result of the false statement, or simply that the person's stature was tangibly diminished in the eyes of friends, business associates and the general public, leading to some economic loss. An exception to the general rule where actual harm need not be shown is where the false statements impugn a person's moral character or falsely accuse the person of having contracted a dreaded disease, such as AIDS or a venereal disease, or being addicted to any drug; false statements about these matters are deemed harmful in themselves because of the serious harm they pose to a person's reputation and ability to earn a living.

A problem with defamation actions relates to defamation aimed at a group of people. The larger the group, the more difficult it becomes to prove that any one individual in it is harmed by the statements, regardless of their falsity, maliciousness or even viciousness. A perfect example is the maligning of entire professions by such statements as: "All lawyers are thieves," "All doctors are quacks," or "All accountants are cheats." The mere size of these groups of professionals makes it impossible to show that any one person is harmed by such statements, even though taken together and repeated often enough, they might indeed tend to damage the reputation of the group. If a group is so small that its individual members are readily identifiable, such general false statements can be the source of libel actions. Thus, "All lawyers are liars, cheats and immoral cretins" is not actionable, since no one lawyer can show significant damage to his or her reputation from a statement aimed at an entire profession; but "All lawyers in Smalltown are liars, cheats and immoral cretins" *can* be the basis of a defamation suit by one or all lawyers in Smalltown if there are only a handful of legal practitioners there.

## FRAUD

*Fraud* occurs whenever one person intentionally misleads another into undertaking some action that causes the defrauded party some harm. In order for this tort to arise, the following five elements must be proven by the defrauded party:

1. a misrepresentation by the defendant to the plaintiff;
2. about a material fact (a significant, important, relevant fact); or
3. made in order to induce the defendant to take some action;
4. reliance by the plaintiff on the misrepresentation; and
5. harm suffered by the plaintiff as a result of his or her reliance on the defendant's misrepresentation.

Fraud typically arises in the context of contract negotiations, where one party purposely lies to another about some material fact relating to the contract in order to induce the defrauded party to enter into the contract. But fraud is not limited to the inducement of a contract. The inducement of any act by a material misrepresentation that is calculated to induce that act can be the basis of a legal action for fraud. The following examples should illustrate:

- *Barbara tells Howard that her 1992 Toyota Corolla has 25,000 miles on it in order to induce him to purchase the car. Howard believes her and agrees to purchase the automobile, which actually has 125,000 miles on it but has had its odometer tampered with to show only 25,000 miles.*

- *Bob tells Sandra that he is collecting funds for hurricane relief after a bad storm causes extensive damage to the Northeast. Sandra makes a generous cash contribution, which Bob happily invests in his retirement fund.*

- *Tom tells his parents that he needs a $2,000 computer to help with his studies at State University. The parents believe their son and buy the computer, which Tom promptly sells for $1,500 to another student. He then books a Caribbean cruise with his girlfriend with the proceeds.*

The tort of fraud has been committed by Barbara, Bob and Tom, even though only the first example involves a contractual situation. In each case, the defrauded parties would be able to sue for damages arising from the fraudulent misrepresentations.

## INTENTIONAL TORTS AGAINST PROPERTY  . . . . . . . . . . . . . . . . .

A second type of common torts involves interference with or damage to individuals' rights to exclusively enjoy their personal and real property.

### TRESPASS TO LAND

*Trespass to land* involves an intentional physical act that results in an unjustified intrusion onto another's land without the owner's consent. The tort is complete as soon as the trespass occurs; there is no requirement that any actual harm be done to the land—the tort seeks to compensate not damage to real estate, but rather the intrusion into another's land and the attendant interference with the true owner's right to exclusively possess and enjoy his or her property. Remember from the previous chapter that trespass is also a crime, and is also punishable as such *in addition to* the tort liability imposed on the trespasser.

Where no actual damage is caused to the land, the measure of damages awarded is usually slight, and may include only *nominal damages* (damages in name only—usually one dollar). When the nature of the trespass is continuing or when damage is actually done to the land, substantial damage awards are likely. A property owner may also ask the judge for an *injunction*—an order prohibiting the trespasser from continuing to trespass in the future. Injunctive relief is typically awarded by judges when trespass is of a continuing nature. Failing to observe an injunction can lead to stiff penalties (including jail time) for contempt of court.

As you will see in Chapter 28, "Real Property," ownership of land extends to the land itself, to any permanent structures on it and to the space above and below the land. For purposes of the tort of trespass to land, any physical intrusion into another's real estate can give rise to the tort; walking on another's land, purposely throwing a ball on it, tunneling underneath it or firing a gun or arrow over it all constitute the tort of trespass.

Where the trespass is innocent (e.g., the person did not realize he or she was entering another's land) or is the result of an emergency situation, such as fleeing a dangerous wild animal or entering land to assist someone in danger, the trespass is deemed excused, but the trespasser must leave upon learning he or she is trespassing or as soon as the emergency situation ends, or be subject to tort liability for the trespass.

### TRESPASS TO PERSONAL PROPERTY

Just as the owner of real estate has the right to exclusively possess and enjoy his or her real property, the owner of personal property also has the exclusive right to enjoy and use his or her property free of outside interference. Any willful interference with that right results in the tort of *trespass to personal property*. As with trespass to real property, it is not necessary to prove that any damage was done to the property before a trespass action can be brought. The following example will illustrate:

> *Bill, a good neighbor, wishes to surprise Sam, a sour old malcontent whose sole existence seems to re-volve around being miserable. Without Sam's permission or knowledge, Bob goes into Sam's garage and removes his old lawn mower, intending to tune it up and sharpen its blade before the mowing season starts. A week later, he returns the mower to its rightful place, cleaned, sharpened and tuned up as good as new. When he informs Sam that he has revitalized his old mower, hoping to see the man smile for once in his life, Sam flies into a rage and decides to sue Bill for trespass to land and trespass to per-sonal property. What result?*

Bill will learn that no good deed goes unpunished when he defends himself against this lawsuit, for he is guilty of trespass to both land and personal property. Alas, his good intentions are irrelevant; the only issue is whether he willfully and without permission entered Sam's real estate (he did) and likewise willfully and without per-mission removed the lawn mower from Sam's garage, thereby depriving him tem-porarily of the exclusive right to its use and enjoyment (he did that, too). What damages is a court likely to award in this case? Nominal damages only: one dollar for the tres-pass to land and one dollar for the trespass to personal property.

## CONVERSION

The tort of *conversion* consists of permanently depriving the owner of personal property of its use and enjoyment through theft or destruction of the personal property. Where theft or willful destruction of the property are involved, the wrongdoer is also subject to criminal liability. If the destruction of the personal property is accomplished through mere carelessness, as opposed to willful conduct, tort damages are still available, though no criminal liability would attach to the act. The following examples will illustrate:

> *José borrows Fernando's Legal Environment of Business book. While using the book, he accidentally drops a glass of grape juice over it, badly staining the pages. José is guilty of the tort of conversion, and liable to Fernando for the cost of the book. He is not, however, guilty of any crime since the conduct was unintentional.*

> *Cindy borrows Yetunde's camcorder and sells it to Wendy (an innocent buyer), telling Yetunde that the camcorder was stolen. Cindy is guilty of conversion and of the crime of theft.*

> *Ben borrows Martha's snowblower and accidentally damages it beyond repair when he comes across large rocks buried under the snow in his driveway. He is guilty of conversion of the snowblower and must pay its reasonable worth to Martha if it cannot be repaired. He is not, however, guilty of any crime because the damage was caused unintentionally.*

## QUESTIONS

1. What is the basic difference between tort law and criminal law?
2. Can a failure to act lead to tort liability? Explain.

3. What is a basic prerequisite to tort liability?

4. List the four invasion-of-privacy torts.

5. What is the basic difference between false light and defamation?

6. What are the requirements of the tort of defamation?

7. When does malice need to be proven in a defamation action? How is malice defined?

8. What are the requirements for proving fraud?

9. Name three torts against property.

# H Y P O T H E T I C A L     C A S E S

1. Pamela Prankster, a practical joker who delights in subjecting her friends to sophomoric pranks, decides to dress up as a burglar and scare her friend Mohammed as an April Fool's prank. She arrives at Mohammed's door at midnight, dressed in typical cat-burglar garb, including a stocking over her face, and sporting a realistic-looking plastic toy gun. She breaks into Mohammed's home by opening his ground-level bedroom window and climbing in. She then accosts the sleeping man, points the gun at his head and yells, "Wake up, handsome!" at the top of her voice. He wakes up agitatedly and is immediately struck by a terror that leaves him unable to move or speak. After enjoying her friend's confusion and fear for a full minute, she removes the stocking from her face and yells out good-naturedly, "Gotcha! April Fool!" Mohammed, who is not amused, decides to sue Pamela for civil damages.
   a. What torts can he sue for? What is the likely result of his case?
   b. If Pamela, while she is pointing the fake gun at Mohammed but before waking him, decides the joke is a bad idea and leaves the way she entered, is she guilty of any tort? Explain fully.

2. Dana borrows Vince's laptop computer over the weekend in order to complete a term paper for her composition class. While using the system, she runs a pirated game she had gotten from a friend on a disk that, unbeknownst to her, contains a computer virus. The virus causes the laptop's hard disk to be reformatted, and rewrites the computer's CMOS chip so that it no longer recognizes any peripherals and cannot be booted, even from a floppy disk. Vince takes the computer to a local technician who informs him that repairing the damage and re-installing the software will cost more than the computer's $550 market price. Under what theory, if any, can Vince successfully sue Dana for the computer's market price? Is Dana guilty of any crime with regard to the incident?

3. Bob, a prominent state politician with aspirations to federal office, confides his marital infidelity to his friend Maurice, asking him to keep the matter secret, since its disclosure could harm his election chances. Five years later, when Bob is a candidate for national office, Maurice decides that fame and money are preferable to friendship and signs a lucrative book deal with Seedy Press to write a book on

Bob's extramarital affair. Bob, furious at his friend's infidelity to him, sues Maurice for the tort of libel. What will he need to prove in order to prevail over Maurice? Will he prevail? Under what other tort should Bob sue Maurice?

## ETHICS AND THE LAW: QUESTIONS FOR FURTHER STUDY  . . . . . . . . . . . . . . . . . . . . . . . . . . . . . . . . .

1. In this chapter, we have seen that some types of behavior can be both a crime and a tort, thus subjecting persons who engage in such behavior to both criminal and civil penalties. Do you think such double punishment is justifiable, or unduly harsh? Explain your answer fully.

2. Minors are generally held to be responsible for their own torts in most states, with some states exacting limited responsibility for minors' torts to their parents up to a set limit, such as $500 to $1,500. What is your view on this issue? Should parents be held accountable for their minor children's torts? If so, should there be any limits set? If not, is it fair to the victims of minors' willful or negligent torts that they often have no immediate viable recourse against penniless minors? Explain.

# NEGLIGENCE AND STRICT LIABILITY

As we've seen in the previous chapter, there can be no tort liability unless a duty of care owed by the defendant to the plaintiff has been breached, resulting in some injury to the defendant's rights. Chapter 6 introduced some of the more common intentional torts. In this chapter, we will explore two types of torts that can give rise to liability for harm that was not intended by the tort feasor: negligence and strict liability.

## NEGLIGENCE ...................................................

Every member of society is charged with a duty to act with reasonable care at all times in order to avoid possible injury to others. The law imposes a duty on all of us to take the precautions that an imaginary *reasonably prudent person* would take in order to prevent inflicting foreseeable injury to others as we go about our daily routines. If a person falls short of this standard of care, thus bringing about foreseeable injury to others, liability for the tort of *negligence* will arise. A defendant to the tort of negligence is charged not with willful conduct, but rather with failing to observe reasonable care under the circumstances—with failing to take the precautions to avoid the injury that a reasonably prudent person would have taken under similar circumstances. The *reasonable person* standard is an objective one; it is a requirement that each member in society act at least in keeping with a reasonably prudent person—a fictional member of society that represents the *average citizen* (a person of average intellect, average common sense and average skills).

In order to bring a successful suit for negligence, the plaintiff must show that:

1. the defendant breached a duty of care owed him or her;
2. the breach brought about *foreseeable* harm to the plaintiff; and
3. the breach was the *proximate cause* (direct, actual cause) of that harm.

The first requirement, breach of a duty of care, is shown by convincing the *trier of fact* (usually a jury, or a judge where the right to trial by jury is waived) that the defendant failed to exercise the care that a reasonably prudent person would have exercised under the circumstances. In other words, one establishes negligence by proving carelessness—failure of the duty to observe due care under the circumstances. The following instances all represent negligent action by the parties involved:

- *Deidre, while driving on an icy road at forty miles per hour, fails to come to a complete stop at a red light and is struck by another car crossing the intersection.*

- *Paula does not shovel her sidewalk after a snowstorm, and a neighbor walking on it slips and falls, fracturing a leg.*

- *John, a jogger, rounds a corner of a busy city street without stopping and crashes into Tom, who falls to the ground and chips two teeth.*

- *Peter, a New York City resident who likes to read* The New York Times *on his way to the subway every morning, crashes against a legal street vendor's table on the sidewalk and causes extensive damage to the vendor's wares.*

In each of these examples, the persons involved failed to observe due care under the circumstances, and breached the duty of care to the victims of their negligence of not exercising the care that a reasonably prudent person would have exercised under the circumstances. The next question to be asked is whether the breach of that duty of care brought about foreseeable harm. The answer for each of the above is yes. Deidre should have realized that driving too fast over slick roads could result in her failure to stop in time at a light and, ultimately, cause an accident; Paula, likewise, should have known that failure to shovel and sand or salt an icy sidewalk could lead to someone falling on it; John should also have realized that running around a corner could result in slamming against an innocent pedestrian, and that the person might then fall and injure himself; and Peter should have realized that reading the paper while walking could cause him to bump into one of the street vendors common in New York City.

The final test for negligence is whether the harm was proximately caused by the negligent act. In order to meet this test, the plaintiff must show that the loss was directly caused by the defendant's negligence and would not have been caused *if not for* that negligence. Proximate cause requires a direct link between the cause of the harm and the negligent act. If there are any intervening circumstances that contribute to the events leading to the injury, then negligence is not the cause of the injury in the eyes of the law. Intervening causes include any outside circumstance not caused by the defendant and not within the defendant's control. In addition, there must be a close link in space and time to the injury and the negligent act; if the person injured by the defendant's negligence is an unreasonably long distance away from the defendant's negligent act, or if an unreasonably long period of time passes between the negligent act and the resulting injury, the injury is not deemed to be proximately caused by the defendant's negligence. The following example should illustrate:

> • *Leona, a bad driver, runs a red light at an intersection. Leon, an even worse driver, sees Leona run the*
> • *red light two blocks away and panics; he swerves right, steps hard on the accelerator (mistaking it for*
> • *the brake) and crashes through the display window of a department store.*

Despite the fact that Leona was clearly negligent in her failure to stop at the red light, she is not responsible for Leon's accident since her negligence was not its proximate cause, Leon was too far away (two blocks) to be in any danger when Leona crossed the intersection; his accident was the direct cause of his overreaction, not of Leona's negligence. Had he been only fifty feet away when Leona ran the light, he probably would have been within the zone of danger and his actions might have been traced to Leona's negligence. But two city blocks away is simply too far, and the accident must be attributed to a separate intervening cause: Leon's poor driving skills.

## DEFENSES TO NEGLIGENCE . . . . . . . . . . . . . . . . . . . . . . . . . . .

Even when negligence is established, it is still possible for a defendant to avoid tort liability by raising and proving one of three defenses: contributory negligence, comparative negligence or assumption of the risk. The effect of these three defenses is to limit or completely avoid a defendant's tort liability.

### CONTRIBUTORY NEGLIGENCE

At common law, a person suing another under a negligence theory could recover only if he or she were free of any negligence. If a plaintiff was found to have been even slightly negligent in the events leading up to his or her injuries, he or she was barred from recovering any damages from the other person, even if the defendant's negligence far outweighed the plaintiff's. When you consider that, in almost every accident, all parties are to blame to some extent for allowing the accident to happen (are *contributorily negligent*), the harshness of this rule becomes clear: Even the slightest negligence on the part of a person injured by another's negligence bars him or her from recovering any damages—regardless of the extent of the other person's negligence. Over time, a number of technical rules were developed to permit recovery by parties who were partially negligent under certain circumstances. Today, most jurisdictions have abandoned contributory negligence as a complete defense to negligence actions in favor of a comparative negligence defense.

### COMPARATIVE NEGLIGENCE

A *comparative negligence* defense allows plaintiffs who are contributorily negligent to sue negligent defendants successfully, but limits their recovery to the percentage of their damages not caused by their negligence. To put it another way, comparative negligence allows a reduction in a plaintiff's recovery proportional to his or her negligence. In the majority of jurisdictions that recognize comparative negligence, a jury (or a judge acting as trier of fact, if the parties waive a jury trial) is asked to assign a percentage of fault to each party in a negligence action—to decide, in essence, how negligent each person was in contributing to the accident. After a jury assigns the proper percentage of culpability to each party, each party is entitled to recover from the other party damages equal to their actual damages minus a setoff for their negligence equal to the percentage of their damages attributable to their negligence. If this sounds confusing, the following example will clarify matters:

> *Tom, Dick and Harriet are involved in a three-car accident in which they each share a part of the fault. A jury, after hearing all the evidence, assigns the following percentages of responsibility to each party for bringing about the accident: 60 percent to Tom, 30 percent to Dick and 10 percent to Harriet. If each party suffered $10,000 in property damages, they would each be entitled to recover the amount of their damages set off by the percentage of fault they shared in the accident. Tom, Dick and Harriet, then, would each recover as follows:*
> - Tom will receive $10,000 minus 60% of his damages ($10,000 − $6,000 = $4,000);
> - Dick will receive $10,000 minus 30% of his damages ($10,000 − $3,000 = $7,000); and
> - Harriet will receive $10,000 minus 10% of her damages ($10,000 − $1,000 = $9,000).

Comparative negligence jurisdictions today are divided into two camps: those that recognize *pure comparative negligence* and those that recognize *modified comparative negligence*. Pure comparative negligence jurisdictions allow plaintiffs to recover no matter what their percentage of negligence, while modified comparative negligence jurisdictions allow plaintiffs to recover only if they are less than 50 percent negligent themselves. In the minority of jurisdictions that recognize pure comparative negligence, such as New York, a plaintiff who is 99 percent responsible for causing an accident can still recover 1 percent of his or her damages from a defendant who was only 1 percent negligent in bringing about the accident. This can cause some interesting problems (and a legal dilemma) of its own, as the following example will illustrate:

> *Dan Dunderhead, the proud owner of a brand-new Ferrari, drives his automobile at 135 miles per hour down the interstate. Sally Slowpoke, a good, cautious driver, merges into Dan's lane with her 1974 Chrysler Valiant, not realizing Dan's excessive speed. Dan, unable to stop in time or to swerve out of the way, rear-ends Sally, totally destroying his car and Sally's. At trial, a jury finds Dan 90 percent negligent and Sally 10 percent negligent (for failing to better estimate Dan's excessive speed before merging into the highway). If Dan's car is worth $200,000 and Sally's is worth $500, Dan will have to pay Sally 90 percent of her loss ($500 × 90% = $450) for a total of $450, while Sally will have to pay Dan 10 percent of his loss ($200,000 × 10% = $20,000) for a whopping $20,000!*

## ASSUMPTION OF THE RISK

A third defense, and a total bar to a recovery in a negligence or in a willful tort action, is *assumption of the risk*. A plaintiff who engages in an activity he or she knows to be dangerous cannot sue for any injury sustained as a result of engaging in such an activity. The key here is whether the plaintiff knew or should have known the inherent danger in engaging in the activity in question, and whether he or she voluntarily assumed that risk. One who voluntarily engages in a dangerous sport such as boxing or auto racing, for example, cannot successfully sue for any reasonably foreseeable injury received from engaging in that activity. The same holds true for a person who knowingly uses a defective product or participates in an activity known to carry some risk. In each of the following examples, the injured party would be barred from recovering damages based on a defense of assumption of risk:

- A spectator along the first-base line who is hit by a line-drive foul.
- A person who borrows a car he knows to have badly worn brakes and who is later injured when the car's brakes fail.
- A driver who drives with a badly worn tire that blows out and causes him to lose control of his car.
- A person who plays with a dog known to bite and is bitten by it.
- A golfer who is hit on the head by a golf ball during a game.

Keep in mind that the defenses of assumption of the risk and its close cousin, product misuse, are available to defendants in any tort action, including the strict liability torts that we will discuss next.

## STRICT LIABILITY · · · · · · · · · · · · · · · · · · · · · · · · · · · · · · · · ·

Under certain circumstances, a person who is neither negligent nor guilty of an intentional tort may still be required to pay damages for injuries that result from his or her activities. Strict liability (also called *liability without fault*) is imposed by law for injuries that result from certain kinds of activities that by their nature are highly dangerous. Strict liability torts arise out of three main situations: ultrahazardous activities, product liability and damage done by wild animals. We will examine each of these areas in turn.

### ULTRAHAZARDOUS ACTIVITIES

Some activities are by their very nature highly dangerous, and no amount of care can make them safe. Such activities are considered to be ultrahazardous, and anyone who is injured as a direct result of the activity is entitled to compensation as a matter of law, regardless of the level of care employed by the defendant to ensure safety. *Ultrahazardous activities* such as manufacturing or handling explosives, for example, can never be made completely safe because of the nature of the materials involved. Anyone who engages in such activity is strictly liable for foreseeable injury to third parties that results directly from the activity. A person who suffers an injury as a result of an ultrahazardous activity is entitled to compensation without needing to show the defendant's fault or negligence; once harm is linked to an ultrahazardous activity, liability is automatic, and what compensation to award plaintiffs for their damages becomes the only issue.

As with other torts, the defense of assumption of the risk may be available to defendants in strict liability actions if they can show that the plaintiff assumed the risk through specific action in a given case. Thus, while a defendant is normally strictly liable for foreseeable injuries that stem directly from an ultrahazardous activity such as blasting or demolition work, a plaintiff who willfully walks into a building that is being demolished, ignoring obvious warnings to keep out, would be held to have assumed the risk of his or her injuries and would be barred from recovering damages for them.

## PRODUCT LIABILITY

*Product liability* places strict liability in tort on manufacturers for defects in the design or manufacturing of products that render such products *unreasonably dangerous* to intended users. Examples of unreasonably dangerous products due to design or manufacturing defects would include spoiled food, automobile tires that experience blowouts due to a manufacturing defect during normal use and a car that ignites when rear-ended because of a design defect.

In order for strict product liability to attach, the product must reach the consumer in unaltered form; products that are customized or otherwise changed after their manufacture and before they are sold to consumers are not subject to product liability claims (consumers injured by such altered products can still sue either the manufacturer or the customizer under a negligence theory, however).

It should be noted that the mere fact that a product is dangerous will not subject its manufacturer to a product liability claim; the product must be *unreasonably* dangerous due to a design or manufacturing *defect*. Knives, guns, razor blades and power tools all pose a danger even when properly used; before consumers can sue for product liability relating to these or any other product, they must show that the product was not merely dangerous, but unreasonably dangerous. Thus, a gun that explodes when fired, a drill that short-circuits and shocks the user when properly used or a chain saw whose chain flies off during proper use would all qualify as strict product liability examples, provided they were properly used and were delivered to the consumer from the manufacturer in unaltered form.

## WILD ANIMALS

The keeping of wild animals is deemed to be such a dangerous activity that anyone injured by them is entitled to recover from the animal's owner under a strict liability theory. In order for strict liability to attach, the animal in question must be a *wild animal*—an animal which by its nature is not fully domesticable. Wolves, tigers, elephants, lions, pythons and gorillas have been known to be kept as pets by some people; any personal injury or property damage caused by these animals, however, will subject the owner to strict liability in tort.

Note that the tort applies only to nondomestic animals. The law relating to domestic animals is somewhat different; in most states, owners of domestic animals such as dogs, cats, horses, cattle and the like are responsible only for personal injury these animals cause, based on a negligence theory. As for the property damage these pets cause, owners are generally strictly liable for it if the damage is of a type that is reasonably foreseeable. Thus, if Fido attacks a neighbor, Fido's owner is liable for the attack only if the neighbor can show that Fido's owner was negligent in preventing the attack. If Fido kills the neighbor's cat, however, Fido's owner will be strictly liable to the neighbor for the damage (assuming that dogs can be expected to attack cats sometimes).

Note that all three types of strict liability torts are closely related, and that the thread that binds them is the unreasonable danger posed to innocent third parties, be it from engaging in an ultrahazardous activity, creating an unreasonably dangerous product or keeping a dangerous animal.

## QUESTIONS · · · · · · · · · · · · · · · · · · · · · · · · · · · · · · · · · · · · · · ·

1. What is the essential breach of duty involved in the tort of negligence?
2. Is the *reasonable person* standard an objective or subjective standard for evaluating an individual's behavior?
3. What must a plaintiff prove in a negligence action in order to prevail over the defendant?
4. Define the concept of *proximate cause*.
5. Define *contributory negligence*.
6. At common law, what was the effect of a finding that the plaintiff was contributorily negligent?
7. What is the difference between contributory negligence and comparative negligence?
8. Distinguish *pure* from *modified* comparative negligence.
9. What are some defenses to tort liability?
10. What are the requirements for a product liability suit?

## H Y P O T H E T I C A L    C A S E S

1. Harold and Harriet get into an automobile accident and sue each other for damages. At trial, it is determined that both parties were negligent. A jury finds that Harold's responsibility for the accident was 60 percent and Harriet's was 40 percent. The jury also finds that Harold suffered total damages in the amount of $10,000 and assesses Harriet's damages at $5,000.
   a. Assuming a pure comparative negligence jurisdiction, what will be each party's recovery in this case, if any?
   b. Assuming a modified comparative negligence jurisdiction, what will each party recover in this case?
   c. Assuming a contributory negligence jurisdiction, what result?
2. Bob asks Bernice if he may borrow her bicycle to run a quick errand. Bernice consents to Bob's request, but warns him that the brakes are weak and asks him to test the brakes thoroughly before driving off. Bob agrees and takes the bike. He fails to heed Bernice's warning about the brakes and finds himself unable to stop the bike from careening into a busy intersection at the end of a steep hill. He

suffers serious injuries and sues Bernice for negligence, claiming $5,000 in provable damages. Bernice counterclaims for negligence for $200, the cost of repairing or replacing her bike. You are the judge hearing this case without a jury. How do you decide this case? Explain your answer fully.

3. Sandra and Althea are spectators in a midsummer baseball game. During the game, Sandra is hit on the head by a foul ball and Althea is knocked on the head by a beer bottle thrown by a rowdy drunken fan who purchased and drank a dozen beers from the concession stand during the game. In addition to the minor head injury, both women suffer bad sunburns during the game. Because of their head injuries and bad sunburns, both women miss three days of work the following week and endure substantial pain and suffering. You are their attorney. (Time flies! You've graduated from college, attended law school for three years and passed the bar of your state—all in the span of this question.) Advise each woman of her possible claims against the ball club, the bottle thrower and the player who hit the foul ball, respectively.

4. Martha's dog, Spot, has always been a loving, well-adjusted pet who has not so much as growled at a stranger in his life. Today, however, he ran up to the letter carrier and bit her on the leg after watching a dog perform a similar act on a network comedy show. The letter carrier sues Martha and the network that broadcast the show on a negligence theory. What result?

5. Would your answer to the preceding question be the same if Spot were a wolf? Explain.

## ETHICS AND THE LAW: QUESTIONS FOR FURTHER STUDY  . . . . . . . . . . . . . . . . . . . . . . . . . . . . . . . . . .

Although the law imposes no duty to act on members of society to help one another out of difficult situations, in most states good Samaritans who take it upon themselves to render assistance to someone in need open themselves to liability for both intentional and negligent torts to the people they assist. Many jurisdictions have enacted legislation to protect medical personnel, such as doctors, nurses and medical technicians who administer assistance at accident sites. Such personnel are liable in many (but not all) jurisdictions only for gross negligence or willfully tortious conduct. But in many jurisdictions, these "good Samaritan" statutes do not apply to non–medical personnel who render assistance to accident victims. Thus, it is possible for a person who saves an accident victim's life by rushing him or her to the hospital but causes some other injury in the process to be successfully sued for a tort by the ungrateful victim once he or she recovers. Is there an ethical problem here in your view? If so, how should it be resolved?

# II

# CONTRACTS

A *contract* can be defined as an agreement between two or more parties that is enforceable in the courts. In order to rise to the level of an enforceable contract, an agreement must meet certain criteria: There must be a valid offer and acceptance, the agreement must be supported by consideration, the parties must have the legal capacity to enter into a contract, the agreement must be genuinely assented to by the parties involved, it must be for a legal purpose and (in some cases) the agreement must be evidenced by a signed writing. If any one of these necessary elements of a contract is missing from an agreement, a valid contract will not be formed.

In this unit, we will examine the types of contracts (Chapter 8) and each element of a valid contract (Chapters 9 through 14). We will also explore the rights of persons with regard to contracts that affect them directly but to which they are not parties (Chapter 15). Finally, we will examine the various means through which parties can discharge their contractual obligations, and we will explore the consequences that flow from a breach of contract (Chapter 16) and the remedies available to compensate parties who suffer a breach (Chapter 17).

CHAPTER

# GENERAL INTRODUCTION
# TO CONTRACTS

As previously noted, a contract is an enforceable agreement between two or more parties. All of us enter into dozens of binding contracts on a daily basis without any conscious awareness that we do so. Buying a subway token, ordering a cup of coffee at a diner, taking a suit to the cleaners, buying a movie ticket and renting a car for a weekend trip all involve valid contracts that give rise to certain rights and responsibilities to the parties involved. We may not think of casual business transactions as contracts, in great part because such transactions are usually carried out to the mutual satisfaction of the parties involved: you pay the agreed-upon fee and get your suit back after it is cleaned, or drink your coffee after it is served, or hop on the subway and eventually reach your destination (more or less on time). The significance of these contracts is important only in the rare cases when parties do not perform as promised: the coffee the diner serves you makes you sick; the suit you get back from the cleaners has a hole in it; the brakes on the rental car you are driving fail to work. It is at these exceptional times when we need to be concerned about whether or not an underlying contract existed, and to examine the rights and responsibilities of the parties involved.

If a contract is defined as a legally enforceable agreement between two or more people, the very definition of a contract implies that not all agreements rise to the level of contracts. While we may all have a moral obligation to honor our promises, the law recognizes only certain types of promises as enforceable. Only promises that meet certain criteria gain the special significance of a contract. For a valid contract to be formed, each of the following criteria must be present:

1. there must have been a valid offer and acceptance to enter into a contract;
2. there must be valid consideration (something of legal value obtained by each party to the contract);
3. each party to the contract has to have the capacity (legal ability) to enter into a contract;

72

4. each party had to freely assent to enter into the contract;

5. the contract must be for a legal purpose; and

6. in a limited number of cases, the contract must be evidenced by a signed writing in order to be binding on the parties.

In the chapters that follow, we will closely examine in turn each of these prerequisites to a valid contract. For now, let it suffice to say that if even one necessary criterion is missing, the underlying agreement will not rise to the level of a binding contract and will not be enforceable in the courts. A few brief examples will illustrate:

> *John promises to give Ellen his stereo next week, after he buys a new one. Ellen agrees to accept the gift. John then changes his mind and gives the stereo to Rachel. If Ellen sues John for breach of contract she will lose, since John's promise was not supported by consideration and thus no contract was formed by Ellen's acceptance of his promise to make her a gift. (Ellen had not agreed to give anything of legal value in exchange for receiving the stereo.)*

> *Chuck agrees to turn over his Rolex watch to Tina in exchange for $100. The promise is made by Chuck while Tina holds a gun to his head. No contract is formed (Chuck's assent to enter into the contract is not freely given, so that no valid contract is formed for lack of his genuine assent.)*

> *Bob, who has been judicially declared to be incompetent to enter into contracts, orders 100 Napoleon Bonaparte costumes from Costumes-B-Us. The agreement is invalid and no contract is formed because Bob lacks the capacity to enter into a valid contract.*

A popular misconception about contract law is that agreements between parties need to be expressed in writing in order to be enforceable. This has never been true. In fact, with limited exceptions to be covered in Chapter 14, verbal agreements are just as binding as written ones. It is even possible to enter into a binding contract without either party uttering a single word; a contract can be implied from the actions of the parties as well as from their oral or written words. What is crucial in contract law is *the intention of the parties to enter into a binding agreement.* Precisely how that intention is expressed is largely irrelevant to the validity of the underlying agreement.

## CLASSIFICATION OF CONTRACTS . . . . . . . . . . . . . . . . . . . . . . .

Contracts can be classified as express, implied-in-fact, bilateral, unilateral, simple and formal. Each distinct type of contract will be examined next.

### EXPRESS CONTRACTS

An *express contract* is formed by specific oral or written language of the parties. Whenever parties to a contract define the terms of their agreement either orally or in writing, an express contract results, as in the following examples:

> *Allison agrees to install new windows in Bernie's home for $8,000. The parties execute a signed agreement specifying when the work is to be done and how payment is to be made. This is a typical express written contract.*

> *Frank verbally offers to mow Wendy's lawn all summer for $8 an hour. Wendy verbally accepts the arrangement. This is a typical express oral contract.*

## IMPLIED-FACT-CONTRACTS

While most people usually specify contractual terms in some detail, it is possible to enter into a binding contract without uttering a word if the actions of the parties clearly indicate their intention to enter into a binding contract. In these situations, the resulting contract is said to be *implied in fact*, as the following example illustrates:

> *Lenore walks into Barbara's bakery on a particularly busy day. She is in a hurry, so she grabs a loaf of Italian bread from the counter and waves it at Barbara, who nods in her direction and continues serving other customers. A binding implied-in-fact contract exists between Lenore and Barbara for the purchase of the bread on credit (Lenore will be obligated to pay Barbara the selling price of the bread within a reasonable time).*

## BILATERAL CONTRACTS

A *bilateral contract* is formed by a mutual exchange of promises between the contracting parties. In a bilateral contract, both parties make enforceable promises to each other as part of their contractual agreement. Consequently, a bilateral contract has two *promisors* (persons making contractual promises) and two *promisees* (persons to whom a contractual promise is made). To put it another way, a bilateral contract is one which contains an exchange of promises for present or future performance by all contracting parties, as the following examples will illustrate:

> *Janice agrees to purchase Frank's guitar for $50.*
>
> *Brenda agrees to wash Sam's windows in exchange for his fixing her lawn mower.*
>
> *Phil agrees to work for ABC Corporation in exchange for a weekly salary of $600.*

These three examples all involve bilateral contracts since there is a mutual exchange of promises by both parties to each contract. Janice promises to pay $50 in exchange for Frank's promise to turn over his guitar to her; Brenda promises to wash the windows in exchange for Sam's promise to fix the lawn mower; Phil agrees to work for ABC Corporation in exchange for ABC's promise to pay him $600 per week. As with all bilateral contracts, these examples show that each contract contains two promisors and two promisees. Once the contract arises, there are two *obligors* (persons obligated to perform contractual promises) and two *obligees* (persons entitled to receive the benefit of the obligor's performance in a contract).

## UNILATERAL CONTRACTS

A *unilateral contract* is formed when one party exchanges a promise of future performance in order to induce another party to take some specific action. In other words, a unilateral contract is an exchange of a *promise* for an *act*. Unlike a bilateral contract, where there is a mutual exchange of promises making each party to the contract both a promisor/obligor and a promisee/obligee, a unilateral contract contains only one promisor/obligor. The promisor in a unilateral contract makes a conditional promise to the promisee in order to induce him or her to undertake some action. Note the following typical examples:

- *Pamela Promisor tells Pepe Promisee that she will pay him $100 if he installs a security light in her back yard over the weekend.*

- *Pascuale Promisor tells Paula Promisee that he will pay her $100 if she will repair his deck over the next week.*

- *Peter Promisor tells Patricia Promisee that he will tune up her car if she cleans out his garage.*

In these three examples, unilateral promises are made by Pamela, Pascuale and Peter, who are trying to induce some specific performance by Pepe, Paula and Patricia. The obligation of these promisors will come into existence *only if* the promisees undertake the desired action. Once the promisees begin rendering the performance in question, the promisors will be obligated to perform as promised. But the promisees are not under any obligation to perform; it is completely up to them whether or not to accept the agreement offered by the promisors by beginning the requested performance.

Note that whether a contract is unilateral or bilateral depends upon the terms offered by the promisor: If the promisor is seeking acceptance through the promisee's performance, then the contract is unilateral; but if the promisor is seeking a present commitment for future performance by the promisee, then the contract is bilateral.

### SIMPLE CONTRACTS

A *simple contract* is any agreement that need not follow a specific format in order to be enforceable. Simple contracts can be oral, written, express or implied in fact. The vast majority of contracts entered into by businesses and individuals are simple contracts.

### FORMAL CONTRACTS

At common law, the most common type of *formal contract* was one that needed to be in writing, signed, witnessed and sealed by the parties. Today, most jurisdictions have abolished the significance of the seal for contracts, but the law still recognizes a number of formal contracts that are required to be in a specific form and contain certain specific language in order to be enforceable. These include negotiable instruments such as checks, drafts, notes, *letters of credit* (promises to honor a certain demand instrument when it is presented for payment) and *recognizances* (formal acknowledgements of indebtedness made in court).

## QUESTIONS . . . . . . . . . . . . . . . . . . . . . . . . . . . . . . . . . . . . .

1. What is the basic definition of a contract?
2. What are the basic elements of a valid contract?

3. Is it true that oral contracts are unenforceable? Explain.
4. What is an implied-in-fact contract?
5. What is a bilateral contract?
6. What is a unilateral contract?
7. What is a formal contract?
8. Are most contracts simple or formal?

## H Y P O T H E T I C A L     C A S E S

1. Dennis tells Gwen, "I'm sick and tired of eating fast food every day. If you prepare one of your gourmet dinners for me tomorrow, I'll gladly pay you $100." Gwen does not respond.
   a. Is Dennis's offer to Gwen a unilateral or bilateral contract?
   b. Assume that Gwen wants to accept the offer under Dennis's terms. What must she do? Explain.

2. Sandra tells Lenny, "If you agree to provide me with all the firewood I need for next winter, I will agree to take care of all your gardening needs this spring and summer." Lenny promptly accepts Sandra's offer.
   a. Assume that a valid contract is formed. Is it express or implied in fact?
   b. Is this an offer for a unilateral or a bilateral contract? Explain.

3. Mark agrees to tutor Bill in accounting for three hours per week at $8 per hour throughout the semester. Both parties reduce their agreement to a writing that each signs in turn.
   a. Is this a simple or formal contract?
   b. Is it a bilateral or unilateral contract?
   c. Is this an express or an implied-in-fact contract?

4. Letisha, while browsing at a busy flea market, sees a vase she likes. The proprietor is busy several feet away, but she manages to get his attention by waving a $5 bill and pointing to the vase. The proprietor nods in her direction, and she takes the vase, leaving $5 on the table, in clear view of the proprietor. The proprietor smiles at her and waves.
   a. Under the facts given, was a contract formed?
   b. Is this a simple or formal contract?
   c. Is this an express or an implied-in-fact contract?

CHAPTER

# OFFER AND ACCEPTANCE

As we have already seen, a contract is a legally enforceable agreement between two or more parties. As this definition implies, a contract depends upon the consent of the parties to enter into a binding agreement. Assuming that the other requisite criteria are present (consideration, capacity, genuine assent, legality and, where required, specific form), a binding contract is formed at the moment that a *valid offer* to enter into a contract is *accepted*. As soon as a valid offer is accepted, the parties involved are bound to carry out the terms of their agreement and can be sued for breach of contract if they fail to do so.

## REQUIREMENTS OF A VALID OFFER ....................

A valid offer must contain an unambiguous promise to enter into a contract and must be communicated by the *offeror* (the person making the offer) to the *offeree* (the person to whom the offer is made). An offer that contains the requisite *unambiguous promise* to enter into a contract and is communicated to the offeree can be accepted by the offeree to form a binding contract. While this seems clear enough, it is not always easy to determine whether an offer is unambiguous, or whether it contains a valid promise, or even, in some cases, whether it has been communicated to the offeree. The following examples will illustrate:

- *Rachel tells Ron, "I am considering selling my house for $100,000." Ron immediately replies, "I accept your offer."*

- *Stacy, angry that her motorcycle has broken down for the third time in two months, cries out, "I will sell this junk heap to the first person that gives me a nickel." Helen, who hears the statement, promptly offers Stacy five cents for the motorcycle.*

- *Arthur tells his friend Ranji, "I'll sell you my portable television set for $50." Before Ranji has a chance to reply, Sandy, who overheard the statement, cries out, "I accept your offer."*

77

Although each of these three examples seems to contain a valid offer, in fact none will form a valid contract if accepted under the facts given. In the first example, Rachel's statement does not contain a valid offer because it does not contain an unequivocal promise: Rachel says that she is *considering* selling her house, not that she promises to sell her house. Her statement is not a clear offer, therefore, and no contract will be formed when Ron tries to accept it. In the second example, Stacy's statement certainly seems clear enough, yet under the circumstances it too is not an unequivocal offer, because the statement is made in anger or frustration and should not be interpreted as seriously intended by any offeree. In the last example, Arthur's statement is a clear, unequivocal offer, but it cannot be accepted by Sandy because it was not communicated to *her,* but rather was made to Ranji. Only a person to whom an offer is communicated can accept it. (In this example, Ranji has the power of accepting Arthur's offer, since it is an unambiguous promise that was communicated to him.)

## REVOCATION OF AN OFFER  · · · · · · · · · · · · · · · · · · · · · · · · · · · ·

In general, a valid offer can be accepted at any time until it is either revoked or lapses by the passage of time. The offeror may revoke the offer at any time before it is accepted by communicating his or her intention to revoke to the offeree; notice of revocation is effective when it is received by the offeree. The offer is also revoked if the offeree receives information from any source that clearly indicates the intention of the offeror to revoke the offer; an example of this is an offeree learning that a car that the offeror had offered to sell him has been sold to another party.

An offer may also be made to expire after a set period of time; if that is the case, the offeree must accept the offer during the time period that it is held open in order to form a contract. If Art tells Barbara, "I will sell you my stereo for $75. Take twenty-four hours to think about it," then Barbara must act within the stated time period or the offer will expire. Even when a time period is specified, however, the offeror may still revoke the offer at any time before it automatically expires by communicating his or her wish to revoke to the offeree.

When no time period is specified for acceptance by the offeree, an offer will terminate after a reasonable time passes, even if the offeror does not revoke it. What constitutes a reasonable time period depends on the surrounding circumstances, and hinges largely on the nature of the subject matter of the contract. If the subject matter of the contract is something with a fairly constant value, such as real estate, a reasonable time might be six months or more. On the other hand, when the subject matter of the contract is susceptible to swift market fluctuations or has a limited useful life, the time period for acceptance of the offer can be very short, ranging from less than an hour, when something as volatile as pork belly or soybean futures is involved, to a day or so, when perishables such as fruits and vegetables are the subject of the offer.

Finally, an offer may automatically lapse by operation of law in a number of instances, such as the accidental destruction of the subject matter of the offer before it is accepted, or the death or incapacity of the offeror prior to acceptance of the offer by the offeree. Thus, if Jenine offers to sell her sailboat to Jemal for $10,000 and the sailboat sinks in a storm before Jemal accepts the offer, it automatically lapses; likewise, if Jemal offers to paint Jenine's portrait for $500 and Jemal dies or becomes permanently incapacitated before Jenine accepts the offer, that offer also lapses.

## ACCEPTANCE

An offer is *accepted* when the offeree signals his or her unambiguous assent to the terms of the offeror's offer. In order for the acceptance to be valid, the offeree must communicate the acceptance to the offeror. In addition, the offeree must accept the offer under the exact terms offered by the offeror; the terms in the acceptance must exactly mirror the terms in the offer for the acceptance to be valid. This requirement is commonly referred to as the common-law *mirror image rule,* which holds that any material deviation in the acceptance from the terms of the offer constitutes a *rejection* of the offer. The following example will illustrate:

- *Bob offers to sell Bernice his English racer for $350. Bernice can accept the offer only by agreeing to buy the bicycle under the offered terms. ("I accept," "Your terms are acceptable," "I'll take the bicycle," "Agreed," or any similar unequivocal response would constitute valid acceptance.)*

In this example, any of the following answers would violate the mirror image rule and automatically reject the offer, since each contains either additional or different terms from the original offer:

- "I'll take the bike for $300."
- "I'll take the bike provided you agree to coach me on racing for ten hours at no additional cost."
- "I accept if you put new tires on the bike."

A *counteroffer* also serves as a rejection of the offer. Once a counteroffer is made, the original offeror now becomes the offeree of the counteroffer and can choose to either accept the counteroffer or reject it. A counteroffer has the effect of automatically rejecting the original offer; once a counteroffer is made, the original offeree loses his or her ability to accept the original offer, as the next example illustrates:

- *John offers to sell Jane his comic book collection for $1,500. Jane says she'll take it for $1,250. John now has the right to accept Jane's counteroffer on her terms, reject it, or make another counteroffer of his own. If he rejects the counteroffer, Jane will no longer be able to accept the original offer to buy the comics for $1,500, since a counteroffer serves as a rejection of the original offer.*

Like an offer, an acceptance must be unambiguous. Although the word *accept* need not be used in a valid acceptance, the intent to accept must be unequivocal in order for a contract to be formed. Such responses as "I'm interested," "That sounds good," or "I could go for that" are all too ambiguous to form a valid acceptance.

## MODES OF ACCEPTANCE

An offer can be accepted through any reasonable means that communicates to the offeror the offeree's assent to the terms of the offer. As previously noted, acceptance of a valid offer immediately gives rise to a contract, provided that the other requirements for a valid contract are also present. This is not a problem in face-to-face negotiations, since the acceptance is immediately communicated to the offeror by the offeree and both parties are aware that a contract is formed. But what if an offeree decides to communicate his acceptance through the mail, by telegraph or by use of e-mail? In such cases, the acceptance is effective as of the moment that it is sent, regardless of when or even whether it is received by the offeror. This is commonly referred to as the *mailbox rule*: when acceptance is made by letter, it is effective as soon as a properly stamped and addressed envelope is dropped in a mailbox or handed over to a postal employee for delivery. In most states, the same rule applies to letters carried by carrier services, telegraphs and electronic or voice mail.

The fact that an acceptance is valid when sent, rather than when received, can cause potential problems for offerors, as in this example:

> *James calls ten friends offering to sell them his piano for $450—a bargain, since its market value is $5,000. He tells them each to let him know within a week if they want to accept his offer. The next day, four of his friends write their acceptances in letters that they deposit in a mailbox, properly addressed to James and containing the proper postage; three other friends leave him messages of acceptance on his answering machine at home; one sends him an electronic mail message of acceptance, one leaves an acceptance message with James's secretary and one calls him at work and personally signals her acceptance.*

James had better hope that his friends are very understanding, for he has ten valid contracts to sell his one piano. While only one of his friends will be able to sue successfully for the actual piano (the one who can prove that he or she accepted first), the other nine friends are entitled to money damages (the difference between what they would have paid for the piano and its market value, in this case $4,550 *each*). This example illustrates the danger of making multiple general offers. How can James protect himself? By limiting acceptance to a specific means, such as: "I will sell my piano to the first person who accepts my offer in person at my home."

## ACCEPTANCE OF A UNILATERAL CONTRACT

As previously noted, an offer for a unilateral contract is an exchange of a promise for an act. What the offeror in a unilateral contract wants is not a promise by the offeree in exchange for a promise, but rather for the offeree to accept the contract by performing some specific act. Acceptance of a unilateral contract, then, is made by the offeree beginning performance of the act requested by the offeror. Once performance begins by the offeree, the offeror cannot withdraw the offer and must allow the offeree to complete the task that is the subject matter of the contract. Acceptance by the offeree is complete when the task is finished, and the offeree is at that time entitled to enforce the offeror's promised performance under the contract, as in this example:

*Sherman offers to pay Sari $500 if she paints his garage within the next seventy-two hours. Sari says nothing, but goes out to purchase the required supplies and begins performing the work the next morning. Once Sari begins her performance by purchasing the supplies (even before she actually begins painting the garage), Sherman may not withdraw the offer and must give Sari the opportunity to complete the work. If Sari does not complete the work on time, she will not be entitled to any payment, since she can accept the offer for a unilateral contract only by her full timely performance. On the other hand, if she completes the work on time, she will have accepted Sherman's offer and will be entitled to payment of the $500.*

## QUESTIONS

1. What are the requirements of a valid offer?
2. What are four ways in which a valid offer can be revoked?
3. What effect does a counteroffer have on an offer?
4. What are the elements of a valid acceptance?
5. What means can be used by an offeree to communicate acceptance to the offeror?

## H Y P O T H E T I C A L     C A S E S

1. Harry, while walking down the street, tells his friend Harriet, "I would seriously consider selling you my antique gold Longines watch for $1,000." Harriet does not answer. A month later, she writes Harry a letter stating that she accepts his offer to sell his Longines watch for $1,000.
   a. Is a contract formed? Explain fully.
   b. Would it make a difference if Harriet had accepted the offer the next day? Do you think that a thirty-day period is reasonable to accept an offer for the sale of an antique gold watch?

2. Barbara tells Bob, "If you agree to fix my leaky gutters next week, I will agree to babysit your daughter next weekend for up to ten hours." Bob replies, "You've got a deal, provided that you give me $10 for the parts I'll need to do the work." Under the facts given, is there a valid contract? Explain.

4. Lenny, an accountant, tells Luisa, "I'll gladly keep the books for your business for a yearly fee of $1,000." Lew, who overhears the offer, promptly answers, "I accept, Lenny."
   a. Is there a valid contract between Lenny and Lew? Explain.
   b. What is the proper legal term for Lew's statement?
   c. If Luisa writes Lenny a letter of acceptance and mails it the next day but forgets to put a stamp on the envelope, will a valid contract be formed?

CHAPTER

# 10

# CONSIDERATION

*Consideration* can be defined as something of legal value given or received as an inducement to enter into a contract. For our purposes, you may think of consideration as the *price* of the contract. There are two elements to consideration: (1) a bargained-for exchange, and (2) something of legal value to the receiver or of legal detriment to the giver. To put it another way, consideration is whatever is given and received as the basis of the contract, and must represent something of legal value to the recipient or of legal detriment to the giver. Nearly anything that meets these two criteria can be the basis of consideration for a contract.

In a bilateral contract, both parties must give consideration in order for the contract to be valid, as this example shows:

- *Dan offers to wash Denise's car if she will run an errand for him. If Denise accepts the offer, a valid contract will be formed. The consideration each gets is as follows: Denise gets her car washed (something of value to her) and Dan gets Denise to run an errand for him (something of value to him).*

Notice that consideration does not have to be money, although money is certainly valid consideration. There is also no requirement that the consideration exchanged be of equal value; all that courts generally look for is the existence of consideration that was freely agreed to. If one or both of the parties make a bad bargain, they will find no relief from the courts. For instance, if Dan offers to wash Denise's car for $200 and she freely accepts his offer, a valid contract is formed. That $200 is an excessive amount to pay for a car wash is irrelevant; if the consideration is legal and freely agreed to by the parties, the courts will enforce contracts without weighing the relative value of the consideration each party is obligated to give under the contract.

While consideration usually entails something of value to the receiver, it can also consist of something of detriment to the giver. If the giver of consideration agrees to do some legal act that he or she is not obligated to do, or give up the right to engage in activity that he or she has the legal right to engage in, this constitutes consideration whether or not there is any tangible benefit to the receiver of the act or forbearance. This may seem confusing at first glance, but a brief example will illustrate:

- *Glenda offers to pay Glenn $1,000 if he will stop biting his nails for six months. Glenn accepts the offer in this unilateral contract by not biting his nails for the six-month period. He is entitled to payment of the $1,000. Although his having refrained from nail biting has not conferred a benefit on Glenda, it nonetheless constitutes valid consideration because he has given up engaging in conduct that he had a legal right to engage in (nail biting), and has thus suffered a detriment.*

As this example illustrates, *forbearance*—the giving up of one's right to engage in legal conduct as the basis of a contract—is valid consideration. The only caveat is that the forbearance must be of *legally permissible conduct* in order to constitute valid consideration. If Glenn had given up smoking marijuana for six months in exchange for Glenda's promise of the $1,000 payment, he would not have given valid consideration; giving up conduct one has no legal right to engage in is, not surprisingly, not considered valid consideration.

## ILLUSORY PROMISES

In order for there to be valid consideration in a contract, each party must give something of value to the other, or of detriment to themselves. If the promised performance or forbearance is so vague as to be uncertain or if it is phrased in such a way as to make performance optional, rather than mandatory, then the promised consideration is invalid. Promises that on the face appear to obligate one of the parties to render some performance but in fact do not obligate the party to perform are deemed *illusory promises*; such promises offer only the illusion of consideration. Promises that contain language such as the following are illusory: "I promise to buy all the gasoline I want"; "I promise to let you do any plumbing work I might desire"; or "I promise to take my auto to your shop for repair any time I wish." The key words here are *want, desire,* and *wish.* The problem with these three examples is that the promisor is not obligated to do anything, since he or she might not wish, desire or want any of the noted goods or services.

On the other hand, *requirement contracts*, which obligate one party to purchase all the goods or services they will *need* over a specific period of time, are valid. If, for example, ABC Corporation agrees to purchase all the heating oil it needs to heat its business from Independent Oil Company for the next year at eighty-nine cents a gallon, this is *not* an illusory promise but a valid contract. Even though there is no way to know exactly how much oil ABC will need over the next year, it is clear that it will need *some* oil, and it will have to purchase it from Independent Oil Company at the agreed-upon price.

The same holds true for *output contracts,* in which a manufacturer agrees to sell all the manufactured goods it produces to a specific reseller for a stated price. Even though it may not be possible to know exactly what a manufacturer's output will be from one year to the next, it is enough to know that it will produce *something,* and whatever it produces, that is what it is obligated to sell at the agreed-upon price.

As you might suspect, requirement contracts and output contracts can easily be illusory contracts if one of the parties exercises bad faith; for instance, if oil becomes too expensive in its requirement contract, ABC could always convert to gas heat; likewise, if the price for the goods that a manufacturer produces under an output contract falls precipitously, the manufacturer might be tempted to cut back production significantly in order to ameliorate its losses. What prevents both requirement contracts and output contracts from being illusory is that the courts will impose a *good-faith requirement* on parties to all such contracts. What this means is that the parties cannot take unfair advantage of the requirement contract or output contract, but must exercise good faith in dealing with such contracts. It would be a breach of contract, for example, for ABC to convert from oil to gas heat, if it has a requirement contract for heating oil, until the expiration of the contract. (It could, however, engage in reasonable conservation measures to lessen its need for fuel if the price rises, such as lowering the thermostat to a *reasonable* lower temperature.) In determining reasonableness and good faith when requirement contracts or output contracts are involved, courts look at performance in previous years, as well as normal practices in the industry involved.

# PAST CONSIDERATION

As previously noted, consideration is defined as something of legal value given or received as an inducement to enter into a contract. As this definition implies, consideration must have some *present* value for the parties. A contract that cites consideration given in the past is unenforceable. To put it another way, past consideration is not valid consideration because nothing of present value is given as inducement to enter into a contract, as the next three examples illustrate:

- *Nelson tells Nellie, "In consideration for your having been the best friend I've ever had over the past ten years, I hereby promise to buy you a brand-new diamond bracelet for Christmas."*

- *Lydia tells Larry at his retirement party, "In consideration for your fifty years of faithful service to Happy Company, we are pleased to award you a stipend of $500 per month above your normal pension benefit for as long as you live."*

- *Tomás tells Tanya, "In consideration of your having risked your life to save me from drowning, I hereby promise to place $50,000 in trust for your son's future education."*

Even though the word *consideration* is used in these three examples, and even though there was certainly legal value in the services provided by Nellie, Larry and Tanya, none of these promises is enforceable in court since the consideration cited is past consideration and none of these individuals is obligated to do anything further under the terms of these agreements. If the promisees were obligated to render some *new* performance (even if minor), however, then there would be valid consideration and a contract would be formed.

# PRE-EXISTING DUTY

The *pre-existing duty rule* states that it is not valid consideration for a party to agree to do that which he or she is already obligated to do. While this may seem obvious, the rule has wide-ranging applications. In most states, for example, the pre-existing duty rule makes modifications to existing contracts invalid unless they are accompanied by additional consideration or unless there is a good-faith dispute as to the meaning of contract terms. Let's look at an example that illustrates the application of the rule:

> *Alice borrows $5,000 from Andy and agrees to repay it in two years with 7 percent interest. After six months, she loses her job and wants to renegotiate the loan with Andy to make it payable in three years at 7 percent interest. Even if Andy agrees to the terms, the changes to the contract are unenforceable since Alice is not giving any additional value to Andy in exchange for the modification to the contract; she has a pre-existing duty to pay the loan in two years and, since Andy is getting nothing he is not already entitled to by agreeing to the new contract, the contract is unenforceable and Alice must pay the loan off in two years under the terms of the original contract if Andy asks for payment at that time.*

If the parties wish to change the terms of the contract in this example, Alice must give some additional consideration to Andy in order for the changed contract not to run afoul of the pre-existing duty rule. She can do this by paying a higher interest rate, by changing the terms of payment to a monthly basis (so that Andy gets payments earlier than he would otherwise be entitled to), by paying Andy twenty dollars for agreeing to the change or by giving any other legal consideration to Andy in exchange for the change in the terms of the original contract.

Note that regardless of problems with the pre-existing duty rule, past consideration or illusory promises, parties are always free to honor agreements that they enter into, even if these are not legally enforceable; if they do so, they are in essence conveying a gift on the recipient of the contract's benefit. The point is that these agreements are *not enforceable* in the courts if the promisors change their mind and refuse to honor them.

## QUESTIONS

1. Define *consideration*.
2. Is *consideration* synonymous with *money*? Explain.
3. Explain how forbearance can be valid consideration.
4. What are illusory promises?
5. What is a requirement contract?
6. What is an output contract?
7. Are output and requirement contracts considered illusory and therefore void? Explain fully.
8. What is past consideration? Why is it invalid?
9. What is the basic thrust of the pre-existing duty rule?

## HYPOTHETICAL CASES

1. Bob tells Barbra, "If you kiss me, I'll give you five dollars." Barbra replies, "Are you serious, or are you pulling my leg?" whereupon Bob assures her that he is

serious. She immediately kisses him and is informed by Bob that he was, after all, pulling her leg. Barbra is not amused and decides to sue Bob in small-claims court "for the sake of the principle." Bob defends on the grounds that there was no written contract and that even if there was, it was unenforceable, since he received no legal consideration from Barbra. You're the judge. Decide the case and give your legal analysis.

2. Ken, grateful that Keisha performed lifesaving CPR on him after he had suffered a heart attack, executes a contract with the following language:

> "In consideration of Keisha Washington's having saved my life, I hereby promise to pay her $100 per week for life. Signed [Ken Smith]"

For the next three years, he faithfully makes the weekly payments, and then stops. Keisha, upset that Ken broke his word to her, sues him, seeking to reinstate his payments. Once again, you are the judge. Decide the case and state your legal reasoning for your decision.

3. Mark agrees to purchase from Martha's farm stand "all the fruit I want, all the vegetables I desire, and all the apple cider I wish for the next two years" in exchange for Martha's giving him a 10 percent discount off her normal retail price on his purchases. He also enters into a separate agreement with Slippery Oil Corporation to purchase "all the home heating fuel I need for the next two years at a price of ninety-four cents per gallon." During the next two years, he buys no fruits, vegetables or cider from Martha and no home heating oil from Slippery Oil. Is he in breach of either contract? Explain.

4. Greg Greedy, a very popular but avaricious college lecturer, has a two-year contract with State University in which he agrees to teach twelve credits per semester during that period in exchange for a yearly salary of $35,000. After his first year, he negotiates with the administration for an additional $5,000 payment to be made to him at the end of the second year in exchange for his finishing out his two-year term. He also gets his students to agree to pay him ten dollars at the end of the semester in every class he teaches in exchange for his agreeing to remain as their instructor. In addition, he separately enters into an agreement with five of his students to tutor them individually after class in the evenings for a modest fee of ten dollars an hour each. If, at the end of his last semester, the college refuses to pay him the $5,000 raise for having completed his contract, the students in his class refuse to pay him the ten dollars they had each promised and the students he had tutored also refuse to pay him for the agreed-upon tutorial sessions, what are Mr. Greedy's rights with respect to each of the three separate contracts?

# ETHICS AND THE LAW: QUESTIONS FOR FURTHER STUDY    . . . . . . .

It is sometimes easy to confuse what is *legal* with what is *right*. In a perfect world, the terms would be synonymous; alas, in the real world they often are not. Examine the following examples from both a legal and an ethical perspective. What are the legal rights of the people involved? What are the ethical implications for each case? Do the law and ethics coincide? Would you suggest any changes to the law? Might changing the law create more problems than it solves?

- *Fred Firebug, an arsonist, is trapped by his own blaze after setting fire to an occupied apartment building. Frieda Firefighter is the first person on the scene. She rescues several victims from the burning building, then notices Fred on the roof, yelling for help—loudly admitting his crime and begging to be rescued. Frieda, exhausted, yells at him to wait for a helicopter that is on the way and will arrive in time to save him. Fred, who enjoys fire only when other people are being consumed by it, pleads with her to rescue him and offers to give her $25,000 in cash if she risks her life to extricate him from the flames. After much pleading on Fred's part, she re-enters the burning building and manages to rescue Fred from the flames. As thanks, Fred tells her he was hoping she'd burn on the way to rescuing him, and that he has no intention of giving her the $25,000 he'd promised.*

- *Samantha, the owner of a restaurant, enters into a requirement contract with Pamela, a farmer, to supply all the fruits and vegetables that she needs in her business for a five-year period at a 20 percent discount off Pamela's normal retail price. Over the five-year period, Samantha always buys produce in quantity during seasonal periods when the price is low and stores it in huge freezers she purchased for that purpose. The result over the five-year period is a net loss of $25,000 to Pamela, whose farm loses money every year, and phenomenal success for Samantha, whose business prospers in great part due to the variety of excellent produce in her all-vegetarian menu. Pamela suspects that Samantha is abusing their contract, but will not bring legal action because "I gave my word and if I made a bad bargain, it's my own fault."*

# 11

# CAPACITY

Contracts involve a consensual relationship; in order for a valid contract to be formed, the parties must freely give their consent to enter into a contract. To put it another way, there must be a meeting of the minds between contracting parties before a binding agreement is formed. Before consent to enter into a contract can be given, two elements must be present: (1) each party to the contract must have contractual *capacity* (the legal ability and power to enter into a contract), and (2) there must be *genuine assent* (consent that is freely given) by each party to enter into a contract. We will examine contractual capacity in this chapter, and the closely related element of genuine assent in Chapter 12.

## DEFINITION OF CAPACITY

Capacity is defined as the legal qualification, competence or fitness to enter into a contract. In order to have the capacity to enter into a contract, a person must have the mental competence to understand the nature of a contract and have reached the age of consent at the time the contract is entered into. Problems with capacity, then, center on two basic areas: agreements entered into by persons lacking the mental capacity to enter into a contract and contracts entered into by minors. We'll examine each of these areas in turn.

## CONTRACTS BY INCOMPETENTS

Contracts entered into by persons who have been judicially declared to be incompetent to handle their own affairs and have had a guardian appointed by the court are *void* (invalid and unenforceable). Persons who are judicially declared to be incompetent lose their capacity to enter into valid contracts, and any contracts they attempt to enter into are unenforceable. This is the case even when the other contracting party is unaware of the incompetence and acts in good faith in entering into the agreement. The only exception involves contracts for *necessaries*—items or services essential for the sustenance of life, such as food, shelter, clothing and medical care. Thus, if an incompetent person enters into a department store and buys a pair of jeans and a box of cookies on credit, a valid contract for the sale of these goods would exist since both food and clothing are necessary for the sustenance of life. But there would be no valid contract if the incompetent person purchased a television set, a computer or a $20,000 fur coat; these would be deemed luxury items, and the person's guardian could have the purchase agreement declared void and, upon return of the goods, be entitled to the return of whatever consideration the incompetent person paid for them.

Contracts entered into by persons who suffer from some mental defect that prevents them from understanding the nature of a contract but who have not been declared to be incompetent are not void but *voidable* at the option of the incompetent person or his or her guardian. The distinction between void and voidable contracts is that a void contract can never be binding, whereas a voidable contract is binding unless the guardian for the incompetent person sues to have the contract *rescinded* (declared invalid from its inception). The option to rescind must be exercised within a reasonable time of the guardian's learning of the contract, or the right to rescind the voidable contract will be lost.

It should be noted that if a person suffers from some mental infirmity or defect, it does not necessarily mean that the person cannot enter into a fully binding contract. In order for a contract to be voidable because of a mental defect, it must be shown that the party seeking to avoid the contract did not understand the nature of a contract *because of* the mental infirmity. A person who suffers from a multiple personality disorder, for example, would be fully capable to enter into a contract as long as the disorder does not impair that person's ability to understand the nature of a contract. Whether or not a person's ability to understand the nature of a contract is impaired by a specific disorder is a question of fact to be determined by the trier of fact at trial (usually the jury).

## CONTRACTS BY INTOXICATED PERSONS · · · · · · · · · · · · · · · · · · · ·

A person who enters into a contract while under the influence of alcohol or any other drug is treated exactly the same as a person suffering from a mental disability who has not been judicially declared incompetent. In other words, contracts of intoxicated persons are generally voidable by such persons if they can show that their intoxication prevented them from understanding the nature of a contract at the time that they entered into the agreement. Most courts require some physical manifestation of inebriation at the time of entering into a contract before they will allow such contracts to be avoided by reason of intoxication. The clearer the manifestation of intoxication at the time of the agreement, the likelier it is that a court will invalidate a contract if the trier of fact finds that the party seeking to invalidate the contract was so intoxicated that he or she did not understand the nature of a contract when consenting to the agreement.

# CONTRACTS BY MINORS   · · · · · · · · · · · · · · · · · · · · · · · · · · · · · ·

Every jurisdiction has a minimum age of consent for entering into binding agreements. While the age of consent varies among the states, it is usually eighteen or twenty-one years of age. When minors enter into a contract before attaining the age of consent, such contracts are voidable in every jurisdiction at the option of the minor. As is the case for contracts of incompetents, there is an exception for contracts involving necessaries—items or services essential to the maintenance of human life.

In most states, a minor has the option of avoiding a contract entered into while a minor at any time during his minority. A minor who wishes to exercise the right to annul a voidable contract must exercise that right before reaching the age of consent or the contract will be deemed automatically ratified and the minor will lose the right of *disaffirmance* (the technical term for declaring a voidable contract void).

Some states limit a minor's right to disaffirm a contract by statute to a specific period of time, usually one year from the date that the contract is entered into. In such states, the minor must disaffirm the contract within the specified time period or it will be deemed to have been ratified.

In most states, the right of minors to disaffirm contracts is absolute. If the consideration received under the contract has been damaged or worn from use, the minor is obligated only to return the consideration he or she received *in whatever condition it is in* and, in so doing, is entitled to a refund of whatever consideration he or she paid under the terms of the contract. Thus, if Paolo buys a car at sixteen in a state that recognizes eighteen as the age of consent, he can return the car at any time until he reaches his eighteenth birthday, or a reasonable time thereafter (usually a week or so from his eighteenth birthday) and be entitled to a *full refund* of whatever consideration he paid for the car. It is irrelevant that a car is not worth the same after being used for two years as it was when purchased; it is not even relevant in most states if the car is damaged or even wholly destroyed; the minor may still return the remains of the auto and be entitled to a full refund of its purchase price!

In some states, adults who deal with children are protected to some extent from situations such as the one just described by being able to sue in tort to recover whatever damage has been done to the underlying subject matter of the contract, as well as for the value of its use. But this is a minority view. In a majority of states, no such recovery is possible.

What if a minor lies about his or her age in order to induce an adult to enter into a contract? When that is the case, there is a split of opinion among the states. Some states would allow the adult to recover damages from the minor on a theory of fraud, while others would *still* allow the minor to disaffirm, despite the lying about his or her age and the fraud perpetrated on the adult.

While this rule may seem harsh, keep in mind that it was developed at common law in order to protect children from being taken advantage of by unscrupulous adults. Whether or not the average child today needs such protection is highly debatable; nevertheless, most states still retain a very paternalistic attitude toward protecting minors from themselves. How, then, can businesses protect themselves from the potential of minors' disaffirmance? Essentially, in two ways: (1) by requiring minors to obtain an adult cosigner for any contract they enter into, or (2) by refusing to deal with minors altogether. The latter option is seldom exercised because minors represent a very important market for most vendors. And, with the exception of big-ticket items, the first option is also often impractical. Why, then, do merchants deal with minors? Because the benefit of courting this segment of the purchasing public far outweighs the potential cost of disaffirmance.

As has been previously noted, minors may not disaffirm contracts for necessaries. Food, clothing, shelter, medical care, and educational expenses have all been held to qualify as necessaries in most states. Credit arrangements are also generally exempt from dis-affirmance by minors. Courts generally look at a child's needs in relation to his or her upbringing and the relative wealth of the child's parents; thus, if the typical college professor's child purchases a $40,000 fur coat, it would clearly be deemed a luxury, rather than a necessary. But if the child of very wealthy parents purchases the same coat, it might well be deemed a necessary in that the child might be used to extravagant clothing. Keep in mind that while this double standard might seem unfair, all it means as applied here is that children of wealthy parents are held to a higher standard in disaffirming contracts; they are not allowed to disaffirm contracts for items that might be a luxury to most people but might not be deemed a luxury to them.

## CONTRACTS BY EMANCIPATED MINORS

Contracts entered into by minors who are self-supporting and living apart from their parents are generally exempted from disaffirmance. Most courts treat emancipated minors as adults for all purposes, including entering into fully binding contracts.

## BUSINESS CONTRACTS BY MINORS

As is the case with emancipated minors, business contracts entered into by nonemancipated minors are also exempt from disaffirmance by the minor. The rationale here is clear: A minor who is mature enough to run his or her own business is also mature enough to be held responsible for contracts entered into on behalf of that business. If the child is not emancipated (e.g., is still a dependent of parents or guardians) but runs his or her own business, the child is still free to disaffirm personal contracts entered into that are unrelated to the business.

## QUESTIONS

1. Define *contractual capacity*.
2. What is the effect of contracts entered into by persons who have been judicially declared to be incompetent?
3. What is the effect of contracts entered into by persons who have some mental defect that does not permit them to understand the nature of a contract but who have not been judicially declared to be incompetent?

4. What is the effect of contracts entered into by persons who suffer from some mental infirmity that does not prevent them from understanding the nature of a contract?

5. What are necessaries?

6. Give five examples of necessaries.

7. How are contracts with intoxicated persons treated?

8. What is the significance of minors' contracts?

9. May emancipated minors disaffirm contracts they enter into with adults?

10. What is the significance of minors' business contracts?

# H Y P O T H E T I C A L     C A S E S

1. Leon believes himself to be Napoleon Bonaparte. Other than that one mental quirk, he is happy, healthy and quite a successful businessperson. He has not been judicially declared to be incompetent and is currently undergoing therapy to address his delusion. At a business lunch, he enters into a million-dollar agreement with Lena, a supplier of raw materials for one of his business ventures. At the time of signing the agreement, Leon was dressed in his normal attire—that of a nineteenth-century French general, and was quite sober. Lena consumed three martinis and two glasses of wine during the two-hour lunch meeting, but was showing absolutely no sign of intoxication and seemed quite lucid and sober at the time that she signed the contract. Discuss fully whether either party (or both) would be able to rescind the agreement the next day based on a claim of incapacity.

2. Bernice is a sixteen-year-old high school student who runs a part-time document preparation service after school. She purchases an IBM-compatible computer for her business and uses the same for almost two years quite successfully. On the day before her eighteenth birthday, she decides she'd like to upgrade her computer system and attempts to disaffirm the original contract. She contacts the original supplier from whom she'd purchased her computer system, informs them she was a minor at the time and demands that they issue her a check for $2,000—the amount she had originally paid for the computer. She also tells them that she will, of course, return the computer to them, even though the hard disk no longer works. The supplier has a good laugh on the phone and then hangs up on her. She sues.
   a. What result? Explain fully.
   b. Assume that Bernice purchases the computer system for her home use when she is 16 and begins using the computer for business use only a month before she decides to disaffirm. What result? Explain fully.

3. Nancy is a seventeen-year-old college student. She enters into a written contract with Norman, an adult, for the purchase of Norman's 1964 Corvette for $2,000 in one week, when she reaches her eighteenth birthday. The day after signing the agreement, it dawns on Norman that he made a bad deal, since the car is worth

many times his asking price. He calls Nancy and informs her that he wishes to disaffirm the contract. Nancy is furious and says she expects him to keep his word and turn over the car when promised.

a. If Norman refuses to turn over the car as promised, may she successfully sue him for damages, or will Norman be able to assert his disaffirmance of the contract successfully?

b. Would your answer be the same if Norman thought Nancy was eighteen at the time that he entered into the contract, but Nancy had not mentioned her age?

c. What if Nancy had lied to Norman about her age and even shown him fake ID? Would your answer be the same? Explain fully.

## ETHICS AND THE LAW: QUESTIONS FOR FURTHER STUDY    . . . . . . .

The special protection that the law affords to minors when it comes to disaffirming contracts stems from the common-law notion that children need special protection—that they are innocent, gullible and easily taken advantage of by adults. While this may be true of very young children, it is difficult to make that argument for the average sixteen- or seventeen-year-old in the 1990s. Should the law be changed? Is there still a need for offering special protection to minors? What of the adults who are victimized by savvy "children" who take advantage of the system? At one time, women were afforded the very same protection as children under the same paternalistic attitude that "the weaker sex needs protection from itself." Thankfully, those days are past. Is it not as condescending to knowledgeable young men and women to be treated as needing special protection when dealing with adults? What about gullible adults? Are they any less deserving of protection? What do you think? Make an argument for a just solution to this dilemma.

# CHAPTER

# 12

# GENUINE ASSENT

As noted in the last chapter, there must be a meeting of the minds of contracting parties before a valid contract can arise. This presupposes that the contracting parties have the capacity to enter into a binding contract, as discussed in Chapter 11, and that the parties give their genuine assent to enter into a binding agreement. Genuine assent, as the term implies, is the requirement that the assent given to enter into a binding agreement be sincere and freely given by both contracting parties.

In this chapter, we will examine the circumstances that can undermine genuine assent and turn a seemingly enforceable contract into either a void or voidable agreement. These include mutual mistake, duress, fraud in the inducement, fraud in the execution and undue influence.

## MUTUAL MISTAKE · · · · · · · · · · · · · · · · · · · · · · · · · · · · · · · · · · · · · · · ·

If both parties to a contract are mistaken as to a material aspect of the contract, the contract is void. There can be no binding agreement if the parties make a significant *mutual mistake* as to an assumption both had made in entering into the agreement, as the following examples will illustrate:

- *Gertrude offers to sell Gary her television set for $100. Gary accepts the offer. Normally a contract would result, but Gertrude owns two sets and Gary knows this; she intends to sell her twelve-inch set but Gary believes she means to sell her twenty-five-inch set. No contract results because the parties were laboring under a mutual mistake of fact as to the subject matter of the contract.*

- *Gertrude offers to sell Gary her twenty-five-inch television set for $100. Gary accepts, without asking any information about the set. At the time of accepting the offer, he assumed the set was a color one, but in fact it is black and white. This is not a mutual mistake of fact, since only Gary is mistaken as to the nature of the set, and the resulting contract is perfectly valid.*

In order for a contract to be invalidated by reason of a mutual mistake as to a material fact relating to the contract, the mistake must relate to an assumption held in common by both parties to the contract. Again, if only one of the parties is mistaken, or if both parties are mistaken as to a nonmaterial fact, the contract is perfectly valid. Whether a fact is material or immaterial is determined by whether the parties relied on the fact in making their decision to enter into the contract. If both parties are mistaken as to a fact that was not a determining factor in the parties' decision to enter into the contract, the contract is fully binding. Thus, if two color-blind individuals enter into a contract for the sale of an automobile thinking it is blue, but in fact it is red, whether or not this is a material defect that would invalidate the contract is dependent upon whether the color of the auto was a relevant consideration for the parties at the time of entering into the agreement. Given the fact that a blue car is worth the same as a red one and that the parties are color-blind, the color of the car is probably not a material factor to this contract.

# DURESS

*Duress* is perhaps the easiest factor to comprehend as invalidating a party's genuine assent. It is clear that if a person has a gun pointed at his or her head when agreeing to enter into a contract, the assent given is not genuine, but is motivated by fear. Under such circumstances, it will come as no surprise that the contract is void.

While a gun to the head may be the simplest form of duress to grasp, duress can take many forms, each equally invalidating a contract. Physical coercion, such as the force or threat of force, constitutes duress, but so do threats of economic or social reprisals. What is important in determining whether a party acted under the threat of duress is whether the agreement to enter into the contract was motivated by the genuine desire to enter into a contract or was motivated by fear of some threat made by the other contracting party. Each of the following examples constitutes duress that would invalidate genuine assent:

- *Bertha tells Benny, "If you don't sign this agreement, I'm going to punch your lights out." Benny believes the threat is real and signs the agreement.*

- *Benny tells Bertha, "Unless you sign this agreement, I will tell your husband that we are lovers." Bertha, believing Benny to be serious, signs the agreement.*

- *Roy tells Rowena, "If you sign this partnership agreement, I won't tell everyone that you have AIDS." Rowena, who has AIDS but wants to keep the information secret, signs the agreement.*

- *Rowena tells Roy, "Unless you hire me as your assistant, I'm going to tell everyone that you wear a hairpiece." Roy, afraid of being ridiculed by his associates, agrees to hire Rowena.*

Courts generally apply an objective test in determining whether a threat constitutes duress. Under an objective standard, a threat constitutes duress only if a reasonable person under the same circumstances would have deemed the threat believable and would have been motivated to action in order to avoid the threat. Thus, if a 90-pound unarmed salesman tells a 300-pound football player, "Unless you buy this television set right now for $300, I'm going to beat you up," that would not constitute a believable threat to a reasonable person, and if the football player agrees to the contract, he will not be able to invalidate it on grounds of duress.

## FRAUD IN THE INDUCEMENT

As we saw in our discussion of intentional torts in Chapter 6, fraud occurs whenever one person intentionally misleads another into undertaking some action that causes the defrauded party some harm. It stands to reason that if one of the parties to a contract gives assent to enter into the agreement because he or she is the victim of a fraud perpetrated by the other party, the assent given is not genuine and the contract can be invalidated.

The effect of fraud on a contract depends on whether *fraud in the inducement* or *fraud in the execution* is involved. Fraud in the inducement occurs whenever a party is misled into a contract by the intentional misrepresentation relating to a material fact made by the other party. In other words, whenever one party purposely lies to another about important matters relating to the contract in order to induce the other party to enter into the contract, fraud in the inducement is involved. The effect of fraud in the inducement is to make the resulting contract voidable at the option of the defrauded party. Whenever fraud in the inducement is involved, the party who has been intentionally misled into entering into the agreement has the option of having the agreement declared void in court. But the guilty party who perpetrated the fraud may not have the agreement declared void; if the defrauded party wishes to go through with the agreement upon learning of the fraud, he or she has the right to fully enforce the agreement. The following example should illustrate:

> *Jasra offers to sell Jason her used VCR for $150. In order to induce him to buy it, she tells him that the VCR has four heads and Dolby stereo. In fact, the VCR has four heads but no Dolby stereo. If Jason purchases the VCR based on the misrepresentations, he may have the contract avoided at his option when he learns that the VCR is not a stereo model. If he is still willing to keep the VCR despite Jasra's misrepresentations about it, however, he is free to do so; Jasra will not be able to invalidate the contract based on her fraudulent statements.*

## FRAUD IN THE EXECUTION

When fraud in the execution is involved, the defrauded party has been intentionally induced to execute a legal instrument by a misrepresentation as to the nature of the instrument being signed. Unlike fraud in the inducement, where one party is misled as to a material fact involving the contract, when fraud in the execution is concerned, one party unknowingly signs a contract believing it to be something else. The following example will illustrate:

> *Norma, a famous sports personality, is given a folded piece of paper by Nat, a fan, who asks her to sign her autograph. She complies. Unknown to her, the piece of paper contains a contract wherein Norma agrees to hire Nat as her manager for a five-year term.*

Norma was misled not as to an aspect of the contract, but as to the very nature of the agreement itself. Her intent in signing her name to the paper was to give a fan an autograph, not to enter into a binding contract. She is a victim of fraud in the execution, since she was willfully misled into executing an agreement she never intended to actuate. She clearly did not genuinely assent to enter into the agreement; in fact, she was unaware that she was entering into an agreement at all when she signed her name to the paper.

Whenever fraud in the execution is involved, the victim does not intend to enter into an agreement at all; thus, the agreement that appears to result from the fraud is not merely voidable at the victim's option, but completely void and unenforceable by either party.

## UNDUE INFLUENCE

*Undue influence*, also known as *overreaching*, is involved when the contracting parties share a relationship based on trust and confidence and one of the parties abuses that position to gain an unfair advantage over the other. Undue influence generally involves a *fiduciary relationship* (a relationship based on trust) such as attorney–client or doctor–patient. Other common instances of overreaching involve parties with close personal or familial ties. The law recognizes that when such relationships are involved, parties are particularly vulnerable to manipulation because they are likely to let their guard down and allow the nature of the relationship to cloud their judgment.

A contract induced by undue influence is voidable at the option of the party who can show that he or she was induced to enter into a disadvantageous agreement because of the special relationship. A plaintiff seeking to avoid a contract based on undue influence needs to show that the assent given to enter into the contract was not genuine, but rather was clouded by the other party's taking unfair advantage of the fiduciary relationship in inducing the plaintiff to enter into the contract. As with fraud in the inducement, contracts involving undue influence by one of the parties are voidable only by the victim of the undue influence.

## QUESTIONS

1. Define *genuine assent.*
2. What is the effect of a mutual mistake of fact on a contract?
3. Will every mutual mistake of fact invalidate a contract?
4. What constitutes duress?
5. Is duress generally determined based on a subjective or objective test?
6. Define *fraud in the inducement.*
7. How is fraud in the execution different from fraud in the inducement?
8. What is the legal effect of fraud in the inducement and fraud in the execution on a contract?

# H Y P O T H E T I C A L        C A S E S

1. William enters into a contract with Wanda, whereby Wanda agrees to ship 1,000 square yards of silk from India aboard the S. S. *Freedom* when the ship next sails. Unknown to the parties at the time of entering into the contract, there are two S. S. *Freedoms* that sail from India to U.S. ports; the first sails in January and the second in March. William meant for the goods to be shipped via the S.S. *Freedom* that sails in January, but Wanda agreed to the contract based on the March sailing date of the S.S. *Freedom* she knew of. When the goods do not arrive at the end of January, when he expected them, William sues Wanda for breach of contract. You are the judge. What result?

2. Sari, while engaging in negotiations for the lease of Sam's commercial property for her new business, is upset by what she perceives to be Sam's unreasonable stubbornness in refusing to accept what she feels is an eminently fair offer for a five-year lease. After an hour of fruitless negotiation, she turns to Sam and says, "You know, you are the most pig-headed person I've ever had the unfortunate experience of dealing with. Unless you accept my offer, I'm going to beat you senseless." Sam promptly accepts the offer and signs a commercial lease agreement with Sari. A month later, unhappy with the arrangement, Sam wants to avoid the contract based on duress.
   a.  Assume that Sam is a 300-pound ex-linebacker for the New York Giants and Sari is a slender, petite woman. Is Sam likely to succeed? Explain.
   b.  Would your answer be different if Sari had threatened to have Sam killed if he did not sign the agreement and Sam believed her to be serious?

3. Alisha, an attorney, enters into a contract with Clint, her client, whereby Clint agrees to sell her 10,000 shares of XYZ Company at $20 per share, the market value of the shares at the time of the contract. A month after the transfer of the shares, the price of the stock climbs to $40 per share due to conditions that were not foreseeable by Alisha or Clint at the time of their contract. Clint, upon learning of the doubling in value of the shares, decides that Alisha took advantage of their relationship and sues to have the contract voided. What result?

4. Assume the same facts as the last question, except that Alisha pays $17 for the stock when it has a market value of $20 per share. If Clint sues seeking to invalidate the contract, what result? What if, after the stock is purchased for $17, it drops to $5 per share and Alisha sues to declare the contract avoided?

# CHAPTER

# 13

# LEGALITY

It should come as no surprise that agreements that involve the commission of a crime are void and unenforceable in the courts. In general, the courts will refuse to arbitrate disputes between parties to illegal contracts, leaving such parties without legal recourse. In this chapter, we will examine some common types of illegal contracts that courts will refuse to enforce and explore the consequences for parties to such contracts.

## CONTRACTS INVOLVING THE COMMISSION OF A TORT OR A CRIME · · · · · · · · · · · · · · · · · · · · · · · · · · · · · ·

When the underlying subject matter of the contract involves the commission of a tort or the violation of a state or federal statute, the agreement is void for illegality and the parties are left with no legal recourse. The courts will not even entertain petitions for a return of whatever consideration was given by the parties to such contracts, leaving the parties to the illegal contract in whatever position it finds them. Thus, if Albert pays Betty $10,000 to kill Charlie and Betty performs her part of the agreement, Betty would not be able to sue Albert for breach of contract since the contract involves a clearly illegal act. If Albert had paid the money to Betty who then refused to carry out the murder of Charlie, Albert would also be prevented from suing Betty for breach of contract. In the latter example, Betty would be able to keep the $10,000 knowing that Albert had no *legal* recourse. In short, criminals who fail to honor their agreements are left to fend for themselves.

## RESTRAINT OF TRADE · · · · · · · · · · · · · · · · · · · · · · · · · · · · · ·

A common type of illegal contract involves agreements in restraint of trade. The purpose of such contracts is to interfere with free competition in the marketplace. Contracts in restraint of trade include agreements involving price fixing, the establishment of monopolies, predatory trade practices or other agreements whose purpose is to thwart competition and subvert the operation of the free market. As with most other illegal agreements, parties to contracts involving restraint of trade cannot sue for redress of grievances arising from such contracts. (The *victims* of such agreements can, of course, seek redress in the courts.) Thus, if Gary and Genrette conspire to drive Gertrude out of business by a price-fixing scheme, neither Gary nor Genrette would be able to sue one another if they breached their illegal agreement. (But Gertrude would be free to sue both parties for tort damages she suffered as a result of the illegal price-fixing scheme.)

## GAMBLING CONTRACTS

Perhaps the most common type of illegal contract involves gambling. At common law, gambling was perfectly legal in all forms. Today, in every jurisdiction, gambling is strictly controlled by statute. The extent to which gambling is allowed in each state varies widely. Some states actively welcome gambling as both a form of entertainment and an important source of state revenue; this includes not only the casino gambling of Nevada and New Jersey, but also the racetrack gambling and offtrack betting allowed in many states, as well as the state-run lotteries prevalent in most states today. But even in states with liberal gambling policies, legal gambling is limited to that allowed by law and is strictly controlled. Whenever gambling not sanctioned by state law occurs, it is treated as any other illegal contract in most states; the result is that the parties to the illegal gambling agreement are not allowed to seek redress for breach of contract in the courts. Thus, if Martha and Matt bet $500 on the outcome of the next Super Bowl game and the loser refuses to honor the illegal gambling agreement, the winner has no recourse in the courts.

## USURIOUS CONTRACTS

At common law, parties were free to enter into contracts for the borrowing and lending of money at any interest rate they freely agreed to pay. Today, the maximum rate of interest that can legally be charged for credit transactions is strictly regulated by law. While the maximum rate allowed in states differs, most states impose a limit of between 16 and 22 percent per year on most consumer credit transactions (rates that lenders can charge businesses are usually somewhat higher). If a credit agreement is entered into which involves a rate of interest higher than the state law allows, the agreement is said to be *usurious* and void. A usurious contract is simply one that calls for payment of a higher interest rate than the law allows.

Unlike most illegal contracts, which the courts treat as void and completely unenforceable by the parties, agreements that involve usury are treated as enforceable in the vast majority of states; the courts *reform* the contract by rewriting it to exclude the usurious rate of interest. In most states, the courts rewrite usurious contracts to make them fit within the legally allowed rate of interest in the state by lowering the illegal rate of interest stated in the contract to the highest rate of interest the law allows. This, if a state allows a maximum 20 percent annual interest rate and a contract calls for a 30 percent interest rate, the courts would enforce the contract by reforming it so that 20 percent interest is payable—the highest legal rate allowed in that state.

In a few states, usurious contracts are enforced by the courts by rewriting them so that *no* interest is payable; usurious contracts in such states are reformed by calculating payments during the agreed-upon credit term based upon the repayment of principal only.

## CONTRACTS CONTRARY TO PUBLIC POLICY . . . . . . . . . . . . . . . . .

All courts have the right to hold contracts that are otherwise legal to be void and unenforceable if they violate the public policy of the state. Courts will refuse to enforce contracts that they deem harmful to the fabric of society or so unfair as to "shock the conscience of the court." The avoidance of contracts that a court finds offensive to public policy or unconscionable is within every court's *equitable jurisdiction*—the power of the court to award an extraordinary remedy when no just legal remedy exists.

There are no hard-and-fast rules as to what types of agreements the courts of any given state will find unconscionable or contrary to public policy. These determinations are made by judges on a case-by-case basis. As a general rule, however, courts are leery of exercising their equitable powers of holding agreements to be void and unenforceable as either unconscionable or against public policy, and exercise such powers only in exceptional cases. That parties made a bad bargain or that some persons in society might deem an agreement objectionable are not grounds for declaring an otherwise valid agreement void. What type of agreements, then, is a court likely to hold void as against public policy or unconscionable? Agreements that are shockingly unfair or grossly unethical are usually declared void, as the following examples will illustrate:

- *Jane, an expectant mother, agrees to turn over her baby at birth to ABC Adoption Service in exchange for a fee of $25,000.*

- *Paul agrees to pay Paula $10,000 plus all medical expenses if she agrees to be artificially inseminated with his sperm and bear a child that she will then turn over to him for adoption.*

- *Tomás, a non-English-speaking resident alien, agrees to purchase a refrigerator from Enrique, who makes a sales presentation in Spanish and then asks Tomás to sign an agreement in English for the purchase of the refrigerator at $1,200 (including interest at the highest rate the law allows) for a refrigerator with a fair market value of $300.*

The first two examples are typical of contracts void as against public policy, because they involve, essentially, thinly disguised baby-selling agreements. The third example is typical of agreements that courts often find unconscionable. Note that the disparity in price and value in a contract of itself is *not* grounds for holding an agreement unconscionable; there must be additional factors that make the agreement shockingly unfair. In the last example, the fact that the sale was made in one language and the agreement was signed in another coupled with the disparity in the price paid for the appliance and its actual worth are what make it unconscionable.

## QUESTIONS · · · · · · · · · · · · · · · · · · · · · · · · · · · · · · · · · · · ·

1. What is the general effect of illegality on a contract?
2. What is the purpose of contracts in restraint of trade?
3. What is the legal effect of a contract in restraint of trade?
4. Were gambling contracts illegal at common law?
5. What determines the legality of a gambling contract today?
6. What is a usurious contract?
7. What is the effect of a usurious contract?
8. What are contracts contrary to public policy?

## H Y P O T H E T I C A L       C A S E S

1. Carmen, Karen and Cisco agree to pool their money to play their state's legal lottery every week. Each person agrees to pay five dollars a week toward playing the same numbers that they all agree to for a whole year. Karen, who lives next to a lottery agent, agrees to play the numbers every week. After six months, one of the numbers picked by the group wins the lottery. Karen, who has been holding the tickets for the group, then refuses to share the proceeds with her new ex-friends, who sue her for breach of contract. What result? Explain fully.

2. Frank asks Fina to place an illegal bet of $500 with her bookie on an upcoming baseball game, and promises to give her 10 percent of his winnings for her service if his team wins. Fina takes the money and makes the bet. Frank's team wins, but Fina's bookie, who has been arrested since she placed the bet with him, cannot be found to make payment on the bet. Frank, furious at the turn of events, sues Fina for $1,000 (the amount he would have recovered from her bookie); Fina, on the other hand, counterclaims for $100, the amount Frank had promised to pay her if he won. You are the judge. What result on both claims? Explain.

3. Wannabee Famous, a mediocre but aggressive figure skater, agrees to pay her bodyguard a salary of $100,000 per year in exchange for his services as bodyguard, and his promise to assault all of her competitors a few days before major matches. After a few matches, Wannabee decides that there's just too much competition and too little time, so she retires from skating, embarks on a new career as a college lecturer on sports ethics and writes a book titled *How to Make the Most of What Little Talent You Have*. Her bodyguard, furious at Wannabee's career change, sues for breach of contract. What result? Explain fully.

4. Desirée, a wealthy industrialist with failing eyesight and bad kidneys, enters into a contract with David wherein he agrees to sell one of his eyes and a kidney to her in exchange for a payment of $1,000,000 in cash plus all medical expenses. A week

after the successful organ transplant, Desirée informs David that she's changed her mind about the agreed-upon payment and will pay him only $25,000 plus all medical expenses. David, furious, sues for breach of contract. You are the judge. What result? Explain fully.

## ETHICS AND THE LAW: QUESTIONS FOR FURTHER STUDY    . . . . . . .

As noted in this chapter, courts have the power under their equity jurisdiction to refuse enforcement of legal contracts that go against the public policy of the state. A problem that arises when judges exercise this right is that they substitute their own sense of ethics (albeit acting for the common good) in place of the state legislature—the elected body entrusted with passing laws for the protection of the public safety and public morals—and the contracting parties themselves. It is legal to sell one's blood, no matter how the average person may feel about those who do so, so why not also be able to sell a kidney that you do not need to live, or an eye? Why should a woman not be able to rent her womb for a price to incubate another woman's fertilized egg? Why not allow surrogate mothering agreements when all parties consent to the practice and no undue influence is exerted on the mother? In cases where there is no direct effect on anyone outside of the contracting parties and the contracting parties freely agree to the terms of a contract, why not let those terms be carried out? What do you think?

# CHAPTER
# 14

# STATUTE OF FRAUDS

As we've previously noted, most contracts do not need to be expressed in a signed writing or follow any specific form in order to be enforceable. From early common law, an inherent problem with oral contracts has been their potential for fraud; parties to oral contracts can easily lie about the specific terms of the agreement, or even about the existence of an agreement itself in order to defraud innocent parties. Because of the potential for fraud inherent in oral contracts, the British Parliament enacted a statute in 1677 entitled *Act for the Prevention of Frauds and Perjuries*. The statute required certain types of contracts to be evidenced by some note or memorandum signed by the party being charged with a breach of contract. The thrust of this statute has been nearly universally adopted by the states in their own versions of a *Statute of Frauds*. Like the original British statute, the Statute of Frauds in most states requires that certain types of contracts be evidenced by a *signed writing* by the party being charged with breach of contract. Contracts that fall within the statute are unenforceable unless the party bringing the legal action can produce a signed memorandum of the contract by the defendant. While the writing does not generally have to be very detailed, it must clearly show that a contract exists between the parties and the nature of the subject matter involved. Not every aspect of the contract needs to be covered by the writing; if sale of goods is involved, for example, it is enough that a general description of the goods and their quantity is stated in the signed writing. Once the contract is established, specific terms such as price or terms of delivery can be shown by oral testimony or through other written evidence.

The Statute of Frauds applies only to *executory contracts*—contracts which have not yet been fully performed by the parties. Once a contract is fully *executed* by each party fully discharging all contractual obligations, the Statute of Frauds is inapplicable. Thus, if parties fully perform an oral contract that under the statute should have been evidenced by a signed writing, they can no longer raise the Statute of Frauds as a defense to the enforceability of the contract.

The Statutes of Frauds in most jurisdictions today are quite similar and cover only the following types of contracts:

- contracts that by their terms cannot be performed within one year;
- contracts for the transfer of an interest in real estate;
- contracts for the sale of goods worth $500 or more;
- contracts promising to answer for the debt of another;
- contracts of executors and administrators; and
- contracts in consideration of marriage.

## DEFINITION OF A SIGNED WRITING

For purposes of the Statute of Frauds, the requirements of both a writing and a signature are very broadly interpreted. As previously noted, the writing itself can be very broad and must merely evidence the existence of a contract in the broadest of terms. The writing can be made on paper or any other portable surface of any kind and with any type of equipment, including a typewriter, computer, pen, pencil, crayon, lipstick or, for that matter, by carving words on a piece of wood with a nail. Likewise, the requirement of a signature is broadly interpreted to mean any symbol or mark made by the contracting party intending it as his or her signature. Thus, a valid signature can be an X mark, the initials of the party, the party's typewritten name, or, of course, the party's name printed or signed by the party. In addition, a writing on paper containing a party's letterhead, bill of sale, purchase order or any other preprinted form is deemed to have been signed by that party if the writing is shown to be genuine.

Keep in mind as you read the material in this chapter that it is possible for only one party to be bound by a signed writing. There is no requirement that the signatures of both parties appear in a writing in order for the contract to be enforceable—only that there be a signed writing *by the party being sued*. The importance of this distinction is illustrated in the following example:

> *Zoreka and Zap discuss a large order for goods that Zap is considering buying from Zoreka's company. During the meeting, Zap borrows Zoreka's eyeliner and scribbles on a cocktail napkin, "I agree to purchase 10,000 gizmos from Zoreka at $99.99 each for delivery June 8, 1996." He then initials the napkin and hands it over to Zoreka. If Zap fails to honor this agreement, his signed writing, represented by the memorandum scribbled on the napkin, will be enough to allow Zoreka to sue him. On the other hand, since Zoreka did not sign or initial the agreement, Zap will not be able to bind her to it if she refuses to perform as promised.*

## CONTRACTS THAT BY THEIR TERMS CANNOT BE PERFORMED WITHIN ONE YEAR

If a contract by its terms cannot be performed within the space of one year, it must be evidenced by a signed writing to be enforceable. Common contracts that require more than one year to complete would include multiyear leases on real or personal property, employment contracts that run for more than one year and construction contracts that by their terms cannot be completed in one year. If it is possible to perform a contract fully within a one-year term, no signed writing is required for it to be fully enforceable. Thus, a contract calling for the building of a bridge within the next twelve to fourteen months need not be in writing, since it is possible for the builder to complete the project within a one-year term. Interestingly enough, the same holds true for a contract that is to run for a person's lifetime—since it is *possible* that the person may die within a year and thus fully discharge his or her contractual obligations. Ironically, a two-year employment contract must be evidenced by a signed writing in order to be enforceable, since by its terms it cannot be completed within one year. (The inference is that a person who dies before a year is up on a multiyear contract is in breach of contract, even though the agreement will be discharged by operation of law for impossibility of performance if it is a personal service-contract.)

## CONTRACTS TRANSFERRING AN INTEREST IN REAL ESTATE

Contracts that transfer any interest in real property must be evidenced by a signed writing in order to be enforceable. As we will see in our coverage of real property law in Chapter 28, interests in real property include transfers of fee interests in real estate, the creation of life estates, easements and *profits à prendre*. Transfers of mere possessory or occupancy rights to real estate, such as leases and licenses, need not be evidenced by a signed writing *unless* they run for a period longer than one year. The reason for this distinction is that leases and licenses do not give their holders a legal interest in real estate, but merely the right to occupy real estate.

## CONTRACTS FOR THE SALE OF GOODS FOR $500 OR MORE

As we will see in Chapters 18 and 22, *goods* can be defined as personal property that is tangible and movable. Nearly anything that can be owned other than real estate qualifies as goods. Books, electronic equipment, clothing, food, boats, cars, planes, pets, livestock and other items with a physical existence that can be moved (or, to put it another way, that are not real estate or anything permanently attached to real estate) all constitute goods. Whenever a contract for the sale of goods with a total price of $500 is entered into, it must be evidenced by a signed writing in order to be enforceable. For purposes of the statute, shipping costs or taxes paid in connection with the sale are not included in the price of the goods. On the other hand, the prices of multiple goods purchased as part of a single transaction are added together to determine the price of the goods for purposes of the statute. Thus, an oral contract for a $300 television set and a $200 VCR purchased at the same time is unenforceable because the total cost of the goods in the transaction is $500. But an oral contract for a $499 fax machine that costs $30 to ship and has $35 in sales taxes attached to it is perfectly binding, since neither sales taxes nor shipping costs are considered in the sale price.

## CONTRACTS PROMISING TO ANSWER FOR THE DEBT OF ANOTHER ..............................

A contract wherein the promisor agrees to answer for another's debt is unenforceable unless it is evidenced by a signed writing. This includes all surety, guarantee and security interests given in consideration of a lender extending credit to any third party. It does not, however, include contracts entered into for another's benefit where the beneficiary of the contract is not the obligor. The following examples will illustrate:

> *Alex agrees to guarantee payment on a loan by Albert to Althea. Alex cannot be bound to this guarantee unless Albert can produce a signed writing by Alex that evidences that promise.*
>
> *Bart purchases a computer printer for $400 from Bertha to give as a gift to Bernice. If this is an oral contract, it is fully enforceable against Bart by Bertha because it is not a contract to answer for the debt of another, but rather a gift purchased by Bart for Bernice's benefit. The obligor here is Bart, not Bernice, and no writing is required.*

## CONTRACTS OF EXECUTORS AND ADMINISTRATORS ..........

Executors of decedents' estates and administrators of incompetents' estates enter into contracts on behalf of the estates they serve on a regular basis. If they agree to be personally bound for contracts that benefit the estates, however, such an agreement must be evidenced by a signed writing before the promise is enforceable. Such contracts are, in effect, contracts promising to answer for the debt of another and are treated as such.

## CONTRACTS IN CONSIDERATION OF MARRIAGE ..............

The final type of contract that is required to be evidenced by a signed writing in order to be enforceable involves contracts wherein the consideration promised by one of the parties is marriage. This includes contracts made by prospective brides and grooms between themselves, as well as contracts between prospective brides and grooms and third parties. Perhaps the most common type of agreement that falls within this section of the Statute of Frauds is prenuptial, or antenuptial, agreements, wherein the parties agree prior to their marriage how property will be distributed in the event that the marriage ends up in divorce. These agreements are perfectly legal in most states, but they must be evidenced by a signed writing in order to be enforceable.

While contracts involving marriage as a consideration between prospective brides and grooms and third parties are not as common, these too are generally legal and enforceable provided they are evidenced by a signed writing. For example, prospective in-laws could offer to pay the bride and groom $1,000,000 if they marry and stay together for at least ten years; as long as the agreement is evidenced by a signed writing by the prospective in-laws, they would have to pay the agreed-upon consideration if the marriage lasts for the agreed-upon term. On the other hand, an oral agreement to that effect would not be binding.

## QUESTIONS . . . . . . . . . . . . . . . . . . . . . . . . . . . . . . . . .

1. What types of contracts are covered under the Statute of Frauds?
2. What is the significance of the Statute of Frauds?
3. Would a contract written with a crayon on a brown paper bag satisfy the requirement of a writing?
4. What constitutes a signature for purposes of the statute?
5. Does a contract that is to run for a person's lifetime have to be evidenced by a signed writing? Explain.
6. Does a six-month lease need to be evidenced by a signed writing? Explain.
7. Does a contract for the purchase of a $450 camera and $75 worth of film have to be evidenced by a signed writing?
8. What types of contracts are considered contracts promising to answer for the debt of another?

## H Y P O T H E T I C A L    C A S E S

1. Annette orally agrees to teach at State University for a two-year term. State University gives her a written memorandum of the agreement, signed by the college president. The agreement states that Annette will be required to teach six credits per semester and be entitled to a salary of $45,000 per year. Annette is not asked to sign the agreement and does not do so. Six months into the contract, Annette receives a better offer from Private University and gives notice to State University that she will leave after completing the first year of her contract. Is Annette in breach of contract if she leaves after one year? If State University wished to fire Annette after one year because it found another instructor willing to teach the same courses for $35,000 per year, can it do so without being in breach of contract? Explain.
2. Henry orally promises to sell his house to Hanna for $125,000. On the day after the agreement is entered into, Hank offers Henry $135,000 for the house, and Henry orally agrees to sell him the house. The next day, Howard offers to rent the house from Henry for one year at $1,000 per month and Henry orally agrees to the lease. If Hanna, Hank and Howard sue Henry to enforce their respective agreements, what will a court decide?
3. Wanda, the wealthy mother of Wendy, a spoiled brat, orally agrees to pay William Wonderful, a movie star, $10,000,000 if he will marry her daughter. William agrees to the arrangement and marries Wendy. If Wanda then refuses to pay him the agreed-upon sum, can William sue for breach of contract? If

William had scribbled on a notepad, "I hereby agree to marry Wendy in consideration of Wanda agreeing to pay me $10,000,000, Signed [William Wonderful]," would your answer be the same? Explain.

4. Jerry, a young person with no previous credit history, asks his father to cosign a car loan. The father, who does not want to be bound by the agreement but wants the son to get the loan, illegibly scribbles his name on the loan application as guarantor, making sure that nobody will be able to make heads or tails of what the signature says. The loan is approved and six months later, Jerry misses a few payments. The bank now wants to force Jerry's father to pay the loan on Jerry's behalf. He defends on grounds that his signature is illegible and does not look at all like his signature, and that he is therefore not liable as a guarantor. What result?

CHAPTER

# 15

# ASSIGNMENT OF CONTRACTS AND THIRD-PARTY BENEFICIARIES

Although contracting parties usually perform their mutual obligations under contracts exactly as agreed upon, there are instances where parties may wish to assign their rights under a contract to an outside party, or may wish to have an outside party discharge their contractual obligations on their behalf. When all parties agree to such alterations in their original agreements, there is, of course, no problem. In this chapter, we will examine the rights of contracting parties to delegate their duties under contracts and to assign their contractual rights in cases where agreement to the assignment and delegation is not reached with the other contracting party. We will also explore the rights of individuals to enforce contracts that they have an interest in but to which they are not a party.

## ASSIGNMENT OF CONTRACT RIGHTS . . . . . . . . . . . . . . . . . . . . .

As we have seen previously, in every bilateral contract each party is obligated to render some type of performance in the form of whatever consideration is required under the contract, and is also entitled to receive whatever consideration the other party has promised as part of the contract. In other words, each party to a bilateral contract is an *obligor* (obligated to give the promised consideration) and an *obligee* (entitled to receive the consideration promised by the other party). Thus, each party to a bilateral contract has both certain rights as well as certain obligations that flow from the agreement.

*Assignment* of contract rights occurs when a party to a contract transfers whatever rights he or she has under a contract to one or more third parties. In general, contractual rights are freely assignable provided that the following conditions are met:

- the rights to be assigned do not involve the performance of unique, nonstandardized personal services such as those rendered by physicians, attorneys, artists and other professionals who exercise a high degree of personal judgment and discretion in rendering services for clients (standardized services, such as those performed by electricians, plumbers or masons in adhering to a building code are freely assignable);
- the assignment of contract rights does not place a significantly greater burden or risk on the obligor in rendering the promised performance;
- the contract itself does not prohibit assignment; and
- the assignment is not prohibited by law. (Many states, for example, prohibit parties from assigning more than a set percentage of their wages, such as 25 percent, to third parties.)

When a permissible assignment of contract rights is involved, the consent of the obligor need not be obtained. Once the obligor is notified of the assignment of contract rights, he or she must perform whatever obligation is owed the *assignor* (the party who assigned his or her contract rights) to the *assignee* (the party to whom the assignor assigned his or her contract rights).

## DELEGATION OF CONTRACT DUTIES . . . . . . . . . . . . . . . . . . . . . .

Just as there are times when parties to a contract may wish to assign their contract rights, there are also times when parties may wish to *delegate* their contract duties. Delegation of duties occurs when an obligor obtains a third party to perform the obligor's responsibilities under a contract in his or her stead. As is the case with assignment of contractual rights, delegation of contractual duties is generally allowed, provided that the following conditions are met:

- the contractual obligations being delegated do not involve unique, nonstandardized personal services such as those rendered by physicians, attorneys, artists and other professionals who exercise a high degree of personal judgment and discretion in rendering services for clients;
- the performance by the *delegatee* (the person to whom the obligor delegates his or her duties) is substantially the same as would have been given by the *delegator* (the party who wishes to delegate his or her duties to a delegatee);
- the contract itself does not prohibit delegation; and
- the delegation is not prohibited by law.

## RIGHTS AND RESPONSIBILITIES OF PARTIES
## AFTER ASSIGNMENT OR DELEGATION . . . . . . . . . . . . . . . . . . . . .

After a valid assignment of contract rights by an assignor to an assignee, the assignee is entitled to performance by the obligor and can sue him or her directly if the obligation is not satisfactorily discharged. The assignee can also sue the assignor if the assignment was made to satisfy an obligation of the assignor to the assignee. The following example will illustrate:

- *Alma owes Benedict $100. Benedict, in turn, owes Danielle $100. In order to extinguish his debt to Danielle, Benedict assigns his right to collect $100 from Alma to Danielle and notifies Alma of the assignment. Alma is now legally obligated to pay Danielle. In the event that Alma refuses to pay Danielle, Danielle has the right to sue either Alma or Benedict to collect the $100 owed her. In the event that Alma only partially discharges her obligation by, say, paying Danielle only $90, Danielle can sue Alma for the remaining $10, or she can choose to sue Benedict for the remaining $10.*

When a valid delegation of duties is involved, the same rules apply: The delegator remains obligated to the obligee until the delegatee fully performs. If the delegatee does not perform at all, or renders an unacceptable performance of the delegator's contractual obligation, the obligee can sue either the delegator or the delegatee, at his or her option, as the following example illustrates:

- *Ed, a general contractor, agrees to build a house for Frank for $100,000. Ed hires Gertrude as his painting contractor. If Gertrude does a poor job of painting the house, Frank can sue either Ed, the delegator of the duty to paint the house, or Gertrude, the delegatee of that duty. Ed's duty to Frank is discharged only after Gertrude renders an acceptable performance.*

## NOVATION

When contracts cannot be assigned or delegated because of contractual provisions prohibiting assignment or delegation, or because the contract is of a type that is not assignable or delegable, the parties may still agree to substituted performance through a *novation*, the substituting of one contract for another. When a novation is involved, both contracting parties agree that their original contract will be canceled and replaced by a new agreement that substitutes a third party for one of the original contracting parties. When a novation occurs, the original contract is canceled by the mutual consent of the parties, and replaced by a new contract involving the substitution of a new party for one of the original contracting parties. The following example will clarify the distinction between an assignment or delegation and a novation:

- *Lina, a lawyer, agrees to represent Albert, an accused arsonist, in a criminal trial. This is a type of contract that is not delegable by Lina or assignable by Albert since unique, nonstandardized professional services are involved. Nevertheless, if Lina is unable to meet her obligation to defend Albert because of other commitments, she can, with Albert's consent, appoint her friend Luis to take over the case. If Lina and Albert both freely agree to the arrangement, then Lina's contract with Albert will be canceled and replaced with a new contract between Luis and Albert. The crucial distinction between assignment or delegation and novation is that novation can never be accomplished unless both parties freely agree to the arrangement. If Albert demands that Lina defend him herself, the novation will not take place and Lina will be liable for breach of contract to Albert if she fails to defend him due to other commitments.*

When a valid novation takes effect, the original contract between the parties is discharged, and so are the duties of the original obligor, who is *not* liable for any breach of contract by the third party who takes over his or her obligations under the new contract.

## RIGHTS OF THIRD-PARTY BENEFICIARIES TO CONTRACTS · · · · · · · · · · · · · · · · · · · · · · · · ·

It is not uncommon for persons who are not parties to a contract to have an interest in its performance. When a third party is intended to benefit from a contract to which he or she is not a party, the third party is termed an *intended beneficiary* of the contract. The typical example of an intended beneficiary is a beneficiary in a life insurance policy. When a third-party beneficiary is not intended by the parties to a contract to benefit from the contract, the third party is termed an *incidental beneficiary.* An example of incidental beneficiaries is employees; they may have a great personal stake in the contracts that their employer enters into, since their livelihood depends on them, but they are not directly intended to benefit from such contracts by the contracting parties. The distinction between incidental and intended beneficiaries is of crucial importance because only intended beneficiaries can bring suit to enforce contracts to which they are not a party.

## QUESTIONS · · · · · · · · · · · · · · · · · · · · · · · · · · · · · · ·

1. What is the difference between an assignment and a delegation?
2. What is an obligor?
3. What is an obligee?
4. How many obligors and obligees are there in every bilateral contract involving two parties?
5. What is an assignor?
6. What is an assignee?
7. Can contract rights be assigned by an assignor without the obligor's permission? If so, under what circumstances?
8. May contract duties be delegated under a contract without the obligee's permission? If so, under what circumstances?
9. Does an obligor who delegates his or her contractual duties to a third party remain liable to the obligee if the third party does not perform in accordance with the contract? Explain.
10. When may third-party beneficiaries sue to enforce a contract to which they are not a party but under which they stand to benefit?

## H Y P O T H E T I C A L     C A S E S

1. Ted, a plumber, owes Teresa $500 for a used computer he purchased from her recently but has not yet paid for. Tim owes Ted $500 for a new shower stall that

Ted installed in his house. If Ted tells Tim to send a check for $500 to Teresa rather than to him in paying for the plumbing work, must Tim honor the request? Explain.

2. Ted, a plumber, agrees to install a shower stall in Teresa's home for a fee of $500. After entering into the contract, Ted subcontracts the work to Tina, an equally qualified and licensed plumber, who agrees to do the work for Ted for $400. When Teresa learns of the delegation of contract duties by Ted, she is furious and wants to invalidate the contract. What result? If Teresa accepts performance by Tina but is not satisfied with the work she performs, who can she sue for damages?

3. High Flying Industries, an airplane manufacturing company, enters into a contract with Western Air, a large carrier, for forty new Super Duper Humongous Jets. After entering into the contract, but before accepting delivery of the planes, Western Air experiences financial difficulties and a protracted labor dispute that threaten to bankrupt the airline. In view of its financial difficulties, Western Air asks High Flying Industries to postpone the plane deliveries until next year. Although unhappy about the arrangement, High Flying Industries agrees to the change because it wants Western Air to stay in business, and believes that the airline can turn its troubles around within a year if it is not forced to accept the delivery of the planes now. Several of High Flying's subcontractors are not so understanding, however; if the contract is postponed, some may go out of business, or, at the very least, will have to lay off large numbers of employees, since their business is dependent on High Flying Industries' contracts for new planes. Several of these subcontractors band together and sue Western Air for breach of contract. What result?

4. Larkin, an attorney, agrees to draft a will for Lorraine in exchange for a fee of $125. Before Larkin has an opportunity to draft the will, she is retained by Killer Kong as a defense attorney in a multiple murder case that has gained national attention. Preparing Killer's defense will take all of Larkin's resources and time over the next several months, so she would like to delegate all of her other business to Lenny, a friend and fellow legal practitioner in the same area. Can she delegate the preparation of Lorraine's will to Lenny without Lorraine's consent? Explain. Assuming that delegation is not possible, how can Larkin still validly have Lenny prepare the will?

## ETHICS AND THE LAW: QUESTIONS FOR
## FURTHER STUDY . . . . . . . . . . . . . . . . . . . . . . . . . . . . . . . . . . . .

As we've seen in this chapter, there are instances in which delegation of duties can take place without the consent of the obligee. The law assumes that certain types of standardized services are identical, regardless of who performs them; the rationale is that plumbers, electricians, masons, roofers, carpenters and other skilled workers who perform services according to some standard code or plans all perform substantially identical work. Anyone who has hired any of these skilled professionals will quickly attest that this is nonsense; there is a wide range of difference in acceptable performance among skilled professionals, and a wide range of pride in workmanship and professionalism among them as well. It is arguable that a fairly simple legal service such as the preparation of a will or the drafting of a power of attorney are in fact much more standardized than the wiring or framing of a house in terms of the uniformity of results that can be expected in these areas, given equally well-trained professionals. When you further consider that much of the routine work performed by lawyers is delegated to paraprofessionals who work under the direct supervision of an attorney, the distinction between standardized and nonstandardized professional services seems to blur even further. How do you feel about the distinction? Should it be abolished? Does it serve a valid function? What do you think underlies the rationale for the distinction? Is it fair? How can you protect yourself from an unwanted delegation or assignment of a contract to which you are a party?

# CHAPTER
# 16

# PERFORMANCE AND BREACH

The vast majority of contracts end when all parties satisfactorily discharge their obligations. But in the performance of contracts, as in nearly all human endeavors, problems do crop up from time to time that result in a failure by one or both contracting parties to perform as promised. At times, such failure to perform is justified; at others, it is not. In this chapter, we will examine the various ways in which a contract can be discharged, as well as the consequences that result from unexcused failure to render the performance promised in a valid contract.

## DISCHARGE THROUGH PERFORMANCE · · · · · · · · · · · · · · · · · · · · ·

As previously noted, parties to contracts fully perform as promised in the vast majority of cases. Once each party renders the agreed-upon consideration, the contract is deemed to be *discharged through performance*. When a contract is discharged through performance, the parties have done all that they have promised to do under the contract and their obligations to one another end. In order for a contract to be discharged through performance, there must be no substantial deviation from the performance promised to that which was actually rendered, and the performance must have been rendered on a timely basis. *Nonconforming performance* (performance that is materially different than what was promised under the contract) or conforming performance that is not rendered on a timely basis constitutes a breach of contract and will subject the breaching party to liability under the contract.

## DISCHARGE THROUGH IMPOSSIBILITY
## OF PERFORMANCE · · · · · · · · · · · · · · · · · · · · · · · · · · · · · · · ·

There are times when parties who make a good-faith attempt to discharge their contractual obligations are unable to do so due to circumstances beyond their control. In such cases, the contract is deemed to be *discharged through impossibility of performance*, and the performance of all contracting parties is excused. In order for a contract to be discharged through impossibility of performance, two criteria must be met: (1) the circumstances that make performance impossible must be beyond the control of the parties, and (2) the parties must be objectively unable to perform. Common examples of circumstances that cause a contract to be discharged through impossibility of performance include the following:

- destruction of the subject matter of the contract through circumstances outside the control of the parties;
- changes in the law that make performance illegal when such performance was legal at the time that the parties originally entered into the contract; and
- breaking out of hostilities between the countries of the contracting parties.

Parties whose contracts are discharged through impossibility of performance may not sue one another for breach of contract, since the failure to perform is deemed to be excusable. If the external conditions that prevent the performance are of a temporary nature, then the duty to perform is merely suspended, rather than the contract being discharged. Likewise, if the external circumstances only partially impair the ability of one of the parties to perform, the party will be obligated to offer whatever performance it can under the circumstances and its duties under the contract will be discharged when it has done so. The following examples should help to clarify the applicable rules:

- *Albert contracts with Betty to import 1,000 widgets a month for the next year. A month after they enter into the agreement, Congress passes a law restricting imports from Betty's country to a maximum of 500 widgets per month for any U.S. importer. Albert's obligation under the contract will be discharged if he purchases from Betty the 500 widgets per month the law allows.*

- *Albert contracts with Betty to import 1,000 widgets a month for the next year. A month later, Congress passes a law outlawing the importation of widgets. Albert's contract with Betty is fully discharged through impossibility of performance. (The subsequent illegality of the transaction makes it impossible to perform the terms of the contract.)*

- *Albert contracts with Betty to import 1,000 widgets a month for the next year. A month later, Congress passes a law placing a three-month moratorium on the importation of widgets. Albert is excused from performance for a three-month period due to impossibility of performance, but must resume the monthly purchases for the remaining term of the contract once the moratorium is lifted.*

## DISCHARGE THROUGH COMMERCIAL IMPRACTICABILITY OF PERFORMANCE

There are instances when unforeseen changes in circumstances between the time that a contract is entered into and the time when performance is due make the contract possible to perform but so difficult or costly as to be impractical. At such times, performance is excused. In order for a contract to be *discharged through commercial impracticability*, the party seeking to have the contract discharged needs to show that (1) the condition that arose after the contract was entered into was *unforeseeable* by the parties at the time of entering into the contract, and (2) the expense or problems incident to performance are so great as to make performance *unreasonable*. The mere fact that performance is more costly than anticipated by the parties will not cause a contract to be discharged; the cost of performance must be both unreasonable and unforeseeable by the parties at the time that they entered into the contract. Whether or not performance in a given circumstance is commercially impracticable is a question of fact for the trier of fact to decide; it should be clear, however, that the costlier and the more difficult performance is, the likelier a jury is to find it commercially impracticable.

Note that labor strikes and reasonable increases in the cost of goods or materials needed to perform the contract, while perhaps unexpected by the parties, are always deemed to be foreseeable. Thus, a party that is unable to perform because it suffers a labor strike is in breach of contract.

## DISCHARGE THROUGH FRUSTRATION OF PURPOSE   . . . . . . . . . . .

It is possible for conditions to change so drastically from the time that a contract is entered into to the time that performance is due that it becomes unreasonable to force the parties to go through with their agreement in view of the changed circumstances. When that happens, the contract is deemed *discharged through frustration of purpose*. For frustration of purpose to be relied upon as the basis of discharging a contract, the party seeking to have the contract discharged needs to show that (1) a basic assumption made by the parties to the contract has been affected through no fault of the parties, and (2) that there is no useful purpose to be served by allowing the contract to continue. A typical example of frustration of purpose would be a homeowner who contracts to have an attached garage built on his land, only to have the house struck by lightning and burned to the ground before the garage is built. While the contractor may be willing and able to perform (indeed, he may insist on it!), a court would be unlikely to allow the contractor to perform over the homeowner's objections since a basic assumption both parties made in entering into the contract—that there would be a house on which to attach the garage—is no longer true. If the court feels that allowing the contract to be performed under the circumstances is wasteful, it may declare the contract discharged and excuse all performance by the parties involved.

## DISCHARGE THROUGH RELEASE   . . . . . . . . . . . . . . . . . . . . . . . . . .

A *release* is a contract not to sue that parties can enter into in order to discharge their contractual or tort obligations with one another. As with any contract, a release must be supported by new consideration. With regard to both tort and contract liability, the consideration given in exchange for the release can be anything of legal value, including a release by one party given in exchange for a release from the other. Thus, two persons who are involved in a minor automobile accident and do not wish to involve their insurance companies to avoid the inevitable rate increases that would result can simply exchange signed releases of liability with one another; both releases in that case are supported by consideration—a promise by each party not to bring legal action against the other. The same is true for a release that relates to a contractual obligation. After a valid contract is entered into but before the parties have performed their obligations, either party can obtain from the other a signed release that excuses them from performance. If both parties want to get out of the contract, mutual releases can be executed and they will be deemed to be supported by consideration, since both parties will give up their right to enforce the contract as consideration for the release from the other contracting party.

## DISCHARGE THROUGH NOVATION   . . . . . . . . . . . . . . . . . . . . . .

As noted in the last chapter novation is the substituting of one contract for another. When a novation is involved, both contracting parties agree that their original contract will be canceled and replaced by a new agreement that substitutes a third party for one of the original contracting parties. Once a valid novation of an existing contract is accomplished, the original contract is discharged and the responsibilities of the parties under that agreement end.

## BREACH OF CONTRACT   . . . . . . . . . . . . . . . . . . . . . . . . . . . .

The failure of any party to a binding contract to discharge their contractual obligations either through rendering the promised performance or through any of the other means of obtaining a valid discharge of contract discussed in this chapter constitutes a *breach of contract*. A party who suffers a breach of contract is entitled to sue for money damages or other remedies as will be discussed in the following chapter. A breach of contract can result either from a failure to perform the agreed-upon duties under a contract, or from the rendering of unacceptable, substandard performance in attempting to perform the duties under a contract. Thus, failing to perform at all or rendering imperfect performance can both constitute a breach of contract. The nature and extent of the breach, as we will see in the next chapter, will affect the damages the nonbreaching party is entitled to collect, as well as the specific remedies from which such a party may be able to choose.

## QUESTIONS   . . . . . . . . . . . . . . . . . . . . . . . . . . . . . . . . . . .

1. How is a contract discharged though performance?
2. What is nonconforming performance?
3. What is discharge through impossibility of performance?
4. What are the requirements for impossibility of performance?
5. When can commercial impracticability be used to discharge a contract?
6. What must the party seeking to have a contract discharged through commercial impracticability need to show?

7. What is a party required to show for a contract to be discharged through frustration of purpose?
8. What is a release?
9. How is a contract discharged through novation?
10. What is a breach of contract?

# H Y P O T H E T I C A L    C A S E S

1. Damon enters into a contract with Dolores wherein he agrees to build a garage within sixty days for $10,000. After entering into the contract, it dawns on Damon that he lacks the necessary skills to perform the agreed-upon task, and institutes an action to have the contract invalidated through impossibility of performance, claiming it is impossible for him to perform as agreed.
   a. What result?
   b. Assume that Damon performs as promised but takes ninety days to complete the job instead of the sixty days agreed upon due to a labor strike by his workers. What result? What if Damon's lateness in completing the job is caused by an unforeseen flash flood that makes it impossible to work for thirty days?
2. Jemal, an artist, agrees to paint a portrait of Jenny for $1,000. After entering into the contract but before either party has performed, Jenny is dismissed from her job and would like to cancel a contract that is now, for her, an unaffordable luxury.
   a. If Jemal refuses to cancel the contract, can Jenny claim her impossibility to pay as circumstances that will discharge the contract?
   b. If Jemal agrees to let Jenny off the hook, how should the parties go about discharging the contract?
   c. If both parties verbally agree not to sue one another, is there any real reason for executing a release?
   d. If Jenny still wants her portrait painted but Jemal would like to get out of the contract without being in breach, what are his options for doing so?

CHAPTER

# 17

# REMEDIES

When a contract is breached, the law provides the nonbreaching parties with a number of remedies whose purpose it is to compensate them for any loss they suffer as a result of the breach. Available remedies can be classified into two distinct categories: *legal remedies* and *equitable remedies*. Legal remedies are readily available to parties who suffer a breach of contract as soon as they establish the breach. In order to be awarded a legal remedy, nonbreaching parties need only establish by a preponderance of the evidence that they suffered a breach and the extent of the damages they suffered as a direct consequence of the breach. Equitable remedies, on the other hand, are not available as a matter of right, but rather may be awarded at the sole discretion of a judge whenever the available legal remedies are insufficient to properly compensate the nonbreaching party for his or her loss. In this chapter, we will examine the basic legal and equitable remedies available to parties who suffer a breach of contract.

## LEGAL REMEDIES · · · · · · · · · · · · · · · · · · · · · · · · · · · · · · · · · · · ·

There are a number of legal remedies that parties who suffer a breach of contract may ask for to compensate them for their loss. These include compensatory damages, nominal damages and, where the parties have so agreed, liquidated damages. Let's take a look at each of these damages in turn.

### COMPENSATORY DAMAGES

The basic purpose of *compensatory damages* is to place the nonbreaching party in the same position he or she would have been in had the breach not occurred. In other words, compensatory damages seeks to offset the loss suffered by the nonbreaching party by a monetary award that will indemnify the party for his or her loss. Compensatory damages are available in four basic forms: loss of the bargain, cost of completion, incidental damages and consequential damages.

121

**Loss of the bargain**    Most parties who sue for breach of contract want to recover *loss of the bargain* damages. This remedy represents the difference between what the nonbreaching party was entitled to under the contract and what he or she actually received, minus any savings the innocent party realized because of the breach. To put it another way, loss of the bargain entails the difference between what the party was entitled to receive under the contract and what he or she actually got, less any cost saved by the innocent party in not having to perform his or her part of the contract. The following examples will illustrate:

> *Carlos agrees to sell Cathy his 1995 Grand Am for $8,000. After entering into the contract, Carlos is offered $9,000 for the car by a third party, Tom, and sells Tom the car. Carlos is in breach of the contract with Cathy and she is entitled to loss of the bargain damages. In this case, assuming that the market price of the car is $9,000, then Cathy's damages would be the difference between what she was entitled to receive (a car worth $9,000), minus what she actually received (nothing, since the contract was breached) minus what she saved as a result of not having to perform her part of the bargain ($8,000, the amount she would have paid for the car). In this case, our formula yields loss of the bargain damages of $1,000 ($9,000 − $0 − $8,000 = $1,000).*

> *Cathy, a general contractor, agrees to build a 10 × 12' addition to Carlos' home for $10,000. Through a mistake, Cathy builds an 8 × 12' addition instead. If Carlos wants to sue for loss of the bargain damages, he is entitled to the difference between the value of what he paid for and the value of what he got, minus any savings he received as a result of the breach. In this case, assume that an 8 × 12' addition is worth $8,500 while a 10 × 12' addition is worth the contract price of $10,000; Carlos is entitled to $1,500 in damages under the loss of the bargain formula.*

**Cost of completion**    Where performance of one party is incomplete or nonconforming, the nonbreaching party may choose to sue for the reasonable cost of curing the defect in the tendered performance by having the performance completed by a third party, or for the reasonable cost of making the nonconforming performance conform to the requirements of the contract. The following example will illustrate:

> *Patrick agrees to paint Pedro's garage for $150. After Patrick paints 99 percent of the garage and only the trim around the garage doors and windows remains to be done, he falls ill and is unable to complete the job. Since the job was substantially completed, Pedro will have to pay the agreed-upon price, but may sue either for his loss of the bargain or for the cost of curing the defective performance, whichever he prefers. If he elects to sue for the cost of curing the defective performance, he is entitled to a setoff in the contract price for the reasonable cost of having a third party complete the work. If a local painter is willing to finish the trim for $35, then Pedro is entitled to a setoff of $35 from the $150 he must pay Patrick. Thus, he will have to pay Patrick $150 − $35 = $115.*

**Incidental damages**    Damages that flow directly from a breach of contract are *incidental damages* and are recoverable by the nonbreaching party. The following example will illustrate:

> *Marion orders fifty bushels of apples from Maria to sell on her fruit stand. Maria mistakenly ships fifty bushels of pears. Since the fruit Maria sent is not what Marion ordered, Maria is in breach of contract for failure to ship conforming goods. Marion is entitled to loss of the bargain damages, and can also recover any incidental expenses that flow directly from the breach, such as the cost of shipping the goods*

- *back to Maria and the cost of storing the goods while awaiting instructions from Maria as to how to*
- *ship them back.*

**Consequential damages**   Damages that are not caused directly by a breach but result as a direct, foreseeable consequence of the breach are *consequential damages*. Typical consequential damages include lost profits and personal injury or property damage flowing as a direct consequence of the breach. The following example will illustrate:

- *Tai orders 200 pounds of soybean burgers to sell in his Veggie Burger establishment from XYZ Foods.*
- *XYZ mistakenly ships 200 pounds of all-beef hamburger patties. As a result of the mixup, Tai has to*
- *close his restaurant for two days, until he can procure the needed ingredients for his veggie burgers*
- *from another source. In addition to loss of the bargain or cost of completion damages, Tai can sue XYZ*
- *Foods for the foreseeable consequential damages of his loss of profits for the two days he had to close*
- *his business, a consequence that flowed directly from the breach.*

Foreseeability of the damages at the time that the parties entered into the contract is a prerequisite to consequential damages being awardable. In addition to showing that the consequential damages were foreseeable by the breaching party at the time of entering into the contract, the party asking for consequential damages must be able to prove those damages with a high degree of certainty; courts will categorically refuse to award damages that are speculative in nature. In the last example, Tai could prove his lost profits by showing the profits made by the business over the past several weeks on the same days of the week that it had to be closed as a result of the breach. Thus, assuming that the business had to be closed on Monday and Tuesday, Tai could prove his lost profits by relying on the average profits he'd made on Monday and Tuesday of the previous week, or on the average profits for Mondays and Tuesdays over the last quarter.

## NOMINAL DAMAGES

Whenever a contract is breached that does not cause any real loss to the non-breaching party, the party is entitled to *nominal damages*. As the name implies, nominal damages are damages in name only—usually one dollar or five cents. It is a way for courts to acknowledge that a legal wrong has been done to one of the parties, but that the party has suffered no real injury. Parties do not ask for nominal damages; these are awarded by a court when a breach of contract is proven but the plaintiff cannot prove any actual damages as a result of the breach.

## LIQUIDATED DAMAGES

In cases where it is expected that actual damages will be difficult to assess in case of a breach, parties often agree ahead of time to a *liquidated damages* provision in the contract that states what damages will be payable by each party in the event of a breach. Generally speaking, liquidated damages may be agreed to between parties to a contract as long as they are reasonable. If the liquidated damages are set at a high value so as to discourage parties from breaching a contract, the courts will universally refuse to enforce them. For such damages to be enforceable, they must be reasonable and related to the actual loss anticipated by one or both parties in the event that the contract is breached.

# EQUITABLE REMEDIES ................................

There are times when none of the available legal remedies will properly compensate a party for the loss of the bargain caused by a breach of contract. In those rare instances, courts have the power to grant some extraordinary remedies based on the court's power to award certain equitable relief when the available legal remedies will not serve the ends of justice. Among a court's equity powers are the ability to award the remedies of specific performance, injunction and quasi-contract. We'll examine each of these in turn.

## SPECIFIC PERFORMANCE

*Specific performance* is an order by a court requiring that the breaching party perform the contract as agreed. Although courts do not generally force parties to honor their contractual obligations, they will do so when the subject matter of the agreement is unique and money damages would not properly compensate the aggrieved party for his or her loss. The types of contracts for which courts often award specific performance include the sale of real estate, antiques, art or other unique subject matter.

It is solely within the discretion of a court whether to allow specific performance; in general, judges are wary of awarding this remedy, preferring to award monetary damages whenever that is a viable remedy. Specific performance is never awarded in cases involving ordinary goods or in personal service contracts.

## INJUNCTION

A second equitable remedy within the discretion of the courts is the power to grant injunctive relief. An *injunction* is a court order that prohibits specific action. In breach-of-contract cases, injunctive relief can be granted to prevent the sale of unique goods or real estate pending the resolution of the breach of contract action. Thus, if a party is seeking specific performance of a sales contract for, say, a rare painting, a court would be asked to issue an injunction preventing the defendant in that action from selling or otherwise disposing of the painting pending the outcome of the case.

## QUASI-CONTRACT

*Quasi-contract* is essentially a legal fiction that courts engage in so as to hold parties liable for nonexistent contracts in order to prevent the unjust enrichment by one party at the expense of the other, or in order to prevent an injustice from being perpetrated. When quasi-contract is invoked, a court imposes an obligation on the parties when none in fact exists at law in order to prevent an injustice from happening. When invoking quasi-contract, the courts treat parties in a particular circumstance as if a contract existed, binding the parties to take an action required to prevent an injustice by creating an obligation where none exists at law. Typical examples where quasi-contract could be invoked involve gross unfairness or a miscarriage of justice, as the following examples illustrate:

- *Harriet agrees to accompany Harold to the prom, and suggests that he rent a limousine and make reservations at an expensive nightclub for the occasion. Harold rents a limousine at a nonrefundable cost of $250, rents a tuxedo for $80 and makes reservations at a hot night spot by paying a nonrefundable fee of $50. The night before the prom, Harriet phones Harold to inform him that she was only kidding and would never assent to going to the prom with the class nerd. Harold, furious, wants to sue to be reimbursed for his expenses in preparation for the evening. Unfortunately, this is not an enforceable contract, since there was no legal consideration given by either party (courts do not consider social obligations such as this one as forming a binding contract). Nevertheless, in this case it would be greatly unjust to not award Harold some relief, since Harriet in fact suggested he rent the limousine and make the arrangements in preparation for the prom. Thus, a court would have the power to hold Harriet liable to Harold for his losses in quasi-contract. (A court would by no means have to do so; it is strictly within the judge's discretion whether or not a sufficient injustice is represented here, justifying the awarding of quasi-contract.)*

- *Martha, while shopping at Marty's Market, gives Marty a $1 bill in exchange for a pack of gum worth 50¢. Marty, who is very nearsighted, believes the $1 bill to be a $20 bill and gives Martha $19.50 in change. Martha says nothing and walks away. Even though there is clearly no contractual duty here from Martha to return the excess $19 mistakenly given to her by Marty, most courts would impose such a duty on her under a quasi-contract theory in order to avoid her unjustly being enriched at Marty's expense.*

## ELECTION OF REMEDIES

Since the basic purpose of awarding remedies for breach of contract is to place the parties in the same position they would have been in had the breach not occurred (or, to put it another way, to compensate parties for their loss), parties are not allowed to have duplicate recoveries, and *punitive damages* (awards intended to punish defendants for their actions) are not awardable in actions for breach of contracts. In suits involving breach of contract, plaintiffs must elect the remedies they believe themselves to be entitled to and prove their damages to the court (with the exception of nominal damages, which a court will award on its own when appropriate). If a plaintiff wants specific performance but asks only for compensatory damages, he or she will be out of luck. Likewise, if a plaintiff is entitled to loss of the bargain damages, as well as incidental and consequential damages, he or she must specifically ask for each remedy or will not be entitled to its award.

Some of the available remedies are mutually exclusive. A person who wishes to sue for money damages for loss of the bargain cannot also receive specific performance. Likewise, a person who sues to recover liquidated damages under a valid liquidated damages provision in a contract cannot also recover other compensatory damages. What damages to ask for is usually an important question of strategy for an attorney, who must decide which of the available remedies are available to his or her client and then select the most advantageous from the ones available. Mutually exclusive remedies can sometimes be asked for in the alternative; this is especially useful when the most beneficial remedy is an equitable one that a court need not award. Thus, a person who wishes specific performance of a contract can ask for that as the primary remedy, and for compensatory damages in the alternative (e.g., in case the court refuses to honor the request for the equitable remedy of choice).

## MITIGATION OF DAMAGES . . . . . . . . . . . . . . . . . . . . . . . . . . . . . .

In most instances, parties who sue for breach of contract are held to have an affirmative duty to *mitigate* their damages; this means that contracting parties must take any steps reasonably necessary to lessen the breaching party's damages when a contract breach occurs. If parties do not attempt in good faith to lessen their damages when a breach occurs, most courts will refuse to compensate nonbreaching parties for the extent of the damages they suffered but could have avoided through a reasonable effort at mitigating the damages. For instance, a tenant who breaches an apartment lease by leaving six months before it expires is liable to the landlord for the remaining six months' rent. But the landlord must try to mitigate the tenant's damages by making a good-faith effort to re-rent the apartment to new tenants. If the landlord makes no such effort, and a court finds that the apartment would have been rented in sixty days if a good-faith effort had been made by the landlord, then the landlord will be able to collect rent only for the sixty-day period during which the apartment had been likely to remain empty had he or she attempted to mitigate the tenant's damages, but will be barred from collecting rent for the months when the apartment would have been rented had the landlord exerted a good-faith effort to find new tenants.

## QUESTIONS   . . . . . . . . . . . . . . . . . . . . . . . . . . . . . . . . . . . . . .

1. What are four basic legal remedies available to parties who suffer a breach of contract?
2. What are three basic equitable remedies available to parties who suffer a breach of contract?
3. How are loss of the bargain damages computed?
4. What is meant by *cost of completion*?
5. What are incidental damages?
6. What are consequential damages?
7. What are nominal damages?
8. What are liquidated damages?
9. What is specific performance and when is specific performance awardable as a remedy?
10. What is an injunction and when is it likely to be awarded in a contract action as a remedy?
11. What is quasi-contract?

# H Y P O T H E T I C A L          C A S E S

1.  Esther agrees to sell her 1995 Ford Taurus to Earl for $7,500. At the time that the parties enter into the contract, the market value of the car is $8,500. When Earl presents a check to Esther for the agreed-upon amount, she informs him that she has changed her mind and will be selling the car to Ezra for $8,500. Earl is furious at Esther's breach and sues her for breach of contract. In his suit, he asks for injunctive relief preventing Esther from transferring the car to Ezra while the suit is pending, as well as specific performance of the contract and, in the alternative, compensatory damages of $1,000. You are the judge. Decide the case and rule on what damages are awardable.

2.  Gary agrees to sell his mint 1954 Ford Thunderbird to Gina for $20,000. After entering into a valid written agreement for the sale of the car, Gary has a change of heart and refuses to part with the automobile. Gina sues. What remedies can she reasonably ask for?

3.  In preparation for the grand opening of his new business, Dan's Diet Delights, Dan orders 1,000 pounds of assorted dietetic sweets. Two days before his scheduled grand opening, his supplier ships 1,000 pounds of rich, high-calorie sweets by mistake. As a result, Dan has to postpone his grand opening for a week (until the right goods arrive) and spend $500 for new advertising and posters with the new grand opening day. He also has to pay one week's salary to two sales employees who have nothing to do in that time, since the goods for the store have not arrived, for a total of $600. In addition, he spends $100 to ship the goods back to the nonconforming supplier, at the supplier's suggestion. After the right goods finally arrive, he sues the supplier. What damages can he ask for and what damages is he likely to receive?

4.  Perry agrees to work as the manager of Patricia's Pet Store for three years in exchange for compensation of $40,000 per year. After the first year of the three-year contract, Perry informs Patricia that he will not complete the remaining two-year term because he has found a more lucrative job elsewhere. Patricia immediately begins interviewing for Perry's replacement and spends approximately $1,000 in search-related expenses before she finds a suitable manager for her store willing to take the job for the same compensation as Perry. If she decides to sue Perry for breach of the employment contract, what, if any, damages will she recover? Would your answer be the same if she finds someone to take Perry's job for $35,000 per year? What if no qualified person can be found to do the same job for under $42,000 per year? Explain fully.

# ETHICS AND THE LAW: QUESTIONS FOR
# FURTHER STUDY . . . . . . . . . . . . . . . . . . . . . . . . . . . . . . . .

It is an unfortunate fact of life that many legal wrongs go unremedied. Most textbooks on law, including this one, focus on the legal rights and duties of citizens in their dealings with one another without paying much attention to real-world realities. It is a fact of life, however unpleasant and unsung, that a sizable percentage of judgments that parties obtain from courts after prevailing in contract or tort actions never get collected. The fact that a court awards damages does not guarantee that defendants will ultimately pay them. And while judgment holders have a number of recourses available to them for collecting outstanding judgments, including attaching the real and personal property of judgment debtors and garnishing wages, for example, collecting through these and other legal means can take time and money in terms of fees charged by attorneys, collection agencies or private investigators to trace the assets of judgment debtors who fraudulently transfer or otherwise attempt to hide their assets, or who flee the jurisdiction in order to avoid paying outstanding judgments. As is often the case, those who violate the law are quite adept at avoiding its consequences. At common law in England, debtors' prison was available as a last resort to punish those who would not pay their debts, including the discharging of outstanding judgments. Even today, in many civil-law jurisdictions throughout the world, jail is a possible consequence of failing to pay one's bills, or of ignoring civil judgments. While indiscriminately jailing debtors would have unacceptable social consequences and certainly have a disproportionate impact on the poor, it is equally true that there is no incentive now for persons who are judgment-proof (e.g., the indigent and persons without traceable income or assets) to act in a responsible manner, since there are no consequences for their refusal to honor financial obligations or judgments. How do you feel about this issue? How do you suggest that a balance be achieved between protecting the truly needy from undue punishment and preventing abuses of the system by those who abuse it?

UNIT

# SALE OF GOODS AND COMMERCIAL PAPER UNDER THE UNIFORM COMMERCIAL CODE

## INTRODUCTION TO THE UNIFORM COMMERCIAL CODE . . . . . . . . . . . . . . . . . . . . . . . . . . . . . . . . . . .

In order to unify laws affecting business, the *Uniform Commercial Code* (UCC) was drafted by the National Conference of Commissioners on Uniform State Laws—a panel comprising preeminent legal experts from throughout the country. By 1967, the UCC was adopted with only minor changes by the legislatures of all the states, with the exception of Louisiana, which has adopted only Articles 1, 3, 4, 5, 7 and 8. (Louisiana law is still heavily influenced by French civil law, and as such, Louisiana law tends to differ markedly from that of the other forty-nine states in a number of important areas.)

Because the UCC effectively unifies the law in key areas in all states, it is a statute of paramount importance to business. Although some differences still exist among the states in areas covered by the UCC, these are generally minor. Thus, the UCC affords to companies that conduct business in more than one state the uniformity and predictability that is essential to commerce.

In this unit, we will examine salient provisions of two key articles of the UCC: Article 2 (Sales) and Article 3 (Commercial Paper).

# 18

# INTRODUCTION TO SALES CONTRACTS

## INTRODUCTION TO ARTICLE 2: SALES · · · · · · · · · · · · · · · · · · · · · ·

Article 2 of the UCC concerns itself with contracts for the sale of goods. In general, the UCC codifies the common law of contracts and makes some significant changes whenever contracts involve the sale of goods.

It is crucial to note from the outset that Article 2 applies only to contracts for the sale of *goods*. As we will see in this chapter, *goods* can be defined as tangible, movable personal property. Contracts for anything other than goods (e.g., service contracts, contracts involving interests in real estate and contracts involving intangible personal property, such as stocks, bonds, patents and copyrights) are not covered by the changes to the common law of contracts provided by Article 2.

In this chapter, we will examine the most significant changes to the law of contracts made by Article 2. Keep in mind as you read the material that follows that what you learned about contract law in chapters 8 through 17 is still applicable when sales contracts are involved *unless* the law has been specifically changed by Article 2. For the most part, this chapter will focus on highlighting the most significant changes to the common law of contracts made by UCC Article 2. As you read the material in this chapter, it will help to understand the changes if you keep in mind two basic principles applicable to Article 2 of the UCC: (1) a major purpose of Article 2 is to simplify the law and to make it easier for parties to enter into binding contracts, and (2) Article 2 will often hold merchants to a higher standard than nonmerchants. Section 2-104 (1) of the UCC defines a merchant as follows:

> "Merchant" means a person who deals in goods of the kind or otherwise by his occupation holds himself out as having knowledge or skill peculiar to the practices or goods involved in the transaction or to whom such knowledge or skill may be attributed by his employment of an agent or broker or other intermediary who by his occupation holds himself out as having such knowledge or skill.

Thus, a merchant is one who either (1) deals in goods of the type involved in the contract in question, or (2) has specific expertise in the type of goods involved either through specialized personal knowledge or through the hiring of persons who have such knowledge to act on his or her behalf.

## APPLICABILITY OF ARTICLE 2

As previously noted, Article 2 applies only to contracts for the sale of goods. Section 2-105 (1) defines *goods* as follows:

> "Goods" means all things (including specially manufactured goods) which are movable at the time of identification to the contract for sale . . . [and] the unborn young of animals and growing crops. . . .

Furthermore, under Section 2-107 (1), *goods* also includes contracts for the sale of minerals, oil and gas if these are *severed* (removed) from the realty by the *seller*; when these items are to be severed from the land by the *buyer*, the contract is not considered one for the sale of goods and is therefore not covered by Article 2.

## FORMAL REQUIREMENTS AND RULES OF CONSTRUCTION

The UCC makes some changes to the common law of contracts with regard to the enforceability of oral contracts and specifies to what extent written agreements may be contradicted by extraneous evidence. The code also does away with the significance of the seal for sales contracts.

### STATUTE OF FRAUDS (§ 2-201)

A contract involving the sale of goods with a price of $500 or more must be evidenced by a signed writing by the party being charged with a breach if it is to be enforceable. Despite the general rule that a signed writing is required in order to enforce contracts for the sale of goods with a price of $500 or more, the UCC relaxes the Statute of Frauds with three important exceptions to its application, as follows:

- Section 2-201 (2) states that when *both* parties are merchants, a signed writing in confirmation of the contract by one of the parties will bind *both* parties unless it is objected to in writing within ten days of receipt by the receiving merchant.
- Section 2-201 (3)(a) further states that if goods are to be specially manufactured for the buyer by the seller and are not resalable by the seller in the regular course of business, the seller can bind the buyer of the specially manufactured goods even without a signed writing by the buyer once the seller has made "either a substantial beginning of their manufacture or commitments for their procurement."
- Section 2-201 (3)(b) additionally states that oral contracts involving the sale of goods with a value of $500 or more are enforceable against a buyer or seller who

admits that an oral contract existed during testimony in open court or in pleadings. Under this exception, however, the contract is enforceable only for the quantity of goods actually admitted to in the pleadings or in the party's testimony.

- Section 2-201 (4)(b) states that the Statute of Frauds cannot be used as a defense to the enforcement of an oral contract to the extent that goods under the contract have been accepted and paid for. In other words, Section 2-201 can be used only to prevent the enforcement of executory oral contracts, but not contracts that have been fully executed and discharged through performance.

## PAROL EVIDENCE RULE (§ 2-202)

The UCC states that when parties have executed a signed writing relating to a contract for the sale of goods that is intended to embody the final agreement of the parties, such written agreements cannot be contradicted by *parol evidence* (oral or extraneous evidence). Terms in such contracts can, however, be explained by *course of dealing, usage of trade, course of performance* and by additional consistent terms (unless a court finds that the written agreement was intended to embody the complete and exclusive agreement between the parties). For purposes of the UCC, course of dealing, usage of trade and course of performance are defined as follows:

- Course of Dealing (§ 1-205 [1]): Previous conduct by the parties establishes a common basis of understanding for interpreting specific contract provisions and the conduct of the parties. The assumption is that when parties do business with one another, an understanding may arise as to the interpretation of common contract provisions from their past experience. Thus, if a buyer and seller have been doing business with each other for ten years on a "net 30 days" credit basis and no specific credit terms are noted on their latest contract, it could be inferred from their course of dealing that a "net 30 days" credit term was assumed to apply.
- Usage of Trade (§ 1-205 [2]): The UCC defines *usage of trade* as "any practice or method of dealing having such regularity of observance in a place, vocation or trade as to justify and expectation that it will be observed with respect to the transaction in question." The UCC recognizes that common language might have special meaning in a given trade or industry, and will allow parol evidence as to such meaning to be introduced in sales contracts. In the lumber industry, for example, an order for "2″ by 4″ by 8′″" wood will in fact not result in wood being shipped that is actually 2″ high by 4″ wide by 8″ in length; the dimensions will be somewhat smaller since it is understood that the 2″ by 4″ by 8′ measurements apply to green wood, which can be expected to shrink as it dries. Thus, in a contract calling for the delivery of lumber, the stated dimensions would be subject to interpretation by what is acceptable in the trade.
- Course of Performance (Practical Construction) (§ 2-208): In a contract for the sale of goods that requires repeated performance over a period of time, the actual performance tendered and accepted is relevant to explaining the terms of a contract. Thus, in a contract that calls for twelve monthly shipments of goods, if the

buyer accepts without complaint the first eleven shipments but refuses the twelfth, acceptance without objection of the first eleven shipments would be relevant in determining the conformity (acceptability) of the goods to the contract.

### INAPPLICABILITY OF SEALS (§ 2-203)

As noted in Chapter 8, at common law a seal had special significance and is still required today in some formal contracts. But the UCC specifically states that seals are inoperative in sales contracts; thus, the presence or absence of a seal on a sales contract has no effect on the contract.

## CONTRACT FORMATION  · · · · · · · · · · · · · · · · · · · · · · · · · · · ·

The UCC makes some significant changes to the common law of contracts in the areas of contract formation, particularly with regard to the requirements of offer and acceptance.

### CONTRACT FORMATION IN GENERAL (§ 2-204)

At common law, a contract was formed at the precise moment that a valid offer was accepted; thus, a clear, unequivocal offer and a clear unequivocal acceptance were prerequisites to the formation of a valid contract. Furthermore, no valid agreement existed unless it was very clear just what it was that the parties were agreeing to. The UCC, however, greatly relaxes these traditional requirements of contract formation by stating that a valid sales contract can exist even if it is impossible to clearly determine the moment of its making. In addition, the UCC makes a sales contract valid even if one or more material terms are omitted or purposely left open, as long as "the parties have intended to make a contract and there is a reasonably certain basis for giving an appropriate remedy." (§ 2-204 [3]).

### OFFER AND ACCEPTANCE IN FORMATION OF CONTRACTS (§ 2-203)

Unless the offer unambiguously states otherwise, the UCC allows acceptance through any reasonable means, and states that an offer for the shipment of goods can be accepted either by a promise to ship or by actual shipment of either conforming or nonconforming goods. If nonconforming goods are shipped, this is simultaneous acceptance and a breach of the sales contract, unless the seller specifically notifies the buyer that the nonconforming goods are being shipped as an accommodation. Thus, if a buyer orders a television set and says he prefers acceptance by letter, the seller can accept either by forwarding the requested acceptance letter, by promising via telegram to ship the set, by shipping the set or even by shipping a stereo (nonconforming goods), in which case the seller would be both accepting the contract for the sale of the television set on the buyer's terms and breaching it at the same time.

Notice that Section 2-203 liberalizes the common-law rules of contract acceptance in favor of making it easier for the parties to enter into binding contracts.

### ADDITIONAL TERMS IN ACCEPTANCE OR CONFIRMATION (§ 2-207)

Another major change to the common law of contracts is effected by Section 2-207, which essentially curtails the mirror image rule. You may remember from Chapter 8 that an acceptance needs to exactly mirror an offer if a contract is to be formed; any material change in the acceptance renders the acceptance a counteroffer and automatically rejects the original offer. The UCC changes this rule by stating that an acceptance that contains additional terms is valid unless it is conditioned on the offeror accepting the offeree's additional terms. The effect of the additional terms varies depending on whether or not the parties are both merchants. If none or only one of the parties is a merchant, the additional terms are ignored. If both parties are merchants, the additional terms become part of the contract unless (1) they are objected to within a reasonable time of receipt of the acceptance, (2) the additional terms materially alter the contract, or (3) the offer specifically limits acceptance to the stated terms. The following examples will illustrate how Section 2-207 works:

- *A seller offers to sell a buyer 100 widgets for $1,000. The buyer accepts through a letter that states: "Please ship the 100 widgets for $1,000. I assume you will ship via Federal Express." If one or none of the parties is a merchant, the additional terms relating to the delivery are simply ignored, and the seller may ship the goods via any commercially reasonable means. If the buyer and the seller are merchants, the additional terms become a part of the contract provided that the seller does not object to them within a reasonable time and further provided that the cost of Federal Express shipping is not substantially higher than that of the other available means of shipment. If it is substantially higher, then the term would not apply, even between merchants, since it would be a material alteration to the terms of the contract.*

- *A seller offers to sell a buyer a boat for $5,000. The buyer accepts the offer as follows: "I agree to purchase your boat provided that you also throw in four life preservers and a water-ski kit." Whether or not the parties are merchants, the acceptance is invalid because it is conditioned on acceptance of the additional terms, making the attempted acceptance into a counteroffer. Words that signal a conditional acceptance include* if, provided that, as long as *and* on condition of.

## UNCONSCIONABLE CONTRACT OR CLAUSE (§ 2-302)    . . . . . . . . . .

The UCC gives courts wide latitude in dealing with contracts that they deem unconscionable as a matter of law. If a court finds a contract or a contract clause unconscionable, it may refuse to enforce the contract, enforce the contract without the unconscionable clause or rewrite the contract to avoid the unconscionable result. For purposes of the UCC, an unconscionable contract can be defined as "one which no man in his senses would make, on the one hand, and which no fair and honest man would accept, on the other." (*Hume v United States*, 132 US 406, 10 S Ct 134) Generally speaking, courts will not invalidate contracts based merely on one party having made a bad bargain or on the bargain being unfair to one party. Gross unfairness of a type that "shocks the conscience of the court" is typically required for a contract to be held voidable on the grounds of unconscionability.

## AUCTION SALES (§ 2-328) . . . . . . . . . . . . . . . . . . . . . . . . . . . . .

Under the UCC, auction sales are deemed to be complete when the auctioneer signals assent to the bidder's offer by the fall of the hammer or in any other customary manner. If a bid is made while the hammer is falling, the auctioneer has the option of deeming the goods sold under the bid for which the hammer was falling or reopening the bidding at his or her discretion.

Auctions can be either *with reserve* or *without reserve*. In auctions with reserve, the auctioneer reserves the right to withdraw any item from the bidding if, in his or her sole discretion, the bids offered are unacceptably low. Auctions without reserve, on the other hand, obligate the auctioneer to sell the item outright for the highest bid. Whether an auction is with or without reserve is in the discretion of the auctioneer; if terms are not stated, the auction is deemed to be with reserve.

Finally, in all bids except during forced sales, such as foreclosures and sheriff's sales, an auctioneer may not knowingly receive a bid on the seller's behalf unless it is made known prior to the bidding that the seller has reserved the right to bid on the auctioned item(s). If a bid is made in violation of this rule, the highest good faith bidder may at his or her option either avoid the sale or take the goods at the highest good-faith bid (the highest bid before a bid was made on the seller's behalf). The reason for this rule should be obvious: to prevent sellers from artificially inflating bids at an auction by bidding against other bidders for their own goods—unless the other bidders are given notice that the seller may be bidding on his or her own goods.

## STATUTE OF LIMITATIONS IN CONTRACTS
## FOR SALE (§ 2-725) . . . . . . . . . . . . . . . . . . . . . . . . . . . . . . . .

The Statute of Limitations for contracts involving the sale of goods is four years from the date that the cause of action *accrues* (a cause of action accrues when the breach occurs). Parties may not extend the period of limitation, but they can reduce it to a period of not less than one year by mutual agreement.

## QUESTIONS . . . . . . . . . . . . . . . . . . . . . . . . . . . . . . . . . . . . .

1. What type of transaction does Article 2 of the UCC apply to?
2. Define *goods*.
3. Does Article 2 of the UCC do away with the common law of contracts?
4. Under what circumstances will a written and signed confirmation of a contract bind both parties to a contract?
5. Under the Statute of Frauds section of the UCC (Section 2-201), when are oral contracts for goods with a value of $500 or more enforceable?
6. What is parol evidence?
7. What type of parol evidence can be used to explain written agreements?
8. What is the significance of a seal under Article 2 of the UCC?

9. What is the effect of shipping nonconforming goods in response to a sales order?

10. In general, what is the affect of nonmaterial additional terms on an acceptance?

11. What is an unconscionable contract?

12. What is the difference between an auction with reserve and one without reserve?

# H Y P O T H E T I C A L      C A S E S

1. Ben Buyer calls Sally Seller by phone and orders a color ink-jet computer printer for $300, two sets of ink cartridges for $49.99 and a Super VGA monitor for $150. The total price of the order is $499.99, plus $35 in sales taxes and $25 for shipping, for a grand total of $559.99. A day after placing the order, Ben has a change of heart and calls Sally to cancel. Sally informs him that she has already shipped the goods and that it is, therefore, too late for him to cancel the order. When the goods arrive five days later, Ben refuses delivery, whereupon Sally sues him in small-claims court to recover loss of the bargain damages plus the incidental expenses of paying for the goods. You are the judge. Decide this case and give the legal justification for your decision.

2. Bernice Buyer sends a purchase order to Sam Seller that reads as follows: "Ship 20 PCs with the following configuration at $1,500 each: 250 MB hard disk, 8 MB RAM, 1.44 MB floppy drive, VGA graphics card with 1 MB RAM, and 250 MB internal tape backup drive." When the purchase order arrives, Sam promptly ships twenty Apple computers with the noted configuration. When the computers arrive, Bernice rejects their delivery, claiming that the term *PCs* clearly implied IBM-compatible machines, rather than Apple Macintosh computers. Sam, on the other hand, claims that since no actual *type* of computer was specified, he was free to ship any commercially reasonable system that met Bernice's specifications. The parol evidence rule notwithstanding, what type of extraneous evidence, if any, can both parties provide in court to bolster their arguments?

3. Bart Buyer, the owner of Bart's Bargain Basement, sends a purchase order to Salena Seller for 1,000 My Little Autopsy toy sets—the season's hottest-selling toy that, to the dismay of parents everywhere, allows children to simulate the thrills and chills of performing a real autopsy on an anatomically correct doll whose body parts can be removed with real gore action. Salena, who does not have the popular toy in stock, ships 1,000 My Undead Mummy dolls to Bart with a note that states: "These are shipped as an accommodation to your order at a 10 percent reduction off our regular wholesale price." When the dolls arrive, Bart rejects them (they are not gory enough to suit the tastes of discriminating five-year-olds) and sues Salena for breach of contract. What result?

4. Benigno Buyer writes Francene Farmer a letter that states he is willing to purchase 1,000 pounds of apples at a price of 33¢ per pound.
   a. How can Francene accept this contract?

b. If Francene writes back, stating, "Your terms are agreeable, provided you purchase a minimum of 1,200 pounds of apples," what is the effect of Francene's statement? Will it matter whether or not Benigno is also a merchant?

c. Assume that the wholesale price of apples is 66¢ per pound at the time that the offer is made. If Francene accepts it, will she be likely to successfully assert a defense of unconscionability if she later refuses to honor the contract's terms?

# 19

# RIGHTS AND DUTIES OF PARTIES IN THE PERFORMANCE AND BREACH OF THE SALES CONTRACT

In this chapter, we will cover the basic rules set out by the UCC affecting the rights and responsibilities of parties to a sales contract both during its performance and after its breach. As is usually the case with the UCC, these rules generally apply in the absence of parties' agreement to the contrary. With few exceptions, parties are free to modify nearly all of the provisions that follow through specific language in the sales contract; if they do not do so, the UCC spells out some key rights and responsibilities of parties in an attempt to reflect their probable intent. As previously noted, one of the main purposes of the UCC is to facilitate commerce and make it easier for people to enter into binding agreements. Because sales contracts are often not very detailed (although they certainly can be), the code provides a basic framework of key rights and duties of the parties that are incorporated into every sales agreement unless the parties agree otherwise.

## DELIVERY OF GOODS (§ 2-308) . . . . . . . . . . . . . . . . . . . . . . . . . . . . .

Unless the parties agree otherwise, the place for delivery of goods by the seller to the buyer is the seller's place of business or, if he or she has no place of business, the seller's residence. If, at the time of entering into a contract, both parties know that the goods are in another place, then delivery is to be made at the place where the goods are.

## TIME FRAME FOR DELIVERY OF GOODS AND NOTICE OF TERMINATION (§ 2-309) . . . . . . . . . . . . . . . . . . . . .

If no specific time for delivery is set, delivery must be within a reasonable time. With regard to contracts that have an indefinite duration, they are valid for a reasonable time but are subject to termination by either party at any time. In order to terminate such agreements, notification of termination must be received before the contract is terminated; parties *cannot* contract away the need for notification of termination.

## CONTRACT OPTIONS AND DUTY OF COOPERATION (§ 2-311) . . . . . . . . . . . . . . . . . . . . . . . . . . . .

A sales contract that allows one of the parties to specify the particulars of performance is valid if it otherwise meets the requirements for a valid sales contract. In such cases, the party with the right to specify the particulars relating to performance has to exercise good faith and be bound by the limits of commercial reasonableness. In addition, the party with the right to specify the performance must exercise the option on a timely basis. Failure to do so constitutes a breach of the sales contract.

## SHIPMENT BY COMMON CARRIER (§ 2-311) . . . . . . . . . . . . . . . . . .

Sales contracts very often require goods to be shipped by the seller to the buyer through a *common carrier* (a company that offers transportation services to the general public, such as UPS, Federal Express, the U.S. Postal Service, and air, train and bus transportation companies). The type of method chosen for delivery of goods can have an effect on such factors as the risk of loss of goods in transit, the time when the buyer obtains an insurable interest, the buyer's right to inspect and reject the goods and who bears the cost of delivery, as we will see from the analysis of the following code sections.

### FOB AND FAS SHIPMENT TERMS AND RISK OF LOSS (§ 2-319)

*FOB* and *FAS* are shipping terms that mean *free on board* and *free alongside* a vessel, respectively. When FOB and FAS are involved, the seller bears the responsibility (and cost, if any) of placing the goods in the possession of the carrier. If the contract calls for FOB or FAS at a specific destination (e.g., FOB buyer's plant or FAS buyer's port), then the seller bears the cost and risk of loss of getting the goods to the named destination.

With simple FOB and FAS contracts, the seller's risk of loss for the goods ends as soon as the seller discharges his or her responsibility of delivering the goods over to the carrier. At that point, if the goods are lost, stolen or damaged in transit, the loss is borne by the buyer (who can then sue the carrier for the loss of goods in transit).

When FOB or FAS to a specific location other than the seller's plant or seller's home port is involved, the seller retains the risk of loss for goods which are lost, stolen or damaged in transit until the delivery of the goods is tendered to the buyer. Once delivery is tendered, it is the buyer's responsibility (and expense) to get the goods loaded off the common carrier.

### CIF AND C&F TERMS (§ 2-320)

The acronyms *CIF* and *C&F* in sales contracts relate to shipping terms and stand for *cost, insurance and freight* and *cost and freight*, respectively. In a CIF contract, the cost of shipping and insurance are included in the sale price; in a C&F contract, the cost of shipping (freight) is included in the sales price, but the cost of insurance is not, and the buyer must procure and pay for insurance on his or her own, if desired.

## SALE ON APPROVAL, SALE OR RETURN AND CONSIGNMENT SALES (§ 2-326)  . . . . . . . . . . . . . . . . . . . . . . . .

A *sale on approval* occurs whenever a seller gives the buyer the right to return goods after delivery is made even if conforming goods are involved. Purchases made by a consumer for goods that include a "free home trial" for a specified period of time, for example, are considered a sale on approval. A *sale or return* involves goods sold to a merchant buyer for resale with the understanding that if they are not resold by the buyer, they can be returned to the seller for credit. The distinction between a sale on approval and a sale or return is of importance when the buyer is insolvent. Goods purchased by a buyer for personal use on a sale-on-approval basis are not subject to attachment by the buyer's general creditors while the goods are in his or her possession until the buyer clearly evidences the intent to keep the goods. When a sale or return is involved, however, the goods that are the subject matter of the sale *are* considered the buyer's property and can be reached by the buyer's general creditors if the buyer becomes insolvent after purchasing the goods.

For purposes of the UCC, *consignment sales* are deemed to be sale-or-return sales unless the goods are clearly labeled as being consigned goods. (In a consignment sale, the owner of goods places them in the hands of a merchant who normally deals in the sale of the type of goods involved, and the merchant then sells the goods for a fee.)

## RISK OF LOSS WITH REGARD TO SALE ON APPROVAL AND SALE OR RETURN (§ 2-327)  . . . . . . . . . . . . . . . . . . . . . . .

In a sale on approval, unless the parties agree otherwise, the risk of loss does not pass to the purchaser until he or she has accepted the goods, and the cost of shipping the goods back to the seller by the buyer if acceptance is refused is borne by the seller. Failure to notify the seller of acceptance after the trial period expires constitutes acceptance. Return of goods in a sale-or-return contract is at the buyer's risk and expense. Thus, if a seller ships goods to a buyer for a fifteen-day free trial and the buyer keeps them for fifteen days without shipping them back, the buyer has accepted the goods and the risk of their loss shifts to him or her. But if goods are stolen, lost or destroyed while in a buyer's possession during the trial period in a sale on approval, the risk of loss is the seller's, and the buyer need not pay for the lost, stolen or destroyed goods. (If the buyer purposely or negligently destroys the goods, however, such destruction will constitute acceptance of the goods and the buyer must pay for them.) On the other hand, if a seller ships goods to a merchant buyer for sale or return and the goods are lost, stolen or accidentally destroyed in transit or while in the buyer's possession, the buyer must pay for them, since the risk of loss for goods in a sale or return is with the buyer.

## PASSING OF TITLE TO GOODS (§ 2-401) . . . . . . . . . . . . . . . . . . . .

In general, title to goods passes to the buyer at the time and place where the seller completes his or her performance of the physical delivery of the goods, but parties may modify when and where title passes by mutual agreement. This means, in part, that *when* title passes depends upon the delivery terms specified in the contract. In carrier cases involving FOB seller's plant, for example, title passes to the buyer as soon as the goods are placed in the hands of the carrier, but in FOB buyer's plant, title will not pass to the buyer until the goods arrive at the buyer's plant. In cases in which the seller is required to actually deliver the goods to the buyer as part of the sales contract (as opposed to an FOB or FAS contract in which the buyer has the burden of unloading the goods from the carrier), such as with the usual in-home delivery customarily available for consumer sales transactions, the title to the goods passes upon tender of delivery of the goods at their final destination.

## INSURABLE INTEREST ON GOODS (§ 2-501) . . . . . . . . . . . . . . . . .

A buyer obtains an *insurable interest* on goods that are in existence at the time of entering into the contract. When *future goods* (goods that are not in existence at the time of entering into the contract, such as goods to be manufactured or ordered by the seller for the buyer) are involved, the buyer obtains an insurable interest as soon as the goods are "shipped, marked or otherwise designated by the seller as goods to which the contract refers." (§ 2-501 [1][b]) If the future goods are crops or the unborn young of animals, the buyer obtains an insurable interest as soon as the crops are planted or the animals are conceived. Sellers, on the other hand, retain an insurable interest in goods for as long as they have title in the goods or for as long as they retain a security interest in them.

## SELLER'S TENDER OF DELIVERY (§ 2-503) . . . . . . . . . . . . . . . . . .

A seller must tender conforming goods to the buyer and give the buyer reasonable notice that the goods are available for delivery. Unless the parties agree otherwise, *tender of delivery* (the notification to the buyer by the seller or his or her agent that goods are available for delivery or pickup) must be at a reasonable hour and the buyer must be given sufficient time to pick up or request delivery of the goods once tender of delivery is made. When goods are in the possession of a bailee and will be delivered to the buyer without actually being moved (such as when they are in the possession of a warehouse from which the buyer will pick them up), the seller must tender delivery by tendering a negotiable instrument of title (such as a warehouse receipt) or by otherwise notifying the bailee (the person to whom property is bailed) of the buyer's right to take delivery of the goods. The following examples will illustrate:

> *A buyer orders a gas stove from a JC Penney catalog for in-store delivery. When the stove arrives, J C Penney must tender delivery by notifying the customer that the stove is available for pickup, then give the customer a reasonable amount of time to pick up the stove. Notification by a postcard would be sufficient, as would a phone call. But if the customer is notified by phone, a single call at 1:00 P.M. on Sunday would not be reasonable tender of delivery if the customer is not at home. Likewise, contacting the customer and telling her that she must pick up the stove within the next two hours would also not be reasonable tender of delivery.*

> *A buyer orders an automobile in New Jersey and agrees to take delivery of the car from the manufacturer's plant in Michigan. If the automobile is available in one of the seller's warehouses in Detroit, the seller must either tender a negotiable instrument of title to the buyer or notify its warehouse of the buyer's right to pick up the car within a reasonable time and then give the buyer a reasonable opportunity to pick up the car.*

> *A buyer purchases a forty-inch television set from Hi-Tech Video Sales. Under the terms of the contract, Hi-Tech will have its delivery department deliver the set to the buyer's home and set it up within two weeks. If the set is ready for delivery a week after entering into the contract, Hi-Tech must make a reasonable effort to notify the buyer that delivery is available and can be made at a reasonable time. If Hi-Tech phones the buyer at 1:00 P.M. on Monday, at 1:02 P.M. on Monday and at 1:05 P.M. on Monday and is unable to reach the buyer, a proper tender of delivery has not been made (calling three times to attempt delivery may be reasonable, but not within a five-minute period on the same day!).*

## SHIPMENT BY SELLER (§ 2-504)

When the seller, under the terms of the sales contract, will not personally deliver the goods to the buyer but rather will ship them via carrier, the seller must place the goods in the hands of the carrier and make arrangements for their delivery in accordance with the terms of the sales contract. If applicable, the seller must also promptly send any required documents of title that the buyer may need to claim the goods from the carrier and promptly notify the buyer of the goods' shipment.

## EFFECT OF SELLER'S TENDER OF DELIVERY (§ 2-507)

Once the seller properly tenders delivery of the goods to the buyer, the buyer is obligated to accept and pay for the goods. Failure of the buyer to accept or pay for conforming goods once they are tendered constitutes a breach of contract.

## RISK OF LOSS (§ 2-509) · · · · · · · · · · · · · · · · · · · · · · · · · · · · · · ·

In the absence of agreement to the contrary, the exact moment at which the risk of loss for goods being shipped by carrier passes to the buyer from the seller depends upon the terms of the contract. When FOB seller's plant or FAS seller's port shipping terms are involved, the risk of loss passes to the buyer as soon as the seller turns over the goods to the carrier for shipment or as soon as the goods are placed alongside a vessel for loading. If the shipping terms call for shipping to a specific destination by carrier, such as FOB buyer's plant or FAS buyer's port, then the risk of loss for the goods shifts from the seller to the buyer as soon as the goods are *tendered* at their final destination. Remember that *tendered* does not mean the same as *delivered*; goods are tendered as soon as the buyer is notified that the goods are ready to be picked up or ready to be delivered at their final destination. Thus, if FOB buyer's plant is involved in a contract, the seller will bear responsibility for any loss occurring during transit from loss, theft or any damage to the goods, but the risk for such loss will shift to the buyer as soon as the goods arrive at their destination and the buyer is notified of their arrival and given a reasonable opportunity to pick them up. On the other hand, if goods are purchased FOB seller's plant, the risk of loss will pass to the buyer as soon as the seller turns the goods over to the carrier (usually in the seller's loading dock).

In cases in which goods are in the possession of a third-party bailee and no movement of the goods is intended by the parties, the risk of loss passes to the buyer as soon as the buyer receives a negotiable document of title (such as a negotiable warehouse receipt) or when the buyer is notified by the bailee of the goods that he or she may pick them up.

Finally, in cases in which goods are not shipped by carrier, but rather delivered directly to the buyer by the seller or picked up directly by the buyer from the seller, the risk of loss passes to the buyer when he or she picks up the goods if the seller is a merchant, or when the goods are tendered to the buyer if the seller is not a merchant. As is often the case, this means that merchant sellers are held to a higher duty of care than nonmerchants, since merchants will bear the loss of any goods they sell until they are actually delivered or picked up by their customers, but nonmerchant sellers bear the risk of loss for such goods only until tender of delivery is made. If this distinction seems a bit confusing, the following example should clarify it nicely:

> *Ines sells a used bicycle to Irving for fifty dollars. Irving pays for the bike but asks Ines if she will hold it for him until the next day. That evening, the bicycle is stolen from Ines' premises. If Ines is in the business of selling bicycles, the risk of loss passes to Irving only upon actual physical delivery of the bike, so that Ines bears the risk of loss and must return the money to Irving if she cannot deliver the goods as promised. But if Ines is not a merchant in bicycles, the risk of loss passes to Irving as soon as the goods are tendered for delivery; in this case, the bike was tendered when it was bought, since he could have taken it at that time, and Irving would bear the loss of its subsequent theft.*

Keep in mind that the parties are always free to reallocate the risk of loss any way they wish by mutual agreement, and also that these rules are relevant only in the event that the goods are either lost, stolen or damaged in transit. Furthermore, these rules are effective only assuming that conforming goods are tendered. If there is a breach of contract involved and the goods tendered are nonconforming because they do not meet the requirements of the contract (e.g., wrong or defective goods), then the risk of loss remains with the seller either until they are accepted by the buyer despite the nonconformity or until the defect is cured by the seller. (§ 2-510)

## BUYER'S RIGHT TO INSPECT GOODS (§ 2-507) · · · · · · · · · · · · · · · ·

In general, a buyer has the right to inspect goods before paying for them to insure that they conform to the requirements of the contract. Any expense for inspecting the goods must be borne by the buyer, but are recoverable from the seller if the goods turn out to be nonconforming and the buyer rejects them. In cases where goods are shipped *COD* (cash on delivery), however, a buyer must pay for the goods without first inspecting them. (If there is a defect in goods ordered COD, the buyer can, of course, demand that the seller rectify the defect and sue the seller for breach of contract if he or she refuses to do so.)

## BUYER'S RIGHTS ON IMPROPER DELIVERY (§ 2-601) · · · · · · · · · · ·

Whenever any delivery contains nonconforming goods, in whole or in part, the buyer has the right to reject the whole delivery, accept the whole delivery, or accept any commercial unit or units and reject the rest. Thus, if a liquor store owner orders ten cases of Cabernet Sauvignon wine and the distributor mistakenly ships one case of Cabernet Sauvignon and nine cases of blush wine, the buyer may accept only the one case of conforming goods and reject the nine cases of nonconforming goods, reject the whole shipment or accept the whole shipment despite the nonconformity.

If the nonconforming shipment is a part of an *installment contract*, where a number of individual deliveries are made over a period of time as part of a larger contract, Section 2-612 of the code makes it harder to reject the shipment. In such cases, the buyer may reject an installment for nonconformity only "if the nonconformity substantially impairs the value of that installment and cannot be cured or if the nonconformity is a defect in the required documents [of title]." If the nonconformity of any single shipment in an installment contract *can* be cured by the seller, the buyer must accept the shipment and then allow the seller to cure the defect.

## MERCHANT BUYERS' DUTIES AS TO RIGHTFULLY REJECTED GOODS (§ 2-603) · · · · · · · · · · · · · · · · · · · · · · · · · · ·

As is often the case with the UCC, merchant buyers are held to a higher duty of care with respect to goods that they rightfully reject as nonconforming than are nonmerchants. A merchant buyer who rightfully refuses to accept nonconforming goods in his or her possession must follow the reasonable instructions of the seller with regard to the goods and, if no instruction is given by the seller, must make a reasonable effort to sell them on behalf of the seller if the goods are perishable or otherwise likely to decrease rapidly in value. The reasonable incidental costs incurred by the buyer in caring for and disposing of the nonconforming goods on behalf of the seller are reimbursable by the seller. In addition, where the buyer is under a duty to sell the goods for the seller in order to prevent their spoilage or loss of value, the buyer is entitled to a reasonable commission for his or her services.

## ANTICIPATORY REPUDIATION (§ 2-610) . . . . . . . . . . . . . . . . . . .

At common law, a breach of contract was not deemed to occur until a party obligated to render performance under a contract refused to do so. For that reason, when one party gave notice to the other that he or she would not or could not discharge performance of his or her obligations under the contract, the other party could not obtain any legal remedy until the actual deadline for the performance had passed. Thus, if a buyer contracted with a seller on January 1 for shipment of 1,000 widgets on July 1, and the seller informed the buyer on January 2 that he could not or would not honor the contract, the buyer could not sue the seller or pursue any other remedy until after July 1—the day when the performance was due. The UCC changes this rule by giving aggrieved parties various options when they are informed by sellers of an *anticipatory repudiation* (notice by one party to the other that the promised performance in a contract will not be given when due). When anticipatory repudiation occurs, the aggrieved party (either the buyer or seller) can await performance by the repudiating party for a reasonable time or opt to resort immediately to any available remedy for breach and simultaneously suspend his or her own performance.

## CASUALTY TO IDENTIFIED GOODS (§ 2-613) . . . . . . . . . . . . . . . . .

When goods identified for shipment or delivery under a sales contract are damaged or destroyed without the fault of either contracting party, the contract is avoided if the loss to the goods is total. If the loss is only partial or if the goods have deteriorated so that they no longer conform to the contract, the buyer has a choice of either treating the contract as avoided or accepting the goods with an adjustment in price for the deterioration or partial loss. If acceptance with price adjustment is elected, the buyer may not assert any other remedy against the seller. (If, for example, 25 percent of goods are damaged due to a fire and the buyer elects to take delivery of the remaining 75 percent of nondamaged goods with a reduction of 25 percent in the contract price, the buyer cannot then ask the seller to ship another 25 percent of goods at the contract price.)

## SUBSTITUTED PERFORMANCE (§ 2-614) . . . . . . . . . . . . . . . . . . . .

Whenever an agreed-upon common carrier for shipment or the facilities for loading or unloading goods becomes unavailable due to circumstances beyond the control of the contracting parties, a commercially reasonable substitute may be made and must be accepted. If, for example, the agreed-upon carrier is unavailable because of a labor dispute, the seller can select a commercially reasonable alternative and the buyer must accept that substitution.

This section also provides for substitute methods of payment in cases where foreign or domestic governmental regulations make the agreed-upon method of payment unavailable. If this happens before goods are delivered, the seller may stop delivery until the buyer provides a commercially acceptable substitute method of payment. If delivery has already been made, then the seller must accept payment in the method provided for in the governmental regulation.

## QUESTIONS . . . . . . . . . . . . . . . . . . . . . . . . . . . . . . . . . . . . . . . . . .

1. Unless the parties agree otherwise, where must goods be delivered by the seller to the buyer?
2. What is a common carrier?
3. What do the acronyms *FOB* and *FAS* stand for?
4. In an FOB seller's plant or FAS seller's port shipping contract, who bears the risk of loss for the goods while they are in transit to the buyer and in the hands of the carrier?
5. What do the acronyms *CIF* and *C&F* stand for?
6. Define the terms *sale on approval*, *sale or return* and *consignment sale*.
7. Who bears the risk of loss for goods that are in a buyer's possession under a sale-on-approval contract during the trial period before the buyer accepts the goods?
8. In general, when does title to goods pass from the seller to the buyer in a sales contract?
9. When does a buyer obtain an insurable interest to goods in a sales contract?
10. Define *tender of delivery*.

## H Y P O T H E T I C A L    C A S E S

1. Beatrice Buyer orders 2,000 square yards of material from Sandra Seller. The contract calls for shipment FOB buyer's plant. Based on these facts, answer the following questions.
   a. Who bears the risk of loss for the goods when they are placed in the hands of the carrier?
   b. Who pays for the shipment of the goods?
   c. Assuming that these goods are in existence in the seller's warehouse when the contract is made, when does the buyer obtain an insurable interest in the goods?
2. Bubba Buyer orders 1,000 cartons of grade A jumbo eggs from Sandy Seller. Sandy ships 100 cartons of grade A jumbo eggs and 900 cartons of grade A medium eggs. Answer the following questions based on these facts.

    a. If Bubba spends $50 to have the eggs inspected and then discovers that 900 cartons do not conform to the requirements of the contract, who is ultimately responsible for the cost of the inspection? Explain.

    b. What are Bubba's options with regard to the goods?

    c. If the shipment were part of an installment contract calling for a delivery of 1,000 cases of eggs every month for a year, will Bubba be able to reject the whole shipment? Explain.

3. Bertha Buyer orders five bushels of oranges from Sal Seller. Sal sends his truck out to deliver five bushels of tangerines. Since Bertha is not home at the time that the delivery is attempted, the driver unloads the tangerines onto Bertha's front porch and leaves them there, along with the bill. A day later, Bertha arrives home to find the tangerines rapidly spoiling in the sun. If she is not a fruit merchant, what are her responsibilities with regard to the fruit? Would your answer be the same if she were a fruit merchant? Explain.

4. Fred Farmer agrees to sell three tons of wheat stored in one of his silos to Betty Buyer. Under the terms of the contract, the wheat is to be delivered in three months, but Betty agrees to pay 50 percent of the sales price at the current market rate in thirty days, with the remaining 50 percent of the price payable upon delivery at the then-prevalent market rate. A week after entering into the contract, a fire breaks out in the grain silo containing the wheat and 20 percent of the wheat is completely destroyed before the fire is put out. In addition, 30 percent of the wheat is damaged by the fire (but is still marketable at a reduced price) and 50 percent of the wheat is unaffected. When Fred informs Betty of the loss, what are her rights with regard to the contract?

CHAPTER

# 20

# WARRANTIES

In every sales transaction, warranties can arise either by the express words or actions of the seller concerning the goods being sold (*express warranties*) or by operation of law as a part of every sales contract (*implied warranties*). In this chapter, we will briefly examine the general provisions of the UCC relating to the creation, application and waiver of warranties in contracts for the sale of goods.

## EXPRESS WARRANTIES (§ 2-313) . . . . . . . . . . . . . . . . . . . . . . . .

Section 2-313 of the UCC states that express warranties can be created by sellers in any of the following ways.

### EXPRESS STATEMENT OR PROMISE ABOUT GOODS

Any express affirmation of fact or promise made by the seller to the buyer about the goods being sold creates an express warranty that the goods will conform to the statement or promise. In order for a warranty to arise, the statement or promise has to be made during the bargaining process; statements made after goods are purchased do not qualify as warranties. Likewise, the statement or promise has to be specific. General statements about the quality of goods (even if exaggerated) do not qualify as warranties. If a salesperson says to a buyer, "This blender represents a great value," "This car gets great mileage," or "This is the best toaster on the market," these statements are too general to constitute warranties and are considered mere sales puffery of the products. But statements such as "This car gets twenty-five miles to the gallon in city driving," "This toaster will toast bread in thirty seconds," or "We will repair or replace the blender within two years if it breaks down," are all clear and specific enough to constitute warranties.

## DESCRIPTION OF THE GOODS

Any description of the goods made as part of the basis of the bargain creates an express warranty that the goods will conform to the description. In order for a description of the goods to rise to the level of a warranty, it must be concrete and made by the seller to the buyer during the bargaining process for the goods. There is no requirement that the words *guarantee* or *warranty* be used in order for an express warranty to arise. As with express statements and promises, general statements about the quality or value of the goods that merely express the seller's opinion or constitute sales puffery are excluded. The following examples will illustrate:

- *"This is a marvelous car and a great value. It gets wonderful gas mileage and goes quite fast on the open road. In addition, it is a sturdy car in solid condition. And not only that, but it looks absolutely terrific—sheer poetry in motion." No express warranties are made in this description. It is merely subjective, overbroad sales puffery that, in typical fashion, says absolutely nothing concrete about the car.*

- *"This car is a 1995 Nissan 240SX with 50,000 miles, a five-speed standard transmission, air conditioning and antilock brakes." Every one of the descriptive statements in this sentence creates a warranty of the used car being sold as to the car's make, model, mileage, transmission, air conditioning and brakes.*

## USE OF SAMPLE OR MODEL DURING SALE

Whenever a model or sample is used by a salesperson trying to make a sale, an express warranty arises that the goods delivered will conform to the model or sample shown the buyer. In order for this warranty to arise, the buyer must actually have inspected the sample or model of the goods before agreeing to the purchase. If the buyer is clearly told or knows that there are differences between the goods being purchased and the model he or she is being shown, however, the warranty will not arise. Thus, purchasing a car after inspecting the showroom model which includes a compact disc player and on-board navigational computer does not mean that a warranty is made that the model delivered will also have the expensive optional equipment, *if* the buyer is told or should realize that the equipment is optional. But if a salesperson tells prospective buyers, "You can have a car just like that one for $20,000," and points to a car loaded with options, a buyer who inspects it prior to agreeing to the sale will have been made a warranty by the salesperson that the car ordered will be equipped exactly as the sample.

# IMPLIED WARRANTIES · · · · · · · · · · · · · · · · · · · · · · · · · · · · · · · ·

In addition to express warranties that can arise from the noted circumstances, a number of implied warranties also attach automatically to every sale, while others arise only in sales involving merchant sellers. We'll examine these in turn.

## WARRANTY OF TITLE AND AGAINST INFRINGEMENT (§ 2-312)

Every seller (merchant or nonmerchant) makes a warranty of title that guarantees he or she has good title to the goods and that the transfer is rightful. The warranty also guarantees that the goods are transferred free from any security interest, lien or other encumbrance that the buyer is not aware of as of the time of entering into the contract.

In addition to the warranty of title, a merchant seller also guarantees that the goods are free of any claim of copyright or patent infringement or similar claim by third parties. An exception is granted to the warranty against infringement to merchant sellers who manufacture goods to specifications furnished by the buyer; such specially manufactured goods are not warranted against claims of infringement by third parties, since it is the buyer's responsibility to furnish specifications that do not infringe on other's patents, copyrights or similar intellectual property rights. The following example will illustrate:

> *ABC Company buys 100 television sets from Sam Seller. Unknown to either ABC or Sam at the time of the sale, the manufacturer of the sets has misappropriated trade secrets and infringed on numerous patents from XYZ Company in the manufacture of the sets. If XYZ sues ABC seeking an injunction against the resale of the sets or for any other damages, ABC can recover any incidental or consequential damages from Sam for breach of the implied warranty against infringement which Sam, as a merchant seller, made to ABC as part of the sale. (Sam could then sue the manufacturer of the sets for his damages caused by its infringement.)*

The warranty of title and against infringement can be waived only by specific language or by circumstances which give the buyer notice that the seller does not claim title to the goods being sold. Purchasing goods from a sheriff's sale, for example, would give notice to the buyer that the goods are sold subject to possible liens or other claims by others.

## WARRANTY OF FITNESS FOR A PARTICULAR PURPOSE (§ 2-315)

In any sale where the seller knows that the buyer is relying on the seller's skill or judgment in selecting goods suitable to the buyer's specific needs, a warranty arises that the goods sold will be suitable to the buyer's special needs. This warranty is made by both merchant and nonmerchant sellers. In order for the warranty to arise, it is imperative that the buyer rely on the seller's superior skill in selecting goods suitable to his or her needs *and* that the seller be aware that the buyer is relying on the seller's superior knowledge or skill with regard to the goods being sold, as the following example illustrates:

> *Ron, who has never skied before, notices a pair of cross-country skis in Rhonda's garage sale. He asks Rhonda if the skis are suitable for downhill skiing, a sport he has been considering taking up. Rhonda, who wants to sell the skis, assures him that they will be perfectly suitable for that purpose. Rhonda has breached the warranty of fitness for a particular purpose in making a recommendation to Ron knowing that he was relying on her superior knowledge of skiing. (Notice that she is also guilty of fraud in the inducement.) As a consequence, she will have to refund Ron's money on demand and will be liable for any damage that Ron suffers as a consequence of her breach of warranty.*

### WARRANTY OF MERCHANTABILITY (§ 2-314)

In every sale by a merchant, an implied warranty is made that the goods will be *merchantable,* which is to say that they will pass without objection in the trade under the contract description, be fit for the ordinary purposes for which such goods are used, are adequately packaged and labeled (if appropriate) and, if labeled, conform to the description or promises made in the label. If the goods are *fungible* (of a type where one part is substantially identical to other parts, such as grain, vegetables and oil), then they must be of at least fair, average quality within their description.

## EXCLUSION OR MODIFICATION OF WARRANTIES (§ 2-316)  . . . . . . . . . . . . . . . . . . . . . . . . . . . . . . . . . . . .

Generally speaking, warranties may be modified or completely excluded either orally or in writing. All that the UCC requires is that the exclusion or limitation be clear. With regard to the warranty of merchantability, it can be excluded only by language that specifically mentions merchantability, and, if in writing, must be conspicuous. In addition, an exclusion of the warranty of fitness for a particular purpose must be in writing and conspicuous.

All implied warranties may be excluded by such language as "There are no warranties which extend beyond the face hereof" (§ 2-316 [2]) and by expressions such as *as is, with all faults* "or other language which in common understanding calls the buyer's attention to the exclusion of warranties and makes plain that there is no implied warranty." (§ 2-316 [3][a])

A buyer who is given the opportunity to examine a sample prior to entering into a contract and examines the goods or refuses to do so cannot claim a breach of an implied warranty with regard to "defects which an examination ought in the circumstances to have revealed to him." (§ 2-316 [3][b]) In addition, "an implied warranty can also be excluded or modified by course of dealing or course of performance or usage of trade." (§ 2-316 [3][c])

## THIRD-PARTY BENEFICIARIES OF WARRANTIES, EXPRESS OR IMPLIED (§ 2-318)  . . . . . . . . . . . . . . . . . . . . . . . .

Section 2-318 of the UCC expressly extends warranty coverage to anyone who is injured by defective goods, regardless of whether the injured person purchased the goods involved. This section in effect addresses the common-law *privity of contract* problems that prevented people from suing to recover for injuries suffered from defective products unless they had actually purchased the products themselves (were in privity of contract with the manufacturer or reseller of the product by being a party to the sales transaction). The code liberally extends coverage to anyone who is injured by a defective product if the person could have been reasonably foreseen to use, consume or be affected by the product. The section reads:

A seller's warranty whether express or implied extends to any natural person if it is reasonable to expect that such person may use, consume or be affected by the goods and who is injured in person by breach of the warranty. A seller may not exclude or limit the operation of this section.

For purposes of the section, *natural person* simply means a human being, as opposed to a corporation or other business organization. Notice that unlike all other warranties, this implied warranty cannot be waived or excluded by any seller. Although not specifically limited to it, this section is of particular importance with regard to the warranty protection afforded by a merchant's warranty of merchantability, since third-party injuries caused by defective products nearly always involve a breach of this warranty. But third-party protection can also extend to other warranties, such as the warranty of title if a gift is made by a buyer to a third party, or the warranty of fitness for a particular purpose when a buyer relies on the seller's expertise in selecting goods intended as a gift for a third party.

## QUESTIONS . . . . . . . . . . . . . . . . . . . . . . . . . . . . . . . . . . . . . . . . . .

1. What are three ways in which express warranties can come into existence?
2. Name four implied warranties.
3. Generally speaking, how do implied warranties come into existence?
4. Which implied warranties are made only by merchant sellers?
5. Can implied warranties be modified or waived? If so, how? If not, why not?
6. Which warranty protection can never be waived?
7. Who makes a warranty of title and what does it guarantee?
8. What is the warranty against infringement and how does it arise?

## H Y P O T H E T I C A L     C A S E S

1. Benito Buyer purchases a screwdriver at a garage sale for fifty cents from Sandra Seller, who is not a merchant in screwdrivers. What warranties, if any, are made as part of this transaction?

2. Benito Buyer purchases a screwdriver for two dollars from Sally's Hardware Store. He lends the screwdriver to his neighbor, Dan Dimwit, who uses the screwdriver as a chisel to break up a piece of crumbling cement in his back yard in order to rebuild it. While Dan is hammering at the screwdriver with a sledgehammer, it breaks and a piece of the handle flies into his eye, causing him a minor eye injury. Explain which warranties attach to this sale and then analyze Dan's chances of suing Sally's Hardware Store for breach of warranty.

3. Botswain Buyer asks the proprietor of his local home building center for advice on thawing a water pipe in his home that froze during a particularly nasty winter cold spell. The seller recommends an oxygen-acetylene torch to do the job—a tool that is not well suited to the job. Botswain, relying on the advice, purchases

a $500 welding kit and proceeds to melt part of the water main into his house in an attempt to defrost it, and in the process turns his basement into an unwanted indoor swimming pool. He wants to sue the seller to recover his damages under a theory of breach of contract, breach of the implied warranty of merchantability and breach of the implied warranty of suitability for a particular purpose. What result? Explain fully.

4. Bruce Buyer purchases a used electric drill at a hardware store. The drill is in a basket with other assorted hardware items and tools. Over the basket, a large sign clearly reads: "All of the items in this basket are sold *as is*." Bruce reads the sign before purchasing the drill. After taking the drill home, he plugs it in and receives a tremendous shock which nearly kills him and requires brief hospitalization. He now wants to sue the seller for breach of warranty. Will he succeed? If so, which warranty in particular was breached by the seller? If not, why not?

CHAPTER

# 21

# REMEDIES FOR BREACH OF THE SALES CONTRACT

As with other areas of contract law, the UCC has made some important modifications to the common-law remedies available to contracting parties who suffer a breach of contract. While the basic common-law remedies for breach of contract discussed in Chapter 17 are still available when a breach of a sales contract occurs, these have been both expanded and limited in varying degrees by the UCC, as we will see in this chapter in our examination of the specific remedies available to both sellers and buyers under the code.

## SELLER'S REMEDIES ........................................

The UCC specifies in substantial detail the specific remedies available to sellers in Sections 2-703 through 2-710. We'll examine the most significant of these code sections next in our discussion.

### SELLER'S REMEDIES IN GENERAL (§ 2-703)

After a buyer's wrongful rejection of goods, revocation of acceptance of goods, failure to pay for goods when due, or wrongful repudiation, a seller may withhold delivery of goods, stop delivery of the goods in the hands of a third party (shipping or warehouse delivery contracts), cancel the contract or pursue any of the other remedies provided under the code.

### SELLER'S RIGHT TO SALVAGE UNFINISHED GOODS (§ 2-704)

When a buyer breaches a contract calling for specially manufactured goods after the seller has begun the manufacturing process but before the manufacture of the goods has been completed, the seller may either sell the partially manufactured goods for their salvage or

154

scrap value or may elect to complete the manufacture of the goods and resell them to another buyer. Any amount recovered by the seller from such a sale would help offset the seller's damages against the buyer if another remedy is pursued against the buyer.

## SELLER'S RIGHT TO STOP DELIVERY (§ 2-705)

A seller may stop delivery of goods in the hands of a carrier or other bailee (such as a warehouse) upon learning of the buyer's insolvency, or if the seller refuses to pay for the goods prior to delivery if payment is then due.

## SELLER'S RIGHT TO RESELL GOODS (§ 2-706)

After a breach by the buyer, the seller may resell the goods to another buyer and recover the difference between the resale price and the contract price, along with any incidental and consequential damages.

## SELLER'S DAMAGES FOR NONACCEPTANCE OR REPUDIATION (§ 2-708)

The measure of damages for the buyer's wrongful nonacceptance or repudiation of goods is the difference between the market price at the time and place that delivery is tendered and the contract price, along with incidental and consequential damages less any expenses the seller saves due to the buyer's breach. Thus, if a buyer, on October 1, agrees to take delivery of goods on January 1 in New York from a seller in California, and then breaches the contract on October 2, the seller's damages will be the market price of the goods in New York on January 1 minus the contract price (the amount payable for the goods under the contract) minus any expenses saved by the seller as a consequence of the breach (such as the cost of shipping to New York if it was an FOB buyer's plant contract). If there are any additional incidental and consequential damages suffered by the seller as a result of the breach, these too are recoverable from the buyer.

In cases where the market-price-minus-contract-price differential does not adequately compensate the seller for the breach, the seller can opt to recover his or her lost profits from the sale along with any incidental and consequential damages.

## ACTION FOR THE PRICE (§ 2-709)

The seller may recover the contract price from a buyer for goods which the buyer has accepted or goods which have been lost, damaged or destroyed in transit after the risk for their loss had shifted to the buyer. A seller may also recover the contract price for goods which he or she cannot resell after a reasonable effort (when there is no ready market for the goods, for example).

## SELLER'S INCIDENTAL DAMAGES (§ 2-710)

A seller's incidental damages recoverable from a buyer after a breach include any "commercially reasonable charges, expenses or commissions incurred in stopping delivery, in the transportation, care and custody of goods after the buyer's breach, in connection with return or resale of the goods or otherwise resulting from the breach." (§ 2-710)

# BUYER'S REMEDIES    · · · · · · · · · · · · · · · · · · · · · · · · · · · · · · · · ·

As with seller's remedies, the UCC details the specific remedies available to buyers in Sections 2-711 through 2-717. We'll examine the most significant of these code sections next.

### BUYER'S REMEDIES IN GENERAL; BUYER'S SECURITY INTEREST IN REJECTED GOODS (§ 2-711)

Upon a seller's breach, a buyer may elect to cancel the contract and recover any money paid to the seller as well as exercise any other remedy allowed by the code. In addition, the buyer has a security interest for goods in his or her possession after a rightful reduction or revocation to the extent of any money paid to the buyer for their sale.

### COVER; BUYER'S PROCUREMENT OF SUBSTITUTE GOODS (§ 2-712)

After a breach, a buyer may cover his or her damages by procuring in good faith and without unreasonable delay the purchase of substitute goods from another seller. *Cover* can be defined as the right of a buyer after a breach of contract to purchase goods from a third party in substitution for the goods he or she was entitled to receive from the original seller. If this remedy is selected, the buyer may recover from the seller the difference between the contract price and the cover price plus incidental and consequential damages, minus any expense saved as a result of the breach.

Cover is an optional remedy, and the failure of a buyer to elect to cover his or her damages within a reasonable period of time will not bar the buyer from pursuing other available remedies.

### BUYER'S DAMAGES FOR NONDELIVERY OR REPUDIATION (§ 2-713)

The measure of damages for nondelivery or repudiation by the seller is the difference between the market price and the contract price at the time that the buyer learned of the breach. The market price is to be based on the place where tender of delivery was due under the contract. As usual, incidental and consequential damages are also recoverable, and any expenses saved by the buyer as a result of the breach are deducted from his or her damages.

### BUYER'S DAMAGES FOR BREACH IN REGARD TO ACCEPTED GOODS (§ 2-714)

After accepting nonconforming goods, the buyer may recover for any reasonable loss resulting from the nonconformity. The measure of damages is the difference in value at the time and place of acceptance between the accepted nonconforming goods and the value of conforming goods. Incidental and consequential damages are also recoverable, if appropriate.

### BUYER'S INCIDENTAL AND CONSEQUENTIAL DAMAGES (§ 2-715)

The buyer's incidental and consequential damages resulting from the seller's breach include reasonable costs incurred in inspecting, receiving, transporting and caring for rightfully rejected goods, as well as commercially reasonable charges incurred in connection with obtaining cover for nonconforming goods. Consequential damages include any loss resulting from the general or particular circumstances of the buyer which the seller at the time of entering into the contract had reason to know and which could not be reasonably prevented through cover or otherwise, and include personal injury or property damage directly caused by and resulting from the breach of any sales warranty.

### BUYER'S RIGHT TO SPECIFIC PERFORMANCE OR REPLEVIN (§ 2-716)

A court may award specific performance where the goods are unique or in other proper circumstances. A buyer may also sue for *replevin* (an action at law requiring the turning over of goods by the person who has them in his or her possession to their rightful owner) when the buyer is unable to effect cover for goods identified in the contract.

### DEDUCTION OF DAMAGES FROM THE PRICE (§ 2-717)

A buyer may, after duly notifying the seller of his or her intent to do so, deduct part or all of the damages from any payment still due from the buyer to the seller for the same contract. A buyer cannot, however, deduct damages for one sales contract from money due the seller for other contracts not involved in the breach.

## GENERAL RULES AFFECTING BOTH BUYERS AND SELLERS . . . . . . .

In addition to the sections affecting buyers' and sellers' remedies that we have just examined, the UCC provides a number of rules relating to remedies that apply equally to both the buyer and the seller in sales contracts. We'll look at these next.

### LIQUIDATION OF DAMAGES (§ 2-718)

Parties may provide for liquidated damages for both buyers and sellers in sales contracts as long as these are reasonably calculated to compensate the parties for their actual anticipated losses in the event of a breach. Unreasonably large liquidated damages provisions are void as penalties.

### CONTRACTUAL MODIFICATION OR LIMITATION OF REMEDIES (§ 2-719)

Parties are free to limit or provide remedies in addition to those in the code by mutual agreement. But if parties limit the available remedies and the exclusive remedy selected fails in its essential purpose, the parties may resort to any remedy provided by the UCC.

In other words, if the remedy selected by the parties through mutual agreement turns out to be unreasonable under the circumstances, a court will ignore the limitation-of-remedies provision in the contract and award another remedy provided by the code. In addition, the parties may limit or exclude incidental or consequential damages through mutual agreement, but this provision will also be ignored by the courts if it is found to be unconscionable.

## QUESTIONS · · · · · · · · · · · · · · · · · · · · · · · · · · · · · · · · · · · · · ·

1. What is the seller's right to salvage unfinished goods?
2. What is the measure of seller's damages after the buyer's nonacceptance or repudiation of goods?
3. What are the incidental damages that a seller may recover after a breach by the buyer?
4. What is cover?
5. What are the buyer's incidental and consequential damages?
6. When may a court award specific performance?
7. Are liquidated damage provisions valid in sales contracts?
8. Are agreements to limit remedies in sales contracts enforceable?

## H Y P O T H E T I C A L    C A S E S

1. A buyer orders 1,000 widgets from a seller to be manufactured to the buyer's specifications. After the seller orders the necessary raw materials to manufacture the widgets but before the manufacture of the goods is completed, the buyer informs the seller that he will not accept delivery of the goods because he has found a cheaper supplier. The seller wishes to sue for breach of contract. What remedies are available to the seller?

2. A Nevada corporation agrees to sell 1,000 widgets to a Colorado company for $100 each under a contract signed January 1. Under the terms of the agreement, the goods are to be delivered to the buyer on February 1. On January 15, the seller informs the buyer that it will be unable to ship the widgets. The market price for widgets in Colorado and Nevada is given in the following table. What are the buyer's exact cover damages, given these facts?

MARKET PRICE OF WIDGETS

| Date | Nevada price | Colorado price |
|------|-------------|----------------|
| January 1 | $ 95 | $ 97 |
| January 15 | $105 | $110 |
| February 1 | $135 | $150 |

3. A buyer agrees to purchase a Picasso from a seller for $5,000,000. At the time of the contract, the market price of the painting is $4,800,000. After entering into the contract but before delivering the painting, the seller has a change of heart and informs the buyer that he will not honor his agreement. At the time that the seller informs the buyer of his intention to breach the contract, the market price of the painting is unchanged. What remedy may the buyer successfully demand in court?

4. A Michigan company orders 1,000 widgets from a Mississippi corporation on January 1 for delivery on February 1 at a price of $100 each. At the time that the contract is entered into, widgets are selling for $95 in Michigan and $100 in Mississippi. When the seller tenders delivery of conforming goods to the buyer in Mississippi on February 1 as promised, the buyer wrongfully rejects the goods. The price of widgets on February 1 was $95 in Michigan and $95 in Mississippi. What is the measure of the seller's damages?

# CHAPTER

# 22

# COMMERCIAL PAPER

## INTRODUCTION TO ARTICLE 3: AN INTRODUCTION TO COMMERCIAL PAPER ·····························

Although it is technically possible to carry out business strictly on a cash basis, the realities of commerce necessitate the use of readily acceptable substitutes for cash as well as financial instruments that make it easy to lend and borrow money. It's simply not practical—or safe—to carry what can often be very large sums of paper money needed for business transactions. It should come as no surprise, then, that approximately 90 percent of all business transactions are carried out by check.

Article 3 of the UCC concerns itself with *commercial paper* in its four basic forms: drafts, checks, notes and certificates of deposit. These serve both as substitutes for cash (drafts and checks) and as a means of facilitating the extension of credit (notes and certificates of deposit). While these instruments have been around for centuries, the UCC has consolidated the common law into a single comprehensive code, updating and modernizing the law as needed.

In order for commercial paper to be readily accepted as a substitute for money or as a means of extending credit, persons accepting such instruments must have some clear assurance that these will be honored when presented for payment. As an incentive to make commercial paper attractive to persons who accept it in the normal course of business, the law provides certain guarantees to those who accept such instruments in good faith and pay value for them in the regular course of business. It is essential to understand the fundamental distinction of commercial paper from other financial or contractual instruments, or the significance of these instruments will not be apparent. The distinguishing characteristic of a *negotiable instrument* is that it can give special protection to persons to whom it is legally negotiated in the course of business. Provided certain conditions for due negotiation are met, persons who take negotiable instruments in good faith and give some value for them take such instruments free of most defenses against their payment. We will discuss at length the requirements for negotiation and holder-in-due-course status both in this and in the following chapter, but keep in mind from the outset that the reason we need to study commercial paper and distinguish it from other legal instruments is that negotiable instruments provide greater assurance that they will be paid when due than do other instruments, for reasons that will soon become apparent.

## FORMS OF NEGOTIABLE INSTRUMENTS (§ 3-104) . . . . . . . . . . . . . .

As previously noted, there are four basic forms of negotiable instruments: drafts, checks, notes and certificates of deposit. Regardless of its form, a negotiable instrument must meet the following criteria:

- the instrument must be in writing;
- it must be signed by the *maker* or *drawer* (the person executing the instrument);
- it must contain an unconditional promise or order to pay a sum certain in money;
- it must contain no other promise or obligation;
- it must be payable on demand or at a definite time; and
- it must be payable to order or bearer.

An instrument which meets all of the noted criteria qualifies as a negotiable instrument; an instrument which fails to meet one or more of the noted criteria may still be a valid instrument, but it will not qualify for the special status of a negotiable instrument.

A negotiable instrument will take one of the four previously noted forms: a draft, a check, a note or a certificate of deposit. Note carefully the basic characteristics of each of these instruments.

### DRAFT

A *draft* is an order by a *drawer* (the person who *draws*, or executes, the draft) to a *drawee* (the person ordered by the drawer to pay the draft) to pay a sum certain in money on demand or at a specified date to the order of a specified *payee* (the person the drawer orders the drawee to pay) or to *bearer* (anyone in possession of the draft). Clearly, a draft is used as a substitute for money. (For an example of a draft, see Figure 22.1.)

---

Date: 7/1/96

To: Drawer Industries

Pay to the order of Paul and Pamela Payees one thousand dollars ($1,000.00).

[Signed] Dick Drawer
President
Drawer Inds.

---

**FIGURE 22.1**  Sample draft

## CHECK

A *check* is nothing more than a draft that is drawn on a bank. In other words, the drawer of a check is a depositor who orders the drawee (his or her bank) to pay the payee a specific amount of money. As with a draft, a check is also a substitute for money. (For an example of a check, see Figure 22.2.)

## NOTE

Unlike drafts and checks which serve as substitutes for money, a *note* serves as evidence of debt. The drafter of the note is called the *maker*, and the person for whose benefit the note is drafted is called the *payee*. Invariably, the maker of a note drafts it in exchange for having received something of present value (a loan for the purchase of a home or the purchase of a car, for example) for which he or she agrees to pay the payee in the future under terms specified by the note. (For an example of a note, see Figure 22.3.)

## CERTIFICATE OF DEPOSIT

Like a note, a *certificate of deposit* (CD) is also an instrument that evidences debt. The only difference between a note and a CD is that a CD is issued only by a bank or other financial institution as evidence of its debt to a named creditor/depositor. Whenever you invest in a bank CD you might think of the transaction as a deposit of money; in reality, however, you are lending the bank money under the terms specified by the CD, for which the bank issues you its promise to repay you, at a stated time in the future, your principal plus interest at a specified rate. (For an example of a certificate of deposit, see Figure 22.4.)

| | |
|---|---|
| Darlene and Darren Drawer | Date: *January 1, 1996* |
| 111 Happy Lane | |
| Joyville, NY 00000 | |

Pay to the order of: *Pamela Payee*

*One hundred twenty and 00/100* ———————————————— Dollars   $120.00

FIRST BANK OF EREHWON
Main Street
Erehwon, New York 00000

*Darren Drawer*

Memorandum
20 00153 43724 07954 : 09573-09

**FIGURE 22.2**   Sample check

---

### PROMISSORY NOTE

DATE: October 15, 1996

For value received, the undersigned jointly and severally promise to pay to Linda Lender or her assigns the principal sum of Ten Thousand Dollars ($10,000.00) with interest from date at the rate of eight percent (8.00%) *per annum*. The said principal and interest shall be payable in lawful money of the United States of America at 123 Any Street, in the State of New York, County of Otsego, or at such place as may hereafter be designated by written notice from the holder to the makers hereof upon demand one year from the date hereof.

Maker's Address                                 [Signed] Margaret Maker
123 Any Street
Oneonta, NY 13820                          [Signed] Mark Maker

---

**FIGURE 22.3**   Sample note

---

### CERTIFICATE OF DEPOSIT

DATE: June 15, 1996

For value received, the LAST BANK OF EREHWON promises to pay to Dennis and Denise Depositors the principal sum of Ten Thousand Dollars ($10,000.00) with interest eighteen months (18 months) from the date hereof at the rate of Six and One Quarter Percent (6.25%) *per annum* compounded daily. The said principal and interest shall be payable in lawful money of the United States of America at 123 Main Street, in the State of Erehwon, or at any branch of the LAST BANK OF EREHWON in the state.

LAST BANK OF EREHWON                  [Signed] Orlando Officer
123 Main Street                                    Senior Vice President
Anytown, EH 12345

---

**FIGURE 22.4**   Sample certificate of deposit

## SPECIFIC REQUIREMENTS FOR NEGOTIABLE INSTRUMENTS . . . . . . . . . . . . . . . . . . . . . . . . . . . . . . . . . .

As we've already seen, an instrument must meet certain specific requirements in order to qualify for the special status of a negotiable instrument. The qualifying criteria bear a closer look, since each one is essential for an instrument to gain the status of a negotiable instrument.

## THE REQUIREMENT OF A SIGNED WRITING

The UCC does not define what constitutes a writing for purposes of creating a negotiable instrument, but the requirement has been liberally construed by the courts to include words written on nearly any portable surface that affords some permanence. No specific words need to be used in creating a negotiable instrument as long as the writing meets all the requirements for negotiability. Thus, even though most checks are routinely written on preprinted forms supplied by the financial institution at which the drawer maintains a checking account, a check can technically be written on nearly any surface capable of accepting writing. A valid draft, check, note or even a CD can be written on a legal pad, looseleaf paper, a shirt or even a coconut shell (though it might take some convincing to get someone to accept such an instrument!). Likewise, the writing can be created with a typewriter, computer printer (impact, inkjet or laser will all do nicely), pen, crayon, pencil or even lipstick. Using any medium that is easy to erase, however, can lead to problems if the instrument is later altered. And, as with a negotiable coconut, using an exotic writing implement may well make the instrument unacceptable to most payees.

As is the case with the type of paper or writing implement used to create a negotiable instrument, the requirement of a signature is rather liberally construed by the courts. The UCC specifically states: "A signature is made by use of any name, including any trade or assumed name, upon an instrument, or by any word or mark used in lieu of a written signature." (§ 3-401 [2]) An X on paper, a scanned signature and a signature reproduced on a rubber stamp are all perfectly valid, as is the signed or printed name or initials of any signer, as long as these are used intentionally as a signature.

## THE REQUIREMENT OF AN UNCONDITIONAL PROMISE

In order to be negotiable, an instrument must on its face make an unconditional, no-strings-attached promise to pay a specific amount of money by a drawer or maker to a named payee or to bearer. With some limited exceptions noted in Section 3-105 of the code, a conditional promise destroys the negotiable nature of an instrument. Hence, a check that reads, "Pay to the order of Paul Payee $200 if the United States wins the 1998 Soccer World Cup," is not a negotiable instrument, since the promise to pay is conditioned on the happening of a future event.

## THE REQUIREMENT OF A SUM CERTAIN IN MONEY

A negotiable instrument must be payable in cash and the amount payable on the instrument must be ascertainable from the instrument itself. The requirement that the instrument be payable in money is met if it is payable in the legal tender of any country; thus a draft payable in yen, pesetas, marks or francs is perfectly negotiable if it meets all the other requirements of a negotiable instrument. An instrument payable in a foreign currency, unless otherwise noted on the instrument itself, can be paid in the U.S. equivalent of the currency at the time of its presentment for payment. (§ 3-107 [2]) In addition, the fact that an instrument is payable with interest, or subject to different interest rates depending on the date when it is paid, will not affect negotiability. (§ 3-106 [a–b])

## THE REQUIREMENT OF NO OTHER PROMISE OR OBLIGATION

Negotiable instruments must contain only one unconditional promise to pay a sum certain in currency. If there are other obligations of promises cited in the instrument along with the promise to pay money, the instrument will not be negotiable. For example, an instrument that promises to pay the payee "one hundred dollars and two ounces of gold" is nonnegotiable, as is a promise by a carpenter to "Pay fifty dollars and build a deck." The additional promises of payment of gold and the building of a deck make the respective instruments nonnegotiable.

## THE REQUIREMENT THAT THE INSTRUMENT BE PAYABLE ON DEMAND OR AT A SPECIFIC TIME

Negotiable instruments must be payable either on demand or at a specifically ascertainable date. Instruments such as checks that are not usually payable at a specific time are demand instruments and are payable at any time on demand as soon as they are issued. For instruments that are payable on or after a specific date, all that is required is that it be clear from the instrument itself when it is payable. Thus, an instrument that is payable "thirty days from today" or "on July 1, 1999" is a *time instrument* and satisfies the requirement of specificity as to the date when it is payable. The mere fact that an instrument is subject to acceleration upon the happening of an event (such as the maker's late payment of an instrument payable on a monthly basis) will not destroy negotiability, nor will the fact that the instrument is subject to an extension upon the request of one or more of the parties. (§ 3-109 [1][d]) But if the instrument is payable only upon an event uncertain to occur, such as "when the Yankees next win the World Series," then it is not negotiable. (§ 3-109 [2])

## THE REQUIREMENT THAT THE INSTRUMENT BE PAYABLE TO ORDER OR TO BEARER

An instrument must be payable either to the order of a specific person (or persons) or company or to bearer. An instrument is *payable to order* if it states that it is payable to a specifically ascertainable person, company or group of people. An instrument is *payable to bearer* if it is payable to no specifically ascertainable person, but rather can be paid to anyone who lawfully has it in his or her possession. An instrument is made payable to bearer by such terms as "Pay to bearer," "Pay to the order of bearer," "Pay to cash," "Pay to the order of cash," or any language which makes the instrument payable to no specifically ascertainable person or company. A check made payable to "life, the universe and everything," for example, is a bearer instrument, since it names no specifically ascertainable person; its effect is the same as drawing a check to the order of cash as a payee. On the other hand, a check made payable to the order of "the owner of the automobile with the New York license number 1234-XYZ" would be payable to the registered owner or owners of such an automobile and would be a negotiable order instrument, since there is sufficient information on the face of the instrument with which to identify the specific payee or payees.

## PARTIES TO COMMERCIAL PAPER . . . . . . . . . . . . . . . . . . . . . . . .

Before we continue our discussion of commercial paper, it will be helpful to introduce the major parties who play a role in the creation, negotiation and payment of negotiable instruments. We will encounter these parties throughout the rest of this unit and it will be helpful if we become familiar with the basic role of each party now.

Drawer: The party who makes or executes a draft.

Drawee: The party who is directed to pay a draft or a note. (If the draft is a check, the drawee is always a bank or other financial institution.)

Maker: The party who makes or executes a note.

Payee: The party to whom a note or draft is made payable.

Bearer: The party in possession of a note or draft made out to him or her as payee or made out to bearer.

Accommodation Party: A party who indorses a note or draft that is not made payable to him or her in order to guarantee payment if the note or draft is dishonored when presented for payment.

Acceptor: A drawee of a draft who binds himself or herself to pay the payee the face value of the draft when it is presented for payment by signing as acceptor on the face of the draft.

Guarantor: A party who signs a note or draft on its face guaranteeing payment in case the note or draft is dishonored when it is presented for payment.

Indorser: The party who signs his or her name on the back of a note or draft naming himself or herself as payee in order to obtain payment on it or negotiate it to a third party.

Indorsee: The party to whom a negotiable instrument is indorsed as the new payee.

## GENERAL RULES APPLICABLE TO COMMERCIAL PAPER  . . . . . . . . .

### ANTEDATING AND POSTDATING NEGOTIABLE INSTRUMENTS (§ 3-114)

The negotiability of an instrument is unaffected by postdating or antedating. For example, if a check issued on August 1 is postdated for September 1, it is still a negotiable instrument.

## INCOMPLETE INSTRUMENTS (§ 3-115)

A negotiable instrument that has not been completely filled out by the maker or drawer cannot be enforced until it is complete. But it is permissible for the holder of an incomplete instrument to complete it by filling in missing information as long as the completion is authorized. If a completion is unauthorized, the instrument is generally void. The burden of proving an unauthorized material alteration is on the party making the assertion that the instrument has been materially altered without his or her consent.

The significance of this section is that good-faith additions to negotiable instruments by persons who have the instrument in their possession are generally lawful unless they are unauthorized. A person receiving a check on which the date has been omitted, for example, may safely insert the date that the check was negotiated to him or her. In addition, a *blank check* (a check that is signed by the maker but is otherwise incomplete) can also lawfully be filled out by the person to whom it is given as long as the drawer intended to authorize the person to do so.

## INSTRUMENTS PAYABLE TO TWO OR MORE PERSONS (§ 3-116)

An instrument payable to two or more parties in the alternative can be negotiated by any of the named parties alone. If an instrument is negotiated to two or more parties jointly, however, the signature of both parties is necessary to effect lawful negotiation. If, for example, a check is made payable to "Jane or John Doe" (payable in the alternative), either John or Jane may cash the entire check. However, if the check is made out to "John and Jane Doe" (payable jointly), *both* John's and Jane's signatures would be required to negotiate the check.

## AMBIGUOUS TERMS AND RULES OF CONSTRUCTION (§ 3-118)

The UCC attempts to resolve the common ambiguities that arise in the course of drafting negotiable instruments by providing rules for the resolution of such common ambiguities and inconsistencies in commercial paper. The most notable of these are as follows:

- If there is doubt as to whether an instrument is a note or a draft, the holder of the instrument may treat it as either one or the other.
- Typewritten terms take precedence over preprinted terms; handwritten terms take precedence over typewritten or preprinted terms.
- Words take precedence over figures (numbers) unless the words are ambiguous, in which case the figure will control.
- If an instrument calls for payment of interest at an unspecified rate, the interest payable is at the *judgment rate* (set by statute in every jurisdiction) from the date of the instrument or, if undated, from the date of issue.

## QUESTIONS    . . . . . . . . . . . . . . . . . . . . . . . . . . . . . . . . . . . . .

1. What are the four basic types of negotiable instruments?

2. What is the fundamental difference between a note and a certificate of deposit? What function do these two instruments serve?

3. What is the fundamental difference between a draft and a check and what purpose do both instruments serve?

4. What are the basic requirements that every instrument must meet in order to be a negotiable instrument?

5. What is the effect of antedating or postdating a check?

6. How must an instrument that is made payable to "Tom, Dick and Harriet Jones" be negotiated?

7. What type of instrument is a check made payable to "a billion grains of sand"? Is such an instrument valid?

8. A check made payable to "Jane Doe" has $100 written in figures in the box provided for the amount, but states "one thousand Dollars" in writing on the space provided to state the amount of the check in words. Is the check valid? If so, for what amount? If not, why not?

9. Peter Payee receives a check as a birthday gift from his grandmother. The check is made out for fifty dollars to him as payee, but his grandmother neglected to write in a date on the space provided and also forgot to write in the amount in words in the space provided on the check. Peter, eager to buy two computer games on sale that week only for fifty dollars, fills in the missing date and the words "fifty and 00/100 Dollars" on the check and negotiates it to his local software dealer. Is the check valid? Has Peter committed an unlawful act in completing the check?

10. Mark Maker issues a note to Percival Payee for $500. The note is made payable one year from the date of issue with interest, but no interest rate is specified. Is the instrument valid and, if so, what interest rate is payable?

## H  Y  P  O  T  H  E  T  I  C  A  L        C  A  S  E  S

1. Bob borrows $500 from his friend Bernadette. In exchange for the money, he gives her a piece of paper like the one that follows. Is this a negotiable instrument? Explain.

Date: May 1, 1996

I, Bob Borrower, hereby acknowledge that I owe Bernadette Lender the sum of $500.

[Signed] Bob Borrower

2. Albert and Betty find themselves shipwrecked on a deserted island in the Pacific when their small boat capsizes. Fearing that they will not be rescued and wishing to alleviate his guilty conscience, Albert decides to pay off a long-standing debt to Betty of $10,000. Feeling generous in his certainty that the two will have to spend the rest of their lives alone on the island, he tells Betty that he would like to give her $20,000 as payment of the debt and the interest that has accrued over the past ten years. Since the parties have neither paper nor writing implements handy, Albert tears off a piece of board from the remains of their boat and uses a rusty nail to scratch out the following message on its surface:

---

Date: July 4, 1996

To: Citibank
    A/C 123-456-09

Pay to the order of Betty Lender $20,000 (twenty thousand and XX/100 dollars).

Albert Debtor

---

The next day, much to Albert's surprise, they are rescued by a passing cruise ship. Is the instrument that Albert executed valid? If so, what type of an instrument is it?

---

Date: 1/1/96

To: Sam Shoemaker
    ABC Industries

One year from today, pay to the order of Sandy Jones $1,000.00 (two thousand dollars) plus simple interest at 7% per annum.

[Signed] Benjamin Brewster

Payment Guaranteed: [Signed] Rhoda Roberts

---

3. On June 1, 1996, Darlene issues a check to Daniel that is dated July 1, 1996. The instrument is made payable to Daniel's order "if the New York Mets win the National League East pennant." Is the instrument negotiable? Explain.

4. Answer the questions that follow based on this instrument:
   a. What type of instrument is this?
   b. What is Benjamin Brewster's function in relation to the instrument?

   c. What is Sam Shoemaker's (of ABC Industries) function in relation to the instrument?
   d. What is Sandy Jones' function in relation to the instrument?
   e. What is Rhoda Roberts' function in relation to the instrument?
   f. Is the instrument valid as written and, if so, exactly how much will be payable under the instrument when it is presented for payment on January 1, 1997?

CHAPTER

# 23

# TRANSFER AND NEGOTIATION OF COMMERCIAL PAPER AND RIGHTS OF HOLDERS

Unlike the transfer of an ownership interest in most tangible personal property, which can be accomplished without any specific formalities, the transfer of negotiable instruments requires the following of a set procedure in order for the *transferee* (the person to whom the instrument is transferred) to gain the special status of a holder of the instrument. In this chapter, we will delve into the statutory requirements for transferring commercial paper.

## TRANSFER OF NEGOTIABLE INSTRUMENTS AND THE TRANSFEREE'S RIGHT TO AN INDORSEMENT  . . . . . . . . . . . . . . . .

Generally speaking, the legal transfer of an interest in a negotiable instrument from one person to another is accomplished by an *indorsement* (a signature placed by the holder of the instrument on the back of the instrument) and the delivery of the instrument to the person intended to be the instrument's new holder. The accomplishment of such a transfer is termed a *negotiation* of the instrument and generally transfers to the new holder whatever rights the transferor had in the instrument. If the transferor of a negotiable instrument neglects to indorse the instrument, Section 3-201 (3) gives the transferee the right to demand specific performance of the transferor's indorsement if the instrument was transferred for value.

## NEGOTIATION  . . . . . . . . . . . . . . . . . . . . . . . . . . . . . . . .

*Negotiation* is defined as "the transfer of an instrument in such form that the transferee becomes a holder." (§ 3-202 [1]) An instrument payable to the order of a specific person or company is negotiated by the physical transfer of the instrument containing all necessary indorsements. A bearer instrument (one that is payable to cash, to bearer or to the order of no specifically identifiable party), on the other hand, is negotiated merely through its delivery, without the requirement that it be indorsed by the transferor.

# INDORSEMENTS

We have already seen that the order of the drawer of a draft to the drawee to pay the payee, as well as the promise of the maker of a note to pay the payee, must be unconditional. But the indorser of a negotiable instrument can make the indorsement conditional without destroying its negotiation. Thus, an indorsement that reads "Pay to Jane Doe if the Yankees win the World Series" is a valid indorsement and does not destroy the negotiability of the instrument. (We'll take a look at special and restrictive indorsements in the following two sections of this chapter.)

The UCC provides that an indorsement must be written by the indorser, or on his or her behalf, on the instrument or on a separate piece of paper that is permanently attached to the instrument. (§ 3-202 [2]) Stapling, gluing or otherwise permanently affixing a separate sheet of paper to a negotiable instrument for indorsements when the space in the back of the instrument is used up is perfectly valid. An additional sheet of paper attached to a negotiable instrument for additional indorsements is called an *allonge*.

In the event that an instrument is made payable to a person with the payee's name misspelled or even with a mistaken name, it is lawful for the payee to indorse the instrument either under his or her correctly spelled or true name or under the misspelled or incorrect name. A person accepting transfer of the instrument, however, can demand that the indorsee in such circumstances sign with both the correct and misspelled or incorrect names. (§ 3-203)

## SPECIAL AND BLANK INDORSEMENTS

A *special indorsement* specifies the person or persons to whom the instrument is made payable. When an instrument is specially indorsed to a specifically identifiable person or company, the instrument cannot be further negotiated without that party's indorsement. (§ 3-204 [1]) For example, if Albert makes out a check to Betty and Betty indorses it "Pay Carmen" or "Pay to the order of Carmen," the check is specially indorsed and Carmen will need to indorse it next before it can be further negotiated to any other person.

A *blank indorsement*, on the other hand, does not specify any specific person but merely consists of a signature *or* a signature preceded by words such as "Pay to cash," "Pay bearer" or "Pay anybody." A check that is indorsed in blank is a bearer instrument and can be further negotiated merely by transferring it to a third party. (§ 3-204 [2]) (Remember that no indorsement is necessary to negotiate a bearer instrument.)

The nature of a negotiable instrument is determined by examining the instrument's last indorsement. An instrument indorsed in blank is *bearer paper*, whereas a specially indorsed instrument is *order paper*.

## RESTRICTIVE INDORSEMENTS

Section 3-205 of the UCC provides that a *restrictive indorsement* is one which fits *one* of the following criteria:

- a conditional indorsement (such as "Pay to Jane Doe if a Democrat wins the next presidential election");
- an indorsement that purports to prohibit further transfer of the instrument (such as "Pay Jane Doe and only Jane Doe." Such indorsements are ignored by the courts, however, and the named indorsee is free to further negotiate the instrument should he or she wish to do so);
- an indorsement that signals a purpose of deposit or collection by the indorsee in negotiating the instrument (such as "for deposit," "Pay any bank" or "for collection"); or
- an indorsement that claims to be for the benefit or use of the indorser or of another person (such as "Pay Jane Doe as a birthday present" or "deposit into my checking account #123-4567").

## RIGHTS OF A HOLDER . . . . . . . . . . . . . . . . . . . . . . . . . . . . .

The UCC defines a *holder* as "a person who is in possession of a document of title or an instrument or a certificated investment security drawn, issued or indorsed to him or his order or to bearer or in blank." (§ 1-201 [20]) Thus, the original payee of a note or draft is a holder when the instrument is delivered to him or her, as are all persons to whom instruments are transferred to them with special indorsements in their benefit or with blank indorsements.

A person who obtains the status of a holder of a negotiable instrument gains the right to further transfer or negotiate it, and to enforce its payment whether or not he or she is the instrument's true owner. (§ 3-301) Anyone may transfer a negotiable instrument once he or she achieves the status of holder. This can present problems, especially when bearer instruments are involved, since anyone (even a thief) can negotiate them. Even though persons who wrongfully cash or otherwise negotiate instruments breach the presentment and transfer warranties of title (as we'll see later), it can still be a problem when such persons cannot be found or are found to be insolvent after a wrongful transfer, since the rightful issuer or owner of the instrument may not be able to sue successfully for the loss resulting from the wrongful negotiation.

When a holder transfers an instrument, however, he or she does so subject to any claims that can be asserted to payment of the instrument by third parties, as well as all normal claims and defenses based on breach of contract. (§ 3-306) Thus, even though a holder might have the legal right (or power, if you prefer) to transfer an instrument, he or she will generally be subject to liability if the transfer is wrongful. For example, a thief who finds a check indorsed in blank can negotiate it to an innocent third party or cash it at his or her bank, but will be subject to civil liability (as well as criminal penalties) for the wrongful transfer if he or she is sued by the drawer of the check or any person to whom he or she wrongfully transferred it. Likewise, a person who receives a check as consideration under a contract will be able to cash the check, but will be subject to liability to the drawer for the value of the check if he or she does not properly perform his or her end of the bargain.

## RIGHTS OF A HOLDER IN DUE COURSE  . . . . . . . . . . . . . . . . . . . .

A person is a *holder in due course* under the definition of Section 3-302 if he or she takes a negotiable instrument:

- for value;
- in good faith; and
- without notice that it is overdue or has been dishonored, or of any defense against it or claim to it on the part of any person.

The significance of holder-in-due-course status is that a holder in due course takes an instrument free from most defenses to its payment. A payee or indorsee who qualifies for holder-in-due-course status is in an excellent position when demanding payment of a negotiable instrument, since only defenses making the instrument void can prevent holders in due course from being paid when they present a negotiable instrument for payment. Section 3-305, which deals with the rights of a holder in due course, states that a holder in due course takes an instrument free from all claims to it on the part of any person, and free from all defenses of any party to the instrument with whom the holder in due course has not dealt. Only the following defenses are assertable against a holder in due course as provided in Section 3-305 (2)(a–e):

- infancy, to the extent that it is a defense to a simple contract;
- incapacity, duress or illegality that render the obligation of the party void;
- misrepresentation that induces a party to sign a negotiable instrument without understanding its nature or its terms (fraud in the execution);
- discharge in insolvency proceedings; or
- any other discharge of which the holder has notice when he or she takes the instrument.

The following example will illustrate the significance of holder-in-due-course status:

*A buyer gives a seller a check for $1,000 in exchange for the seller's promise to ship a thirty-one-inch television set. As soon as he receives the check, the seller indorses it to XYZ Oil Company to pay for a delivery of fuel oil in that amount. XYZ in turn indorses the check and deposits it in its account at Second National Bank. If the television set that eventually arrives at the buyer's home is a twenty-five-inch set, can the buyer demand that either XYZ or Second National Bank refund the amount they were paid upon negotiation of the check?*

The answer here depends on whether or not XYZ Oil Company and Second National Bank are holders in due course. Since they each accepted the negotiable instrument for value, in good faith and without notice that there were any claims against it, they qualify as holders in due course and are not subject to the defense of breach of contract that the buyer has against the seller—the original payee and subsequent transferor of the instrument. Does the original payee also qualify for holder-in-due-course status, or can the buyer force him to refund the amount he received from negotiating the check? Clearly, the seller is not a holder in due course, since he was obviously aware that there would be a claim against payment of the check for breach of contract.

## QUESTIONS  . . . . . . . . . . . . . . . . . . . . . . . . . . . . . . . . . . . . . . . .

1. What are the two steps required to transfer a negotiable instrument?
2. What is a negotiation?
3. Is a conditional indorsement valid?
4. If a drawer misspells a payee's name, how can the payee negotiate the instrument?
5. What are special and blank indorsements?
6. What are restrictive indorsements?
7. What is the UCC definition of the term *holder*?
8. How does a person become a holder in due course?
9. What is the significance of holder-in-due-course status?
10. What defenses are valid even against a holder in due course?

## H Y P O T H E T I C A L    C A S E S

1. Danielle Drawer writes a check payable to Pablo Payee for $50. Pablo, who owes Inga Indorsee $50, signs his name on the reverse of the check and hands it to her. Answer the following questions based on these facts.
   a. What type of indorsement did Pablo make?
   b. After Pablo's indorsement, is the instrument order paper or bearer paper?
   c. If a thief were to steal the check after Pablo's blank indorsement, would the thief be able to cash the check?
2. Don Drawer gives a check to his friend Pamela Payee as a birthday gift. Pamela indorses the check "Pay any bank, [Signed] Pam Payee." Answer the following questions based on these facts.
   a. Is Pamela a holder of the instrument when Don gives her the check?
   b. Is Pamela a holder in due course of the instrument? Explain.
   c. Is Pamela's bank a holder in due course after it accepts the check and credits her account? Explain.
   d. What type of indorsement is involved?
   e. Is the negotiation from Pamela to her bank valid, given that she signed her name as Pam Payee rather than Pamela Payee?

3. Matthew Maker drafts a note payable to Sam Slimy for $1,000, payable on demand. At the time that Matthew drafts the note, Sam is holding a gun to his head. A day later, Sam indorses the note to Irene Innocent in exchange for $1,000 in cash. When Irene tries to cash the note with Matthew, will Matthew have to pay it? Would your answer be the same if Irene had taken the note in exchange for $200 in cash? Explain fully.

# 24

# LIABILITY OF PARTIES TO COMMERCIAL PAPER AND WARRANTIES OF TRANSFER AND PRESENTMENT

As we've already seen, the primary purpose of negotiable instruments is to facilitate commercial transactions by acting as a substitute for cash or as evidence of debt and a guarantee of its repayment. We've also seen that there is an element of risk to persons who issue negotiable instruments, since they must generally pay holders in due course under the terms of the instrument and are barred from asserting most defenses to its payment. If we ended our discussion of commercial paper here, it might well seem that the risk inherent in the negotiation of these instruments is an unacceptable one. Fortunately, the makers and drawers of negotiable instruments do have a measure of protection against most adverse circumstances that can arise out of the transfer of these instruments through the contractual and signature liability that arises from the transfer of a negotiable instrument and from the warranties that automatically attach when such instruments are negotiated or presented for payment to the drawees or makers. In this chapter, we will explore the liability of parties to commercial paper, as well as the warranties of transfer and presentment that arise from their negotiation.

## LIABILITY OF PARTIES TO COMMERCIAL PAPER . . . . . . . . . . . . . . .

There are essentially two types of liability that parties to commercial paper can have: *signature liability* and *contractual liability*. Signature liability arises from the act of signing a negotiable instrument in order to create or transfer it, while *contractual liability* attaches based on the relationship that parties have to one another with regard to the instrument being created or negotiated. We'll examine both types of liability in turn.

## SIGNATURE LIABILITY

Before a person can be found to have any liability on a negotiable instrument, the person's signature must appear on the instrument. (§ 3-401 [1]) As we've previously seen, the code is rather liberal in determining what a signature is, essentially holding any mark made by a party with the intention of having it serve as a signature to be a valid signature. (§ 3-401 [2]) Since no person is liable on an instrument unless his or her signature appears on it, the drawee of a draft or check is not liable on the instrument at the time that the drawer draws the instrument, but becomes liable to pay it upon signaling his or her intention to do so by signing on the face of an instrument as an acceptor. Thus, if you write a check to a named payee, your bank is not liable on the instrument unless and until it accepts the check by certifying it.

The mere fact that a person's signature appears on commercial paper can subject the signer to liability for the instrument. It is not necessary that the signer receive any consideration for signing or have any relationship to the instrument; all that is required is that the signature be genuine and that the signer intentionally placed it on the instrument. If, for example, Albert asks Betty to carry a check over to Charlie, who is ten feet away, and Betty signs on the reverse of the check before giving it to Charlie, she has signature liability as an indorser of the check—even though she was not asked to sign, had no need to sign, and certainly received no consideration for signing her name on the check.

## CONTRACTUAL LIABILITY

Parties who sign commercial paper incur contractual liability for payment of an instrument that can be either primary or secondary, depending on the relation of the party to the instrument.

The maker of a note or certificate of deposit and the acceptor of a draft or check have primary liability for payment of the instrument. (§ 3-413 [1]) The drawer of a draft or check, on the other hand, has secondary liability for its payment that does not arise unless the drawee refuses to pay the check when it is presented for payment. In addition, Section 3-413 (2) allows the drawer to limit his or her contractual liability for payment of an instrument by drawing the instrument "without recourse," which limits the right of the payee to seek payment on the instrument *only* from the drawee.

Indorsers of negotiable instruments are all secondarily liable for payment of the instrument if the primarily liable parties fail to discharge the instrument when it is presented for payment. If an instrument is dishonored, an indorser must pay any person who has indorsed the instrument after him or her, after being given proper notice by such subsequent indorsers that dishonor of the instrument has occurred. But an indorser can disclaim his or her contractual liability by indorsing the instrument "without recourse." (§ 3-414 [1]) Where there are multiple indorsers of an instrument that is negotiated a number of times before ultimately being presented to the maker or drawee for payment, Section 3-414 (2) provides that indorsers are liable to one another in the order that they indorse the instrument, and the order of indorsement is presumed to be the same as the order in which the signatures appear on the back of the instrument.

In addition to drawers and indorsers, guarantors who guarantee payment of the instrument are secondarily liable if the drawee or maker does not pay. (§ 3-416 [1]) A guarantor who signs an instrument with the words "collection guaranteed" has secondary liability for payment of the instrument, but need not pay it until it has been dishonored and the payee or other party seeking payment on it has successfully sued the maker or drawer and received a judgment against him or her.

Finally, an accommodation party who signs an instrument only to lend his or her name to it in order to bolster its acceptance by a payee or indorser is either primarily or secondarily liable depending upon whether he or she signs the instrument as an indorser or on its face as a primary party. (§ 3-415 [2]) The accommodation party has no interest in the instrument but signs it (often as a favor to a drawer or maker with questionable credit) in order to enhance the acceptability of the instrument to payees or indorsers who might otherwise refuse to accept it.

The contractual liability of parties to an instrument can be summarized as follows:

Drawer: Secondarily liable on a check or draft he or she has drawn (pays if the drawee refuses to pay).

Drawee: Primarily liable on a check or draft he or she has accepted.

Maker: Primarily liable on a note or CD he or she has executed.

Accommodation Party: Secondarily liable for payment of a note or draft he or she has indorsed in order to guarantee its payment. Primarily liable on a note or draft he or she has signed as a primary party (such as co-maker).

Guarantor: Secondarily liable for payment of a note or draft for which he or she has guaranteed payment by signing as guarantor on its face.

Indorser: Secondarily liable to all parties to whom a note is negotiated after he or she negotiates a note or draft. Must refund whatever consideration he or she received for negotiating the draft if it is dishonored by the primarily liable parties.

## WARRANTIES ON PRESENTMENT AND TRANSFER  . . . . . . . . . . . . .

In addition to the contractual liability of parties to commercial paper, there are implied warranties that attach to the transfer of a negotiable instrument and to its presentment for payment.

### PRESENTMENT WARRANTIES

Section 3-417 (1) of the UCC specifies that any person who receives payment or acceptance of a negotiable instrument makes the following implied warranties to every person who pays or accepts the instrument:

- that he or she has good title to the instrument or is authorized to obtain payment or acceptance of the instrument on behalf of one who has good title;

- that he or she has no knowledge that the signature of the maker or acceptor is unauthorized (but this warranty is *not* given by a holder in due course acting in good faith to a maker or drawer with regard to his or her own signatures or to an acceptor of a draft if the holder in due course took the draft without knowledge that the signature was not genuine); and
- that the instrument has not been materially altered (but this warranty is also not made by a holder in due course to the maker of a note, to the drawer of a draft or to the acceptor of the draft).

## TRANSFER WARRANTIES

Section 3-417 (2) of the code provides that any person who transfers a negotiable instrument for consideration makes the following five warranties to the transferee:

- that he or she has good title to the instrument or is authorized to obtain payment or acceptance of the instrument on behalf of one who has good title, and that the transfer is rightful;
- that all signatures are genuine or authorized;
- that the instrument has not been materially altered;
- that no defense of any party is good against the transferor (if the instrument is transferred without recourse, this warranty is limited to the transferor having no knowledge of any defense by any party to the instrument); and
- that he or she has no knowledge of any insolvency proceeding against a maker or acceptor (or the drawer of an unaccepted draft or check).

# PRESENTMENT, NOTICE OF DISHONOR AND PROTEST  . . . . . . . . . .

*Presentment* of an instrument involves the furnishing of a negotiable instrument to the drawee for his or her *acceptance* (an acknowledgement that the instrument is valid and will be paid when due) or to the drawee or acceptor for payment. In general, presentment of an instrument to the primarily liable party for acceptance is a prerequisite to invoking secondary liability on an instrument. Drafts that are payable at other than the drawee's residence or place of business must be presented for acceptance before the drawer's or indorser's secondary liability arises (§ 3-501 [1][a]), and presentment for payment is necessary to charge any indorser with payment of the draft. If a draft is payable at a bank, presentment for payment is necessary, and failure to make such presentment can discharge the drawer, acceptor or maker of a draft or note if it is drawn or appears to be payable outside of the United States or its possessions. (§ 3-501 [1][c] and [3])

## TIME OF PRESENTMENT (§ 3-503)

Presentment is defined in Section 3-504 (1) as "a demand for acceptance or payment made upon the maker, acceptor, drawee or other payor by or on behalf of the holder."

When an instrument does not specify when presentment is to be made, the code provides for presentment as follows:

- Instruments payable on or after a specific date: Presentment for acceptance (if desired or necessary) must be made on or before the due date. Presentment for payment must be on the due date.
- Instruments payable on sight: Must be presented for acceptance or negotiated within a reasonable time of their issue.
- Instruments whose payment is accelerated due to an acceleration clause: Must be presented for payment within a reasonable time of the acceleration.

The definition of *a reasonable time* depends on the instrument involved and the customary trade and banking usage. When an uncertified check drawn on a U.S. bank other than by the bank itself is involved, a reasonable time for presentment of the instrument for collection or payment is presumed to be thirty days. A check presented after that time is still valid, but the drawer's liability on it is discharged. (An indorsee or payee who tries to negotiate a check after thirty days from the date of its issue is able to collect only from the drawee and cannot sue the drawer if the check is dishonored.) Presentment is deemed reasonable with respect to the indorser's liability within seven days of the indorsement. (§ 3-503 (2)[a]–[b])

## TIME ALLOWED FOR ACCEPTANCE OR PAYMENT (§ 3-506)

Acceptance of an instrument presented for acceptance may be deferred up to the close of the business day after the presentment is made. If the instrument is not accepted by that time, it is deemed to be dishonored. An instrument presented for payment, on the other hand, may be held for a reasonable time for inspection prior to its payment, but must be paid by the close of the business day on which it is presented for payment. Failure to pay an instrument by the close of the business day in which it is presented for payment constitutes a dishonor of the instrument.

## NOTICE OF DISHONOR (§ 3-508)

Notice of dishonor may be given by any person who may be liable under the instrument, by the holder of the instrument (or by anyone on his or her behalf), by any party who has received notice of the instrument's dishonor or by anyone who may be compelled to pay the instrument. When a bank is the party giving notice of dishonor, it must do so by midnight of the day in which it dishonors the instrument or receives notice that the instrument has been dishonored. Persons who dishonor an instrument (other than banks) must give notice of dishonor prior to midnight of the third business day after dishonor or receipt of notice of dishonor. Notice may be given in any reasonable manner, either orally or in writing. When notice is given in writing, it is effective when it is *sent* (whether or not it is ever received).

## PROTEST (§ 3-509)

*Protest* is a "certificate of dishonor made under the hand and seal of the United States consul or vice consul or a notary public or other person authorized to certify dishonor by the law of the place where the dishonor occurs." (§ 3-509 [1]) The formal requirement of protest is necessary before secondary liability can arise under the instrument. Protest is required only when negotiable instruments are payable outside of the United States as a means of certifying that dishonor has occurred.

## QUESTIONS . . . . . . . . . . . . . . . . . . . . . . . . . . . . . . . . . . . . . . . .

1. What are the two types of liability that parties to commercial paper have?
2. What parties to commercial paper have primary liability for its payment?
3. What parties have secondary contractual liability for payment of commercial paper?
4. What two basic types of warranties are involved in commercial paper transactions?
5. What are the warranties of presentment and when are they available?
6. What are the warranties of transfer and to whom do they apply?
7. When must presentment be made when the instrument does not specify a time for presentment?
8. What is the time frame within which an instrument presented for acceptance must be accepted? What about an instrument presented for payment?
9. What is the time frame within which notice of dishonor needs to be given by a bank? By a party who is not a bank?
10. What is protest?

## H Y P O T H E T I C A L     C A S E S

1. Examine the sample negotiable instrument that follows and answer the questions that relate to it.

> July 8, 1998
> Two years from date, I promise to pay Ed Biosca two thousand dollars ($2,000.00) with interest at the rate of 8.50% per annum compounded daily.
>
> [Signed] Beulah Borrower
> Payment Guaranteed: [Signed] Nat Toobright

a. What type of instrument is this?
b. Who is/are the primarily liable party or parties to this instrument?
c. Is there a secondarily liable party to this instrument? If so, who is it?

2. Assume the same facts as in the previous question. Assume further that on July 8, 1998, Ed Biosca presents this note to Beulah Borrower.
   a. When must Beulah pay the instrument?
   b. Assume that Beulah is unable or unwilling to pay the instrument when it is presented. What must Ed do?
   c. Does protest have to be made of this instrument?
3. Sam Slick, a crook, finds a check made out to Pamela Payee in the amount of $10 on Pamela's desk at work. He steals the check, changes the amount to $100, forges Pam's signature and specially indorses the check to himself as indorsee. The next day, Sam negotiates the instrument to Ignacio Innocent, a coworker, who does not know of the theft or alteration of the check and who pays Sam $100 for the instrument.
   a. What transfer warranties has Sam breached in negotiating the check to Ignacio?
   b. Which transfer warranty or warranties has Sam not breached in negotiating the instrument?

4. Examine the sample instrument that follows and then answer the questions that relate to it.

| | |
|---|---|
| Diana Drawer | Date: July 9, 1998 |
| 123 Any Street | |
| Happyville, NE 12345 | |

Pay to the order of Pedro Payee

One hundred and xx/100——Dollars    $100.00

Ultimate National Bank
Happyville, Nebraska

MEMO: _____    [Signed] D. Drawer
123 4567 8901:0001

a  What type of instrument is this?
b. What length of time will be presumed reasonable for this instrument to be presented for payment or acceptance?
c. If Pedro deposits the check in his account and it turns out that Diana did not have sufficient funds to cover the check, how long does Pedro's bank have to notify him of the dishonor when it learns of it?
d. How must the bank notify Pedro of the dishonor?
e. If the bank sends Pedro notification of the dishonor by mail and he never receives the letter, is the notification valid?

U N I T

# IV

# PROPERTY

## INTRODUCTION TO PROPERTY · · · · · · · · · · · · · · · · · · · · · · · · · ·

The term *property* is used to describe anything that is capable of being owned. An ownership right in property, regardless of its nature, gives the owner a whole bundle of rights that the government sanctions and protects. For instance, the owner of real estate or personal property has the right to use it, sell it, give it away, rent it, possess it, prevent others from possessing or interfering with it and, with few exceptions, even to destroy it. Ownership of property carries with it the exclusive right to use, possess and dispose of the thing in which one has an ownership interest. The government sanctions property rights by recognizing the rights of individuals to private property ownership, and protects those rights by enacting and enforcing criminal statutes that make interfering with the property rights of others a punishable offense (e.g., theft, arson, criminal mischief), as well as by allowing individuals to use the courts to defend their property rights and to seek civil damages against those who interfere with them (e.g., actions in tort and contract).

Property can be divided into two basic types: real and personal. *Real property* essentially consists of land and anything permanently attached to it, while *personal property* consists of anything else that is capable of being owned. Personal property can be further divided into both *tangible* and *intangible* types. We have already been exposed to tangible personal property (also called *goods* and *chattels*) in our discussion of Article 2 of the Uniform Commercial Code covering the sale of goods. Intangible personal property, on the other hand, includes things which do not have physical existence, such as intellectual property (copyrights, patents, trademarks and the like), stocks, bonds, contract rights and commercial paper.

In this unit, we will explore both personal and real property rights, as well as the rights and responsibilities of parties incidental to owning, renting, borrowing and giving away real and personal property during the owner's life and after death.

# 25

# INTRODUCTION TO PERSONAL PROPERTY

As you are doubtless aware, nearly everything on earth is capable of being owned. Even at early common law, where all real property and wild animals in England were deemed to belong to the crown (which in turn could give parts of it to favored nobles as it saw fit), serfs were allowed limited rights to own personal property. Then, as now, there were five basic ways in which rights to personal property could be acquired: by possession, purchase, manufacture, *accession* (the adding of value to the property by one's labor) and gift. In this chapter, we will examine the creation and transfer of rights to both tangible and intangible personal property.

## ACQUIRING TITLE TO PERSONAL PROPERTY THROUGH POSSESSION · · · · · · · · · · · · · · · · · · · · · · · · · · · · · · ·

While the oft-repeated phrase, "Possession is nine-tenths of the law," is generally untrue, like most clichés it contains some truth, for possession alone can convey a property interest in at least two instances: the lawful killing or capture of wild animals and the finding of abandoned property.

### WILD ANIMALS

Under current personal property law, wild animals belong to no one while they are free. A wild animal can, however, become personal property if it is lawfully killed and retrieved by a hunter or lawfully trapped or captured alive. Thus, a hunter who kills a deer using an approved means and pursuant to a valid big-game hunting license owns the deer as soon as he or she takes possession of it. Likewise, fish swimming in a pond, river or ocean are subject to personal ownership if they are caught by an angler with a valid fishing license (if one is required). If fish or game are illegally killed or caught, however, ownership does not pass to the hunter or angler; rather, the ownership vests in the state. Thus, deer killed out of season by a hunter without a license or by a hunter using an unapproved weapon (e.g., a rifle in a jurisdiction that allows the taking of deer only by the use of a shotgun or a bow and arrow) or fish that do not meet the required size or weight all belong to the state. The same is generally true of game accidentally killed, such as a deer struck by an automobile; in most jurisdictions, the deer belongs to the state, but many states allow the driver of the auto that struck the animal to claim it for his or her own use if the motorist so desires.

A wild animal which is captured alive and then escapes is considered personal property only as long as it was in captivity; as soon as it regains its freedom, the property interest of its captor ends and the animal can become the property of anyone who ultimately kills and takes possession of it or recaptures it alive. Note too that the mere lawful killing of a wild animal does not convey a property interest; the animal becomes personal property only when the hunter takes possession of it. The traditional common-law rule holds that the person taking possession of a dead wild animal owns it, regardless of who killed it (as long as the killing was lawful and the person taking possession of the animal has a hunting license, if one is required). Keep in mind, however, that states are free to modify the traditional common law through judicial decisions or legislative enactments.

## ABANDONED PROPERTY

The finder of abandoned property obtains ownership of it by taking possession of the property. Property is deemed abandoned if its true owner clearly relinquishes the interest to such property through a clearly manifested intention to divest himself or herself of the property. A homeowner who puts an old television set by the curb next to the garbage for collection on the day that garbage is normally picked up, for example, has clearly abandoned the television set and it may be claimed by any passerby who takes it. In determining whether property is abandoned, the intent of the owner is of paramount importance; that property merely *appears* to be abandoned does not mean that it necessarily is. A wallet that falls into a wastebasket, for example, is not abandoned property, but rather qualifies as lost property, even though it might appear to be abandoned property to a person who later picks it out of the wastebasket. The same would be true of property placed by the curb for pickup as refuse or in a garbage pail by someone who does not own it; only the true owner can relinquish property rights to personal property. Whether or not property was actually abandoned by its true owner is a question of fact that must be resolved by the trier of fact if the issue is litigated at trial.

It is important to distinguish between abandoned property and lost or mislaid property for purposes of ownership by possession, for the finder of lost or mislaid property does *not* gain ownership of it. Mislaid property is property that the true owner purposely placed somewhere and then forgot to retrieve. Leaving a briefcase in a cab, for example, or forgetting a pocketbook at a restaurant table are both examples of mislaid property. Lost property, on the other hand, is property that the owner involuntarily lost custody of, by accident or negligence, and does not know where to find. A wallet dropped by accident in the middle of the street or a camera that drops inadvertently from the neck of its owner when the strap breaks are both examples of lost property. As we'll see in our discussion of bailments in Chapter 27, the finder of lost or mislaid property does not become its owner, but rather an involuntary bailee of it who has a responsibility to make a reasonable attempt to find its true owner. (See Figure 25.1 for a typical example of a statute that defines the rights and responsibilities of finders of lost property.)

## ACQUIRING TITLE TO PROPERTY THROUGH PURCHASE   . . . . . . . .

The most common means of acquiring both tangible and intangible personal property is through its purchase. As we've already seen from our discussion of the sale of goods, title to tangible personal property generally passes upon delivery of the property from the buyer to the seller pursuant to a sales contract. When you go to a bakery and pay for a loaf of Italian bread, you gain ownership over the bread as soon as it is handed to you by the bakery attendant and you pay for it. The same is true for any other tangible or intangible property. once property is delivered and paid for pursuant to a binding agreement for its sale, the item's ownership passes from the seller to the buyer, and the buyer acquires whatever ownership interest the seller had to give. This is true whether a cash, credit or barter transaction is involved. If an electrician agrees to purchase a painter's painting in exchange for wiring the painter's home, title to the painting will pass as soon as it is turned over to the electrician, subject to the electrician's keeping her end of the bargain and properly wiring the painter's home. The same would be true if the electrician paid $500 in cash for the painting, gave a check for $500 for it or charged the painting on her Visa or MasterCard.

When title is acquired through purchase, the purchaser acquires exactly whatever title the seller had to give; thus, if the seller is a thief, the purchaser will generally acquire no title to the goods (one exception is goods sold by a merchant to whom the goods were entrusted by the true owner, as we'll see in the next chapter in our discussion of bailments). The general rule is that a seller passes exactly the title he or she has to the goods being sold; since a thief has no title to the goods sold, he or she passes no title to them.

## ACQUIRING TITLE TO PERSONAL PROPERTY
## THROUGH MANUFACTURING  . . . . . . . . . . . . . . . . . . . . . . . . . . .

The act of creation conveys a property interest in the creator in the fruits of his labor. Thus, a person who combines paint and paper to manufacture a painting owns the painting; likewise, a person who writes a poem or the lyrics or music to a song acquires an ownership interest in these intangible intellectual properties. If goods are manufactured with materials not owned by the manufacturer, however, then ownership will not vest in the creator but rather will remain with the owner of the materials used by the

While traditional wisdom may hold that the finder of lost property may keep it for his or her own use, the law has never supported that point of view. Ownership rights to personal property can be transferred only through one of the traditional means discussed in this chapter and are not lost through the negligence of the owner who negligently leaves behind or inadvertently drops personal property. From early common law, the finder of lost or mislaid property had a legal duty to make some effort to find the true owner of the property, and was held to be holding the property as a bailee or caretaker for the true owner until the owner could be found. The finder of lost property could use the property after conducting a reasonable search for its true owner, but had to return it should the true owner show up in the future and claim the property. Both at common law and today, one who finds lost or mislaid property and immediately puts it to his or her own use without a reasonable effort to find the true owner is guilty of a crime (theft) and a tort (conversion).

Many states have codified the responsibility of the finder of lost property into a statute. In New York, such a statute can be found in Article 7-B of the Personal Property Law. Under the statute, the finder of property must take one of the following steps, depending upon the value of the property found:

- Property worth under $10: The finder of such property must make a reasonable effort to find its true owner. If the search is unsuccessful, title to the property vests in the finder after one year from the date that the property was found.
- Property worth $10 or more and commercial paper: The finder of such property must find the property's true owner within ten days or turn over the property to police, who will then have the responsibility of finding its true owners. If police cannot find the true owners and the property is unclaimed, title will vest in the finder after a period of time that varies with the value of the property as follows:

  For property worth less than $100, in three months;
  For property worth $100 to $500, in six months;
  For property worth $500 to $5,000, in one year; and
  For property worth more than $5,000, in three years.

**FIGURE 25.1**   Finders Keepers?

person who created the new substance. If, for example, a thief steals lumber and other building supplies from a construction site and uses them to construct a house on his land, the thief will *not* obtain title to the finished home despite the fact that he manufactured it; rather, the title to the house (if it can be moved from the land) or to its value (if it cannot) will remain with the true owner of the building supplies.

## ACQUIRING TITLE TO PERSONAL PROPERTY
## THROUGH ACCESSION · · · · · · · · · · · · · · · · · · · · · · · · · · · ·

*Accession* can be defined as an increase to the value of property one owns through either one's own input or some external force. For example, if you purchase an old, unseaworthy boat for $50 and restore it into a splendid vessel worth $5,000, the boat will have $4,950 added to its value and your property will have benefited from an accession brought about by your work. Likewise, if you own a cow that becomes pregnant, you will own the calf it eventually bears and the milk it produces. This may all be obvious, but the issue of who owns property that benefits from an accession can become clouded when the property of one person is improved—either willfully or through a mistake—by the work of another.

   Whenever accession is made by one person to the property of another, the question of who should benefit from the accession depends upon the surrounding circumstances. When the accession is made by one person in bad faith, with the knowledge that the property belongs to another, the property in its improved form belongs to the true owner and there is no need to compensate the person who added to its value. Thus, a thief who paints a stolen car and puts a new engine in it will not be compensated by the car's true owner for the value added to the vehicle. When the accession is innocently made, which is to say under circumstances when the person adding value to another's property did so in good faith, under a mistaken assumption as to the ownership of the property or the owner's intention to abandon it, the person making the accession is entitled to compensation by the true owner of the property. In most instances, the true owner is entitled to keep the property but must return either the improvement to the property or its reasonable value. In cases where the property is transformed from its original form into something of far superior value because of the accession, the person who innocently transformed the property is entitled to keep it but must pay its true owner the reasonable value of the property in its original form. The following examples will illustrate:

* *Elizabeth, an artist, finds a very bad oil painting in front of Elijah's house and, believing that he intends to throw it out, takes it home with her. She then sets to work on it and imbues the painting with new life—and a new aesthetic and material value. When Elijah learns of Elizabeth's mistake, he demands that she return the painting and claims that the accession she has caused to his property rightfully belongs to him. Elizabeth counters that the painting belongs to her, since she acted in good faith and reasonably believed the painting had been abandoned.*

* *Elizabeth, an artist, sees a painting hanging in Elijah's living room of the type created in assembly-line fashion that are sometimes sold in shopping malls and department stores. She finds the painting so bad as to be offensive and an insult to art lovers the world over. She rips it down from the wall in disgust and (without Elijah's knowledge or consent) takes it home and paints over it with fresh oils, transforming a $50 eyesore into a $5,000 work of art. When Elijah learns of Elizabeth's actions, he demands that she turn over his painting, claiming that the accession to it rightfully belongs to him. Elizabeth refuses to turn over her artwork, but offers to pay him the $50 his original oil painting was worth.*

In the first example, Elizabeth innocently transforms the painting into something of great value. Because the accession was done in good faith and under the reasonable belief that the painting had been abandoned, Elizabeth may keep the painting but must pay Elijah whatever the original painting was worth. In the second example, however, Elizabeth acts with the knowledge that the painting belongs to Elijah and is, therefore, not entitled to any compensation for its accession.

## ACQUIRING TITLE TO PERSONAL PROPERTY THROUGH A GIFT  · · · · · · · · · · · · · · · · · · · · · · · · · · · · · ·

The final means by which title can be obtained to personal property is by being the recipient of a gift. In order for title to personal property to pass by gift, the following criteria must be met:

- the giver of the gift (the *donor*) must intend to part with the property for the benefit of the receiver (the *donee*) out of detached, disinterested generosity;
- there must be a delivery of the property from the donor of the gift to the donee; and
- there must be an acceptance of the gift by the donee.

In order for the donor to have the requisite state of mind to make a gift, he or she must have the legal capacity to dispose of property and must make the gift with no strings attached. With regard to the competence of the donor, the same rules apply as do to contracts; gifts by judicially declared incompetents are void, while gifts by minors or persons with diminished capacity who have not been adjudged incompetent are voidable. If the donor expects to receive some consideration in return for making the "gift," then there is no valid gift, but rather a contract, and standard contract law applies to the transaction.

The requirement of delivery normally entails the physical transfer of the property from the donor to the donee either directly or through an agent (such as delivery by messenger or common carrier). In cases where physical delivery is impossible or impractical, a valid constructive delivery can be made by the donor's taking some affirmative step to deliver either the property itself or the means of obtaining the property to the donee. For example, if a donor wishes to make a gift to the donee of a gold watch that is in the donor's safety deposit box in a bank, giving the donee the key to the safety deposit box along with written authorization to the bank to allow the donee access to the safety deposit box would construe a valid constructive delivery of the watch itself. Likewise, giving the keys and signed title to a car by a donor to the donee constitutes constructive delivery of the automobile, regardless of where the automobile itself is located at the time that the keys and title are transferred. Acceptance of a gift by the donee requires words or actions that clearly and unequivocally evidence the intent to accept the gift.

### *INTER VIVOS* GIFTS

When the subject matter of the gift is transferred during the lifetime of the donor to the donee, the transfer is termed an *inter vivos* gift (a gift between the living). *Inter vivos* gifts are generally irrevocable. Thus, when a donor with the intention of making a gift delivers it to the donee and the donee accepts it, the gift is complete and the title to the property passes from the donor to the donee. Once the transfer is effectuated, the donor cannot change his or her mind and recall the property, for it no longer belongs to the donor. The donor can, however, change his or her mind at any time before all three conditions to a valid gift are met.

Since a valid *inter vivos* gift requires an intention to make a valid gift by the giver, gifts that are the product of undue influence or fraud or are made by a person without the capacity to enter into a contract are voidable at the option of the giver.

### *CAUSA MORTIS* GIFTS

A *causa mortis* gift is one made during the donor's lifetime in contemplation of death. When a *causa mortis* gift is involved, the donor intends to make a gift only out of fear that he or she is about to die. Such a gift is valid, but, unlike a normal *inter vivos* gift, is revocable by the donor if he or she does not die of the cause he or she contemplates dying from at the time of making the gift. A typical *causa mortis* gift would include a person who is about to undergo surgery giving a ring to a loved one and saying, "I want you to have this ring now, since I fear I'll die during the operation." If the person dies, the gift is effective. If the person survives the operation, however, he or she can reclaim the gift from the donee within a reasonable time of recovery.

### TESTAMENTARY GIFTS

A *testamentary* gift is one which the donor intends not to take effect until after his or her death. Unlike *inter vivos* gifts, which require no specific formalities as long as they meet the three criteria for a valid gift, testamentary gifts are typically made through a will and must conform to the formalities for such instruments. (We'll discuss wills in detail in Chapter 31.) Testamentary gifts are revocable during the lifetime of the *testator* or *testatrix* (the man or woman, respectively, who drafts a will in order to make testamentary gifts to take effect upon his or her death).

## QUESTIONS    . . . . . . . . . . . . . . . . . . . . . . . . . . . . . . . . . . . . . . . .

1. How does one obtain title to wild animals?
2. To whom does a deer killed out of season by a poacher belong?
3. How does one obtain title to abandoned property?
4. Does the finder of lost or mislaid property automatically become its owner?
5. What is accession?
6. What is an *inter vivos* gift?

7. What are the three requirements that must be met for a valid *inter vivos* gift?

8. What is a *causa mortis* gift?

9. Are either *causa mortis* gifts or *inter vivos* gifts revocable? If so, under what circumstances?

10. What are testamentary gifts?

# H Y P O T H E T I C A L    C A S E S

1. Andrea, Andy and Althea notice a bunny while walking in the woods. Andrea immediately yells out, "I'm gonna get that rabbit and make a couple of lucky rabbit's feet!" Andy cries out, "Over my dead body! I saw it first and I'm gonna grab it and have it stuffed!" Althea exclaims, "I'll brain the first idiot who lays a hand on that adorable bunny! I want it for a pet!" The three then run toward the poor bunny, which tries its best to elude them. Andrea catches it first, loudly proclaiming her victory; but the bunny bites her thumb and she drops it unharmed. Andy grabs at the poor creature next and tries to stuff it in his pocket, but drops it when Althea tackles him from behind. Althea then grabs at the bunny and manages to capture and hold it, taking it home with great care. Andrea and Andy, nursing their bruises and egos, solemnly vow revenge. Andrea and Andy both sue Althea for the return of the bunny that they claim rightfully belongs to them. Assume that rabbits are considered pests in the state where all this occurred and that there are no laws relating to the killing or live taking of rabbits. Whose bunny is it, anyway? Explain.

2. Michael buys an auto from Terry for $500. Unknown to him, the auto was stolen by a thief who had sold it to Terry six months earlier. Michael buys and installs a $500 sound system for the car and spends 100 hours of his time and $50 in materials to restore the automobile. By the time he is finished, the car is worth $5,000. On the first day that he puts the car on the road, its true owner appears and claims the car. Michael claims that the car rightfully belongs to him, since he was a good-faith purchaser of the automobile and paid its fair market price for it. The case ends up in small-claims court and you are the judge. Decide this case and justify your decision with sound legal reasoning.

3. Assume the same facts as in the previous case, except that Michael installs a $500 sound system and does no other work to the car before the owner surfaces and claims the vehicle. What result?

4. George purchases a thirty-five-inch color television set for his friend Gina and has it shipped to her home as a surprise gift. On the day that the set is to be delivered, George has a falling out with Gina and tells her, "I had bought a large-screen TV as a birthday gift for you that was supposed to be delivered today, but I've changed my mind and I'm going to have the delivery canceled." Gina immediately retorts, "Too late, I accept your gift."
   a. Can George cancel the delivery, or is he too late to rescind the gift? Explain.

b. If the television set had already been delivered and accepted by Gina before the falling out and George stopped payment on the check he'd used to pay for the set, would the gift be revoked?

## ETHICS AND THE LAW: QUESTIONS FOR FURTHER STUDY    . . . . . . .

The law requires the finder of lost or mislaid property to make a reasonable search for its true owner or risk prosecution for theft, regardless of the value of the item that is lost. In addition, there is no requirement that the finder be compensated by the true owner when the item is claimed (other than for any reasonable expenses incurred in relation to the care of the item or advertisements relating to its loss). This imposes an arguably unfair burden on finders of lost property and might even encourage persons who find the property to refuse to pick it up so as not to have to fulfill the legal obligation of searching for the property's true owner. Should the law force the true owner of lost or mislaid property to compensate the finder for the reasonable value of the finder's services in attempting to locate the owner? Might this encourage persons who find lost or mislaid goods to turn them in to police or attempt to search for the property's true owners? Aren't we in fact encouraging persons who find such property to keep it and break the law by giving them no incentive to "do the right thing"? What do you think?

# CHAPTER

# 26

# INTELLECTUAL PROPERTY

As we've already seen in the last chapter, the very act of creation can convey a property interest to the creator in the object of his or her creation. This is true for tangible personal property, such as manufactured goods, as well as for intangible personal property, such as an inventor's idea, a writer's work or an actor's performance. In the eyes of the law, a wordsmith's work is as much worthy of protection as a silversmith's creations. But intellectual property is harder to protect against theft and infringement than is tangible personal property. It is easier to prove interference with tangible property rights than with intangible ones. For instance, if a carpenter's creation, say a chair, is stolen, damaged or used by another without the carpenter's consent, the carpenter will have relatively little trouble proving the infringement. But a songwriter whose song or music is stolen or inappropriately "borrowed" by another who claims it to be his or her own creation will have a harder time making a case. Interference with intangible property rights is often easily accomplished and difficult to trace. Indeed, most people infringe on other's intangible property rights on a regular basis, often unaware that they are doing so. Copying commercial software from a friend, giving someone a tape of a favorite compact disc and using the ideas of others in term papers or other writing without giving credit all constitute unlawful interference with intangible property rights. In this chapter, we will examine the basic laws that protect intellectual property rights in the United States in the form of patents, copyrights, trademarks and service marks.

The U.S. Constitution gives to Congress in Article I, Section 8, the power to "promote the Progress of Science and useful Arts, by securing for limited Times to Authors and Inventors the exclusive Right to their respective Writings and Discoveries." Congress has secured these rights through appropriate legislation and the creation of the U.S. Patent and Trademark Office to regulate the issuance of patents, copyrights, trademarks and service marks in accordance with congressional guidelines.

## PATENTS

A *patent* is an exclusive right granted to an inventor by the federal government to profit from the use of his or her invention for a period of seventeen years. During the seventeen-year period that the inventor alone is given the exclusive right to exploit the invention covered by the patent, the patent itself is deemed intangible personal property; as such, it can be sold, given away or leased to anyone the inventor chooses for whatever consideration is mutually agreed upon. After the patent expires, the invention becomes public domain and may be used by anyone without the need to compensate the inventor.

In order to qualify for patenting, the subject matter for which a patent is sought must be new and must not infringe on any other existing patent. While most patents involve some type of device, it is also possible to patent new chemical substances, such as a new drug or a better lubricant. New compositions of matter, such as genetically engineered microorganisms with special properties, are also patentable. Novel manufacturing techniques or processes are also patentable provided they are both new and useful. For example, if a better process for extracting sap from maple trees in order to make maple syrup were discovered, the process could be patented, as could a new method of extracting oil from shale rock.

Application for a patent is made to the U.S. Patent and Trademark Office. In his or her application, the inventor must show how the invention works, including detailed technical drawings and other supporting evidence of how the device can be manufactured, as well as provide a narrative detailing the novelty and usefulness of the object that make it worthy of patenting.

Upon the grant of a patent, the inventor is protected from any infringement during the patent's useful life. Any unauthorized use of the patented idea by a third party will result in a valid civil suit for damages by the inventor against the infringing party, regardless of the infringer's good faith or lack of actual knowledge of the existence of the patent. If the infringement is malicious, a court is empowered to award both actual damages (such as lost royalties) as well as punitive damages equal to three times the actual damages caused by the infringement, as well as court costs and attorneys' fees if the judge deems it appropriate. Where patent infringement is not malicious, but rather caused by negligence or ignorance of the infringer, the typical damages awarded are a reasonable royalty for use of the inventor's patent.

## COPYRIGHTS

The Federal Copyright Act provides protection to authors of literary, dramatic, musical, choreographic and artistic works, including motion pictures and other audiovisual works. The act is very broad in scope and is intended to cover any original work or authorship, regardless of the medium. The act also includes computer software (both electronic programs and written program listings).

Any qualifying work can be *copyrighted* by registering with the U.S. Patent and Trademark Office in Washington, D.C., but registration is not necessary in order to invoke copyright protection. A work is deemed copyrighted as soon as it is expressed in some tangible form, such as by writing it down or typing it into a computer. Nevertheless, it is a good idea to formally register copyrighted work one deems important because it adds a measure of protection in the event of a future dispute as to the origination date of the work.

Copyright protection lasts throughout the author's life and for an additional fifty years after the author's death. During the copyright period, the author (and his or her estate for fifty years after the author's life) has the exclusive right to reproduce the work or to make any derivative works based on it. Authors are also entitled to royalty payments upon public use of copyrighted works, such as the broadcasting of a song or music video over the airwaves or the public performance of a play.

Limited *fair use* of copyrighted work for educational purposes can be made without constituting copyright infringement, as well as for news reporting and literary criticism. To qualify as fair use, the portion of the copyrighted work must be relatively small and not unduly infringe on the work as a whole. For example, quoting from one page of a novel for purposes of literary criticism or copying one article from a newspaper for classroom distribution are allowed under fair use. But if the amount of material used is excessive, a copyright infringement occurs. In determining whether a specific instance of alleged copyright infringement is covered by the fair use doctrine, and is thus exempt from liability, the courts perform a balancing test between the author's right to profit from his or her work and the educational or literary value of the infringement. Courts in recent years have shown decreasing tolerance for allowing a fair-use exception to copyright infringement actions, even in not-for-profit educational settings.

# TRADEMARKS

A *trademark* is any symbol, picture, design or words adopted by a manufacturer to distinguish its products from other similar products in the market. In order to be capable of being registered with the U.S. Patent and Trademark Office, a trademark must be unique and cannot be a generic name. Product names, such as *Coca-Cola* and *Coke*, can be registered trademarks, as well as slogans adopted to identify a product ("the real thing" relating to Coke, for example). But the generic words *Cola* or *Soda*, by themselves, cannot be trademarks, since they are not unique but rather descriptive of a type of product. Company logos and graphic designs are also capable of being registered trademarks. Thus, *7-Up* and *the Uncola* are trademarks for the well-known soft drink, and so is the red dot used by the soft-drink maker in its advertising and as part of its product's name. Likewise, the distinctive design in product labels can be covered by a trademark.

When a trademark is registered, it may be contested by any company which claims an infringement of its own trademark for a period of five years. If a new trademark is not contested within that time period, it becomes incontestable. Once issued, a registered trademark is valid for a period of ten years, but may be renewed at the expiration of each ten-year period upon a showing that the trademark is still in use by the registrant and has not been abandoned. Application to renew a trademark must be made within three months of its expiration. In addition, evidence that a trademark is still in use by its registered holder must be furnished after six years of its first being issued. Like all personal property, a trademark may be sold or assigned by its owner.

## SERVICE MARKS, CERTIFICATION MARKS AND COLLECTIVE MARKS . . . . . . . . . . . . . . . . . . . . . . . . . . . . . . . .

Service marks, certification marks and collective marks are closely related to trademarks and treated in exactly the same way for purposes of registration and renewal. A *service mark* is any distinctive mark used by a service industry for purposes of advertising or sales. The radio and television network designations of ABC, NBC, CBS and Fox, for example, are all service marks, as are the CBS eye symbol, and the NBC peacock. Likewise, the symbols used by book publishers along with their names on book spines, such as Bantam Books' rooster, Random House's home symbol and Prentice Hall's walking man, are also service marks.

*Certification marks*, on the other hand, are specific words or symbols adopted by a group of companies or government agencies to denote the quality, origin or some other attribute relating to the goods. Typical certification marks include USDA Choice, UL (Underwriter's Laboratories) Approved, and the Union Label attached to goods manufactured in the United States by union workers.

*Collective marks* are trademarks or service marks used by members of collective groups, cooperatives or associations such as labor unions and trade associations to denote membership in the group.

## REMEDIES FOR INFRINGEMENT OF A REGISTERED MARK . . . . . . .

It is an infringement of a registered mark to reproduce such a mark or an imitation of such a mark, without the consent of the registrant, by any means for a commercial purpose whenever doing so would tend to confuse or deceive the public as to the genuineness of the goods involved. This means not only that third parties cannot misappropriate the registered mark (trademark, service mark or certification mark) of another, but also that even a misleading approximation of such a mark cannot be used for commercial purposes if the public may be misled as to the identity of the goods. So that not only can't a new soft drink maker use the name *Pepsi-Cola* or any registered mark associated with the nationally known soft drink, but it can't even use a name or adopt a logo that is close enough to confuse the general public. *Peppy Cola*, for example, *might* be an allowable trade name for such a drink, but if the manufacturers adopt a lettering style or can design that approximates Pepsi's own trademarks, it would constitute trademark infringement. Whether a particular trade name or trademark is sufficiently similar to the existing registered marks of a product is a question of fact for the trier of fact to determine.

The damages allowable for infringement of a registered mark vary, depending on the nature of the infringement. Where an infringement is innocently made by a printer who manufactures literature, packaging or any other material to be used in the sale or marketing of the product, the only remedy available against the printer is an injunction to prevent it from continuing to create such infringing material. Injunctive relief is likewise the only remedy available against a television station, newspaper or other medium which innocently runs commercials containing infringing material. Where the infringement is intentional, however, and made for the purpose of confusing or deceiving the public, the party that suffers an infringement of a registered mark may not only be awarded injunctive relief, but may also recover any profits made by the infringer from the infringement, as well as any damages sustained by the holder of the infringed registered mark as a result of the infringement. *Treble damages* (three times the actual damages or the infringer's actual profits made from the infringement) may also be awarded, as well as court costs and attorneys' fees.

# TRADE SECRETS

*Trade secrets* include business plans, mechanisms, manufacturing techniques and compiled data that give a business an advantage over its competitors. Although some trade secrets, such as formulas for the manufacture of products, could be patented, they often are not, in order to extend the useful life of the formula and to keep it secret. If, for example, the formula for making Coca Cola were patented, its ingredients would be a part of the public record and would give the company only a seventeen-year monopoly on its manufacture. By maintaining a formula as a trade secret, the company can maintain its monopoly over the manufacture of a given product indefinitely or until its competitors can duplicate the formula themselves. Likewise, customer lists and other information vital to the running of a business are considered trade secrets.

The significance of trade secrets is that they are protected in two ways. First, employees who have access to such information are under an obligation not to divulge it and can be enjoined from doing so, as well as sued for breach of their *fiduciary duty* (duty of loyalty and utmost good faith) to their employer if they do. Second, because trade secrets are considered personal property of a company, any illegal access to or interference with such secret information is both a crime and a tort and carries criminal as well as civil liability. If the information contained in a trade secret is discovered through lawful means, however, the discoverer is free to use it. If a new company stumbles upon another's secret manufacturing techniques or formulas by chance or by its own independent research into the product, it is free to use those formulas or manufacturing techniques itself unless they are covered by a patent.

# QUESTIONS

1. What is a patent?
2. What government office is in charge of granting patents?
3. Can a state grant patents?

4. Are sculptures, paintings, photographs and choreographed dances protected by copyright? Explain.
5. How does a work become copyrighted?
6. How long does copyright protection last?
7. What is a trademark?
8. What is a service mark?
9. What are certification marks?
10. How long do registered marks (trademarks, service marks, certification marks, and collective marks) last?

# H Y P O T H E T I C A L    C A S E S

1. Imalia Inventor invents the proverbial better mousetrap. She promptly begins its manufacture in her garage and starts selling the mousetraps to local businesses and private individuals through a direct-marketing campaign. Sales are brisk and she soon turns her invention into a profitable business that catches the attention of other mousetrap manufacturers throughout the world. Within six months, mousetraps identical to hers flood the market at a much lower price and drive her out of business. Furious at this injustice, she wants to sue for patent infringement and for interference with trade secrets. What result?

2. Wanda Writer compiles a book of her poetry as well as a rough draft of a novel using her computer. She never prints the material because she considers it a work in progress, preferring to do all revisions on her computer. Every week, she performs a backup of the material onto two floppy disks. When the work is completed, she takes the disks to work, intending to use her laser printer to print the material out to send to selected publishers for their consideration. On her way to work, however, she has her purse stolen by a thief in the subway. The thief keeps her valuables, but throws the disks away, having no need of these. They are later found by chance by an English professor who is impressed with the work and, unable to determine its rightful owner, publishes the novel in his own name and copies two of the 100 poems for distribution in his class. Wanda eventually learns of the professor's actions and decides to sue him for copyright infringement both for the publication of the novel in his own name and for the unauthorized use of her poetry in the classroom. What result on both claims? Explain fully.

3. The makers of a new toothpaste called West launch their new product on the market with a heavy ad campaign in newspapers, magazines and television stations across the nation. The ads feature a western theme that revolves around cowboys, gunfighters and similar characters endorsing the product. While the commercials are unique, the packaging and lettering of the toothpaste is very similar to another leading dentifrice, Crest. Based upon these facts, answer the following questions:
   a. Does there seem to be a trademark infringement here? What will the makers of Crest need to show in order to succeed in a trademark infringement action?

b. Assuming that the lettering and designs are found to infringe on Crest's registered trademark, what damages should be assessed against the manufacturer of West toothpaste?

c. What damages can the makers of Crest seek against the media for running the infringing commercials?

4. A food-service company invents an artificial sweetener that tastes exactly like sugar, has no calories and is cheaper than sugar to produce. The company seeks a patent for its new invention and begins manufacturing the new product. Answer the following questions based upon these facts.

a. If the company wants to register the product under the name *Sugar*, will it succeed?

b. Assume that the company obtains a registered trademark for the product under the name *Natural Sweet*. Six years later, when the product has captured a 90 percent share of the artificial sweetener market, a competitor sues for trademark infringement, claiming that the product is too closely linked to its own trademark, both in the name and in the appearance of the lettering in the registered trademark's logo. Assume that both of these allegations are true. What result?

c. Eighteen years after the introduction of the product into the market, a competitor clones the product and markets it under its own trademark. The inventor of the product sues to protect its product, claiming both an infringement of its patent and a violation of its valuable trade secrets by the appropriation of its formula. What result?

# CHAPTER

# 27

# BAILMENTS

In the previous two chapters, we discussed ownership interests to personal property. In this chapter, we will explore the rights and responsibilities of parties to personal property that is transferred by an owner to a third party for temporary custody.

## INTRODUCTION TO BAILMENTS

When possession of personal property is transferred by its true owner to a third party for temporary custody with the understanding that the property must be returned to its true owner at some time in the future, a *bailment* occurs. The owner of the property who gives over custody of it to a third party is called the *bailor*, and the person to whom custody of goods is temporarily entrusted is called the *bailee*. In order for a valid bailment to occur, personal property (either tangible or intangible) must be involved, and the following must occur:

- there must be a transfer of property from the bailor to the bailee;
- the transfer must be of a temporary nature with the understanding that the bailed property will be returned to the bailor in the future;
- there must be a willful acceptance of the bailed property by the bailee.

When these conditions are met, a bailment arises that conveys certain rights and obligations to the parties involved that depend in part on the type of bailment involved. The three basic types of bailments that parties can enter into are (1) bailments for the sole benefit of the bailor, (2) bailments for the sole benefit of the bailee and (3) mutual-benefit bailments.

### BAILMENTS FOR THE SOLE BENEFIT OF THE BAILOR

A bailment for the sole benefit of the bailor, as the name implies, is one which benefits only the bailor (owner) of the bailed property. This type of bailment is *gratuitous* (the bailee is not paid for his services and derives no benefit from the bailment) and places on the bailee only a slight duty of care with regard to the bailed goods. When this type of bailment is involved, the bailee is not responsible for any damage or loss of the bailor's property unless the bailee was grossly negligent in caring for it or damages the property himself or herself.

A bailment for the sole benefit of the bailor typically occurs in situations where the bailor asks the bailee as a favor to temporarily look after his or her property. Each of the following situations entails a bailment for the sole benefit of the bailor:

- Sam asks Samantha to keep an eye on his books in the student cafeteria while he goes to the men's room.
- Pam asks Peter to hold her camera and snap her picture.
- Bernard asks Beatrice to keep an eye on several bags of groceries while he goes to get his car from the parking lot.

Each of these situations involves the bailee doing a favor for the bailor. Since the bailee is not deriving any benefit from the bailment, his or her duty of care with regard to the bailed goods is slight. In these examples, the bailees would not be responsible for any theft or damage to the bailed goods unless they themselves stole or damaged them or unless they were grossly negligent with regard to their care for the goods. In all three instances, leaving the goods completely unattended would constitute gross negligence, as would moving so far away from the goods as to be unable to watch them. As long as the three bailees stayed within a reasonable distance from the goods and made some effort to watch them, they would not be responsible for their loss or theft should the goods be stolen or damaged by a third party. Note, too, that the bailment in the examples will not arise unless the bailees agree to look after the goods. Thus, if Cindy asks Chuck to look after her pocketbook while she goes to the women's room and leaves before he agrees to do so by his word or deed, no bailment occurs and Chuck has absolutely no responsibility with regard to the pocketbook.

## BAILMENTS FOR THE SOLE BENEFIT OF THE BAILEE

A bailment for the sole benefit of the bailee is also a gratuitous bailment from which only the bailee derives a benefit. However, unlike bailments for the sole benefit of the bailor, where the bailee's duty of care is slight, the bailee's duty of care with regard to the bailed goods in a bailment for the sole benefit of the bailee is great. In such a bailment, the bailee has an absolute duty to ensure the safety and integrity of the bailed goods and will be liable to the bailor for any damage to them while they are in his or her care, no matter how slight the damage or that it could not have been prevented by the bailee. In other words, bailees in bailments for the sole benefit of the bailee are strictly liable for any damage to the bailed goods. Common examples of such bailments include the following:

- Henry borrows Hannah's automobile to go on a shopping trip.
- Martha borrows Muhammad's camcorder to tape her daughter's wedding.
- Ranji borrows Rhoda's boat to go on a fishing trip.

## MUTUAL-BENEFIT BAILMENTS

A mutual-benefit bailment is one in which both the bailor and bailee derive some legal benefit from the bailment of the goods involved. Typical mutual-benefit bailments include (but are not limited to) rental agreements involving personal property. When such bailments are involved, one person typically pays money to another in exchange for the temporary use of the other's personal property. But money need not be the consideration given by the bailee; anything of legal value given by the bailee as consideration for being allowed to use the bailed property will suffice to make the bailment one of mutual benefit. Thus, the routine car-rental and videotape-rental agreements clearly involve mutual-benefit bailments, but so do the following situations:

- Liv borrows Lenny's power saw to work on a home construction project with the understanding that she will buy Lenny three new blades for the saw when she returns it.
- Pamela agrees to look after Pascuale's car while he goes on a two-month vacation abroad in exchange for being allowed to use the car during that time period.
- Teresa allows Tai to borrow her snowblower during the winter in exchange for Tai's agreement to clear her driveway after every snowstorm.

The duty of care involved in a mutual benefit bailment is one of reasonable care under the circumstances. To put it another way, the duty of care for such bailments is greater than that of bailments for the sole benefit of the bailor, but not as great as that of bailments for the sole benefit of the bailee. In practical terms, this means that ordinary wear and tear with regard to the bailed goods is permissible in such bailments, but the bailee has a duty to take reasonable care of the bailed property and is responsible for any damage above reasonable wear and tear that could have been prevented through reasonable care of the bailed goods. As always, what is reasonable care under the circumstances is a question of fact to be determined by the trier of facts.

## BAILOR'S RIGHTS AND DUTIES  . . . . . . . . . . . . . . . . . . . . . . . . . .

Bailors in all bailments have certain rights and responsibilities arising from the bailment. The principal rights of bailors include the right to have the property returned by the bailee when the bailment ends and the right to receive the agreed-upon consideration from the bailee for the bailment (unless, of course, a gratuitous bailment is involved). The responsibilities of the bailor, on the other hand, include turning over the bailed property to the bailee as agreed and either warning the bailee of any known defects in the property that might cause injury or other loss to the bailee. The duty to warn the bailee depends in part on the nature of the bailment. Where bailments for the sole benefit of the bailee are involved, the duty of the bailor to warn the bailee extends only to known hidden defects in the goods of which he or she is aware and which would not be obvious to the bailee. When mutual-benefit bailments are involved, the bailor is responsible for warning the bailee not only of any known defects, but also of any defect which the bailee *could* have discovered through a reasonable inspection. The bailor must also indemnify the bailee for any reasonably necessary expense incurred in the care of the goods while in the bailee's possession.

## BAILEE'S RIGHTS AND DUTIES · · · · · · · · · · · · · · · · · · · · · · · · ·

The bailee has the right to possess the bailed property and, if the bailment agreement so provides, to use it during the term of the bailment. The bailee also has the right to be indemnified for any reasonable cost incurred with respect to caring for the property, and for any injury he or she sustains as a result of the bailor's failure to warn him or her of defects in the bailed property. The bailee's duties with regard to the bailed property include caring for it in accordance with the nature of the bailment and returning the bailed property to the bailor at the end of the bailment.

## LIMITATIONS OF RIGHTS AND DUTIES
## OF PARTIES TO BAILMENTS · · · · · · · · · · · · · · · · · · · · · · · · · · ·

Parties to bailments are generally free to limit or alter their respective rights and duties through their contractual agreement. The express agreement between the parties will control with regard to their rights and responsibilities. Contractual provisions that limit or increase the responsibility of one or both parties are generally enforceable as long as they are not unconscionable and as long as they are freely agreed to by both parties. Waiver-of-liability clauses by bailees, for example, are generally binding, as are clauses imposing strict liability on bailees for damage to the bailed goods. Thus, a bailment agreement concerning an automobile which is entrusted to a parking attendant at a garage can limit the liability of the garage for loss or injury to the vehicle or its contents which is not caused by garage employees. For such a waiver to be valid, however, the bailor must be made aware of it at the time of the bailment. If no notice of the waiver is given but rather is included on the back of the parking stub in small print, the waiver would be invalid. But if there are legible signs stating the garage's waiver of liability that are clearly visible to the bailor at the time that he or she entrusts the car to the garage, the waiver would be valid.

## SPECIAL BAILMENTS · · · · · · · · · · · · · · · · · · · · · · · · · · · · · · ·

Certain types of bailments are treated differently with regard to the bailee's liability for goods entrusted to his or her care, making the bailee strictly liable for damage or loss of such goods. The most common types of special bailments involve common carriers and innkeepers. A *common carrier* is any company in the business of transporting people or cargo that offers its services to the general public, while *innkeepers* include all companies in the hospitality industry providing lodging services. Whenever a special bailment is involved, the bailee is strictly liable for theft, loss or damage to bailed goods regardless of the level of care it extended in caring for the goods or the lack of fault in their loss. Innkeepers are generally strictly liable for the personal property of their guests in the hotel's premises, as are common carriers for the property of passengers and the goods it ships. Restaurants, on the other hand, are liable only for the property of guests specifically placed in the restaurant's care, as through a coat check; restaurant guests who hang their own clothing in a restaurant area provided for that purpose, however, do so at their own risk since the property is not entrusted to a restaurant employee. At common law, the liability of the special carrier was absolute, regardless of the value of the bailed goods; today, the liability has been limited by federal and state legislation to a set dollar amount in most cases. In addition, hotels may limit their liability for guests' property by providing a safe in which guests may place their valuables and advising their guests of the availability of the safe.

## CONSTRUCTIVE BAILMENTS

Although bailments require that the owner of personal property willfully give up control of the property and place it in the hands of the bailee for his or her temporary control, and likewise require the acceptance of the bailed property by the bailee, there are times when the courts will treat property in the hands of a person who does not own it as a constructive bailment. A *constructive bailment* is a legal fiction used by the courts to hold persons who have property lawfully belonging to others in their possession responsible for the reasonable care of such property. Finders of lost or mislaid property, for example are constructive bailees of the property until the true owner can be found or until ownership to the property passes to them by operation of law. Likewise, thieves and embezzlers are also held to be constructive bailees of the property they wrongfully possess. In much the same vein, a person who mistakenly takes the property of another thinking it his or her own is also a constructive bailee of that property until he or she returns it to its true owner.

## QUESTIONS

1. What is a bailment?
2. What are the necessary criteria for a bailment to arise?
3. What is a bailment for the sole benefit of the bailor?
4. What is a bailment for the sole benefit of the bailee?
5. What is the duty of care for the bailee in a mutual-benefit bailment? A bailment for the sole benefit of the bailor? A bailment for the sole benefit of the bailee?
6. What are the principal rights of the bailor with regard to bailed property?
7. What are the principal rights of the bailee with regard to bailed property?
8. What are the two most common types of special bailments?
9. What is the significance of a special bailment?
10. What are innkeepers? What is an innkeeper's liability for bailed goods?

# H Y P O T H E T I C A L    C A S E S

1. Sari asks Steve to look after her dog as a favor while she goes on vacation for two weeks, and Steve agrees to care for the dog during that time. During the two-week period, Steve spends $30 on dog food and $25 on a visit to the vet when the dog becomes violently ill for undetermined reasons. In addition, Sam spends $200 in lumber to build the dog a custom-made doghouse. After Sari returns home, Steve presents her with a bill for each of the noted expenses, including $250 for his time in building the doghouse and $100 for his services as a "doggie sitter" during the period in question. Sari refuses to pay any of the charges, claiming that Steve was supposed to look after the dog as a favor and that any money spent by him on the dog was merely a gift. You are the judge. What result? Explain your decision fully.

2. Karl lends his VCR to Karen so that she can dub a tape of her daughter's wedding from her VCR to Karl's. In exchange for borrowing the VCR over the weekend, Karen promises to have the video heads professionally cleaned before returning it to Karl. While the VCR is in her care, it is accidentally scratched. What type of bailment was involved here? Is Karen responsible for the damage to the VCR? Explain fully.

3. Priscilla parks in a private parking lot in the downtown area of her city which charges $12.99 plus tax for all-day parking. She pulls into the lot and is directed by the parking attendant to park in parking space number 125. She does so and then goes to the attendant to pay the parking fee. The attendant does not ask for, nor does Priscilla offer, her car keys. At the attendant's booth, a large sign in bold red letters reads: "ATTENTION: Customers park here at their own risk. Lock your car and take all valuables from it. Management assumes no risk for losses of any kind to customers' cars or their contents while in this lot." She reads the sign and gives the attendant the required fee, taking from him a parking stub which contains the same language. When she returns to her car later that evening, she finds that it has been broken into, the upholstery has been ripped in various places, two windows have been smashed and her radio, cellular phone and pocketbook (which she'd left in the car's glove compartment) have been stolen. Furious, she sues the parking lot owners, alleging failure to observe the reasonable care required to avoid the damage to her vehicle as required under a mutual-benefit bailment. What result? Explain fully.

4. Frank and Fiona go into a restaurant inside a hotel at which they are not staying as guests. On their way in, Frank hangs up his coat and hat in a coat rack by the entrance to the restaurant. After they are seated, a busboy offers to check Fiona's fur coat for her, and she assents. A short time later, the busboy returns with a coat-check ticket which he gives to Fiona. After a wonderful meal, Frank discovers that his hat and coat are missing from the coat rack, as is the fur that was checked by the busboy into the hotel's coat-check room. They sue the restaurant for breach of the bailment agreement with regard to both articles of clothing and for strict liability, claiming a special bailment existed. Will either theory of liability be successful? Explain fully.

# 28

# REAL PROPERTY

*Real property* can be defined as land and anything that is permanently attached to land, including buildings, trees and growing crops. What distinguishes real from personal property is that real property is fixed and unmovable, whereas personal property (both tangible and intangible) is movable. Whenever personal property is permanently affixed to real property, its nature changes from personal to real property and it becomes a part of the real property to which it is attached.

The owner of real estate owns not only the land itself and anything permanently attached to it, but also everything below the land, including minerals and precious metals, as well as the space above the land up to a height set by local ordinances (typically up to several hundred feet above the highest structure in the land). With few exceptions, such as easements (discussed later in this chapter), the owner of real estate has the exclusive right to use the property and to prevent others from using it without permission. We have already seen in our discussions of criminal law and torts that willful entry into the real estate of another without the owner's assent can constitute trespass.

Real property by its nature is eternal; land has existed since the earth's birth and will endure until its demise. This contrasts sharply with personal property, which by its nature has a finite existence. Tangible personal property wears out or is used up over a period of time, and even intangible personal property such as patents and copyrights usually has a finite existence. In part because real property lasts forever, the law has come to recognize a number of varying degrees of interests in real estate that range from absolute present and future ownership of real estate forever (fee simple absolute) to a number of lesser interests that will be examined in this chapter. In addition, we will explore the means of obtaining and transferring interests to real property that, as we will see, require far greater formalities than does the acquisition and transfer of title to personal property.

# ESTATES IN LAND · · · · · · · · · · · · · · · · · · · · · · · · · · · · · · · · · · ·

Interests in real property are classified in accordance with the rights they convey to the real estate involved. These can range from absolute ownership of property to the mere right to occupy property for a preset period of time or to gain access to property for a limited purpose. Ownership interests in land that last forever or for an undetermined period of time (including a person's lifetime) are called *freehold estates,* while interests that are limited to a specific period of time are called *leasehold estates.* A freehold estate is a right of title to land, as distinguished from a leasehold estate, which is a mere *possessory* interest in land, without title.

## FREEHOLD ESTATES

**Fee simple absolute**    *Fee simple absolute* is the most complete ownership interest in land that can be possessed. It conveys to the owner of the land the absolute, unqualified right to own, possess and dispose of land forever.

**Determinable fee**    A *determinable fee* (also referred to as a *base fee* or *qualified fee*) is a fee estate with some qualification or limitation attached to it. Typically, such estates are conferred only upon the happening of a future event, or are subject to termination upon some future circumstance. For instance, if land is transferred by a father to his daughter subject to her not marrying before his death, a determinable fee estate is created. Whether or not the property will pass to the daughter depends upon whether or not the condition attached to its grant is met; if the daughter marries during the grantor's lifetime, her interest in the property is terminated; but if the grantor dies before the daughter has married, then a fee simple absolute interest in the land would vest in the daughter.

**Life estate**    A *life estate* is a fee interest that lasts during the life of a specific individual. The holder of a life estate interest in land has a proprietary interest in the land during the life of a specific individual. Usually, the estate runs for the lifetime of the grantee (the person to whom the life estate is granted), but a life estate can also be based on the life of a third person other than the grantee. For example, a mother can grant a life estate to her son that lasts for the son's lifetime, or the mother's lifetime, or the lifetime of any other person.

Because the life estate has a limited duration, the owner of a life estate does not enjoy the same rights to the land as does the owner of a fee simple absolute. The owner of a life estate is entitled to the exclusive possession of the realty during the life of the person on whose life the estate is based. During that lifetime, the owner of the life estate may exclusively possess the realty, put it to any lawful use, and lease or even sell outright his or her interest in the realty to any third person. But owners of life estates are prohibited from unreasonably interfering with or limiting the value of the real estate to the future holders of a fee interest in the estate. An owner of a life estate who abuses his or her rights with respect to the realty by destroying its future value to the prejudice of a future heir to the property is guilty of waste and can be sued for damages by any parties whose future interests in the land are damaged. The holder of a life estate may benefit from all that the land has to offer, including mining the land for its mineral or precious metal content, farming the land and using timber on the land during the duration of the life estate, as long as such use does not unreasonably hamper the rights of subsequent owners of the land. If, for example, land covered by a life estate has a gold mine in it that produces 100 ounces of gold every month before the grant of the life estate, the grantee of the life estate may continue to mine the land and retrieve from it 100 ounces of gold per month during the duration of his or her estate, but may not significantly increase the mining operations. Likewise, the owner of a life estate containing timber may make reasonable use of the timber for his or her own needs, but may not sell all the timber on the land to a logging company.

**Dower**    *Dower* is a special type of life estate reserved for a widow to property owned by the husband during his life. At common law, a widow had a one-third interest for her lifetime in any land that her deceased husband owned in fee in order to provide for her sustenance and that of any children of the marriage. Upon the wife's death, the land would typically pass in fee to her children by the deceased husband, if any survived her, or otherwise as provided for by the husband in his will. Dower has been modified or abolished in nearly all jurisdictions today, but an analogous statutory provision is made in many states' intestacy statutes and in provisions that make it impossible to deny a surviving spouse at least a one-third interest in the estate of the deceased spouse.

**Curtesy**    *Curtesy* is provision for widowers analogous to dower, giving them either a fee interest or a life estate in their wives' land provided that the marriage produced at least one child. Like dower, curtesy has been either modified or abolished in most jurisdictions. In most states, husbands and wives are given some inalienable right to at least a portion of the property of the deceased spouse—typically a one-third life estate or fee simple interest in the deceased spouse's estate.

# NONFREEHOLD ESTATES

It is possible to have the legal right to use and occupy real estate without having a fee ownership interest in it. Such is the nature of nonfreehold or leasehold estates which only provide a possessory interest in realty. The three most common of these leasehold estates include estates for years, periodic tenancies and tenancies at will.

## LEASEHOLD ESTATES

**Estate for years**    An *estate for years* is a possessory interest in land that grants its holder the right to occupy land for a set period of time. As is the case with all leasehold estates, an estate for years conveys only a possessory interest in the grantee and does not convey a fee or ownership interest.

**Periodic tenancy**    A *periodic tenancy,* like an estate for years, is a nonfee possessory interest in real estate that lasts for a specified period of time, such as week-to-week or month-to-month, and is renewable at the end of each period by the mutual consent of the landlord and tenant.

**Tenancy at will**    A tenancy at will is a tenancy that has no fixed term of duration and can be ended at any time by either the landlord or the tenant.

# FUTURE INTERESTS · · · · · · · · · · · · · · · · · · · · · · · · · · · · · · ·

Future interests in real property are possessory or ownership interests which do not exist at present but rather will or might arise in the future. When a present interest in a life estate is granted, for example, a future fee interest is retained in the property after the end of the life estate. With regard to fee interests in real property, there are two main future interests that we need to be aware of: reversions, and remainders, which can be either absolute or contingent upon the happening of an event, both of which we will look at next.

### REVERSIONARY INTERESTS

A *reversionary interest* is a future interest in real estate that is retained by a grantor of real property by granting to a grantee something less than a fee simple absolute interest in the real estate involved. When a reversionary interest is retained, real property transferred by the grantor will vest once again in the grantor, or his or her estate, at some time in the future. If a grantor grants a fee simple absolute interest in real estate, he or she retains no interest in the property, since by definition such a grant involves an absolute transfer of whatever ownership interest the grantor has in the property to the grantee forever. If less than a fee simple absolute interest in land is transferred, such as by a life estate or an estate for years, then the grantor retains an interest in the land which will *revert* to him or her upon the natural termination of the grantee's interest in the land. If, for example, Ted transfers a life estate in Blackacre to Tanya, Ted retains a reversionary interest in Blackacre, since he will regain a fee simple absolute interest in the land as soon as Tanya dies. The same would be true if Ted transferred the land to Tanya for a period of ten years.

In these last two examples, an *absolute* reversionary interest is retained by Ted, since the land is certain to revert to him in the future (upon Tanya's death in the first example and the expiration of the ten-year period in the second). It is also possible to retain a *contingent* reversionary interest in land (also called *the possibility of a reverter*) through the transfer of a determinable fee interest. If, for example, Ted transfers to Tanya his interest in Blackacre subject to her successfully completing college before her twenty-second birthday, Ted retains the possibility of a reverter to Blackacre since it will revert to him in the event that Tanya fails to graduate from college by the required age.

### REMAINDER INTERESTS

A *remainder interest* is a future interest to real estate that is given to a third party by a grantor by an express grant to a grantee of less than a fee simple interest in property with a provision that the property will or may vest in a third party upon the passage of time or happening of an event in the future. As is the case with a reversionary interest, a remainder interest may be either absolute or contingent. If, for example, Ted grants Blackacre "to my daughter, Darlene, for life, then to my son, Sam," a present life estate is given to Darlene with Sam receiving an absolute remainder interest. (Darlene is certain to die at some point in the future, and Sam or his heirs will then inherit Blackacre in fee simple absolute.) A contingent remainder interest could be conveyed to Sam by a grant such as the following: "To my daughter, Darlene, for life, then to my son, Sam, if he is then alive." In the last example, Sam receives only a grant of a contingent remainder interest, since he will receive the property in question in fee simple only if he outlives his sister. Assuming that Sam dies before Darlene in the last example, what will happen to Blackacre? Why it will then revert to Ted's estate, of course. (The grantor has retained a contingent reversionary interest in the property under the last example in the event that the son dies before the daughter.)

## NONPOSSESSORY INTEREST IN LAND  . . . . . . . . . . . . . . . . . . . . .

The fee and leasehold interests we've discussed thus far are all possessory interests in real property, since the holder of any of these interests has either a present or a future contingent or absolute right to occupy or possess real property. In addition to these possessory interests in real property, the law recognizes a number of nonpossessory interests giving the holder the right not to occupy land, but rather to make some limited use of it. Such nonpossessory interests include easements, *profits à prendre* and licenses.

### EASEMENTS

An *easement* is a right to use the property of another for a limited purpose. The most common kinds of easements involve the right to travel over the property of another to gain access to one's land, as well as those granting public utilities the right to transport power, water, gas or phone lines over or under land in order to provide needed services. When an easement is granted over one piece of land for the benefit of another, the benefited land is called the *dominant tenement* and the land which is burdened by the easement is called the *servient tenement*. Generally speaking, easements can have perpetual existence or be created to last for a specified period of time.

**Affirmative easements**  An *affirmative easement* is one which grants to its holder the right to pass over the land of another or otherwise gain access into it for the permitted purpose named in the easement. If the owner of Whiteacre has an easement over Greenacre to gain access to his property from a main road, for example, such an easement would be considered an affirmative easement, with Whiteacre as the dominant tenement and Greenacre the servient tenement.

**Negative easements**    A *negative easement* is one which prohibits certain kinds of lawful activity from being carried out in the servient tenement in order to benefit the owner of the dominant tenement. If, for example, the owner of Redacre is concerned that the owner of Blueacre next door might decide to plant tall trees or build a tall structure on Blueacre and thereby obstruct the view from Redacre, he can try to obtain a negative easement from the owner of Blueacre preventing him from planting trees or erecting any structure higher than one story on his land. Negative easements can be procured for any agreed-upon consideration and are often included in land that is sold by developers as part of a planned community for the benefit of the community as a whole. For example, lots sold by a developer might contain a negative easement prohibiting purchasers from putting trailers on the land where trailers are otherwise allowed by law.

**Easement appurtenant**    *Easements appurtenant* are easements attached to one piece of land for the benefit of another. An easement appurtenant runs with the land forever (passes with transfer of the land), unless it is canceled by the owner of the dominant tenement, and is transferred to any subsequent owners of both the servient and dominant tenements. For example, if Ben, the owner of Blackacre, grants an easement appurtenant to Wilma, the owner of Whiteacre, granting her the right to gain access to Whiteacre through Ben's land, the easement will attach to both Blackacre and Whiteacre and pass with all subsequent transfer of both tracts. Once the easement is created, it can only be extinguished by Wilma (the owner of the dominant tenement) or any subsequent owners of Whiteacre to whom she transfers her land.

**Easement in gross**    Unlike easements appurtenant, which attach to the land and are transferred with its sale, an *easement in gross* is personal in nature and gives its holder the right to make a limited use of another's land for his or her personal benefit. Easements in gross benefit an individual rather than a dominant tenement. Thus, if Ben, the owner of Blackacre, grants "to Wilma, personally, and only to Wilma, the right to walk or drive over Blackacre to gain access to State Route 1," Wilma will be the beneficiary of an easement in gross which will last for her lifetime but will not be transferable. Such an easement can be granted to Wilma whether or not she owns land adjoining Blackacre, since an easement in gross does not attach itself to or run with the land.

## CREATION OF AN EASEMENT

Easements are considered nonpossessory interests in real property and as such are subject to the same formalities of creation as any other transfer of an interest in real property. We will examine the transfer of interests in real property in the next chapter, but for now, it should be noted that easements can arise in a number of ways. An easement can arise from an *express grant* by the grantor executing a valid deed containing the terms of the easement and transferring it to the grantee. An easement can also arise by *reservation* when the transferor of real property reserves to himself or herself in the deed the right to use the property for a particular purpose, or by transferring the property by a deed containing a negative easement. Easements can also arise by *implication* through the transfer of property under circumstances where the clear intention of the parties was to reserve an easement but they neglected to do so expressly in transferring the property. Finally, an easement can arise out of *necessity* in instances where, for example, there is no means of gaining access to a person's land other than through the land of another.

## PROFITS À PRENDRE

A *profit à prendre* is another nonpossessory right in real estate that gives its holder the right to go onto the land of another and to remove something from it or to make some use of the soil of another. Common *profits à prendre* involve mining rights, logging rights and water rights to another's land. The distinguishing characteristic of a *profit à prendre* versus an easement is that the former involves the right to remove something from the land, whereas the latter merely involves the right to go onto or pass through the land of another for a specific purpose. Because *profits à prendre* confer an interest in real property, they must be created subject to the same formalities as any other real property interest.

## LICENSES

A *license* is a revocable, temporary privilege to go onto another's land for a specific purpose. Unlike easements and *profits à prendre,* licenses are *not* considered interests in land. Like easements and *profits à prendre,* licenses can be conferred free of charge or for a fee. Because they are not interests in real estate, licenses can be created and revoked orally or in writing without any special requirements or formalities.

Because a license is revocable at any time by the owner or a person in lawful possession of the real property, a person who is on another's land as a licensee must leave as soon as the license expires or is revoked; otherwise he or she becomes a trespasser. This is true even when a fee was paid for the license. Thus, guests in your home must leave as soon as you tell them to, or *revoke their license* to be in your home, and patrons of a movie theater must leave whenever management asks them to do so—with or without just cause. Licensees who have given consideration for their license (such as patrons of a movie theater) and are asked to leave the premises without cause are entitled to a refund of whatever consideration they paid for the license under a theory of breach of contract. If a license for which a fee has been paid is revoked for cause, such as for theater patrons who talk loudly during a movie or throw popcorn, then no refund need be made by the grantor of the license since no breach of contract is involved.

# QUESTIONS · · · · · · · · · · · · · · · · · · · · · · · · · · · · · · · · · · · · · · · · ·

1. What are freehold estates?
2. What is the most complete ownership interest in land that can be possessed?
3. What is a determinable fee?

4. What is a reversionary interest?
5. What is a remainder interest?
6. What is the distinction between affirmative and negative easements?
7. What is an easement appurtenant?
8. What is an easement in gross and how is it different from an easement appurtenant?
9. What is the main distinction between easements and *profits à prendre?*
10. What is a license?

# H Y P O T H E T I C A L      C A S E S

1. Leroy Landowner transfers title to real estate he owns by a deed that contains the following transfer language:

   To my son, Leon, for life, then to Leon's children. If Leon should die childless, then to my daughter, Lyssandra.

   a. What type of interest does Leon have to the land?
   b. What interest do Leon's unborn children have with regard to this transfer of land?
   c. What is Lyssandra's interest in the land?
   d. What interest, if any, has Leroy reserved for himself or his estate? Explain fully.

2. Timothy, a college student at State University, agrees to rent a studio apartment from Tasha and to pay her $100 per week. The parties make no other provision in their agreement and the agreement is not reduced to a writing.
   a. What kind of interest in real estate does Timothy have as a result of this agreement? Be specific.
   b. Does Timothy gain a fee interest as a result of this agreement? Explain.
   c. How long will this arrangement last? What if either Timothy or Tasha is unhappy with the arrangement after a few months go by?

3. Ben, the owner of Blackacre, would like to obtain permission to fish in Gwendolyn's pond on Greenacre, a property that adjoins his own. He would also like the right to cross over Greenacre with his car to avoid a lengthy traffic light on the main road on which his property is situated. In addition, he would like to obtain assurances from Gwendolyn that she will never build any structure within 300 feet of his property line or within 1,000 feet of her pond. He negotiates a deal with Gwendolyn giving him precisely what he wants in exchange for an undisclosed dollar amount. Gwendolyn executes a deed granting Ben the right to fish on her pond throughout his life, and the right for Ben or any person who purchases Blackacre from him in the future to cross over Greenacre in order to get access to a secondary road. The deed also grants to Ben and any future owners of Blackacre the assurance that no structure will ever be built on Greenacre within 300 feet of Blackacre, and that no structure will be built within 1,000 feet of Greenacre's pond

during Ben's life. State in precise language the nature of the interest in Greenacre that Ben has procured under these terms. Be specific.

4. A group of college students go on a club-sponsored trip to a theme park in their state. Each of the students pays the $25 access fee to the park and enters after being given a set of rules that apply to patrons' conduct while in the park. The rules prohibit alcoholic beverages from being taken into the park or consumed by patrons in the park and require patrons to wear shoes at all times in the park. No other rules are posted. Before the day is over, one of the students is kicked out of the park for drinking a beer that she had brought into the park (she was twenty-one and of legal drinking age in the state involved), a second student is ejected for wandering about the park in his underwear (but wearing sneakers) and a third student is expelled for using obscene and abusive language to one of the park's employees and repeatedly pulling the ears of the victim's rabbit costume. The park refuses to refund the money of any of the three students, and they decide to sue in small-claims court for a refund of their $25 fees and for other incidental and consequential damages flowing from an alleged breach of contract.

a. With regard to real-property law, what was the status of the three students while they were visiting the park?

b. Did the park have the legal authority to eject all three students from its premises? Explain.

c. Will any of the students succeed in their claims against the park? Explain.

# CHAPTER

# 29

# CREATION AND TRANSFER OF INTERESTS IN REAL PROPERTY

Interests in real property can be created and transferred in two ways. The first and most common is through the execution and transfer of a *deed*, and the second is by *adverse possession* (obtaining possession to the property of another and holding onto it to the exclusion of all others, while claiming it as one's own for a period of time typically ranging from five to twenty years).

## TRANSFER BY DEED . . . . . . . . . . . . . . . . . . . . . . . . . . . . . . . . .

The creation and transfer of an interest in land is almost always accomplished by the execution and delivery of a valid deed to the property from the *grantor* (the seller and transferor of the property) to the *grantee* (the buyer and transferee of the property). When a valid deed is delivered to the grantee, title to the underlying real estate passes; delivery of the deed is the legal equivalent of delivering the land itself.

In order to be valid, a deed must meet certain requirements. It must (1) be in writing, (2) list the name or names of the grantor(s) and the grantee(s), (3) contain words that unequivocally show an intent to transfer land, (4) offer a clear description of the land being transferred, and (5) contain the signature(s) of the grantee(s). As long as these five requirements are met, a deed will be valid. Even though nearly all deeds are executed by filling in the blanks of ready-made forms, there is no requirement that a specific form be used in most jurisdictions, and a handwritten deed is perfectly valid as long as it contains the five noted requirements.

A deed can be used to transfer any present or future interest in realty, including fee interests such as fee simple and life estate transfers, as well as nonfee interests such as easements and *profits à prendre*.

## WARRANTY DEED

A *warranty deed* is a deed in which the grantor gives assurances to the grantee that he or she has valid title to the land being transferred and obligates himself or herself to make reparations to the grantee or anyone to whom the grantee may subsequently transfer the land if the title was somehow defective. (See Figure 29.1 for a sample warranty deed.)

## QUITCLAIM DEED

A *quitclaim deed* is a deed in which the grantor transfers whatever title he or she has to a given piece of land (if any) to the grantee. Unlike a warranty deed, a quitclaim deed contains no assurance that the grantor has good title and no promise to make any future reparations if the title is defective. Such deeds are typically granted when a defect in the title of the transferor is suspected or when the transferor purchases the land as an agent for a third party and subsequently needs to transfer title to the third party. As you might

---

*WARRANTY DEED*

Warranty deed made this _____ day of _____, 19___,
between _____, whose address is
[Seller's full name]

_____, City of
[Seller's street address]

_____, County of _____, State of _____,
for the consideration of _____ Dollars ($_____)
received from _____, whose address
[Buyer's full name]

is _____, City of
[Buyer's street address]

_____, County of _____, State of _____,
does hereby transfer all of his or her interest in the following
real property situated in the County of _____, State
of _____: _____
[Legal description of land]

_____, the address to which is
_____ , together
[Street address of property]

with the tenements, hereditaments and appurtenances thereunto belonging, and the rents, issues and profits thereof and warrants the title to same.

In witness whereof, _____ has hereunto
[Buyer's name]

agreed this day and year as set forth above.

_____
[Signature of grantor(s)]

_____
[Acknowledgment by notary public]

---

**FIGURE 29.1** Sample warranty deed

---

### QUITCLAIM DEED

This quitclaim deed is made this _____ day of _____, 19___, between _____, whose address is
<small>[Seller's full name]</small>

_____, City of
<small>[Seller's street address]</small>

_____, County of _____, State of _____, and _____, whose address
<small>[Buyer's full name]</small>

is _____, City of
<small>[Buyer's street address]</small>

_____, County of _____, State of _____. That for and in the consideration of _____ Dollars ($_____), the receipt of which is hereby acknowledged, _____ does hereby release, remise and
<small>(Seller's full name)</small>

forever quitclaim unto _____ all of his
<small>(Buyer's full name)</small>

or her interest, if any, in that certain real property commonly known as _____, County of _____,
<small>(Street address of property)</small>

State of _____, described as follows: _____ _____,
<small>(Legal description of land)</small>

_____, together with the tenements, heredi-
<small>(Street address of property)</small>

taments and appurtenances thereunto belonging, and the rents, issues and profits thereof, to have and to hold, all and singular the premises, with the appurtenances, unto _____ and his or her heirs and assigns forever.
<small>[Buyer's name]</small>

In witness whereof, _____ has hereunto
<small>[Buyer's name]</small>

agreed this day and year as set forth above.

_____
<small>[Signature of grantor(s)]</small>

_____
<small>[Acknowledgment by notary public]</small>

**FIGURE 29.2**   Sample quitclaim deed

suspect, there is an element of risk in purchasing property with a quitclaim deed, which usually affects its selling price. In addition, title insurance is generally unavailable for property purchased with a quitclaim deed, and most banks will not issue a standard mortgage for such property. (See Figure 29.2 for a sample quitclaim deed.)

## CONTRACT OF SALE . . . . . . . . . . . . . . . . . . . . . . . . . . . . . . .

Although a contract of sale is not necessary to the transfer of real estate, contracts of sale are invariably found in transactions involving the purchase and sale of real estate.

Such contracts are ruled by the applicable contract law in the jurisdiction where the contract is entered into or where the real estate is situated. Because contracts involving the sale of real estate obviously involve an interest in real estate, such contracts must be evidenced by a writing signed by the buyer(s) and seller(s) in order to be enforceable by both parties under the Statute of Frauds. If a verbal contract for the sale of real estate is involved, the parties may still honor their agreement and validly transfer the property upon the execution and delivery of a valid deed, but such a contract would not be enforceable in the courts if either party refuses to go through with the verbal agreement. On the other hand, because real estate is unique, written, signed contracts by parties are enforceable in the courts to secure damages for breach if either party reneges on the agreement, and the equitable remedy of specific performance is also available to buyers who wish to force sellers to transfer a deed pursuant to a valid contract of sale.

## TITLE THROUGH INTER VIVOS AND TESTAMENTARY GIFTS

As previously noted, a contract is unnecessary as a means of conveying real estate. While the purchase of real estate is the most common means of obtaining title to it, title can also be obtained by means of a gift. An *inter vivos* transfer of an interest in realty can occur by gift from the transfer of a deed for which no money or, more commonly, a nominal fee of one dollar is paid. As with all transfers of real estate, the delivery of a valid deed by the transferor to the transferee accomplishes the transfer. If a grantor makes a testamentary disposition of real estate by a provision in a will, it is the *executor* or *executrix* (the legal representative of the deceased testator or testatrix) who executes and delivers a valid deed to the person for whose benefit the testamentary gift was made.

## TITLE THROUGH EMINENT DOMAIN

Another means of effectuating a transfer of real estate without need for a contract of sale is a transfer to the state or federal government under its powers of eminent domain. *Eminent domain* is the state's power to condemn or *expropriate* private property for public use upon paying its owner the property's market price. In the United States, the federal government is given the power of eminent domain by the Fifth Amendment to the U.S. Constitution. Such a power is also found in the constitutions of the individual states. If the government wishes to use private land for public use, its owners with few exceptions have no choice but to deed over to the government all or whatever part of the land the government requires. Typical exercises of the government's eminent domain powers extend to the building of roads, expansion of parks and the construction of similar public projects. Not only individuals but entire towns may be called upon to transfer their land to the government (usually quite unhappily) for such projects as new construction or expansion of reservoirs, dams and similar public works.

Eminent domain is also relied upon in granting necessary easements for power and telephone lines that must pass over private lands. The same is true for government expropriation of partial real estate rights, such as the subsurface rights to private land in order to build a subway system. When such a partial taking of private land for public use is involved, the landowner is compensated for the partial taking at market value and is otherwise free to use or sell whatever portion of the land was not seized for public use.

# RECORDING STATUTES . . . . . . . . . . . . . . . . . . . . . . . . . . . . . . . . . .

Every jurisdiction provides for a means of *recording* deeds in order to give notice to subsequent purchasers of the property of previous transfers of the property. While most states do not require that deeds be recorded in order to effectively pass title to land, recording a deed offers protection to the purchaser of property from previous or subsequent fraudulent transfers of property to the same land by a previous owner or by a single grantor. A typical problem in this area arises when a grantor executes multiple deeds to the same property, with the intention of defrauding the grantees. Since there can be only one true owner of real estate in such circumstances, the question becomes who has the greater interest. At common law, the answer was simple: first in time, first in right, so that the first grantee of the land would be entitled to it. Today, the problem has been addressed by states through the adoption of recording statutes that provide a simple means of giving notice to third parties of owners of record to real estate, and provide for a means of resolving multiple claims by innocent grantees to the same land. There are three basic types of recording statutes in use today: notice acts, race acts and race-notice acts.

## NOTICE ACTS

Jurisdictions that use *notice acts* as their recording statutes prevent persons with actual notice of a previous transfer of the property from having a greater interest in the property than the previous transferee of the property who has not recorded its deed. In other words, in such jurisdictions a transferee takes property subject to any previous ownership interests that he or she has *constructive* knowledge of (because the deeds detailing these interests have been officially recorded), as well as subject to any previous transfer of the property that he or she has *actual* knowledge of, regardless of whether or not such transfer has been recorded.

## RACE ACTS

Under *race acts*, the first person to record a deed has the greater right to the underlying property, regardless of any actual knowledge of previous unrecorded transfers of the property. Race acts get their name from the fact that new transferees or property must race to the recording office to have their interest in the property protected from previous or subsequent transfers; where more than one transfer has been made to the same property, the person who wins the race to the recording office gets the superior interest to the land, regardless of whether or not he or she was aware that other prior transfers had been made.

## RACE-NOTICE ACTS

As the name implies, *race-notice acts* combine the provisions of both the race and notice acts by providing that the first person to record a deed without notice of any prior recorded or unrecorded transfers of property obtains the greater interest to the underlying property. In other words, race-notice acts require a transferee of property to take it without any actual or constructive knowledge of any previous transfers of the property by the same grantor that would conflict with the grantee's interest.

# TITLE THROUGH ADVERSE POSSESSION  . . . . . . . . . . . . . . . . . . . .

*Adverse possession* is a means of acquiring property by maintaining possession of it during a statutorily defined period and meeting certain additional criteria. Unlike more common means of obtaining property that require the transfer of a deed, with adverse possession title is obtained by meeting the statutorily defined criteria which include the following:

- the possession must be open and notorious;
- the possession must be continuous for the entire statutory period (usually five to twenty years);
- the possession must be adverse and exclusive; and
- the possession must be with claim of right.

To put it another way, in order for title to property to pass by adverse possession, the possession must be actual, open, notorious and exclusive during the statutory period and the possessor of the property must show that he or she held it without the owner's permission.

The requirement that possession be open and notorious means that the adverse possessor must openly maintain his or her possession of the land. The requirement that the possession be continuous means that there can be no breaks in the time of possession; if, for example, an adverse possessor holds land for five years, moves to another state for a year and then returns to the land, the possession would not be continuous, and the statutory period would begin to run anew when the adverse possessor returns to the land. The requirement that the possession be adverse and exclusive means that it must be against the owner's interests, and that the adverse possessor must not permit anyone—including the land's true owner—to use or possess the land during the period that he or she maintains adverse possession of it. Finally, the requirement that the possession be with claim of right necessitates that the adverse possessor tell others that he or she is the owner of the land, or claims the land as his or her own; this requirement can be met by statements to third persons or by posting visible notices on the land, such as a sign proclaiming "Harry's Homestead," or the posting of "No Tres-passing" signs with the adverse possessor's name on them.

Adverse possession presents a particularly serious problem for absentee landowners, especially in states with relatively brief statutory periods, such as five to ten years. The law requires property owners to take some affirmative steps to protect their property from infringement by taking timely action against trespassers before they can perfect their interest in the land under the adverse possession statute. To put it another way, adverse possession is really a Statute of Limitations that requires landowners to protect their property rights within a certain period of time or risk losing them. Keep in mind that not all adverse possession claims are nefarious in nature, and that many arise out of honest mistakes, such as a landowner mistakenly building a structure on a neighbor's land. In any case, whether the adverse possession is inno-cent or willful, the claim of the adverse possessor extends only to the land actually oc-cupied and used by him or her during the period of adverse possession. Thus, if Henrietta builds a homestead on one acre of Harry's ten-acre land, she will eventually own only the one acre she has exclusively used throughout the statutory period, and not the entire ten-acre tract.

## CONCURRENT OWNERSHIP . . . . . . . . . . . . . . . . . . . . . . . . . . . . . . .

Like personal property, real property can be owned individually or jointly by two or more persons or companies. There are three distinct types of joint ownership options of which you should be aware: joint tenancy, tenancy in common and tenancy by the entirety.

### JOINT TENANCY

*Joint tenancy* is a means of two or more persons owning real estate together. The most significant feature of joint tenancy is that the property owned by the joint tenants passes automatically to the survivors upon the death of any joint tenant. If two people own real estate as joint tenants, then the survivor automatically owns the whole upon one joint tenant's death. If more than two people own real estate as joint tenants, the share of any joint tenant who dies is distributed equally among the survivors, so that if four friends own a home equally as joint tenants and one dies, the share of each survivor in the property increases from a 25 percent interest to a 33.3 percent interest.

It is not necessary that each joint tenant have an equal share in the property. It is possible to have two joint tenants with vastly different ownership interests in the un-derlying real estate; nevertheless, if any one of them dies, his or her share passes to the survivors in equal shares. Thus, if two friends own property as joint tenants in which one holds a 95 percent interest and the other a 5 percent interest, a surviving tenant would automatically obtain title to the whole property, regardless of his or her invest-ment in it.

Joint tenants share in the responsibility for upkeep of a home, payment of taxes and other expenses that naturally result from the ownership of real property in proportion to their ownership interest of the property. Thus, a 10 percent joint owner of property pays 10 percent of the property's expenses. But the right of joint tenants to occupy or use real estate is not related to their ownership interest of it; a 10 percent owner has the right to occupy 100 percent of the house at all times. This potential problem is resolved by a separate contractual agreement between the joint owners detailing their rights of occupancy.

The interest of a joint tenant to real property is freely transferable during the joint tenant's life. It can be sold, leased or given away at will. This presents another potential problem for joint tenants, since all of them have the power to freely dispose of their property interest to any person or persons they wish. For this reason, joint tenants often have a separate contract detailing restrictions on the transfer of the property and/or a right of first refusal of the co-tenants to purchase the interest of a joint tenant who wishes to sell his or her interest in the property before an offering is made to the general public. A joint tenancy is severable at any time by any one joint tenant who can petition a court to partition the property or to force its sale.

### TENANCY IN COMMON

*Tenancy in common* is similar in all respects to joint tenancy with one important exception: the interest of a tenant in common who dies passes to his or her estate, rather than to the surviving tenants in common. In other words, tenants in common enjoy the same rights and responsibilities as joint tenants except that there is no survivorship provision in the tenancy.

### TENANCY BY THE ENTIRETY

*Tenancy by the entirety* is a form of joint tenancy reserved for husbands and wives. The main difference between joint tenancy and tenancy by the entirety is that a tenant by the entirety cannot transfer his or her interest in the underlying property without the signature of the co-tenant.

## PUBLIC AND PRIVATE RESTRICTIONS ON LAND USE . . . . . . . . . . . .

Generally speaking, the owner of real estate has the right to use the land in any way he or she sees fit, provided that the use is permitted by law. But there are limits to this right that can be imposed by the government and through private agreements among landowners.

### ZONING

The government exerts control over the private use of land through zoning regulations. A state's power to control the private use of land is found in its general police powers, under which a state may regulate private conduct in order to promote the public good in the areas of health, safety and ethics and to promote the general welfare of its citizens. Public land use regulation is carried out primarily at the local level, with the state empowering local city or town zoning boards to pass regulations relating to land use. Zoning regulations relate to architectural and structural building designs, as well as limiting the allowed uses of lands in certain divisions or districts within a community, such as by dividing communities into areas that permit farming, heavy and light industry and residential use of real estate, or any combination of these and similar land use classifications.

When an existing land use classification is changed by a zoning board, persons who had previously used their property in a way which now becomes illegal are typically allowed to continue their *nonconforming use* of their land at least for a period of time—usually as long as the existing owner retains title to the land and continues to use it in the nonconforming way. In addition, zoning authorities have the power to grant a *variance* to any person who petitions the authority for an exemption to the zoning regulations—usually by claiming hardship or special circumstances. Variances permitting deviation from the zoning ordinance are typically not granted unless the petitioner can convince the authority that the zoning ordinance represents an undue hardship for him.

## PRIVATE RESTRICTIONS ON LAND USE

In addition to the zoning ordinances in a given area, individuals also have the ability to restrict otherwise permissible uses of land through their private agreements. We have already seen one way of accomplishing such voluntary restrictions on land use by means of negative easements. For instance, if members of a given community want to make sure that some permissible land uses they find disagreeable are not carried out by any of its members, they can execute a negative easement preventing such use of their land. As has been previously noted, this is often done in new subdivisions and in planned communities. Such restrictive *covenants* can be included in the original deeds to land and made to run with the land, so that all subsequent owners of the property will be bound by them.

## QUESTIONS ·······································

1. What are the requirements for a valid deed?
2. What is a warranty deed?
3. What is a quitclaim deed?
4. May property be transferred without a contract of sale?
5. What purpose do recording statutes serve and what are the three types of recording acts in use today?
6. What is adverse possession? What are the criteria for establishing title through adverse possession?
7. Define *joint tenancy, tenancy in common* and *tenancy by the entirety*.
8. What is a variance?

9. What is generally required for a variance to be granted?

10. What is a private means of effecting a restriction of land use?

# H Y P O T H E T I C A L    C A S E S

1. Greg Grantor wishes to make a gift of a one-acre tract of land he owns to his friend Gina. He orally tells her in front of ten reliable witnesses that the land is hers forever and that she may dispose of it at will. Gina promptly accepts the gift and takes possession of the land. A month later, Greg dies and his executor serves notice on Gina that she must vacate the land. Gina refuses to do so, claiming the land is rightfully hers. What result?

2. Assume the same facts as in the last question except that after making the oral statement of his intention to give Gina the land, Greg writes the following on a piece of paper with a pen:

   I, Greg Grantor, hereby give to Gina Grantee all my rights and interest in the one-acre tract of land I own called Blackacre with the intent that she be the owner of the land forever.

   [Signed] Greg Grantee.

   Greg then gives the paper to Gina and dies a month later.
   a. Based on these facts, if Greg's executor demands that Gina quit the premises, what result?
   b. What interest, if any, does Gina have after the transfer of the paper to her?
   c. Will she be able to record the instrument as a deed? If so, what type of deed is it?

3. Francene Fink, a not-very-nice person with a long history of defrauding innocent persons, executes ten valid quitclaim deeds to a piece of property she owns at ten separate closings during a two-day period. She then leaves the country for a warmer climate in a country with no extradition treaty. If her state has a recording statute based on a race-notice act, answer the following questions based on these facts.
   a. Who will ultimately have the best title to the property?
   b. Does the fact that a quitclaim deed was given by Francene preclude any of the ten grantees from acquiring a valid title to the land?
   c. Assuming that Francene is apprehended before she could flee the country, would any of the grantees be able to successfully sue her for damages? If so, under what theory? If not, why not?

4. Sam Slick moves into a 100-acre tract of land belonging to Irma Innocent, an absentee landowner. He builds a log home on the land and builds a barbed wire fence around a one-acre tract of land surrounding his home. He tells everyone he meets that he owns the entire 100 acres of land, even though he actually takes possession of only the one-acre tract. Whenever anyone attempts to approach his home, he drives them away. After nine years of living on Irma's land, he decides to move to another state and leaves his homestead for a six-month period, telling

everyone that he will return in six months and posting "No Trespassing" signs around the perimeter of the one-acre land surrounding his home.

a. If the state of Sam's homestead requires a five-year period of adverse possession, who owns Sam's homestead after Sam returns to the state? Assuming that Sam would be the owner under adverse possession, how much land would he own?

b. If the state involved has a ten-year requirement for adverse possession, how long must Sam wait before he actually owns the homestead after he returns from his six-month trip?

c. If Sam had moved onto the land with Irma's consent but, once in it, he began telling everyone (except Irma) that he owned it and met the other requirements for adverse possession, would he own the land after the required time period expired? Explain.

## ETHICS AND THE LAW: QUESTIONS FOR FURTHER STUDY . . . . . . . .

It can be argued that adverse possession rewards criminal conduct by allowing a trespasser who illegally seizes the land of another eventually to become its true owner. Can adverse possession be justified on moral grounds as the valid public policy of a state? Or is this an outmoded wrinkle in the fabric of real-property law that states should iron out? Take a stand on the issue that is ethically defensible.

# CHAPTER

## 30

# LANDLORDS' AND TENANTS' RIGHTS AND RESPONSIBILITIES

Agreements involving the rental of real property carry with them certain rights and obligations for the landlord and tenant that are imposed by law. Generally speaking, however, the parties are free to modify these implied rights and duties, as well as to create different ones by express agreement. In this chapter, we will focus primarily on these implied rights and obligations which operate in the absence of a contrary agreement by the parties.

## CREATION OF THE LANDLORD-TENANT RELATIONSHIP . . . . . . . . .

As we've seen in Chapter 28, there are three basic leasehold estates that can be created which convey to the tenant the right to possess real property without a freehold interest in such property. Whether the tenancy involved is a tenancy for years, a periodic tenancy or a tenancy at will, the same rules apply to its formation. Such tenancies can be created either orally or by a written agreement between the parties that can be as detailed or as brief as the parties wish. Where the agreement is detailed, as is the case with rental agreements involving standard leases (see Figures 30.1 and 30.2), the rights and responsibilities of the parties are primarily determined by the agreement itself; where it is brief or nonexistent, the common law of real property steps in and defines the rights and duties of the parties.

While standard forms for leases are quite similar to one another, there is no requirement that a lease agreement be in any particular form. The Statute of Frauds requires any estate for years with a duration greater than one year to be in writing. For tenancies that run a year or less, verbal agreements are perfectly valid and binding.

## *RESIDENTIAL LEASE*

LEASE AGREEMENT made between _____ (Landlord) and _____ (Tenant).

For good consideration it is agreed between the parties as follows:

1. Landlord hereby leases and rents to Tenant the premises described as follows:

_____

2. This Lease shall be in effect for a term of _____ years, commencing on _____, 19__ and terminating on _____, 19__.

3. Tenant shall pay Landlord the annual rent of $_____ during said term, in monthly payments of $_____, each, payable monthly in advance.

4. Tenant shall at its own expense provide the following utilities:

_____

5. Tenant further agrees that:

a) Upon the expiration of the lease it will return possession of the leased premises in its present condition, reasonable wear and tear and fire casualty excepted. Tenant shall commit no waste to the leased premises.

b) It shall not assign or sublet or allow any other person to occupy the leased premises without Landlord's prior written consent.

c) It shall not make any material or structural alterations to the leased premises without Landlord's prior written consent.

d) It shall comply with all building, zoning and health codes and other applicable laws for said leased premises.

e) It shall not conduct a business deemed extra hazardous, a nuisance or requiring an increase in fire insurance premiums.

f) In the event of any breach of the payment of rent or any other allowed charge, or other breach of this Lease, Landlord shall have full rights to terminate this Lease in accordance with state law and re-enter and claim possession of the leased premises, in addition to such other remedies available to Landlord arising from said breach.

6. This Lease shall be binding upon and inure to the benefit of the parties, their successors, assigns and personal representatives.

7. Additional Lease terms: _____

_____

Signed and sealed this _____ day of _____, 19__.

_____
Landlord

_____
Tenant

**FIGURE 30.1**    Sample residential lease (short form)

## COMMERCIAL LEASE

This Lease (*Lease*) is made this _____ day of _____, 19__ by and between _____ (hereinafter *Landlord*) and _____(hereinafter *Tenant*).

In consideration for the mutual promises and covenants contained herein, and for other good and valuable consideration, the parties hereby agree as follows:

     1. The Landlord leases to the Tenant, and the Tenant rents from the Landlord the following described premises: _____

     2. The term of the Lease shall be for _____ commencing _____, 19__ and ending _____, 19__.

     3. The Tenant shall pay to Landlord as rent $_____ per year in equal monthly installments of $_____ payable in advance at _____.

     4. This Lease is subject to all present or future mortgages affecting the premises.

     5. Tenant shall use and occupy the premises only as a _____ subject at all times to the approval of the Landlord.

     6. The Tenant shall not make any alterations in, additions to or improvements to the premises without the prior written consent of the Landlord.

     7. The Landlord, at his own expense, shall furnish the following utilities or amenities for the benefit of the Tenant: _____.

     8. The Tenant, at his own expense, shall furnish the following:

_____

_____

     9. The Tenant shall purchase at his own expense public liability insurance in the amount of $_____ as well as fire and hazard insurance in the amount of $ _____ for the premises and shall provide satisfactory evidence thereof to the Landlord and shall continue same in force and effect throughout the Lease term hereof.

     10. The Tenant shall not permit or commit waste to the premises.

     11. The Tenant shall comply with all rules, regulations, ordinances codes and laws of all governmental authorities having jurisdiction over the premises.

     12. The Tenant shall not permit or engage in any activity which will effect an increase in the rate of insurance for the Building in which the premises is contained nor shall the Tenant permit or commit any nuisance thereon.

     13. The Tenant shall not sublet or assign the premises nor allow any other person or business to use or occupy the premises without the prior written consent of the Landlord, which consent may not be unreasonably withheld.

     14. At the end of the term of this Lease, the Tenant shall surrender and deliver up the premises in the same condition (subject to any additions, alterations or improvements, if any) as presently exists, reasonable wear and tear excluded.

     15. Upon default in any term or condition of this Lease, the Landlord shall have the right to undertake any or all other remedies permitted by Law.

     16. This Lease shall be binding upon, and inure to the benefit of, the parties, their heirs, successors, and assigns.

     Signed this _____ day of _____, 19__.

_____          _____
Tenant                                                    Landlord

**FIGURE 30.2**   Sample commercial lease (short form)

## TERMINATION OF THE LANDLORD-TENANT RELATIONSHIP · · · · · · · · · · · · · · · · · · · · · · · · · · · · · ·

A landlord-tenant relationship can be terminated in one of three ways: by the expira-tion of the specified period involved in a tenancy for years, by either the landlord or tenant serving notice on the other that he or she wishes to terminate a periodic tenancy or a tenancy at will, or by a breach of the tenancy agreement by either the landlord or the tenant.

A tenancy at will can be terminated at any time by either party serving notice upon the other of his or her intention to terminate the tenancy. A periodic tenancy, how-ever, requires a one-period notice to be provided prior to termination by the landlord or the tenant; if, for example, the tenancy is from month to month, then one month's notice is required prior to termination, while one week's notice would be required for a tenancy from week to week.

## UNLAWFUL TERMINATION OF THE LANDLORD-TENANT RELATIONSHIP · · · · · · · · · · · · · · · · · · · · · · · · · · · · ·

A tenancy unlawfully terminates upon a breach by either the landlord or tenant of a material duty they owe one another. Upon the unlawful termination of a lease by a ten-ant, the tenant remains liable for payment of rent throughout the remaining lease period. But the landlord must make a reasonable effort to mitigate or lessen the tenant's liability by attempting to rent the premises as quickly as possible to another tenant. As soon as the premises are rented to another tenant, the rent paid by the new tenant is used to set off the previous tenant's obligation, and the breaching tenant is required to pay any shortfall between the due rent and the rent paid by the new tenant. In addi-tion, the landlord is entitled to recover from the breaching tenant any incidental and consequential expenses caused by the breach, such as the cost of advertising for new tenants or the charges paid to a realtor for listing the apartment.

## LANDLORD'S RIGHTS AND RESPONSIBILITIES · · · · · · · · · · · · · · · ·

The landlord's primary responsibility is to provide habitable premises to the tenant throughout the lease period, and to protect the right of the tenant to quietly and ex-clusively possess the premises during the rental period. In addition, the landlord is ob-ligated to make necessary repairs to common areas and to rental premises on a timely basis when needed, and to provide necessary essential services, such as heat and hot water (unless, of course, the tenant is responsible for such services under the rental agreement).

The landlord's rights include the right to be paid the rent promptly when it is due and the right to have the tenant maintain reasonable care of the premises during the tenancy. The landlord is also entitled to have the tenant quit the rental premises at the end of the tenancy, as well as to any other rights the landlord has expressly reserved to himself or herself in the rental agreement.

## TENANT'S RIGHT AND RESPONSIBILITIES  . . . . . . . . . . . . . . . . . .

The tenant's primary responsibility is to pay the agreed-upon rent on a timely basis. In addition, the tenant has the responsibility not to unreasonably disturb other tenants. The tenant is also responsible for making minor repairs to the rental property and warning the landlord of the need for any major repairs should the tenant become aware of such a need; minor repairs would include unstopping a clogged sink or fixing a leaking faucet, while major repairs would include structural repairs to the building, such as fixing a roof or repairing a sagging floor. In addition, the tenant must refrain from unduly harming the rental property; any damage done to rental property beyond normal and reasonable wear and tear is the responsibility of the tenant. The tenant is also responsible for quitting the rental premises upon the termination of the rental period. Although these are the main responsibilities of tenants, other responsibilities can be, and usually are, spelled out in the rental agreement.

The tenant's rights, on the other hand, include the right to exclusive possession and use of the premises under the terms of the lease. In addition, the tenant is entitled to quiet enjoyment of the rental premises, and the landlord must take affirmative steps to remove any impediment to such quiet enjoyment that is reasonably within his or her power to remove. For example, unduly noisy tenants or tenants who engage in illicit activities such as prostitution or drug sale must be evicted by the landlord upon any other tenant's request and proof of such activity. The tenant is also entitled to premises that are reasonably safe and habitable; a landlord who provides rental premises that contain unreasonable safety hazards or who fails to provide necessary services such as heat and hot water is in breach of the rental agreement, and such a breach constitutes a wrongful constructive eviction of the tenant. Unless the rental agreement states otherwise, the tenant also has the right to sublet or assign the right to occupy the rental premises to third parties during the lease period. If premises are sublet, the tenant and the sublessee are jointly responsible for the payment of rent and for any damage done to the rental premises; the same is true for leases that are assigned to lessees by tenants. Other rights may be provided by state laws and the actual rental agreement.

## LANDLORDS' REMEDIES UPON BREACH OF A
## RENTAL AGREEMENT  . . . . . . . . . . . . . . . . . . . . . . . . . . . . .

Landlords have wide latitude in the remedies that they may reserve to themselves upon a tenant's breach by expressly providing for remedies in the lease. Unless a lease provision is deemed to be unconscionable, it will generally be enforced. This is particularly the case in commercial leases, where courts are much less likely to hold a remedy reserved by the landlord unconscionable if it is freely agreed to by the tenant. Even provisions that would be void as penalties in residential leases are often upheld in commercial leases, such as rent acceleration clauses that require a tenant to pay the rent due for the entire long-term lease immediately upon any breach of the lease, including a late rent payment. In addition, leases can contain valid forfeiture clauses that annul the tenant's rights to occupy the property upon any breach of the lease, including nonpayment of rent or failure to maintain the premises in a reasonable state of repair. In addition, a landlord can include a clause in a lease to the effect that the lease automatically terminates upon any breach by the tenant. When such clauses are contained in a lease, a landlord can bring an action for a summary judgment against the tenant and an order of eviction merely by proving that a breach has occurred. Some jurisdictions also allow landlords to forcibly re-enter the premises after a breach by a tenant who refuses to quit the premises; such a remedy, termed *self-help*, is not universally available, however. In jurisdictions that provide an expedited method for landlords to reclaim property from tenants who wrongfully retain it after breaching a lease, self-help is not available.

In addition to extraordinary remedies that landlords may reserve to themselves in leases, every landlord has the power to treat a lease as terminated after a breach by the tenant and to sue the tenant for damages (including incidental and consequential damages) caused by the breach. In addition, a landlord may opt to continue a lease in force after a tenant's breach and recover from him or her any damages that are caused from the breach.

Regardless of which remedy a landlord pursues after a tenant's breach, he or she has a duty to mitigate the tenant's damages. If, for example, a tenant with a two-year lease leaves after one year without the landlord's permission, the landlord can treat the lease as still in force and sue the tenant for damages, but the landlord must make a reasonable effort to re-rent the premises within a reasonable time after the breach. In other words, the landlord cannot sit back and continue to collect rent from the tenant for the remaining year without making some attempt to re-rent the property to another tenant.

## TENANT'S REMEDIES UPON BREACH OF A RENTAL AGREEMENT · · · · · · · · · · · · · · · · · · · · · · · · · · · · · ·

A tenant's remedies for a landlord's breach of a material duty owed under a lease include the right to either terminate the lease and recover damages or continue the lease and recover damages. A tenant wishing to terminate for a landlord's failure to live up to a material obligation must first give the landlord notice and provide him or her with the opportunity to remedy the situation within a reasonable time. If a landlord fails to remedy his or her breach within a reasonable time of having been notified of it, the tenant may treat the lease as terminated and sue the landlord for any actual damages suffered as a result of the breach (including incidental and consequential damages). If a tenant does not wish to treat the lease as terminated upon a landlord's failure to live up to his or her contractual obligations, the tenant may continue the lease and seek any of the following equitable and legal remedies: (1) recover money damages (typically the difference between the value of the premises as promised and the value of the premises after the landlord's breach), (2) seek a rent abatement until the situation is remedied, (3) use the rent money to perform the landlord's obligations, and (4) withhold rent from the landlord by depositing it in an escrow account until the breach is remedied. Court intervention is often required before a tenant can resort to any self-provisions such as using rent money to perform the landlord's obligations.

## QUESTIONS · · · · · · · · · · · · · · · · · · · · · · · · · · · · · · · · · · · · · · · · ·

1. Must lease agreements be in any specific form?
2. What are the three lawful means by which a landlord-tenant relationship can be terminated?
3. What are the basic responsibilities of a tenant?
4. What are the tenant's basic rights with regard to the rental property?
5. What are the landlord's basic duties?
6. What are the landlord's essential rights?
7. Are lease provisions that provide specific remedies to landlords generally enforced in the courts?
8. What remedies are available to a landlord who does not specifically provide for extraordinary remedies in a lease?
9. What must a landlord do to mitigate damages if a tenant leaves the premises after six months in a two-year lease?
10. What remedies are available to a tenant who wishes to remain in the rental property after a material breach of the lease by the landlord?

## H Y P O T H E T I C A L    C A S E S

1. Ted is a tenant of Leopold. He has never entered into a formal lease agreement, but has been living in Leopold's house for ten years. He pays his rent on the first of every month and has done so (with several rent increases) in a timely basis throughout his tenancy.
   a. What type of tenancy do Ted and Leopold have?
   b. If Ted wants to leave his apartment because he intends to purchase a home, what must he do?
   c. What if Leopold wants to oust Ted in order to rent to someone else?
   d. What if Leopold wants to allow Ted to remain as a tenant but also wants to increase his rent by $100 per month?
2. Timmy is a tenant in Liana's apartment building and has a two-year lease. Timmy would like to sublet part of his apartment to Tawana in order to help with the rent payments. When Liana finds out about the arrangement, she is furious and wants to evict Timmy and Tawana on grounds that he breached the lease.
   a. If the lease made no provisions as to subletting, what result?
   b. What if Timmy had subleased the entire apartment to Tawana without Liana's permission and the lease was likewise silent on the issue of subleasing?
   c. If Timmy subleases the apartment to Tawana after one month of the two-year lease, who will be responsible for the rent payments when they are due? What will be the effect of Tawana's breaking the lease?

3. Tasha, a tenant in Leon's two-family home, has a two-year lease that specifies she must pay for the utilities she uses in her apartment, but that Leon is responsible for providing heat and hot water. In January, during a particularly cold period, the boiler breaks, leaving Tasha without heat or hot water for three days. Leon, who is also without heat or hot water during that period, has the furnace looked at immediately, but is told by the company that has his service contract that the repair will take three days due to the need to have a replacement part shipped from a supplier. Tasha, who hates the cold, immediately moves to another apartment and sues Leon for breach of the lease, seeking compensatory damages of $300 (for the unused month's rent) and incidental and consequential damages of $1,000 ($800 in moving expenses and a $200 fee she had to pay a realtor to help find her a new apartment). Leon, on the other hand, counterclaims for damages for breach of the lease, claiming Tasha had no right to quit the premises under the circumstances. You are the judge. Resolve this dispute based on your knowledge of the applicable law.

## ETHICS AND THE LAW: QUESTIONS FOR FURTHER STUDY   . . . . . . .

Generally speaking, courts are likelier to enforce extraordinary remedies written into commercial leases than they are to enforce the same remedies written into residential leases. Why do you think this is so? From an ethical perspective, is it fair?

# 31

# WILLS

In our discussion of property thus far, we have seen that it is possible to transfer both real and personal property in a variety of ways, including by gift. Up until now, we have only discussed *inter vivos* and *causa mortis* gifts, which constitute a present transfer of both title to property as well as of the property itself. It is also possible to make future transfers of gifts of real or personal property through the use of a will. In this chapter, we will examine the basic laws relating to wills and learn how they can be used to convey interests to real and personal property. We will also examine how the property of a person who dies without leaving a valid will is distributed.

## AN INTRODUCTION TO WILLS . . . . . . . . . . . . . . . . . . . . . . . . . .

A *will* is an instrument that allows a person to make a distribution of his or her property that will become effective upon the person's death. A will is by its nature revocable at any time by the person who creates it until the person's death. There are five main functions that a valid will can serve: (1) making positive dispositions of real and personal property, (2) directing how property is *not* to be distributed (e.g., disinheriting individuals in whole or in part who would otherwise be entitled to a distribution of property under intestacy), (3) making arrangements for the disposing of one's body after death, (4) providing for the guardianship of minor children, and (5) naming a person to act as executor or executrix of the estate. (See Figure 31.1 for a sample will.)

## DEFINITIONS . . . . . . . . . . . . . . . . . . . . . . . . . . . . . . . . . . .

In order to understand the law relating to wills, it is important that you become familiar with the terminology on page 239.

*WILL*

LAST WILL AND TESTAMENT OF_____

I, _____, a resident of _____ County, in the state of _____, declare that this is my will.

FIRST:

I revoke all Wills and Codicils that I have previously made.

SECOND:

I am not currently married. I have no children now living, nor have I any deceased children who died and left issue.

THIRD:

I give all my jewelry, clothing, household furniture and furnishings, personal automobiles and other tangible articles of a personal nature, or my interest in any such property not otherwise disposed of by this will or in any other manner together with any insurance on the property, to _____, who presently resides at _____, _____ if he or she survives me by thirty (30) days, and if he or she does not so survive me, then I give said property to _____, who presently resides at _____, and if she or he does not survive me by thirty (30) days, then to _____, who presently resides at _____, otherwise to pass with the residency of my estate.

FOURTH:

I give the residue of my estate as follows:

1. To _____, who presently resides at _____, should he or she survive me by thirty (30) days.

2. If _____, who presently resides at _____, does not survive me by thirty (30) days, I give his or her interest to _____, who presently resides at _____, and if she does not survive me by thirty (30) days, then to _____, who presently resides at _____, should he or she survive me by thirty (30) days, and if he or she should not so survive me, then I give the rest and residue of my estate to those persons who would have taken said property under the intestacy laws of the state of _____.

FIFTH:

I nominate _____, who shall be represented by _____, as Executor of this Will, to serve without bond. If he or she shall for any reason fail to qualify as Executor, I nominate _____, who shall be represented by _____, as Executor to serve without bond. The term "my Executor" as used in this Will shall include any personal representative of my estate.

I authorize my Executor to sell, with or without notice, at either public or private sale, and to lease any property belonging to my estate, subject only to such confirmation of court as may be required by law.

**FIGURE 31.1**   Sample will (simple form)

I authorize my Executor to invest and reinvest any surplus money in the Executor's hands in every kind of property, real, personal, or mixed and every kind of investment, specifically including but not limited to interest-bearing accounts, corporate obligations of every kind, preferred or common stocks, shares of investment trusts, investment companies, mutual funds or common trust funds, including funds administered by the Executor, and mortgage participations, that men of prudence, discretion, and intelligence acquire for their own account.

SIXTH:

I direct that all inheritance, estate or other death taxes (excluding any additional tax imposed under Internal Revenue Code Section 2032A or any generation-skipping transfer tax) that may by reason of my death be attributable to my probate estate or any portion of it, or to any property or transfers of property outside my probate estate, shall be paid by my Executor out of the residue of my estate disposed of by this Will, without adjustment among the residuary beneficiaries, and shall not be charged against or collected from any beneficiary of my probate estate, or from any transferee or beneficiary of any property outside my probate estate.

SEVENTH:

If any beneficiary under this Will in any manner, directly or indirectly, contests or attacks this Will or any of its provisions, any share or interest in my estate given to the contesting beneficiary under this Will is revoked and shall be disposed of in the same manner provided herein as if that contesting beneficiary had predeceased me without issue.

I subscribe my name to this Will on _____,19__, at _____.

_____

On the date written below, _____ declared to us, the undersigned, that this instrument, consisting of these few pages including the page signed by us as witnesses, was his or her Will and requested us to act as witnesses to it. He or she thereupon signed this Will in our presence, all of us being present at the same time. We now, at his or her request, in his or her presence and in the presence of each other, subscribe our names as witnesses.

Each states that the testator is not a minor and appears to be of sound mind and that we have no knowledge or any facts indicating that the foregoing instrument, or any part of it, was procured by duress, menace, fraud or undue influence.

We, each of himself or herself, declare that each of us is over the age of majority, and that each of us is, and the others appear to be, of sound mind.

We, each for himself or herself, declare under penalty of perjury that the foregoing is true and correct and that this attestation and this declaration are executed on the _____ day of _____, 19__, at _____, _____.

_____, residing at _____.
_____, residing at _____.
_____, residing at _____.

**FIGURE 31.1**  Continued

Decedent: A person who has died (with or without a valid will).

Testator:  A man who executes a valid will.

Testatrix: A woman who executes a valid will.

Executor: A man appointed by a testator or testatrix to carry out the wishes and provisions expressed in a will, and to dispose of property in accordance with the testamentary provisions after the death of the testator or testatrix.

Executrix: A woman appointed by a testator or testatrix to carry out the wishes and provisions expressed in a will, and to dispose of property in accordance with the testamentary provisions after the death of the testator or testatrix.

Intestacy: The state of dying without having executed a valid will.

Intestate: Without a valid will. A person dies intestate when he or she has not left a will, or has left a will that is invalid because it fails to meet the technical requirements for a valid will.

Intestate Succession: The laws in a state that determine how a decedent's property is to be distributed when the decedent has died without having left a valid will.

Intestacy Statute: A state's statute that determines how a decedent's property is to be distributed when the decedent has died without having left a valid will.

Distributee: A person entitled to take or to share in a decedent's property under the laws governing intestacy.

Issue: Descendants in any degree from a common ancestor (includes adopted children).

*Per Capita:* A distribution made to named individuals or to a class of individuals in which each takes an equal share. Literally means a distribution "by the heads" on a "share and share alike" basis.

*Per Stirpes:* A distribution made "by the roots," or by lineage, where interested individuals take a proportionate share of a distribution that a deceased ancestor would have been entitled to had he or she been alive. When a distribution is made *per stirpes*, as is the case in intestacy statutes, descendants of a common ancestor by blood or through adoption share in any distribution intended for the deceased ancestor. Thus, if a distribution is made for two sisters *per stirpes* and one had died before the testator, the dead distributee's share would pass to her direct descendants on a *per stirpes* basis, rather than vesting on the surviving codistributee, as would be the case in a *per capita* distribution.

Bequest: A gift of personal property by will (also called a *legacy*).

Devise: A gift of real property by will.

Codicil: A supplement to a will that either alters any provision in the will or reaffirms it. A codicil must be executed in exactly the same way as a will in order to be valid.

# REQUIREMENTS OF A VALID WILL    · · · · · · · · · · · · · · · · · · · · · ·

Although laws relating to the creation of a valid will vary somewhat among the fifty states, the requirements for the creation of a valid will tend to be relatively uniform. With the exception of holographic and nuncupative wills, which we will discuss shortly, all wills must meet the following criteria in order to be valid:

- the testator or testatrix must be of legal age;
- the testator or testatrix must have the legal capacity to dispose of property;
- the will must be written (unless it is a nuncupative will) and signed by the testator or testatrix at its end (a signature appearing before the end of the will invalidates any provisions in the will that appear after the signature);
- the will must be signed before witnesses or acknowledged before witnesses by the testator or testatrix who must then sign as witnesses to the will (two or three witnesses are required, depending on the jurisdiction); and
- in some jurisdictions, the will needs to be published.

## REQUIREMENT OF LEGAL AGE

A testator or testatrix must be of legal age (eighteen years of age in most jurisdictions) in order to execute a valid will. A will executed by a minor is void and is *not* deemed ratified when the minor reaches legal age.

## REQUIREMENT OF LEGAL CAPACITY

In order for a will to be valid, the testator or testatrix must have the legal capacity to dispose of property at the time of executing the will. Wills drafted by incompetents, like those drafted by minors, are void. Competence is measured as of the time that the will is drafted. That a legally competent person becomes incompetent subsequent to drafting the will does not invalidate the instrument.

Fraud, duress, and undue influence can invalidate a testator's or testatrix's capacity in much the same way as they serve to invalidate genuine assent to a contract. Thus, a will that is shown to have been drafted as a result of fraud, duress or undue influence is void.

## REQUIREMENT OF A SIGNED WRITING

There is no special form that needs to be used in drafting a valid will, and writing of any sort on any type of paper with any type of writing instrument is acceptable if the writing conforms to the requirements for a valid will. The signature of the testator or testatrix must appear at the end of the will, following all of its provisions. If by some mistake it appears otherwise than at the end of the will, any provisions following the signature are ignored, but the will is still valid minus such provisions in most jurisdictions.

The requirement of a signature is liberally construed, as is generally the case in other legal instruments. Any mark made by the testator or testatrix on the will intended as a signature will satisfy the requirement of a signature.

## REQUIREMENT OF WITNESSING THE WILL

Most jurisdictions require that wills be witnessed by at least two or three witnesses who sign either after seeing the testator or testatrix sign before them or after having the testator or testatrix acknowledge his or her signature on the will to them. If the testator or testatrix does not sign immediately before the witnesses, the witnessing of the will must usually take place within a set time of the testator's or testatrix's signing of the will. (In New York, for example, a will must be witnessed within thirty days of its execution by the testator or testatrix.)

Witnesses are not required to know what is in the will and, in fact, ought not to be allowed to read it unless the testator or testatrix expresses the wish that they do so, since witnesses are not acknowledging the contents of the will, but rather that the testator or testatrix signed with the intention of creating the will.

If more than the required number of witnesses sign the will, any excess witnesses are referred to as *supernumeraries*. The presence of supernumeraries does not affect the validity of the will; in fact, supernumeraries can be useful when witnesses are required to testify as to their witnessing the will or to the testator's or testatrix's state of mind (especially in cases involving contests of the will) since witnesses can die, move from a jurisdiction or have lapses of memory.

A problem can arise with witnesses who are also entitled to receive a bequest or devise under the will. Generally speaking, such witnesses do not invalidate the will, but are barred from taking under the terms of the will unless they are also entitled to take under the laws of intestacy. If that is the case, then an interested witness may take the *lesser* of his or her intestate share or the bequest or devise provided for in the will. If there is a conflict involving an interested witness, but the will can be validated without the interested witness's signature because of the existence of a supernumerary, then the interested witness may take his or her full share under the terms of the will.

## REQUIREMENT OF PUBLICATION OF THE WILL

Some jurisdictions require that a will be not only witnessed but also published by the testator or testatrix. The publication requirement is fulfilled, however, merely by the communication of the testator or testatrix to the witnesses that the instrument they are asked to sign is the last will and testament of the testator or testatrix. For example, a will is published by the testator or testatrix asking each of the witnesses to sign as follows: "This is my last will and testament. Please acknowledge my signature and sign as a witness in the space provided." Any similar words that clearly convey to the witnesses that the instrument is the last will and testament of the testator or testatrix will generally suffice as fulfilling the requirement of publication, where one exists.

# HOLOGRAPHIC AND NUNCUPATIVE WILLS  . . . . . . . . . . . . . . . . .

As previously noted, there are two types of wills recognized in many states that represent a departure from the traditional will format and do not require the same formalities as traditional wills: holographic wills and nuncupative wills.

## HOLOGRAPHIC WILLS

A *holographic will* is one that is completely written out in the testator's handwriting. In states that recognize such wills as having a special status, the requirements of a signature, witnessing and publication are dispensed with. The rationale for treating holographic wills differently from traditional wills is that it is far less likely for a holographic will to be forged than is the case for a traditional form will. In states that do not recognize holographic wills as such, a will that is entirely written in the testator or testatrix's own hand is still perfectly valid, but must also be signed and witnessed as any other will.

## NUNCUPATIVE WILLS

A *nuncupative will* is an oral will that is dictated by the testator or testatrix to two or more witnesses. Many states recognize such wills, but place strict limitations on their validity, usually recognizing them as valid only if they are dictated by a soldier during active duty in an armed conflict or by a mariner at sea. For this reason, such wills are also commonly referred to as "soldier's and sailor's wills."

States that recognize nuncupative wills also place a time limit on their effectiveness. Typically, a nuncupative will dictated by a soldier is valid until one year after the cessation of the hostilities in which the soldier was taking part at the time of dictating the will. In cases of mariners at sea, a nuncupative will is also limited in duration to a set period after the sailor reaches land. (In New York, for example, such wills are valid for three years from the time of their making.)

The purpose for these wills is obvious: to allow persons to make relatively informal wills at a time when they might be otherwise unable to execute a traditional will due to their special circumstances. If an oral will is not re-executed as a valid traditional will within the time specified in the state's statute, then it expires and the testator's or testatrix's estate will be distributed under the intestacy statute when he or she dies.

Since these wills are not reduced to a writing by the testator or testatrix, they are proven by the testimony of the witnesses as to the wishes of the testator or testatrix. Interested witnesses to a nuncupative will are treated exactly the same as interested witnesses to a traditional will and generally cannot benefit from the will.

# REVOCATION OF A WILL   . . . . . . . . . . . . . . . . . . . . . . . . . . . .

A will is revocable at any time prior to the death of the testator or testatrix, and may be revoked by any unequivocal act that clearly shows an attempt to revoke the will. Thus, a testator or testatrix who writes "VOID" across all pages of a will and initials each page will effectively cancel the will, as does one who tears it up with the intent of destroying it. But the cancellation of part of a will is generally ineffectual; thus, crossing out a single will provision and initialing it will generally not result in a cancellation of the provision or of the entire will. (A codicil is needed to effectuate such a change.) Although the destruction of a will does not necessarily imply its revocation, if a will that was last known to be in the hands of the decedent is not found upon his or her death, a revocation of the will is presumed.

The subsequent writing of a will automatically revokes any previous wills if it includes a blanket revocation to that effect. If the drafter of a new will neglects to revoke prior wills specifically, then to the extent that the new will changes any of the provisions of an earlier will, these are deemed to have been revoked. But consistent provisions in both wills are read together. For this reason, the revocation of all prior wills is always the first clause in every will.

Marriage does not in itself revoke a prior will, except that a wife or husband cannot be disinherited. A will made prior to marriage will be subject to a spouse's intestate share should the testator or testatrix die without having changed the will. Divorce, on the other hand, does sever the prior spouse's rights to take any part of the decedent's estate, both under intestacy and under any unrevoked will provision. Upon a final divorce decree, a will's provisions in favor of a divorced spouse are automatically revoked; if the divorced spouses subsequently remarry each other, the revoked bequests or devises in the unrevoked will are reinstated, as are the spousal intestacy rights.

## DISINHERITANCE OF SPOUSES AND CHILDREN . . . . . . . . . . . . . . . .

As previously noted, two of the five main functions that a valid will can serve include making positive dispositions of real and personal property and directing how property is *not* to be distributed. While a testator or testatrix is free to dispose of his or her property in any way he or she sees fit, there are limits on a testator's or testatrix's right to disinherit his or her spouse and children. In every state, it is impossible to wholly disinherit a spouse to whom one is legally married at death. If an attempt to disinherit a spouse is made, the spouse will be able to assert his or her rights to a statutory minimum portion of the estate.

Under English common law, a spouse was absolutely entitled to a portion of a decedent spouse's estate. If the surviving spouse was a widow, she was entitled to *dower*—a life estate in one-third of all the husband's real property upon his death in order to assure her sustenance and that of her children. A surviving widower was likewise entitled to assert his right of *curtesy*—a life estate in all of a deceased wife's real property if the marriage had produced a legitimate child which was born alive and might inherit the estate. While dower and curtesy have been largely abolished or modified in the vast majority of states, a similar right for both husbands and wives is retained today in the form of an *inalienable intestacy* share. In every state, a surviving spouse is entitled to at least a life interest in the estate of the dead spouse.

Children are not given protection from disinheritance in most states. While some states require that a nominal sum (such as one dollar) be awarded to a surviving child or that the child be specifically named in order to be disinherited, in most states parents can disinherit children simply by failing to make any provisions for them in a will.

## INTESTACY

Whenever a decedent has died without leaving a valid will, he or she is said to have died *intestate*, and the state determines how the decedent's property will be distributed to the decedent's family. Every state has an intestacy statute that details how a decedent's estate is to be distributed after death. While such statutes generally reflect an attempt to distribute a decedent's assets in accordance with what a state's legislature believes to be the wishes of most residents in the state, the contents of your state's intestacy statute might surprise you; the basic assumptions you might make as to who will get your property upon your death might well not coincide with your state's intestacy statute. (See Figure 31.2 for a sample intestacy statute.) If that is the case, the only way to ensure that your wishes are followed is to execute a valid will.

## QUESTIONS

1. What is a will? What basic functions do wills serve?
2. What is the effect of a will drafted by a child?
3. How many witnesses are typically required for a valid will?
4. What is a supernumerary?
5. Do witnesses generally need to know what is in the will? Is there an exception to this rule?
6. In jurisdictions that require the publication of a will, does the will have to be published in a newspaper of general circulation? Explain.
7. What are holographic and nuncupative wills?
8. How can a valid will be revoked?
9. Can children and spouses be disinherited? Explain.
10. What is intestacy and what is the net result of dying intestate?

## H Y P O T H E T I C A L    C A S E S

1. Sandy Soldier, while at her barracks in time of peace, decides it would be a good idea to make a will. She asks three friends to be witnesses to her will and she tells them that it is her intent to leave all of her personal and real property to her parents, share and share alike, except that she wants her valuable stamp collection to go to her brother, Benny. While she speaks, one of the three witnesses, William,

*Estates, Powers and Trusts Laws*

Article 4

### Section 4-1.1 Descent and distribution of a decedent's estate

The property of a decedent not disposed of by will shall be distributed as provided in this section. In computing said distribution, debts, administration expenses and reasonable funeral expenses shall be deducted but all estate taxes shall be disregarded, except that nothing contained herein relieves a distributee from contributing to all such taxes the amounts apportioned against him or her under [Section] 2-1.8.

Distribution shall then be as follows:

(a) If a decedent is survived by:

(1) A spouse and issue, fifty thousand dollars and one-half of the residue to the spouse, and the balance thereof to the issue by representation.

(2) A spouse and no issue, the whole to the spouse.

(3) Issue and no spouse, the whole to the issue, by representation.

(4) One or both parents, and no spouse and no issue, the whole to the surviving parent or parents.

(5) Issue of parents, and no spouse, issue or parent, the whole to the issue of the parents, by representation.

(6) One or more grandparents or the issue of grandparents (as hereinafter defined), and no spouse, issue, parent or issue of parents, one-half to the surviving paternal grandparent or grandparents, or if neither of them survives the decedent, to their issue, by representation, and the other one-half to the surviving maternal grandparent or grandparents, or if neither of them survives the decedent, to their issue, by representation; provided that if the decedent was not survived by a grandparent or grandparents on one side or by the issue of such grandparents, the whole to the surviving grandparent or grandparents on the other side, or if neither of them survives the decedent, to their issue, by representation, in the same manner as the one-half. For the purposes of this subparagraph, issue of grandparents shall not include issue more remote than grandchildren of such grandparents.

(7) Great-grandchildren of grandparents, and no spouse, issue, parent, issue of parents, grandparent, children of grandparents or grandchildren of grandparents, one-half to the great-grandchildren of the paternal grandparents, per capita, and the other one-half to the great-grandchildren of the maternal grandparents, per capita; provided that if the decedent was not survived by great-grandchildren of grandparents on one side, the whole to the great-grandchildren of grandparents on the other side, in the same manner as the one-half.

(b) For all purposes of this section, decedent's relatives of the half blood shall be treated as if they were relatives of the whole blood.

(c) Distributees of the decedent, conceived before his or her death but born alive thereafter, take as if they were born in his or her lifetime.

(d) The right of an adopted child to take a distributive share and the right of succession to the estate of an adopted child continue as provided in the domestic relations law.

(e) A distributive share passing to a surviving spouse under this section is in lieu of any right of dower to which such spouse may be entitled.

**FIGURE 31.2**    Sample intestacy statute [New York State]

takes notes. When Sandy notices that William has taken notes, she reads them and, finding them an accurate reflection of her wishes, she initials them at the end. Six months later, Sandy dies in an automobile accident.

   a. Did she effectively create a will by dictating it under the circumstances? Explain fully.

   b. Did Sandy create a valid will by initialing William's notes? Explain.

   c. How will Sandy's property be distributed?

2. Tiffany Testatrix, a young woman of sixteen, wants to create a will after learning of a friend's tragic death. She does a little bit of background reading on the subject, and then writes out the following document completely in her own hand:

I, Tiffany Testatrix, being of sound and disposing mind hereby make my last Will and Testament.

I leave my porcelain doll collection to Jane Jones, my best friend. I also leave all of my personal papers and collection of photographs to Jane.

I leave the money in my bank accounts to my parents *per stirpes*.

I name my brother, Michael, to act as my executor. If Michael is unable or unwilling to act in that capacity, then I name my father as executor of my estate.

I wish my eyes, kidneys, liver and heart to be donated to a local hospital for use in transplants that might give others a second chance at life. I wish the remainder of my remains to be cremated and scattered at sea.

The rest, residue and remainder of my estate is to go to the American Red Cross.

[Initialed] T. T.

   a. What type of will is involved here?

   b. Is the will valid?

   c. Do the initials suffice as a signature in this will?

   d. If Tiffany dies upon reaching her ninetieth birthday without having drafted another will, how will her property be distributed?

3. Assume the same facts as in the previous question, except that Tiffany is eighteen and of legal age at the time that she executed the instrument.

   a. Is this a valid will? Explain fully.

   b. Assuming that Tiffany's state recognizes the type of will involved here, does the fact that it has not been witnessed invalidate it?

   c. Assume for the sake of this question that the instrument is valid and that upon her death Tiffany has amassed a billion-dollar real-estate empire, that her collection of porcelain dolls is worth $1,000,000 and that she has $250,000 in savings and checking accounts. Further assume that Tiffany's parents have died before her, but that her childhood friend, Jane, and her brother, Michael, are still alive. How will her assets be distributed?

   d. Assume that Michael is unhappy with the will and wishes to contest its validity. In the event that he is successful in showing that Tiffany did not have the requisite state of mind to dispose of property or that the will was not seriously intended, thus invalidating the instrument, how is the property likely to be distributed?

4. Thomas Testator drafts a valid will when he is thirty years old and single in which he leaves all of his estate to his parents, or, if they predecease him, to various charities. At thirty-five, Thomas marries Tawana and remains married to her until his death at the ripe old age of 100, with Tawana surviving him. He never changes his will, and at his death both parents have predeceased him.
   a. Who gets his estate? Be specific.
   b. Assume that soon after marrying, Thomas takes out his will and crosses out the provision giving his property to his parents and replaces Tawana's name where the will had previously read to the parents if they survived him, else to the named charities. What is the effect of this change?
   c. What if Thomas writes "VOID" across each page of the will and initials each page after doing so?

## ETHICS AND THE LAW: QUESTIONS FOR FURTHER STUDY · · · · · · · · · · · · · · · · · · · · · · · · · · · · · · · · · ·

Most states permit children to be disinherited, but not spouses. The prohibition against disinheriting a spouse is absolute, regardless of the underlying relationship between the parties, the length of the marriage, or the support (or lack thereof) that the spouses provided to one another during their married lives. Would you characterize this as a just and ethical law? How about the ability to disinherit children, regardless of the underlying relationship or support that children might have given to the parent throughout their lives? Should a bad marriage convey greater interests in the estate of a deceased spouse than the interest that a good, nurturing, supportive and loving child obtains as a birthright and by affinity of blood? What arguments based on sound ethical principles can you make for the maintenance of the current law or for its change? Should the same rights apply to live-in partners who are not married?

# CHAPTER

# 32

# TRUSTS

Up until now, our discussion has focused on transfers of property that involve ownership interests. But it is also possible to transfer less than a full ownership right in property by giving or selling to someone the right to benefit from property owned by another. We have already been exposed to this concept in our study of real property, where we've seen that it is possible to give or sell to someone less than a full fee simple interest in property, such as by the transfer of a life estate or an estate for years, where the recipient of the property interest obtains the right to benefit from it for life or for a set period of time, but not full ownership of the property. The same concept applies to a *trust*, where the actual property is held by a third party (the *trustee*) who is its legal owner but must manage the property for the benefit of the trust beneficiary, as well as income that the property produces.

A trust is an arrangement whereby property is transferred by its owner to some third party or parties who are entrusted with its management for the benefit of a named beneficiary. A trust involves a *fiduciary relationship* (a confidential relationship based on trust) in which the trustee (the person entrusted with the property) must exercise the highest duty of care and honesty in exercising his or her duties, and place the interests of the beneficiary of the trust above his or her own.

Before we continue with our discussion, it might be wise to define some terms.

Trust: An arrangement whereby real or personal property is held by one person entrusted with its management and care for the benefit of another.

Trustee: A person entrusted with the care of property for the benefit of another.

Beneficiary: A person who receives the income or other benefits derived from property under the care of a trustee.

Trust Corpus: The underlying property that forms the basis of the trust. (Literally *the body of the trust.*)

Trust Settlor: The creator of a trust who gives the trust corpus over to the trustee for the benefit of the beneficiary. (The settlor is also commonly referred to as the trustor or creator.)

Express Trust: A trust created by the express wishes of the settlor.

Resulting Trust: A trust that arises by implication of law or the requirements of equity from the implied intent of the settlor in creating a trust. The most common resulting trust is a trust in favor of the settlor when an express trust fails or upon the death of an express beneficiary when the settlor had not expressly named secondary beneficiaries of the trust.

Constructive Trust: A fictional trust deemed by courts to exist as an equitable remedy to avoid unjust enrichment in cases where property is obtained through unlawful means such as fraud or duress.

Private Trust: An express trust for the benefit of specific beneficiaries.

Charitable Trust: A trust for a religious, educational or other philanthropic purpose that does not benefit specific individual beneficiaries, but rather charitable organizations or the public at large.

*Inter vivos* Trust: A trust created by the settlor during his or her lifetime.

Testamentary Trust: A trust created by a provision in a will that is not to take effect until the settlor's death.

## CREATION OF EXPRESS TRUSTS · · · · · · · · · · · · · · · · · · · · · · · · · ·

The creation of an *express trust* requires that the trust settlor deliver to the trustee (or trustees) the trust corpus with the intention of creating a trust for the benefit of the trust beneficiary. When an *inter vivos* trust is involved, the settlor personally delivers the trust corpus to the trustee; in a testamentary trust, it is the executor of the estate who is charged with delivering the trust corpus to the trustee.

In order for a valid trust to be created, the trust must be for a lawful purpose. As long as the noted requirements are met, a trust can be created orally or through a signed writing. But if an interest in real estate is involved as the trust corpus, a signed writing is required in order to satisfy the statute of frauds.

## REQUIREMENTS, RIGHTS AND RESPONSIBILITIES OF TRUSTEES · · · · · · · · · · · · · · · · · · · · · · · · · · · · · · · · · · · ·

Individuals who wish to serve as trustees must be of legal age and cannot be incompetent. States often impose other requirements on trustees, such as that they not be convicted felons or unable to execute their duties due to alcohol or drug addiction. A residency requirement may also be imposed by states on trustees.

During the period that the trust is in force, the trustee is the legal owners of the trust corpus. If more than one trustee is named in a trust, then the trustees own property as joint tenants. Trustees must use reasonable care in the management of trust property and can be sued for any loss resulting from mismanagement of the trust that arises out of negligence or incompetence. Because trustees perform a valuable service to the trust beneficiary, they are entitled to reasonable compensation for their services unless they specifically agree to serve gratuitously.

Upon the termination of a trust that is either revocable by its nature or set to automatically expire upon the happening of an event or the passage of time, the trust corpus revests in the settlor or otherwise as provided in the trust instrument, and the trustees' interest in the trust corpus ends.

## REVOCABLE AND IRREVOCABLE TRUSTS    . . . . . . . . . . . . . . . . . .

A trust is irrevocable unless the settlor specifically reserves the power to revoke the trust. In a typical revocable trust, the settlor retains the right to revoke the trust or to alter its beneficiaries, trustees or the trust's income provisions during the settlor's lifetime. A settlor can also reserve the right to appoint the remainder interest in the trust by will. In addition, a trust can be set up to automatically terminate at a future date or upon the happening of an event. If the power to revoke is retained by the settlor, then he or she also retains a reversionary interest in the trust corpus, called a *resulting trust by reversion*, which vests the trust corpus in the settlor if the power of revocation is exercised in the future, or if the corpus is set to revest in the settlor upon the happening of an event or the expiration of a set period of time. For example, a settlor who creates a trust for the benefit of a child that is to run for the child's lifetime reserves for himself or herself a resulting trust by reversion upon the child's death. (See Figures 32.1 and 32.2 for samples of irrevocable and revocable trusts.)

## TOTTEN TRUSTS  . . . . . . . . . . . . . . . . . . . . . . . . . . . . . . . . . . .

A *Totten trust* gets its name from the case that led to its recognition in New York (*Matter of Totten*, 179 NY 112 [1904]), but such trusts are also recognized in many other states. In a Totten trust, the settlor opens a bank account in his or her own name in trust for a named beneficiary. During the settlor's life, the trust is freely revocable by the settlor in whole or in part by either closing the account or removing money from it. If the settlor has not revoked the account at his or her death, however, the funds in the account vest in the beneficiary.

In addition to being subject to revocation by the settlor during his or her life, a Totten trust can also be revoked by a will in which the testator or testatrix gives the money in the account to a beneficiary other than the account's named trustee. In order to revoke a Totten trust by will (in New York, at least), the testator or testatrix must specifically name the bank account, give its account number, state the bank at which the account is held and the name of the beneficiary named in the account.

### IRREVOCABLE TRUST

TRUST AGREEMENT made this _____ day of _____, 19___, be-tween _____ (the "Grantor") and _____ and _____(the "Trustees").

1. TRUST PROPERTY. The Grantor, desiring to create trusts for the benefit of his adult children and for other good and valuable consideration, irrevocably assigns to the Trustees the property described in attached Schedule A (the "Trust Property"), in trust, for the purposes and on the conditions hereinafter stated.

2. DISPOSITIVE PROVISIONS. The Trustees shall hold the property for the primary benefit of _____ and _____ (the "Beneficiaries"), and the Trustees shall hold, manage and invest the trust property, and shall collect and receive the income, and after deducting all necessary expenses incident to the administration of the trusts, shall dispose of the corpus and income of the trusts as follows:

(a) The Trustees shall pay the entire net income of the trust, quarter-annually, to the beneficiaries of the trust, provided that there shall be paid over absolutely to the beneficiaries at age _____ the corpus of the trust.

(b) If any of the beneficiaries shall die before attaining the age of _____ years, the trust for his or her benefit shall cease, and the corpus, together with any undistributed income, shall be paid over absolutely to the issue of the beneficiary then living per stirpes; but if there be no issue, then to the other beneficiaries if living, either outright, or, if the other beneficiary shall not have then attained the age of ____ years, in trust, to be added to, held, administered, and distributed as part of the trust for the other beneficiary; but if the other beneficiary is not then living, then absolutely to the then-living issue of the other beneficiary per stirpes; and if there is no issue, then to the estate of the beneficiary for whom the trust was being held originally.

(c) Notwithstanding anything contained to the contrary, if at any time while the trusts are in force any financial emergency arises in the affairs of either of the primary beneficiaries of the trusts, or if the independent income of either of the beneficiaries (exclusive of the income from any trust created for his or her benefit by the Grantor) and all other means of support are insufficient for the support of the beneficiary, in the judgment of the Trustees, the Trustees shall pay over to the beneficiary, solely out of the corpus of the trust for his or her benefit, at any time and from time to time, the sum or sums as the Trustees shall deem necessary or appropriate in their discretion.

3. TRUSTEES' POWERS. In the administration of the trusts, the Trustees shall have the following powers, all of which shall be exercised in the fiduciary capacity, primarily in the interest of the beneficiaries:

(a) To hold and continue to hold as an investment the property, or any additional property which may be received by them, so long as they deem proper, and to invest and reinvest in any securities or property, whether or not income-producing, deemed by them to be for the best interest of the trusts and the beneficiaries.

(b) To rent or lease any property of the trusts for the time and upon the terms and for the price or prices as in their discretion and judgment may seem just and proper and for the best interest of the trusts and the beneficiaries.

(c) To sell and convey any of the property of the trusts or any interest, or to exchange it for other property, for the price or prices and upon the terms as in their discretion and judgment may be deemed for the best interest of the trusts and the beneficiaries.

(d) To make all repairs and improvements at any time deemed necessary and proper to and upon real property constituting a part of the trusts.

(e) To deduct, retain, expend, and pay out of any money belonging to the trusts any and all necessary and proper expenses in connection with the operation and conduct of the trusts.

**FIGURE 32.1**    Sample irrevocable trust

(f) To vote upon all securities belonging to the trusts, and to become a party to any stockholders' agreements deemed advisable by them in connection with the securities.

(g) To consent to the reorganization, consolidation, merger, liquidation or readjustment of, or other change in, any corporation, company, or association.

(h) To compromise, settle, arbitrate or defend any claim or demand in favor of or against the trusts.

(i) To incur and pay the ordinary and necessary expenses of administration, including (but not by way of limitation) reasonable attorneys' fees, accountants' fees, investment counsel fees, and the like.

(j) To act through an agent or attorney-in-fact, by and under power of attorney duly executed by the Trustees, in carrying out any of the authorized powers and duties.

(k) To borrow money for any purposes of the trusts, or incidental to their administration, upon their bond or promissory note as trustees, and to secure their repayment by mortgaging, creating a security interest in, or pledging or otherwise encumbering any part or all of the property of the trusts.

(l) To lend money to any person or persons upon the terms and in the ways and with the security as they may deem advisable for the best interest of the trusts and the beneficiaries.

(m) To engage in business with the property of the trusts as sole proprietor, or as a general or limited partner, with all the powers customarily exercised by an individual so engaged in business, and to hold an undivided interest in any property as tenant in common or as tenant in partnership.

(n) To determine the manner in which the expenses incidental to or in connection with the administration of the trusts shall be apportioned as between corpus and income.

(o) The Trustees may freely act under all or any of the powers by this Agreement given to them in all matters concerning the trusts, after forming their judgment based upon all the circumstances of any particular situation as to the wisest and best course to pursue in the interest of the trusts and the beneficiaries, without the necessity of obtaining the consent or permission of any interested person, or the consent or approval of any court.

The powers granted to the Trustees may be exercised in whole or in part, from time to time, and shall be deemed to be supplementary to and not exclusive of the general powers of trustees pursuant to law, and shall include all powers necessary to carry them into effect.

4. LIMITATION ON POWERS. Notwithstanding anything contained to the contrary, no powers enumerated or accorded to trustees generally pursuant to law shall be construed to enable the Grantor, or the Trustees or either of them, or any other person, to sell, purchase, exchange, or otherwise deal with or dispose of all or any parts of the corpus or income of the trusts for less than an adequate consideration in money or monies worth, or to enable the Grantor to borrow all or any part of the corpus or income of the trusts, directly or indirectly, without adequate interest or security.

5. CORPUS AND INCOME. The Trustees shall have the power to determine the allocation of receipts between corpus and income and to apportion extraordinary and share dividends between corpus and income.

6. TRUSTEES' AUTHORITY AND THIRD PARTIES. No person purchasing, renting, or leasing any of the property of the trusts, or in any manner dealing with the trusts or with the Trustees, shall be required to inquire into the authority of the Trustees to enter into any transaction, or to account for the application of any money paid to the Trustees on any account.

7. ADDITIONAL PROPERTY. The Grantor reserves the right to himself or to any other person at any time, by deed or will, to add to the corpus of either or both of the trusts, and any property added shall be held, administered, and distributed as part of the trust or trusts. The additional property shall be allocated between the trusts in accordance with any directions given in the instrument of transfer.

**FIGURE 32.1**    Continued

8. ACCOUNTING BY TRUSTEES. The Trustees may render an accounting at any time to the beneficiaries of the trust, and the written approval of a beneficiary shall be final, binding, and conclusive upon all persons then or thereafter interested in the trust for that beneficiary. The Trustees may at any time render a judicial account of their proceedings for either or both of the trusts.

9. COMPENSATION OF TRUSTEES. The Trustees waive the payment of any compensation for their services, but this waiver shall not apply to any successor trustee who qualifies and acts under this Agreement except that no person who adds to the corpus of either or both of the trusts shall ever be entitled to any compensation.

10. SUCCESSOR TRUSTEES. Either of Trustees shall have the power to appoint his or her successor Trustee. If either of the named Trustees shall die, resign, become incapacitated, or refuse to act further as Trustee, without having appointed a successor Trustee, the other named Trustee may, but shall not be required to, appoint a successor Trustee. The appointment of a successor Trustee shall be made by a duly acknowledged instrument delivered to the primary beneficiaries and to the person, if any, then acting as Trustee.

11. BOND AND LIABILITY OF TRUSTEES. Neither of the two (2) named Trustees shall be required to give any bond or other security. The Trustees shall not be liable for any mistake or error of judgment in the administration of the trusts, except for willful misconduct, so long as they continue to exercise their duties and powers in a fiduciary capacity primarily in the interests of the beneficiaries.

12. IRREVOCABILITY. The trusts shall be irrevocable, and the Grantor expressly waives all rights and powers, whether alone or in conjunction with others, and regardless of when or from what source he may have acquired such rights or powers, to alter, amend, revoke, or terminate the trusts, or any of the terms of this Agreement, in whole or in part. By this instrument the Grantor relinquishes absolutely and forever all his possession or enjoyment of, or right to the income from, the trust property, and all his right and power, whether alone or in conjunction with others, to designate the persons who shall possess or enjoy the trust property, or the income.

13. SITUS. This trust has been executed and delivered in the State of _____ and shall be construed and administered according to the laws of that state.

In witness whereof the Grantor and the Trustees have executed this Agreement in the City of_____, County of _____.

_____
Grantor

_____
Trustee

_____
Trustee

**FIGURE 32.1**    Continued

*REVOCABLE TRUST*

_____, SETTLOR, of _____ in the County of _____, has this day conveyed and transferred to _____, a _____ located at and of _____, State of _____, TRUSTEE, the property as listed and set forth in Schedule A attached hereto and made a part hereof, and the said Trustee hereby makes and executes this Declaration of Trust and hereby agrees for itself and its successors in effect, to hold said property and any property from time to time added hereto IN TRUST NEVERTHELESS upon the following uses and benefits, that is to say:

FIRST: The property shall be held, managed, invested and reinvested by the Trustee, and its successor or successors, with all the powers to the Trustee as herein provided.

SECOND: The Trustee shall divide the Trust Property into equal shares for each of the beneficiaries, namely _____, and shall pay to, or apply for the benefit of, said named beneficiaries such amount, or amounts, of the net income and/or principal from each of said shares as the Trustee in its uncontrolled discretion may determine, any net income in any year which is not paid to, or applied for the benefit of, the beneficiary of each said share shall be added to the principal of said share at the end of the year.

THIRD: The Trustee shall pay to each of said beneficiaries the principal of the share held for his or her benefit, free and discharged from any Trust in or within one (1) year from the date of the death of the last surviving settlor unless this trust is sooner revoked.

FOURTH: In extension and not in limitation of the powers given them by law or other provisions of this instrument, the Trustee and any successor or successors shall have the full power with respect to any property in any Trust established hereunder, to deal with the same as if he or she were the owner thereof without order or license of any Court.

FIFTH: The interest of each beneficiary in the income and principal of a trust under this instrument shall be free from the control or interference of any creditor of the beneficiary or any spouse of a married beneficiary and shall not be subject to attachment or susceptible of anticipation or alienation.

SIXTH: This Declaration of Trust is revocable and the Settlor retains the power to alter, amend or revoke this instrument either in whole or in part at any time. Revocation shall be accomplished by a certificate of the Settlor delivered to the Trustee personally or by certified mail.

IN WITNESS WHEREOF _____ and _____, Settlors, and _____, Trustee, have hereunto set their hands and seals this ____ day of _____, 19___.

In presence of: _____        _____

_Notary Public_                                          _Settlor_

_____          _ _____

_Notary's Seal_                                          _Settlor_

_____

                                                              _Trustee_

**FIGURE 32.2**   Sample revocable trust

In addition to being revocable during the settlor's lifetime, Totten trusts are subject to attachment by creditors of the settlor after death, and are subject to the surviving spouse's elective share (the one-third inalienable intestacy share that a spouse is entitled to) if the surviving spouse has not been provided with at least the minimum required share by the decedent's will.

Finally, if a beneficiary of a Totten trust predeceases the settlor of the trust, the trust is automatically revoked and the corpus revests in the settlor.

## CREATION OF TESTAMENTARY TRUSTS · · · · · · · · · · · · · · · · · · ·

As previously noted, *testamentary trusts* are created by a provision in a will and do not take effect until the testator's death. It is the responsibility of the executor or executrix to turn over the trust corpus to the trustee after the death of the testator/settlor after the will has been probated.

## CREATION OF A RESULTING TRUST · · · · · · · · · · · · · · · · · · · · · ·

A *resulting trust* is a trust implied from the intentions of the settlor when an express trust fails. Thus, a resulting trust arises by operation of law and is not expressly created by the settlor. As previously noted, the most common type of resulting trust is a trust that results in favor of the settlor when an express trust fails and no other provisions are made by the settlor for the disposition of the trust corpus. For instance, if Andrew creates a trust in favor of Benita but makes no provisions for what is to happen to the trust corpus upon Benita's death, a resulting trust in favor of Andrew or Andrew's estate will be created by implication when Benita dies, the assumption being that the settlor intends to retain a future interest in the property once an express trust ends or fails.

## CREATION OF A CONSTRUCTIVE TRUST · · · · · · · · · · · · · · · · · · ·

Like a resulting trust, a *constructive trust* arises automatically by operation of law. A constructive trust, in fact, is not a trust at all but rather a legal fiction that the courts engage in so as to prevent unjust enrichment (much like the equitable quasi-contract we have seen in contract law). Whenever a person illegally obtains property that belongs to another, such as by theft, fraud, duress or undue influence, a constructive trust comes into effect and holds the person in possession of the property to be a trustee (albeit an unwilling one) for the benefit of the true owner of the property, who is both the constructive settlor and the constructive beneficiary of the trust. A constructive trust is, in effect, a legal remedy available to anyone who is illegally or fraudulently parted from his or her property to obtain both the return of the property and any gains made to it by the wrongdoer/"trustee" while the property was in his or her possession.

## TERMINATION OF TRUSTS ...........................

When a trust terminates depends on such factors as its terms and whether it is a revocable or an irrevocable trust. Both revocable and irrevocable trusts automatically terminate upon the accomplishment of their stated purpose, as, for example, the expiration of a set time period or the end of the beneficiary's life (if the trust was set to last for the beneficiary's lifetime). In addition, both revocable and irrevocable trusts end upon the trust corpus being depleted. Finally, revocable trusts can be terminated at any time by the settlor.

## QUESTIONS ...................................

1. What is a trust?
2. How is a trust created?
3. Does the creation of a trust require a writing?
4. Are trusts generally revocable or irrevocable?
5. How is a Totten trust created?
6. Are Totten trusts revocable? If so, how?
7. How are testamentary trusts created?
8. What is a resulting trust?
9. What is a constructive trust? How does such a trust come into existence?
10. How does a revocable trust terminate?

## H Y P O T H E T I C A L    C A S E S

1. Alissa verbally tells Barry that she would like him to manage her stock portfolio for Charlie's benefit while Charlie attends college. She signs over all of her stocks to Barry, who agrees to make periodic distributions to Charlie out of the earnings from those stocks, and to reconvey these stocks to Alissa when Charlie graduates.
   a. Is a trust created by the above agreement? Assuming for the moment that a trust is created, what type of trust is it?
   b. How would you characterize Alissa, Barry and Charlie with respect to the agreement (assuming for the moment that a valid trust is created)?
   c. Assuming a trust is created, what would happen if Charlie dies prior to completing college?
   d. Assume for the moment that no trust is created here because a writing is required. If Alissa transfers the stock certificates to Barry under an oral agreement, how would you characterize the arrangement and Barry's obligation thereunder?

2. Michelle opens a savings account with $500 in her own name in trust for Michael. In the year that follows, she gets into a bit of a financial bind and withdraws $495 from the account. But when her financial situation improves, she deposits vari-

ous amounts into the account, with the result that at her death the account contains $150,000. Michelle's only other significant assets at her death are a checking account with $500 in it and an automobile with a market value of $500.

   a. If Michelle dies leaving no living relatives entitled to an intestate distribution, what will Michael be entitled to receive from the account?

   b. If Michelle dies leaving only a daughter and no other living relatives, what will Michael receive? What about the daughter?

   c. What if Michelle has a husband and no other living relatives upon her death?

3. Simeone Settlor calls her attorney and tells him that she wishes to create a trust in

favor of her nephew, Simon, for $200,000. She instructs the lawyer (who is also to be the trustee) that she wants Simon to benefit from the income of the trust during his life, with the corpus to be divided among Simon's children at his death, or, if he dies childless, to the American Heart Association. She further authorizes the lawyer, who has a valid power of attorney to act on her behalf, to withdraw the funds from one of her accounts at State Bank. If she dies an hour after the communication with the lawyer, is a valid trust created? Explain fully.

4. Vinnie Victim is swindled out of $10,000 by a con man who invests the money in a speculative venture that results in a ten-fold increase of his investment. Vinnie wants to sue the swindler. What are his rights?

U N I T

# AGENCY AND EMPLOYMENT

## INTRODUCTION TO AGENCY AND LABOR LAW . . . . . . . . . . . . . . .

In business as well as in our personal lives, it is often necessary to have others act on our behalf in order to carry out routine tasks that we may not have the time or expertise to carry out ourselves. An entrepreneur might go into business for himself or herself and initially perform all of the required tasks personally while the enterprise is in its early stages. But if the business is successful and the owner wants to expand his or her operations, it will be impossible to do so without hiring additional help to take on some of the responsibilities of the expanding venture. As new employees are hired, they become *agents* of the owner and are empowered by him or her to carry out certain tasks in his or her stead. To put it another way, the owner of a business delegates some duties to agents, whom we normally call employees, and empowers these agents to act on his or her behalf in accordance with the terms of the employment. Thus, a used-car salesman hired by the owner of a used-car lot is empowered to sell cars on the owner's behalf, and can bind the owner to sales contracts he enters into on the owner's behalf with third parties (used-car buyers). Similarly, an individual can authorize another to act as his or her agent for the purpose of carrying out any legal task by executing a valid power of attorney. In both of these instances, if the agent acts on behalf of the *principal* (the person on whose behalf the agent acts) with the principal's authority, the acts of the agent bind the principal exactly as if the principal had acted himself or herself. This simple principle forms the basis of agency law, and is of critical importance to the formation of the business organizations we will discuss in the next unit (partnerships, limited partnerships and corporations).

In this unit, we will explore the basic principles of the law of agency and explore its application in employment relationships. We will also delve into an overview of labor law and probe current legal issues and legislation affecting employment.

CHAPTER

# 33

# AGENCY

*Agency* is a consensual relationship that comes into existence when one person authorizes another to act on his or her behalf to conduct some lawful business. An agent acts as a stand-in for the person he or she represents (called the *principal*) and is empowered to conduct most any legal business on the principal's behalf. When a duly authorized agent acts on behalf of a principal, it is as if the principal had acted himself or herself.

## CREATION OF AN AGENCY · · · · · · · · · · · · · · · · · · · · · · · · · · · · · · ·

Agency is a consensual relationship. As such, it requires that the principal have the mental capacity to enter into a contract with the agent. Thus, incompetents and minors can disaffirm agency agreements, and judicially declared incompetents cannot enter into agency agreements at all (the same rules apply as to contractual capacity).

Interestingly, there is no requirement that the agent be competent. In most states, any person may be an agent, including incompetents and children. Principals are free to chose whomever they wish to act on their behalf, and this includes persons lacking full mental capacity.

Generally speaking, no formalities are necessary for the creation of a valid agency. Oral instructions as well as written ones will lead to the creation of an agency. The only exception is when the agent is empowered to take some action on the principal's behalf that will require a written, signed contract to be executed under the requirements of the Statute of Frauds. In such instances, the agency agreement must also be represented by a signed writing if it is to be enforceable. This requirement is commonly referred to as the *equal dignities rule*. Simply stated, the equal dignities rule requires an agency agreement to conform to the same formalities as any agreement that the agent will subsequently enter into on the principal's behalf. Thus, if a principal hires an agent to purchase real estate, the agency agreement must be evidenced by a signed writing, since real estate cannot be purchased without execution of a signed writing. Perhaps the most common means of creating an agency relationship is by the execution of a valid power of attorney, whereby the principal authorizes the holder of the power of attorney (called the *attorney in fact*) to act as his or her agent with respect to matters specified in the power of attorney. (See Figure 33.1 for an example of a power of attorney.)

# AGENT'S AUTHORITY  . . . . . . . . . . . . . . . . . . . . . . . . . . . . . . . .

Agents may act on behalf of their principals in accordance with their actual or apparent authority. Agents who act under the aegis of any such authority will bind their principals to contracts entered into on their behalf.

## AGENT'S ACTUAL AUTHORITY

An agent acts with *actual authority* if he or she acts pursuant to the express or implied instructions of the principal. *Actual express authority* can be found in any oral or written instructions given the agent by the principal, while *actual implied authority* includes any reasonable steps that an agent takes in order to carry out the express authority granted by the principal. For example, if Peter Principal instructs Angela Agent to purchase a used Japanese-built automobile with less than 70,000 miles for a price not to exceed $5,000, Angela would have the express authority to purchase any vehicle in her discretion that meets the conditions expressed by the principal. In addition, Angela would have the implied authority to take any additional reasonable steps to carry out her instructions. Under this example, Angela could purchase a 1994 Toyota Corolla with 50,000 miles for $5,000, since doing so would clearly come within her actual express authority. She should also pay the required taxes and registration fee for such a vehicle and arrange its transportation at a commercially reasonable cost; her authority to perform these tasks would be implied from her express authority, since it is commercially reasonable (necessary, in fact) to pay sales taxes and registration fees and to transport an automobile after its purchase.

In determining an agent's implied authority, one must look to the actual express authority granted by the principal. Any steps that are reasonably required for the agent to carry out the actual express authority granted by the principal will generally be deemed to have been implicitly authorized by the principal. For example, the express authority granted by a principal who hires an agent to act as general manager of his or her business enterprise would include the implied authority to hire, train, supervise and fire employees, as well as to contract for necessary services—all of which are implicitly necessary for the agent to carry out his or her expressly granted authority to manage the business.

## AGENT'S APPARENT AUTHORITY

Like implied authority, an agent has *apparent authority* that flows directly from an express grant of actual authority by the principal. Apparent authority can be defined as the authority that an agent seems (or appears) to have to a reasonably prudent person under the circumstances. Such authority generally flows from the custom and practice

## POWER OF ATTORNEY

STATE OF _____  ⎫
                                      ⎬
COUNTY OF _____  ⎭

KNOW ALL PERSONS BY THESE PRESENTS:

_____, hereinafter referred to as PRINCIPAL, do(es) appoint
_[Name of individual(s) granting the power of attorney]_

_____ his (her) true and lawful attorney.
_[Name of person to act as attorney-in-fact]_

In principal's name, and for principal's use and benefit, said attorney is authorized hereby:

(1) To demand, sue for, collect and receive all money, debts, accounts, legacies, bequests, interest, dividends, annuities and demands as are now or shall hereafter become due, payable or belonging to principal, and take all lawful means for the recovery thereof and to compromise the same and give discharges for the same;

(2) To buy and sell land, make contracts of every kind relative to land, any interest therein or the possession thereof, and to take possession and exercise control over the use thereof;

(3) To buy, sell, mortgage, assign, transfer and in any manner deal with goods, wares and merchandise, choses in action, certificates or shares of capital stock and other property in possession or in action, and to make, do and transact all and every kind of business of whatever nature;

(4) To execute, acknowledge, and deliver contracts of sale, escrow instructions, deeds, leases including leases for minerals and hydrocarbon substances and assignments of leases, covenants, agreements and assignments of agreements, mortgages and assignments of mortgages, conveyances in trust, to secure indebtedness or other obligations, and assign the beneficial interest thereunder, subordinations of liens or encumbrances, bills of lading, receipts, evidences of debt, releases, bonds, notes, bills, requests to reconvey deeds of trust, partial or full judgments, satisfactions of mortgages, and other debts, and other written instruments of whatever kind and nature, all upon such terms and conditions as said attorney shall approve.

Giving and granting to said attorney full power and authority to do all and every act and thing whatsoever requisite and necessary to be done relative to any of the foregoing as fully to all intents and purposes as principal might or could do if personally present.

All that said attorney shall lawfully do or cause to be done under the authority of this power of attorney is expressly approved.

Signed before me this _____ day of _____, 19_____          _____ (L.S.)

_____
    Notary's Signature

_____
    Notary's Seal

**FIGURE 33.1**    Sample Power of Attorney

of an industry or the general assumptions about a person's position that a reasonably prudent person might make. For example, since it is generally true that a personnel manager has the power to hire new employees, an interviewee who is offered a job by a company's personnel manager can accept such an offer and bind the principal to honor it even if that specific personnel manager was not authorized by management to make employment offers. The same is true of contracts entered into by employees who have been fired on behalf of their previous employers. If, for instance, the purchasing manager for XYZ Corporation enters into a million-dollar equipment purchase contract on the day after he is fired by XYZ, the company would be bound by the contract unless the supplier with whom the ex-purchasing manager contracted was aware of the employee's lack of actual authority.

## AGENCY BY ESTOPPEL

There are instances in which a principal who has not actually empowered an agent to act on his or her behalf can be bound by acts of the agent under an *estoppel* theory (a person who misleads another into believing certain facts to be true is estopped, or prevented, from denying the truth of those facts when they are relied upon in good faith by the person who has been misled to his or her detriment). If the principal misleads a third party into believing that a person who is not an agent is in fact the principal's agent, then the principal will be unable to disavow acts of the agent under grounds of lack of authority if the third party relies on the false agent's misrepresentations and suffers some tangible loss as a consequence. For instance, if a sole proprietor leads an innocent third party to believe that a specific person is his or her agent when no actual agency exists, any contracts entered into by the third party with the false agent in reliance on the principal's misrepresentations will bind that principal as if the false agent were in fact a duly authorized agent.

# TERMINATION OF AN AGENCY    . . . . . . . . . . . . . . . . . . . . . . . . . .

An agency can be terminated in one of three ways: by consent of the parties, by completion of the agency purpose or expiration of the agency period or by operation of law.

## TERMINATION BY CONSENT OF THE PARTIES

Generally speaking, an agency can be terminated at any time by the mutual consent of the principal and agent, or by the unilateral wish of either party. This is true even in cases where a contract exists between the parties that prevents an agency from being dissolved or states that the agency will run for a specified period of time. If an agency is wrongfully terminated by one of the parties unilaterally, damages may be available to the aggrieved party. Thus, if a person agrees to serve as agent for a principal for a period of five years and quits at the end of the first year, the principal may be able to recover compensatory damages (e.g., the difference between what he or she would have paid the agent under their agreement and what he or she must pay a replacement agent for the remaining period in the breached agency agreement). But the agency itself will be effectively terminated upon the wish of either the principal or the agent.

## TERMINATION BY COMPLETION OF AGENCY PURPOSE OR EXPIRATION OF AGENCY PERIOD

An agency automatically terminates upon the completion of its stated purpose when the agency is entered into in order to complete a single purpose. For example, an agency that is created for the purpose of the agent purchasing a specific piece of real estate for the principal automatically expires when the agent completes his or her assigned task. Likewise, an agency that is set up to expire after a set period of time or upon the happening of a given event automatically terminates when the specified time period is met or the specified event happens.

## TERMINATION BY OPERATION OF LAW

An agency automatically terminates by operation of law upon the death, incompetence or bankruptcy of the principal, or upon the death of the agent. (Note that incompetence or bankruptcy of the agent does not automatically terminate the agency.) Subsequent illegality and impossibility of performance also cause an agency to be terminated by operation of law, since the purpose of the agency cannot be fulfilled. If the impossibility of performance or illegality is only temporary, then the agency resumes (unless it is otherwise terminated by either party) as soon as the impediment to the completion of the agency purpose is removed. For example, if XYZ Corporation hires Adam Agent to purchase electronics goods from a specific country for resale in the United States during the next ten years at a set salary, and Congress places an embargo on that country for alleged civil rights abuses a year after the contract was entered into, the agency terminates by operation of law. But if Congress removes the sanctions a year later because of an improvement in that country's civil rights record, then the agency would resume for the remaining eight-year period called for in the original agreement.

# PRINCIPAL'S DUTIES IN AN AGENCY AGREEMENT    . . . . . . . . . . . . .

A principal owes certain duties to the agent in every agency. These include the duty to compensate the agent for his or her services (unless compensation is waived by the agent), the duty to indemnify the agent for any reasonable costs incurred or losses suffered as a result of the agency and the duty to cooperate with the agent in carrying out the purposes of the agency. In addition to these duties that arise by operation of law in every agency, the principal can have other duties specified in the agency agreement. A principal who breaches any duty owed his or her agent will be liable to the agent for damages.

## DUTY TO COMPENSATE AGENT

Unless it is clear that a gratuitous agency was intended, the agent is entitled to be compensated for his or her service to the principal. If compensation is not discussed, the agent is entitled to compensation for the reasonable value of the services rendered.

## DUTY OF REIMBURSEMENT AND INDEMNIFICATION

Agents will often need to expend money on behalf of the principal in order to carry out the duties of the agency. If these expenditures are reasonable and necessary to further the interests of the principal, the agent is entitled to reimbursement from the principal for these expenses upon giving an accounting of them. In addition, agents can sometimes suffer personal losses while engaged in the business of the agency. As long as these losses were reasonably foreseeable by the principal at the time of entering into the agency and were not caused by the willful acts of the agent, the agent is entitled to indemnification for such losses. For example, if an agent is injured through no fault of his or her own while conducting agency business, the principal must indemnify the agent for all medical expenses and related losses resulting from the injury. Likewise, an agent whose personal property is damaged or destroyed while carrying out agency business is generally entitled to indemnification by the principal for such losses.

## DUTY OF COOPERATION

A principal must render any reasonable assistance necessary to allow the agent to carry out the responsibilities of the agency. This duty extends to providing the agent with any necessary information or resources needed to perform the assigned agency duties, and also includes a duty of the principal not to interfere with the agent while the agent attempts to carry out the duties of the agency.

# AGENT'S DUTIES IN AN AGENCY AGREEMENT  . . . . . . . . . . . . . . . . .

Like the principal, the agent has certain obligations that flow from the agency agreement by operation of law and by the express terms of the agency agreement. The agent's duties arising by operation of law include the duty of loyalty, the duty of obedience, the duty to inform the principal of relevant facts relating to the agency learned by the agent, the duty to exercise due care in carrying out the responsibilities of the agency and the duty to render an accurate accounting of expenses incurred or income received by the agent in conducting the principal's business.

## DUTY OF LOYALTY

The duty of loyalty requires the agent to place the interests of the principal above his or her own and to deal honestly and in good faith in carrying out his or her duties as assigned by the principal. Agency is a fiduciary relationship based on trust in which the agent must exercise absolute good faith in his or her dealings on behalf of the principal. An agent can breach this duty in a number of ways, including the obvious means of stealing or misappropriating funds from the principal and the much more subtle means of unfairly competing with the principal or using information learned by means of the agency relationship to further the agent's interests rather than those of the principal. An agent cannot even keep gifts or illicit bribes received in the normal course of conducting agency business on the principal's behalf; such gains are considered the rightful property of the principal and must be turned over to him or her by the agent who receives them.

## DUTY OF OBEDIENCE

The agent's duty of obedience to the principal requires him or her to follow the reasonable instructions of the principal relating to the agency. Failure to do so will subject the agent to liability for any resulting loss suffered by the principal.

## DUTY TO COMMUNICATE TO THE PRINCIPAL RELEVANT INFORMATION LEARNED ABOUT THE AGENCY

A principal is deemed to have knowledge of any relevant information that the agent learns during the course of performing his or her duties under the agency. Because of the principal's implied knowledge of information at the disposal of the agent, the agent must communicate any relevant facts he or she learns relating to the agency to the principal immediately. If the agent fails to do so, he or she can be held responsible for any losses suffered by the principal as a result of the agent's failure to disclose the relevant information.

## DUTY TO EXERCISE DUE CARE IN CONDUCTING AGENCY BUSINESS

Agents must exercise the duties of their agency with reasonable care. Failure to do so can result in tort liability for negligence. Agents who have special skills, such as attorneys, physicians or architects, must exercise a level of professionalism and expertise that is acceptable in their profession; failure to do so can result in liability for malpractice.

## DUTY TO RENDER AN ACCOUNTING

Agents must keep accurate records of expenses incurred on behalf of their principals for which they are entitled to reimbursement or indemnification, as well as of any income or other benefit derived from the agency to which the principal is entitled. Agents must render a formal accounting to their principals from time to time, whenever an accounting is reasonably requested by the principal or as otherwise provided by their agency agreement.

# LIABILITY OF PRINCIPAL FOR AGENT'S TORTS  . . . . . . . . . . . . . . . . .

Principals are liable for the torts committed by their agents during the scope of their agency. The agent, of course, is also liable for his or her own torts with regards to third parties whom the agent injures while engaged in agency business. In order for the principal to be held liable for the agent's torts, two tests must be met: (1) there must be a *master-servant* relationship, wherein the agent is under the direct control of the principal (e.g., the agent must be an employee of the principal), and (2) the tort must have been committed by the agent while engaged in conducting agency business. If, for example, an innocent person is injured by the driver of a delivery truck while the driver is making a delivery, the injured person can hold the driver's employer liable for injuries suffered; but not so if the driver injures someone while driving his or her own car on the way to work, since he or she would not at that time have been engaged in conducting agency business.

Independent contractors are not deemed agents of their employers, but rather are deemed to be self-employed and solely responsible for their own torts. In determining whether a given person is an employee or an independent contractor, courts weigh a number of factors, including the level of control exerted by the principal over the details of the work performed by the person, the number of hours worked by the person on the principal's behalf every week, whether the person has other clients, and whether the person exerts independent judgment in carrying out his or her duties. Thus, a gardener who works for the Jones family two hours per week and has thirty other clients in the area is not an employee, but an independent contractor; but a gardener who works exclusively for the Joneses for thirty hours per week and has no other clients probably *is* an employee. The difference can be crucial if the gardener injures someone during the course of his or her employment, for the Joneses would not be responsible for such injuries in the former case but *would* be liable for them in the latter.

## LIABILITY OF AGENT FOR CONTRACTS ENTERED INTO ON PRINCIPAL'S BEHALF · · · · · · · · · · · · · · · · · · · · · · · ·

Agents are not generally personally liable on contracts they enter into on behalf of their principals within the scope of their authority. When an authorized agent enters into a contract on behalf of a principal, it is as if the principal had entered into the contract personally. The agent is merely a facilitator and not a party to the contract. A problem arises, however, when an agent enters into an unauthorized contract or when an agent acts on behalf of a principal who wishes to keep his or her identity secret from the other contracting party. In such instances, the agent may be solely liable under the resulting contract, or may be jointly liable with the principal, depending on the circumstances.

### AGENT'S UNAUTHORIZED CONTRACTS

If an agent enters into a contract with a third party on behalf of a principal without having either actual or implied authority to do so, the principal is not bound under the resulting agreement, and the agent is personally liable under the contract. For example, if Alec Agent is authorized by Pamela Principal to bid up to $10,000 at auction for a piece of real estate and Alec bids $20,000 on the property, Pamela is not bound by the resulting agreement, since Alec acted without express or implied authority, but Alec *is* bound by it and liable to the third party with whom he contracted (e.g., the auctioneer) for breach of contract if he does not purchase the land at the agreed-upon price.

Principals are free to honor unauthorized contracts entered into by their agents if they choose, but are under no obligation to do so. If a principal elects to honor an unauthorized contract entered into on his behalf by an agent, he or she *ratifies* the agreement and is afterwards bound by it. Ratification involves an affirmation by the principal of a previously unauthorized act by the agent. Once an unauthorized contract is ratified by the principal, the agent is no longer liable under it, since the liability for performing the contract is assumed by the principal upon its ratification.

### AGENT'S AUTHORIZED CONTRACTS ON BEHALF OF A FULLY DISCLOSED PRINCIPAL

An agent has no liability for authorized contracts entered into on behalf of a fully disclosed principal. A principal is fully disclosed when the party with whom the agent deals on the principal's behalf is aware that the agent is acting as an agent for a particular principal and is aware of the principal's identity. As previously noted, the agent in such instances is merely a facilitator and does not become a party to the contract. If either the principal or the third party subsequently breaches the contract, they can sue only each other (and not the agent) for the breach.

### AGENT'S AUTHORIZED CONTRACTS ON BEHALF OF A PARTIALLY DISCLOSED PRINCIPAL

When a partially disclosed principal is involved, the agent discloses to the third party that he or she is acting on behalf of a principal, but refuses to disclose the identity of the principal. Such contracts are common in instances where the principal fears that the third party might be unwilling to deal with the principal, or where the identity of the principal might drive up the price of the contract if it is known. In such contracts, both the principal and the agent have joint liability under the contract and both can be sued if the contract is breached.

### AGENT'S AUTHORIZED CONTRACTS ON BEHALF OF AN UNDISCLOSED PRINCIPAL

In contracts involving an undisclosed principal, the third party with whom the agent contracts is unaware that the agent is acting on behalf of any principal. As far as the third party is concerned, the agent acts solely on his or her own behalf and is thus clearly personally liable for the performance of the contract if the undisclosed principal fails to perform. If the third party later learns the undisclosed principal's identity, the third party may hold *both* the agent and the undisclosed principal liable under the contract.

# QUESTIONS  . . . . . . . . . . . . . . . . . . . . . . . . . . . . . . . . . .

1. What is agency?
2. What formalities are necessary in order to enter into an agency agreement?
3. How does the equal dignities rule apply?

4. What are the three basic means by which an agency can be terminated?

5. What effect does the death of the agent have on an agency? The death of the principal?

6. What effect does the bankruptcy of the agent have on an agency? The bankruptcy of the principal?

7. What are the basic duties owed by the principal to the agent in every agency relationship?

8. What are the basic duties of all agents to their principals?

9. What is the contractual liability of agents who enter into unauthorized contracts on behalf of their principals?

10. What is the agent's contractual liability in contracts entered into with third parties on behalf of a disclosed principal? A partially disclosed principal? An undisclosed principal?

# H Y P O T H E T I C A L    C A S E S

1. Marsha asks Muhammad, a fellow student at State University who is a computer whiz, to purchase a computer for her that in his best judgment would best meet her needs. She tells him that he can spend up to $1,500 on a complete system, including an inexpensive printer. Muhammad, after many hours of research to put together the most cost-effective system at the lowest possible price for Marsha, places an order with Computer World on Marsha's behalf and asks that the complete system be shipped to Marsha.

   a. Is Muhammad Marsha's agent under the facts given? If so, does he need written authorization before he can purchase the system on Marsha's behalf?

   b. If Muhammad orders a system for $1,500 from Computer World after identifying himself as acting as an agent for Marsha, is Muhammad liable on the contract if Marsha refuses the computer system when it is delivered? Explain.

   c. If Muhammad gets carried away and orders a $2,000 system for Marsha, who is liable on the contract if Marsha refuses to accept it when the system is delivered? Explain.

   d. If payment for Muhammad's services was not discussed when Marsha asked him to purchase the computer system, will Muhammad nevertheless be entitled to be paid for his services? Explain.

   e. If Muhammad purchases a system that is inappropriate for Marsha's needs, what recourse will she have?

2. Barbara hires Enrique as a consultant to set up and maintain her computer network. Enrique works at Barbara's business site approximately five to ten hours per week and bills Barbara at a rate of $60 per hour for his work. He does not have an office in Barbara's place of business and is not on the payroll. He works unsupervised and sets his own schedule and hours on an as-needed basis. In addition to working for Barbara, Enrique does consulting work for several other clients on a rotating basis.

    a. Is Enrique an employee or an independent contractor?

    b. What practical difference does it make whether Enrique is an independent contractor or an employee?

    c. Would Enrique be considered an employee under the previous facts if he worked twenty hours per week for the past three years for Barbara and had no other clients?

3. Jasmine hires Jemal to run her business as general manager under a three-year contract. After six months, they have a falling out and Jemal gives Jasmine notice of his intention to resign from his position and expresses the willingness to stay on for up to sixty days to allow Jasmine to recruit a suitable successor.

    a. If Jasmine is unwilling to release Jemal from his contractual obligation, can she force him to stay on as her agent for the contractual three-year term?

    b. If Jasmine cannot convince Jemal to stay on as her general manager, what recourse does she have against him? Explain.

    c. Assuming that Jasmine can find several suitable replacements for Jemal for a lesser salary than she had agreed to pay him, what recourse will she have against Jemal?

# CHAPTER

# 34

# LABOR LAW

At early common law, labor law did not exist as a separate field of law. The relationship between employers, or *masters*, and employees, or *servants*, was governed by the law of agency and contracts. It will come as no surprise that the law generally favored the employer rather than the employee on most matters relating to the employment relationship. Employees' rights under employment contracts were generally limited to the terms of the employment contract itself; since the terms of employment were generally dictated by the employer, employment contracts contained little legal protection for employees beyond the guarantee of receiving the bargained-for wages, with rare exception. More often than not, the sole remedy available to an employee who felt unjustly treated by an employer was to sever the contract and seek employment elsewhere.

Today, agency and contract law are still at the heart of labor law, but a significant amount of federal and state legislation has been enacted that helps to define the rights and responsibilities of employers and employees in a number of key areas, including collective bargaining, occupational safety and protection from discrimination based on sex, race, color, religion, national origin or physical disability.

## RIGHTS AND RESPONSIBILITIES OF EMPLOYERS AND EMPLOYEES BASED ON AGENCY · · · · · · · · · · · · · · · · · · · · · ·

Employees are considered agents of the employers for whom they work and, as such, have the rights and responsibilities of agents discussed in the last chapter. Thus, an employer owes the employee the duties of compensation, reimbursement and indemnification as well as the duty of cooperation, while the employee owes the employer the duties of loyalty and obedience, the duty to make an accounting and the duty to exercise due care in the performance of employment responsibilities.

The rights and responsibilities dictated by the law of agency for employers and employees do not extend to employers and independent contractors. Unlike employees, who are deemed to be agents of their employers, independent contractors are

271

considered to be self-employed and owe no duty to their employers beyond those dictated by the employment contract. The distinction between employees and independent contractors can be crucial when a third party is injured through the negligence of the independent contractor, or when the independent contractor suffers injury or other loss while working for the employer. Since an agency relationship does not exist between independent contractors and those who employ them, independent contractors are solely responsible for their torts (including their negligence) and they are not given the protection available to employees when they suffer injury or other loss while performing their contractual responsibilities. At times, a thorny issue develops as to whether a given person is an independent contractor or an employee; in deciding such questions, courts weigh a number of factors in an attempt to determine the nature of the relationship. Relevant factors include the extent of control exercised by the employer over the individual's performance of contractual duties (the greater the control, the likelier it is that the worker is an employee rather than an independent contractor), the duration of the employment contract and the exclusiveness of the relationship (the longer the relationship, the likelier an employee is involved; the more clients a person works for, the less likely it is that he or she is an employee of any of them), whether or not the worker works out of the employer's premises and whether or not the worker uses his or her own tools are also a factor in determining whether an individual is an employee or an independent contractor.

## RIGHTS AND RESPONSIBILITIES OF EMPLOYERS AND EMPLOYEES BASED ON CONTRACT LAW . . . . . . . . . . . . . . . . .

As previously noted, at common law the precise rights and responsibilities of the employer and employee were almost exclusively dictated by general agency law and the employment contract. While other factors come into play today, the employment contract is still of critical importance in determining the rights and responsibilities of the parties. Parties are free to define the nature of the employment relationship through oral or written contracts as long as these do not conflict with federal or state law. Length of employment, precise duties, compensation and benefits package are all typically defined in the employment contract. In most cases, the employer as offeror of the employment contract defines these terms and the employee as offeree either accepts or rejects the offer on the employer's terms. Employees can, of course, bargain for better terms than those offered by the employer, but most employees in reality have little bargaining power, especially in tight job markets or in positions requiring few specialized skills.

To a large extent, both the federal and state governments' attempts to regulate labor law through legislation can be seen as an effort to level the playing field between employers and employees by setting limits on the terms that employers (and, to a lesser extent, unions) may impose on employees through the employment contract. Throughout the remainder of this chapter, we'll spotlight a cross-section of the more salient legislative efforts in the area of labor law in order to gain an overview of the limits that have been placed on employers in dictating terms of employment for their employees. Keep in mind from this point on that employment is still (at least technically) *at will*, which is to say that employers and employees are free to negotiate the terms of employment within the boundaries of the law and that an employer or employee may unilaterally terminate any employment contract that does not have a fixed duration at any time with or without just cause, as long as no federal or state law is violated by the termination.

## GOVERNMENTAL REGULATION OF LABOR-MANAGEMENT RELATIONS · · · · · · · · · · · · · · · · · · · · · · · · · · · · ·

The history of labor-management relations in the United States through the first three decades of this century was not an auspicious one from the workers' perspective. There was no formal protection for workers' rights to form unions or bargain collectively with management. While these rights had long been recognized in Europe, where a greater emphasis on workers' rights had been (and remains) a focal point of that continent's industrialized democracies, in the United States most organized labor activities were deemed to violate either criminal or civil laws. The most effective tools for collective bargaining by workers were not sanctioned by law. The mere act of joining a union could (and often did) result in the firing of an employee. Likewise, employees who banded together and instituted boycotts against an employer could be prosecuted for criminal antitrust violations under the 1914 Clayton Act, which made illegal all conspiracies to restrain trade or interfere with commerce. Organizers of boycotts or strikes could also be sued in many states for civil damages under a tort theory (such as willful interference with contract rights). Most state courts readily granted injunctions, at management's request, preventing employees from engaging in illegal boycotts. In addition, since workers had no protected right to join a union or to engage in collective bargaining, employers were free to insist on including a clause in employment contracts that prevented employees from joining a union as a condition of being hired. These contractual provisions, which came to be known as *yellow-dog contracts* by union sympathizers, were usually enforced by the courts and served to effectively deny workers the ability to join unions. But by 1932, the political climate had begun to change and what had been very effective roadblocks to the labor movement were slowly removed through a series of acts passed by Congress granting some measure of protection to workers and curtailing the most egregious abuses of power by management.

### NORRIS–LA GUARDIA ACT (1932)

The Norris–La Guardia Act of 1932 accomplished two important goals: it declared yellow-dog contracts (agreements prohibiting workers from joining unions as a condition of being hired) illegal as against public policy and unenforceable, and restricted the power of federal judges to issue injunctions against union boycotts. While the act did not prevent employers from seeking injunctive relief against employee boycotts in state courts, many states in effect extended the act by also preventing their courts from issuing such injunctions.

## NATIONAL LABOR RELATIONS ACT (1935)

The National Labor Relations Act of 1935 (also known as the Wagner Act) granted to employees for the first time the right to organize, to bargain collectively through representatives of their own choosing and to engage in activities for the purpose of collective bargaining or other mutual aid or protection. The act also prohibited five types of unfair labor practices by employers: (1) interference with attempts of employees to unionize or join unions, (2) domination or interference with the formation or administration of any labor union or contributing financial or other support to it, (3) discrimination in hiring, tenure of employment or any term or condition of employment to encourage or discourage membership in any labor organization, (4) discharge of or discrimination against an employee for filing charges or giving testimony under the act, and (5) refusal to bargain collectively with the chosen representatives of the employees.

The act also prohibited *closed-shop* agreements that required employers to hire only union workers. *Union-shop* agreements, where employees need not be a union member when hired but must join the union a short time after being hired, were *not* made illegal by the act, however. In addition, the act established the National Labor Relations Board to hear and adjudicate complaints from employees about employers' unfair labor practices. Board decisions on such matters were automatically reviewed by district courts of appeals, which issued orders of enforcement if they concurred with the findings of the National Labor Relations Board.

## FAIR LABOR STANDARDS ACT (1938)

The Fair Labor Standards Act of 1938 fixed for the first time minimum wage and maximum hours provisions. The act set the maximum work week at forty-four hours for the first year after its adoption, forty-two hours after one year and forty hours per week thereafter, requiring employers to pay all hourly employees time-and-a-half for any work required beyond the stated maximum. The act also set minimum wage provisions on a sliding scale that increased from 25¢ an hour for the first year to 30¢ per hour for the next six years and 40¢ per hour thereafter. The minimum wage requirements have been raised periodically thereafter, starting with an increase to 75¢ per hour in 1949 and culminating in a minimum wage of $4.25 as of April 1, 1991.

## LABOR-MANAGEMENT RELATIONS ACT (1947)

The Labor-Management Relations Act of 1947 (also known as the Taft-Hartley Act) essentially modified the 1935 National Labor Relations Act (the Wagner Act) in a number of significant areas. Chief among these modifications was the extension of the prohibition of unfair labor practices to include unions as well as employers. The act made it an unfair labor practice for unions to engage in any of the following prohibited activities: (1) coercing or restraining employees in their choice of a union to represent them, or coercing or restraining employers in the choice of their own bargaining representatives, (2) compelling an employer to fire an employee in a union shop for other than nonpayment of dues, and (3) refusing to bargain in good faith.

The act also gave the president the right to seek an injunction forcing striking workers back to work for a period of up to sixty days in strikes that in the president's view imperil national health or safety. If the dispute is not settled during the sixty-day cooling-off period, the president can ask for a twenty-day extension of the injunction if the strike threatens a national emergency.

## LABOR-MANAGEMENT REPORTING AND DISCLOSURE ACT (1959)

The Labor-Management Reporting and Disclosure Act of 1959 (also known as the Landrum-Griffin Act), like the Labor-Management Relations Act (the Taft-Hartley Act) before it, further modified the National Labor Relations Act of 1935 (the Wagner Act), primarily tightening up control of unions' internal affairs. The act imposed fiduciary duties on union leadership and provided for criminal punishment of union officials who violated the trust of their office. Federal monitoring of unions' financial status was imposed and unions were required for the first time to report both to the federal government and to their members how union funds were used. The act also regulates union elections, including instituting the requirement that union elections be run through secret ballots. Furthermore, protection is extended to members who state their opposition to union leadership or policies, making it illegal for the union to punish such dissenting members. Finally, unions are required under the act to provide members with copies of collective bargaining agreements and to make members aware of their rights under the act.

# ADDITIONAL FEDERAL REGULATION AFFECTING EMPLOYMENT  . . . . . . . . . . . . . . . . . . . . . . . . . . . . .

In addition to the labor-specific federal acts just noted, other federal (and, to a lesser extent, state) legislation has had a crucial role in redefining the employer–employee relationship. From the early 1930s through the late 1950s, Congress set into place the foundation of American labor law through the landmark acts we've just briefly discussed. In so doing, Congress set itself up as the primary source of law relating to employment, preempting state legislation and regulation of labor in areas Congress elects to regulate. From the 1960s through the 1990s, Congress has maintained its leadership role in legislation affecting employment by passing several important acts that further define the rights and responsibilities of employers and employees in a number of key areas that we will examine next.

## EMPLOYMENT DISCRIMINATION

Title VII of the 1964 Civil Rights Act is the single most important legislation protecting workers from illegal discrimination on the job. The act makes it an unlawful employment practice for an employer:

> (1) to fail or refuse to hire or to discharge any individual, or otherwise to discriminate against any individual with respect to his compensation, terms, conditions, or privileges of employment, because of such individual's race, color, religion, sex, or national origin; or

(2) to limit, segregate, or classify his employees or applicants for employment in any way which would deprive or tend to deprive any individual of employment opportunities or otherwise adversely affect his status as an employee, because of such individual's race, color, religion, sex, or national origin.

The 1964 Civil Rights Act created the Equal Employment Opportunity Commission (EEOC) and empowered it to enforce the act. The EEOC, an independent commission made up of five members appointed by the president, investigates charges of discrimination and enforces the law against covered employers, labor unions and employment agencies it believes to be guilty of unlawful discrimination.

In order for employers, unions and employment agencies to be covered by the act, they must be engaged in activities that have an impact on interstate commerce (as we have previously seen, nearly any activity can be seen as having an impact in interstate commerce) and employ at least an average of fifteen persons for a minimum of twenty weeks during the year. Employers who do not meet these criteria do not come within the act because their activities are deemed too insignificant to have an impact on interstate commerce, and thus fall outside of congressional regulatory power. (Remember that as we saw from Chapter 1, Congress must base all social legislation on the commerce clause since it does not possess general regulatory powers under the constitution.)

Not all forms of discrimination are prohibited by the act. Discrimination is permissible if it is pursuant to a *bona fide* occupational qualification reasonably necessary to the operation of the business enterprise. Thus, the Catholic Church may choose to ordain only male Catholics for the priesthood, since being both male and Catholic are both necessary qualifications for being a Catholic priest. Likewise, a motion-picture producer who wishes to make a film about the life of Nelson Mandela or Dr. Martin Luther King may recruit only black males for the role. On the other hand, an airline may not hire only female flight attendants merely because its customers prefer female attendants.

The act's prohibition against discrimination based on sex has been interpreted by the courts to date only as preventing unjustified discrimination based on a person's biological gender. Discrimination based on sexual preference, however, is not covered as such.

## SEXUAL HARASSMENT

Sexual harassment on the job can constitute employment discrimination within the 1964 Civil Rights Act under certain circumstances. This is an area of the law that is still evolving. As such, an authoritative definition of sexual harassment has yet to evolve. The EEOC has issued guidelines for defining sexual harassment as follows:

Unwelcome sexual advances, requests for sexual favors, and other verbal or physical conduct of a sexual nature constitute sexual harassment when (1) submission to such conduct is made either explicitly or implicitly a term or condition of an individual's employment, [or] (2) submission [to] or rejection of such conduct has the purpose or effect of unreasonably interfering with an individual's work performance or creating an intimidating, hostile or offensive working environment. (EEOC Guidelines § 1604.11 [f])

While the EEOC guidelines do not have the force of law, they have persuasive power for judges who must ultimately define the types of conduct that comprise sexual harassment as they decide cases where such harassment is alleged to have occurred. The bulk of decided cases up to the present have been concerned with the first definition of sexual harassment under the EEOC guidelines. Primarily, these involve instances of a supervisor abusing his or her position of authority in attempting to exact sexual favors from a subordinate employee. Such conduct is universally held to be an unfair labor practice and a violation of Title VII of the 1964 Civil Rights Act. A much harder question involves the second definition of sexual harassment under the EEOC guidelines, since it is not as clear what types of conduct constitute "unreasonably interfering with an individual's work performance" or what constitutes "creating an intimidating, hostile or offensive working environment." For example, is it sexual harassment for a supervisor to keep a pinup calendar in his office if an employee finds it offensive? What about a print of a nude painting, such as Goya's *La Maja Desnuda*? Arguably, allowing any sexually explicit language in the workplace—even by other employees—might constitute sexual harassment if any employee finds that such language creates an "intimidating, hostile or offensive working environment." These issues are certain to be litigated in the future, and the courts will be forced to grapple with the free speech and free expression implications as they define the limits of acceptable behavior in the workplace.

## AGE DISCRIMINATION

The Age Discrimination in Employment Act of 1986 (ADEA) protects men and women over the age of forty against discrimination because of their age in hiring or promotion. Like Title VII of the 1964 Civil Rights Act, the ADEA applies to employers, unions and employment agencies. The act also effectively outlaws mandatory retirement solely because of age, with few exceptions.

## UNEMPLOYMENT BENEFITS

States provide unemployment insurance benefits to workers who lose their jobs through no fault of their own under programs coordinated by the federal government. All such plans are funded by mandatory contributions by employers and employees. Funds collected by the states to finance their unemployment insurance programs are turned over to the federal government and kept in a trust fund. Applications for unemployment insurance and payments to unemployed workers are handled by a state unemployment insurance agency under federal guidelines. The administrative costs of each state's unemployment insurance program is borne by the federal government. Requirements for eligibility of benefits, duration of benefits and the amount of benefits payable are controlled by local laws, though states tend to adopt similar regulations in these areas. Railroad workers, farm workers, domestic workers and federal workers are not covered, although railroad and federal employees have coverage under separate federal legislation.

In general, employees must work a minimum number of weeks per calendar year in order to be eligible for coverage, and only employees who are dismissed from their jobs without just cause are entitled to receive benefits; employees who quit a job out of choice are not eligible for unemployment insurance, nor are employees who are fired for wrongful conduct, such as embezzlement or illegal drug use on the job.

## HEALTH AND SAFETY

The Occupational Safety and Health Act of 1970 was passed by Congress in order to ensure employee health and safety on the job. Under the act, the Secretary of Labor is given the responsibility of promulgating standards for ensuring workers' health and safety on the job as well as the power to enforce these standards in the courts.

The act imposes on employers a duty to furnish to all employees a workplace free from recognized hazards that are likely to cause death or serious injury. Employers are also required to keep records of all occupational injuries or illness that result in death, loss of consciousness, the loss of one or more work days, or medical treatment other than first aid.

The act created a dedicated agency within the Department of Labor, the Occupational Safety and Health Administration (OSHA), to handle matters relating to administration and enforcement of the act. The agency is charged with conducting safety inspections of workplaces with a poor safety record and to force compliance with the act through the courts when employers do not voluntarily resolve safety or health problems identified by the agency. OSHA also investigates allegations of safety or health violations at the request of employees, who are protected against reprisals for making such allegations or otherwise asserting their rights under the act.

## WORKERS' COMPENSATION

Every state has adopted a workers' compensation statute that provides compensation for employees for job-related injuries. Coverage varies from state to state, with some states limiting coverage to employees engaged in manual labor while others cover nearly all employees regardless of the nature of the employment. Covered employees who suffer injuries arising out of the course of their employment are guaranteed compensation for their loss as well as payment of medical bills, but give up the right to sue the employer under a tort or contract theory for damages resulting from the injury. States generally limit damages recoverable by injured employees to statutorily provided amounts that are generally modest when compared to jury awards for similar injuries. States' workers' compensation statutes, thus, provide some measure of protection to employees who suffer injuries on the job by guaranteeing them prompt medical care at no cost to them (even if the injury is caused by their own negligence), but also serve to effectively limit the common-law rights of employees to later sue the employer for damages for the same injury.

## FAMILY AND MEDICAL LEAVE ACT

The Family and Medical Leave Act of 1993 allows public- and private-sector employees who have worked for the same employer for one year and a minimum of 1,250 hours to take up to twelve weeks of unpaid leave in any twelve-month period for any of the following reasons: (1) the birth or adoption of a child; (2) acquiring a foster child; (3) the serious illness of a spouse, child or parent; or (4) the serious illness of the employee. The act applies to any employee who works for an employer with fifty or more employees and who lives within seventy-five miles of the work site. Employers may require and employees may elect to include paid leave (such as vacation or sick time) as a part of the twelve-week period. Employees are under obligation to provide thirty days' notice prior to taking leave in cases where the need for leave is foreseeable. In addition, the employer is entitled to demand proof of the underlying reason for the leave (such as medical certification of illness or legal proof of adoption or birth of a child). In cases where a husband and wife both work for the same employer, the *combined* period of leave taken by the couple may not exceed twelve weeks per calendar year.

## AMERICANS WITH DISABILITIES ACT

The Americans with Disabilities Act of 1990 (ADA) contains two principal parts. Title I of the ADA forbids discrimination against qualified individuals with physical or mental disabilities in hiring, firing or promotion and requires employers to make reasonable accommodations for disabled employees. Title III of the ADA mandates accessibility for the disabled to new and existing public and private facilities that are open to the general public.

This landmark legislation expands the 1973 Rehabilitation Act, which prohibited discrimination in hiring on the basis of handicap in federal employment and by federal contractors and companies receiving federal assistance. The ADA is enforced by the EEOC and, as of July 25, 1994, applies to all employers engaged in interstate commerce who employ at least fifteen employees per day for at least twenty weeks per year. The United States or corporations wholly owned by the United States are excluded from the act, as are Indian tribes, social clubs and employers who do not employ fifteen or more workers per day for twenty weeks during any given year. The specific provisions of Title I of the ADA include the following:

- it forbids discrimination against *qualified* disabled individuals based upon the disability in hiring, retention or promotion;
- it mandates that *reasonable accommodations* be made for qualified disabled individuals by employers unless such accommodations would impose an *undue hardship* on the business operation;
- it allows private individuals to bring lawsuits to enforce the act through injunction (but not for damages); and
- it also allows the U.S. attorney general to bring legal action, including injunctions, fines and/or damages, against employers who violate the act (including attorneys' fees, court costs, reinstatement and treble damages).

In its regulations relating to the ADA, the EEOC defines an individual as qualified for a specific job if he or she "satisfies the requisite *skill, experience, and education re-*

*quirements* of the employment position." (italics added) (29 CFR § 1630.2 [m]) The ADA does not require lesser-qualified disabled individuals to be hired; it only forbids discrimination against otherwise qualified individuals merely because of their disability.

Under the ADA, an individual is considered to be disabled if he or she suffers from a physical or mental impairment that *substantially limits* one or more *major life functions.* (29 CFR § 1630.2 [j]) Major life functions are essential functions such as walking, thinking, seeing, hearing or reproducing. In addition, the impairment must be permanent in nature and substantial. For instance, a person who sprains an ankle while jogging would not be considered to be disabled for purposes of the act even if he or she is unable to walk as a result of the sprain, since it is a temporary condition. Likewise, someone suffering from mild arthritis who can get around well but is somewhat slowed down by the disease is not disabled (a person suffering from severe arthritis whose mobility is substantially impaired would be disabled, however).

Title III of the ADA requires greater accessibility by all to places open to the public. The act mandates in great detail changes to existing and new construction to make it accessible to the physically challenged. The detailed regulations require greater accessibility through a number of means, including detailed building code changes mandating the height of tables at restaurants, the number of restrooms in buildings and the installation of elevators in all new construction taller than two stories or with more than 3,000 square feet per floor. The regulations go as far as to detail the number of parking spaces that must be set aside for handicapped drivers and the number of theater seats that must be made handicapped accessible. In addition, telephone companies are mandated to provide telecommunications devices for the deaf. All new construction must comply with the ADA guidelines, and existing structures must also be made handicapped accessible unless doing so would prove an undue hardship.

Social clubs, religious institutions, residential facilities covered by fair housing laws and owner-occupied inns with fewer than six rooms to rent are all exempt from the act. The ADA also covers accessibility to public transportation by the handicapped.

# QUESTIONS

1. From which two branches of law does labor law primarily stem?
2. What are the two most significant provisions of the Norris–La Guardia Act of 1932?
3. What are the basic provisions of the National Labor Relations Act of 1935 (the Wagner Act)?
4. What are the basic provisions of the Fair Labor Standards Act of 1938?
5. What are the basic provisions of the Labor-Management Relations Act of 1947 (the Taft-Hartley Act)?
6. What are the basic provisions of the Labor-Management Reporting and Disclosure Act of 1959 (the Landrum-Griffin Act)?
7. The 1964 Civil Rights Act makes what type of discrimination in employment illegal?

8. How does the Equal Employment Opportunity Commission define *sexual harassment* in its guidelines?

9. What federal act was passed by Congress in 1970 to oversee employees' health and safety on the job? What federal agency is charged with enforcement of the act?

10. What are the two main areas covered by the 1990 Americans with Disabilities Act?

# H Y P O T H E T I C A L    C A S E S

1. Devon hires Rex to do odd jobs around his house on a fairly regular basis. Over the next year, Rex works an average of six hours per week for Devon performing a variety of tasks which include gardening, house painting, snow removal and minor household repairs. Devon also works for a number of other homeowners in the community performing similar tasks for them on a regular basis. He is paid a flat hourly fee by Devon and uses both his own tools and tools provided by Devon in the performance of his job.

   a. During a late October afternoon while performing leaf pickup for Devon, Rex decides to gather leaves in a large steel drum and burn them, without Devon's knowledge or consent. A gust of wind carries a burning leaf to Angela's house next door, starting a fire that causes extensive property damage. Is Devon responsible for the damage? What is the main issue on which this answer depends? Explain.

   b. Would it make a difference in the last question if Rex worked twenty hours per week exclusively for Devon? Explain.

2. Benny Bigot owns a small business that employs ten part-time and three full-time workers throughout the year. He places an ad in a local paper for a full-time receptionist. He subsequently interviews a number of applicants and refuses to hire a number of otherwise qualified applicants for the following reasons: Barbara because she is Jewish, David because he is male, Linda because she is black and Harry because he is gay.

   a. All are outraged when Benny tells them the reasons he will not hire them and file complaints with the Equal Employment Opportunity Commission. What result under federal law?

   b. If Benny expands his business and hires twenty full- and part-time workers year round, what result? Explain fully.

   c. What would be the result under the preceding facts if Benny ran a seasonal business employing 100 persons for three months every year?

3. Samantha, the general manager of ABC Corporation, asks Sam, her secretary, out for drinks after work. Sam believes this to be a sexual advance on Samantha's part and is deeply insulted by it. He immediately calls the EEOC to file a sexual harassment complaint. What result?

4. Martha, an automobile mechanic, is injured when an article of loose clothing becomes entangled in the generator pulley of an engine she is diagnosing. She

suffers severe injuries requiring her to be hospitalized for a week and to undergo several surgical procedures. After the operation, she is unable to return to work for two months.

a. If she is found to have been negligent in wearing loose clothing while working on a running engine in violation of the shop's safety guidelines, who will bear the cost of her medical injuries and her time lost from work?

b. If she is unhappy with the award given her by the Workers' Compensation Board in her state in compensation for her injuries, can Martha sue her employer under a contract or tort theory?

5. Frank, a legally blind attorney who has just been admitted to practice in his state, applies for a position as an associate at a law firm, answering an advertisement that lists a minimum of five years' experience as one of the requirements of the job. In his letter of application, he notes that he is legally blind but claims to be capable of performing the necessary duties with only minor accommodations by the employer. He is not granted an interview and decides to sue, claiming that the employer discriminated against him in violation of the Americans with Disabilities Act.

a. What result?

b. If, instead of having just been admitted to practice, Frank had been employed as an attorney by another firm for ten years, would your answer to the last question change? Explain.

c. Assuming that Frank has a stronger case in the last example, what will he need to establish in order to succeed in his claim of unlawful discrimination?

d. Assume that Frank is one of the finest attorneys in his state who has recently begun to lose his vision due to irreversible glaucoma. Further assume that his current employer dismisses him, claiming he can no longer perform his regular job duties. If Frank can show that he would be able to continue performing his job if the employer purchases a larger computer monitor for him to use and furnishes better lighting in his office, would he be likely to succeed in his case if the total cost of the new equipment would be $1,000 for the employer and the employer were a large law firm? What if the cost were $10,000 and the employer were a small law firm with limited resources?

U N I T

# BUSINESS ORGANIZATIONS

## INTRODUCTION TO BUSINESS ORGANIZATIONS · · · · · · · · · · · · · ·

One of the first decisions that a person or persons seeking to establish a new business venture must make is the basic organization of the business. The basic types of business organizations include sole proprietorships, partnerships, limited partnerships and corporations. As we will see in the following four chapters, each type of business organization offers certain benefits as well as drawbacks that should be carefully weighed by the proponent of the new business venture before deciding which form is best suited to the new business. The requirements for organizing a business under each of the available forms of business organization vary widely. The formalities required for a sole proprietorship are minimal; a person wishing to go into business for himself or herself need do little more than start the business. A partnership also requires few formalities prior to the startup of the business. Limited partnerships and corporations, on the other hand, must meet strict requirements set out by each state's limited partnership act or business corporation law. In this unit, we explore each form of business organization in order to understand its fundamental makeup, and examine the benefits and liabilities of structuring a business under each of the available types of business organization.

283

# 35

# SOLE PROPRIETORSHIP

The oldest and simplest form of business organization is the *sole proprietorship*. Under this form of business organization, the owner of a business personally operates the business himself or herself and is solely responsible for all aspects of the enterprise.

## FORMATION OF A SOLE PROPRIETORSHIP  . . . . . . . . . . . . . . . . .

The greatest benefit of the sole proprietorship form of business organization is that no formalities are required for its formation. A person wishing to start a business that carries his or her own name can start the enterprise at any time without the need to seek state approval. Of course, if the business is one that the state chooses to regulate in order to protect the safety, health or welfare of the general public, then the sole proprietorship must meet whatever licensing criteria the state sets for the operation of such a business; for example, only a person who has been duly admitted to a state's bar may go into the business of practicing law in the state, and only a person who procures a liquor license may sell liquor. Likewise, if the business will be involved in the sale of goods or the providing of services subject to a state or local sales tax, the sole proprietor will need to fulfill the state's requirements for tax collection. As long as the enterprise complies with all applicable state and federal regulations applicable to all business concerns, the sole proprietorship needs no additional formalities for its formation.

Persons who wish to do business under an assumed name must apply for a permit from the appropriate state office (typically the office of the secretary of state) and pay a nominal fee for the privilege of doing business under a business name. The purpose of this requirement is to prevent persons from doing business under the same name in the same area when consumer confusion might ensue. Thus, Rick Carpenter needs no special permission to start a carpentry business under the name Rick Carpenter or even Rick's Carpentry Service, but he would need to get what is commonly termed a *doing business as* (DBA) certificate from the appropriate office in his state if he wants to call his business Good Homes Carpentry, Expert Carpentry Works or any other similar business name.

## BENEFITS OF THE SOLE PROPRIETORSHIP   . . . . . . . . . . . . . . . . . .

As previously noted, the greatest benefit of the sole proprietorship is that it requires no formalities for its inception. As a result, one can begin doing business as a sole proprietorship at a moment's notice. Contrast this with limited partnerships or corporations which, as we will discuss in later chapters, require drafting detailed agreements and filing them with appropriate state agencies before the business can get off the ground—a process that can be time-consuming and expensive.

Another benefit of sole proprietorship is that the proprietor need not share decision-making authority for his or her business with others and can thus make business decisions quickly. Partnerships and corporations, on the other hand, require the reaching of a consensus and, in the case of corporations, the meeting of onerous formalities before some major business decisions (such as the sale of business assets or the acquisition of business property) can be made—processes which can interfere with the smooth operation of some businesses and make the institution of major changes a slow and often tedious process.

Just as important as the autonomy that sole proprietorship permits the business owner to enjoy is the freedom from liability for the negligent acts or bad business decisions of others. General partners in a partnership are deemed to be agents of one another, and directors and officers of a corporation are deemed to be agents of the corporation. Under the law of agency, as we saw in Chapter 33, principals can be bound by the authorized acts of their agents and are also liable for the negligent acts of their agents committed during the course of the agency. Thus, partners in a partnership can be held liable for contracts entered into on behalf of the partnership by any other partner, as well as for the negligent acts of any partner that injures a third party. Likewise, a corporation can be held liable for the authorized acts of its officers and directors, as well as their negligence. A sole proprietor, however, need never worry about being responsible for the bad judgment, negligence or bad faith of a joint owner, but is responsible only for his or her own acts and those of any subordinate employees he or she hires.

There are also some financial advantages for a sole proprietorship in terms of tax savings and lower administrative costs. Unlike most corporations, for example, the sole proprietorship does not pay federal, state or local income taxes as a business entity; all income earned by the enterprise is taxed merely as simple income to the owner. Because bookkeeping and legal formalities for the business are simplified, administrative costs are usually lower than for other forms of business organizations; for example, there is often less need for legal and accounting services for a sole proprietorship when compared with other business organizations.

## LIABILITIES OF THE SOLE PROPRIETORSHIP  . . . . . . . . . . . . . . . . .

While there are many benefits rooted in the simplicity of the sole proprietorship, a number of tangible liabilities also stem from this form of business organization. Chief among these is the unlimited personal liability of the sole proprietor for all debts incurred by the business. The sole proprietorship is not recognized as a separate entity from its owner; as a consequence, the debts of the business are deemed to be the *personal* debts of the owner. The sole proprietor has unlimited personal liability for all debts incurred by the business. If the business fails, its owner can lose not only the capital invested in the business, but also faces the prospect of having business debts satisfied out of his or her other personal assets if the business assets are insufficient to cover business debts. Creditors of a sole proprietorship are entitled to satisfy business debts not only from business assets but also from the personal assets of the business owner.

Another down side of the sole proprietorship is that the owner must rely solely on his or her own assets and expertise in running the business. While the business owner need not share profits or consult with others on business decisions, neither can he or she count on others to lend their expertise, share business losses or shoulder part of the responsibilities for the daily operation of the business. This can be a particularly important drawback when the business owner needs to raise capital for expansion or to cover extraordinary operational expenses.

## PROPERTY STATUS OF THE SOLE PROPRIETORSHIP  . . . . . . . . . . . .

A sole proprietorship is considered personal property. As such, it can be transferred in whole or in part at any time by its owner through sale or *inter vivos* or testamentary gift. If a business concern that is organized as a sole proprietorship is sold or otherwise transferred by its owner, its nature can change depending on both the terms of its transfer and the wishes of the new business owner. A sole proprietorship transferred to a single person who continues to run the business as a sole proprietor, for example, retains its previous status, while one transferred to two or more persons as joint owners becomes a partnership. A sole proprietorship can also be reorganized as a corporation if its new owners so desire. The type of business organization can also be changed by a present owner by reorganizing it from a sole proprietorship to a partnership or corporation.

## TERMINATION OF THE SOLE PROPRIETORSHIP  . . . . . . . . . . . . . . .

Just as there are no formalities for starting a sole proprietorship, there are none for ending one. The sole proprietorship can terminate as a business concern at any time upon the will of the sole proprietor, or it can end by operation of law upon the death, incapacity or bankruptcy of the owner. When the business ends, its owner will remain personally liable for completing any outstanding contracts and for meeting any other business obligation of the sole proprietorship. If the business ends due to the death or incapacity of its owner, the owner's estate or guardian will be responsible for paying the business's creditors out of estate funds.

## QUESTIONS   . . . . . . . . . . . . . . . . . . . . . . . . . . . . . . . . . . . . .

1. What are the basic types of business organizations available?
2. What is the simplest form of business organization?
3. What formalities are necessary for the formation of a sole proprietorship?
4. What are the basic benefits of doing business as a sole proprietorship?
5. What is the greatest drawback of the sole proprietorship?
6. Is it easier or harder to raise capital as a sole proprietorship than it is as a partnership? Explain.
7. What is the property status of a sole proprietorship and how can a sole proprietorship be transferred?
8. What are the formalities for terminating a sole proprietorship?
9. What is the owner's liability for business debts upon the termination of a sole proprietorship?
10. What is the effect of the owner's death or incapacity on the liabilities of a sole proprietorship?

## H Y P O T H E T I C A L   C A S E S

1. Harold would like to start his own business copying and selling shareware and public-domain software disks. He already owns a sizable collection of shareware and public-domain software on CD-ROM and believes that there is a market for his services in his area. He purchases 500 floppy disks, labels and mailing supplies and then makes up flyers that he distributes at colleges and posts on local bulletin boards advertising his services.
   a. Will Harold be in violation of the law if he starts doing business without first seeking a permit from the state?
   b. Can Harold call his business Harold's Software without getting a state permit?
   c. Can Harold call his business Software Works without state approval?
2. Assume the same facts as in the last case. If Harold's state has a sales tax that applies to the sale of software, can he go into business without informing the state?
3. Sandra, a house painter, decides to go into business for herself as an independent contractor. She prints up flyers advertising the availability of her services, has letterhead printed with the name Sandra's Paint Works and places a small ad in her local newspaper announcing the opening of her new business. After several days, calls start coming in and she contracts her services for a few jobs to private homeowners and general contractors. She soon earns a reputation for her reasonable fees and professional work, and her business experiences tremendous growth in a short period of time.
   a. Assuming her net income for the first year is $60,000, will she have to pay any business income tax under the facts given?
   b. Given the fact that her business is successful, should Sandra be concerned about her potential liability if the business fails?

c. After five years in business, Sandra has managed to increase her income to $200,000 per year. She has also purchased a new home, a small boat and various other personal assets with a value in excess of $500,000. The assets of her business, however, amount only to $10,000 in office equipment. If she is sued for $1,000,000 for negligently causing severe property damage and personal injury when scaffolding from her last job collapsed, what is her potential personal liability?

d. If Sandra wants to incorporate her business in order to protect herself against the threat of unlimited personal liability, may she do so?

e. If Sandra wants to sell her business and retire after ten years, may she do so?

f. Sandra decides to leave her business to her son Samuel and daughter Samantha after her death. When she dies, what will be the nature of the business after it passes to her children?

# CHAPTER

# 36

# PARTNERSHIP

Section 6 of the Model Partnership Act, a statute proposed by the National Conference of Commissioners of Uniform State Laws for adoption by all states, defines a partnership as "an association of two or more persons to carry on as co-owners a business for profit." To put it another way, a partnership consists of an association by two or more persons to conduct a business for profit as co-owners.

Although most states have adopted the Model Partnership Act in some form, partnership as a form of business organization was well established at common law; the Model Partnership Act largely codifies the common law in an effort to bring greater uniformity to states that adopt it. The real foundation of partnership law rests in the law of agency and contracts.

## FORMATION OF A PARTNERSHIP · · · · · · · · · · · · · · · · · · · · · · · ·

Like the sole proprietorship, the partnership form of business organization does not require specific formalities for its formation. Oral and written agreements to enter into a partnership are generally equally binding. A partnership can also arise by operation of law even without a specific agreement; any voluntary association by two or more persons to conduct a business for profit as joint owners automatically results in the formation of a partnership by operation of law, whether or not the joint owners specifically intended it.

If two or more persons go into a business for profit together without making specific provisions for the type of business organization the business will take, a partnership automatically results, and the rights and responsibilities of the parties are dictated by the law of partnership. In most cases, however, persons wishing to go into business together draw up a formal *partnership agreement*, a contract detailing the rights and obligations of each party. (See Figure 36.1 for a sample partnership agreement form.)

## PARTNERSHIP AGREEMENT

AGREEMENT made _____, 19___ between _____, of
(Name of partner #1)

_____, and _____, of _____.
(Address of partner #1)　　　　　　　　　(Name of partner #2)　　　　　　　　　(Address of partner #2)

    1. NAME AND BUSINESS. The parties hereby form a partnership under the name of _____ to conduct the following business: _____.
(Business name)　　　　　　　　　　　　　　　　　　　　(Description of partnership business)

The principal office of the business shall be at _____.
(Principal business address of partnership)

    2. TERM. The partnership shall begin on _____, 19___, and shall continue until terminated as herein provided.

    3. CAPITAL. The capital of the partnership shall be contributed in cash by the partners as follows: _____.
(Description of partners' capital contribution)

    A separate capital account shall be maintained for each partner. Neither partner shall withdraw any part of his capital account. Upon the demand of either partner, the capital accounts of the partners shall be maintained at all times in the proportions in which the partners share in the profits and losses of the partnership.

    4. PROFIT AND LOSS. The net profits of the partnership shall be divided equally between the partners and the net losses shall be borne equally by them. A separate income account shall be maintained for each partner. Partnership profits and losses shall be credited or charged to the separate income account of each partner. If a partner has no credit balance in his income account, losses shall be charged to his capital account.

    5. SALARIES AND DRAWINGS. Neither partner shall receive any salary for services rendered to the partnership. Each partner may, from time to time, withdraw the credit balance in his income account.

    6. INTEREST. No interest shall be paid on the initial contributions to the capital of the partnership or on any subsequent contributions of capital.

    7. MANAGEMENT DUTIES AND RESTRICTIONS. The partners shall have equal rights in the management of the partnership business, and each partner shall devote his entire time to the conduct of the business. Without the consent of the other partner neither partner shall on behalf of the partnership borrow, lend, make, deliver or accept any commercial paper, or execute any mortgage, security agreement, bond or lease, or purchase or contract to purchase, or sell or contract to sell any property for or of the partnership other than the type of property bought and sold in the regular course of its business.

    8. BANKING. All funds of the partnership shall be deposited in its name in such checking account or accounts as shall be designated by the partners. All withdrawals therefrom are to be made upon checks signed by either partner.

    9. BOOKS. The partnership books shall be maintained at the principal office of the partnership, and each partner shall at all times have access thereto. The books shall be kept on a fiscal-year basis, commencing _____ and ending _____, and shall be closed and balanced at the end of each fiscal year. An audit shall be made as of the closing date.

    10. VOLUNTARY TERMINATION. The partnership may be dissolved at any time by agreement of the partners, in which event the partners shall proceed with reasonable promptness to liquidate the business of the partnership. The partnership name shall be sold with the other assets of the business. The assets of the partnership business shall be used and distributed in the following order: (a) to pay or provide for the payment of all partnership liabilities and liquidating expenses and obligations; (b) to equalize the income accounts of the partners; (c) to discharge the balance of the income accounts

**FIGURE 36.1**   Sample partnership agreement form

of the partners; (d) to equalize the capital accounts of the partners; and (e) to discharge the balance of the capital accounts of the partners.

11. DEATH. Upon the death of either partner, the surviving partner shall have the right either to purchase the interest of the decedent in the partnership or to terminate and liquidate the partnership business. If the surviving partner elects to purchase the decedent's interest, he shall serve notice in writing of such election, within three months after the death of the decedent, upon the executor or administrator of the decedent, or, if at the time of such election no legal representative has been appointed, upon any one of the known legal heirs of the decedent at the last-known address of such heir.

(a) If the surviving partner elects to purchase the interest of the decedent in the partnership, the purchase price shall be equal to the decedent's capital account as at the date of his death plus the decedent's income account as at the end of the prior fiscal year, increased by his share of partnership profits or decreased by his share of partnership losses for the period from the beginning of the fiscal year in which his death occurred until the end of the calendar month in which his death occurred, and decreased by withdrawals charged to his income account during such period. No allowance shall be made for goodwill, trade names, patents, or other intangible assets, except as those assets have been reflected on the partnership books immediately prior to the decedent's death; but the survivor shall nevertheless be entitled to use the trade name of the partnership.

(b) Except as herein otherwise stated, the procedure as to liquidation and distribution of the assets of the partnership business shall be the same as stated in paragraph 10 with reference to voluntary termination.

13. ARBITRATION. Any controversy or claim arising out of or relating to this Agreement, or the breach hereof, shall be settled by arbitration in accordance with the rules, then obtaining, of the American Arbitration Association, and judgment upon the award rendered may be entered in any court having jurisdiction thereof.

In witness whereof the parties have signed this Agreement.

_____
(Signature of partner #1)

_____
(Signature of partner #2)

**FIGURE 36.1**    Continued

# RELATIONSHIP OF PARTNERS TO THE PARTNERSHIP AND TO ONE ANOTHER  · · · · · · · · · · · · · · · · · · · · · · · · · · · · · ·

The relationship between partners in a partnership is largely dictated by the law of agency and contracts.

## AGENCY RIGHTS AND DUTIES OF PARTNERS

Partners are agents of the partnership when they act within the scope of their authority. As such, they bind the partnership to any contracts they enter into on the partnership's behalf within the regular course of business. As is true of all agents, partners owe fiduciary duties to the partnership. As co-owners of the business, partners also have the interests of principals in the enterprise; since each partner is essentially both an agent of the partnership as well as a principal of the same, each partner also owes every other partner the duties of a fiduciary. As such, partners must place partnership interests above their own personal gain and must execute their duties as partners with the utmost good faith.

The general duties owed by agents to their principals, as discussed in Chapter 33, apply to each partner in the partnership. Thus, partners owe the partnership and one another not merely the duty of loyalty, but also the duties of obedience (they must carry out the rightful requests of the majority partners), the duty to exercise reasonable care and diligence in the exercise of their partnership duties, the duty to notify the partnership of any facts learned that are relevant to the partnership and the duty to make an accounting to the partnership of any benefits derived from conducting partnership business as well as any expenses incurred on the partnership's behalf. By the same token, the partnership owes each individual partner the duty of reimbursement and indemnification, as well as the duty of cooperation.

## CONTRACTUAL RIGHTS AND DUTIES OF PARTNERS

Partners are free to control the nature of their relationship to one another and the precise reciprocal duties they owe one another and the partnership through the partnership agreement. In the absence of provisions to the contrary in the partnership agreement (the basic contract that dictates the rights and responsibilities of the partners in relation to the partnership and one another), partners have an equal right to manage the business and to share in the profits of the business. The mere fact that one partner makes a greater capital contribution to the partnership will not give that partner a greater voice in the management of the business or a greater share in its profits unless it is otherwise provided in the partnership agreement. Unless the partnership agreement provides otherwise, partners must share in the losses of the business in accordance with the share of profits they receive from it. Thus, if partners share profits equally, they will also share losses equally, but if a formula is adopted for the sharing of profits, the same formula will apply to the sharing of losses between the partners, unless they specifically agree otherwise.

## ADDITIONAL RIGHTS AND DUTIES OF PARTNERS IMPOSED BY LAW · · · · · · · · · · · · · · · · · · · · · · · · · · · · · · · · · · ·

### LIMITATIONS OF PARTNERS' ABILITY TO BIND THE PARTNERSHIP

Despite the fact that partners can individually bind the partnership to contracts entered into on its behalf during the regular course of business, the unanimous consent of all partners is required to undertake certain acts that are especially dangerous for the partnership, including assigning partnership property for the benefit of creditors, disposing of the partnership's goodwill, confessing a judgment (voluntarily acknowledging existing debt and submitting to a judgment being entered without a judicial proceeding), submitting a partnership claim to arbitration or any other act which would make it impossible to carry out the ordinary business of the partnership. (Uniform Partnership Act, § 9 [3][a–e])

## LIMITATION ON PARTNERS' RIGHT OF COMPENSATION

Unless otherwise agreed, partners serve without compensation for their services beyond the distribution of partnership profits to which they are entitled.

## PARTNERS' CAPITAL CONTRIBUTIONS

Each partner is entitled to repayment of the capital contributions (cash and/or property) made to the partnership upon death or withdrawal from the partnership, or upon the dissolution of the partnership. Payments or advances to the partnership by any partner above and beyond the agreed-upon initial capital contribution will earn interest for the partner as of the date it is made.

## ADMISSION OF NEW PARTNERS

Admission of new partners into an existing partnership agreement can be made only with the unanimous consent of all partners.

## PARTNERS' RIGHT TO INSPECT PARTNERSHIP'S BOOKS

Every partner has the right to inspect the books of the partnership at any time. The books must be kept at the principal office of the partnership and made available to every partner at all times for inspection and copying.

# PARTNERS' LIABILITY FOR PARTNERSHIP DEBT . . . . . . . . . . . . . . .

All partners are jointly and severally liable for all partnership debts. This means that partners can be sued individually or together by any person to whom the partnership owes a debt. This includes (but is not limited to) debts that arise from contracts, tort liability or liability to the state and federal governments for taxes or fees connected to the running of the business. Thus, each partner is subject to unlimited personal liability for partnership debts. If a single partner is sued by a creditor, he or she must fully discharge the debt out of his or her personal assets, but can then seek reimbursement from the other partners for their individual share of the liability.

Persons who misrepresent themselves as partners to a partnership when they are in fact not partners can also be held fully liable for debts of the partnership by persons to whom the misrepresentation of partnership was made. Likewise, persons who are misrepresented as being partners by actual partners in the partnership will be able to bind the partnership under a theory of equitable estoppel.

Incoming partners are fully liable for any pre-existing liability of the partnership when they become partners, but their liability is limited to the extent of their capital contribution made to the partnership. With regard to liability incurred by the partnership *after* a new partner is admitted, the new partner will share unlimited liability for such debt with all other partners.

## PARTNERS' PROPERTY RIGHTS    . . . . . . . . . . . . . . . . . . . . . . . . .

Each partner is a co-owner of partnership property and holds such property as a *tenant in partnership* with all other partners. Tenancy in partnership gives partners the right to possess all partnership property, be it real or personal, jointly with all other partners for partnership purposes only. A partner may not possess any partnership property for any other purpose without the consent of all other partners. Unlike other property interests, a tenancy in partnership is nonassignable other than through a transfer agreed to by all partners. Likewise, a partner's right to partnership property is not attachable by personal creditors of the partner; it is only subject to attachment by creditors of the partnership. Upon the death or incompetence of a partner, personal and real property held by him or her as a partner in partnership automatically vests in the surviving partners. (The estate of the deceased or incompetent partner is, of course, paid the value of the partner's share.)

While physical property owned by the partners as tenants in partnership is not assignable by any partner, each partner *can* freely assign his or her partnership interests to third parties. Such a conveyance, however, transfers only the partner's right to share in the profits of the business. Partners' duties to the partnership, including the duty to perform personal services and to manage the partnership, are nondelegable. A partner who sells, assigns or otherwise transfers his or her interest in the partnership is still obligated to assist in the running of the business.

## DISSOLUTION OF A PARTNERSHIP AND WINDING UP    . . . . . . . . . .

A partnership can end at any time for a number of reasons, including by the mutual agreement of the parties, the withdrawal of any one partner or the expiration of a preset time period for the partnership's duration. Where there is no agreement to the contrary, partnerships are deemed to be voluntary and subject to dissolution at any time by the will of any one partner. Even in cases where partners agree not to dissolve the partnership for a specific period of time, any one partner may still cause the partnership to dissolve by voluntarily withdrawing from it. If this happens, the withdrawing partner may be liable to the other partners for breach of contract, but the partnership will nevertheless be dissolved.

A partnership can also end by operation of law by the death or decreed insanity of a partner, or by a partner's bankruptcy. A partnership can also be dissolved if a court decrees that any one partner is otherwise incapable of carrying out partnership duties (such as through illness or other disability), or if a partner is found to be guilty of misconduct that prejudices the carrying out of the partnership business, or if the business can be carried out only at a loss.

After dissolution, a partnership enters the winding-up period. During this time, the partners may continue to carry out business as long as is reasonably necessary to complete existing contracts that are in progress and to otherwise bring the business affairs to an orderly close. Upon dissolution of a partnership, partners lose their authority to bind the partnership to new contracts. If a partner enters into new contracts on behalf of the partnership during the winding-up period, the partnership and other partners will not be bound by such contracts; rather, the partner acting without express authority will be personally bound to these contracts in the same way as any agent who exceeds his actual authority.

Even after dissolution and winding up, partners retain unlimited personal liability for partnership debts. If the assets of a dissolved partnership are insufficient to cover partnership debts, creditors of the partnership can sue partners individually or jointly for any shortfall.

## NOTICE TO THIRD PARTIES UPON DISSOLUTION · · · · · · · · · · · ·

When a partnership is dissolved other than by operation of law (such as by the death or bankruptcy of a partner), partners still have apparent authority to bind the partnership with respect to persons who had previously extended credit to the partnership or known of its existence. For this reason, it is essential that notice be given to such persons that the partnership has been dissolved. Until such notice is received, persons who knew of the partnership's existence or who had extended credit to the partnership in the past may still enter into binding contracts with the partnership through any of its partners. In order to effectively revoke partners' apparent authority to bind the partnership to new contracts, persons who have previously extended credit to the partnership must be personally notified of the partnership's dissolution by any reasonable means (e.g., by letter, telephone or telegraph, or in person). If such notification is mailed, it is effective when it is received (even if it is never read). Notification to persons who might have known of the existence of the partnership but had not extended credit to it previously is sufficient if it is published in a newspaper of general circulation in the area or areas where the partnership did business.

## QUESTIONS   · · · · · · · · · · · · · · · · · · · · · · · · · · · · · · · · · · · · · · · ·

1. Define the term *partnership*.
2. What specific requirements are there to the formation of a partnership?
3. What is the importance of the law of agency to the law of partnerships?
4. What duties do partners owe the partnership?
5. What duties are owed all partners by the partnership?
6. In the absence of agreement to the contrary, how are profits in a partnership shared? What about expenses?

7. Partners may generally unilaterally bind the partnership to contracts they enter into with third parties on the partnership's behalf in the regular course of business. But some types of acts require unanimous assent by all partners in a partnership. What are they?

8. Can new members be admitted to an existing partnership? If so, how? What liability do such members have with respect to the debts of the partnership incurred before they joined it?

9. What is the liability of partners for partnership debt?

10. What types of activities can a partnership engage in during the winding-up period?

# H Y P O T H E T I C A L    C A S E S

1. Daniel, Denise and Donald, three college students, decide it would be a good idea to provide research and word-processing services for other students at State University for a fee. They advertise their business in the college newspaper under the name Daniel, Denise and Donald Research and Writing Service. Daniel contributes $250 in cash towards the venture, while Denise provides an old computer system with software and Donald provides a laser printer. Neither Denise nor Donald makes any other cash contributions. The friends do not discuss the nature of the business and do not enter into any type of written or oral agreement relating to the business; they merely begin working together in the hope of earning enough money to defray the latest in a series of tuition increases at their college over the past few years.
   a. What is the nature of the business?
   b. Assume that the value of the students' contribution to the business is as follows: Daniel, $250; Denise, $1,250; Donald $750. How will the profits of the business be distributed?
   c. How will business losses be shared?
   d. How will losses be shared if the friends agree that Dan is to receive 20 percent of the profits, Denise 50 percent and Donald 30 percent?
   e. If the friends agree in writing that they will work at the business throughout their college careers and Donald quits the business after an unsuccessful semester, what will the effect be on the business organization? What can Daniel and Denise do if they are unwilling to dissolve the arrangement?
   f. Assuming that a partnership exists here, who owns the equipment given over to the business by Denise and Donald? May they each take their equipment home with them for their own use as a matter of right over holidays and weekends if they choose to do so? Explain fully.

2. Harry and Harriet enter into an agreement to start an antique dealership business as equal partners. Harry agrees to make a $50,000 capital contribution to the business and Harriet agrees to provide a commercial building that she has inherited, worth $150,000, as her capital contribution. The agreement between the

partners specifically states that business profits and losses will be shared equally. After successfully running the business for a number of years, the partners decide they would like to hire someone to manage the daily operation of the business for them. They hire Helen as the general manager of the business. Although Helen is not a part-owner of the business, her salary will be based on a share of the business profits. And, although all fundamental business decisions are made by Harry and Harriet, they often ask her advice before implementing new policies.

   a. Is Helen a partner? Explain fully.

   b. If the business goes bankrupt and its debts exceed its assets by $200,000 after dissolution, what will the responsibility of Harry, Harriet and Helen be with regard to the debts?

   c. Assume that after dissolution, the debts of the business exceed its assets by $100,000 and that Harry is insolvent, but Harriet has personal assets (including her family home) well in excess of $100,000. How much of the debt could creditors ask Harriet to bear? Explain.

3. Evelyn and Edward open a used-car dealership together. Evelyn makes a capital contribution of $100,000 to the business, and Edward, who has no money to contribute but who has a great deal of business sense and a willingness to work hard, agrees to manage all affairs of the business. No contract is entered into by the two, who are longtime friends and implicitly trust each other.

   a. Is Edward entitled to receive a salary for his services? Explain.

   b. If the business is slow in getting off the ground, may Edward work part-time for another auto dealership without Evelyn's consent in order to pay his rent? Explain.

   c. Assume that the venture is successful and, ten years later, Evelyn dies. What will be the effect of her death?

   d. If the business is worth $1,000,000 at the time of Evelyn's death, how will the proceeds from the sale of the business be distributed between Evelyn's estate and Edward?

   e. After Evelyn's death, what exactly must Edward do in terms of the business?

# 37

# LIMITED PARTNERSHIP

A *limited partnership* is a type of partnership made up of one or more general partners who manage the business and have unlimited personal liability for partnership debts, and one or more limited partners who contribute capital to the business and share in its profits, but whose liability for partnership obligations is limited to the extent of their investment in the business.

Unlike the sole proprietorship and partnership forms of business organization that were recognized at common law, the limited partnership is a creation of statute. As such, a limited partnership can be created only in accordance with the specific requirements of a state's limited partnership act. Most states have adopted the Model Limited Partnership Act promulgated by the National Conference of Commissioners of Uniform State Laws in some form.

The limited partnership form of business organization was created to address one of the worst shortcomings of the traditional partnership form: the unlimited personal liability of all partners for financial obligations incurred by the partnership. While such liability on partners protects the general public against losses when dealing with a partnership, thus encouraging business with such organizations, the unlimited personal liability can have a negative effect on the willingness of persons to become partners. As we have seen from the last chapter, partners must be willing to bear the risk of unlimited personal liability for partnership losses. This is a risk that is unacceptable to many investors—in particular those of substantial means, for whom the risk of unlimited personal liability is greatest. What the limited partnership form of business organization accomplishes is the creation of a special class of partner who is merely an investor and does not become involved in the actual running of the business, while retaining unlimited personal liability for the traditional partners (general partners) of the business. As an investor, the limited partner places the money invested in the partnership through his or her capital contribution at risk in the event that the enterprise fails, but is insulated from personal liability beyond the extent of that investment. Thus, limited partnerships encourage investment by putting limited partners in an analogous position to stockholders in a corporation. (This will become clear as we examine corporations in the next chapter.)

## FORMATION OF A LIMITED PARTNERSHIP    . . . . . . . . . . . . . . . . . .

In order to form a limited partnership, a certificate of limited partnership needs to be executed and filed with the appropriate state office (usually the office of the secretary of state). Article 2, Section 201 of the Uniform Limited Partnership Act sets out the requirements for the information that must be contained in the certificate of limited partnership as follows:

(1) the name of the limited partnership;

(2) the address of the office and name and address of the agent for service of process . . . ;

(3) the name and business address of each general partner;

(4) the latest date upon which the limited partnership is to dissolve;

(5) any other matters the general partners determine to include therein.

As should be apparent from these requirements, the main purpose of requiring the limited partnership certificate to be executed and filed is to give notice to the general public of the existence of the partnership and the identity of its general partners. As we will see shortly, general partners retain unlimited personal liability for partnership debt, so that forcing disclosure of the identity and address of such partners is important to preserving the rights of the general public to sue such partners in the event that partnership debts are not properly discharged in the regular course of business. Likewise, the requirement that an agent be named for service of process (e.g., notice that a lawsuit is instituted) is intended to facilitate suing the partnership by clearly identifying the name and address of a person in the state authorized to receive service of process on behalf of the partnership.

Once a certificate of limited partnership is filed, it can be amended by duly notifying the secretary of state of any desired changes. Amendments to the certificate are mandatory and must be made within thirty days after the admission or withdrawal of a general partner or the continuation of the business after the happening of an event that requires its dissolution, such as the death or bankruptcy of a general partner.

## RIGHTS AND OBLIGATIONS OF GENERAL
## AND LIMITED PARTNERS    . . . . . . . . . . . . . . . . . . . . . . . . . . . . .

The rights and obligations of general partners in a limited partnership are identical to those of partners in a traditional partnership. General partners are co-owners of the business who owe the business the fiduciary duties of agents and who share in the management and in the profits of the business, as well as in its debts. Limited partners, on the other hand, share only in the profits of the business and are liable for its debts only up to the limit of their capital investment. Unlike general partners, limited partners cannot have a voice in the management of the business; limited partners who become involved in the running of the business lose their special status and are subject to unlimited liability for the debts of the business to persons who believe limited partners to be general partners because of their involvement in the management of the business. In other words, limited partners who become involved in the management of the business are estopped from denying that they are general partners with regard to persons who might have reasonably believed them to be general partners because of their involvement in managing the business. In addition, a limited partner who allows his or her name to be used in the name of the partnership will be liable as a general partner to any person who extends credit to the partnership without actual knowledge that the partner so named is a limited partner.

Despite the prohibition on limited partners managing the partnership, some or all limited partners *can* be granted the right to vote along with general partners on partnership matters by express provision in the limited partnership agreement. Thus, limited partners can have a voice through their vote on policy matters and business decisions affecting the partnership, as long as they do not directly assume the reins of managerial power over the partnership.

In most states, corporations are allowed to be general or limited partners in limited partnerships. When a corporation, rather than a natural person (live human being), is involved as a partner, the liability of the corporation for partnership debts will encompass either all assets of the corporation (if the corporation is a general partner) or the capital invested in the partnership (if the corporation is a limited partner). As you will see in the next chapter, the corporate shareholders (the owners of the corporation) in either case will be insulated from personal liability beyond their investment in the corporation.

## WITHDRAWAL BY GENERAL AND LIMITED PARTNERS    . . . . . . . . . .

A general partner may withdraw from a limited partnership at any time by giving written notice to the other partners. If the partnership agreement prohibits withdrawal, a general partner may still withdraw, but will be in breach of the partnership contract and can be sued for damages by the other partners. Upon the withdrawal of a general partner, the partnership will be dissolved unless the partnership agreement makes provisions for continuation by the remaining partners in such an event.

Limited partners may also withdraw at any time by giving less than six months' written notice of their intention to all partners. If the limited partner's right to withdraw is limited in the partnership contract and the limited partner withdraws in violation of such a contract, then the withdrawing partner may be liable for breach-of-contract damages. The withdrawal of a limited partner will not automatically dissolve the partnership unless the limited partnership agreement so provides.

# DISSOLUTION OF A LIMITED PARTNERSHIP · · · · · · · · · · · · · · · · · ·

A limited partnership will be dissolved under any of the following circumstances:

(1) at the time specified in the certificate of limited partnership [e.g., after ten years in a partnership set up to last ten years];

(2) upon the happening of events specified in writing in the limited partnership agreement;

(3) by the written consent of all partners;

(4) by the withdrawal of a general partner unless the limited partnership agreement specifically allows the business to continue upon such an event and there is at least one remaining general partner;

(5) by the entry of a decree of judicial dissolution. (Uniform Partnership Act, Article 8, § 801)

With regard to number (4), if the partnership will be dissolved due to the withdrawal of a general partner when no provision was made for the continuation of the business in such an event, or due to the withdrawal of a general partner leaving no other general partners in the partnership, the remaining partners can continue in business as a partnership provided they all sign a written agreement to continue in business and name at least one general partner. A decree of judicial dissolution as described in number (5) will be granted when a court finds it reasonably impractical to carry out the business in conformity with the terms of the limited partnership agreement.

# FOREIGN LIMITED PARTNERSHIP · · · · · · · · · · · · · · · · · · · · · · ·

A limited partnership is considered a *domestic limited partnership* when doing business in the state in which it is organized, and a *foreign limited partnership* when doing business in every other state. Foreign limited partnerships must register with the appropriate office in every state they wish to do business in (generally the office of the secretary of state) and pay the requisite fees before doing business in any state other than the one in which they are organized. In order to register as a foreign limited partnership, a general partner must submit a form in duplicate to the secretary of state of every state in which the partnership wishes to do business (other than the state in which it is organized). The form must contain the following information:

(1) the name of the foreign limited partnership and, if different, the name under which it proposes to register and transact business in this state;

(2) the state and date of its formation;

(3) the name and address of any agent for service of process on the foreign limited partnership whom the foreign limited partnership elects to appoint. [The act further specifies that "the agent must be an individual resident of this state, a domestic corporation, or a foreign corporation having a place of business, and authorized, to do business in this State"];

(4) a statement that the Secretary of State is appointed the agent of the foreign limited partnership for service of process if no agent has been appointed under paragraph (3), or if appointed, the agent's authority has been revoked or if the agent cannot be found or served with the exercise of reasonable diligence;

(5) the address of the office required to be maintained in the state of its organization by the laws of that state or, if not so required, of the principal office of the foreign limited partnership;

(6) the name and business address of each general partner;

(7) the address of the office at which is kept a list of the names and addresses of the limited partners and their capital contributions, together with an undertaking by the foreign limited partnership to keep those records until the foreign limited partnership's registration in this State is canceled or withdrawn. (Uniform Limited Partnership Act, Article 9, § 902)

The registration requirements just stated are meant to protect the citizens of the state in the event that they have claims against a foreign limited partnership by making it easy to sue both the partnership and its individual members. In addition, the registration fee is a source of income for states. You might have noticed that there is no analogous requirement of registration for sole proprietorships or traditional partnerships. The reason is the equal protection clause of the Fourteenth Amendment, which requires a state to treat citizens of other states exactly as it treats its own citizens. Thus, individuals who wish to do business in other states cannot be subjected to registration requirements or fees that those states do not impose on their own citizens. But the courts have been a bit more lenient in cases of states imposing additional licensing requirements to foreign corporations and limited partnerships which are creatures of statute and thus not entitled to quite the same protection as natural persons.

If an application to register as a foreign limited partnership is properly completed and accompanied by the appropriate fee (which varies from state to state), the secretary of state issues a certificate of registration to transact business to the applicant, returning a copy of the application to the applicant and keeping one on file.

In the event that a foreign limited partnership does business in a state without filing the required certificate, it will not be allowed to bring any lawsuit in the state seeking civil relief for alleged breaches of contract or torts committed against it until it completes the registration process. It can, however, enter into valid contracts notwithstanding the failure to register, and can also be sued by third parties in the state's courts.

# RIGHT OF LIMITED PARTNERS TO BRING DERIVATIVE ACTIONS    . . .

Like shareholders of a corporation, limited partners in a partnership have the right to bring derivative actions on behalf of the limited partnership if the general partners refuse to do so. A *derivative action* is an action by a limited partner to enforce a partnership cause of action that the general partners are unwilling to enforce themselves.

If a derivative action by a limited partner on behalf of the partnership is successful, a court has the power to award reasonable costs, including attorneys' fees, to the limited partner bringing the lawsuit on the partnership's behalf. Any recovery above the costs of litigating the case is then turned over to the partnership.

A derivative action can be brought only by a limited partner while he is still a partner for any action that accrued after he was admitted as a partner to the limited partnership. In order to bring a derivative action, the limited partner must show that the general partners have been unwilling to bring the action themselves on behalf of the limited partnership, and that they are unlikely to do so on their own.

## QUESTIONS  . . . . . . . . . . . . . . . . . . . . . . . . . . . . . . . .

1. What is a limited partnership?
2. Did limited partnerships exist at common law?
3. How is a limited partnership formed?
4. What information must be contained in the certificate of limited partnership?
5. What is the basic difference between a limited partner and a general partner in a partnership?
6. May a corporation be a limited or general partner in most states?
7. If the partnership agreement is silent as to the withdrawal of members, what is the effect of a general partner withdrawing from the partnership? What is the effect of a limited partner withdrawing?
8. What are the circumstances upon which a limited partnership will be dissolved?
9. Define *foreign limited partnerships* and *domestic limited partnerships.*
10. May foreign limited partnerships do business in states other than the one they were organized in? If so, do they need to follow any specific procedures before they can do business?

## H Y P O T H E T I C A L    C A S E S

1. Tom, Dick and Harriet start a new tax preparation and financial planning business together. Their state does not require any special licensing for such businesses, and, since the three partners are good friends, they do not draw up any specific agreement relating to the business. They do, however, verbally agree that all profits of the business are to be shared equally, and so are all losses, except that Harriet will be responsible only up to the extent of her capital contribution in the business. They further agree that Harriet will not have any direct role in the management of the business, but rather will be an investor.
   a. What form of business organization do the friends have? Explain.
   b. Is Harriet a limited partner, since that is obviously the role that the parties intended for her to play in the business?
   c. Assume that Harriet had invested $50,000 in the business, while Tom and Dick had invested $5,000 each in the venture. What is each party's potential liability should the business fail?
2. Abel, Betty and Charlene want to purchase a bookstore to compete with the campus bookstore in their university. They believe that they can make a nifty profit by instituting a 10 percent markup on everything they sell—including the used books they buy back from students at a fair price. They are afraid, though, of the

unlimited liability posed by the partnership form of business organization and would like to minimize their risk.

a. Can they set up a limited partnership where all three are limited partners? Explain.

b. If one of the three volunteers to be a general partner provided that business insurance is purchased to cover any potential liability, could the business be set up as a limited partnership?

c. Assume that the business is set up as a limited partnership and is very successful. After a year in business, a problem arises with one of their suppliers who fails to ship a large order in time for the beginning of the semester, costing the business thousands of dollars in lost profits. If Abel and Betty refuse to sue the supplier, who is a relative of Abel and a very close friend of Betty, what can Charlene, the limited partner, do?

3. Dominick, Enrique and Frances are partners in a general partnership involving a lucrative used-automobile dealership in northern Pennsylvania. Because of the success of their business, they want to expand their operations to New York and New Jersey, opening two new dealerships in those states.

a. Can they reorganize the general partnership into a limited partnership to attract new investors?

b. What requirements would have to be met by the limited partnership before it could start doing business in New York or New Jersey?

CHAPTER

# 38

# CORPORATIONS

Like the limited partnership, the corporate form of business organization owes its existence to statutory law. In 1811, New York was the first state to enact a corporate statute, with other states following soon thereafter. Today, every state has enacted a business corporation statute, and the National Conference of Commissioners of Uniform State Laws has promulgated a Model Business Corporation Act. In this chapter, we will first concentrate on how a corporation is created and managed and then explore the unique nature of the corporate entity and explore its advantages and disadvantages over the partnership and sole proprietorship forms of business organization.

## FORMATION OF A CORPORATION · · · · · · · · · · · · · · · · · · · · · · · ·

Because a corporation is a creature of statute that owes its existence to a state's business corporation law, it must be organized in accordance with the requirements of that statute.

### ARTICLES OF INCORPORATION

Under the Revised Model Business Corporation Act (which most state business corporation statutes resemble closely), the corporation's incorporators must deliver to the state's secretary of state corporate articles of incorporation which *must* contain the following information:

1. The corporate name for the corporation;

2. the number of shares of stock that the corporation is authorized to issue;

3. the address of the corporation's registered office and the name of the corporation's registered agent; and

4. the name and address of each incorporator. (Revised Model Business Corporation Act, § 2.02 [a])

In addition to the above mandatory minimum information, articles of incorporation *may* also contain some or all of the following types of information:

1. the names and addresses of individuals who are to serve as the initial directors;

2. provisions not inconsistent with law regarding:

    (i) the purpose or purposes for which the corporation is organized;

    (ii) managing the business and regulating the affairs of the corporation;

    (iii) defining, limiting, and regulating the powers of the corporation, its board of directors, and shareholders;

    (iv) a par value for authorized shares or classes of shares;

    (v) the imposition of personal liability on shareholders for the debts of the corporation to a specified extent and upon specified conditions; and

3. any provision that under this Act is required or permitted to be set forth in the bylaws. (Revised Model Business Corporation Act § 2.02 [b])

As you can see, the articles of incorporation have similar requirements to the certificate of limited partnership and a similar purpose: to give notice to the public at large of the existence of the corporation and to provide an agent on whom process can be served by anyone seeking to initiate legal action against the corporation.

## CORPORATE NAME

There are two requirements that incorporators must meet in selecting a corporate name. First, with few exceptions, the name may not currently be in use by another corporation in the same state. Second, the corporate name must include one of the following words in its title: *corporation, incorporated, company* or *limited,* or one of the following abbreviations for such words: *corp., inc., co.* or *ltd.*

## CORPORATE EXISTENCE

Under the Revised Model Business Corporation Act, a corporation's existence begins as soon as the articles of incorporation are filed by the secretary of state. Articles of incorporation that meet the statutory criteria and are accompanied by the appropriate filing fee are stamped by the secretary of state and filed upon their receipt. A stamped copy of the articles of incorporation is then returned to the corporate office, along with a stamped receipt for the paid filing fee. If there is a defect in the articles of incorporation submitted for filing, the secretary of state rejects them without filing and returns the documents with a written explanation of the defect.

## DEFECTIVE INCORPORATION

A corporation that has been formed in strict compliance with a state's business corporation act is said to be a *de jure corporation*, or a corporation by virtue of law. When the incorporators file articles of incorporation that do not meet all the requirements of the state's business corporation act, a *de jure corporation* cannot be formed. Nevertheless, if a good-faith effort has been made to comply with the act and the proposed corporation qualifies for corporate status under the state's laws, the business enterprise can be considered a *de facto corporation*, or a corporation in fact, and treated as a valid corporation. For a corporation to qualify as a *de facto* corporation, its incorporators must have made a good-faith effort to comply with the state's business corporation act, the business concern must be otherwise eligible for corporate status, and the business must be in operation as a corporation when the defect in its application is discovered. *De facto* corporate status typically results when necessary information is negligently omitted from the articles of incorporation, such as by omitting an incorporator's address or providing an incorrect name for the registered agent.

In states that adhere to the Revised Model Business Corporation Act, there can be no *de facto* corporations, since all corporations classify as *de jure* as soon as the articles of incorporation are accepted by the secretary of state. Errors can simply be corrected once they are discovered after filing in such states, and the certificate is returned without acceptance or filing (thus, the corporation does not come into existence) if the error is discovered by the secretary of state.

## PROMOTERS' LIABILITY FOR PREINCORPORATION CONTRACTS · · · · · · · · · · · · · · · · · · · · · · · · · · · · · · · · ·

Before a corporation is formed, one or more persons are usually involved in obtaining stock subscriptions from investors and in laying the groundwork for the creation of the corporation. In helping to get the new business enterprise off the ground, *promoters* enter into contracts with third parties on behalf of the corporation that they are attempting to form. Because promoters act on behalf of a nonexistent entity when they begin their work on the corporation's behalf, they are not held to be agents of the corporation; a corporation that is not yet in existence cannot be a principal and, thus, cannot consent to the agency. What this means is that promoters are personally liable for any contracts they enter into on the corporation's behalf before the corporation comes into existence. In most instances, this does not present a problem for promoters because the new corporation ratifies any contracts promoters enter into on its behalf at the first meeting of the board of directors, thus taking the promoters off the hook with regard to liability for such contracts. But there is a very real element of risk for promoters when they carry out their preincorporation duties, since there is no guarantee that the board of directors of the company will ratify the promoters' contracts on the corporation's behalf. In fact, the corporation may never even be formed. In such cases, promoters can find themselves in the very uncomfortable position of retaining personal liability for contracts entered into on the corporation's behalf and monies extended on behalf of the corporation for such necessary preincorporation activities as hiring lawyers or accountants to assist in getting the corporation off the ground, paying filing fees, and arranging commercial leases or employment contracts for necessary office space and key employees of the corporation while it is still in its embryonic preincorporation stage.

Once the promoters' initial groundwork for the corporation is completed, one or more persons must be selected to act as *incorporators* by the promoters (or the promoters can act as incorporators themselves). The incorporator has the responsibility of filing the articles of incorporation with the secretary of state and calling the first organizational meeting for the new corporation once it is formed. In most states, the secretary of state issues a certificate of incorporation signaling the birth of the new company after accepting and filing the articles of incorporation submitted by the incorporators. The Revised Model Business Corporation Act, however, does not require the issuance of a certificate of incorporation, but rather states that a corporation is formed as soon as the secretary of state accepts and files the articles of incorporation. As a result, it is likely that the number of states which actually issue a certificate of incorporation will decline in the future.

## FIRST ORGANIZATIONAL MEETING OF THE CORPORATION  . . . . . .

If the corporation's directors are named in the articles of incorporation, an organizational meeting is called by a majority of the directors. The primary purpose of this meeting is to appoint corporate officers and to adopt the corporate *bylaws*—the internal rules governing the operation of the corporation. During this first meeting, the directors also typically ratify any contracts entered into on the corporation's behalf by the promoters.

In the event that the directors are not listed in the articles of incorporation, then a majority of the incorporators call the organizational meeting. At this meeting, the first order of business is the appointment of directors by the incorporators. Once appointed, the directors appoint the corporate officers, adopt the corporate bylaws, and ratify the promoters' preincorporation contracts entered into on the corporation's behalf.

## MANAGEMENT OF THE CORPORATION  . . . . . . . . . . . . . . . . . . .

The owners of a corporation are its shareholders. Each shareholder owns a part of the corporation equal to the number of shares owned divided by the total number of shares issued and outstanding. As an example, if a corporation has 100 shares issued and outstanding and a shareholder owns ten of those shares, he or she would own a one-tenth interest in the corporation.

Despite being the corporation's owners, shareholders do not have the right to directly participate in the management of the company. Like limited partners in a limited partnership, corporate shareholders can only indirectly participate in the corporation's management through exercising their right to vote at shareholders' meetings. Shareholders vote for the board of directors at annual shareholders' meetings. The responsibility for managing the corporation falls to the directors, who in turn hire corporate officers to implement their policies and manage the day-to-day operation of the corporate enterprise.

## CORPORATE DIRECTORS

Directors have a fiduciary responsibility to the corporations they serve. As such, they must exercise their responsibilities in good faith using reasonable care and must make a good-faith effort to further the best interests of the corporation. Directors are personally liable to the corporation if they breach these duties.

As previously noted, shareholders vote for directors at annual shareholders' meetings. Shareholders can also remove directors by calling a meeting for that purpose at any time and then voting them out of office. The articles of incorporation can require that removal be only for cause; if the articles of incorporation are silent as to removal of directors, then they can be removed with or without cause (e.g., with or without a valid reason).

In corporations having nine or more directors, the articles of incorporation can specify that the board can be elected in two or three staggered groups that are as nearly equal as possible. If such a scheme is selected, the board members in the first group would serve for one year, the ones in the second for two years, and the ones in the third for three years.

For all corporations, the term of the first board of directors named in the articles of incorporation or by the incorporators expires at the first shareholders' meeting.

## CORPORATE OFFICERS

Corporate officers are appointed by the board of directors and serve at the pleasure of the board. The specific duties of corporate officers can be set out in the corporate bylaws or prescribed by the board of directors. The board of directors, acting in a manner consistent with the corporate bylaws, can also appoint an officer to prescribe the duties of other officers.

Like directors, officers serve in a fiduciary capacity and must also exercise their responsibilities in good faith using reasonable care and must make a good-faith effort to further the best interests of the corporation.

The precise number and titles of corporate officers can be spelled out in the corporate bylaws, but every corporation must have an officer whose duty it is to keep records of directors' and shareholders' meetings and to authenticate records of the corporation (e.g., a secretary). Under the Revised Model Business Corporation Act, a single person can act in various capacities as an officer, so that it is possible to have one officer who acts as president and secretary of the corporation. Some states, though, require there to be at least two corporate officers in every corporation.

# CLASSIFICATION OF CORPORATIONS  . . . . . . . . . . . . . . . . . . . . . .

Corporations are commonly classified in accordance with their purpose, the nature of their activities and their ownership.

## PUBLIC AND PRIVATE CORPORATIONS

The corporate form serves both private and public interests equally well. Public corporations are organized by federal, state or local governments in order to carry out necessary public services. Municipalities, such as cities and towns, are often organized as public corporations, as are companies entrusted with the administration of public services. Private corporations, on the other hand, are organized by private individuals to carry out private business.

## FOR-PROFIT AND NONPROFIT CORPORATIONS

Corporations can be created for profit and nonprofit purposes. Public corporations are by nature nonprofit, since their purpose is not to make money but rather to advance the public good in some way. Private corporations, on the other hand, can be either for-profit or nonprofit, depending on their purpose. A nonprofit corporation is one that is organized for the purpose of achieving some artistic, humanitarian or philanthropic purpose or the rendering of some public service, as opposed to a traditional business organized to make a profit. Like Chapter S corporations (which will be discussed later in this chapter), nonprofit corporations are tax exempt.

## DOMESTIC, FOREIGN AND ALIEN CORPORATIONS

Corporations are classified as *domestic, foreign* or *alien* depending on where they were organized and where they do business. Like limited partnerships, corporations are deemed to be domestic when they do business in the state where they were incorporated and are considered foreign in all other states. Corporations organized under the laws of another country are considered alien corporations when they do business anywhere in the United States.

As is true of limited partnerships, corporations wishing to transact business in states other than that of their incorporation must register with the secretary of state of each such state. The address of a registered office in the state and the name and address of a registered agent of the corporation for the state must be provided to the secretary of state as part of the registration process and accompanied by the appropriate fee required by each state.

## CLOSELY HELD AND PUBLICLY TRADED CORPORATIONS

A *closely held corporation* is one whose shares are not traded to the general public in any stock exchange. Such corporations are usually (but not always) small companies owned by a few investors. A *publicly traded corporation*, on the other hand, is one whose shares are traded in any stock exchange.

## PROFESSIONAL CORPORATIONS

Professional corporations are for-profit corporations organized to provide a professional service. Physicians, lawyers, architects, accountants and engineers are but a few of the professions whose members commonly form professional corporations. A professional corporation must have the words *Professional Corporation* or the letters *P.C.* following the corporate name *instead of* the normal words or abbreviations appended to corporate names (e.g., *Corp., Inc., Co.* or *Ltd.*).

## THE CORPORATION AS AN ENTITY   · · · · · · · · · · · · · · · · · · · · · · ·

Unlike other business organizations, the corporation is viewed as a separate entity from its owners. The law grants a corporation status as an *artificial being*, much like a person, for most purposes. This means that the corporation has certain rights and responsibilities that other business organizations do not.

As an artificial being, a corporation has rights not enjoyed by other business organizations. It can own property in its own name, borrow or lend money, sue and be sued and is entitled to the protection of most laws the same as natural persons. On the other hand, like a natural person, a corporation must pay taxes (although at a lesser rate than individuals) and can be found guilty of crimes if the punishment is a fine (obviously, you can't put a corporation in prison). In addition, a corporation can be set up to enjoy perpetual existence, unlike sole proprietorships and partnerships, which are dissolved upon their owners' death.

Because a corporation is deemed to be an entity separate from its owners, the owners of a corporation (its stockholders) are *not* personally liable for corporate debts beyond their investment in the company. All that a shareholder risks in purchasing a share of stock is the money paid for its purchase. The limited liability offered by a corporation to its owners is its greatest appeal. On the other hand, stockholders pay a premium for this protection. As already noted, corporations pay taxes in their own right, including federal income taxes (as well as state income taxes, where applicable). This means that the profits of the corporation are subject to double taxation: The corporation pays income taxes on corporate profits, and then the shareholders pay personal income taxes on corporate profits distributed to them as dividends.

### PIERCING THE CORPORATE VEIL

If shareholders are to enjoy the limited liability offered by the corporate form of business organization, it is crucial that the separate-entity status of the corporation be maintained. Failure to meet the formalities required of a corporation can result in a court ignoring the corporate entity and holding its owners subject to unlimited personal liability for all corporate debt. A court will "pierce the corporate veil" in instances where a corporation is created to defraud creditors, where corporate funds or property are not kept separate from that of the corporation's shareholders or where required formalities (such as the keeping of minutes of directors' and shareholders' meetings) are not met.

### CHAPTER S CORPORATIONS

The greatest disadvantage of organizing a business as a corporation is the double taxation to which corporate profits are subject. The Internal Revenue Code, however, grants a tax exemption to certain qualifying corporations. In order to qualify as a Subchapter S *small-business corporation* and enjoy the benefit of tax exemption, a corporation must meet the following requirements:

- there can be no more than fifteen shareholders;
- every shareholder must be a natural person or an estate or trust whose income is taxed to the grantor;
- no stockholder can be a nonresident alien;
- the corporation must have only one class of stock;
- shareholders must unanimously consent to have the corporation treated as a small-business corporation under Subchapter S;
- the corporation must not derive more than 20 percent of its income from passive investment activities such as rents, royalties or income derived from the sale of stocks;
- undistributed corporate income must be treated as taxable income to the shareholders (such income is not treated as taxable income in a regular corporation until it is actually distributed to shareholders such as by cash dividends); and
- shareholders are allowed to deduct net operating losses from their gross income. (Shareholders in a standard corporation may not take such deductions.) (Internal Revenue Code, §§ 1371–1374)

The purpose of Subchapter S is to allow small, closely held businesses that would otherwise be organized as partnerships or limited partnerships to take advantage of the corporate form of business organization without being subjected to double taxation.


## QUESTIONS  . . . . . . . . . . . . . . . . . . . . . . . . . . . . . . . . . . . . . .

1. What information must be contained in a corporation's articles of incorporation?
2. What are the requirements to which the selection of a corporate name must conform?
3. Under the Revised Model Business Corporation Act, when does a corporation's existence begin?
4. Define the terms *de jure corporation* and *de facto corporation.*
5. Is a corporation responsible for the preincorporation contracts of its promoters once it comes into existence? Explain.
6. Are promoters agents of the corporation? Explain.
7. What is the primary purpose of holding a corporation's first organizational meeting?
8. Who owns a corporation and who manages it?
9. What is the difference between domestic, foreign and alien corporations?
10. What are the basic benefits that a corporation enjoys over other forms of business organizations because of its status as a legal entity in the eyes of the law?

**11.** What are the basic liabilities that a corporation faces above those of other business organizations due to its status as an entity?

**12.** What does the term *piercing the corporate veil* mean?

**13.** What requirements must a business meet before it can file as a Subchapter S corporation?

**14.** What is the main benefit of Subchapter S status?

# H Y P O T H E T I C A L    C A S E S

1. Leon, Lonnie and Lenore wish to start a band. They call their group MCP (Musically Challenged Persons) and begin booking gigs at local parties. Worried about the potential liability to which they may be subjected as a partnership, the three friends agree to incorporate their business. They sign an agreement that states, "We the undersigned hereby establish the MCP Corporation, an entertainment company devoted to filling the needs of musically challenged audiences everywhere." Each person then signs the agreement.
   a. Is a corporation formed by the agreement? Explain.
   b. Under these facts, what type of business organization is involved?
   c. Assume for the moment that a *de jure* corporation is not formed under the facts given. Is a *de facto* corporation formed? Explain.
   d. What procedure should the three artistic entrepreneurs follow in order to incorporate their business?
   e. If the requirements for incorporation are met, when will the corporation actually be formed if the state in question follows the Revised Model Business Corporation Act?
   f. If the three friends want to expressly provide in the articles of incorporation a prohibition against playing country or rap music, may they do so? Explain.

2. Able and Arlene are directors of XYZ Corporation, a company involved in the petrochemical business. Both are also major stockholders of the company and serve on other corporations' boards of directors. Arlene is also XYZ's president and chief executive officer.
   a. Are Able and Arlene legally able to serve as board members of a corporation in which they are also shareholders?
   b. If Exxon, Mobil and Amoco would like Arlene to serve on their boards of directors also, may she do so? Explain.
   c. If Able would like to accept an offer to join the board of a large charitable organization and a food-service company, may he do so?

3. Cathy, an electrical contractor, sets up a corporation in which she is the sole stockholder and president. Her husband, Carlos, is the secretary and both she and her husband serve on the corporation's board of directors as its only two members. Cathy, who was a sole proprietor before incorporating her company, continues to run her business exactly as before. She pays company debts out of her personal bank account and deposits all checks payable to the company in her personal bank

account. In addition, she does not consult Carlos on any business decisions or hold regular meetings of the board of directors. She does, however, hold yearly stockholder's meetings and votes to re-elect herself and Carlos as directors; Carlos dutifully records the minutes of these meetings.

a. Does the fact that there is only one shareholder invalidate this corporation?

b. If the corporation goes bankrupt, will Cathy be sheltered against personal liability from the debts of the corporation? Explain fully.

c. Assume that Cathy and Carlos run the corporation as a *bona fide* organization, keeping proper records of all necessary meetings and carefully avoiding the commingling of corporate and private funds. How would you classify this corporation in the state that it is organized and in which Cathy does business?

4. José, John and Josephine are partners in a very successful restaurant business in New Jersey. José is a citizen of Mexico who is a legal resident alien in the United States. John is a Canadian National who lives in Toronto, Canada, but travels frequently to the United States on business. Josephine is an American citizen who lives in Elizabeth, New Jersey. The partners have recently decided that they would like to expand their business to numerous other sites in the state and would like to incorporate to lessen their personal liability risks.

a. May the partners opt to file as a Subchapter S corporation? Explain fully.

b. What is the downside of creating a standard corporation for the partners?

UNIT

# VII

# BANKRUPTCY

## INTRODUCTION TO BANKRUPTCY · · · · · · · · · · · · · · · · · · · · · · ·

Bankruptcy law provides legal relief to both debtors and creditors when debtors are either unable or unwilling to pay their legal debts. The United States Constitution, under Article I, Section 8, Clause 4, grants to Congress the right to "establish . . . uniform Laws on the subject of Bankruptcies throughout the United States." Congress passed a number of laws relating to bankruptcy from 1800 to 1874. These were first consolidated into a comprehensive Bankruptcy Act (also known as the Nelson Act) on July 1, 1898. The Bankruptcy Act was next materially amended in 1938 by the Chandler Act. The most significant revision of bankruptcy laws was made in 1978, when the existing bankruptcy laws were significantly revised and enacted as Title 11 of the United States Code—our current Bankruptcy Act. Some significant changes were again made to Title 11 in 1984, and the act has undergone minor periodic revisions since then on a fairly regular basis. (The Bankruptcy Act of 1978 and its subsequent amendments are referred to as the Bankruptcy Code.)

Out current Bankruptcy Code is divided into eight chapters, seven of which are odd-numbered (Chapters 1, 3, 5, 7, 9, 11 and 13) one of which is even-numbered (Chapter 12). The content of each chapter is as follows:

Chapter 1: General Provisions (starting with § 101)

Chapter 3: Case Administration (starting with § 301)

Chapter 5: Creditors, the Debtor, and the Estate (starting with § 501)

Chapter 7: Liquidation (starting with § 701)

Chapter 9: Adjustment of Debts of a Municipality (starting with § 901)

Chapter 11: Reorganization (starting with § 1101)

Chapter 12: Adjustment of Debts of Family Farmers with Regular Annual Income (starting with § 1201)

Chapter 13: Adjustment of Debts of an Individual with Regular Income (starting with § 1301)

Chapters 1, 3 and 5 concern themselves with basic definitions and procedural matters that apply to all bankruptcy proceedings. Chapter 7 deals with simple bankruptcy or liquidation of the debts of an insolvent individual or business; it applies to all debtors except banks, railroads, insurance companies and savings and loans. Chapter 9 applies to insolvent municipalities. Chapter 11 concerns itself with the reorganization of business debts in order to allow an insolvent enterprise to continue in business. Chapter 12 deals with the insolvency of family farmers (farmers who obtain at least 50 percent of their income from farming and who have not more than $1,500,000 in debts, 80 percent of which are related to their farm business). Chapter 13 concerns itself with the adjustment of debt (similar to Chapter eleven reorganization for businesses) for individuals who have a steady income and owe less than $100,000 in unsecured debt and less than $350,000 in secured debt.

In this unit, we will concentrate on the three major types of bankruptcy proceedings under Title 11 of the United States Code: Chapter 7 liquidation, Chapter 11 reorganization and Chapter 13 adjustment of debts.

# CHAPTER

# 39

# LIQUIDATION, REORGANIZATION AND ADJUSTMENT OF DEBTS

The heart of the Bankruptcy Code is contained in Chapters 7, 11 and 13. Chapter 7 deals with straight bankruptcy or *liquidation*, which involves the discharge of a debtor's debts upon the collection and sale at auction of all the debtor's nonexempt property for the benefit of creditors. Chapter 11 concerns itself not with the liquidation or forgiveness of debt, but rather its *reorganization* or restructuring in order to allow the debtor to continue in business, and Chapter 13 involves the *adjustment* of debt of an individual. Under Chapters 11 and 13, the debtor's debts are satisfied not from the sale of his or her nonexempt assets, but rather from future earnings to be realized by an individual or business.

## CHAPTER 7: LIQUIDATION . . . . . . . . . . . . . . . . . . . . . . . . . . . .

A Chapter 7 liquidation proceeding allows individuals and businesses who are unable to meet their financial obligations to have their debts discharged by turning over substantially all of their property to a trustee in order that it may be sold for the benefit of the debtor's creditors. In essence, Chapter 7 allows a debtor to make a fresh start by removing the burden of debts that are beyond the debtor's ability to repay. A measure of protection is also awarded to the debtor's creditors who may force liquidation proceedings under certain circumstances when a debtor is unable or unwilling to repay his or her debts.

### WHO MAY BRING CHAPTER 7 PROCEEDINGS

Chapter 7 applies to all debtors other than railroads, insurance companies, banks, savings and loan associations, homestead associations and credit unions, which are specifically excluded. (11 USC § 109 [b]). Individuals, corporations and partnerships can avail themselves of bankruptcy protection.

Liquidation proceedings under Chapter 7 may be brought by the debtor (*voluntary liquidation*) or by the debtor's creditors (*involuntary liquidation*). In order for creditors to force liquidation on a debtor, the debtor must have a minimum combined unsecured debt of $5,000. If the total number of creditors is twelve or more, three creditors must join in the petition for involuntary liquidation. If there are fewer than twelve creditors with an aggregate debt of at least $5,000 in unsecured debt, then a single creditor may file a petition for involuntary liquidation.

## APPOINTMENT OF INTERIM TRUSTEE

After a voluntary or involuntary petition for relief is filed, the court issues an order for relief and may appoint an interim trustee if there is a showing that a trustee is necessary to preserve the property of the estate for the benefit of the debtors. If an interim trustee is appointed, all property of the debtor not specifically exempted from attachment must be turned over to the trustee, who is entrusted with managing the property until a final determination is made by the court in the bankruptcy proceedings. Debtors who wish to retain possession of property ordered turned over to a trustee may do so if they can post a sufficient bond to cover the creditors' interest in the property. If an interim trustee is requested by the debtor and deemed warranted by the court, the debtor then has an opportunity to select a trustee of his or her own choosing.

## BANKRUPTCY DECREE

Finally, a trial is held, the purpose of which is to determine whether the debtor has been unable or unwilling to meet his or her financial obligations as they become due. If it is found that he or she has not (such as by generally failing to pay bills when due), the court enters a bankruptcy decree and orders the debtor's property to be sold at auction to satisfy the debts. In the event that the debtor is insolvent (that liabilities exceed assets), the creditors are paid a *prorata* share of the proceeds from the liquidation of the debtor's estate and the debtor's debts are then discharged in the following priority order:

- secured creditors to the extent of their security interest;
- administrative expenses of the estate (such as trustees' and attorneys' fees);
- *gap creditors* (a gap creditor is one who became a creditor in the normal course of business after the filing of the bankruptcy petition but before the appointment of a trustee);
- wages, salaries or commissions earned by employee creditors within ninety days prior to the filing for bankruptcy or ninety days of the cessation of business (each employee may claim up to a maximum of $2,000 in such claims);
- claims for contributions to employee benefit plans (health, life and pension benefits) within 180 days of the filing for bankruptcy or the cessation of business,

whichever occurred first (up to a maximum of $2,000 *in combination with* wages, salaries or commissions);

- Farmers for grain in a debtor's silo and fishermen for up to $2,000 in fish in the hands of a debtor fish storage or fish processing facility;
- consumer creditors who have deposited money in connection with the purchase, rental or lease of property, or who have paid for undelivered goods up to a maximum of $900;
- unpaid taxes; and
- the debtor's estate (e.g., the excess of property remaining after all previous debts are satisfied is returned to the debtor).

In the event that there are insufficient funds to pay all of the members of a class their full debt, the debt is prorated for the members of the class. For example, if an estate has only $1,000 left when it comes time to pay the holders of the second lowest priority claim (tax liens) and the debtor owes $1,000 to the state in unpaid income taxes and $500 to the local; government in unpaid real-property taxes (assume for the moment that both have an equal priority), the state would get two-thirds of the remaining sum and the local government would get one-third ($666.67 to the state and $333.33 to the local government). In the event that the money runs out prior to claims in all priority classes being discharged (as is usually the case), all debts are nevertheless generally discharged and the debtor need not repay any balance on the debts owed the creditors even if the debtor is financially able to do so at a later date. On the downside, a judgment of bankruptcy goes on the debtor's credit report for seven years and will make it very difficult for the debtor to reestablish a good credit rating.

## DEBTORS' PROPERTY EXEMPT FROM ATTACHMENT

The basic principle behind Chapter 7 is that debtors turn in to the court whatever real and personal property they own to be sold for the benefit of their creditors, and in return have their debts forgiven to the extent that their assets are insufficient to cover them. Forcing debtors to turn in all of their worldly possessions in order to be granted the protection of Chapter 7 might cause a severe hardship for debtors who would be left penniless and possibly without a means of earning a living. The Bankruptcy Act, therefore, allows debtors to keep some of their property after a voluntary or an involuntary Chapter 7 proceeding by statutorily exempting certain types of property from attachment. (For a complete list of property that is statutorily exempt from attachment, see Figure 39.1.)

## CHAPTER 11: REORGANIZATION . . . . . . . . . . . . . . . . . . . . . . . . .

Under Chapter 11, businesses that have gotten into financial difficulties are given the opportunity to restructure their debts and formulate a plan for their repayment. Unlike Chapter 7 liquidation, which allows for the forgiveness of debt beyond an individual's or business's ability to repay it, Chapter 11 permits the repayment of debt to be made under different terms than those under which the debt was originally

(1) The debtor's equity in his primary residence and/or a burial plot up to $7,500;

(2) The debtor's interest, not to exceed $1,200 in value, in one motor vehicle;

(3) The debtor's interest, not to exceed $200 in value in any particular item or $4,000 in aggregate value, in household furnishings, household goods, wearing apparel, appliances, books, animals, crops, or musical instruments, that are held primarily for the personal, family, or household use of the debtor or a dependent of the debtor;

(4) The debtor's aggregate interest, not to exceed $500 in value, in jewelry held primarily for the personal, family, or household use of the debtor or a dependent of the debtor;

(5) The debtor's aggregate interest in any property, not to exceed in value $400 plus up to $3,750 of any unused amount of the exemption provided under paragraph (1) of this subsection;

(6) The debtor's aggregate interest, not to exceed $750 in value, in any implements, professional books, or tools, of the trade of the debtor or the trade of a dependent of the debtor;

(7) Any unmatured life insurance contract owned by the debtor, other than a credit life insurance contract;

(8) The debtor's aggregate interest, not to exceed in value $4,000 less any amount of property of the estate transferred in the manner specified in section 542(d) of this title, in any accrued dividend or interest under, or loan value of, any unmatured life insurance contract owned by the debtor under which the insured is the debtor or an individual of whom the debtor is a dependent;

(9) Professionally prescribed health aids for the debtor or a dependent of the debtor;

(10) The debtor's right to receive—

(A) a social security benefit, unemployment compensation, or a local public assistance benefit;

(B) a veterans' benefit;

(C) a disability, illness, or unemployment benefit;

(D) alimony, support, or separate maintenance, to the extent reasonably necessary for the support of the debtor and any dependent of the debtor;

(E) a payment under a stock bonus, pension, profit sharing, annuity, or similar plan or contract on account of illness, disability, death, age, or length of service, to the extent reasonably necessary for the support of the debtor and any dependent of the debtor, unless—

(i) such plan or contract was established by or under the auspices of an insider that employed the debtor at the time the debtor's rights under such plan or contract arose;

(ii) such payment is on account of age or length of service; and

(iii) such plan or contract does not qualify under section 401(a), 403(a), 403(b), 408, or 409 of the Internal Revenue Code of 1986 (26 USC. 401(a), 403(a), 403(b), 408, or 409).

(11) The debtor's right to receive, or property that is traceable to—

(A) an award under a crime victim's reparation law;

**FIGURE 39.1**   Property exempt from attachment in Chapter 7 liquidation [11 USC § 522 (d) (1–11)]

(B) a payment on account of the wrongful death of an individual of whom the debtor was a dependent, to the extent reasonably necessary for the support of the debtor and any dependent of the debtor;

(C) a payment under a life insurance contract that insured the life of an individual of whom the debtor was a dependent on the date of such individual's death, to the extent reasonably necessary for the support of the debtor and any dependent of the debtor;

(D) a payment, not to exceed $7,500, on account of personal bodily injury, not including pain and suffering or compensation for actual pecuniary loss, of the debtor or an individual of whom the debtor is a dependent; or

(E) a payment in compensation of loss of future earnings of the debtor or an individual of whom the debtor is or was a dependent, to the extent reasonably necessary for the support of the debtor and any dependent of the debtor.

**FIGURE 39.1**   Continued

incurred. The reorganization of debt often involves changing the way debt is repaid, such as by extending the debt's term, in an attempt to provide a business with financial difficulties some needed breathing room in an effort to keep it afloat and prevent Chapter 7 liquidation.

## WHO MAY BRING CHAPTER 11 PROCEEDINGS

Any person or entity who qualifies for Chapter 7 protection may also file under Chapter 11, except for stockbrokers and commodity brokers who are specifically excluded. In addition, railroads may also file for Chapter 11 protection, even though they are excluded from filing for Chapter 7 protection.

## APPOINTMENT OF COMMITTEE OF CREDITORS

After the court enters an order of relief, a committee of creditors holding unsecured claims against the debtor is appointed. The court is also empowered to appoint other committees of creditors if it deems it appropriate (such as when there are many creditors with different classes of claims). This committee "shall ordinarily consist of the persons, willing to serve, that hold the seven largest claims against the debtor of the kinds represented on such committee. . . . " (11 USC § 1102 [b][1]). This committee (or committees, where two or more are appointed) serves as the primary negotiating body in formulating the reorganization plan. The committee is specifically empowered:

(1) to consult with the trustee or debtor in possession concerning the administration of the case;

(2) to investigate the acts, conduct, assets, liabilities, and financial condition of the debtor, the operation of the debtor's business and the desirability of the continuance of such business, and any other matter relevant to the case or to the formulation of a plan;

(3) to participate in the formulation of a plan, advise those represented by such committee of such committee's determinations as to any plan formulated, and collect and file with the court acceptances or rejections of a plan;

(4) to request the appointment of a trustee or examiner under Section 1104 of this title; and

(5) to perform such other services as are in the interest of those represented. (11 USC § 1103 [c])

As you can see, the committee of creditors has broad powers to investigate the debtor and to study the feasibility of a reorganization plan. If such a plan is deemed feasible by the debtors, the committee is then primarily responsible for creating and submitting a specific plan of reorganization for the debtor.

## APPOINTMENT OF TRUSTEE OR EXAMINER

After the case is started but before the court approves a final reorganization plan, a trustee or examiner is appointed. The court can appoint a trustee for cause if it believes that there has been fraud, dishonesty, incompetence or gross mismanagement of the affairs of the debtor by current management, either before or after the commencement of the case, or simply if the court believes such an appointment to be in the best interests of the creditors. If a trustee is not appointed and the debtor is allowed to continue managing the business, then any interested party may request the appointment of an examiner (1) to investigate any allegations of fraud, dishonesty, incompetence, misconduct, mismanagement, or irregularity in the management of the affairs of the debtor of or by current or former management of the debtor; (2) if the court believes the appointment of an examiner will be in the interest of any interested party; or (3) if the debtor's unsecured debts exceed $5,000,000.

## DUTIES OF TRUSTEE

If a trustee is appointed, he or she is given the following duties: (1) accountability for all property received; (2) keeping all interested parties informed as to their findings; (3) investigating the acts, conduct, assets, liabilities and financial condition of the debtor, the operation of the debtor's business, and the desirability of the continuance of the business and any other matter relevant to the case or to the formulation of a plan; (4) reporting the results of his or her investigation to the court and to creditors' committees, equity security holders' committees, indenture trustees and any other entity the court designates; and (5) filing a plan or reporting why a plan cannot be formulated, or recommending conversion to liquidation, an individual repayment plan, or dismissal. (If the trustee formulates a plan or reorganization, he or she will do so in consultation with the debtors.) (11 USC § 1106 [a][1–7])

## DUTIES OF EXAMINER

If an examiner is appointed instead of a trustee, the examiner has the following duties: (1) investigating the acts, conduct, assets, liabilities and financial condition of the debtor, the operation of the debtor's business, the desirability of the continuance of the business, and any other matter relevant to the case or to the formulation of a plan; and (2) reporting the results of his or her investigation to the court and to creditors' committees, equity security holders' committees, indenture trustees and any other entity the court designates. (11 USC § 1106 [b])

## FILING OF REORGANIZATION PLAN

As is true of liquidation, reorganization may be voluntary or involuntary. A Chapter 11 case may be begun voluntarily by a debtor filing a plan of reorganization at any time (even after an involuntary case is begun). The debtor is given an exclusive right to file a plan within the first 120 days from the court's order of relief granted upon the proper filing of a case under this chapter. Other interested parties may also propose a plan if a trustee has been appointed, if the debtor does not meet the 120-day deadline, or if the debtor meets the 120-day deadline but fails to obtain approval of the plan by the creditors within 180 days of the filing of the petition.

## ACCEPTANCE OF REORGANIZATION PLAN

Before it becomes effective, a reorganization plan must be accepted by the members of each class of debtors that the plan will affect. For a class of creditors to accept the plan, not less than half of the members of a class who together hold a minimum of two-thirds of the total debt for the entire class must vote to accept the plan.

## CONFIRMATION OF REORGANIZATION PLAN

After acceptance of a reorganization plan, it must be confirmed by the court. A plan will be confirmed by the court only if it is found to meet the following criteria: (1) it meets all the legal requirements of Chapter 11; (2) it has been offered in good faith; (3) the debtors in each class either have accepted the plan or will be guaranteed a minimum claim under the reorganization, the same as they would have received under Chapter 7 liquidation; and (4) confirmation of the plan is not likely to be followed by liquidation or further financial reorganization in the future.

## EFFECT OF REORGANIZATION PLAN'S CONFIRMATION

Once a plan is confirmed, the debtor and all creditors are bound by the terms of the plan. Debts of the debtor that arose before the filing for Chapter 11 reorganization are excused, except as specifically provided for in the reorganization plan or under the provisions of the Bankruptcy Act (e.g., some tax liability is nondischargeable for corporate debtors under Chapter 11). Unlike in Chapter 7 proceedings, the debtor in Chapter 11 proceedings retains ownership of his or her property and may continue in business under the specific guidelines of the reorganization plan.

# CHAPTER 13: ADJUSTMENT OF DEBTS . . . . . . . . . . . . . . . . . . . .

Chapter 13 allows an individual with regular income to file a plan with the court for the adjustment of debt. If the plan is approved, the individual's debts will be forgiven if he or she honors the repayment plan approved by the court.

## WHO MAY BRING CHAPTER 13 PROCEEDINGS

Chapter 13 proceedings may be brought by any individuals (other than stockbrokers or commodity brokers) who have a stable income from wages or other reliable sources that would allow them to meet their obligations under a repayment plan. For purposes of this chapter, persons on fixed incomes, including pensions, social security, disability or public assistance, all qualify as persons having a regular income. Such income can be derived from self-employment in a business (provided such income is steady and reliable), but the business entity itself cannot be the subject of the reorganization. (As we've just seen, business reorganization would, of course, be covered by Chapter 11 of the Bankruptcy Code.)

In addition to the requirement of a regular income, the total unsecured debt for an individual (or an individual and a spouse filing jointly) must be less than $100,000, and the total secured debt must be less than $350,000.

## INSTITUTING CHAPTER 13 PROCEEDINGS

Unlike Chapter 7 and Chapter 11 proceedings, which may be instituted voluntarily at the request of the debtor or involuntarily at the request of the creditors, Chapter 13 proceedings may be brought only voluntarily by the debtor. The rationale for not permitting involuntary Chapter 13 cases is perhaps best expressed in the Senate's own report on Section 303 of the Bankruptcy Act governing the commencement of involuntary cases:

> Involuntary chapter 13 cases are not permitted. . . . To do so would constitute bad policy, because chapter 13 only works when there is a willing debtor that wants to repay his creditors. Short of involuntary servitude, it is difficult to keep a debtor working for his creditors when he does not want to pay them back. (Senate Report No. 95-989)

Lest it seem unfair to deny creditors the ability to bring an involuntary case under Chapter 13, keep in mind that they *can* bring either an involuntary Chapter 7 or Chapter 11 action. The purpose of Chapter 13 is to make it simpler for debtors who meet the eligibility criteria for Chapter 13 to come up with a voluntary plan to reorganize their debts without having to jump through all the hoops required by the standard Chapter 11 reorganization.

## FILING AND CONTENTS OF THE PLAN

Since Chapter 13 allows only voluntary petitions for relief to be filed, it stands to reason that only the debtor may file a plan for the adjustment of his debts. The debtor's plan must contain the following provisions:

1. the debtor must provide for the submission of all future income (or as much of it as necessary to effectuate the plan) to the plan trustee;
2. it must provide for the deferred payment of all claims entitled to a priority under section 507 of the Bankruptcy Code (See Figure 39.2);
3. requires identical treatment for all claims of a particular class;

11 USC Chapter 5 – § 507: Priorities

(a) The following expenses and claims have priority in the following order:

(1) First, administrative expenses allowed under section 503(b) of this title, and any fees and charges assessed against the estate under chapter 123 of title 28.

(2) Second, unsecured claims allowed under section 502(f) of this title.

(3) Third, allowed unsecured claims for wages, salaries, or commissions, including vacation, severance, and sick leave pay—

(A) earned by an individual within 90 days before the date of the filing of the petition or the date of the cessation of the debtor's business, whichever occurs first; but only

(B) to the extent of $2,000 for each such individual.

(4) Fourth, allowed unsecured claims for contributions to an employee benefit plan—

(A) arising from services rendered within 180 days before the date of the filing of the petition or the date of the cessation of the debtor's business, whichever occurs first; but only

(B) for each such plan, to the extent of—

(i) the number of employees covered by each such plan multiplied by $2,000; less

(ii) the aggregate amount paid to such employees under paragraph (3) of this subsection, plus the aggregate amount paid by the estate on behalf of such employees to any other employee benefit plan.

(5) Fifth, allowed unsecured claims of persons—

(A) engaged in the production or raising of grain, as defined in section 557(b)(1) of this title, against a debtor who owns or operates a grain storage facility, as defined in section 557(b)(2) of this title, for grain or the proceeds of grain, or

(B) engaged as a United States fisherman against a debtor who has acquired fish or fish produce from a fisherman through a sale or conversion, and who is engaged in operating a fish produce storage or processing facility— but only to the extent of $2,000 for each such individual.

(6) Sixth, allowed unsecured claims of individuals, to the extent of $900 for each such individual, arising from the deposit, before the commencement of the case, of money in connection with the purchase, lease, or rental of property, or the purchase of services, for the personal, family, or household use of such individuals, that were not delivered or provided.

(7) Seventh, allowed unsecured claims of governmental units, only to the extent that such claims are for—

(A) a tax on or measured by income or gross receipts—

(i) for a taxable year ending on or before the date of the filing of the petition for which a return, if required, is last due, including extensions, after three years before the date of the filing of the petition;

(ii) assessed within 240 days, plus any time plus 30 days during which an offer in compromise with respect to such tax that was made within

**FIGURE 39.2**     Priority order for creditors' claims under Chapters 7, 11 and 13 [11 USC § 507]

240 days after such assessment was pending, before the date of the filing of the petition; or

(iii) other than a tax of a kind specified in section 523(a)(1)(B) or 523(a)(1)(C) of this title, not assessed before, but assessable, under applicable law or by agreement, after, the commencement of the case;

(B) a property tax assessed before the commencement of the case and last payable without penalty after one year before the date of the filing of the petition;

(C) a tax required to be collected or withheld and for which the debtor is liable in whatever capacity;

(D) an employment tax on a wage, salary, or commission of a kind specified in paragraph (3) of this subsection earned from the debtor before the date of the filing of the petition, whether or not actually paid before such date, for which a return is last due, under applicable law or under any extension, after three years before the date of the filing of the petition;

(E) an excise tax on—

(i) a transaction occurring before the date of the filing of the petition for which a return, if required, is last due, under applicable law or under any extension, after three years before the date of the filing of the petition; or

(ii) if a return is not required, a transaction occurring during the three years immediately preceding the date of the filing of the petition;

(F) a customs duty arising out of the importation of merchandise—

(i) entered for consumption within one year before the date of the filing of the petition;

(ii) covered by an entry liquidated or reliquidated within one year before the date of the filing of the petition; or

(iii) entered for consumption within four years before the date of the filing of the petition but unliquidated on such date, if the Secretary of the Treasury certifies that failure to liquidate such entry was due to an investigation pending on such date into assessment of antidumping or countervailing duties or fraud, or if information needed for the proper appraisement or classification of such merchandise was not available to the appropriate customs officer before such date; or

(G) a penalty related to a claim of a kind specified in this paragraph and in compensation for actual pecuniary loss.

**FIGURE 39.2**    Continued

4. the plan may not provide a payment period longer than three years (although the court may extend the period to four years).

**CONFIRMATION OF THE PLAN**

A court will confirm the debtor's plan for the repayment of his or her debts if it meets the following criteria:

- it meets the legal requirements of the Bankruptcy Act in general and Chapter 13 in particular;

- it is proposed in good faith by the debtor;
- it provides payments to unsecured creditors which are not less than they would be entitled to under Chapter 7 liquidation proceedings;
- it provides for the full payment of secured debts;
- the plan is feasible; and
- all required fees and charges under Chapter 13 have been paid.

## PAYMENTS BY DEBTOR

Unless a court orders otherwise, a debtor is required to commence making payments to the court-appointed trustee within thirty days of filing the proposed plan. If the plan is confirmed, the trustee will continue to receive payments as provided for under the plan and distribute these to the creditors in accordance with the provisions of the plan. If the plan is not approved by the court, the trustee must return all monies received from the debtor to him or her (minus the trustee's allowable fee).

## EFFECT OF CONFIRMATION

After confirmation, the debtor must make payments to the trustee as provided for in the plan. The property in the debtor's estate, however, will vest in him or her, free of creditors' claims, as long as the accepted repayment plan is adhered to by the debtor.

## DISCHARGE

After the debtor makes the final payment under the terms of the plan, the court will issue an order discharging the debtor from all debt covered by the plan. A court may also grant a discharge even before the debtor completes the agreed-upon payments under the plan if the court finds that the debtor's failure to keep making payments is brought about by circumstances for which the debtor should not be held accountable, as long as all creditors have been paid an amount equal to what they would have received under a Chapter 7 liquidation or a Chapter 11 reorganization of the debtor's estate.

# LIMITATION ON REFILING FOR PROTECTION UNDER THE BANKRUPTCY ACT

Debtors may not avail themselves of the protection of the Bankruptcy Act more frequently than once every six years. A voluntary or involuntary petition for liquidation or reorganization filed within six years of a discharge in bankruptcy under Chapter 7 or the acceptance of a reorganization plan under Chapters 11 or 13 will be dismissed by the court.

# QUESTIONS

1. Which chapters of the Bankruptcy Act concern themselves with basic definitions and procedural matters?

2. What is the subject matter of Chapters 7, 11 and 13 of the Bankruptcy Act?

3. What is the difference between voluntary and involuntary proceedings under the Bankruptcy Act?

4. What are the requirements for bringing involuntary liquidation proceedings against a debtor under Chapter 7?

5. What chapter of the Bankruptcy Act does not allow for involuntary proceedings to be instituted against creditors?

6. What property of the debtor is exempt from attachment under liquidation proceedings?

7. What is the basic difference between Chapter 7 and Chapter 11?

8. What types of debtors may bring a Chapter 7 liquidation proceeding?

9. What types of debtors may bring a Chapter 11 reorganization proceeding?

10. What are the duties of a trustee under Chapter 11 reorganization proceedings?

11. What is the procedure for acceptance of a Chapter 11 reorganization plan?

12. What are the criteria for confirmation of a Chapter 11 plan by the court?

13. Who may bring a Chapter 13 proceeding?

14. May a debtor's creditors institute a Chapter 13 proceeding? If so, under what circumstances?

15. What provisions must be contained in a debtor's plan under Chapter 13?

# H Y P O T H E T I C A L    C A S E S

1. Beautiful Homes, Inc., a closely held company in the business of providing home decorating services that is wholly owned by Jenny Chang, finds itself in financial difficulties. Its assets, including the goodwill of the business, its long-term commercial lease and its receivables, total $150,000, and the total debts of the business are $250,000. Although the business is generally healthy, Jenny's problems stem primarily from her having financed a recent expansion through short-term, variable-interest loans just before interest rates began to rise. The result is that she can no longer meet her monthly payments.

   a. Under the facts given, would Jenny be wise to file for Chapter 7 protection of her business? Explain fully.

   b. Should Jenny file for Chapter 11 protection of her business? Explain fully.

   c. Could Jenny file for Chapter 13 protection of her business enterprise? Explain.

2. Debby Debtor has just been informed that her $50,000-per-year middle-management position is being eliminated as part of her company's downsizing. Debby's basic assets include a car worth $20,000, $30,000 equity in her home, $10,000 in CDs and $2,000 in savings. Her monthly payments on her home, car, credit cards, utilities and property taxes total $2,500. Her total unsecured debt is $20,000, and her secured debt (primarily her home and auto financing) is $300,000. Afraid that she will need many months to find another job and that

selling her home in the present real estate market in her area would not be feasible, she is considering filing for protection under the Bankruptcy Act.

   a. May Debby file under Chapter 7? Should she?

   b. May she file under Chapter 11? Should she?

   c. May she file under Chapter 13? Explain fully.

3. Don Broke has managed to obtain $100,000 in unsecured loans (mostly from unsolicited credit cards with high credit lines and even higher interest rates). He also owes $20,000 on a homeowner's loan secured by a mortgage on his home. (He took out that loan in a vain attempt to pay off his credit-card debt.) Don's only source of income is his job at a fast-food restaurant in which he makes the current minimum wage of $4.25 per hour, for total gross earnings of approximately $734 per month. He owns a house, worth $60,000, that he inherited from his parents. He also owns a classic car, valued at $15,000, that he inherited from his grandmother. Finally, he owns approximately $5,000 worth of personal property and household goods, including a $2,000 big-screen television set. After being unable to pay his monthly bills for several months, Don decides he must avail himself of the protection offered by the Bankruptcy Code.

   a. Does Don qualify for Chapter 13 protection?

   b. Should Don file for liquidation or reorganization? Explain.

   c. Assume that Don files for liquidation under Chapter 7. How much of his personal or real property will he be able to keep? (To put it another way, how much of his property will be exempt from attachment under Chapter 7?)

4. Peter Penniless files for bankruptcy under Chapter 7. At the time of filing, his assets subject to attachment totaled $3,000. His debts included the following: $2,500 in allowed administrative expenses in bringing the case; and $5,000 to Visa, $4,000 to Mastercard and $1,000 to American Express in unsecured debt.

   a. How much of the administrative expense claim will be paid? Explain fully.

   b. How much of the unsecured debt will be paid to the credit-card creditors? Explain fully.

U N I T

# CONSUMER PROTECTION

## INTRODUCTION TO CONSUMER PROTECTION · · · · · · · · · · · · · · ·

We have already explored the issue of government regulation of business in our discussions of the regulatory environment of business in Chapter 3, administrative law in Chapter 4 and of labor law in Chapter 34. In this unit we will take a closer look at consumer protection legislation, an area where significant regulation has been imposed at the state and federal levels in recent years.

# 40

# CONSUMER PROTECTION

Consumer protection is a concept that did not exist at common law. Contract law assumes that parties to contracts bargain with one another at arm's length, with each party looking out for his or her own best interests in a detached, businesslike manner. As long as a business transaction involved no fraud or overreaching (taking advantage of a confidential relationship in order to gain a business advantage) by one of the parties, the courts offered no relief to a contracting party that had simply made a bad bargain or bought defective goods without some type of warranty from the seller. *Caveat emptor* (let the buyer beware) was the operative principle underlying all consumer transactions from early common law through much of this century.

Today, a number of federal and state statutes have greatly restricted the doctrine of *caveat emptor* with regard to transactions between merchants and nonmerchant consumers. The rationale for these regulatory statutes is that merchants have an unfair advantage over consumers in business transactions and that it is too easy for consumers to be taken advantage of by unscrupulous merchants, especially in situations where they are most vulnerable, such as when entering into contracts involving the sale of goods or services pursuant to a home solicitation by a salesperson.

In this chapter we will examine some of the salient consumer protection legislation at the federal level. Most states have additional consumer protection regulations that often go beyond the protection guaranteed by the federal statutes. Bear in mind that the material presented here is merely representative of current consumer protection legislation and is but the tip of a very large regulatory iceberg. Unless otherwise stated in the discussion that follows, the regulatory statutes apply only to transactions involving a consumer and a merchant. Transactions in which both parties are merchants or in which both parties are consumers typically are not covered by consumer protection regulatory statutes; for those transactions, *caveat emptor* is still the operative principle.

## FEDERAL TRADE COMMISSION ACT
## (15 USCA § 41 *ET SEQ.*) · · · · · · · · · · · · · · · · · · · · · · · · · · · ·

The Federal Trade Commission Act declares unlawful "[u]nfair methods of competition in or affecting commerce, and unfair or deceptive acts or practices in or affecting commerce." (15 USC § 45) The act gives the Federal Trade Commission (FTC) the power to issue cease-and-desist orders when it finds instances of unfair competition or unfair or deceptive trade practices affecting interstate commerce. Export commerce is specifically exempt from regulation by the FTC *unless* such methods of competition have a direct, substantial, and reasonably foreseeable effect on interstate commerce or on import commerce with other nations or on export commerce with other nations. In other words, export commerce with individual countries is generally not regulated by the FTC unless it has a potential to affect export commerce generally or interstate commerce in particular. When the FTC has reason to believe that a person, partnership or corporation is engaging in unfair competition or unfair or deceptive trade practices, it can serve a complaint giving the accused at least thirty days to appear at a hearing and show cause why a cease-and-desist order should not be issued by the commission mandating that the illegal conduct be stopped. Cease-and-desist orders issued by the FTC can be appealed to the district courts of appeals within sixty days from the date of the service of such orders. Violations of FTC cease-and-desist orders can result in penalties of up to $10,000 for each violation. For purposes of the act, every day that a cease-and-desist order is violated constitutes a separate offense, so that a fine of $10,000 per day may be assessed against persons or companies who violate an FTC order. The FTC may also ask a federal district court to issue an injunction mandating that the offending trade practices be stopped. Violation of a duly issued injunction can result in additional penalties for contempt of court.

To date, the Federal Trade Commission Act has been used primarily as a means of preventing false or misleading advertisement.

## TRUTH-IN-LENDING ACT OF 1968
## (15 USCA § 1601 *ET SEQ.*) · · · · · · · · · · · · · · · · · · · · · · · · · · ·

The Truth-in-Lending Act of 1968 was intended by Congress to make consumers aware of the terms of credit agreements by requiring full disclosure of relevant credit terms by lenders to consumers and to protect consumers from unfair and inaccurate billing practices. The act and its numerous amendments represent an important cornerstone in the area of consumer protection.

The Truth-in-Lending Act applies to any credit transaction affecting the sale of goods or services by a seller on credit to a consumer for primarily personal, family or household purposes. Credit transactions that are primarily for a business purpose, as opposed to a personal purpose, are not covered by the act.

## DISCLOSURE REQUIREMENTS

The act requires that certain terms in the credit agreement be conspicuously disclosed to consumers in writing. Terms that must be disclosed in such a way as to be clearly visible to the consumer include the following:

- Finance charge: All charges above and beyond the cash price of the transaction must be disclosed, including interest, loan fees, carrying charges, credit report fees and credit life insurance fees, if applicable.
- Annual percentage rate: The actual annual percentage rate of interest payable on the credit transaction must be disclosed in accordance with a formula approved by the Board of Governors of the Federal Reserve System.

The Board of Governors of the Federal Reserve System publishes sample disclosure forms that lenders must substantially adhere to in order to comply with the act. Willful failure to comply with the act can result in criminal penalties for lenders, including a fine of up to $5,000 and/or imprisonment for up to one year for each violation. Because the act does not preempt state regulation of consumer credit transactions, states are free to enact additional legislation protecting consumers' rights in consumer credit transactions.

## RIGHT OF RESCISSION

In cases involving borrowing by a consumer in which the lender is given a security interest in the consumer's primary residence, the consumer is given the right to unilaterally rescind the credit agreement up until midnight of the third business day following the day that the consumer receives the required disclosure statement by the lender. A consumer who exercises the right to rescind cannot be charged any fee in connection with the credit agreement.

In the event that a consumer is not given the disclosure statement by the lender, he or she retains the right to rescind not just for three days, but for a full three years from the date of the sale of the property or of the consummation of the transaction, whichever occurred first.

Once the consumer exercises the right to rescind, the consumer must return to the lender whatever consideration was received in exchange for the credit agreement, and the lender must arrange to pick up the property in the consumer's possession within twenty days of the consumer offering to return such property. (Property that has not been picked up within twenty days of its good-faith tender by the consumer will vest in the consumer, who may keep it without cost.)

Note that the right of rescission is enjoyed only by consumers who give a security interest to lenders involving their home in exchange for a consumer credit transaction. In such transactions, a consumer wishing to rescind after the statutorily provided three-day period will have to prove that the lender never provided the required disclosure statement since Section 1635 (c) of the act provides a "[r]ebuttable presumption of delivery of required disclosures."

In addition, the right of rescission is specifically exempted from transactions involving residential mortgages, loan consolidations or refinancing agreements, as well as transactions with a state agency. Advances under revolving credit accounts that are secured by a mortgage on the consumer's primary residence do come within the act, but the right of rescission is available to the consumer only when he or she first opens the account; subsequent purchases made with funds advanced from the same revolving credit account would not be covered.

### RESTRICTIONS ON THE GARNISHMENT OF WAGES

The Truth-in-Lending Act was amended in 1970 to limit the garnishment of an employee's wages to the *lesser of* 25 percent of the employee's weekly wages or the employee's weekly wages minus 30 times the prevailing federal minimum hourly wage. Using this formula, a worker who in 1995 earned a salary of $400 per week could have his or her disposable salary garnished up to the lesser of the following two figures:

- 25 percent of his or her disposable weekly salary ($400 × 25% = $100 per week), or
- his or her disposable weekly salary minus 30 times the prevailing federal minimum wage of $4.25 per hour ($400 − [30 × $4.25] or $400 − $127.50 = $272.50 per week).

Since the lesser amount under these formulas is $100, the consumer earning $400 per week could have up to $100 of his or her salary garnished in total by all of his or her creditors to pay for outstanding credit debt.

A number of exceptions to the garnishment restriction just noted are listed in Section 1673 (b) of the act. These include:

- orders of support granted by a court of competent jurisdiction;
- bankruptcy proceedings under Chapter 13 of the Bankruptcy Act; and
- debts due to any state or to the federal government.

The act further provides that where orders of support are involved, garnishment of wages cannot exceed 50 percent of disposable earnings per week when the garnishee has a spouse or dependent child in addition to the spouse or child he or she is paying support for. Where the garnishee does not have a dependent spouse or child other than the ones to whom support is due, then a maximum of 60 percent of the individual's disposable weekly earnings may be garnished to pay for support.

## CONSUMER LEASING ACT OF 1976 (15 USCA § 1667 *ET SEQ.*)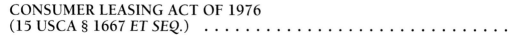

The Consumer Leasing Act of 1976 amends the Truth-in-Lending Act of 1968 to require the disclosure of key terms in contracts for the leasing of personal property to consumers. The act defines a consumer lease as a "contract in the form of a lease or bailment for the use of personal property by a natural person for a period of time exceeding four months, and for a total contractual obligation not exceeding $25,000, primarily for personal, household or family purposes. . . . " (15 USCA § 1667[1]) Leases for personal property that are not covered by the act, such as short-term leases of less than four months' duration or leases of luxury items with a total contract price in excess of $25,000, are governed by standard contract law and do not require any special disclosure.

Consumer leases that by their terms are governed by the Act must contain the following disclosure provisions:

1. A brief description or identification of the leased property;
2. The amount of any payment by the lessee required at the inception of the lease;
3. The amount paid or payable by the lessee for official fees, registration, certificate of title, license fees or taxes;
4. The amount of other charges payable by the lessee not included in the periodic payments, a description of the charges and a statement that the lessee shall be liable for the differential, if any, between the anticipated fair market value of the leased property and its appraised actual value at the termination of the lease, if the lessee has such liability;
5. A statement of the amount or method of determining the amount of any liabilities the lease imposes upon the lessee at the end of the term and whether or not the lessee has the option to purchase the leased property and at what price and time;
6. A statement identifying all express warranties and guarantees made by the manufacturer or lessor with respect to the leased property, and identifying the party responsible for maintaining or servicing the leased property together with a description of the responsibility;
7. A brief description of insurance provided or paid for by the lessor or required of the lessee, including the types and amounts of the coverages and costs;
8. A description of any security interest held or to be retained by the lessor in connection with the lease and a clear identification of the property to which the security interest relates;
9. The number, amount, and due dates or periods of payments under the lease and the total amount of such periodic payments;
10. Where the lease provides that the lessee shall be liable for the anticipated fair market value of the property on expiration of the lease, the fair market value of the property at the inception of the lease, the aggregate cost of the lease on expiration and the differential between them; and
11. A statement of the conditions under which the lessee or lessor may terminate the lease prior to the end of the term and the amount or method of determining any penalty or other charge for delinquency, default, late payments or early termination. (15 USCA § 1667 [a])

The required disclosure can be made on the lease contract itself, and the lessor is allowed to provide a good-faith estimate of terms that he or she cannot know with certainty at the inception of the lease.

# FAIR CREDIT REPORTING ACT OF 1970 (15 USCA § 1681 *ET SEQ.*) . . . . . . . . . . . . . . . . . . . . . . . . . .

The Fair Credit Reporting Act of 1970 amends the 1968 Truth-in-Lending Act to place limits on credit reporting agencies. Section 1681 (b) limits credit reporting agencies to furnishing consumer credit reports *only* under one of the following circumstances:

1. in response to the order of a court having jurisdiction to issue such an order;
2. in accordance with the written instructions of the consumer to whom it relates; or
3. to a person who it has reason to believe
   a. intends to use the information in connection with a credit transaction involving the consumer on whom the information is to be furnished and involving the extension of credit to, or review or collection of an account of, the consumer;
   b. intends to use the information for employment purposes;
   c. intends to use the information in connection with the underwriting of insurance involving the consumer;
   d. intends to use the information in connection with a determination of the consumer's eligibility for a license or other benefit granted by a governmental instrumentality required by law to consider an applicant's financial responsibility or status; or
   e. otherwise has a legitimate business need for the information in connection with a business transaction involving the consumer.

The clear intention of the act is to limit the dissemination of credit information about consumers by credit reporting agencies to only individuals who have a good reason for requiring such information.

## OBSOLETE INFORMATION IN CREDIT REPORTING AGENCY FILES

The act also prohibits credit reporting agencies from maintaining obsolete information in their files. Section 1681 (c) requires credit reporting agencies to remove the following types of information from their files:

- suits and adverse judgments after seven years or upon the expiration of the applicable statute of limitations, whichever is less;
- paid tax liens seven years after the date of payment;

- accounts placed for collection more than seven years prior to the date of the report;
- records of arrest, indictment or convictions seven years after release or parole; and
- any other adverse information antedating the date of the report by more than seven years.

The act in effect institutes a seven-year Statute of Limitations on carrying negative information about a consumer in a credit report in order to protect consumers from having their credit affected by stale information. But the prohibitions on stale information in consumer credit reports does *not* apply to credit reports prepared in connection with one of the following:

- a credit transaction involving $50,000 or more;
- the underwriting of life insurance for a face value of $50,000 or more; or
- the employment of any individual at an annual salary of $20,000 or more.

If a credit report is being prepared in connection with one of the three special circumstances just noted, a credit reporting agency may include information older than seven years in its credit report.

## DISCLOSURE TO CONSUMERS OF CREDIT REPORT PREPARATION

Before an investigative credit report is prepared in connection with a consumer, the lender who wishes to order the report must disclose this fact to the consumer in writing within three days of requesting the report. The notification must also inform the consumer of his or her right to request additional disclosure information under the act by making a written request. If a written request is made by the consumer for additional information, the credit reporting agency must mail to the consumer a written disclosure stating the nature and scope of the investigation requested within five days of receiving the request.

The act also provides that all credit reporting agencies must provide to consumers upon request a full and accurate disclosure of the following types of information in their files:

1. The nature and substance of all information (except medical information) in its files on the consumer at the time of the request.
2. The sources of the information—except that the sources of information acquired solely for use in preparing an investigative consumer report and actually used for no other purpose need not be disclosed, provided that in the event an action is brought under this subchapter, such sources shall be available to the plaintiff under appropriate discovery procedures in the court in which the action is brought.
3. The recipients of any consumer report on the consumer which it has furnished—
   (a) for employment purposes within the two-year period preceding the request, and
   (b) for any other purpose within the six-month period preceding the request. (§ 1681 [g][a])

## CONSUMERS' RIGHT TO DISPUTE INFORMATION IN CREDIT REPORTS

A consumer who wishes to challenge the accuracy or completeness of any information held in the files of a credit reporting agency can notify the agency of any information he or she wishes to dispute. Once notified by the consumer, the agency must reinvestigate the information within a reasonable time. If it finds the information to be inaccurate or can no longer verify the information, it must promptly delete such information from its records. If it finds the disputed information to be accurate, it can retain such information in its records but must allow the consumer to add a statement of dispute setting forth the nature of the dispute in writing. (The agency can limit the statement to not more than 100 words if it provides the consumer with assistance in accurately summarizing the material.)

If information is deleted from a consumer's record pursuant to a dispute or if the consumer elects to add a notation as to disputed information in his or her record, the agency must issue an updated report to any person designated by the consumer who has received a report containing the disputed information within two years preceding the dispute.

## CRIMINAL PENALTIES

Criminal penalties of up to $5,000 and/or imprisonment for up to one year are imposed under the act for willfully obtaining information from a consumer reporting agency under false pretenses or for any officer of employee of a credit reporting agency who knowingly and willfully provides information about a consumer to any person not authorized to receive such information.

## CIVIL PENALTIES

In cases of willful noncompliance with the requirements of this act by a consumer credit reporting agency, the consumer may recover any actual damages caused by the noncompliance, as well as reasonable court costs, attorneys' fees and any punitive damages that a court may deem reasonable. In cases of negligent noncompliance, a consumer may recover actual damages, court costs and attorneys' fees. Consumers may not, however, successfully sue for defamation for any incorrect information reported by a credit reporting agency unless the false information was furnished with malice by the agency or with a willful intent to injure the consumer.

# EQUAL CREDIT OPPORTUNITY ACT OF 1976
# (15 USCA § 1691 *ET SEQ.*) . . . . . . . . . . . . . . . . . . . . . . . . . . .

The Equal Credit Opportunity Act of 1976 makes it unlawful to discriminate against any applicant (not merely consumers) with respect to any credit transaction:

1. on the basis of race, color, religion, national origin, sex or marital status, or age (provided the applicant has the capacity to contract);

2. because all or part of the applicant's income derives from any public assistance program; or

3. because the applicant has in good faith exercised any right under this chapter. (§ 1691[a])

For purposes of the Act, the following activities do *not* constitute discrimination:

1. to make an inquiry of marital status if such inquiry is for the purpose of ascertaining the creditor's rights and remedies applicable to the particular extension of credit and not to discriminate in a determination of credit-worthiness;

2. to make an inquiry of the applicant's age or of whether the applicant's income derives from any public assistance program if such inquiry is for the purpose of determining the amount and probable continuance of income levels, credit history, or other pertinent element of credit-worthiness as provided in regulations of the Board;

3. to use any empirically derived credit system which considers age if such system is demonstrably and statistically sound in accordance with regulations of the Board, except that in the operation of such system the age of an elderly applicant may not be assigned a negative factor or value; or

4. to make an inquiry or to consider the age of an elderly applicant when the age of such applicant is to be used by the creditor in the extension of credit in favor of such applicant. (§ 1691[b])

The act permits discrimination based on race or age when it is to the advantage of applicants in certain situations, such as in programs targeted at certain disadvantaged groups (e.g., low-cost loans for minority-owned businesses) or programs that grant preferential treatment to the elderly (e.g., a senior-citizen discount on a bank loan).

The act provides civil remedies to aggrieved applicants to whom credit is denied in violation of the act that include actual damages as well as punitive damages of up to $10,000 per person in individual suits, as well as court costs and reasonable attorneys' fees. In case of class actions by borrowers against lenders, actual damages and attorneys' fees are also recoverable, but punitive damages are limited to the lesser of $500,000 or 1 percent of the creditor's net worth.

## FAIR DEBT COLLECTION PRACTICES ACT OF 1977 (15 USCA § 1692 *ET SEQ.*) ·····························

The Fair Debt Collection Practices Act of 1977 provides protection to consumers against unfair debt collection practices by creditors or collection agencies. The Act places strict guidelines on the types of communication that creditors or debt collectors may engage in with consumer debtors. The act places the following general restrictions on debt collectors:

- Any communication with the consumer must take place between the hours of 8:00 A.M. and 9:00 P.M. (local time at the consumer's location);
- The debt collector may not speak directly to the consumer if he or she knows that the consumer is represented by an attorney with respect to the collection of the debt in question;
- The debt collector is prohibited from contacting the consumer at work if he or she knows or suspects that the employer prohibits the consumer from receiving such communication;
- The debt collector may not contact any third person with regard to the collection of debt other than the consumer, his or her attorney, a consumer credit reporting agency, the creditor's attorney or the debt collector's attorney.

Debt collectors are also prohibited from harassing the consumer through any of the following types of actions:

- Making threats of physical harm to any person or to anyone's property or reputation;
- Using obscene or profane language;
- Publishing a list of consumers who allegedly refuse to pay their debts, other than to debt collection or consumer credit reporting agencies;
- Advertising the sale of a debt to coerce its payment;
- Causing a phone to ring or repeatedly engaging a consumer in conversation in order to annoy, abuse or harass the consumer;
- Placing telephone calls without disclosing the caller's identity (except when calling third persons in a good-faith effort to locate the debtor, in which case the identity of the caller as a collection agency cannot be disclosed).

In addition to the foregoing, debt collectors are also expressly prohibited from making false, deceptive or misleading representations in connection with the collection of a debt. Debt collectors who fail to comply with the requirements of the act are liable to the consumer debtor for any actual damages suffered by the consumer as a result of the debt collector's failure to comply with the requirements of the act, court costs and reasonable attorneys' fees and any additional damages the court deems appropriate up to $1,000 (e.g., punitive damages). If a class action is involved, the additional damages are limited to the lesser of $500,000 or 1 percent of the debt collector's net worth.

# CONSUMER PRODUCT SAFETY ACT OF 1972 (15 USCA § 2051 *ET SEQ.*)

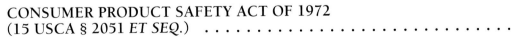

The Consumer Product Safety Act of 1972 was created by Congress in order to meet four purposes:

1. to protect the public against unreasonable risks of injury associated with consumer products;

2. to assist consumers in evaluating the comparative safety of consumer products;

3. to develop uniform safety standards for consumer products and to minimize conflicting state and local regulations; and

4. to promote research and investigation into the causes and prevention of product-related deaths, illnesses, and injuries. (§ 2051[b])

In order to implement its stated purposes, the act created the Consumer Product Safety Commission as an independent regulatory agency empowered to do the following:

- set safety standards for consumer products;
- conduct research into product safety;
- investigate product safety;
- collect and disseminate data on injuries and deaths caused by consumer products;
- work with manufacturers toward instituting voluntary consumer safety standards;
- issue recall notices of unsafe products; and
- ban products it deems pose an unreasonable safety risk to consumers.

## AUTOMOBILE INFORMATION DISCLOSURE ACT OF 1958 (15 USCA § 1231 *ET SEQ.*) . . . . . . . . . . . . . . . . . . . . . . . . . . . .

The Automobile Information Disclosure Act of 1958 requires new car manufacturers to affix to the windshield or side window of every new car offered for sale a label containing the following information:

(a) the make, model, and serial or identification number or numbers;

(b) the final assembly point;

(c) the name, and the location of the place of business, of the dealer to whom it is to be delivered;

(d) the name of the city or town at which it is to be delivered to such dealer;

(e) the method of transportation used in making delivery of such automobile, if driven or towed from final assembly point to place of delivery; and

(f) the following information:

(1) the retail price of such automobile suggested by the manufacturer;

(2) the retail delivered price suggested by the manufacturer for each accessory or item of optional equipment, physically attached to such automobile at the time of its delivery

to such dealer, which is not included within the price of such automobile as stated pursuant to paragraph (1);

(3) the amount charged, if any, to such dealer for the transportation of such automobile to the location at which it is delivered to such dealer;

(4) the total of the amounts specified pursuant to paragraphs (1), (2), and (3). (§ 1232)

Willful failure to affix or endorse the required label as required by the act results in a fine of up to $1,000 for the manufacturer for each occurrence. Altering, removing or rendering the label illegible by anyone prior to its delivery to the car's ultimate purchaser can also result in a fine of up to $1,000 for each occurrence and/or imprisonment for up to one year.

## NATIONAL TRAFFIC AND MOTOR VEHICLE SAFETY ACT OF 1966 (15 USCA § 1381 *ET SEQ.*) . . . . . . . . . . . . . . . . . . . . . . .

Congress passed the National Traffic and Motor Vehicle Safety Act of 1966 in order to reduce deaths and injuries caused by traffic accidents by establishing automobile safety standards. The act charges the Secretary of Transportation with carrying out its provisions through the National Highway Traffic Safety Administration. Violations of the act are punishable by a fine of up to $1,000 per violation up to a maximum fine of $800,000 for any related series of violations. In addition, the federal district courts are given the power to grant injunctions against the sale or importation of automobiles that do not meet the safety standards promulgated under the act.

## MOTOR VEHICLE INFORMATION AND COST SAVINGS ACT OF 1972 (15 USCA § 1901 *ET SEQ.*) . . . . . . . . . . . . . . . . . . . . .

The purpose of the Motor Vehicle Information and Cost Savings Act of 1972 is to allow the Secretary of Transportation to set safety standards for passenger automobile bumpers and to gather and disseminate data on the crashworthiness of passenger automobiles. The act provides for a fine on manufacturers of up to $1,000 per occurrence and up to a maximum of $800,000 for any related series of violations for failure to comply with the bumper safety requirements once these are disseminated. State and local governments are specifically preempted from passing their own bumper safety regulations.

In order to assist the Secretary of Transportation in gathering data on the crash characteristics of passenger automobiles, the act gives him or her subpoena power to force automobile manufacturers to testify and turn over data relating to the crash data of their vehicles. The secretary is also charged with publishing the findings of crash tests and related data to the public in a simplified form that may be useful in comparing the crash characteristics and general safety of passenger automobiles.

## FAIR PACKAGING AND LABELING ACT OF 1967
## (15 USCA § 1451 *ET SEQ.*)  . . . . . . . . . . . . . . . . . . . . . . . . .

The goal of the Fair Packaging and Labeling Act of 1967 is to "enable consumers to obtain accurate information as to the quantity of the contents and should facilitate value comparisons." (§ 1451) In order to achieve this goal, the act makes it illegal for anyone engaged in the labeling or distribution of consumer commodities to distribute such packaged goods in violation of the act. Common carriers and wholesalers and retailers of consumer goods are exempt from the act, however, unless they are involved in the packaging or labeling of the goods prior to their sale or transportation.

The act prohibits the distribution of packaged goods unless they conform to the following regulations:

(1) The commodity shall bear a label specifying the identity of the commodity and the name and place of business of the manufacturer, packer, or distributor;

(2) The net quantity of contents (in terms of weight, measure, or numerical count) shall be separately and accurately stated in a uniform location upon the principal display panel of that label;

(3) The separate label statement of net quantity of contents appearing upon or affixed to any package—

(A)(i) if on a package containing less than four pounds or one gallon and labeled in terms of weight or fluid measure, shall, unless subparagraph (ii) applies and such statement is set forth in accordance with such subparagraph, be expressed both in ounces (with identification as to avoirdupois or fluid ounces) and, if applicable, in pounds for weight units, with any remainder in terms of ounces or common or decimal fractions of the pound; or in the case of liquid measure, in the largest whole unit (quarts, quarts and pints, or pints, as appropriate) with any remainder in terms of fluid ounces or common or decimal fractions of the pint or quart;

(ii) if on a random package, may be expressed in terms of pounds and decimal fractions of the pound carried out to not more than two decimal places;

(iii) if on a package labeled in terms of linear measure, shall be expressed both in terms of inches and the largest whole unit (yards, yards and feet, or feet, as appropriate) with any remainder in terms of inches or common or decimal fractions of the foot or yard;

(iv) if on a package labeled in terms of measure of area, shall be expressed both in terms of square inches and the largest whole square unit (square yards, square yards and square feet, or square feet, as appropriate) with any remainder in terms of square inches or common or decimal fractions of the square foot or square yard;

(B) shall appear in conspicuous and easily legible type in distinct contrast (by topography, layout, color, embossing, or molding) with other matter on the package;

(C) shall contain letters or numerals in a type size which shall be (i) established in relationship to the area of the principal display panel of the package, and (ii) uniform for all packages of substantially the same size; and

(D) shall be so placed that the lines of printed matter included in that statement are generally parallel to the base on which the package rests as it is designed to be displayed.

(4) The label of any package of a consumer commodity which bears a representation as to the number of servings of such commodity contained in such package shall bear a statement of the net quantity (in terms of weight, measure, or numerical count) of each such serving.

(5) For purposes of paragraph (3)(A)(ii) of this subsection the term "random package" means a package which is one of a lot, shipment, or delivery of packages of the same consumer commodity with varying weights, that is, packages with no fixed weight pattern. (§ 1453 [a])

The Secretary of Health and Human Services is empowered by the act to promulgate additional labeling regulations. The Secretary of the Treasury is charged with enforcing the requirements of the act with regard to imported goods.

State regulation over labeling of consumer goods is preempted by the act where such regulation would be less stringent or require different information than does the act. Additional regulation by the states above and beyond that required by the act, however, is not prohibited.

# POISON PREVENTION PACKAGING ACT OF 1970 (15 USCA § 1471 *ET SEQ.*) . . . . . . . . . . . . . . . . . . . . . . . . . . .

The Consumer Product Safety Commission is empowered by the Poison Prevention Packaging Act of 1970 to promulgate regulations for the labeling and packaging of household products that pose a danger to children. The commission is empowered to require special labeling and packaging, where it deems it feasible for products that pose a serious illness danger for children. The commission is also empowered to prevent products it deems dangerous to children from being packaged in a way that it determines is unnecessarily attractive to children.

Where childproof packaging is required under the act, it is permissible for alternate packaging to be made available for households that do not have children, as long as such packaging is clearly labeled as such; this is an accommodation to elderly people who might have difficulty opening medicines or other consumer goods contained in childproof packaging.

# ADDITIONAL REGULATION . . . . . . . . . . . . . . . . . . . . . . . . . . . . .

The sample federal acts discussed in this chapter represent only the very tip of a colossal regulatory iceberg not only in the area of consumer protection, but also in such areas as environmental law, public health and safety, labor and employment and many others. In the area of consumer protection alone, such agencies as the Food and Drug Administration, the Consumer Product Safety Commission, the Office of Consumer Affairs, and the National Highway Safety Administration are only some of the federal agencies that issue and enforce regulations affecting consumers. In addition, most states also independently oversee consumer protection through state regulatory agencies and/or statutory provisions.

## QUESTIONS

1. "Congress has reserved to itself the exclusive power to legislate in the area of consumer protection." Is this statement true or false? Explain.

2. Which federal act declares unfair or deceptive trade practices affecting commerce unlawful?

3. What is the basic purpose of the Truth-in-Lending Act of 1968?

4. Under what circumstances does a consumer have the right to rescind a credit transaction under the Truth-in-Lending Act? What period of time is a consumer given to exercise this right? Under what circumstances may a consumer have up to three years to exercise the right of rescission?

5. What restrictions are imposed on the garnishment of wages by the Truth-in-Lending Act?

6. What limits are placed on the federal government's garnishment of employee wages?

7. What is the basic function of the Consumer Leasing Act of 1976?

8. Under the Fair Credit Reporting Act of 1970, what are the only circumstances under which credit reporting agencies may furnish a credit report on a consumer?

9. Generally speaking, after how many years is negative information in a consumer report considered to be obsolete?

10. Under what special circumstances may stale information be used in a consumer credit report?

11. What are a consumer's basic rights under the Fair Credit Reporting Act if he or she wishes to dispute information contained in his or her credit report?

12. What criminal penalties are imposed by the Fair Credit Reporting Act?

13. What are the civil penalties available for willful and negligent noncompliance with the Fair Credit Reporting Act?

14. What types of discrimination does the Equal Credit Opportunity Act prohibit?

15. What types of discrimination does the Equal Credit Opportunity Act allow?

16. Under the Fair Debt Collection Practices Act of 1977, a collection agency wishing to contact a debtor must do so at what time during the day?

17. What are the four stated purposes of the Consumer Product Safety Act of 1972?

18. What congressional act requires manufacturers of automobiles to affix a label to the car stating, among other things, the car's make, model and serial number, its

manufacturer's suggested retail price and the cost of all optional equipment attached to the automobile?

19. What is the basic purpose of the Motor Vehicle Information and Cost Savings Act of 1972?

20. What federal act regulates the types of goods that must be sold in childproof containers?

# H Y P O T H E T I C A L     C A S E S

1. Carmen Consumer reads a newspaper advertisement from XYZ Computer Company for a Pentium 90 complete computer system for $2,000. The advertisement claims that the computer "boasts a huge hard drive, a printer, lots of RAM, a color monitor and comes with all the software you'll ever need preinstalled." After seeing the computer on display at XYZ's showroom, she purchases a system on credit extended by XYZ. The credit agreement states that Carmen must pay $100 per month for 36 months, and that the monthly payments "include interest, a loan initiation fee of $50 and credit life insurance for the life of the loan." The loan is not secured by any real or personal property owned by Carmen. After taking the computer home, Carmen learns that the brand name of the computer is Pentium 90, but that the computer's central processing unit is an Intel 80386 DX running at 33 MHz—a much inferior system worth less than half the price of a Pentium 90–based system. She also learns that the "huge hard drive" is a puny 30 MB drive that is less than one-tenth the size of drives offered in typical business computer systems. In addition, the computer comes with only 2 MB of RAM—inadequate for most modern applications. The computer also features an obsolete CGA graphics card and monitor. Based on these facts, answer the following questions.

   a. What consumer protection statute has the seller likely violated in its deceptive advertisement?

   b. What could the appropriate federal agency do to immediately stop the seller from continuing its deceptive advertisement practices? What penalty could the agency impose if the practice continues after its attempt to stop it?

   c. With regard to the credit agreement, what federal act, if any, has the seller violated? Explain.

   d. May Carmen rescind the sale contract based upon the fact that she was not given proper disclosure of the credit terms as required by federal law? Explain fully.

   e. Regardless of whether Carmen can rescind the contract under federal law, under what theory may she still avoid the contract under the facts given?

2. Bob Borrower enters into an agreement to lease a living-room set and an entertainment system from Consumer Rental Company for a price of $85 per week. He signs a contract with Consumer Rental Company in which he agrees to allow Consumer Rental to assign $85 per week from his salary at Fast Food Company

as an automatic wage garnishment in the event that he ever fails to make a payment on time. He further agrees to rent the goods for a minimum of two years. After making two payments, Bob realizes that he is unable to afford the contract price for the goods on his net salary of $200 per week.

a.  Assuming that Consumer Rental Company properly provided Bob with the necessary disclosure statement and that there is no defect with the contract or its formation, may Consumer Rental enforce the garnishment of Bob's wages for the contracted amount assuming a minimum wage of $4.25 per hour? Explain fully.

b.  Assume that Bob's salary is $400 per week. Would your answer be different? Explain.

c.  Assume that Bob nets $600 per week and is quite able to make the rental payments. Unfortunately, he has been cheating on his federal and state taxes and owes thousands of dollars to both the IRS and his state. What is the maximum amount of salary subject to attachment by the IRS or his state's tax collector?

3.  Chuck Consumer leases a new Mercedes automobile for $650 per month on a lease that is to run for five years. He also enters into a one-year business lease on a state-of-the-art computer to be used exclusively in his business. In addition, he also leases a small yacht for $2,500 per month for three years. Feeling a bit guilty about providing new toys for himself, he also leases a Lincoln for his wife for three years at $500 per month and rents a motor home for his parents to take a cross-country trip in for a three-month period. Based on these facts, answer the following questions.

a.  Which of the leases comes within the Consumer Leasing Act of 1976? Explain fully.

b.  For which of the leases involved must Chuck be given a disclosure statement under the Consumer Leasing Act of 1976?

c.  After signing the lease agreements just discussed, Chuck is turned down for the yacht lease because of a poor medical report in his credit history. May he claim that the lessor has violated the Equal Credit Opportunity Act of 1976 by discriminating against him because of a physical disability? Explain.

d.  Assume that Chuck is not in fact suffering from the health problem that appeared in the credit report, but that the credit agency reported it as such due to having received inaccurate information from Chuck's physician. May Chuck sue the credit reporting agency for libel for falsely publishing the information? Explain.

e.  After learning of the error in his credit report, Chuck writes the agency requesting that the information be deleted. The agency ignores the request and continues to report the erroneous data for several years. If Chuck suffers some loss due to the incorrect data in the future, what damages is he entitled to demand from the agency?

## ETHICS AND THE LAW: QUESTIONS FOR FURTHER STUDY   . . . . . . .

1. Federal law offers protection against excessive garnishment of wages to consumers who are unable or unwilling to repay loans or otherwise live up to their contractual obligations without regard to the motivation or state of mind of the consumer when he or she entered into a credit agreement. Thus, a working single mother with an excellent credit history who is unable to repay a debt because she has lost her job or because her ex-spouse has illegally stopped making support payments has the same protection against excessive wage garnishment as an incorrigible deadbeat who never meets his financial obligations and perpetually enters into credit agreements without any intent of fulfilling his legal obligations. Since the cost of bad debts is ultimately borne by everyone through higher interest rates and loan origination fees, is it fair to allow the law to shelter individuals who behave irresponsibly from their own folly and to effectively shift the economic burden to the honest, responsible members of society who pay their bills on time and never take on more credit than they can afford? Do we not encourage irresponsible behavior by effectively removing the element of risk for irresponsible behavior? What do you think?

2. While the garnishment of wages in order to ensure the repayment of debt provides an important weapon in the battle against recalcitrant debtors, one can argue that garnishment of wages can remove a debtor's incentive to work and thus prove counterproductive. This is particularly true for debtors in relatively low-paying jobs who are faced with a garnishment of a significant portion of their disposable income; for such persons, it can often prove more financially rewarding to obtain public assistance than to work at a subsistence wage since most forms of public assistance, unlike wages, are not subject to attachment or garnishment. Thus, for a person of modest means faced with a substantial attachment of wages to pay creditors, child support or alimony, relying on public assistance and/or working "off the books" in the underground economy can be more financially rewarding than honest work. There is currently no viable system in place to force individuals to work in order to pay off debts or meet their lawful obligations of supporting their families. Should the law be changed to address this problem? Or is the present system generally working well with only minor problems in your view? Defend the current status quo or make suggestions for meaningful change based on the best interests of society.

# THE MAYFLOWER COMPACT: NOVEMBER 11, 1620

In the name of God, Amen. We, whose names are underwritten, the loyal subjects of our dread sovereigne Lord King James, by the Grace of God, of Great Britaine, France, and Ireland king, defender of the faith, etc., having undertaken for the glory of God, and advancement of the Christian faith, and the honor of our king and country, a voyage to plant the first colony in the Northerne parts of Virginia, doe, by these presents, solemnly and mutually in the presence of God and one another, covenant and combine ourselves together into a civill body politick, for our better ordering and preservation, and furtherance of the ends aforesaid; and by virtue hereof do enact, constitute, and frame, such just and equall laws, ordinances, acts, constitutions, and offices, from time to time, as shall be thought most meete and convenient for the generall good of the Colonie unto which we promise all due submission and obedience. In witness whereof we have hereunto subscribed our names at Cap-Cod the 11th of November, in the raigne of our sovereigne lord, King James of England, France, and Ireland, the eighteenth and of Scotland, the fiftie-fourth. Anno. Domini, 1620.

| | |
|---|---|
| Mr. John Carver | Mr. Stephen Hopkins |
| Mr. William Bradford | Digery Priest |
| Mr. Edward Winslow | Thomas Williams |
| Mr. William Brewster | Gilbert Winslow |
| Isaac Allerton | Edmund Margesson |
| Miles Standish | Peter Brown |
| John Alden | Richard Bitteridge |
| John Turner | George Soule |
| Francis Eaton | Edward Tilly |

James Chilton

John Craxton

John Billington

Joses Fletcher

John Goodman

Mr. Samuel Fuller

Mr. Christopher Martin

Mr. William Mullins

Mr. William White

Mr. Richard Warren

John Howland

Edward Liester

John Tilly

Francis Cooke

Thomas Rogers

Thomas Tinker

John Ridgate

Edward Fuller

Richard Clark

Richard Gardiner

Mr. John Allerton

Thomas English

Edward Doten

APPENDIX

# B

# DECLARATION OF INDEPENDENCE

In CONGRESS, July 4, 1776.
A DECLARATION
By the REPRESENTATIVES of the
UNITED STATES OF AMERICA,
In GENERAL CONGRESS assembled.

When in the Course of human events, it becomes necessary for one people to dissolve the political bands which have connected them with another, and to assume among the powers of the earth, the separate and equal station to which the Laws of Nature and of Nature's God entitle them, a decent respect to the opinions of mankind requires that they should declare the causes which impel them to the separation.

We hold these truths to be self-evident, that all men are created equal, that they are endowed by their Creator with certain unalienable Rights, that among these are Life, Liberty and the pursuit of Happiness. That to secure these rights, Governments are instituted among Men, deriving their just powers from the consent of the governed, that whenever any Form of Government becomes destructive of these ends, it is the Right of the People to alter or to abolish it, and to institute new Government, laying its foundation on such Principles and organizing its powers in such form, as to them shall seem most likely to effect their Safety and Happiness. Prudence, indeed, will dictate that Governments long established should not be changed for light and transient causes; and accordingly all experience hath shewn, that mankind are more disposed to suffer, while evils are sufferable, than to right themselves by abolishing the Forms to which they are accustomed. But when a long train of abuses and usurpations, pursuing invariably the same Object, evinces a design to reduce them under absolute Despotism, it is their right, it is their duty, to throw off such Government, and to provide new Guards for their future security. Such has been the patient sufferance of these Colonies; and such is now the necessity which constrains them to alter their former Systems of Government. The history of the present King of Great Britain is a history of repeated injuries and usurpations, all having in direct object the establishment of an absolute Tyranny over these States. To prove this, let Facts be submitted to a candid world.

He has refused his Assent to Laws, the most wholesome and necessary for the public good.

He has forbidden his Governors to pass Laws of immediate and pressing importance, unless suspended in their operation till his Assent should be obtained; and when so suspended, he has utterly neglected to attend to them.

He has refused to pass other Laws for the accommodation of large districts of people, unless those people would relinquish the right of Representation in the Legislature, a right inestimable to them and formidable to tyrants only.

He has called together legislative bodies at places unusual, uncomfortable, and distant from the depository of their public Records, for the sole purpose of fatiguing them into compliance with his measures.

He has dissolved Representative Houses repeatedly, for opposing with manly firmness his invasions on the rights of the people.

He has refused for a long time, after such dissolutions, to cause others to be elected; whereby the Legislative powers, incapable of Annihilation, have returned to the People at large for their exercise, the State remaining in the meantime exposed to all the dangers of invasion from without, and convulsions within.

He has endeavoured to prevent the population of these States; for that purpose obstructing the Laws for Naturalization of Foreigners; refusing to pass others to encourage their migrations hither, and raising the conditions of new Appropriations of Lands.

He has obstructed the Administration of Justice, by refusing his Assent to Laws for establishing Judiciary Powers.

He has made Judges dependent on his Will alone, for the tenure of their offices, and the amount and payment of their Salaries.

He has erected a multitude of New Offices, and sent hither swarms of Officers to harass our People, and eat out their substance.

He has kept among us, in times of peace, Standing Armies without the consent of our legislatures.

He has affected to render the Military independent of and superior to the Civil power.

He has combined with others to subject us to a jurisdiction foreign to our constitution, and unacknowledged by our laws; giving his Assent to their Acts of pretended Legislation:

For quartering large bodies of armed troops among us:

For protecting them, by a mock Trial, from Punishment for any Murders which they should commit on the Inhabitants of these States:

For cutting off our Trade with all parts of the world:

For imposing Taxes on us without our Consent:

For depriving us in many cases, of the benefits of Trial by Jury:

For transporting us beyond Seas to be tried for pretended offences:

For abolishing the free System of English Laws in a neighbouring Province, establishing therein an Arbitrary government, and enlarging its Boundaries, so as to render it at once an example and fit Instrument for introducing the same absolute rule into these Colonies:

For taking away our Charters, abolishing our most valuable Laws, and altering fundamentally the Forms of our Governments:

For suspending our own Legislatures, and declaring themselves invested with power to legislate for us in all cases whatsoever.

He has abdicated Government here, by declaring us out of his Protection and waging War against us.

He has plundered our seas, ravaged our Coasts, burnt our towns, and destroyed the lives of our people.

He is at this time transporting large Armies of foreign Mercenaries to compleat the works of death, desolation and tyranny, already begun with circumstances of Cruelty and perfidy scarcely paralleled in the most barbarous ages, and totally unworthy the Head of a civilized nation.

He has constrained our fellow Citizens taken Captive on the high Seas to bear Arms against their Country, to become the executioners of their friends and Brethren, or to fall themselves by their Hands.

He has excited domestic insurrections amongst us, and has endeavoured to bring on the inhabitants of our frontiers, the merciless Indian Savages, whose known rule of warfare, is an undistinguished destruction of all ages, sexes and conditions.

In every stage of these Oppressions We have Petitioned for Redress in the most humble terms: Our repeated Petitions have been answered only by repeated injury. A Prince, whose character is thus marked by every act which may define a Tyrant, is unfit to be the ruler of a free people.

Nor have We been wanting in attention to our British brethren. We have warned them from time to time of attempts by their legislature to extend an unwarrantable jurisdiction over us. We have reminded them of the circumstances of our emigration and settlement here. We have appealed to their native justice and magnanimity, and we have conjured them by the ties of our common kindred to disavow these usurpations, which would inevitably interrupt our connections and correspondence. They too have been deaf to the voice of justice and of consanguinity. We must, therefore, acquiesce in the necessity, which denounces our Separation, and hold them, as we hold the rest of mankind, Enemies in War, in Peace Friends.

We, therefore, the Representatives of the United States of America, in General Congress, Assembled, appealing to the Supreme Judge of the world for the rectitude of our intentions, do, in the Name, and by Authority of the good People of these Colonies, solemnly publish and declare, That these United Colonies are, and of Right ought to be Free and Independent States; that they are Absolved from all Allegiance to the British Crown, and that all political connection between them and the State of Great Britain, is and ought to be totally dissolved; and that as Free and Independent States, they have full Power to levy War, conclude Peace, contract Alliances, establish Commerce, and to do all other Acts and Things which Independent States may of right do. And for the support of this Declaration, with a firm reliance on the protection of divine Providence, we mutually pledge to each other our Lives, our Fortunes and our sacred Honor.

JOHN HANCOCK, President
Attested, CHARLES THOMSON, Secretary

New Hampshire
    Josiah Bartlett,
    Wm. Whipple,
    Matthew Thornton.
Massachusetts-Bay
    Saml. Adams,
    John Adams,
    Robt. Treat Paine,
    Elbridge Gerry.
Rhode-Island and
Providence, &c.
    Step. Hopkins,
    William Ellery.
Connecticut
    Roger Sherman,
    Saml. Huntington,
    Wm. Williams,
    Oliver Wolcott.
Georgia
    Button Gwinnett
    Lyman Hall
    Geo. Walton
Maryland
    Samuel Chase
    William Paca
    Thomas Stone
    Charles Carroll
      Of Carrollton
Virginia
    George Wythe
    Richard Henry Lee
    Thomas Jefferson
    Benjamin Harrison
    Thomas Nelson, Jr.
    Francis Lightfoot Lee
    Carter Braxton

Delaware
    Caesar Rodney,
    Geo. Read,
    Tho. McKean.
North-Carolina
    Wm. Hooper,
    Joseph Hewes,
    John Penn.
South Carolina
    Edward Rutledge
    Thomas Heyward, Jr.
    Thomas Lynch, Jr.
    Arthur Middleton
New Jersey
    Richard Stockton
    John Witherspoon
    Francis Hopkinson
    John Hart
    Abraham Clark
New-York
    Wm. Floyd,
    Phil. Livingston,
    Frans. Lewis,
    Lewis Morris.
Pennsylvania
    Robert Morris
    Benjamin Rush
    Benjamin Franklin
    John Morton
    George Clymer
    James Smith
    George Taylor
    James Wilson
    George Ross

# APPENDIX

# C

# THE CONSTITUTION OF THE UNITED STATES

(Adopted by the delegates to the Constitutional Convention on September 17, 1787; ratified by the required nine states on June 21, 1788; ratified by all of the original thirteen states by 1790.)

## PREAMBLE

WE THE PEOPLE of the United States, in Order to form a more perfect Union, establish Justice, insure domestic Tranquility, provide for the common defence, promote the general Welfare, and secure the Blessings of Liberty to ourselves and our Posterity, do ordain and establish this Constitution for the United States of America.

## ARTICLE ONE

Section 1. All legislative Powers herein granted shall be vested in a Congress of the United States, which shall consist of a Senate and House of Representatives.

Section 2. The House of Representatives shall be composed of Members chosen every second year by the people of the several States, and the Electors in each State shall have the Qualifications requisite for Electors of the most numerous Branch of the State Legislature.

No Person shall be a Representative who shall not have attained to the Age of twenty five Years, and been seven Years a Citizen of the United States, and who shall not, when elected, be an Inhabitant of that State in which he shall be chosen.

Representatives and direct Taxes shall be apportioned among the several States which may be included within this Union, according to their respective Numbers, which shall be determined by adding to the whole Number of free Persons, including those bound to Service for a Term of Years, and excluding Indians not taxed, three fifths of all other Persons. The actual Enumeration shall be made within three Years after the first Meeting of the Congress of the United States, and within every subsequent Term of ten Years, in such Manner as they shall by Law direct. The Number of Representatives shall not exceed one for every thirty Thousand, but each State shall have at Least one Representative; and until such enumeration shall be made, the State of New Hampshire shall be entitled to chuse three, Massachusetts eight, Rhode-Island and Providence Plantations one, Connecticut five, New-York six, New Jersey four, Pennsylvania eight, Delaware one, Maryland six, Virginia ten, North Carolina five, South Carolina five, and Georgia three.

When vacancies happen in the Representation from any State, the Executive Authority thereof shall issue Writs of Election to fill such vacancies.

The House of Representatives shall chuse their speaker and other Officers; and shall have the sole Power of Impeachment.

Section 3. The Senate of the United States shall be composed of two Senators from each State, chosen by the Legislature thereof, for six Years; and each Senator shall have one Vote.

Immediately after they shall be assembled in consequence of the first Election, they shall be divided as equally as may be into three Classes. The Seats of the Senators of the first Class shall be vacated at the Expiration of the second Year, of the second Class at the Expiration of the fourth Year, and of the third Class at the Expiration of the sixth Year, so that one third may be chosen every second Year; and if Vacancies happen by Resignation, or otherwise, during the recess of the legislature of any State, the Executive thereof may make temporary Appointments until the next Meeting of the Legislature, which shall then fill such Vacancies.

No Person shall be a Senator who shall not have attained to the Age of thirty years, and been nine Years a Citizen of the United States, and who shall not, when elected, be an Inhabitant of that State for which he shall be chosen.

The Vice President of the United States shall be President of the Senate, but shall have No vote, unless they be equally divided.

The Senate shall chuse their other Officers, and also a President pro tempore, in the absence of the Vice President, or when he shall exercise the office of President of the United States.

The Senate shall have the sole Power to try all Impeachments. When sitting for that purpose, they shall be on Oath or Affirmation. When the President of the United States is tried, the Chief Justice shall preside: And no Person shall be convicted without the Concurrence of two thirds of the Members present.

Judgment in Cases of Impeachment shall not extend further than to removal from Office, and disqualification to hold and enjoy any Office of honor, Trust or Profit under the United States: but the Party convicted shall nevertheless be liable and subject to Indictment, Trial, Judgment and Punishment, according to law.

Section 4. The Times, Places and Manner of holding Elections for Senators and Representatives, shall be prescribed in each State by the Legislature thereof; but the Congress may at any time by Law make or alter such Regulations, except as to the Places of chusing Senators.

The Congress shall assemble at least once in every Year, and such Meeting shall be on the first Monday in December, unless they shall by Law appoint a different Day.

Section 5. Each House shall be the Judge of the Elections, Returns and Qualifications of its own Members, and a Majority of each shall constitute a Quorum to do Business; but a smaller Number may adjourn from day to day, and may be authorized to compel the Attendance of absent Members, in such Manner, and under such Penalties as each House may provide.

Each House may determine the Rules of its Proceedings, punish its Members for disorderly Behaviour, and, with the Concurrence of two thirds, expel a Member.

Each House shall keep a Journal of its Proceedings, and from time to time publish the same, excepting such Parts as may in their Judgment require Secrecy; and the Yeas and Nays of the Members of either House on any question shall, at the Desire of one fifth of those Present, be entered on the Journal.

Neither house, during the Session of Congress, shall, without the Consent of the other, adjourn for more than three days, nor to any other Place than that in which the two Houses shall be sitting.

Section 6. The Senators and Representatives shall receive a Compensation for their Services, to be ascertained by Law, and paid out of the Treasury of the United States. They shall in all Cases, except Treason, Felony and Breach of the Peace, be privileged from Arrest during their Attendance at the Session of their respective Houses, and in going to and returning from the same; and for any Speech or Debate in either House, they shall not be questioned in any other Place.

No Senator or Representative shall, during the Time for which he was elected, be appointed to any civil Office under the Authority of the United States, which shall have been created, or the Emoluments whereof shall have been encreased during such time; and no person holding any Office under the United States, shall be a Member of either House during his Continuance in Office.

Section 7. All Bills for raising Revenue shall originate in the House of Representatives; but the Senate may propose or concur with Amendments as on other Bills.

Every Bill which shall have passed the House of Representatives and the Senate, shall, before it become a Law, be presented to the President of the United States; If he approve he shall sign it, but if not he shall return it, with his Objections to that House in which it shall have originated, who shall enter the Objections at large on their Journal, and proceed to reconsider it. If after such Reconsideration two thirds of that House shall agree to pass the bill, it shall be sent, together with the Objections, to the other House, by which it shall likewise be reconsidered, and if approved by two thirds of that House, it shall become a Law. But in all such Cases the Votes of both Houses shall be determined by yeas and Nays, and the Names of the Persons voting for and against the Bill shall be entered on the Journal of each House respectively. If any Bill shall not be returned by the President within ten Days (Sundays excepted) after it shall have been presented to him, the Same shall be a Law, in like Manner as if he had signed it, unless the Congress by their Adjournment prevent its return, in which Case it shall not be a Law.

Every Order, Resolution, or Vote to which the Concurrence of the Senate and House of Representatives may be necessary (except on a question of adjournment) shall be presented to the President of the United States; and before the Same shall take Effect, shall be approved by him, or being disapproved by him, shall be repassed by two thirds of the Senate and House of Representatives, according to the Rules and Limitations prescribed in the Case of a Bill.

Section 8. The Congress shall have Power To lay and collect Taxes, Duties, Imposts and Excises, to pay the Debts and provide for the common Defence and general Welfare of the United States; but all Duties, Imposts and Excises shall be uniform throughout the United States;

To Borrow Money on the Credit of the United States;

To regulate Commerce with foreign Nations, and among the several States, and with the Indian Tribes;

To establish an uniform Rule of Naturalization, and uniform Laws on the subject of Bankruptcies throughout the United States;

To coin Money, regulate the Value thereof, and of foreign Coin, and fix the Standard of Weights and Measures;

To provide for the Punishment of counterfeiting the Securities and current Coin of the United States;

To establish Post Offices and Post Roads;

To promote the Progress of Science and useful Arts, by securing for limited Times to Authors and Inventors the exclusive Right to their respective Writings and Discoveries;

To constitute Tribunals inferior to the supreme Court;

To define and punish Piracies and Felonies committed on the high Seas, and Offences against the Law of Nations;

To declare War, grant Letters of Marque and Reprisal, and make Rules concerning Captures on Land and Water;

To raise and support Armies, but no Appropriation of Money to that Use shall be for a longer Term than two Years;

To provide and maintain a Navy;

To make Rules for the Government and Regulation of the land and naval Forces;

To provide for calling forth the Militia to execute the Laws of the Union, suppress Insurrections and repel Invasions;

To provide for organizing, arming, and disciplining, the Militia, and for governing such Part of them as may be employed in the Service of the United States, reserving to the States respectively, the Appointment of the Officers, and the Authority of training the Militia according to the discipline prescribed by Congress;

To exercise exclusive Legislation in all Cases whatsoever, over such District (not exceeding ten Miles square) as may, by Cession of particular States, and the Acceptance of Congress, become the Seat of the Government of the United States, and to exercise like Authority over all Places purchased by the Consent of the Legislature of the State in which the Same shall be for the Erection of Forts, Magazines, Arsenals, dock-Yards, and other needful Buildings;—And

To make all Laws which shall be necessary and proper for carrying into Execution the foregoing Powers, and all other powers vested by this Constitution in the Government of the United States, or in any Department or Officer thereof.

Section 9. The Migration or Importion of such Persons as any of the States now existing shall think proper to admit, shall not be prohibited by the Congress prior to the Year one thousand eight hundred and eight, but a Tax or duty may be imposed on such Importation, not exceeding ten dollars for each Person.

The Privilege of the Writ of Habeas Corpus shall not be suspended, unless when in Cases of Rebellion or Invasion the public Safety may require it.

No Bill of Attainder or ex post facto Law shall be passed.

No Capitation, or other direct, Tax shall be laid, unless in Proportion to the Census or Enumeration herein before directed to be taken.

No Tax or Duty shall be laid on Articles exported from any State.

No preference shall be given by any Regulation of Commerce or revenue to the Ports of one State over those of another: nor shall Vessels bound to, or from, one State, be obliged to enter, clear, or pay Duties in another.

No Money shall be drawn from the Treasury, but in Consequence of Appropriations made by Law; and a regular Statement and Account of the Receipts and Expenditures of all public Money shall be published from time to time.

No Title of Nobility shall be granted by the United States: and no Person holding any Office of Profit or Trust under them, shall, without the Consent of the Congress, accept of any present, Emolument, Office, or Title, of any kind whatever, from any King, Prince, or foreign State.

Section 10. No State shall enter into any Treaty, Alliance, or Confederation; grant Letters of Marque and Reprisal; coin Money; emit Bills of Credit; make any Thing but gold and silver Coin a Tender in Payment of Debts; pass any Bill of Attainder, ex post facto Law, or Law impairing the Obligation of Contracts, or grant any Title of Nobility.

No State shall, without the Consent of the Congress, lay any Imposts or Duties on Imports or Exports, except what may be absolutely necessary for executing it's inspection Laws: and the net Produce of all Duties and Imposts, laid by any State on Imports or Exports, shall be for the Use of the Treasury of the United States; and all such Laws shall be subject to the Revision and Controul of the Congress.

No State shall, without the Consent of Congress, lay any Duty of Tonnage, keep Troops, or Ships of War in time of Peace, enter into any Agreement or Compact with another State, or with a foreign Power, or engage in War, unless actually invaded, or in such imminent Danger as will not admit of delay.

## ARTICLE TWO

Section 1. The executive Power shall be vested in a President of the United States of America. He shall hold his Office during the term of four Years, and, together with the Vice President, chosen for the same term, be elected, as follows

Each State shall appoint, in such Manner as the legislature thereof may direct, a Number of Electors, equal to the whole Number of Senators and Representatives to which the State may be entitled in the Congress: but no Senator or Representative, or Person holding an Office of Trust or Profit under the United States, shall be appointed an Elector.

The Electors shall meet in their respective States, and vote by Ballot for two Persons, of whom one at least shall not be an Inhabitant of the same State with themselves. And they shall make a List of all the Persons voted for, and of the Number of Votes for each; which List they shall sign and certify, and transmit sealed to the Seat of the Government of the United States, directed to the President of the Senate. The President of the Senate shall, in the Presence of the Senate and House of Representatives, open all the Certificates, and the Votes shall then be counted. The Person having the greatest Number of Votes shall be the President, if such Number be a Majority of the whole Number of Electors appointed; and if there be more than one who have such Majority, and have an equal Number of Votes, then the House of Representatives shall immediately chuse by Ballot one of them for President: and if no Person have a Majority, then from the five highest on the List the said House shall in like Manner chuse the President. But in chusing the President, the Votes shall be taken by States, the Representation from each State having one Vote; A quorum for this Purpose shall consist of a Member or Members from two thirds of the States, and a Majority of all the States shall be necessary to a Choice. In every Case, after the Choice of the President, the Person having the greatest Number of Votes of the Electors shall be the Vice President. But if there should remain two or more who have equal Votes, the Senate shall chuse from them by Ballot the Vice President.

The Congress may determine the Time of chusing the Electors, and the Day on which they shall give their votes; which Day shall be the same throughout the United States.

No Person except a natural born Citizen, or a Citizen of the United States, at the time of the Adoption of this Constitution, shall be eligible to the Office of President; neither shall any Person be eligible to that Office who shall not have attained to the Age of thirty five Years, and been fourteen Years a Resident within the United States.

In Case of the Removal of the President from Office, or of his Death, Resignation, or Inability to discharge the Powers and Duties of the said Office, the Same shall devolve on the Vice President, and the Congress may by Law provide for the Case of Removal, Death, Resignation or Inability, both of the President and Vice President, declaring what Officer shall then act as President, and such Officer shall act accordingly, until the Disability be removed, or a President shall be elected.

The President shall, at stated Times, receive for his Services, a Compensation, which shall neither be encreased nor diminished during the Period for which he shall have been elected, and he shall not receive within that Period any other Emolument from the United States, or any of them.

Before he enter on the Execution of his Office, he shall take the following Oath or Affirmation:—"I do solemnly swear (or affirm) that I will faithfully execute the

Office of President of the United States, and will to the best of my Ability, preserve, protect and defend the Constitution of the United States."

Section 2. The President shall be Commander in Chief of the Army and Navy of the United States, and of the Militia of the several States, when called into the actual Service of the United States; he may require the Opinion, in writing, of the principal Officer in each of the executive Departments, upon any Subject relating to the Duties of their respective offices, and he shall have Power to grant Reprieves and Pardons for Offences against the United States, except in Cases of Impeachment.

He shall have Power, by and with the Advice and Consent of the Senate, to make Treaties, provided two thirds of the Senators present concur; and he shall nominate, and by and with the Advice and Consent of the Senate, shall appoint Ambassadors, other public Ministers and Consuls, Judges of the supreme Court, and all other Officers of the United States, whose appointments are not herein otherwise provided for, and which shall be established by Law: but the Congress may by Law vest the Appointment of such inferior Officers, as they think proper, in the President alone, in the Courts of Law, or in the Heads of Departments.

The President shall have Power to fill up all Vacancies that may happen during the Recess of the Senate, by granting Commissions which shall expire at the End of their next Session.

Section 3. He shall from time to time give to the Congress Information of the State of the Union, and recommend to their Consideration such Measures as he shall judge necessary and expedient; he may, on extraordinary Occasions, convene both Houses, or either of them, and in Case of Disagreement between them, with Respect to the Time of Adjournment, he may adjourn them to such Time as he shall think proper; he shall receive Ambassadors and other public Ministers; he shall take Care that the Laws be faithfully executed, and shall Commission all the Officers of the United States.

Section 4. The President, Vice President and all civil Officers of the United States, shall be removed from Office on Impeachment for, and Conviction of, Treason, Bribery, or other High Crimes and Misdemeanors.

## ARTICLE THREE

Section 1. The judicial Power of the United States, shall be vested in one supreme Court, and in such inferior Courts as the Congress may from time to time ordain and establish. The Judges, both of the supreme and inferior Courts, shall hold their Offices during good Behaviour, and shall, at stated Times, receive for their Services, a Compensation, which shall not be diminished during their Continuance in office.

Section 2. The judicial Power shall extend to all Cases, in Law and Equity, arising under this Constitution, the Laws of the United States, and Treaties made, or which shall be made, under their Authority;—to all Cases affecting ambassadors, other public ministers and Consuls;—to all Cases of admiralty and maritime Jurisdiction;—to Controversies to which the United States shall be a Party;—to Controversies between two or more States;—between a State and Citizens of another State;—between Citizens of different States;—between Citizens of the same State claiming Lands under Grants of different States, and between a State, or the Citizens thereof, and foreign States, Citizens or Subjects.

In all Cases affecting Ambassadors, other public Ministers and Consuls, and those in which a State shall be Party, the supreme Court shall have original Jurisdiction. In all the other Cases before mentioned, the supreme Court shall have appellate Jurisdiction, both as to Law and Fact, with such Exceptions, and under such Regulations as the Congress shall make.

The trial of all Crimes, except in Cases of Impeachment, shall be by Jury; and such Trial shall be held in the State where the said Crimes shall have been committed; but when not committed within any State, the Trial shall be at such Place or Places as the Congress may by Law have directed.

Section 3. Treason against the United States, shall consist only in levying War against them, or in adhering to their Enemies, giving them Aid and Comfort. No Person shall be convicted of Treason unless on the Testimony of two Witnesses to the same overt Act, or on Confession in open Court.

The Congress shall have Power to declare the Punishment of Treason, but no Attainder of Treason shall work Corruption of Blood, or Forfeiture except during the Life of the Person attainted.

# ARTICLE FOUR

Section 1. Full Faith and Credit shall be given in each State to the public Acts, Records, and judicial Proceedings of every other State. And the Congress may by general Laws prescribe the Manner in which such Acts, Records and Proceedings shall be proved, and the Effect thereof.

Section 2. The Citizens of each State shall be entitled to all Privileges and Immunities of Citizens in the several States.

A Person charged in any State with Treason, Felony, or other Crime, who shall flee from Justice, and be found in another State, shall on Demand of the executive Authority of the State from which he fled, be delivered up, to be removed to the State having Jurisdiction of the Crime.

No Person held to Service or Labour in one State, under the Laws thereof, escaping into another, shall, in Consequence of any Law or Regulation therein, be discharged from such Service or Labour, but shall be delivered up on Claim of the Party to whom such Service or Labour may be due.

Section 3. New States may be admitted by the Congress into this Union; but no new State shall be formed or erected within the Jurisdiction of any other State; nor any State be formed by the Junction of two or more States, or Parts of States, without the Consent of the Legislatures of the States concerned as well as of the Congress.

The Congress shall have power to dispose of and make all needful Rules and Regulations respecting the Territory or other Property belonging to the United States; and nothing in this Constitution shall be so construed as to Prejudice any claims of the United States, or of any particular State.

Section 4. The United States shall guarantee to every State in this Union a Republican Form of Government, and shall protect each of them against Invasion; and on Application of the Legislature, or of the Executive (when the Legislature cannot be convened) against domestic Violence.

## ARTICLE FIVE

The Congress, whenever two thirds of both Houses shall deem it necessary, shall propose Amendments to this Constitution, or, on the Application of the Legislatures of two thirds of the several States, shall call a Convention for proposing Amendments, which, in either Case, shall be valid to all Intents and Purposes, as Part of this Constitution, when ratified by the Legislatures of three fourths of the several States, or by Conventions in three fourths thereof, as the one or the other Mode of Ratification may be proposed by the Congress; Provided that no Amendment which may be made prior to the Year One thousand eight hundred and eight shall in any Manner affect the first and fourth Clauses in the Ninth Section of the first Article; and that no State, without its Consent, shall be deprived of its equal Suffrage in the Senate.

## ARTICLE SIX

All Debts contracted and Engagements entered into, before the Adoption of this Constitution, shall be as valid against the United States under this Constitution, as under the Confederation.

This Constitution, and the Laws of the United States which shall be made in Pursuance thereof; and all Treaties made, or which shall be made, under the Authority of the United States, shall be the supreme Law of the Land; and the Judges in every State shall be bound thereby, any Thing in the Constitution or Laws of any State to the Contrary notwithstanding.

The Senators and Representatives before mentioned, and the Members of the several State Legislatures, and all executive and judicial Officers, both of the United States and of the several States, shall be bound by Oath or Affirmation, to support this Constitution; but no religious Test shall ever be required as a Qualification to any Office or public Trust under the United States.

## ARTICLE SEVEN

The Ratification of the Conventions of nine States, shall be sufficient for the Establishment of this Constitution between the States so ratifying the Same.

DONE in Convention by the Unanimous Consent of the States present the Seventeenth Day of September in the Year of our Lord one thousand seven hundred and Eighty seven and of the Independence of the United States of America the Twelfth IN WITNESS whereof We have hereunto subscribed our Names,

George Washington—President and deputy from Virginia

| | |
|---|---|
| New Hampshire: | John Langdon, Nicholas Gilman |
| Massachusetts: | Nathaniel Gorham, Rufus King |
| Connecticut: | William Samuel Johnson, Roger Sherman |
| New York: | Alexander Hamilton |
| New Jersey: | William Livingston, David Brearly, William Paterson, Jonathan Dayton |
| Pennsylvania: | Benjamin Franklin, Thomas Mifflin, Robert Morris, George Clymer, Thomas FitzSimons, Jared Ingersoll, James Wilson, Gouverneur Morris |
| Delaware: | George Read, Gunning Bedford, Jr., John Dickinson, Richard Bassett, Jacob Broom |
| Maryland: | James McHenry, Daniel of Saint Thomas Jenifer, Daniel Carroll |
| Virginia: | John Blair, James Madison, Jr. |
| North Carolina: | William Blount, Richard Dobbs Spaight, Hugh Williamson |
| South Carolina: | John Rutledge, Charles Cotesworth Pinckney, Charles Pinckney, Pierce Butler |
| Georgia: | William Few, Abraham Baldwin |

Attest
William Jackson
Secretary

# Amendments to the U.S. Constitution

(NOTE: The first ten amendments to the Constitution, called the Bill of Rights, were proposed by the First Congress in September, 1789, and were ratified by all of the thirteen original states by December 15, 1791.)

## FIRST AMENDMENT

Congress shall make no law respecting an establishment of religion, or prohibiting the free exercise thereof; or abridging the freedom of speech, or of the press; or the right of the people peaceably to assemble, and to petition the Government for a redress of grievances.

## SECOND AMENDMENT

A well regulated Militia, being necessary to the security of a free State, the right of the people to keep and bear Arms, shall not be infringed.

## THIRD AMENDMENT

No soldier shall, in time of peace be quartered in any house, without the consent of the Owner, nor in time of war, but in a manner to be prescribed by law.

## FOURTH AMENDMENT

The right of the people to be secure in their persons, houses, papers, and effects, against unreasonable searches and seizures, shall not be violated, and no Warrants shall issue, but upon probable cause, supported by Oath or affirmation, and particularly describing the place to be searched, and the persons or things to be seized.

## FIFTH AMENDMENT

No person shall be held to answer for a capital, or otherwise infamous crime, unless on a presentment or indictment of a Grand Jury, except in cases arising in the land or naval forces, or in the Militia, when in actual service in time of War or public danger; nor shall any person be subject for the same offence to be twice put in jeopardy of life or limb; nor shall be compelled in any criminal case to be a witness against himself, nor be deprived of life, liberty, or property, without due process of law; nor shall private property be taken for public use, without just compensation.

## SIXTH AMENDMENT

In all criminal prosecutions, the accused shall enjoy the right to a speedy and public trial, by an impartial jury of the State and district wherein the crime shall have been committed, which district shall have been previously ascertained by law, and to be informed of the nature and cause of the accusation; to be confronted with the witnesses against him; to have compulsory process for obtaining witnesses in his favor, and to have the Assistance of Counsel for his defence.

## SEVENTH AMENDMENT

In Suits at common law, where the value in controversy shall exceed twenty dollars, the right of trial by jury shall be preserved, and no fact tried by a jury, shall be otherwise re-examined in any Court of the United States, than according to the rules of the common law.

## EIGHTH AMENDMENT

Excessive bail shall not be required, nor excessive fines imposed, nor cruel and unusual punishments inflicted.

## NINTH AMENDMENT

The enumeration in the Constitution, of certain rights, shall not be construed to deny or disparage others retained by the people.

## TENTH AMENDMENT

The powers not delegated to the United States by the Constitution, nor prohibited by it to the States, are reserved to the States respectively, or to the people.

## ELEVENTH AMENDMENT (ratified Feburary 7, 1795)

The judicial power of the United States shall not be construed to extend to any suit in law or equity, commenced or prosecuted against one of the United States by Citizens of another State, or by Citizens or Subjects of any Foreign State.

## TWELFTH AMENDMENT (ratified June 15, 1804)

The Electors shall meet in their respective states, and vote by ballot for President and Vice-President, one of whom, at least, shall not be an inhabitant of the same state with themselves; they shall name in their ballots the person voted for as President, and in distinct ballots the person voted for as Vice-President, and they shall make distinct lists of all persons voted for as President, and of all persons voted for as Vice-President, and of the number of votes for each, which lists they shall sign and certify, and transmit sealed to the seat of the government of the United States, directed to the President of the Senate;—The President of the Senate shall, in the presence of the Senate and House of Representatives, open all the certificates and the votes shall then be counted;—the person having the greatest number of votes for President, shall be the President, if such number be a majority of the whole number of Electors appointed; and if no person have such majority, then from the persons having the highest numbers not exceeding three on the list of those voted for as President, the House of Representatives shall choose immediately, by ballot, the President. But in choosing the President, the votes shall be taken by states, the representation from each state having one vote; a quorum for this purpose shall consist of a member or members from two-thirds of the states, and a majority of all the states shall be necessary to a choice. And if the House of Representatives shall not choose a President whenever the right of choice shall devolve upon them, before the fourth day of March next following, then the Vice-President shall act as President, as in the case of the death or other constitutional disability of the President.—The person having the greatest number of votes as Vice-President, shall be the Vice-President, if such number be a majority of the whole number of Electors appointed, and if no person have a majority, then from the two highest numbers on the list, the Senate shall choose the Vice-President; a quorum for the purpose shall consist of two-thirds of the whole number of Senators, and a majority of the whole number shall be necessary to a choice. But no person constitutionally ineligible to the office of President shall be eligible to that of Vice-President of the United States.

## THIRTEENTH AMENDMENT (ratified December 6, 1865)

Section 1. Neither slavery nor involuntary servitude, except as a punishment for crime whereof the party shall have been duly convicted, shall exist within the United States, or any place subject to their jurisdiction.

Section 2. Congress shall have power to enforce this article by appropriate legislation.

## FOURTEENTH AMENDMENT (ratified July 9, 1868)

Section 1. All persons born or naturalized in the United States, and subject to the jurisdiction thereof, are citizens of the United States and of the State wherein they reside. No State shall make or enforce any law which shall abridge the privileges or immunities of citizens of the United States; nor shall any State deprive any person of life, liberty, or property, without due process of law; nor deny to any person within its jurisdiction the equal protection of the laws.

Section 2. Representatives shall be apportioned among the several States according to their respective numbers, counting the whole number of persons in each State, excluding Indians not taxed. But when the right to vote at any election for the choice of electors for President and Vice President of the United States, Representatives in Congress, the Executive and Judicial officers of a State, or the members of the Legislature thereof, is denied to any of the male inhabitants of such State, being twenty-one years of age, and citizens of the United States, or in any way abridged, except for participation in rebellion, or other crime, the basis of representation therein shall be reduced in the proportion which the number of such male citizens shall bear to the whole number of male citizens twenty-one years of age in such State.

Section 3. No person shall be a Senator or Representative in Congress, or elector of President and Vice President, or hold any office, civil or military, under the United States, or under any State, who, having previously taken an oath, as a member of Congress, or as an officer of the United States, or as a member of any State legislature, or as an executive or judicial officer of any State, to support the Constitution of the United States, shall have engaged in insurrection or rebellion against the same, or given aid or comfort to the enemies thereof. But Congress may by a vote of two-thirds of each House, remove such disability.

Section 4. The validity of the public debt of the United States, authorized by law, including debts incurred for payment of pensions and bounties for services in suppressing insurrection or rebellion, shall not be questioned. But neither the United States nor any State shall assume or pay any debt or obligation incurred in aid of insurrection or rebellion against the United States, or any claim for the loss or emancipation of any slave; but all such debts, obligations and claims shall be held illegal and void.

Section 5. The Congress shall have power to enforce, by appropriate legislation, the provisions of this article.

## FIFTEENTH AMENDMENT (ratified February 3, 1870)

Section 1. The right of citizens of the United States to vote shall not be denied or abridged by the United States or by any State on account of race, color, or previous condition of servitude.

Section 2. The Congress shall have power to enforce this article by appropriate legislation.

## SIXTEENTH AMENDMENT (ratified February 3, 1913)

The Congress shall have power to lay and collect taxes on incomes, from whatever source derived, without apportionment among the several States, and without regard to any census or enumeration.

## SEVENTEENTH AMENDMENT (ratified April 8, 1913)

The Senate of the United States shall be composed of two Senators from each State, elected by the people thereof for six years; and each Senator shall have one vote. The electors in each State shall have the qualifications requisite for electors of the most numerous branch of the State legislatures.

When vacancies happen in the representation of any State in the Senate, the executive authority of such State shall issue writs of election to fill such vacancies: *Provided,* That the legislature of any State may empower the executive thereof to make temporary appointments until the people fill the vacancies by election as the legislature may direct.

This amendment shall not be so construed as to affect the election or term of any Senator chosen before it becomes valid as part of the Constitution.

## EIGHTEENTH AMENDMENT (ratified January 16, 1919)

Section 1. After one year from the ratification of this article the manufacture, sale, or transportation of intoxicating liquors within, the importation thereof into, or the exportation thereof from the United States and all territory subject to the jurisdiction thereof for beverage purposes is hereby prohibited.

Section 2. The Congress and the several States shall have concurrent power to enforce this article by appropriate legislation.

Section 3. This article shall be inoperative unless it shall have been ratified as an amendment to the Constitution by the legislatures of the several States, as provided in the Constitution, within seven years from the date of the submission hereof to the States by the Congress.

## NINETEENTH AMENDMENT (ratified August 18, 1920)

The right of citizens of the United States to vote shall not be denied or abridged by the United States or by any State on account of sex.

Congress shall have power to enforce this article by appropriate legislation.

## TWENTIETH AMENDMENT (ratified January 23, 1933)

Section 1. The terms of the President and Vice President shall end at noon on the 20th day of January, and the terms of Senators and Representatives at noon on the 3d day of January, of the years in which such terms would have ended if this article had not been ratified; and the terms of their successors shall then begin.

Section 2. The Congress shall assemble at least once in every year, and such meeting shall begin at noon on the 3d day of January, unless they shall by law appoint a different day.

Section 3. If, at the time fixed for the beginning of the term of the President, the President elect shall have died, the Vice President elect shall become President. If a President shall not have been chosen before the time fixed for the beginning of his term, or if the President elect shall have failed to qualify, then the Vice President elect shall act as President until a President shall have qualified; and the Congress may by law provide for the case wherein neither a President elect nor a Vice President elect shall have qualified, declaring who shall then act as President, or the manner in which one who is to act shall be selected, and such person shall act accordingly until a President or Vice President shall have qualified.

Section 4. The Congress may by law provide for the case of the death of any of the persons from whom the House of Representatives may choose a President whenever the right of choice shall have devolved upon them, and for the case of the death of any of the persons from whom the Senate may choose a Vice President whenever the right of choice shall have devolved upon them.

Section 5. Sections 1 and 2 shall take effect on the 15th day of October following the ratification of this article.

Section 6. This article shall be inoperative unless it shall have been ratified as an amendment to the Constitution by the legislatures of three-fourths of the several States within seven years from the date of its submission.

## TWENTY-FIRST AMENDMENT (ratified December 5, 1933)

Section 1. The eighteenth article of amendment to the Constitution of the United States is hereby repealed.

Section 2. The transportation or importation into any State, Territory, or possession of the United States for delivery or use therein of intoxicating liquors, in violation of the laws thereof, is hereby prohibited.

Section 3. This article shall be inoperative unless it shall have been ratified as an amendment to the Constitution by conventions in the several States, as provided in the Constitution, within seven years from the date of the submission hereof to the States by the Congress.

## TWENTY-SECOND AMENDMENT (ratified February 27, 1951)

Section 1. No person shall be elected to the office of the President more than twice, and no person who has held the office of President, or acted as President, for more than two years of a term to which some other person was elected President shall be elected to the office of the President more than once. But this Article shall not apply to any person holding the office of President when this Article was proposed by the Congress, and shall not prevent any person who may be holding the office of President, or acting as President, during the term within which this Article becomes operative from holding the office of President or acting as President during the remainder of such term.

Section 2. This article shall be inoperative unless it shall have been ratified as an amendment to the Constitution by the legislatures of three-fourths of the several States within seven years from the date of its submission to the States by the Congress.

## TWENTY-THIRD AMENDMENT (ratified March 29, 1960)

Section 1. The District constituting the seat of Government of the United States shall appoint in such manner as the Congress may direct:

A number of electors of President and Vice President equal to the whole number of Senators and Representatives in Congress to which the District would be entitled if it were a State, but in no event more than the least populous State; they shall be in addition to those appointed by the States, but they shall be considered, for the purposes of the election of President and Vice President, to be electors appointed by a State; and they shall meet in the District and perform such duties as provided by the twelfth article of amendment.

Section 2. The Congress shall have power to enforce this article by appropriate legislation.

## TWENTY-FOURTH AMENDMENT (ratified January 23, 1964)

Section 1. The right of citizens of the United States to vote in any primary or other election for President or Vice President, for electors for President or Vice President, or for Senator or Representative in Congress, shall not be denied or abridged by the United States or any State by reason of failure to pay any poll tax or other tax.

Section 2. The Congress shall have power to enforce this article by appropriate legislation.

## TWENTY-FIFTH AMENDMENT (ratified February 10, 1967)

Section 1. In case of the removal of the President from office or of his death or resignation, the Vice President shall become President.

Section 2. Whenever there is a vacancy in the office of the Vice President, the President shall nominate a Vice President who shall take office upon confirmation by a majority vote of both Houses of Congress.

Section 3. Whenever the President transmits to the President pro tempore of the Senate and the Speaker of the House of Representatives his written declaration that he is unable to discharge the powers and duties of his office, and until he transmits to them a written declaration to the contrary, such powers and duties shall be discharged by the Vice President as Acting President.

Section 4. Whenever the Vice President and a majority of either the principal officers of the executive departments, or of such other body as Congress may by law provide, transmit to the President pro tempore of the Senate and the Speaker of the House of Representatives their written declaration that the President is unable to discharge the powers and duties of his office, the Vice President shall immediately assume the powers and duties of the office as Acting President.

Thereafter, when the President transmits to the President pro tempore of the Senate and the Speaker of the House of Representatives his written declaration that no inability exists, he shall resume the powers and duties of his office unless the Vice President and a majority of either the principal officers of the executive department, or of such other body as Congress may by law provide, transmit within four days to the President pro tempore of the Senate and the Speaker of the House of Representatives their written declaration that the President is unable to discharge the powers and duties of his office. Thereupon Congress shall decide the issue, assembling within forty-eight hours for that purpose if not in session. If the Congress, within twenty-one days after Congress is required to assemble, determines by two-thirds vote of both houses that the President is unable to discharge the powers and duties of his office, the Vice President shall continue to discharge the same as Acting President; otherwise, the President shall resume the powers and duties of his office.

## TWENTY-SIXTH AMENDMENT (ratified July 1, 1971)

Section 1. The right of citizens of the United States, who are eighteen years of age or older, to vote shall not be denied or abridged by the United States or any state on account of age.

Section 2. The Congress shall have power to enforce this article by appropriate legislation.

## TWENTY-SEVENTH AMENDMENT (ratified May 7, 1992)

No law, varying the compensation for the services of Senators and Representatives, shall take effect until an election of Representatives has intervened.

# APPENDIX

# D

# UNIFORM COMMERCIAL CODE ARTICLE 2—SALES
## (Selected Sections)

### SECTION 2-101. SHORT TITLE.

This Article shall be known and may be cited as Uniform Commercial Code—Sales.

### SECTION 2-102. SCOPE; CERTAIN SECURITY AND OTHER TRANSACTIONS EXCLUDED FROM THIS ARTICLE.

Unless the context otherwise requires, this Article applies to transactions in goods; it does not apply to any transaction which although in the form of an unconditional contract to sell or present sale is intended to operate only as a security transaction nor does this Article impair or repeal any statute regulating sales to consumers, farmers or other specified classes of buyers.

### SECTION 2-103. DEFINiTIONS AND INDEX OF DEFINITIONS.

(1) In this Article unless the context otherwise requires
   (a) "Buyer" means a person who buys or contracts to buy goods.
   (b) "Good faith" in the case of a merchant means honesty in fact and the observance of reasonable commercial standards of fair dealing in the trade.
   (c) "Receipt" of goods means taking physical possession of them.
   (d) "Seller" means a person who sells or contracts to sell goods.
(2) Other definitions applying to this Article or to specified Parts thereof, and the sections in which they appear are:
   "Acceptance." Section 2-606.
   "Banker's credit." Section 2-325.

"Between merchants." Section 2-104.
"Cancellation." Section 2-106 (4).
"Commercial unit." Section 2-105.
"Confirmed credit." Section 2-325.
"Conforming to contract." Section 2-106.
"Contract for sale." Section 2-106.
"Cover." Section 2-712.
"Entrusting." Section 2-403.
"Financing agency." Section 2-104.
"Future goods." Section 2-105.
"Goods." Section 2-105.
"Identification." Section 2-501.
"Installment contract." Section 2-612.
"Letter of Credit." Section 2-325.
"Lot." Section 2-105.
"Merchant." Section 2-104.
"Overseas." Section 2-323.
"Person in position of seller." Section 2-707.
"Present sale." Section 2-106.
"Sale." Section 2-106.
"Sale on approval." Section 2-326.
"Sale or return." Section 2-326.
"Termination." Section 2-106.

(3) The following definitions in other Articles apply to this Article:
"Check." Section 3-104.
"Consignor." Section 7-102.
"Consumer goods." Section 9-109.
"Dishonor." Section 3-507.
"Draft." Section 3-104.

(4) In addition Article 1 contains general definitions and principles of construction and interpretation applicable throughout this Article.

## SECTION 2-104. DEFINITIONS: "MERCHANT"; "BETWEEN MERCHANTS"; "FINANCING AGENCY."

(1) "Merchant" means a person who deals in goods of the kind or otherwise by his occupation holds himself out as having knowledge or skill peculiar to the practices or goods involved in the transaction or to whom such knowledge or skill may be attributed by his employment of an agent or broker or other intermediary who by his occupation holds himself out as having such knowledge or skill.

(2) "Financing agency" means a bank, finance company or other person who in the ordinary course of business makes advances against goods or documents of title or who by arrangement with either the seller or the buyer intervenes in ordinary course to make or collect payment due or claimed under the contract for sale, as by purchasing

or paying the seller's draft or making advances against it or by merely taking it for collection whether or not documents of title accompany the draft. "Financing agency" includes also a bank or other person who similarly intervenes between persons who are in the position of seller and buyer in respect to the goods (Section 2-707).

(3) "Between merchants" means in any transaction with respect to which both parties are chargeable with the knowledge or skill of merchants.

### SECTION 2-105. DEFINITIONS: TRANSFERABILITY; "GOODS"; "FUTURE" GOODS; "LOT"; "COMMERCIAL UNIT."

(1) "Goods" means all things (including specially manufactured goods) which are movable at the time of identification to the contract for sale other than the money in which the price is to be paid, investment securities (Article 8) and things in action. "Goods" also includes the unborn young of animals and growing crops and other identified things attached to realty as described in the section on goods to be severed from realty (Section 2-107).

(2) Goods must be both existing and identified before any interest in them can pass. Goods which are not both existing and identified are "future" goods. A purported present sale of future goods or of any interest therein operates as a contract to sell.

(3) There may be a sale of a part interest in existing identified goods.

(4) An undivided share in an identified bulk of fungible goods is sufficiently identified to be sold although the quantity of the bulk is not determined. Any agreed proportion of such a bulk or any quantity thereof agreed upon by number, weight or other measure may to the extent of the seller's interest in the bulk be sold to the buyer who then becomes an owner in common.

(5) "Lot" means a parcel or a single article which is the subject matter of a separate sale or delivery, whether or not it is sufficient to perform the contract.

(6) "Commercial unit" means such a unit of goods as by commercial usage is a single whole for purposes of sale and division of which materially impairs its character or value on the market or in use. A commercial unit may be a single article (as a machine) or a set of articles (as a suit of furniture or an assortment of sizes) or a quantity (as a bale, gross, or carload) or any other unit treated in use or in the relevant market as a single whole.

### SECTION 2-106. DEFINITIONS. "CONTRACT"; "AGREEMENT"; "CONTRACT FOR SALE"; "SALE"; "PRESENT SALE"; "CONFORMING" TO CONTRACT; "TERMINATION"; "CANCELLATION."

(1) In this Article unless the context otherwise requires "contract" and "agreement" are limited to those relating to the present or future sale of goods. "Contract for sale" includes both a present sale of goods and a contract to sell goods at a future time. A "sale" consists in the passing of title from the seller to the buyer for a price (Section 2-401). A "present sale" means a sale which is accomplished by the making of the contract.

(2) Goods or conduct including any part of a performance are "conforming" or conform to the contract when they are in accordance with the obligations under the contract.

(3) "Termination" occurs when either party pursuant to a power created by agreement or law puts an end to the contract otherwise than for its breach. On "termination" all obligations which are still executory on both sides are discharged but any right based on prior breach or performance survives.

(4) "Cancellation" occurs when either party puts an end to the contract for breach by the other and its effect is the same as that of "termination" except that the canceling party also retains any remedy for breach of the whole contract or any unperformed balance.

## SECTION 2-107. GOODS TO BE SEVERED FROM REALTY, RECORDING.

(1) A contract for the sale of minerals or the like (including oil and gas) or a structure or its materials to be removed from realty is a contract for the sale of goods within this Article if they are to be severed by the seller but until severance a purported present sale thereof which is not effective as a transfer of an interest in land is effective only as a contract to sell.

(2) A contract for the sale apart from the land of growing crops or other things attached to realty and capable of severance without material harm thereto but not described in subsection (1) or of timber to be cut is a contract for the sale of goods within this Article whether the subject matter is to be severed by the buyer or by the seller even though it forms part of the realty at the time of contracting, and the parties can by identification effect a present sale before severance.

(3) The provisions of this section are subject to any third party rights provided by the law relating to realty records, and the contract for sale may be executed and recorded as a document transferring an interest in land and shall then constitute notice to third parties of the buyer's rights under the contract for sale.

## SECTION 2-201. FORMAL REQUIREMENTS; STATUTE OF FRAUDS.

(1) Except as otherwise provided in this section a contract for the sale of goods for the price of $500 or more is not enforceable by way of action or defense unless there is some writing sufficient to indicate that a contract for sale has been made between the parties and signed by the party against whom enforcement is sought or by his authorized agent or broker. A writing is not insufficient because it omits or incorrectly states a term agreed upon but the contract is not enforceable under this paragraph beyond the quantity of goods shown in such writing.

(2) Between merchants if within a reasonable time a writing in confirmation of the contract and sufficient against the sender is received and the party receiving it has reason to know its contents, it satisfies the requirements of subsection (1) against such party unless written notice of objection to its contents is given within ten days after it is received.

(3) A contract which does not satisfy the requirements of subsection (1) but which is valid in other respects is enforceable

(a) if the goods are to be specially manufactured for the buyer and are not suitable for sale to others in the ordinary course of the seller's business and the seller, before notice of repudiation is received and under circumstances which reasonably indicate that the goods are for the buyer, has made either a substantial beginning of their manufacture or commitments for their procurement; or

(b) if the party against whom enforcement is sought admits in his pleading, testimony or otherwise in court that a contract for sale was made, but the contract is not enforceable under this provision beyond the quantity of goods admitted; or

(c) with respect to goods for which payment has been made and accepted or which have been received and accepted (Section 2-606).

## SECTION 2-202. FINAL WRITTEN EXPRESSION, PAROL OR EXTRINSIC EVIDENCE.

Terms with respect to which the confirmatory memoranda of the parties agree or which are otherwise set forth in a writing intended by the parties as a final expression of their agreement with respect to such terms as are included therein may not be contradicted by evidence of any prior agreement or of a contemporaneous oral agreement but may be explained or supplemented

(a) by course of dealing or usage of trade (Section 1-205) or by course of performance (Section 2-208); and

(b) by evidence of consistent additional terms unless the court finds the writing to have been intended also as a complete and exclusive statement of the terms of the agreement.

## SECTION 2-203. SEALS INOPERATIVE.

The affixing of a seal to a writing evidencing a contract for sale or an offer to buy or sell goods does not constitute the writing a sealed instrument and the law with respect to sealed instruments does not apply to such a contract or offer.

## SECTION 2-204. FORMATION IN GENERAL.

(1) A contract for sale of goods may be made in any manner sufficient to show agreement, including conduct by both parties which recognizes the existence of such a contract.

(2) An agreement sufficient to constitute a contract for sale may be found even though the moment of its making is undetermined.

(3) Even though one or more terms are left open a contract for sale does not fail for indefiniteness if the parties have intended to make a contract and there is a reasonably certain basis for giving an appropriate remedy.

## SECTION 2-205. FIRM OFFERS.

An offer by a merchant to buy or sell goods in a signed writing which by its terms gives assurance that it will be held open is not revocable, for lack of consideration, during the time stated or if no time is stated for a reasonable time, but in no event may such period of irrevocability exceed three months; but any such term of assurance on a form supplied by the offeree must be separately signed by the offeror.

## SECTION 2-206. OFFER AND ACCEPTANCE IN FORMATION OF CONTRACT.

(1) Unless otherwise unambiguously indicated by the language or circumstances
  (a) an offer to make a contract shall be construed as inviting acceptance in any manner and by any medium reasonable in the circumstances;
  (b) an order or other offer to buy goods for prompt or current shipment shall be construed as inviting acceptance either by a prompt promise to ship or by the prompt or current shipment of conforming or non-conforming goods, but such a shipment of non-conforming goods does not constitute an acceptance if the seller seasonably notifies the buyer that the shipment is offered only as an accommodation to the buyer.

(2) Where the beginning of a requested performance is a reasonable mode of acceptance an offeror who is not notified of acceptance within a reasonable time may treat the offer as having lapsed before acceptance.

## SECTION 2-207. ADDITIONAL TERMS IN ACCEPTANCE OR CONFIRMATION.

(1) A definite and seasonable expression of acceptance or a written confirmation which is sent within a reasonable time operates as an acceptance even though it states terms additional to or different from those offered or agreed upon, unless acceptance is expressly made conditional on assent to the additional or different terms.

(2) The additional terms are to be construed as proposals for addition to the contract. Between merchants such terms become part of the contract unless:
  (a) the offer expressly limits acceptance to the terms of the offer;
  (b) they materially alter it; or
  (c) notification of objection to them has already been given or is given within a reasonable time after notice of them is received.

(3) Conduct by both parties which recognizes the existence of a contract is sufficient to establish a contract for sale although the writings of the parties do not otherwise establish a contract. In such case the terms of the particular contract consist of those terms on which the writings of the parties agree, together with any supplementary terms incorporated under any other provisions of this Act.

## SECTION 2-208. COURSE OF PERFORMANCE OR PRACTICAL CONSTRUCTION.

(1) Where the contract for sale involves repeated occasions for performance by either party with knowledge of the nature of the performance and opportunity for objection to it by the other, any course of performance accepted or acquiesced in without objection shall be relevant to determine the meaning of the agreement.

(2) The express terms of the agreement and any such course of performance, as well as any course of dealing and usage of trade, shall be construed whenever reasonable as consistent with each other; but when such construction is unreasonable, express terms shall control course of performance and course of performance shall control both course of dealing and usage of trade (Section 1-205).

(3) Subject to the provisions of the next section on modification and waiver, such course of performance shall be relevant to show a waiver or modification of any term inconsistent with such course of performance.

## SECTION 2-209. MODIFICATION, RESCISSION AND WAIVER.

(1) An agreement modifying a contract within this Article needs no consideration to be binding.

(2) A signed agreement which excludes modification or rescission except by a signed writing cannot be otherwise modified or rescinded, but except as between merchants such a requirement on a form supplied by the merchant must be separately signed by the other party.

(3) The requirements of the statute of frauds section of this Article (Section 2-201) must be satisfied if the contract as modified is within its provisions.

(4) Although an attempt at modification or rescission does not satisfy the requirements of subsection (2) or (3) it can operate as a waiver.

(5) A party who has made a waiver affecting an executory portion of the contract may retract the waiver by reasonable notification received by the other party that strict performance will be required of any term waived, unless the retraction would be unjust in view of a material change of position in reliance on the waiver.

## SECTION 2-210. DELEGATION OF PERFORMANCE; ASSIGNMENT OF RIGHTS.

(1) A party may perform his duty through a delegate unless otherwise agreed or unless the other party has a substantial interest in having his original promisor perform or control the acts required by the contract. No delegation of performance relieves the party delegating of any duty to perform or any liability for breach.

(2) Unless otherwise agreed all rights of either seller or buyer can be assigned except where the assignment would materially change the duty of the other party, or increase materially the burden or risk imposed on him by his contract, or impair materially his chance of obtaining return performance. A right to damages for breach of the whole contract or a right arising out of the assignor's due performance of his entire obligation can be assigned despite agreement otherwise.

(3) Unless the circumstances indicate the contrary a prohibition of assignment of "the contract" is to be construed as barring only the delegation to the assignee of the assignor's performance.

(4) An assignment of "the contract" or of "all my rights under the contract" or an assignment in similar general terms is an assignment of rights and unless the language or the circumstances (as in an assignment for security) indicate the contrary, it is a delegation of performance of the duties of the assignor and its acceptance by the assignee constitutes a promise by him to perform those duties. This promise is enforceable by either the assignor or the other party to the original contract.

(5) The other party may treat any assignment which delegates performance as creating reasonable grounds for insecurity and may without prejudice to his rights against the assignor demand assurances from the assignee (Section 2-609).

## SECTION 2-301. GENERAL OBLIGATIONS OF PARTIES.

The obligation of the seller is to transfer and deliver and that of the buyer is to accept and pay in accordance with the contract.

## SECTION 2-302. UNCONSCIONABLE CONTRACT OR CLAUSE.

(1) If the court as a matter of law finds the contract or any clause of the contract to have been unconscionable at the time it was made the court may refuse to enforce the contract, or it may enforce the remainder of the contract without the unconscionable clause, or it may so limit the application of any unconscionable clause as to avoid any unconscionable result.

(2) When it is claimed or appears to the court that the contract or any clause thereof may be unconscionable the parties shall be afforded a reasonable opportunity to present evidence as to its commercial setting, purpose and effect to aid the court in making the determination.

## SECTION 2-303. ALLOCATION OR DIVISION OF RISKS.

Where this Article allocates a risk or a burden as between the parties "unless otherwise agreed," the agreement may not only shift the allocation but may also divide the risk or burden.

## SECTION 2-304. PRICE PAYABLE IN MONEY, GOODS, REALTY, OR OTHERWISE.

(1) The price can be made payable in money or otherwise. If it is payable in whole or in part in goods each party is a seller of the goods which he is to transfer.

(2) Even though all or part of the price is payable in an interest in realty the transfer of the goods and the seller's obligations with reference to them are subject to this Article, but not the transfer of the interest in realty or the transferor's obligations in connection therewith.

## SECTION 2-305. OPEN PRICE TERM.

(1) The parties if they so intend can conclude a contract for sale even though the price is not settled. In such a case the price is a reasonable price at the time for delivery if
    (a) nothing is said as to price; or
    (b) the price is left to be agreed by the parties and they fail to agree; or
    (c) the price is to be fixed in terms of some agreed market or other standard as set or recorded by a third person or agency and it is not so set or recorded.

(2) A price to be fixed by the seller or by the buyer means a price for him to fix in good faith.

(3) When a price left to be fixed otherwise than by agreement of the parties fails to be fixed through fault of one party the other may at his option treat the contract as canceled or himself fix a reasonable price.

(4) Where, however, the parties intend not to be bound unless the price be fixed or agreed and it is not fixed or agreed there is no contract. In such a case the buyer must return any goods already received or if unable so to do must pay their reasonable value at the time of delivery and the seller must return any portion of the price paid on account.

## SECTION 2-306. OUTPUT, REQUIREMENTS AND EXCLUSIVE DEALINGS.

(1) A term which measures the quantity by the output of the seller or the requirements of the buyer means such actual output or requirements as may occur in good faith, except that no quantity unreasonably disproportionate to any stated estimate or in the absence of a stated estimate to any normal or otherwise comparable prior output or requirements may be tendered or demanded.

(2) A lawful agreement by either the seller or the buyer for exclusive dealing in the kind of goods concerned imposes unless otherwise agreed an obligation by the seller to use best efforts to supply the goods and by the buyer to use best efforts to promote their sale.

## SECTION 2-307. DELIVERY IN SINGLE LOT OR SEVERAL LOTS.

Unless otherwise agreed all goods called for by a contract for sale must be tendered in a single delivery and payment is due only on such tender but where the circumstances give either party the right to make or demand delivery in lots the price if it can be apportioned may be demanded for each lot.

## SECTION 2-308. ABSENCE OF SPECIFIED PLACE FOR DELIVERY.

Unless otherwise agreed
    (a) the place for delivery of goods is the seller's place of business or if he has none his residence; but

(b) in a contract for sale of identified goods which to the knowledge of the parties at the time of contracting are in some other place, that place is the place for their delivery; and

(c) documents of title may be delivered through customary banking channels.

## SECTION 2-309. ABSENCE OF SPECIFIC TIME PROVISIONS; NOTICE OF TERMINATION.

(1) The time for shipment or delivery or any other action under a contract if not provided in this Article or agreed upon shall be a reasonable time.

(2) Where the contract provides for successive performances but is indefinite in duration it is valid for a reasonable time but unless otherwise agreed may be terminated at any time by either party.

(3) Termination of a contract by one party except on the happening of an agreed event requires that reasonable notification be received by the other party and an agreement dispensing with notification is invalid if its operation would be unconscionable.

## SECTION 2-310. OPEN TIME FOR PAYMENT OR RUNNING OF CREDIT; AUTHORITY TO SHIP UNDER RESERVATION.

Unless otherwise agreed

(a) payment is due at the time and place at which the buyer is to receive the goods even though the place of shipment is the place of delivery; and

(b) if the seller is authorized to send the goods he may ship them under reservation, and may tender the documents of title, but the buyer may inspect the goods after their arrival before payment is due unless such inspection is inconsistent with the terms of the contract (Section 2-513); and

(c) if delivery is authorized and made by way of documents of title otherwise than by subsection (b) then payment is due at the time and place at which the buyer is to receive the documents regardless of where the goods are to be received; and

(d) where the seller is required or authorized to ship the goods on credit the credit period runs from the time of shipment but post-dating the invoice or delaying its dispatch will correspondingly delay the starting of the credit period.

## SECTION 2-311. OPTIONS AND COOPERATION RESPECTING PERFORMANCE.

(1) An agreement for sale which is otherwise sufficiently definite (subsection (3) of Section 2-204) to be a contract is not made invalid by the fact that it leaves particulars of performance to be specified by one of the parties. Any such specification must be made in good faith and within limits set by commercial reasonableness.

(2) Unless otherwise agreed specifications relating to assortment of the goods are at the buyer's option and except as otherwise provided in subsections (1)(c) and (3) of Section 2-319 specifications or arrangements relating to shipment are at the seller's option.

(3) Where such specification would materially affect the other party's performance but is not seasonably made or where one party's cooperation is necessary to the agreed performance of the other but is not seasonably forthcoming, the other party in addition to all other remedies

    (a) is excused for any resulting delay in his own performance; and

    (b) may also either proceed to perform in any reasonable manner or after the time for a material part of his own performance treat the failure to specify or to cooperate as a breach by failure to deliver or accept the goods.

## SECTION 2-312. WARRANTY OF TITLE AND AGAINST INFRINGEMENT; BUYER'S OBLIGATION AGAINST INFRINGEMENT.

(1) Subject to subsection (2) there is in a contract for sale a warranty by the seller that

    (a) the title conveyed shall be good, and its transfer rightful; and

    (b) the goods shall be delivered free from any security interest or other lien or encumbrance of which the buyer at the time of contracting has no knowledge.

(2) A warranty under subsection (1) will be excluded or modified only by specific language or by circumstances which give the buyer reason to know that the person selling does not claim title in himself or that he is purporting to sell only such right or title as he or a third person may have.

(3) Unless otherwise agreed a seller who is a merchant regularly dealing in goods of the kind warrants that the goods shall be delivered free of the rightful claim of any third person by way of infringement or the like but a buyer who furnishes specifications to the seller must hold the seller harmless against any such claim which arises out of compliance with the specifications.

## SECTION 2-313. EXPRESS WARRANTIES BY AFFIRMATION, PROMISE, DESCRIPTION, SAMPLE.

(1) Express warranties by the seller are created as follows:

    (a) Any affirmation of fact or promise made by the seller to the buyer which relates to the goods and becomes part of the basis of the bargain creates an express warranty that the goods shall conform to the affirmation or promise.

    (b) Any description of the goods which is made part of the basis of the bargain creates an express warranty that the goods shall conform to the description.

    (c) Any sample or model which is made part of the basis of the bargain creates an express warranty that the whole of the goods shall conform to the sample or model.

(2) It is not necessary to the creation of an express warranty that the seller use formal words such as "warrant" or "guarantee" or that he have a specific intention to make a warranty, but an affirmation merely of the value of the goods or a statement pur-

porting to be merely the seller's opinion or commendation of the goods does not create a warranty.

## SECTION 2-314. IMPLIED WARRANTY: MERCHANTIBILITY; USAGE OF TRADE.

(1) Unless excluded or modified (Section 2-316), a warranty that the goods shall be merchantable is implied in a contract for their sale if the seller is a merchant with respect to goods of that kind. Under this section the serving for value of food or drink to be consumed either on the premises or elsewhere is a sale.

(2) Goods to be merchantable must be at least such as
  (a) pass without objection in the trade under the contract description; and
  (b) in the case of fungible goods, are of fair average quality within the description; and
  (c) are fit for the ordinary purposes for which such goods are used; and
  (d) run, within the variations permitted by the agreement, of even kind, quality and quantity within each unit and among all units involved; and
  (e) are adequately contained, packaged, and labeled as the agreement may require; and
  (f) conform to the promises or affirmations of fact made on the container or label if any.

(3) Unless excluded or modified (Section 2-316) other implied warranties may arise from course of dealing or usage of trade.

## SECTION 2-315. IMPLIED WARRANTY: FITNESS FOR PARTICULAR PURPOSE.

Where the seller at the time of contracting has reason to know any particular purpose for which the goods are required and that the buyer is relying on the seller's skill or judgment to select or furnish suitable goods, there is unless excluded or modified under the next section an implied warranty that the goods shall be fit for such purpose.

## SECTION 2-316. EXCLUSION OR MODIFICATION OF WARRANTIES.

(1) Words or conduct relevant to the creation of an express warranty and words or conduct tending to negate or limit warranty shall be construed wherever reasonable as consistent with each other; but subject to the provisions of this Article on parol or extrinsic evidence (Section 2-202) negation or limitation is inoperative to the extent that such construction is unreasonable.

(2) Subject to subsection (3), to exclude or modify the implied warranty of merchantability or any part of it the language must mention merchantability and in case of a writing must be conspicuous, and to exclude or modify any implied warranty of fitness the exclusion must be by a writing and conspicuous. Language to exclude all implied warranties of fitness is sufficient if it states, for example, that "There are no warranties which extend beyond the description on the face hereof."

(3) Notwithstanding subsection (2)

    (a) unless the circumstances indicate otherwise, all implied warranties are excluded by expressions like "as is," "with all faults" or other language which in common understanding calls the buyer's attention to the exclusion of warranties and makes plain that there is no implied warranty; and

    (b) when the buyer before entering into the contract has examined the goods or the sample or model as fully as he desired or has refused to examine the goods there is no implied warranty with regard to defects which an examination ought in the circumstances to have revealed to him; and

    (c) an implied warranty can also be excluded or modified by course of dealing or course of performance or usage of trade.

(4) Remedies for breach of warranty can be limited in accordance with the provisions of this Article on liquidation or limitation of damages and on contractual modification of remedy (Sections 2-718 and 2-719).

## SECTION 2-317. CUMULATION AND CONFLICT OF WARRANTIES EXPRESS OR IMPLIED.

Warranties whether express or implied shall be construed as consistent with each other and as cumulative, but if such construction is unreasonable the intention of the parties shall determine which warranty is dominant. In ascertaining that intention the following rules apply:

    (a) Exact or technical specifications displace an inconsistent sample or model or general language of description.

    (b) A sample from an existing bulk displaces inconsistent general language of description.

    (c) Express warranties displace inconsistent implied warranties other than an implied warranty of fitness for a particular purpose.

## SECTION 2-318. THIRD PARTY BENEFICIARIES OF WARRANTIES EXPRESS OR IMPLIED.

A seller's warranty whether express or implied extends to any natural person if it is reasonable to expect that such person may use, consume or be affected by the goods and who is injured in person by breach of the warranty. A seller may not exclude or limit the operation of this section.

## SECTION 2-319. F. O. B. AND F. A. S. TERMS.

(1) Unless otherwise agreed the term F. O. B. (which means "free on board") at a named place, even though used only in connection with the stated price, is a delivery term under which

    (a) when the term is F. O. B. the place of shipment, the seller must at that place ship the goods in the manner provided in this Article (Section 2-

504) and bear the expense and risk of putting them into the possession of the carrier; or

(b) when the term is F. O. B. the place of destination, the seller must at his own expense and risk transport the goods to that place and there tender delivery of them in the manner provided in this Article (Section 2-503);

(c) when under either (a) or (b) the term is also F. O. B. vessel, car or other vehicle, the seller must in addition at his own expense and risk load the goods on board. If the term is F. O. B. vessel the buyer must name the vessel and in an appropriate case the seller must comply with the provisions of this Article on the form of bill of lading (Section 2-323).

(2) Unless otherwise agreed the term F. A. S. vessel (which means "free alongside") at a named port, even though used only in connection with the stated price, is a delivery term under which the seller must

(a) at his own expense and risk deliver the goods alongside the vessel in the manner usual in that port or on a dock designated and provided by the buyer; and

(b) obtain and tender a receipt for the goods in exchange for which the carrier is under a duty to issue a bill of lading.

(3) Unless otherwise agreed in any case falling within subsection (1)(a) or (c) or subsection (2) the buyer must seasonably give any needed instructions for making delivery, including when the term is F. A. S. or F. O. B. the loading berth of the vessel and in an appropriate case its name and sailing date. The seller may treat the failure of needed instructions as a failure of cooperation under this Article (Section 2-311). He may also at his option move the goods in any reasonable manner preparatory to delivery or shipment.

(4) Under the term F. O. B. vessel or F. A. S. unless otherwise agreed the buyer must make payment against tender of the required documents and the seller may not tender nor the buyer demand delivery of the goods in substitution for the documents.

## SECTION 2-320. C. I. F. AND C. & F. TERMS.

(1) The term C. I. F. means that the price includes in a lump sum the cost of the goods and the insurance and freight to the named destination. The term C. & F. or C. F. means that the price so includes cost and freight to the named destination.

(2) Unless otherwise agreed and even though used only in connection with the stated price and destination, the term C. I. F. destination or its equivalent requires the seller at his own expense and risk to

(a) put the goods into the possession of a carrier at the port for shipment and obtain a negotiable bill or bills of lading covering the entire transportation to the named destination; and

(b) load the goods and obtain a receipt from the carrier (which may be contained in the bill of lading) showing that the freight has been paid or provided for; and

    (c) obtain a policy or certificate of insurance, including any war risk insurance, of a kind and on terms then current at the port of shipment in the usual amount, in the currency of the contract, shown to cover the same goods covered by the bill of lading and providing for payment of loss to the order of the buyer or for the account of whom it may concern; but the seller may add to the price the amount of the premium for any such war risk insurance; and

    (d) prepare an invoice of the goods and procure any other documents required to effect shipment or to comply with the contract; and

    (e) forward and tender with commercial promptness all the documents in due form and with any indorsement necessary to perfect the buyer's rights.

(3) Unless otherwise agreed the term C. & F. or its equivalent has the same effect and imposes upon the seller the same obligations and risks as a C. I. F. term except the obligation as to insurance.

(4) Under the term C. I. F. or C. & F. unless otherwise agreed the buyer must make payment against tender of the required documents and the seller may not tender nor the buyer demand delivery of the goods in substitution for the documents.

## SECTION 2-324. "NO ARRIVAL, NO SALE" TERM.

Under a term "no arrival, no sale" or terms of like meaning, unless otherwise agreed,

    (a) the seller must properly ship conforming goods and if they arrive by any means he must tender them on arrival but he assumes no obligation that the goods will arrive unless he has caused the non-arrival; and

    (b) where without fault of the seller the goods are in part lost or have so deteriorated as no longer to conform to the contract or arrive after the contract time, the buyer may proceed as if there had been casualty to identified goods (Section 2-613).

## SECTION 2-325. "LETTER OF CREDIT" TERM; "CONFIRMED CREDIT."

(1) Failure of the buyer seasonably to furnish an agreed letter of credit is a breach of the contract for sale.

(2) The delivery to seller of a proper letter of credit suspends the buyer's obligation to pay. If the letter of credit is dishonored, the seller may on seasonable notification to the buyer require payment directly from him.

(3) Unless otherwise agreed the term "letter of credit" or "banker's credit" in a contract for sale means an irrevocable credit issued by a financing agency of good repute and, where the shipment is overseas, of good international repute. The term "confirmed credit" means that the credit must also carry the direct obligation of such an agency which does business in the seller's financial market.

## SECTION 2-326. SALE ON APPROVAL AND SALE OR RETURN; CONSIGNMENT SALES AND RIGHTS OF CREDITORS.

(1) Unless otherwise agreed, if delivered goods may be returned by the buyer even though they conform to the contract, the transaction is

    (a) a "sale on approval" if the goods are delivered primarily for use, and

    (b) a "sale or return" if the goods are delivered primarily for resale.

(2) Except as provided in subsection (3), goods held on approval are not subject to the claims of the buyer's creditors until acceptance; goods held on sale or return are subject to such claims while in the buyer's possession.

(3) Where goods are delivered to a person for sale and such person maintains a place of business at which he deals in goods of the kind involved, under a name other than the name of the person making delivery, then with respect to claims of creditors of the person conducting the business the goods are deemed to be on sale or return. The provisions of this subsection are applicable even though an agreement purports to reserve title to the person making delivery until payment or resale or uses such words as "on consignment" or "on memorandum". However, this subsection is not applicable if the person making delivery

    (a) complies with an applicable law providing for a consignor's interest or the like to be evidenced by a sign, or

    (b) establishes that the person conducting the business is generally known by his creditors to be substantially engaged in selling the goods of others, or

    (c) complies with the filing provisions of the Article on Secured Transactions (Article 9).

(4) Any "or return" term of a contract for sale is to be treated as a separate contract for sale within the statute of frauds section of this Article (Section 2-201) and as contradicting the sale aspect of the contract within the provisions of this Article on parol or extrinsic evidence (Section 2-202).

## SECTION 2-327. SPECIAL INCIDENTS OF SALE ON APPROVAL AND SALE OR RETURN.

(1) Under a sale on approval unless otherwise agreed

    (a) although the goods are identified to the contract the risk of loss and the title do not pass to the buyer until acceptance; and

    (b) use of the goods consistent with the purpose of trial is not acceptance but failure seasonably to notify the seller of election to return the goods is acceptance, and if the goods conform to the contract acceptance of any part is acceptance of the whole; and

    (c) after due notification of election to return, the return is at the seller's risk and expense but a merchant buyer must follow any reasonable instructions.

(2) Under a sale or return unless otherwise agreed

(a) the option to return extends to the whole or any commercial unit of the goods while in substantially their original condition, but must be exercised seasonably; and

(b) the return is at the buyer's risk and expense.

### SECTION 2-328. SALE BY AUCTION.

(1) In a sale by auction if goods are put up in lots each lot is the subject of a separate sale.

(2) A sale by auction is complete when the auctioneer so announces by the fall of the hammer or in other customary manner. Where a bid is made while the hammer is falling in acceptance of a prior bid the auctioneer may in his discretion reopen the bidding or declare the goods sold under the bid on which the hammer was falling.

(3) Such a sale is with reserve unless the goods are in explicit terms put up without reserve. In an auction with reserve the auctioneer may withdraw the goods at any time until he announces completion of the sale. In an auction without reserve, after the auctioneer calls for bids on an article or lot, that article or lot cannot be withdrawn unless no bid is made within a reasonable time. In either case a bidder may retract his bid until the auctioneer's announcement of completion of the sale, but a bidder's retraction does not revive any previous bid.

(4) If the auctioneer knowingly receives a bid on the seller's behalf or the seller makes or procures such a bid, and notice has not been given that liberty for such bidding is reserved, the buyer may at his option avoid the sale or take the goods at the price of the last good faith bid prior to the completion of the sale. This subsection shall not apply to any bid at a forced sale.

### SECTION 2-402. RIGHTS OF SELLER'S CREDITORS AGAINST SOLD GOODS.

(1) Except as provided in subsections (2) and (3), rights of unsecured creditors of the seller with respect to goods which have been identified to a contract for sale are subject to the buyer's rights to recover the goods under this Article (Sections 2-502 and 2-716).

(2) A creditor of the seller may treat a sale or an identification of goods to a contract for sale as void if as against him a retention of possession by the seller is fraudulent under any rule of law of the state where the goods are situated, except that retention of possession in good faith and current course of trade by a merchant-seller for a commercially reasonable time after a sale or identification is not fraudulent.

(3) Nothing in this Article shall be deemed to impair the rights of creditors of the seller

(a) under the provisions of the Article on Secured Transactions (Article 9); or

(b) where identification to the contract or delivery is made not in current course of trade but in satisfaction of or as security for a pre-existing claim for money, security or the like and is made under circumstances which under any rule of law of the state where the goods are situated would apart from this Article constitute the transaction a fraudulent transfer or voidable preference.

## SECTION 2-403. POWER TO TRANSFER; GOOD FAITH PURCHASE OF GOODS; "ENTRUSTING."

(1) A purchaser of goods acquires all title which his transferor had or had power to transfer except that a purchaser of a limited interest acquires rights only to the extent of the interest purchased. A person with voidable title has power to transfer a good title to a good faith purchaser for value. When goods have been delivered under a transaction of purchase the purchaser has such power even though

    (a) the transferor was deceived as to the identity of the purchaser, or

    (b) the delivery was in exchange for a check which is later dishonored, or

    (c) it was agreed that the transaction was to be a "cash sale," or

    (d) the delivery was procured through fraud punishable as larcenous under the criminal law.

(2) Any entrusting of possession of goods to a merchant who deals in goods of that kind gives him power to transfer all rights of the entruster to a buyer in ordinary course of business.

(3) "Entrusting" includes any delivery and any acquiescence in retention of possession regardless of any condition expressed between the parties to the delivery or acquiescence and regardless of whether the procurement of the entrusting or the possessor's disposition of the goods has been such as to be larcenous under the criminal law.

(4) The rights of other purchasers of goods and of lien creditors are governed by the Articles on Secured Transactions (Article 9), Bulk Transfers (Article 6) and Documents of Title (Article 7).

## SECTION 2-501. INSURABLE INTEREST IN GOODS; MANNER OF IDENTIFICATION OF GOODS.

(1) The buyer obtains a special property and an insurable interest in goods by identification of existing goods as goods to which the contract refers even though the goods so identified are non-conforming and he has an option to return or reject them. Such identification can be made at any time and in any manner explicitly agreed to by the parties. In the absence of explicit agreement identification occurs

    (a) when the contract is made if it is for the sale of goods already existing and identified;

    (b) if the contract is for the sale of future goods other than those described in paragraph (c), when goods are shipped, marked or otherwise designated by the seller as goods to which the contract refers;

    (c) when the crops are planted or otherwise become growing crops or the young are conceived if the contract is for the sale of unborn young to be born within twelve months after contracting or for the sale of crops to be harvested within twelve months or the next normal harvest season after contracting whichever is longer.

(2) The seller retains an insurable interest in goods so long as title to or any security interest in the goods remains in him and where the identification is by the seller alone he may until default or insolvency or notification to the buyer that the identification is final substitute other goods for those identified.

(3) Nothing in this section impairs any insurable interest recognized under any other statute or rule of law.

## SECTION 2-502. BUYER'S RIGHT TO GOODS ON SELLER'S INSOLVENCY.

(1) Subject to subsection (2) and even though the goods have not been shipped a buyer who has paid a part or all of the price of goods in which he has a special property under the provisions of the immediately preceding section may on making and keeping good a tender of any unpaid portion of their price recover them from the seller if the seller becomes insolvent within ten days after receipt of the first installment on their price.

(2) If the identification creating his special property has been made by the buyer he acquires the right to recover the goods only if they conform to the contract for sale.

## SECTION 2-503. MANNER OF SELLER'S TENDER OF DELIVERY.

(1) Tender of delivery requires that the seller put and hold conforming goods at the buyer's disposition and give the buyer any notification reasonably necessary to enable him to take delivery. The manner, time and place for tender are determined by the agreement and this Article, and in particular

    (a) tender must be at a reasonable hour, and if it is of goods they must be kept available for the period reasonably necessary to enable the buyer to take possession; but

    (b) unless otherwise agreed the buyer must furnish facilities reasonably suited to the receipt of the goods.

(2) Where the case is within the next section respecting shipment tender requires that the seller comply with its provisions.

(3) Where the seller is required to deliver at a particular destination tender requires that he comply with subsection (1) and also in any appropriate case tender documents as described in subsections (4) and (5) of this section.

(4) Where goods are in the possession of a bailee and are to be delivered without being moved

    (a) tender requires that the seller either tender a negotiable document of title covering such goods or procure acknowledgment by the bailee of the buyer's right to possession of the goods; but

    (b) tender to the buyer of a non-negotiable document of title or of a written direction to the bailee to deliver is sufficient tender unless the buyer seasonably objects, and receipt by the bailee of notification of the buyer's rights fixes those rights as against the bailee and all third persons; but risk of loss of the goods and of any failure by the bailee to honor the non-negotiable document of title or to obey the direction remains on the seller until the buyer has had a reasonable time to present the document or direction, and a refusal by the bailee to honor the document or to obey the direction defeats the tender.

(5) Where the contract requires the seller to deliver documents

(a) he must tender all such documents in correct form, except as provided in this Article with respect to bills of lading in a set (subsection (2) of Section 2-323); and

(b) tender through customary banking channels is sufficient and dishonor of a draft accompanying the documents constitutes non-acceptance or rejection.

## SECTION 2-504. SHIPMENT BY SELLER.

Where the seller is required or authorized to send the goods to the buyer and the contract does not require him to deliver them at a particular destination, then unless otherwise agreed he must

(a) put the goods in the possession of such a carrier and make such a contract for their transportation as may be reasonable having regard to the nature of the goods and other circumstances of the case; and

(b) obtain and promptly deliver or tender in due form any document necessary to enable the buyer to obtain possession of the goods or otherwise required by the agreement or by usage of trade; and

(c) promptly notify the buyer of the shipment.

Failure to notify the buyer under paragraph (c) or to make a proper contract under paragraph (a) is a ground for rejection only if material delay or loss ensues.

## SECTION 2-505. SELLER'S SHIPMENT UNDER RESERVATION.

(1) Where the seller has identified goods to the contract by or before shipment:

(a) his procurement of a negotiable bill of lading to his own order or otherwise reserves in him a security interest in the goods. His procurement of the bill to the order of a financing agency or of the buyer indicates in addition only the seller's expectation of transferring that interest to the person named.

(b) a non-negotiable bill of lading to himself or his nominee reserves possession of the goods as security but except in a case of conditional delivery (subsection (2) of Section 2-507) a non-negotiable bill of lading naming the buyer as consignee reserves no security interest even though the seller retains possession of the bill of lading.

(2) When shipment by the seller with reservation of a security interest is in violation of the contract for sale it constitutes an improper contract for transportation within the preceding section but impairs neither the rights given to the buyer by

shipment and identification of the goods to the contract nor the seller's powers as a holder of a negotiable document.

## SECTION 2-507. EFFECT OF SELLER'S TENDER; DELIVERY ON CONDITION.

(1) Tender of delivery is a condition to the buyer's duty to accept the goods and, unless otherwise agreed, to his duty to pay for them. Tender entitles the seller to acceptance of the goods and to payment according to the contract.

(2) Where payment is due and demanded on the delivery to the buyer of goods or documents of title, his right as against the seller to retain or dispose of them is conditional upon his making the payment due.

## SECTION 2-508. CURE BY SELLER OF IMPROPER TENDER OR DELIVERY; REPLACEMENT.

(1) Where any tender or delivery by the seller is rejected because non-conforming and the time for performance has not yet expired, the seller may seasonably notify the buyer of his intention to cure and may then within the contract time make a conforming delivery.

(2) Where the buyer rejects a non-conforming tender which the seller had reasonable grounds to believe would be acceptable with or without money allowance the seller may if he seasonably notifies the buyer have a further reasonable time to substitute a conforming tender.

## SECTION 2-509. RISK OF LOSS IN THE ABSENCE OF BREACH.

(1) Where the contract requires or authorizes the seller to ship the goods by carrier
  (a) if it does not require him to deliver them at a particular destination, the risk of loss passes to the buyer when the goods are duly delivered to the carrier even though the shipment is under reservation (Section 2-505); but
  (b) if it does require him to deliver them at a particular destination and the goods are there duly tendered while in the possession of the carrier, the risk of loss passes to the buyer when the goods are there duly so tendered as to enable the buyer to take delivery.

(2) Where the goods are held by a bailee to be delivered without being moved, the risk of loss passes to the buyer
  (a) on his receipt of a negotiable document of title covering the goods; or
  (b) on acknowledgment by the bailee of the buyer's right to possession of the goods; or
  (c) after his receipt of a non-negotiable document of title or other written direction to deliver, as provided in subsection (4)(b) of Section 2-503.

(3) In any case not within subsection (1) or (2), the risk of loss passes to the buyer on his receipt of the goods if the seller is a merchant; otherwise the risk passes to the buyer on tender of delivery.

(4) The provisions of this section are subject to contrary agreement of the parties and to the provisions of this Article on sale on approval (Section 2-327) and on effect of breach on risk of loss (Section 2-510).

## SECTION 2-510. EFFECT OF BREACH ON RISK OF LOSS.

(1) Where a tender or delivery of goods so fails to conform to the contract as to give a right of rejection the risk of their loss remains on the seller until cure or acceptance.

(2) Where the buyer rightfully revokes acceptance he may to the extent of any deficiency in his effective insurance coverage treat the risk of loss as having rested on the seller from the beginning.

(3) Where the buyer as to conforming goods already identified to the contract for sale repudiates or is otherwise in breach before risk of their loss has passed to him, the seller may to the extent of any deficiency in his effective insurance coverage treat the risk of loss as resting on the buyer for a commercially reasonable time.

## SECTION 2-511. TENDER OF PAYMENT BY BUYER; PAYMENT BY CHECK.

(1) Unless otherwise agreed tender of payment is a condition to the seller's duty to tender and complete any delivery.

(2) Tender of payment is sufficient when made by any means or in any manner current in the ordinary course of business unless the seller demands payment in legal tender and gives any extension of time reasonably necessary to procure it.

(3) Subject to the provisions of this Act on the effect of an instrument on an obligation (Section 3-802), payment by check is conditional and is defeated as between the parties by dishonor of the check on due presentment.

## SECTION 2-512. PAYMENT BY BUYER BEFORE INSPECTION.

(1) Where the contract requires payment before inspection non-conformity of the goods does not excuse the buyer from so making payment unless
    (a) the non-conformity appears without inspection; or
    (b) despite tender of the required documents the circumstances would justify injunction against honor under the provisions of this Act (Section 5-114).

(2) Payment pursuant to subsection (1) does not constitute an acceptance of goods or impair the buyer's right to inspect or any of his remedies.

## SECTION 2-513. BUYER'S RIGHT TO INSPECTION OF GOODS.

(1) Unless otherwise agreed and subject to subsection (3), where goods are tendered or delivered or identified to the contract for sale, the buyer has a right before payment or acceptance to inspect them at any reasonable place and time and in any reasonable manner. When the seller is required or authorized to send the goods to the buyer, the inspection may be after their arrival.

(2) Expenses of inspection must be borne by the buyer but may be recovered from the seller if the goods do not conform and are rejected.

(3) Unless otherwise agreed and subject to the provisions of this Article on C. I. F. contracts (subsection (3) of Section 2-321), the buyer is not entitled to inspect the goods before payment of the price when the contract provides

  (a) for delivery "C. O. D." or on other like terms; or

  (b) for payment against documents of title, except where such payment is due only after the goods are to become available for inspection.

(4) A place or method of inspection fixed by the parties is presumed to be exclusive but unless otherwise expressly agreed it does not postpone identification or shift the place for delivery or for passing the risk of loss. If compliance becomes impossible, inspection shall be as provided in this section unless the place or method fixed was clearly intended as an indispensable condition failure of which avoids the contract.

## SECTION 2-601. BUYER'S RIGHTS ON IMPROPER DELIVERY.

Subject to the provisions of this Article on breach in installment contracts (Section 2-612) and unless otherwise agreed under the sections on contractual limitations of remedy (Sections 2-718 and 2-719), if the goods or the tender of delivery fail in any respect to conform to the contract, the buyer may

  (a) reject the whole; or

  (b) accept the whole; or

  (c) accept any commercial unit or units and reject the rest.

## SECTION 2-602. MANNER AND EFFECT OF RIGHTFUL REJECTION.

(1) Rejection of goods must be within a reasonable time after their delivery or tender. It is ineffective unless the buyer seasonably notifies the seller.

(2) Subject to the provisions of the two following sections on rejected goods (Sections 2-603 and 2-604)

  (a) after rejection any exercise of ownership by the buyer with respect to any commercial unit is wrongful as against the seller; and

  (b) if the buyer has before rejection taken physical possession of goods in which he does not have a security interest under the provisions of this Article (subsection (3) of Section 2-711), he is under a duty after rejection to hold them with reasonable care at the seller's disposition for a time sufficient to permit the seller to remove them; but

  (c) the buyer has no further obligations with regard to goods rightfully rejected.

(3) The seller's rights with respect to goods wrongfully rejected are governed by the provisions of this Article on seller's remedies in general (Section 2-703).

## SECTION 2-603. MERCHANT BUYER'S DUTIES AS TO RIGHTFULLY REJECTED GOODS.

(1) Subject to any security interest in the buyer (subsection (3) of Section 2-711), when the seller has no agent or place of business at the market of rejection a merchant buyer is under a duty after rejection of goods in his possession or control to follow any reasonable instructions received from the seller with respect to the goods and in the absence of such instructions to make reasonable efforts to sell them for the seller's account if they are perishable or threaten to decline in value speedily. Instructions are not reasonable if on demand indemnity for expenses is not forthcoming.

(2) When the buyer sells goods under subsection (1), he is entitled to reimbursement from the seller or out of the proceeds for reasonable expenses of caring for and selling them, and if the expenses include no selling commission then to such commission as is usual in the trade or if there is none to a reasonable sum not exceeding ten percent on the gross proceeds.

(3) In complying with this section the buyer is held only to good faith and good faith conduct hereunder is neither acceptance nor conversion nor the basis of an action for damages.

## SECTION 2-604. BUYER'S OPTIONS AS TO SALVAGE OF RIGHTFULLY REJECTED GOODS.

Subject to the provisions of the immediately preceding section on perishables if the seller gives no instructions within a reasonable time after notification of rejection the buyer may store the rejected goods for the seller's account or reship them to him or resell them for the seller's account with reimbursement as provided in the preceding section. Such action is not acceptance or conversion.

## SECTION 2-605. WAIVER OF BUYER'S OBJECTIONS BY FAILURE TO PARTICULARIZE.

(1) The buyer's failure to state in connection with rejection a particular defect which is ascertainable by reasonable inspection precludes him from relying on the unstated defect to justify rejection or to establish breach
  (a) where the seller could have cured it if stated seasonably; or
  (b) between merchants when the seller has after rejection made a request in writing for a full and final written statement of all defects on which the buyer proposes to rely.

(2) Payment against documents made without reservation of rights precludes recovery of the payment for defects apparent on the face of the documents.

## SECTION 2-606. WHAT CONSTITUTES ACCEPTANCE OF GOODS.

(1) Acceptance of goods occurs when the buyer
  (a) after a reasonable opportunity to inspect the goods signifies to the seller that the goods are conforming or that he will take or retain them in spite of their non-conformity; or
  (b) fails to make an effective rejection (subsection (1) of Section 2-602), but such acceptance does not occur until the buyer has had a reasonable opportunity to inspect them; or
  (c) does any act inconsistent with the seller's ownership; but if such act is wrongful as against the seller it is an acceptance only if ratified by him.
(2) Acceptance of a part of any commercial unit is acceptance of that entire unit.

## SECTION 2-607. EFFECT OF ACCEPTANCE; NOTICE OF BREACH; BURDEN OF ESTABLISHING BREACH AFTER ACCEPTANCE; NOTICE OF CLAIM OR LITIGATION TO PERSON ANSWERABLE OVER.

(1) The buyer must pay at the contract rate for any goods accepted.
(2) Acceptance of goods by the buyer precludes rejection of the goods accepted and if made with knowledge of a non-conformity cannot be revoked because of it unless the acceptance was on the reasonable assumption that the non-conformity would be seasonably cured but acceptance does not of itself impair any other remedy provided by this Article for non-conformity.
(3) Where a tender has been accepted
  (a) the buyer must within a reasonable time after he discovers or should have discovered any breach notify the seller of breach or be barred from any remedy; and
  (b) if the claim is one for infringement or the like (subsection (3) of Section 2-312) and the buyer is sued as a result of such a breach he must so notify the seller within a reasonable time after he receives notice of the litigation or be barred from any remedy over for liability established by the litigation.
(4) The burden is on the buyer to establish any breach with respect to the goods accepted.
(5) Where the buyer is sued for breach of a warranty or other obligation for which his seller is answerable over
  (a) he may give his seller written notice of the litigation. If the notice states that the seller may come in and defend and that if the seller does not do so he will be bound in any action against him by his buyer by any determination of fact common to the two litigations, then unless the seller after seasonable receipt of the notice does come in and defend he is so bound.

(b) if the claim is one for infringement or the like (subsection (3) of Section 2-312) the original seller may demand in writing that his buyer turn over to him control of the litigation including settlement or else be barred from any remedy over and if he also agrees to bear all expense and to satisfy any adverse judgment, then unless the buyer after seasonable receipt of the demand does turn over control the buyer is so barred.

(6) The provisions of subsections (3), (4) and (5) apply to any obligation of a buyer to hold the seller harmless against infringement or the like (subsection (3) of Section 2-312).

## SECTION 2-608. REVOCATION OF ACCEPTANCE IN WHOLE OR IN PART.

(1) The buyer may revoke his acceptance of a lot or commercial unit whose non-conformity substantially impairs its value to him if he has accepted it
   (a) on the reasonable assumption that its non-conformity would be cured and it has not been seasonably cured; or
   (b) without discovery of such non-conformity if his acceptance was reasonably induced either by the difficulty of discovery before acceptance or by the seller's assurances.

(2) Revocation of acceptance must occur within a reasonable time after the buyer discovers or should have discovered the ground for it and before any substantial change in condition of the goods which is not caused by their own defects. It is not effective until the buyer notifies the seller of it.

(3) A buyer who so revokes has the same rights and duties with regard to the goods involved as if he had rejected them.

## SECTION 2-609. RIGHT TO ADEQUATE ASSURANCE OF PERFORMANCE.

(1) A contract for sale imposes an obligation on each party that the other's expectation of receiving due performance will not be impaired. When reasonable grounds for insecurity arise with respect to the performance of either party the other may in writing demand adequate assurance of due performance and until he receives such assurance may if commercially reasonable suspend any performance for which he has not already received the agreed return.

(2) Between merchants the reasonableness of grounds for insecurity and the adequacy of any assurance offered shall be determined according to commercial standards.

(3) Acceptance of any improper delivery or payment does not prejudice the aggrieved party's right to demand adequate assurance of future performance.

(4) After receipt of a justified demand failure to provide within a reasonable time not exceeding thirty days such assurance of due performance as is adequate under the circumstances of the particular case is a repudiation of the contract.

## SECTION 2-610. ANTICIPATORY REPUDIATION.

When either party repudiates the contract with respect to a performance not yet due the loss of which will substantially impair the value of the contract to the other, the aggrieved party may

(a) for a commercially reasonable time await performance by the repudiating party; or

(b) resort to any remedy for breach (Section 2-703 or Section 2-711), even though he has notified the repudiating party that he would await the latter's performance and has urged retraction; and

(c) in either case suspend his own performance or proceed in accordance with the provisions of this Article on the seller's right to identify goods to the contract notwithstanding breach or to salvage unfinished goods (Section 2-704).

## SECTION 2-611. RETRACTION OF ANTICIPATORY REPUDIATION.

(1) Until the repudiating party's next performance is due he can retract his repudiation unless the aggrieved party has since the repudiation canceled or materially changed his position or otherwise indicated that he considers the repudiation final.

(2) Retraction may be by any method which clearly indicates to the aggrieved party that the repudiating party intends to perform, but must include any assurance justifiably demanded under the provisions of this Article (Section 2-609).

(3) Retraction reinstates the repudiating party's rights under the contract with due excuse and allowance to the aggrieved party for any delay occasioned by the repudiation.

## SECTION 2-612. "INSTALLMENT CONTRACT"; BREACH.

(1) An "installment contract" is one which requires or authorizes the delivery of goods in separate lots to be separately accepted, even though the contract contains a clause "each delivery is a separate contract" or its equivalent.

(2) The buyer may reject any installment which is non-conforming if the non-conformity substantially impairs the value of that installment and cannot be cured or if the non-conformity is a defect in the required documents; but if the non-conformity does not fall within subsection (3) and the seller gives adequate assurance of its cure the buyer must accept that installment.

(3) Whenever non-conformity or default with respect to one or more installments substantially impairs the value of the whole contract there is a breach of the whole. But the aggrieved party reinstates the contract if he accepts a non-conforming installment without seasonably notifying of cancellation or if he brings an action with respect only to past installments or demands performance as to future installments.

## SECTION 2-613. CASUALTY TO IDENTIFIED GOODS.

Where the contract requires for its performance goods identified when the contract is made, and the goods suffer casualty without fault of either party before the risk of loss passes to the buyer, or in a proper case under a "no arrival, no sale" term (Section 2-324) then
(a) if the loss is total the contract is avoided; and
(b) if the loss is partial or the goods have so deteriorated as no longer to conform to the contract the buyer may nevertheless demand inspection and at his option either treat the contract as avoided or accept the goods with due allowance from the contract price for the deterioration or the deficiency in quantity but without further right against the seller.

## SECTION 2-614. SUBSTITUTED PERFORMANCE.

(1) Where without fault of either party the agreed berthing, loading, or unloading facilities fail or an agreed type of carrier becomes unavailable or the agreed manner of delivery otherwise becomes commercially impracticable but a commercially reasonable substitute is available, such substitute performance must be tendered and accepted.

(2) If the agreed means or manner of payment fails because of domestic or foreign governmental regulation, the seller may withhold or stop delivery unless the buyer provides a means or manner of payment which is commercially a substantial equivalent. If delivery has already been taken, payment by the means or in the manner provided by the regulation discharges the buyer's obligation unless the regulation is discriminatory, oppressive or predatory.

## SECTION 2-615. EXCUSE BY FAILURE OR PRESUPPOSED CONDITIONS.

Except so far as a seller may have assumed a greater obligation and subject to the preceding section on substituted performance:
(a) Delay in delivery or non-delivery in whole or in part by a seller who complies with paragraphs (b) and (c) is not a breach of his duty under a contract for sale if performance as agreed has been made impracticable by the occurrence of a contingency the non-occurrence of which was a basic assumption on which the contract was made or by compliance in good faith with any applicable foreign or domestic governmental regulation or order whether or not it later proves to be invalid.
(b) Where the causes mentioned in paragraph (a) affect only a part of the seller's capacity to perform, he must allocate production and deliveries among his customers but may at his option include regular customers not then under contract as well as his own requirements for further manufacture. He may so allocate in any manner which is fair and reasonable.

(c) The seller must notify the buyer seasonably that there will be delay or non-delivery and, when allocation is required under paragraph (b), of the estimated quota thus made available for the buyer.

## SECTION 2-701. REMEDIES FOR BREACH OF COLLATERAL CONTRACTS NOT IMPAIRED.

Remedies for breach of any obligation or promise collateral or ancillary to a contract for sale are not impaired by the provisions of this Article.

## SECTION 2-702. SELLER'S REMEDIES ON DISCOVERY OF BUYER'S INSOLVENCY.

(1) Where the seller discovers the buyer to be insolvent he may refuse delivery except for cash including payment for all goods theretofore delivered under the contract, and stop delivery under this Article (Section 2-705).

(2) Where the seller discovers that the buyer has received goods on credit while insolvent he may reclaim the goods upon demand made within ten days after the receipt, but if misrepresentation of solvency has been made to the particular seller in writing within three months before delivery the ten day limitation does not apply. Except as provided in this subsection the seller may not base a right to reclaim goods on the buyer's fraudulent or innocent misrepresentation of solvency or of intent to pay.

(3) The seller's right to reclaim under subsection (2) is subject to the rights of a buyer in ordinary course or other good faith purchaser under this Article (Section 2-403). Successful reclamation of goods excludes all other remedies with respect to them.

## SECTION 2-703. SELLER'S REMEDIES IN GENERAL.

Where the buyer wrongfully rejects or revokes acceptance of goods or fails to make a payment due on or before delivery or repudiates with respect to a part or the whole, then with respect to any goods directly affected and, if the breach is of the whole contract (Section 2-612), then also with respect to the whole undelivered balance, the aggrieved seller may

(a) withhold delivery of such goods;

(b) stop delivery by any bailee as hereafter provided (Section 2-705);

(c) proceed under the next section respecting goods still unidentified to the contract;

(d) resell and recover damages as hereafter provided (Section 2-706);

(e) recover damages for non-acceptance (Section 2-708) or in a proper case the price (Section 2-709);

(f) cancel.

## SECTION 2-704. SELLER'S RIGHT TO IDENTIFY GOODS TO THE CONTRACT NOTWITHSTANDING BREACH OR TO SALVAGE UNFINISHED GOODS.

(1) An aggrieved seller under the preceding section may

(a) identify to the contract conforming goods not already identified if at the time he learned of the breach they are in his possession or control;

(b) treat as the subject of resale goods which have demonstrably been intended for the particular contract even though those goods are unfinished.

(2) Where the goods are unfinished an aggrieved seller may in the exercise of reasonable commercial judgment for the purposes of avoiding loss and of effective realization either complete the manufacture and wholly identify the goods to the contract or cease manufacture and resell for scrap or salvage value or proceed in any other reasonable manner.

## SECTION 2-705. SELLER'S STOPPAGE OF DELIVERY IN TRANSIT OR OTHERWISE.

(1) The seller may stop delivery of goods in the possession of a carrier or other bailee when he discovers the buyer to be insolvent (Section 2-702) and may stop delivery of carload, truckload, planeload or larger shipments of express or freight when the buyer repudiates or fails to make a payment due before delivery or if for any other reason the seller has a right to withhold or reclaim the goods.

(2) As against such buyer the seller may stop delivery until

(a) receipt of the goods by the buyer; or

(b) acknowledgment to the buyer by any bailee of the goods except a carrier that the bailee holds the goods for the buyer; or

(c) such acknowledgment to the buyer by a carrier by reshipment or as warehouseman; or

(d) negotiation to the buyer of any negotiable document of title covering the goods.

(3) (a) To stop delivery the seller must so notify as to enable the bailee by reasonable diligence to prevent delivery of the goods.

(b) After such notification the bailee must hold and deliver the goods according to the directions of the seller but the seller is liable to the bailee for any ensuing charges or damages.

(c) If a negotiable document of title has been issued for goods the bailee is not obliged to obey a notification to stop until surrender of the document.

(d) A carrier who has issued a non-negotiable bill of lading is not obliged to obey a notification to stop received from a person other than the consignor.

## SECTION 2-706. SELLER'S RESALE INCLUDING CONTRACT FOR RESALE.

(1) Under the conditions stated in Section 2-703 on seller's remedies, the seller may resell the goods concerned or the undelivered balance thereof. Where the resale is

made in good faith and in a commercially reasonable manner the seller may recover the difference between the resale price and the contract price together with any incidental damages allowed under the provisions of this Article (Section 2-710), but less expenses saved in consequence of the buyer's breach.

(2) Except as otherwise provided in subsection (3) or unless otherwise agreed re-sale may be at public or private sale including sale by way of one or more contracts to sell or of identification to an existing contract of the seller. Sale may be as a unit or in parcels and at any time and place and on any terms but every aspect of the sale including the method, manner, time, place and terms must be commercially reasonable. The resale must be reasonably identified as referring to the broken contract, but it is not necessary that the goods be in existence or that any or all of them have been identified to the contract before the breach.

(3) Where the resale is at private sale the seller must give the buyer reasonable notification of his intention to resell.

(4) Where the resale is at public sale

    (a) only identified goods can be sold except where there is a recognized market for a public sale of futures in goods of the kind; and

    (b) it must be made at a usual place or market for public sale if one is reasonably available and except in the case of goods which are perishable or threaten to decline in value speedily the seller must give the buyer reasonable notice of the time and place of the resale; and

    (c) if the goods are not to be within the view of those attending the sale the notification of sale must state the place where the goods are located and provide for their reasonable inspection by prospective bidders; and

    (d) the seller may buy.

(5) A purchaser who buys in good faith at a resale takes the goods free of any rights of the original buyer even though the seller fails to comply with one or more of the requirements of this section.

(6) The seller is not accountable to the buyer for any profit made on any resale. A person in the position of a seller (Section 2-707) or a buyer who has rightfully rejected or justifiably revoked acceptance must account for any excess over the amount of his security interest, as hereinafter defined (subsection (3) of Section 2-711).

## SECTION 2-708. SELLER'S DAMAGES FOR NON-ACCEPTANCE OR REPUDIATION.

(1) Subject to subsection (2) and to the provisions of this Article with respect to proof of market price (Section 2-723), the measure of damages for non-acceptance or repudiation by the buyer is the difference between the market price at the time and place for tender and the unpaid contract price together with any incidental damages provided in this Article (Section 2-710), but less expenses saved in consequence of the buyer's breach.

(2) If the measure of damages provided in subsection (1) is inadequate to put the seller in as good a position as performance would have done then the measure of dam-

ages is the profit (including reasonable overhead) which the seller would have made from full performance by the buyer, together with any incidental damages provided in this Article (Section 2-710), due allowance for costs reasonably incurred and due credit for payments or proceeds of resale.

## SECTION 2-709. ACTION FOR THE PRICE.

(1) When the buyer fails to pay the price as it becomes due the seller may recover, together with any incidental damages under the next section, the price

(a) of goods accepted or of conforming goods lost or damaged within a commercially reasonable time after risk of their loss has passed to the buyer; and

(b) of goods identified to the contract if the seller is unable after reasonable effort to resell them at a reasonable price or the circumstances reasonably indicate that such effort will be unavailing.

(2) Where the seller sues for the price he must hold for the buyer any goods which have been identified to the contract and are still in his control except that if resale becomes possible he may resell them at any time prior to the collection of the judgment. The net proceeds of any such resale must be credited to the buyer and payment of the judgment entitles him to any goods not resold.

(3) After the buyer has wrongfully rejected or revoked acceptance of the goods or has failed to make a payment due or has repudiated (Section 2-610), a seller who is held not entitled to the price under this section shall nevertheless be awarded damages for non-acceptance under the preceding section.

## SECTION 2-710. SELLER'S INCIDENTAL DAMAGES.

Incidental damages to an aggrieved seller include any commercially reasonable charges, expenses or commissions incurred in stopping delivery, in the transportation, care and custody of goods after the buyer's breach, in connection with return or resale of the goods or otherwise resulting from the breach.

## SECTION 2-711. BUYER'S REMEDIES IN GENERAL; BUYER'S SECURITY INTEREST IN REJECTED GOODS.

(1) Where the seller fails to make delivery or repudiates or the buyer rightfully rejects or justifiably revokes acceptance then with respect to any goods involved, and with respect to the whole if the breach goes to the whole contract (Section 2-612), the buyer may cancel and whether or not he has done so may in addition to recovering so much of the price as has been paid

(a) "cover" and have damages under the next section as to all the goods affected whether or not they have been identified to the contract; or

(b) recover damages for non-delivery as provided in this Article (Section 2-713).

(2) Where the seller fails to deliver or repudiates the buyer may also

(a) if the goods have been identified recover them as provided in this Article (Section 2-502); or

(b) in a proper case obtain specific performance or replevy the goods as provided in this Article (Section 2-716).

(3) On rightful rejection or justifiable revocation of acceptance a buyer has a security interest in goods in his possession or control for any payments made on their price and any expenses reasonably incurred in their inspection, receipt, transportation, care and custody and may hold such goods and resell them in like manner as an aggrieved seller (Section 2-706).

## SECTION 2-712. "COVER"; BUYER'S PROCUREMENT OF SUBSTITUTE GOODS.

(1) After a breach within the preceding section the buyer may "cover" by making in good faith and without unreasonable delay any reasonable purchase of or contract to purchase goods in substitution for those due from the seller.

(2) The buyer may recover from the seller as damages the difference between the cost of cover and the contract price together with any incidental or consequential damages as hereinafter defined (Section 2-715), but less expenses saved in consequence of the seller's breach.

(3) Failure of the buyer to effect cover within this section does not bar him from any other remedy.

## SECTION 2-713. BUYER'S DAMAGES FOR NON-DELIVERY OR REPUDIATION.

(1) Subject to the provisions of this Article with respect to proof of market price (Section 2-723), the measure of damages for non-delivery or repudiation by the seller is the difference between the market price at the time when the buyer learned of the breach and the contract price together with any incidental and consequential damages provided in this Article (Section 2-715), but less expenses saved in consequence of the seller's breach.

(2) Market price is to be determined as of the place for tender or, in cases of rejection after arrival or revocation of acceptance, as of the place of arrival.

## SECTION 2-714. BUYER'S DAMAGES FOR BREACH IN REGARD TO ACCEPTED GOODS.

(1) Where the buyer has accepted goods and given notification (subsection (3) of Section 2-607) he may recover as damages for any non-conformity of tender the loss resulting in the ordinary course of events from the seller's breach as determined in any manner which is reasonable.

(2) The measure of damages for breach of warranty is the difference at the time and place of acceptance between the value of the goods accepted and the value they would have had if they had been as warranted, unless special circumstances show proximate damages of a different amount.

(3) In a proper case any incidental and consequential damages under the next section may also be recovered.

## SECTION 2-715. BUYER'S INCIDENTAL AND CONSEQUENTIAL DAMAGES.

(1) Incidental damages resulting from the seller's breach include expenses reasonably incurred in inspection, receipt, transportation and care and custody of goods rightfully rejected, any commercially reasonable charges, expenses or commissions in connection with effecting cover and any other reasonable expense incident to the delay or other breach.

(2) Consequential damages resulting from the seller's breach include

(a) any loss resulting from general or particular requirements and needs of which the seller at the time of contracting had reason to know and which could not reasonably be prevented by cover or otherwise; and

(b) injury to person or property proximately resulting from any breach of warranty.

## SECTION 2-716. BUYER'S RIGHT TO SPECIFIC PERFORMANCE OR REPLEVIN.

(1) Specific performance may be decreed where the goods are unique or in other proper circumstances.

(2) The decree for specific performance may include such terms and conditions as to payment of the price, damages, or other relief as the court may deem just.

(3) The buyer has a right of replevin for goods identified to the contract if after reasonable effort he is unable to effect cover for such goods or the circumstances reasonably indicate that such effort will be unavailing or if the goods have been shipped under reservation and satisfaction of the security interest in them has been made or tendered.

## SECTION 2-717. DEDUCTION OF DAMAGES FROM THE PRICE.

The buyer on notifying the seller of his intention to do so may deduct all or any part of the damages resulting from any breach of the contract from any part of the price still due under the same contract.

## SECTION 2-718. LIQUIDATION OR LIMITATION OF DAMAGES; DEPOSITS.

(1) Damages for breach by either party may be liquidated in the agreement but only at an amount which is reasonable in the light of the anticipated or actual harm caused by the breach, the difficulties of proof of loss, and the inconvenience or nonfeasibility of otherwise obtaining an adequate remedy. A term fixing unreasonably large liquidated damages is void as a penalty.

(2) Where the seller justifiably withholds delivery of goods because of the buyer's breach, the buyer is entitled to restitution of any amount by which the sum of his payments exceeds

(a)  the amount to which the seller is entitled by virtue of terms liquidating the seller's damages in accordance with subsection (1), or

(b)  in the absence of such terms, twenty per cent of the value of the total performance for which the buyer is obligated under the contract or $500, whichever is smaller.

(3)  The buyer's right to restitution under subsection (2) is subject to offset to the extent that the seller establishes

(a)  a right to recover damages under the provisions of this Article other than subsection (1), and

(b)  the amount or value of any benefits received by the buyer directly or indirectly by reason of the contract.

(4)  Where a seller has received payment in goods their reasonable value or the proceeds of their resale shall be treated as payments for the purposes of subsection (2); but if the seller has notice of the buyer's breach before reselling goods received in part performance, his resale is subject to the conditions laid down in this Article on resale by an aggrieved seller (Section 2-706).

## SECTION 2-719. CONTRACTUAL MODIFICATION OR LIMITATION OF REMEDY.

(1)  Subject to the provisions of subsections (2) and (3) of this section and of the preceding section on liquidation and limitation of damages,

(a)  the agreement may provide for remedies in addition to or in substitution for those provided in this Article and may limit or alter the measure of damages recoverable under this Article, as by limiting the buyer's remedies to return of the goods and repayment of the price or to repair and replacement of non-conforming goods or parts; and

(b)  resort to a remedy as provided is optional unless the remedy is expressly agreed to be exclusive, in which case it is the sole remedy.

(2)  Where circumstances cause an exclusive or limited remedy to fail of its essential purpose, remedy may be had as provided in this Act.

(3)  Consequential damages may be limited or excluded unless the limitation or exclusion is unconscionable. Limitation of consequential damages for injury to the person in the case of consumer goods is *prima facie* unconscionable but limitation of damages where the loss is commercial is not.

## SECTION 2-721. REMEDIES FOR FRAUD.

Remedies for material misrepresentation or fraud include all remedies available under this Article for non-fraudulent breach. Neither rescission or a claim for rescission of the contract for sale nor rejection or return of the goods shall bar or be deemed inconsistent with a claim for damages or other remedy.

## SECTION 2-723. PROOF OF MARKET PRICE: TIME AND PLACE.

(1) If an action based on anticipatory repudiation comes to trial before the time for performance with respect to some or all of the goods, any damages based on market price (Section 2-708 or Section 2-713) shall be determined according to the price of such goods prevailing at the time when the aggrieved party learned of the repudiation.

(2) If evidence of a price prevailing at the times or places described in this Article is not readily available the price prevailing within any reasonable time before or after the time described or at any other place which in commercial judgment or under usage of trade would serve as a reasonable substitute for the one described may be used, making any proper allowance for the cost of transporting the goods to or from such other place.

(3) Evidence of a relevant price prevailing at a time or place other than the one described in this Article offered by one party is not admissible unless and until he has given the other party such notice as the court finds sufficient to prevent unfair surprise.

## SECTION 2-724. ADMISSIBILITY OF MARKET QUOTATIONS.

Whenever the prevailing price or value of any goods regularly bought and sold in any established commodity market is in issue, reports in official publications or trade journals or in newspapers or periodicals of general circulation published as the reports of such market shall be admissible in evidence. The circumstances of the preparation of such a report may be shown to affect its weight but not its admissibility.

## SECTION 2-725. STATUTE OF LIMITATIONS IN CONTRACTS FOR SALE.

(1) An action for breach of any contract for sale must be commenced within four years after the cause of action has accrued. By the original agreement the parties may reduce the period of limitation to not less than one year but may not extend it.

(2) A cause of action accrues when the breach occurs, regardless of the aggrieved party's lack of knowledge of the breach. A breach of warranty occurs when tender of delivery is made, except that where a warranty explicitly extends to future performance of the goods and discovery of the breach must await the time of such performance the cause of action accrues when the breach is or should have been discovered.

(3) Where an action commenced within the time limited by subsection (1) is so terminated as to leave available a remedy by another action for the same breach such other action may be commenced after the expiration of the time limited and within six months after the termination of the first action unless the termination resulted from voluntary discontinuance or from dismissal for failure or neglect to prosecute.

(4) This section does not alter the law on tolling of the statute of limitations nor does it apply to causes of action which have accrued before this Act becomes effective.

# E

# UNIFORM COMMERCIAL CODE ARTICLE 3—COMMERCIAL PAPER (Selected Sections)

**SECTION 3-101. SHORT TITLE.**

This Article shall be known and may be cited as Uniform Commercial Code—Commercial Paper.

**SECTION 3-102. DEFINITIONS AND INDEX OF DEFINITIONS .**

(1) In this Article unless the context otherwise requires
  (a) "Issue" means the first delivery of an instrument to a holder or a remitter.
  (b) An "order" is a direction to pay and must be more than an authorization or request. It must identify the person to pay with reasonable certainty. It may be addressed to one or more such persons jointly or in the alternative but not in succession.
  (c) A "promise" is an undertaking to pay and must be more than an acknowledgment of an obligation.
  (d) "Secondary party" means a drawer or endorser.
  (e) "Instrument" means a negotiable instrument.

(2) Other definitions applying to this Article and the sections in which they appear are:
  "Acceptance." Section 3-410.
  "Accommodation party." Section 3-415.
  "Alteration." Section 3-407.
  "Certificate of deposit." Section 3-104.
  "Certification." Section 3-411.
  "Check." Section 3-104.
  "Definite time." Section 3-109.

"Dishonor." Section 3-507.
"Draft." Section 3-104.
"Holder in due course." Section 3-302.
"Negotiation." Section 3-202.
"Note." Section 3-104.
"Notice of dishonor." Section 3-508.
"On demand." Section 3-108.
"Presentment." Section 3-504.
"Protest." Section 3-509.
"Restrictive Indorsement." Section 3-205.
"Signature." Section 3-401.

## SECTION 3-103. LIMITATIONS ON SCOPE OF ARTICLE.

(1) This Article does not apply to money, documents of title or investment securities.

## SECTION 3-104. FORM OF NEGOTIABLE INSTRUMENTS; "DRAFT"; "CHECK"; "CERTIFICATE OF DEPOSIT"; "NOTE."

(1) Any writing to be a negotiable instrument within this Article must
    (a) be signed by the maker or drawer; and
    (b) contain an unconditional promise or order to pay a sum certain in money and no other promise, order, obligation or power given by the maker or drawer except as authorized by this Article; and
    (c) be payable on demand or at a definite time; and
    (d) be payable to order or to bearer.
(2) A writing which complies with the requirements of this section is
    (a) a "draft" ("bill of exchange") if it is an order;
    (b) a "check" if it is a draft drawn on a bank and payable on demand;
    (c) a "certificate of deposit" if it is an acknowledgment by a bank of receipt of money with an engagement to repay it;
    (d) a "note" if it is a promise other than a certificate of deposit.
(3) As used in other Articles of this Act, and as the context may require, the terms "draft," "check," "certificate of deposit" and "note" may refer to instruments which are not negotiable within this Article as well as to instruments which are so negotiable.

## SECTION 3-105. WHEN PROMISE OR ORDER UNCONDITIONAL.

(1) A promise or order otherwise unconditional is not made conditional by the fact that the instrument
    (a) is subject to implied or constructive conditions; or
    (b) states its consideration, whether performed or promised, or the transaction which gave rise to the instrument, or that the promise or order is made or the instrument matures in accordance with or "as per" such transaction; or

(c) refers to or states that it arises out of a separate agreement or refers to a separate agreement for rights as to prepayment or acceleration; or

(d) states that it is drawn under a letter of credit; or

(e) states that it is secured, whether by mortgage, reservation of title or otherwise; or

(f) indicates a particular account to be debited or any other fund or source from which reimbursement is expected; or

(g) is limited to payment out of a particular fund or the proceeds of a particular source, if the instrument is issued by a government or governmental agency or unit; or

(h) is limited to payment out of the entire assets of a partnership, unincorporated association, trust or estate by or on behalf of which the instrument is issued.

(2) A promise or order is not unconditional if the instrument

(a) states that it is subject to or governed by any other agreement; or

(b) states that it is to be paid only out of a particular fund or source except as provided in this section.

## SECTION 3-106. SUM CERTAIN.

(1) The sum payable is a sum certain even though it is to be paid

(a) with a stated rate of interest or by stated installments; or

(b) with stated different rates of interest before and after default or a specified date; or

(c) with a stated discount or addition if paid before or after the date fixed for payment; or

(d) with exchange or less exchange, whether at a fixed rate or at the current rate; or

(e) with costs of collection or an attorney's fee or both upon default.

(2) For the purposes of subsection one of this section "a stated rate of interest" shall also include a rate of interest that cannot be calculated by looking only to the instrument but which is readily ascertainable by a reference in the instrument to a published statute, regulation, rule of court, generally accepted commercial or financial index, compendium of interest rates, or announced rate of a named financial institution.

(3) Nothing in this section shall validate any term which is otherwise illegal.

## SECTION 3-107. MONEY.

(1) An instrument is payable in money if the medium of exchange in which it is payable is money at the time the instrument is made. An instrument payable in "currency" or "current funds" is payable in money.

(2) A promise or order to pay a sum stated in a foreign currency is for a sum certain in money and may be satisfied by payment of that number of dollars which the stated foreign currency will purchase at the buying sight rate for that currency on the day on which the instrument is payable, or, if payable on demand, on the day of demand.

## SECTION 3-108. PAYABLE ON DEMAND.

Instruments payable on demand include those payable at sight or on presentation and those in which no time for payment is stated.

## SECTION 3-109. DEFINITE TIME.

(1) An instrument is payable at a definite time if by its terms it is payable

(a) on or before a stated date or at a fixed period after a stated date; or

(b) at a fixed period after sight; or

(c) at a definite time subject to any acceleration; or

(d) at a definite time subject to extension at the option of the holder, or to extension to a further definite time at the option of the maker or acceptor or automatically upon or after a specified act or event.

(2) An instrument which by its terms is otherwise payable only upon an act or event uncertain as to time of occurrence is not payable at a definite time even though the act or event has occurred.

## SECTION 3-110. PAYABLE TO ORDER.

(1) An instrument is payable to order when by its terms it is payable to the order or assigns of any person therein specified with reasonable certainty, or to him or his order, or when it is conspicuously designated on its face as "exchange" or the like and names a payee. It may be payable to the order of

(a) the maker or drawer; or

(b) the drawee; or

(c) a payee who is not maker, drawer or drawee; or

(d) two or more payees together or in the alternative; or

(e) an estate, trust or fund, in which case it is payable to the order of the representative of such estate, trust or fund or his successors; or

(f) an office, or an officer by his title as such in which case it is payable to the principal but the incumbent of the office or his successors may act as if he or they were the holder; or

(g) a partnership or unincorporated association, in which case it is payable to the partnership or association and may be indorsed or transferred by any person thereto authorized.

(2) An instrument not payable to order is not made so payable by such words as "payable upon return of this instrument properly indorsed."

(3) An instrument made payable both to order and to bearer is payable to order unless the bearer words are handwritten or typewritten.

## SECTION 3-111. PAYABLE TO BEARER.

An instrument is payable to bearer when by its terms it is payable to

(a) bearer or the order of bearer; or

(b)  a specified person or bearer; or

(c)  "cash" or the order of "cash", or any other indication which does not purport to designate a specific payee.

## SECTION 3-112. TERMS AND OMISSIONS NOT AFFECTING NEGOTIABILITY.

(1)  The negotiability of an instrument is not affected by

(a)  the omission of a statement of any consideration or of the place where the instrument is drawn or payable; or

(b)  a statement that collateral has been given to secure obligations either on the instrument or otherwise of an obligor on the instrument or that in the case of default on those obligations the holder may realize on or dispose of the collateral; or

(c)  a promise or power to maintain or protect collateral or to give additional collateral; or

(d)  a term authorizing a confession of judgment on the instrument if it is not paid when due; or

(e)  a term purporting to waive the benefit of any law intended for the advantage or protection of any obligor; or

(f)  a term in a draft providing that the payee by indorsing or cashing it acknowledges full satisfaction of an obligation of the drawer; or

(g)  a statement in a draft drawn in a set of parts (Section 3-801) to the effect that the order is effective only if no other part has been honored.

(2)  Nothing in this section shall validate any term which is otherwise illegal.

## SECTION 3-113. SEAL.

An instrument otherwise negotiable is within this Article even though it is under a seal.

## SECTION 3-114. DATE, ANTEDATING, POSTDATING.

(1)  The negotiability of an instrument is not affected by the fact that it is undated, antedated or postdated.

(2)  Where an instrument is antedated or postdated the time when it is payable is determined by the stated date if the instrument is payable on demand or at a fixed period after date.

(3)  Where the instrument or any signature thereon is dated, the date is presumed to be correct.

## SECTION 3-115. INCOMPLETE INSTRUMENTS.

(1)  When a paper whose contents at the time of signing show that it is intended to become an instrument is signed while still incomplete in any necessary respect it can-

not be enforced until completed, but when it is completed in accordance with authority given it is effective as completed.

(2) If the completion is unauthorized the rules as to material alteration apply (Section 3-407), even though the paper was not delivered by the maker or drawer; but the burden of establishing that any completion is unauthorized is on the party so asserting.

### SECTION 3-116. INSTRUMENTS PAYABLE TO TWO OR MORE PERSONS.

An instrument payable to the order of two or more persons
(a) if in the alternative is payable to any one of them and may be negotiated, discharged or enforced by any of them who has possession of it;
(b) if not in the alternative is payable to all of them and may be negotiated, discharged or enforced only by all of them.

### SECTION 3-118. AMBIGUOUS TERMS AND RULES OF CONSTRUCTION.

The following rules apply to every instrument:
(a) Where there is doubt whether the instrument is a draft or a note the holder may treat it as either. A draft drawn on the drawer is effective as a note.
(b) Handwritten terms control typewritten and printed terms, and typewritten control printed.
(c) Words control figures except that if the words are ambiguous figures control.
(d) Unless otherwise specified a provision for interest means interest at the judgment rate at the place of payment from the date of the instrument, or if it is undated from the date of issue.
(e) Unless the instrument otherwise specifies two or more persons who sign as maker, acceptor or drawer or indorser and as a part of the same transaction are jointly and severally liable even though the instrument contains such words as "I promise to pay."
(f) Unless otherwise specified consent to extension authorizes a single extension for not longer than the original period. A consent to extension, expressed in the instrument, is binding on secondary parties and accommodation makers. A holder may not exercise his option to extend an instrument over the objection of a maker or acceptor or other party who in accordance with Section 3-604 tenders full payment when the instrument is due.

### SECTION 3-119. OTHER WRITINGS AFFECTING INSTRUMENT.

(1) As between the obligor and his immediate obligee or any transferee the terms of an instrument may be modified or affected by any other written agreement executed as a part of the same transaction, except that a holder in due course is not affected by any limitation of his rights arising out of the separate written agreement if he had no notice of the limitation when he took the instrument.

(2) A separate agreement does not affect the negotiability of an instrument.

## SECTION 3-121. INSTRUMENTS PAYABLE AT BANK.

A note or acceptance which states that it is payable at a bank is the equivalent of a draft drawn on the bank payable when it falls due out of any funds of the maker or acceptor in current account or otherwise available for such payment.

## SECTION 3-122. ACCRUAL OF CAUSE OF ACTION.

(1) A cause of action against a maker or an acceptor accrues
   (a) in the case of a time instrument on the day after maturity;
   (b) in the case of a demand instrument upon its date or, if no date is stated, on the date of issue.

(2) A cause of action against the obligor of a demand or time certificate of deposit accrues upon demand, but demand on a time certificate may not be made until on or after the date of maturity.

(3) A cause of action against a drawer of a draft or an indorser of any instrument accrues upon demand following dishonor of the instrument. Notice of dishonor is a demand.

(4) Unless an instrument provides otherwise, interest runs at the rate provided by law for a judgment
   (a) in the case of a maker, acceptor or other primary obligor of a demand instrument, from the date of demand;
   (b) in all other cases from the date of accrual of the cause of action.

## SECTION 3-201. TRANSFER; RIGHT TO INDORSEMENT.

(1) Transfer of an instrument vests in the transferee such rights as the transferor has therein, except that a transferee who has himself been a party to any fraud or illegality affecting the instrument or who as a prior holder had notice of a defense or claim against it cannot improve his position by taking from a later holder in due course.

(2) A transfer of a security interest in an instrument vests the foregoing rights in the transferee to the extent of the interest transferred.

(3) Unless otherwise agreed any transfer for value of an instrument not then payable to bearer gives the transferee the specifically enforceable right to have the unqualified indorsement of the transferor. Negotiation takes effect only when the indorsement is made and until that time there is no presumption that the transferee is the owner.

## SECTION 3-202. NEGOTIATIONS.

(1) Negotiation is the transfer of an instrument in such form that the transferee becomes a holder. If the instrument is payable to order it is negotiated by delivery with any necessary indorsement; if payable to bearer it is negotiated by delivery.

(2) An indorsement must be written by or on behalf of the holder and on the instrument or on a paper so firmly affixed thereto as to become a part thereof.

(3) An indorsement is effective for negotiation only when it conveys the entire instrument or any unpaid residue. If it purports to be of less it operates only as a partial assignment.

(4) Words of assignment, condition, waiver, guaranty, limitation or disclaimer of liability and the like accompanying an indorsement do not affect its character as an indorsement.

## SECTION 3-203. WRONG OR MISSPELLED NAME.

Where an instrument is made payable to a person under a misspelled name or one other than his own he may indorse in that name or his own or both; but signature in both names may be required by a person paying or giving value for the instrument.

## SECTION 3-204. SPECIAL INDORSEMENT; BLANK INDORSEMENT.

(1) A special indorsement specifies the person to whom or to whose order it makes the instrument payable. Any instrument specially indorsed becomes payable to the order of the special indorsee and may be further negotiated only by his indorsement.

(2) An indorsement in blank specifies no particular indorsee and may consist of a mere signature. An instrument payable to order and indorsed in blank becomes payable to bearer and may be negotiated by delivery alone until specially indorsed.

(3) The holder may convert a blank indorsement into a special indorsement by writing over the signature of the indorser in blank any contract consistent with the character of the indorsement.

## SECTION 3-205. RESTRICTIVE INDORSEMENTS.

An indorsement is restrictive which either
(a) is conditional; or
(b) purports to prohibit further transfer of the instrument; or
(c) includes the words "for collection," "for deposit," "pay any bank," or like terms signifying a purpose of deposit or collection; or
(d) otherwise states that it is for the benefit or use of the indorser or of another person.

## SECTION 3-206. EFFECT OF RESTRICTIVE INDORSEMENT.

(1) No restrictive indorsement prevents further transfer or negotiation of the instrument.

(2) An intermediary bank, or a payor bank which is not the depositary bank, is neither given notice nor otherwise affected by a restrictive indorsement of any person except the bank's immediate transferor or the person presenting for payment.

(3) Except for an intermediary bank, any transferee under an indorsement which is conditional or includes the words "for collection," "for deposit," "pay any bank," or like terms (subparagraphs (a) and (c) of Section 3-205) must pay or apply any value given by him for or on the security of the instrument consistently with the indorsement and to the extent that he does so he becomes a holder for value. In addition such transferee is a holder in due course if he otherwise complies with the requirements of Section 3-302 on what constitutes a holder in due course.

(4) The first taker under an indorsement for the benefit of the indorser or another person (subparagraph (d) of Section 3-205) must pay or apply any value given by him for or on the security of the instrument consistently with the indorsement and to the extent that he does so he becomes a holder for value. In addition such taker is a holder in due course if he otherwise complies with the requirements of Section 3-302 on what constitutes a holder in due course. A later holder for value is neither given notice nor otherwise affected by such restrictive indorsement unless he has knowledge that a fiduciary or other person has negotiated the instrument in any transaction for his own benefit or otherwise in breach of duty (subsection (2) of Section 3-304).

### SECTION 3-301. RIGHTS OF A HOLDER.

The holder of an instrument whether or not he is the owner may transfer or negotiate it and, except as otherwise provided in Section 3-603 on payment or satisfaction, discharge it or enforce payment in his own name.

### SECTION 3-302. HOLDER IN DUE COURSE.

(1) A holder in due course is a holder who takes the instrument
   (a) for value; and
   (b) in good faith; and
   (c) without notice that it is overdue or has been dishonored or of any defense against or claim to it on the part of any person.
(2) A payee may be a holder in due course.
(3) A holder does not become a holder in due course of an instrument
   (a) by purchase of it at judicial sale or by taking it under legal process; or
   (b) by acquiring it in taking over an estate; or
   (c) by purchasing it as part of a bulk transaction not in regular course of business of the transferor.
(4) A purchaser of a limited interest can be a holder in due course only to the extent of the interest purchased.

## SECTION 3-303. TAKING FOR VALUE.

A holder takes the instrument for value

(a) to the extent that the agreed consideration has been performed or that he acquires a security interest in or a lien on the instrument otherwise than by legal process; or

(b) when he takes the instrument in payment of or as security for an antecedent claim against any person whether or not the claim is due; or

(c) when he gives a negotiable instrument for it or makes an irrevocable commitment to a third person.

## SECTION 3-304. NOTICE TO PURCHASER.

(1) The purchaser has notice of a claim or defense if

    (a) the instrument is so incomplete, bears such visible evidence of forgery or alteration, or is otherwise so irregular as to call into question its validity, terms or ownership or to create an ambiguity as to the party to pay; or

    (b) the purchaser has notice that the obligation of any party is voidable in whole or in part, or that all parties have been discharged.

(2) The purchaser has notice of a claim against the instrument when he has knowledge that a fiduciary has negotiated the instrument in payment of or as security for his own debt or in any transaction for his own benefit or otherwise in breach of duty.

(3) The purchaser has notice that an instrument is overdue if he has reason to know

    (a) that any part of the principal amount is overdue or that there is an uncured default in payment of another instrument of the same series; or

    (b) that acceleration of the instrument has been made; or

    (c) that he is taking a demand instrument after demand has been made or more than a reasonable length of time after its issue. A reasonable time for a check drawn and payable within the states and territories of the United States and the District of Columbia is presumed to be thirty days.

(4) Knowledge of the following facts does not of itself give the purchaser notice of a defense or claim

    (a) that the instrument is antedated or postdated;

    (b) that it was issued or negotiated in return for an executory promise or accompanied by a separate agreement, unless the purchaser has notice that a defense or claim has arisen from the terms thereof;

    (c) that any party has signed for accommodation;

    (d) that an incomplete instrument has been completed, unless the purchaser has notice of any improper completion;

    (e) that any person negotiating the instrument is or was a fiduciary;

    (f) that there has been default in payment of interest on the instrument or in payment of any other instrument, except one of the same series.

(5) The filing or recording of a document does not of itself constitute notice within the provisions of this Article to a person who would otherwise be a holder in due course.

(6) To be effective notice must be received at such time and in such manner as to give a reasonable opportunity to act on it.

(7) In any event, to constitute notice of a claim or defense, the purchaser must have knowledge of the claim or defense or knowledge of such facts that his action in taking the instrument amounts to bad faith.

### SECTION 3-305. RIGHTS OF A HOLDER IN DUE COURSE.

To the extent that a holder is a holder in due course he takes the instrument free from

(1) all claims to it on the part of any person; and

(2) all defenses of any party to the instrument with whom the holder has not dealt except

    (a) infancy, to the extent that it is a defense to a simple contract; and

    (b) such other incapacity, or duress, or illegality of the transaction, as renders the obligation of the party a nullity; and

    (c) such misrepresentation as has induced the party to sign the instrument with neither knowledge nor reasonable opportunity to obtain knowledge of its character or its essential terms; and

    (d) discharge in insolvency proceedings; and

    (e) any other discharge of which the holder has notice when he takes the instrument.

### SECTION 3-306. RIGHTS OF ONE NOT HOLDER IN DUE COURSE.

Unless he has the rights of a holder in due course any person takes the instrument subject to

    (a) all valid claims to it on the part of any person; and

    (b) all defenses of any party which would be available in an action on a simple contract; and

    (c) the defenses of want or failure of consideration, non-performance of any condition precedent, non-delivery, or delivery for a special purpose (Section 3-408); and

    (d) the defense that he or a person through whom he holds the instrument acquired it by theft, or that payment or satisfaction to such holder would be inconsistent with the terms of a restrictive indorsement. The claim of any third person to the instrument is not otherwise available as a defense to any party liable thereon unless the third person himself defends the action for such party.

## SECTION 3-307. BURDEN OF ESTABLISHING SIGNATURES, DEFENSES AND DUE COURSE.

(1) Unless specifically denied in the pleadings each signature on an instrument is admitted. When the effectiveness of a signature is put in issue

    (a) the burden of establishing it is on the party claiming under the signature; but

    (b) the signature is presumed to be genuine or authorized except where the action is to enforce the obligation of a purported signer who has died or become incompetent before proof is required.

(2) When signatures are admitted or established, production of the instrument entitles a holder to recover on it unless the defendant establishes a defense.

(3) After it is shown that a defense exists a person claiming the rights of a holder in due course has the burden of establishing that he or some person under whom he claims is in all respects a holder in due course.

## SECTION 3-401. SIGNATURE.

(1) No person is liable on an instrument unless his signature appears thereon.

(2) A signature is made by use of any name, including any trade or assumed name, upon an instrument, or by any word or mark used in lieu of a written signature.

## SECTION 3-402. SIGNATURE IN AMBIGUOUS CAPACITY.

Unless the instrument clearly indicates that a signature is made in some other capacity it is an indorsement.

## SECTION 3-403. SIGNATURE BY AUTHORIZED REPRESENTATIVE.

(1) A signature may be made by an agent or other representative, and his authority to make it may be established as in other cases of representation. No particular form of appointment is necessary to establish such authority.

(2) An authorized representative who signs his own name to an instrument

    (a) is personally obligated if the instrument neither names the person represented nor shows that the representative signed in a representative capacity;

    (b) except as otherwise established between the immediate parties, is personally obligated if the instrument names the person represented but does not show that the representative signed in a representative capacity, or if the instrument does not name the person represented but does show that the representative signed in a representative capacity.

(3) Except as otherwise established the name of an organization preceded or followed by the name and office of an authorized individual is a signature made in a representative capacity.

## SECTION 3-404. UNAUTHORIZED SIGNATURES.

(1) Any unauthorized signature is wholly inoperative as that of the person whose name is signed unless he ratifies it or is precluded from denying it; but it operates as the signature of the unauthorized signer in favor of any person who in good faith pays the instrument or takes it for value.

(2) Any unauthorized signature may be ratified for all purposes of this Article. Such ratification does not of itself affect any rights of the person ratifying against the actual signer.

## SECTION 3-405. IMPOSTORS; SIGNATURE IN NAME OF PAYEE.

(1) An indorsement by any person in the name of a named payee is effective if
    (a) an impostor by use of the mails or otherwise has induced the maker or drawer to issue the instrument to him or his confederate in the name of the payee; or
    (b) a person signing as or on behalf of a maker or drawer intends the payee to have no interest in the instrument; or
    (c) an agent or employee of the maker or drawer has supplied him with the name of the payee intending the latter to have no such interest.

(2) Nothing in this section shall affect the criminal or civil liability of the person so indorsing.

## SECTION 3-406. NEGLIGENCE CONTRIBUTING TO ALTERATION OR UNAUTHORIZED SIGNATURE.

Any person who by his negligence substantially contributes to a material alteration of the instrument or to the making of an unauthorized signature is precluded from asserting the alteration or lack of authority against a holder in due course or against a drawee or other payor who pays the instrument in good faith and in accordance with the reasonable commercial standards of the drawee's or payor's business.

## SECTION 3-407. ALTERATION.

(1) Any alteration of an instrument is material which changes the contract of any party thereto in any respect, including any such change in
    (a) the number or relations of the parties; or
    (b) an incomplete instrument, by completing it otherwise than as authorized; or
    (c) the writing as signed, by adding to it or by removing any part of it.

(2) As against any person other than a subsequent holder in due course
    (a) alteration by the holder which is both fraudulent and material discharges any party whose contract is thereby changed unless that party assents or is precluded from asserting the defense;

(b) no other alteration discharges any party and the instrument may be enforced according to its original tenor, or as to incomplete instruments according to the authority given.

(3) A subsequent holder in due course may in all cases enforce the instrument according to its original tenor, and when an incomplete instrument has been completed, he may enforce it as completed.

## SECTION 3-408. CONSIDERATION.

Want or failure of consideration is a defense as against any person not having the rights of a holder in due course (Section 3-305), except that no consideration is necessary for an instrument or obligation thereon given in payment of or as security for an antecedent obligation of any kind. Nothing in this section shall be taken to displace any statute outside this Act under which a promise is enforceable notwithstanding lack or failure of consideration. Partial failure of consideration is a defense *pro tanto* whether or not the failure is in an ascertained or liquidated amount.

## SECTION 3-410. DEFINITION AND OPERATION OF ACCEPTANCE.

(1) Acceptance is the drawee's signed engagement to honor the draft as presented. It must be written on the draft, and may consist of his signature alone. It becomes operative when completed by delivery or notification.

(2) A draft may be accepted although it has not been signed by the drawer or is otherwise incomplete or is overdue or has been dishonored.

(3) Where the draft is payable at a fixed period after sight and the acceptor fails to date his acceptance the holder may complete it by supplying a date in good faith.

## SECTION 3-411. CERTIFICATION OF A CHECK.

(1) Certification of a check is acceptance. Where a holder procures certification the drawer and all prior indorsers are discharged.

(2) Unless otherwise agreed a bank has no obligation to certify a check.

(3) A bank may certify a check before returning it for lack of proper indorsement. If it does so the drawer is discharged.

## SECTION 3-413. CONTRACT OF MAKER, DRAWER AND ACCEPTOR.

(1) The maker or acceptor engages that he will pay the instrument according to its tenor at the time of his engagement or as completed pursuant to Section 3-115 on incomplete instruments.

(2) The drawer engages that upon dishonor of the draft and any necessary notice of dishonor or protest he will pay the amount of the draft to the holder or to any indorser who takes it up. The drawer may disclaim this liability by drawing without recourse.

(3) By making, drawing or accepting the party admits as against all subsequent parties including the drawee the existence of the payee and his then capacity to indorse.

## SECTION 3-414. CONTRACT OF INDORSER; ORDER OF LIABILITY.

(1) Unless the indorsement otherwise specifies (as by such words as "without recourse") every indorser engages that upon dishonor and any necessary notice of dishonor and protest he will pay the instrument according to its tenor at the time of his indorsement to the holder or to any subsequent indorser who takes it up, even though the indorser who takes it up was not obligated to do so.

(2) Unless they otherwise agree indorsers are liable to one another in the order in which they indorse, which is presumed to be the order in which their signatures appear on the instrument.

## SECTION 3-415. CONTRACT OF ACCOMMODATION PARTY.

(1) An accommodation party is one who signs the instrument in any capacity for the purpose of lending his name to another party to it.

(2) When the instrument has been taken for value before it is due the accommodation party is liable in the capacity in which he has signed even though the taker knows of the accommodation.

(3) As against a holder in due course and without notice of the accommodation oral proof of the accommodation is not admissible to give the accommodation party the benefit of discharges dependent on his character as such. In other cases the accommodation character may be shown by oral proof.

(4) An indorsement which shows that it is not in the chain of title is notice of its accommodation character.

(5) An accommodation party is not liable to the party accommodated, and if he pays the instrument has a right of recourse on the instrument against such party.

(6) An accommodation party warrants to any subsequent holder who is not the party accommodated and who takes the instrument in good faith that

    (a) all signatures are genuine or authorized; and

    (b) the instrument has not been materially altered; and

    (c) all prior parties had capacity to contract; and

    (d) he has no knowledge of any insolvency proceeding instituted with respect to the maker or acceptor or the drawer of an unaccepted instrument.

## SECTION 3-416. CONTRACT OF GUARANTOR.

(1) "Payment guaranteed" or equivalent words added to a signature mean that the signer engages that if the instrument is not paid when due he will pay it according to its tenor without resort by the holder to any other party.

(2) "Collection guaranteed" or equivalent words added to a signature mean that the signer engages that if the instrument is not paid when due he will pay it according to its tenor, but only after the holder has reduced his claim against the maker or acceptor to judgment and execution has been returned unsatisfied, or after the maker or acceptor has become insolvent or it is otherwise apparent that it is useless to proceed against him.

(3) Words of guaranty which do not otherwise specify guarantee payment.

(4) No words of guaranty added to the signature of a sole maker or acceptor affect his liability on the instrument. Such words added to the signature of one of two or more makers or acceptors create a presumption that the signature is for the accommodation of the others.

(5) When words of guaranty are used presentment, notice of dishonor and protest are not necessary to charge the user.

(6) Any guaranty written on the instrument is enforceable notwithstanding any statute of frauds.

## SECTION 3-417. WARRANTIES ON PRESENTMENT AND TRANSFER.

(1) Any person who obtains payment or acceptance and any prior transferor warrants to a person who in good faith pays or accepts that
    (a) he has a good title to the instrument or is authorized to obtain payment or acceptance on behalf of one who has a good title; and
    (b) he has no knowledge that the signature of the maker or drawer is unauthorized, except that this warranty is not given by a holder in due course acting in good faith
     (i) to a maker with respect to the maker's own signature; or
     (ii) to a drawer with respect to the drawer's own signature, whether or not the drawer is also the drawee; or
    (iii) to an acceptor of a draft if the holder in due course took the draft after the acceptance or obtained the acceptance without knowledge that the drawer's signature was unauthorized; and
    (c) the instrument has not been materially altered, except that this warranty is not given by a holder in due course acting in good faith
     (i) to the maker of a note; or
     (ii) to the drawer of a draft whether or not the drawer is also the drawee; or
    (iii) to the acceptor of a draft with respect to an alteration made prior to the acceptance if the holder in due course took the draft after the acceptance, even though the acceptance provided "payable as originally drawn" or equivalent terms; or
    (iv) to the acceptor of a draft with respect to an alteration made after the acceptance.

(2) Any person who transfers an instrument and receives consideration warrants to his transferee and if the transfer is by indorsement to any subsequent holder who takes the instrument in good faith that

(a) he has a good title to the instrument or is authorized to obtain payment or acceptance on behalf of one who has a good title and the transfer is otherwise rightful; and

(b) all signatures are genuine or authorized; and

(c) the instrument has not been materially altered; and

(d) no defense of any party is good against him; and

(e) he has no knowledge of any insolvency proceeding instituted with respect to the maker or acceptor or the drawer of an unaccepted instrument.

(3) By transferring "without recourse" the transferor limits the obligation stated in subsection (2)(d) to a warranty that he has no knowledge of such a defense.

(4) A selling agent or broker who does not disclose the fact that he is acting only as such gives the warranties provided in this section, but if he makes such disclosure warrants only his good faith and authority.

## SECTION 3-418. FINALITY OF PAYMENT OR ACCEPTANCE.

Except for recovery of bank payments as provided in the Article on Bank Deposits and Collections (Article 4) and except for liability for breach of warranty on presentment under the preceding section, payment or acceptance of any instrument is final in favor of a holder in due course, or a person who has in good faith changed his position in reliance on the payment.

## SECTION 3-501. WHEN PRESENTMENT, NOTICE OF DISHONOR, AND PROTEST NECESSARY OR PERMISSIBLE.

(1) Unless excused (Section 3-511) presentment is necessary to charge secondary parties as follows:

(a) presentment for acceptance is necessary to charge the drawer and indorsers of a draft where the draft so provides, or is payable elsewhere than at the residence or place of business of the drawee, or its date of payment depends upon such presentment. The holder may at his option present for acceptance any other draft payable at a stated date;

(b) presentment for payment is necessary to charge any indorser;

(c) in the case of any drawer, the acceptor of a draft payable at a bank or the maker of a note payable at a bank, presentment for payment is necessary, but failure to make presentment discharges such drawer, acceptor or maker only as stated in Section 3-502 (1)(b).

(2) Unless excused (Section 3-511)

(a) notice of any dishonor is necessary to charge any indorser;

(b) in the case of any drawer, the acceptor of a draft payable at a bank or the maker of a note payable at a bank, notice of any dishonor is necessary, but failure to give such notice discharges such drawer, acceptor or maker only as stated in Section 3-502 (1)(b).

(3)  Unless excused (Section 3-511) protest of any dishonor is necessary to charge the drawer and indorsers of any draft which on its face appears to be drawn or payable outside of the states and territories of the United States and the District of Columbia. The holder may at his option make protest of any dishonor of any other instrument and in the case of a foreign draft may on insolvency of the acceptor before maturity make protest for better security.

(4)  Notwithstanding any provision of this section, neither presentment nor notice of dishonor nor protest is necessary to charge an indorser who has indorsed an instrument after maturity.

## SECTION 3-502. UNEXCUSED DELAY; DISCHARGE.

(1)  Where without excuse any necessary presentment or notice of dishonor is delayed beyond the time when it is due
      (a)  any indorser is discharged; and
      (b)  any drawer or the acceptor of a draft payable at a bank or the maker of a note payable at a bank who because the drawee or payor bank becomes insolvent during the delay is deprived of funds maintained with the drawee or payor bank to cover the instrument may discharge his liability by written assignment to the holder of his rights against the drawee or payor bank in respect of such funds, but such drawer, acceptor or maker is not otherwise discharged.

(2)  Where without excuse a necessary protest is delayed beyond the time when it is due any drawer or indorser is discharged.

## SECTION 3-503. TIME OF PRESENTMENT.

(1)  Unless a different time is expressed in the instrument the time for any presentment is determined as follows:
      (a)  where an instrument is payable at or a fixed period after a stated date any presentment for acceptance must be made on or before the date it is payable;
      (b)  where an instrument is payable after sight it must either be presented for acceptance or negotiated within a reasonable time after date or issue whichever is later;
      (c)  where an instrument shows the date on which it is payable presentment for payment is due on that date;
      (d)  where an instrument is accelerated presentment for payment is due within a reasonable time after the acceleration;
      (e)  with respect to the liability of any secondary party presentment for acceptance or payment of any other instrument is due within a reasonable time after such party becomes liable thereon.

(2)  A reasonable time for presentment is determined by the nature of the instrument, any usage of banking or trade and the facts of the particular case. In the case of an uncertified check which is drawn and payable within the United States and which

is not a draft drawn by a bank the following are presumed to be reasonable periods within which to present for payment or to initiate bank collection:

(a) with respect to the liability of the drawer, thirty days after date or issue whichever is later; and

(b) with respect to the liability of an endorser, seven days after his indorsement.

(3) Where any presentment is due on a day which is not a full business day for either the person making presentment or the party to pay or accept, presentment is due on the next following day which is a full business day for both parties.

(4) Presentment to be sufficient must be made at a reasonable hour, and if at a bank during its banking day.

## SECTION 3-504. HOW PRESENTMENT MADE.

(1) Presentment is a demand for acceptance or payment made upon the maker, acceptor, drawee or other payor by or on behalf of the holder.

(2) Presentment may be made

(a) by mail, in which event the time of presentment is determined by the time of receipt of the mail; or

(b) through a clearing house; or

(c) at the place of acceptance or payment specified in the instrument or if there be none at the place of business or residence of the party to accept or pay. If neither the party to accept or pay nor anyone authorized to act for him is present or accessible at such place presentment is excused.

(3) It may be made

(a) to any one of two or more makers, acceptors, drawees or other payors; or

(b) to any person who has authority to make or refuse the acceptance or payment.

(4) A draft accepted or a note made payable at a bank in the United States must be presented at such bank.

(5) In the cases described in Section 4-210 presentment may be made in the manner and with the result stated in that section.

## SECTION 3-505. RIGHTS OF PARTY TO WHOM PRESENTMENT IS MADE.

(1) The party to whom presentment is made may without dishonor require

(a) exhibition of the instrument; and

(b) reasonable identification of the person making presentment and evidence of his authority to make it if made for another; and

(c) that the instrument be produced for acceptance or payment at a place specified in it, or if there be none at any place reasonable in the circumstances; and

(d) a signed receipt on the instrument for any partial or full payment and its surrender upon full payment.

(2)  Failure to comply with any such requirement invalidates the presentment but the person presenting has a reasonable time in which to comply and the time for acceptance or payment runs from the time of compliance.

## SECTION 3-506. TIME ALLOWED FOR ACCEPTANCE OR PAYMENT.

(1)  Acceptance may be deferred without dishonor until the close of the next business day following presentment. The holder may also in a good faith effort to obtain acceptance and without either dishonor of the instrument or discharge of secondary parties allow postponement of acceptance for an additional business day.

(2)  Except as a longer time is allowed in the case of documentary drafts drawn under a letter of credit, and unless an earlier time is agreed to by the party to pay, payment of an instrument may be deferred without dishonor pending reasonable examination to determine whether it is properly payable, but payment must be made in any event before the close of business on the day of presentment.

## SECTION 3-507. DISHONOR; HOLDER'S RIGHT OF RECOURSE; TERM ALLOWING RE-PRESENTMENT.

(1)  An instrument is dishonored when
    (a)  a necessary or optional presentment is duly made and due acceptance or payment is refused or cannot be obtained within the prescribed time or in case of bank collections the instrument is seasonably returned by the midnight deadline (Section 4-301); or
    (b)  presentment is excused and the instrument is not duly accepted or paid.

(2)  Subject to any necessary notice of dishonor and protest, the holder has upon dishonor an immediate right of recourse against the drawers and indorsers.

(3)  Return of an instrument for lack of proper indorsement is not dishonor.

(4)  A term in a draft or an indorsement thereof allowing a stated time for re-presentment in the event of any dishonor of the draft by nonacceptance if a time draft or by nonpayment if a sight draft gives the holder as against any secondary party bound by the term an option to waive the dishonor without affecting the liability of the secondary party and he may present again up to the end of the stated time.

## SECTION 3-508. NOTICE OF DISHONOR.

(1)  Notice of dishonor may be given to any person who may be liable on the instrument by or on behalf of the holder or any party who has himself received notice, or any other party who can be compelled to pay the instrument. In addition an agent or bank in whose hands the instrument is dishonored may give notice to his principal or customer or to another agent or bank from which the instrument was received.

(2)  Any necessary notice must be given by a bank before its midnight deadline and by any other person before midnight of the third business day after dishonor or receipt of notice of dishonor.

(3) Notice may be given in any reasonable manner. It may be oral or written and in any terms which identify the instrument and state that it has been dishonored. A misdescription which does not mislead the party notified does not vitiate the notice. Sending the instrument bearing a stamp, ticket or writing stating that acceptance or payment has been refused or sending a notice of debit with respect to the instrument is sufficient.

(4) Written notice is given when sent although it is not received.

(5) Notice to one partner is notice to each although the firm has been dissolved.

(6) When any party is in insolvency proceedings instituted after the issue of the instrument notice may be given either to the party or to the representative of his estate.

(7) When any party is dead or incompetent notice may be sent to his last known address or given to his personal representative.

(8) Notice operates for the benefit of all parties who have rights on the instrument against the party notified.

## SECTION 3-509. PROTEST; NOTING FOR PROTEST.

(1) A protest is a certificate of dishonor made under the hand and seal of a United States consul or vice consul or a notary public or other person authorized to certify dishonor by the law of the place where dishonor occurs. It may be made upon information satisfactory to such person.

(2) The protest must identify the instrument and certify either that due presentment has been made or the reason why it is excused and that the instrument has been dishonored by nonacceptance or nonpayment.

(3) The protest may also certify that notice of dishonor has been given to all parties or to specified parties.

(4) Subject to subsection (5) any necessary protest is due by the time that notice of dishonor is due.

(5) If, before protest is due, an instrument has been noted for protest by the officer to make protest, the protest may be made at any time thereafter as of the date of the noting.

## SECTION 3-510. EVIDENCE OF DISHONOR AND NOTICE OF DISHONOR.

The following are admissible as evidence and create a presumption of dishonor and of any notice of dishonor therein shown:

(a) a document regular in form as provided in the preceding section which purports to be a protest;

(b) the purported stamp or writing of the drawee, payor bank or presenting bank on the instrument or accompanying it stating that acceptance or payment has been refused for reasons consistent with dishonor;

(c) any book or record of the drawee, payor bank, or any collecting bank kept in the usual course of business which shows dishonor, even though there is no evidence of who made the entry.

## SECTION 3-602. EFFECT OF DISCHARGE AGAINST HOLDER IN DUE COURSE.

No discharge of any party provided by this Article is effective against a subsequent holder in due course unless he has notice thereof when he takes the instrument.

## SECTION 3-605. CANCELLATION AND RENUNCIATION.

(1) The holder of an instrument may even without consideration discharge any party

    (a) in any manner apparent on the face of the instrument or the indorsement, as by intentionally canceling the instrument or the party's signature by destruction or mutilation, or by striking out the party's signature; or

    (b) by renouncing his rights by a writing signed and delivered or by surrender of the instrument to the party to be discharged.

(2) Neither cancellation nor renunciation without surrender of the instrument affects the title thereto.

## SECTION 3-804. LOST, DESTROYED OR STOLEN INSTRUMENTS.

The owner of an instrument which is lost, whether by destruction, theft or otherwise, may maintain an action in his own name and recover from any party liable thereon upon due proof of his ownership, the facts which prevent his production of the instrument and its terms. The court shall require security, in an amount fixed by the court not less than twice the amount allegedly unpaid on the instrument, indemnifying the defendant, his heirs, personal representatives, successors and assigns against loss, including costs and expenses, by reason of further claims on the instrument, but this provision does not apply where an action is prosecuted or defended by the state or by a public officer in its behalf.

## SECTION 3-805. INSTRUMENTS NOT PAYABLE TO ORDER OR TO BEARER.

This Article applies to any instrument whose terms do not preclude transfer and which is otherwise negotiable within this Article but which is not payable to order or to bearer, except that there can be no holder in due course of such an instrument.

# UNIFORM PARTNERSHIP ACT

## PART I

### SECTION 1. NAME OF ACT.

This act may be cited as the Uniform Partnership Act.

### SECTION 2. DEFINITION OF TERMS.

"Court" includes every court and judge having jurisdiction in the case.

"Business" includes every trade, occupation or profession.

"Bankrupt" includes bankruptcy under the Federal Bankruptcy Act or insolvent under any state insolvent act.

"Conveyance" includes every assignment, lease, mortgage or encumbrance.

"Real property" includes land and any interest or estate in land.

### SECTION 3. INTERPRETATION OF KNOWLEDGE AND NOTICE.

(1) A person has "knowledge" of a fact within the meaning of this Act not only when he has actual knowledge thereof, but also when he has knowledge of such other facts as in the circumstances shows bad faith.

(2) A person has "notice" of a fact within the meaning of this Act when the person who claims the benefit of the notice

    (a) states the fact to such person, or

    (b) delivers through the mail, or by other means of communication, a written statement of the fact to such person or to a proper person at his place of business or residence.

### SECTION 4. RULES OF CONSTRUCTION.

(1) The rule that statutes in derogation of the common law are to be strictly construed shall have no application under this Act.

(2) The law of estoppel shall apply under this Act.

(3) The law of agency shall apply under this Act.

(4) This Act shall be so interpreted and construed as to effect its general purpose to make uniform the law of those states which enact it.

(5) This Act shall not be construed so as to impair the obligations of any contract existing when the Act goes into effect, nor to affect any action or proceedings begun or right accrued before this Act takes effect.

## SECTION 5. RULES FOR CASES NOT PROVIDED FOR IN THIS ACT.

In any case not provided for in this Act the rules of law and equity, including the law merchant, shall govern.

## PART II    NATURE OF A PARTNERSHIP

### SECTION 6. PARTNERSHIP DEFINED.

(1) A partnership is an association of two or more persons to carry on as co-owners a business for profit.

(2) But any association formed under any other statute of this state, or statute adopted by authority, other than the authority of this state, is not a partnership under this act, unless such association would have been a partnership in this state prior to the adoption of this act; but this act shall apply to limited partnerships except in so far as the statutes relating to such partnerships are inconsistent herewith.

### SECTION 7. RULES FOR DETERMINING THE EXISTENCE OF A PARTNERSHIP.

In determining whether a partnership exists, these rules shall apply:

(1) Except as provided by Section 16 persons who are not partners as to each other are not partners as to third persons.

(2) Joint tenancy, tenancy in common, tenancy by the entireties, joint property, common property, or part ownership does not of itself establish a partnership, whether such co-owners do or do not share any profits made by the use of the property.

(3) The sharing of gross returns does not of itself establish a partnership, whether or not persons sharing them have a joint or common right or interest in any property from which the returns are derived.

(4) The receipt by a person of a share of the profits of a business is prima facie evidence that he is a partner in the business, but no such inference shall be drawn if such profits were received in payment:

(a) As a debt by installments or otherwise;

(b) As wages of an employee or rent to a landlord;

(c) As an annuity to a widow or representative of a deceased partner;

(d) As interest on a loan, though the amount of payment varies with the profits of the business;

(e) As the consideration for the sale of a good-will of a business or other property by installments or otherwise.

## SECTION 8. PARTNERSHIP PROPERTY.

(1) All property originally brought into the partnership stock or subsequently acquired by purchase or otherwise, on account of the partnership, is partnership property.

(2) Unless contrary intent appears, property acquired with partnership funds is partnership property.

(3) Any estate in real property may be acquired in the partnership name. Title so acquired can be conveyed only in the partnership name.

(4) A conveyance to a partnership in the partnership name, though without words of inheritance, passes the entire estate of the grantor unless a contrary intent appears.

# PART III    RELATIONS OF PARTNERS TO PERSONS DEALING WITH THE PARTNERSHIP

## SECTION 9. PARTNER AGENT OF PARTNERSHIP AS TO PARTNERSHIP BUSINESS.

(1) Every partner is an agent of the partnership for the purpose of its business, and the act of every partner, including the execution in the partnership name of any instrument, for apparently carrying on in the usual way the business of the partnership of which he is a member binds the partnership, unless the partner so acting has in fact no authority to act for the partnership in the particular matter, and the person with whom he is dealing has knowledge of the fact that he has no such authority.

(2) An act of a partner which is not apparently for the carrying on of the business of the partnership in the usual way does not bind the partnership unless authorized by the other partners.

(3) Unless authorized by the other partners or unless they have abandoned the business, one or more but less than all of the partners have no authority to:
    (a) Assign the partnership property in trust for creditors or on the assignee's promise to pay the debts of the partnership,
    (b) Dispose of the good-will of the business,
    (c) Do any other act which would make it impossible to carry on the ordinary business of a partnership,
    (d) Confess a judgment,
    (e) Submit a partnership claim or liability in arbitration or reference.

(4) No act of a partner in contravention of a restriction on authority shall bind the partnership to persons having knowledge of the restriction.

## SECTION 10. CONVEYANCE OF REAL PROPERTY OF THE PARTNERSHIP.

(1) Where title to real property is in the partnership name, any partner may convey title to such property by a conveyance executed in the partnership name; but the partnership may recover such property unless the partner's act binds the partnership under the provisions of paragraph (1) of Section 9 or unless such property has been conveyed by the grantee or a person claiming through such grantee to a holder for value without knowledge that the partner, in making the conveyance, has exceeded his authority.

(2) Where title to real property is in the partnership name, a conveyance executed by a partner, in his own name, passes the equitable interest of the partnership, provided that the act is one within the authority of the partner under the provision of paragraph (1) of Section 9.

(3) Where title to real property is in the name of one or more but not all the partners, and the record does not disclose the right of the partnership, the partners in whose name the title stands may convey title to such property, but the partnership may recover such property if the partner's act does not bud the partnership under the provisions of paragraph (1) of Section 9, unless the purchaser or his assignee, is a holder for value, without knowledge.

(4) Where the title to real property is in the name of one or more or all of the partners, or in a third person in trust for the partnership, a conveyance executed by a partner in the partnership name, or in his own name, passes the equitable interest of the partnership, provided that the act is one within the authority of the partner under the provisions of paragraph (1) of Section 9.

(5) Where the title to real property is in the name of all the partners a conveyance executed by all the partners passes all their rights in such property.

## SECTION 11. PARTNERSHIP BOUND BY ADMISSION OF PARTNER.

An admission or representation made by any partner concerning partnership affairs within the scope of his authority as conferred by this Act is evidence against the partnership.

## SECTION 12. PARTNERSHIP CHARGED WITH KNOWLEDGE OF OR NOTICE TO PARTNER.

Notice to any partner of any matter related to partnership affairs, and the knowledge of the partner acting in the particular matter, acquired while a partner or then present in his mind, and the knowledge of any other partner who reasonably could and should have communicated it to then acting partner, operate as notice to or knowledge of the partnership, except in the case of a fraud on the partnership committed by or with consent of that partner.

## SECTION 13. PARTNERSHIP BOUND BY PARTNER'S WRONGFUL ACT.

Where, by any wrongful act or omission of any partner acting in the ordinary course of the business of the partnership or with the authority of his co-partners, loss or injury is caused to any person, not being a partner of the partnership, or any penalty is incurred, the partnership is liable therefor to the same extent as the partner so acting or omitting to act.

## SECTION 14. PARTNERSHIP BOUND BY PARTNER'S BREACH OF TRUST.

The partnership is bound to make good the loss:
(a) Where one partner acting within the scope of his apparent authority receives money or property of a third person and misapplies it; and
(b) Where the partnership in the course of its business receives money or property of a third person and the money or property so received is misapplied by any partner while it is in the custody of the partnership.

## SECTION 15. NATURE OF PARTNER'S LIABILITY.

All partners are liable:
(a) Jointly and severally for everything chargeable to the partnership under Sections 13 and 14.
(b) Jointly for all other debts and obligations of the partnership, but any partner may enter into a separate obligation to perform a partnership contract.

## SECTION 16. PARTNER BY ESTOPPEL.

(1) When a person, by words spoken or written or by conduct, represents himself, or consents to another representing him to any one, as a partner in an existing partnership or with one or more persons not actual partners, he is liable to any such person to whom such representation has been made, who has, on the faith of such representation, given credit to the actual or apparent partnership, and if he has made such representation or consented to its being made in a public manner he is liable to such person, whether the representation has or has not been made or communicated to such person so giving credit by or with the knowledge of the apparent partner making the representation or consenting to its being made:
(a) When a partnership liability results, he is liable as though he were an actual member of the partnership.
(b) When no partnership liability results, he is liable jointly with the other persons, if any, so consenting to the contract or representation as to incur liability, otherwise separately.
(2) When a person has been thus represented to be a partner in an existing partnership, or with one or more persons not actual partners, he is an agent of the persons consenting to such representation to bind them to the same extent and in the same

manner as though he was a partner in fact, with respect to persons who rely upon the representation. Where all members of the existing partnership consent to the representation, a partnership act or obligation results; but in all other cases it is the joint act or obligation of the person acting and the persons consenting to the representation.

### SECTION 17. LIABILITY OF INCOMING PARTNER.

A person admitted as a partner into an existing partnership is liable for all the obligations of the partnership arising before his admission as though he had been a partner when such obligations were incurred, except that this liability shall be satisfied only out of partnership property.

## PART IV   RELATION OF PARTNERS TO ONE ANOTHER

### SECTION 18. RULES DETERMINING RIGHTS AND DUTIES OF PARTNERS.

The rights and duties of the partners in relation to the partnership shall be determined, subject to any agreement between them, by the following rules:

(a) Each partner shall be repaid his contributions, whether by way of capital or advances to the partnership property and share equally in the profits and surplus remaining after all liabilities, including those to partners, are satisfied; and must contribute towards the losses, whether of capital or otherwise, sustained by the partnership according to his share of the profits.

(b) The partnership must indemnify every partner in respect to payments made "and personal liabilities reasonably incurred by him in the ordinary and proper conduct of its business, or for the preservation of its business or property.

(c) A partner, who in aid of the partnership makes any payment or advance beyond the amount of capital which he agreed to contribute, shall be paid interest from the date of the payment or advance.

(d) A partner shall receive interest on the capital contributed by him only from the date when repayment should be made.

(e) All partners have equal rights in the management and conduct of the partnership business.

(f) No partner is entitled to remuneration for acting the partnership business, except that a surviving partner is entitled to reasonable compensation for his services in winding up the partnership affairs.

(g) No person can become a member of the partnership without the consent of all the partners.

(h) Any difference arising as to ordinary matters connected with the partnership business may be decided by a majority of the partners; but no act in contravention of any agreement between the partners may be done rightfully without the consent of all of the partners.

## SECTION 19. PARTNERSHIP BOOKS.

The partnership books shall be kept, subject to any agreement between the partners, at the principal place of business of the partnership, and every partner shall at all times have access to and may inspect and copy any of them.

## SECTION 20. DUTY OF PARTNERS TO RENDER INFORMATION.

Partners shall render on demand true and full information of all things affecting the partnership to any partner or the legal representative of any deceased partner or partner under legal disability.

## SECTION 21. PARTNER ACCOUNTABLE AS A FIDUCIARY.

(1) Every partner must account to the partnership for any benefit, and shall hold as trustee for it any profits derived by him without the consent of the other partners from any transaction connected with the formation, conduct, or liquidation of the partnership or from any used by him of its property.

(2) This section applies also to the representatives of a deceased partner engaged in the liquidation of the affairs of the partnership as the personal representatives of the last surviving partner.

## SECTION 22. RIGHT TO AN ACCOUNT.

Any partner shall have the right to a formal account as to partnership affairs:
(a) If he is wrongfully excluded from the partnership business or possession of its property by his co-partners,
(b) If the right exists under the terms of any agreement,
(c) As provided by Section 21,
(d) Whenever other circumstances render it just and reasonable.

## SECTION 23. CONTINUATION OF PARTNERSHIP BEYOND FIXED TERM.

(1) When a partnership for a fixed term or particular undertaking is continued after the termination of such term or particular undertaking without any express agreement, the rights and duties of the partners remain the same as they were at such termination, so far as is consistent with partnership at will.

(2) A continuation of the business by the partners or such of them as habitually acted therein during the term, without any settlement or liquidation of the partnership affairs, is prima facie evidence of a continuation of the partnership.

## PART V    PROPERTY RIGHTS OF A PARTNER

### SECTION 24. EXTENT OF PROPERTY RIGHTS OF A PARTNER.

The property rights of a partner are
(1)  his rights in specific partnership partnership property,
(2)  his interest in the partnership, and
(3)  his right to participate in the management.

### SECTION 25. NATURE OF A PARTNER'S RIGHT IN SPECIFIC PARTNERSHIP PROPERTY.

(1)  A partner is a co-owner with his partners of specific partnership property holding as a tenant in partnership.
(2)  The incidents of this tenancy are such that:
  (a)  A partner, subject to the provision of this Act and to any agreement between the partners, has an equal right with his partners to possess specific partnership property for partnership purposes; but he has no right to possess such property for any other purpose without the consent of his partners.
  (b)  A partner's right in specific partnership property is not assignable except in connection with the assignment of rights of all partners in the same property.
  (c)  A partner's right to specific partnership property is not subject to attachment or execution, except on a claim against the partnership.
  (d)  On the death of a partner his right in specific partnership property vests in the surviving partner or partners, except where the deceased was the last surviving partner, when his right in such property vests in his legal representative. Such surviving partner or partners, or the legal representative of the last surviving partner, has no right to possess the partnership property for any but a partnership purpose.
  (e)  A partner's right in specific partnership property is not subject to dower, curtesy, or allowances to widows, heirs or next of kin.

### SECTION 26. NATURE OF PARTNER'S INTEREST IN THE PARTNERSHIP.

A partner's interest in the partnership is his share of the profits and surplus, and the same is personal property.

### SECTION 27. ASSIGNMENT OF PARTNER'S INTEREST.

(1)  A conveyance by a partner of his interest in the partnership does not of itself dissolve the partnership, nor, as against the other partners in the absence of agreement, entitle the assignee, during the continuance of the partnership to interfere in the management or administration of the partnership business or affairs, or to require any

information or account of partnership transactions, or to inspect the partnership books; but it merely entitles the assignees to receive in accordance with his contract the profits to which the assigning partner would otherwise be entitled.

(2) In case of a dissolution of the partnership, the assignee is entitled to receive his assignor's interest and may require an account from the date only of the last account agreed to by the partners.

## SECTION 28. PARTNER'S INTEREST SUBJECT TO CHARGING ORDER.

(1) On due application to a competent court by any judgment creditor of a partner, the court which entered the judgment, order or decree, or any other order of court, may charge the interest of the debtor partner with repayment of the unsatisfied amount of such judgment debt with interest thereon; and may then or later appoint a receiver of his share of the profits, and of any other money due or to fall due to him in respect of the partnership, and make all other orders, directions, accounts and inquiries which the debtor partner might have made, or which the circumstances of the case may require.

(2) The interest charged may be redeemed at any time before foreclosure, or in the case of a sale being directed by the court may be purchased without thereby causing a dissolution:
 (a) With separate property, by any one or more of the partners, or
 (b) With partnership property, by any one or more of the partners with the consent of all the partners whose interests are not so charged or sold.

(3) Nothing in this Act shall be held to deprive a partner of his right, if any, under the exemption laws, as regards his interest in the partnership.

## PART VI    DISSOLUTION AND WINDING UP

### SECTION 29. DISSOLUTION DEFINED.

The dissolution of the partnership is the change in the relation of the partners caused by any partner ceasing to be associated in the carrying on as distinguished from the winding up of the business.

### SECTION 30. PARTNERSHIP NOT TERMINATED BY DISSOLUTION.

On dissolution the partnership is not terminated, but continues until the winding up of partnership affairs is completed.

### SECTION 31. CAUSES OF DISSOLUTION.

Dissolution is caused:
(1) Without violation of the agreement of the partners:
 (a) By the termination of the definite term or particular undertaking specified in the agreement,

      (b)  By the express will of any partner when no definite term or particular undertaking is specified,

      (c)  By the express will of all the partners who have not assigned their interest or suffered them to be charged for their separate debts,

      (d)  By the expulsion of any partner from the business bona fide in accordance with such a power conferred by the agreement among the partners;

(2) In contravention of the agreement between the partners, where the circumstances do not permit a dissolution under any other provision of this section, by the express will of any partner at any time;

(3) By any event which makes it unlawful for the business of the partnership to be carried on or for the members to carry it on in partnership;

(4) By the death of any partner;

(5) By the bankruptcy of any partner or the partnership;

(6) By decree of the court under Section 32.

## SECTION 32. DISSOLUTION BY DECREE OF COURT.

(1) On application by or for a partner the court shall decree a dissolution whenever:

      (a)  A partner has been declared a lunatic in any judicial proceeding or is shown to be of unsound mind,

      (b)  A partner becomes in any other way incapable of performing his part of the partnership contract,

      (c)  A partner has been guilty of such conduct as tend to affect prejudicially the carrying on of the business,

      (d)  A partner willfully or persistently commits a breach of a partnership agreement, or otherwise so conducts himself, in matters relating to the partnership business that it is not reasonably practicable to carry on the business in partnership with him,

      (e)  The business of the partnership can only be carried on at a loss,

      (f)  Other circumstances render a dissolution equitable.

(2) On the application of the purchaser of a partner's interest under Sections 27 or 28.

## SECTION 33. GENERAL EFFECT OF DISSOLUTION ON AUTHORITY OF PARTNER.

Except so far as may be necessary to wind up partnership affairs or to complete transactions begun but not then finished, dissolution terminates all authority of any partner to act for the partnership,

(1) Except with respect to the partners,

      (a)  When the dissolution is not by the act, bankruptcy or death of a partner; or

(b) When the dissolution is by such act, bankruptcy or death of a partner, in cases where Section 34 so applies.

(2) With respect to persons not partners, as declared in Section 35.

## SECTION 34. RIGHT OF PARTNER TO CONTRIBUTION FROM CO-PARTNERS AFTER DISSOLUTION.

Where the dissolution is caused by the act, death or bankruptcy of a partner, each partner is liable to his co-partners for his share of any liability created by any partner acting for the partnership as if the partnership had not been dissolved unless:

(a) The dissolution being by act of any partner, the partner acting for the partnership had knowledge of the dissolution, or

(b) The dissolution being by the death or bankruptcy of a partner, the partner acting for the partnership had knowledge or notice of the death or bankruptcy.

## SECTION 35. POWER OF PARTNER TO BIND PARTNERSHIP TO THIRD PERSONS AFTER DISSOLUTION.

(1) After dissolution a partner can bind the partnership except as provided in paragraph (3)

(a) By any act appropriate for winding up partnership affairs or completion transactions unfinished at dissolution;

(b) By any transaction which would bind the partnership if dissolution had not taken place, provided the other party to the transaction:

(i) Had extended credit to the partnership prior to dissolution and had no knowledge or notice of the dissolution; or

(ii) Though he had not so extended credit, had nevertheless known of the partnership prior to dissolution and had no knowledge or notice of dissolution, the fact of dissolution had not been advertised in a newspaper of general circulation in the place (or in each place if more than one) at which the partnership business was regularly carried on.

(2) The liability of a partner under paragraph (1)(b) shall be satisfied out of partnership assets alone when such partner had been prior to dissolution:

(a) unknown as a partner to the person with whom the contract was made; and

(b) So far unknown and inactive in partnership affairs that the business reputation could not be said to have been in any degree due to his connection with it.

(3) The partnership is in no case bound by any act of a partner after dissolution:

(a) where the partnership is dissolved because it is unlawful to carry on the business, unless the act is appropriate for winding up partnership affairs; or

(b) Where the partner has become bankrupt; or

(c) Where the partner has no authority to wind up partnership affairs; except by a transaction by one who:

(i) Had extended credit to the partnership prior to dissolution and had no knowledge or notice of his want of authority; or

(ii) Had not extended credit to the partnership prior to dissolution, and, having no knowledge or notice of his want of authority, and the fact of his want of authority has not been advertised in the manner provided for advertising the fact of dissolution in paragraph (1)(b)(ii).

(4) Nothing in this section shall affect the liability under Section 16 of any person who after dissolution represents himself or consents to another representing him as a partner in a partnership engaged in carrying on business.

## SECTION 36. EFFECT OF DISSOLUTION ON PARTNER'S EXISTING LIABILITY.

(1) The dissolution of the partnership does not of itself discharge the existing liability of a partner.

(2) A partner is discharged from any existing liability upon dissolution of the partnership by an agreement to that effect between himself, the partnership creditor and the person or partnership continuing the business; and such agreement may be inferred from the course of dealing between the creditor having the knowledge of the dissolution and the person or partnership continuing the business.

(3) Where a person agrees to assume the existing obligations of a dissolved partnership, the partners whose obligations have been assumed shall be discharged from any liability to any creditor of the partnership who, knowing of the agreement, consents to a material alteration in the nature of time of payment of such obligations.

(4) The individual property of a deceased partner shall be liable for all obligations incurred while he was a partner but subject to the prior payment of his separate debts.

## SECTION 37. RIGHT TO WIND UP.

Unless otherwise agreed the partners who have not wrongfully dissolved the partnership or the legal representative of the last surviving partner, not bankrupt, has the right to wind up partnership affairs; provided, however, that any partner, his legal representative or his assignee, upon cause shown, may obtain winding up by the court.

## SECTION 38. RIGHTS OF PARTNERS TO APPLICATION OF PARTNERSHIP PROPERTY.

(1) When dissolution is caused in any way, except in contravention of the partnership agreement, each partner as against his co-partners and all person claiming through them in respect of their interests in the partnership, unless otherwise agreed, may have the partnership property applied to discharge its liabilities, and the surplus

applied to pay in cash the net amount owing to the respective partners. But if dissolution is caused by expulsion of a partner, bona fide under the partnership agreement and if the expelled partner is discharged from all partnership liabilities, either by payment or agreement under Section 36(2), he shall receive in cash only the net amount due him from the partnership.

(2) When dissolution is caused in contravention of the partnership agreement the rights of the partners shall be as follows:

    (a) Each partner who has not caused dissolution wrongfully shall have

        (i) all the rights specified in paragraph (1) of this section, and

        (ii) the right, as against each partner who has caused the dissolution wrongfully, to damages for breach of the agreement.

    (b) The partners who have not caused the dissolution wrongfully, if they all desire to continue the business in the same name, of the partnership, either by themselves or jointly with others, may do so, during the agreed term for the partnership and for that purpose may possess the partnership property, provided they secure the payment by bond approved by the court, or pay to any partner who has caused the dissolution of the partnership wrongfully, the value of his interest in the partnership at the dissolution, less any damages recoverable under clause (2)(a)(ii) of this section, and in like manner indemnify him against all present or future partnership liabilities.

    (c) A partner who has caused the dissolution wrongfully shall have:

        (i) If the business is not continued under the provisions of paragraph 2(b) all the rights of a partner under paragraph 91), subject to clause (2)(a)(ii) of this section,

        (ii) If the business is continued under paragraph (2)(b) of this section the right as against his co-partners and all claiming through them in respect of their interests in the partnership, to have the value of his interest in the partnership, less any damages caused to his co-partners by the dissolution, ascertained and paid to him in cash, or the payment secured by bond approved by the court, and to be released from all existing liabilities of the partnership, but in ascertaining the value of the partner's interest the value of good-will of the business shall not be considered.

## SECTION 39. RIGHTS WHERE PARTNERSHIP IS DISSOLVED FOR FRAUD OR MISREPRESENTATION.

Where a partnership contract is rescinded on the ground of the fraud or misrepresentation of one of the parties thereto, the party entitled to rescind is, without prejudice to any other right, entitled:

    (a) To a lien on, or right of retention of, the surplus of the partnership property after satisfying the partnership liabilities to third persons for any sum of money paid by him for the purchase of an interest of the partnership and for any capital or advances contributed by him; and

(b) To stand, after all liabilities to third persons have been satisfied, in the pace of the creditors of the partnership for any payments made by him in respect to partnership liabilities; and

(c) To be indemnified by the person guilty of the fraud or making the representation against all debts and liabilities of the partnership.

## SECTION 40. RULES FOR DISTRIBUTION.

In settling accounts between the partners after dissolution, the following rules shall be observed, subject to any agreement to the contrary:

(a) The assets of the partnership are:
  (i) The partnership property,
  (ii) The contributions of the partners necessary for the payment of all the liabilities specified in clause (b) of this paragraph.

(b) The liabilities of the partnership shall rank in order of payment, as follows:
  (i) Those owing to creditors other than partners,
  (ii) Those owing to partners other than for capital and profits,
  (iii) Those owing to partners in respect to capital,
  (iv) Those owing to partners in respect to profits.

(c) The assets shall be applied in the order of their declaration in clause (a) of this paragraph to the satisfaction of the liabilities.

(d) The partners shall contribute, as provided by Section 18, (a) the amount necessary to satisfy the liabilities; but, if any, but not all, of the partners are insolvent, or, not being subject to process, refuse to contribute, the other partners shall contribute their share of the liabilities, and, in the relate proportions in which they share the profits, the additional amount necessary to pay the liabilities.

(e) As assignee for the benefit of creditors or any person appointed by the court shall have the right to enforce the contributions specified in clause (d) of this paragraph.

(f) Any partner or his legal representative shall have the right to enforce the contributions specified in clause (d) of this paragraph.

(g) The individual property of a deceased partner shall be liable for the contributions specified in clause (d) of this paragraph.

(h) When partnership property and the individual properties of the partners are in possession of a court for distribution, partnership creditors shall have priority on partnership property and separate creditors on individual property, saving the rights of lien or secured creditors as heretofore.
  (i) Where a partner has become bankrupt or his estate is insolvent the claims against his personal property shall rank in the following order:
  (ii) Those owing to separate creditors,

(iii)  Those owing to partnership creditors,

(iv)  Those owing to partners by way of contribution.

## SECTION 41. LIABILITY OF PERSONS CONTINUING THE BUSINESS IN CERTAIN CASES.

(1)  When any new partner is admitted into an existing partnership, or when any partner retires and assigns (or the representative of the deceased partner assigns) his rights in the partnership property to two or more of the partners, or to one or more of the partners and one or more of third persons, if the business is continued without liquidation of the partnership affairs, creditors of the first or dissolved partnership are also creditors of the partnership so continuing the business.

(2)  When all but one partner retire and assign (or the representative of a deceased partner assigns) their rights in partnership property to the remaining partner, who continues the business without liquidation of partnership affairs, either alone or with others, creditors of the dissolved partnership are also creditors of the person or partnership so continuing the business.

(3)  When any partner retires or dies and the business of the dissolved partnership is so continued as set forth in paragraphs (1) and (2) of this section with the consent of the retired partners or the representative of the deceased partner, but without any assignment of his rights in partnership property, rights of creditors of the dissolved partnership and of the creditors of the person or partnership continuing the business shall be as if such assignment had been made.

(4)  When all partners or their representatives assign their rights in partnership property to one or more third persons who promise to pay the debts and who continue the business of the dissolved partnership, creditors of the dissolved partnership are also creditors of the person or partnership continuing the business.

(5)  When any partner wrongfully causes a dissolution and the remaining partners continue the business under the provisions of Section 38(2)(b), either alone or with others, and without liquidation of the partnership affairs, creditors of the dissolved partnership are also creditors of the person or partnership continuing the business.

(6)  When a partner is expelled and the remaining partners continue the business either alone or with others, without liquidation of the partnership affairs, creditors of the dissolved partnership are also creditors of the person or partnership continuing the business.

(7)  The liability of a third person becoming a partner in the partnership continuing the business, under this section, to the creditors of the dissolved partnership shall be satisfied out of partnership property only.

(8)  When the business of a partnership after dissolution is continued under any conditions set forth in this section the creditors of the dissolved partnership, as against the separate creditors of the retiring or deceased partner, or the representative of the deceased partner, have a prior right to any claim of the retired partner or partnership continuing the business, on account of the retired or deceased partner's interest in the

dissolved partnership or on account of any consideration promised for such interest or his right in partnership property.

(9) Nothing in this section shall be held to modify any right of creditors to set aside any assignment on the ground of fraud.

(10) The use by the person or partnership continuing the business of the partnership name, or the name of a deceased partner as part thereof, shall not of itself make the individual property of the deceased partner liable for any dents contracted by such person or partnership.

### SECTION 42. RIGHTS OF RETIRING OF ESTATE OF DECEASED PARTNER WHEN THE BUSINESS IS CONTINUED.

When any partner retires or dies, and the business is continued under any of the conditions set forth in Section 41, paragraphs (1), (2), (3), (5), (6) or Section 38, paragraph (2)(b) without any settlement of the accounts as between him or his estate and the person or partnership continuing the business, unless otherwise agreed, he or his legal representative as against such persons or partnership may have the value of his interest at the date of dissolution ascertained, and shall receive as an ordinary creditor an amount equal to the value of his interest in the dissolved partnership with interest, or, at his option or at the option of his legal representative, in lieu of interest, the profits attributable to the use of his rights in the property of the dissolved partnership; provided that the creditors of the dissolved partnership as against the separate creditors, or the representative of the retired or deceased partner, shall have priority on any claim arising out of this section, as provided by Section 48, paragraph (8) of this Act.

### SECTION 43. ACCRUAL OF ACTIONS.

The right to an account of his interest shall accrue to any partner, his legal representative, as against the winding up partners or the surviving partners or the person or partnership continuing the business, at the date of dissolution, in the absence of any agreement to the contrary.

# INDEX